The Airplane in American Culture

The Airplane in American Culture

EDITED BY DOMINICK A. PISANO

THE UNIVERSITY OF MICHIGAN PRESS

Ann Arbor

2006   2005   2004   2003   4   3   2   1

A CIP catalog record for this book is available from the British Library.

Library of Congress Cataloging-in-Publication Data

The airplane in American culture / edited by Dominick A. Pisano.
    p.   cm.
    Includes index.
    ISBN 0-472-09833-0 (Cloth : alk. paper) — ISBN 0-472-06833-4
(Paper : alk. paper)
      1. Aeronautics—United States.   2. Airplanes—United States.
      3. Popular culture—United States.   I. Pisano, Dominick, 1943–

TL521 .A779   2003
629.13′00973—dc21   2003014103

Contents

Acknowledgments

The editor is grateful to the contributors and to the following persons for helping to produce this work: LeAnn Fields, Trish Graboske, James R. Hansen, Mark Hirsch, Kate Igoe, the team at Impressions Book and Journal Services, Peter Jakab, Kristine Kaske, Melissa Keiser, Allison Liefer, Felix Lowe, Ted Maxwell, Heidi Munro, Brian Nicklas, Abigail Potter, Judith Schavrien, Collette Williams, and James I. Wilson.

New Directions in the History of Aviation

DOMINICK A. PISANO

The Airplane in American Culture began to take form during a research visit to the Henry Ford Museum and Greenfield Village.[1] In going through the museum's collections, I came across *The Automobile and American Culture,* edited by David L. Lewis and Laurence Goldstein (a contributor to this volume). It struck me that an analogous volume of essays on the airplane would be possible. Might there not be some value in asking scholars to reflect on how aviation had influenced American culture and society? Coincidentally, during my visit to the Henry Ford Museum, the advisory board of the Smithsonian History of Aviation series had met with Felix Lowe, director of the Smithsonian Institution Press at the time, to discuss the future of historical writing on aviation. The board concluded that there was a need for books that went beyond the narrow concerns of the traditional writing on aviation by exploring its social and cultural implications.[2]

A year later, James R. Hansen's article, "Aviation History in the Wider View," appeared in the July 1989 issue of *Technology and Culture,* the journal of the Society for the History of Technology. Hansen, a member of the Smithsonian History of Aviation Series advisory board, outlined what directions new historical writing on aviation might take. He argued that "books for airplane buffs have been published in great abundance since aviation's rise to military prominence during World War I, and since the end of World War II the number of scholarly monographs on a great variety of essential topics in both civil and military aviation history has grown steadily." Nevertheless, Hansen felt strongly that aviation history "[had] fallen behind other fields . . . wherein broadly synthetic, contextual, and interdisciplinary studies explore the meaning of a particular field of history in terms of what it means to others." He called for historical syntheses that looked at "the social motives, aims, and second-order consequences of the aviation enterprise."[3]

The conclusions of the History of Aviation Series' board of advisors and Hansen's essay reinforced my belief that *The Airplane in American Culture* could be a valuable project. During the time it took to plan and execute the book, other questions arose about Hansen's remarks and the historiography of aviation.

How valid is Hansen's assessment of aviation history? How does a book like *The Airplane in American Culture* fit into the historiographic record? For answers, we must look to the past to see why the history of flight has pursued certain paths and ignored others. The editor's introduction to a book such as this provided the occasion and the opportunity to explore these questions.

A Capsule History of the History of Aviation

The professionalization of the writing of American history is little more than a century old, yet the profession has undergone a profound transformation that reflects the changing cultural, political, and intellectual norms of the past hundred years. Professional history writing grew out of a desire to remove history from the realm of advocacy and move it into the realm of objectivity. *That Noble Dream,* the title of Peter Novick's book on the so-called Objectivity Question and the American historical profession, as well as a literal rendering of the admirable goal of objectivity in the writing of history, has, as Novick suggests, faded into obscurity. While professionalization ran the course of the establishment of graduate studies leading to the Ph.D. degree, creation of a professional organization, the American Historical Association, and a journal, *American Historical Review,* the idea of objectivity has had its share of problems during the course of the last century. World War I and the interwar years introduced a relativist strain into the profession that was eventually incorporated into an objectivist synthesis during and after World War II. But the 1960s saw a breakdown in the synthesis, leading to what Novick characterizes as "the present period of confusion, polarization, and uncertainty, in which the idea of historical objectivity has become more problematic than ever before."[4]

The writing of the history of aviation in the United States (which can be characterized variously as intersecting with the areas of military history, the history of technology, and public history) has run no such course. It has, as its critics have claimed, remained virtually static in its aims and methods over the course of its history, which originated with the first systematic gathering of information about military aviation during World War I. The so-called Gorrell's History (after Edgar S. Gorrell, chief historian of the U.S. Air Service, American Expeditionary Forces [AEF]) was a monumental attempt to document the work of the air service in World War I. Gorrell's intent was to be comprehensive; "to include a report of every activity undertaken or accomplished in the AEF, of every battle fought, of every production problem met, of every success or failure—in fact a complete story." Gorrell later lamented that his work languished "in the vaults of the War Department in Washington, some of the pages torn, some yellowing, many hard to read," and that "small use had been made of it . . . because of its inaccessibility."[5]

Ernest L. Jones, who before being commissioned in the Air Service in 1917 had been editor of *Aeronautics,* one of the first periodicals devoted to aviation in the United States, assisted Gorrell. Jones had established the organization that became the Information Section of the Air Service, AEF. Since Jones was an intelligence officer, he was adept at collecting information. He established the historical reporting system by which each Air Service unit was to write its own history, with emphasis on operations, and submit it to headquarters. In these reports, Jones desired "picturesque accounts of notable air battles and the human story of their participants" . . . "to please the public who will be eager for authentic stories of the deeds of American soldiers." Units were asked to make every effort "to present facts of dramatic, comic, or tragic interest, tales of obstacles overcome, of discouraging conditions, of problems of personnel, equipment, supplies, transportation or maintenance, or tests that may have historical value." Jones has to be credited with being one of the first chroniclers of the history of flight in America, and he spent a lifetime compiling a chronology of aviation and collecting materials on the history of aeronautics.[6]

Another slightly different attempt to document the history of flight in the years before World War II was made by the predecessor of the American Institute of Aeronautics and Astronautics, the Institute of the Aeronautical Sciences (IAS). Two years after the organization was formed in 1932, it received a small donation of several hundred books from members, the beginnings of an institutional library. In 1935, the IAS, in cooperation with the Works Progress Administration (WPA), compiled an index of aeronautics, with two thousand main headings, which included biographical and bibliographic material, chronologies, a digest of technical articles, company files, and photographic files. Eventually, the index increased to more than two million entries. In 1939, the IAS began an aeronautical archives and lending library in New York City, based on a loan of books, magazines, and pamphlets from William A. Burden, a private collector, who would later become Assistant Secretary of Commerce for aeronautics. Other contributors were Hart O. Berg, the agent in contract negotiations for the sale of Wright brothers' aircraft in Europe, who added his collection of documents, photographs, and books. Harry Guggenheim contributed rare aeronautical prints, engravings, and etchings. Bella Landauer donated aeronautical sheet music, trade cards, posters, bookplates, and prints.[7]

The result of "Gorrell's History," Jones's chronology, and the IAS collection was a systematic gathering of material on aeronautics. The undertakings did not result in a formalized historical publication, however, although the Office of Air Force History published parts of Gorrell's compilation in the late 1970s. A professionally written book would not appear until after World War II. In 1948, Wesley Frank Craven and James Lea Cate published the first of seven volumes of *The Army Air Forces in World War II*. Craven, a professor of history at New

York University (he later taught at Princeton), and Cate, from the University of Chicago, held commissions in the U.S. Army Air Forces (USAAF) and were part of the USAAF's Historical Division (later called Historical Office) in World War II. In December 1945, Craven and Cate opened discussions with the University of Chicago, which had expressed interest in publishing a military history "written without suppression or distortion of significant facts." The University of Chicago "agreed to sponsor the project on the understanding that the authors would be given access to all pertinent documents and would enjoy perfect freedom of interpretation."[8]

Although the Craven and Cate series is exhaustive, it reveals the unquestioning attitude of the men who wrote it and the concerns of the time in which it was written. As Richard Kohn points out in his foreword to the new imprint, published by the Office of Air Force History in 1983, "the strategic bombing campaigns received the primary emphasis, not only because of a widely-shared belief in bombardment's contribution to victory but also because of its importance in establishing the United States Air Force as a military service independent of the Army. The huge investment of men and machines and the effectiveness of the combined Anglo-American bomber offensive against Germany had not been subjected to the critical scrutiny they have since received. Nor, given the personalities involved and the immediacy of the events, did the authors question some of the command arrangements. In the tactical area, to give another example, the authors did not doubt the effect of aerial interdiction on both the German withdrawal from Sicily and the allied landings at Anzio."[9]

Academic historians also had been recruited to chronicle the AAF during the war, but AAF officials often held them at some distance, denying access to sensitive documents because they feared the contents could embarrass them. In 1944, for example, General Ira Eaker wrote to the assistant chief of air staff for intelligence that no criticism of the war's conduct should be allowed in official correspondence without the approval of headquarters. There was, Eaker cautioned, "a mass of historians at both ends watching all this correspondence . . . and these things cannot but creep into the official record unless we are all on guard." John E. Fagg, one of the contributors to the work, claimed that access to documents was limited and that while the history was being written, "we were still basking in the great victory of the war and aware that the account had to be cleared before publication . . . [h]ence the conclusions and intimations here and there were not as sharp" as those he had drawn in other professional historical work. Fagg admitted also that the team of historians was impressed with the leadership qualities of air force leaders and that this affected the writing of the official history. Wesley Frank Craven held similar views, saying that "working as I did . . . with high ranking officers of the AAF who understood our professional problem and gave us tremendous support, I learned to respect the professional soldier for his intelligence and his patriotism, if I may put it that way." It is conceivable that the attitudes of its leaders toward a favorable chronicling of the events involving the Army Air Forces was influenced by the fact that the service was intent on becoming independent of the U.S. Army. Anything unfavorable, especially if it had to do with the effectiveness of the AAF to carry out its mission, might diminish its attempts to break away from the army.[10]

In addition to the attention paid to official history by the AAF, aviation's legitimization as a historical subject was brought about in large part by federal history programs, especially the U.S. Air Force History Office, a direct descendent of the AAF's Historical Office, and the Air Force Historical Research Agency (formerly the Albert F. Simpson Historical Research Center). The U.S. Air Force's current history program is directed primarily toward commanders and leaders; thus, much of its work is suspect as being an apologia for organization points of view.

Other federal history programs also contributed to the writing of aviation-aerospace history. For example, the National Aeronautics and Space Administration (NASA), which came into being in 1958, produced a spate of historical work on the early space program. These were produced under the aegis of NASA historian Eugene Emme, a professional historian, who wrote that "clearly the history of rocket technology and space exploration must pass into the domain of dispassionate and non-participant historians. Those who helped to make history, albeit intimate to many happenings, will consistently possess a perspective dominated by their own experiences. Only with detachment can the totality of history emerge as a coherent body of knowledge." Although the NASA histories were written primarily by trained, credentialed historians, they were by and large uncritical and tended to stick rather closely to an internalist viewpoint without much regard for historical context.[11]

The formation of the Society for the History of Technology (SHOT) in 1958 and the publication of its journal *Technology and Culture* in 1959 provided further legitimation for writing aviation history. SHOT made aviation part of its larger context for the history of technology by providing a place in its journal for publication of scholarly articles and reviews of books on the subject. An assessment of *Technology and Culture* for the first quarter century of its existence, however, indicates that, although little in the way of scholarly writing on aviation appeared there during this period, many books on the subject ranging from the popular to the scholarly were reviewed. Few of these could be said to adhere to the society's expressed concern "not only with the history of technological devices and processes, but also with the relations of technology to science, politics, social change, economics and the arts and humanities." In fact, former engineers or members of the community undertook the great majority of the book reviews, and these were written from an internalist position that viewed aviation as technologically progressive. Moreover, "aeronautics," as it is referred to in the publication's index, has never held a prominent place in *Technology and Culture*. A scan of this journal's index over a twenty-five-year period indicates that subjects such as electricity, engineering, science, industrial history, railroads, and the military's relationship with technology have received far greater attention in its pages.[12]

Nearly one hundred years after the invention of the airplane, and with time to evaluate its social, cultural, and political effects on our lives, the writing of the history of the subject has not progressed as far as it could or should. Unlike other areas of historical endeavor, the history of aviation and space flight has rarely been caught up in the titanic historiographical debates that have characterized the writing of American history over the past century. Although there have been exemplary attempts over the years to gather information on the subject, there has until recently been little attempt to analyze and make sense of that information historically. Attempts to subsume the history of air and space into the rubric of the history of technology have failed. Attempts to establish history programs under the aegis of federal agencies have not been entirely successful because it is always tempting for so-called public history to (at best) promote the organization's interests and (at worst) become a public relations platform for the organization's political agenda.[13]

A Reverence for the Airplane

While the traditions of preferring to collect historical materials rather than analyze them and to write the history from an internalist, progressive viewpoint are important in explaining the narrow focus of the history of aviation, these factors ignore some rather important underlying cultural explanations. In *The Winged Gospel*, Joseph J. Corn has analyzed the treatment of the airplane as an object of reverence, indeed, worship. Corn captured the flavor of the cultural debate concerning the representation of aviation when he wrote that "as Americans searched for language appropriate to the excitement they felt for the airplane, they inevitably borrowed from [the] Christian tradition. They often spoke of themselves as 'disciples,' 'apostles,' and 'prophets,' and thought of aviation as a 'winged gospel' or 'holy cause,' one that would literally transform the conditions of life." Corn's hypothesis could well account for the iconographic manner in which the history of aviation has been written.[14]

Corn argues that these evangelizing attitudes toward aviation are rooted in American ideas and ideals about progress, especially faith in technology. "This concept of progress," Corn says,

> beholden to intellectual currents generated by the Enlightenment, took a new direction in the nineteenth century as Americans experienced the coming of industrialization. Noting the dramatic improvements wrought in manufacturing,

transportation, and agriculture, it was hard not to conclude that mechanical innovation, not simply rationalism, was the primary catalyst of social and moral improvement. Machines produced not only other machines, it seemed, but also progress itself. More than that, nineteenth-century commentators also viewed machines as moving society toward the millennium. Technology and the Saviour, they thought, both were working toward the same purpose. This perspective reflected the pervasive Protestantism of nineteenth-century American culture and suffused the winged gospel in the twentieth century.

Corn points out that as time went on, the exaggerated promise of the airplane did not materialize. "By 1950 few believed any longer that the airplane pointed to anything like a reordering of human society. The airplane had ceased to symbolize a future of unlimited individual mobility, of world peace, of enlightenment and culture, or of greater democracy and equality. It was simply a weapon or a vehicle, and as this realization sunk in the winged gospel faded out."[15]

Nevertheless, sufficient vestiges of the "winged gospel" remain to substantiate James R. Hansen's idea that the writing of aviation history is infused with enthusiasms of all kinds, but especially for the artifact over other important considerations. The American Aviation Historical Society (AAHS) is the largest formal organization of enthusiast-writers in the United States. The AAHS was founded in 1956 with an avowed antiquarian perspective. In the introduction to the first volume of its journal, published in spring 1956, Secretary William T. Larkins wrote that the audience for the publication was made up of

> a growing number of enthusiasts and scale model builders whose hobby, or non paying interest, lies in collecting books, photographs, plans, and information about airplanes and aviation. . . . The second group, composed of professional pilots, aircraft engineers, and others who have made their living in aviation during the same period, is equally important and adds the first hand information of personal experience to that which the first group has produced.

From the beginning, the emphasis was mostly on the airplane as principal artifact. "Our subject," Larkins wrote, "anything that happened in American aviation history, is intended to be understood in the broadest sense. Specifically to use airplanes as an example, this includes not only the design, construction, and life history of American built planes in the United States, but also all data relating to any use or service in any foreign country." Regardless, Larkins's airplane example has been predominant throughout the history of the organization, which has been in existence for nearly a half century.[16]

Hansen corroborates this viewpoint:

> One likely reason for the treatment of aircraft as an independent and autonomous force in history has been the deeply rooted human notion that there is

something either "magical" or "organic" about the machine, and about the this especially wonderful machine in particular. In an attempt to adjust psychologically to the growing presence of powerful new machines in our world, we have given them human names and endowed them with the most familiar qualities of life.

But this "inclination to breathe life into the machine has been misleading," Hansen says. "We have treated aircraft as if they were alive, and as if each type of aircraft, like a species of bird, possessed its own distinct vital force. . . . The airplane itself tends to make the history. The people who design, build, and use the airplane, and all of the social institutions that go along with those activities, play a subordinate role, as if they were all passengers in a plane that flies itself."[17]

Corn's and Hansen's ideas about the sacredness of the machine could account for the hundreds of popular books and articles that appear each year in which aircraft are the focal point to the exclusion of all other considerations. This perspective prevails despite the fact that the period of the "winged gospel" is long since over. But criticism of this sort applies not only to popular writers. Enthusiasts, Hansen wrote, "fall into two groups: those 'well intentioned and often talented individuals whose work suffers from the lack of professional training in a demanding craft,' and those who have the requisite professional training but who nonetheless become caught up emotionally in the subject they are supposed to be examining critically." This may be because the subject matter lends itself to an iconographic, progressive interpretation—record-setting flights, heroic pilots flying higher and faster, bold designers building better and better aircraft—without much critical analysis or deep probing.[18]

Complaints about the writing of the history of aviation are not new. A decade before Hansen's article appeared in *Technology and Culture,* and five years before Corn's *Winged Gospel,* Alex Roland pointed to another deficiency. There is, Roland wrote, "a folklore of aeronautical development—or rather several folklores—to which all of the insiders seem to subscribe. A conventional wisdom grows up about how this or that invention evolved, and most everyone embraces this received opinion, no matter how at variance it may be with documented facts." Roland goes on to say that standard accounts of aviation technology differ as to whether military or civilian influences "had a greater effect on aeronautical development." I. B. Holley agreed with Roland's assessment, saying that instead of an "intellectual history of aeronautics," we get "descriptions of hardware, what we most need is a great deal more attention to the creative process behind the hardware. How are the goals, the performance specifications, defined, and by whom? What are the assumptions, conscious and unconscious, of the formulators? What are the prevailing constraints, and why do these constraints act as they do? In this connection, one would do well to consider the broader implications of unwitting psychological restraints."[19]

These statements ring especially true today. We still do not understand basic lines of technological development, because few historians of aviation, as Roland suggested, have done "serious and comprehensive research in the primary documentation." In some cases, primary sources of information are extremely difficult to find or no longer exist, but Roland's point about received wisdom being perpetuated and reperpetuated is still valid. Historians simply have not done enough of the hard work of primary source research to answer basic questions about the history of aviation. Associated with these deficiencies are the lack of authoritative histories of various significant aviation manufacturers, government sponsored research and development facilities, industrial processes and labor practice. Nor is there an understanding of how aviation became part of a larger technological "system building" in Thomas P. Hughes's terminology (e.g., the formation of an imposing organizational structure for its research and development, manufacture, and use, or the establishment of values of order, system, and control within its institutional framework). Beyond these subjects, others such as the psychological, anthropological, and sociological meanings of man's dream to fly and their effect on the airplane's political, social, and technological development might be explored in a comprehensive work that dealt with the airplane's effect on American culture. In the history of aviation, the examination of such large questions has all too frequently been ignored; instead, the internalist, technologically deterministic, and progressive approach has prevailed.[20]

New Directions for the History of Aviation

Current editor-in-chief of *Technology and Culture* John M. Staudenmaier's comments on the conflicts that currently exist within the history of technology aptly summarize the situation in the history of aviation. Staudenmaier says that technological narratives are fiercely debated because of "the West's love affair with progress" and progress's association with science and technology, as well as "the marketing importance of an upbeat image for current technologies." He argues that historians of technology "interact with their colleagues in a social context that is deeply biased, on both the popular and the academic level, toward the very whig history that vitiates their profession." Moreover, Staudenmaier believes that "the master narrative of technological progress operates as a bias within the profession." Staudenmaier sees historians of technology as lining up in two distinct camps: on the one side are those who are "comfortable with rationality," and, on the other, those "who are comfortable with complexity, ambiguity, con-

flict, and unresolved issues." Staudenmaier contends that the first group per-
ceives progress as quantifiable, tangible, and good. The second group discourses
about technology "in terms of symbol and power," and inquires as to "who creates the symbols that constitute the pervasive, multivalent, and ambiguous moral
presence of the various dominant technologies resident in Western societies."
For this group, "ambiguity is not a bad thing, unresolved questions are healthy,
and differences between various actors (and victims) in technological stories constitute the stuff of the historical record."[21]

The Airplane in American Culture, then, is in some measure a response to
Hansen's call for a "wider view," Corn's observations about the fervor akin to
worship attendant to aviation, Roland and Holley's complaints about received
wisdom's precedence over archival research, and description over analysis, and
Staudenmaier's remarks about the Whiggishness of the history of technology.
The essays herein are the beginnings of a dialogue about the social and cultural
ramifications of aviation that will perhaps redress to some extent the imbalance
that now exists in the literature. Decisions as to the choice of topics were simple:
so few scholars are even remotely interested in the cultural history of aviation
that their names came readily to mind. The categories grew partly from my own
interests, but were greatly influenced by the scholarly concerns of the contributors. The essays represent areas that might be appealing to social and cultural
historians, historians of aviation, historians of technology, and a general audience. Ultimately, this book is an attempt to delineate areas of interest for in-
depth research in the cultural history of aviation.

Why are these aspects of the history of aviation important? Because without
them we cannot understand the story in all of its complexity, and because social-
cultural context has become so important to the writing of the history of technology. Steve Lubar suggests that historians of American culture (whatever their
subject area focus is) must "better understand some bigger issue, whether it be,
on the one hand, cultural change, social change, class, ethnicity, gender, race—
the big questions of American history—or, on the other hand, the nature of technological knowledge, the relations of science and technology, or the processes of
technological change or technological creativity and design—the key issues of
the history of technology." This is especially true for the narrowly focused writing of the history of aviation.[22]

An Overview of This Volume

This collection begins with an overview essay, "The Airplane and the American
Experience," in which Roger E. Bilstein provides a survey of public engagement
with the airplane from its origins to the present and also suggests neglected areas
of study in the scholarship of aviation. The rest of the book consists of four areas

of investigation: public perception of the airplane and how that perception was formed; the airplane's role in issues of race and gender; the airplane's importance in forming perceptions of the landscape and its influence in art and literature; and the airplane's significance in the culture of war.

An important aspect of public perception of the airplane is how aviation's image was molded to fit what industry promoters believed was appropriate for it to appear safe in the minds of thousands of potential consumers. In "The Greatest Show Not on Earth: The Confrontation between Utility and Entertainment in Aviation," Dominick A. Pisano examines the origins of American aeronautics as entertainment and shows how culturally based biases helped define a useful purpose for aviation. He also shows how changes in attitudes toward aviation's purpose reflected the broader cultural viewpoints of the periods in which these changes took place. A variation on this theme was how the image of the pilot was formed. In "The Man Nobody Knows: Charles A. Lindbergh and the Culture of Celebrity," Charles L. Ponce de Leon shows how, in a very large sense, Lindbergh's image was manufactured to suit public opinion. Lindbergh's well-publicized confrontations with the press provide a unique way of analyzing the cult of celebrity in the United States during the early twentieth century.

Although public perception of aviation has been formulated to show that it fostered democratic ideals, the reality has been less encouraging. African Americans have been (and to a large extent still are) disenfranchised from flying in the United States. In "'Great Shadow in the Sky': The Airplane in the Tulsa Race Riot of 1921 and the Development of African American Visions of Aviation, 1921–1926," Jill D. Snider examines the ambivalence of blacks in the United States toward the airplane. Snider concludes that, while the shapers of popular attitudes toward flying in the early 1920s—reporters, editors, and pilots—"often arrived at conflicting conclusions concerning the role of aeronautics in the race's future, they all were compelled to grapple with the implications of the airplane as a white-controlled technology in a world increasingly divided by race." Like African Americans, women have had to settle for second place in the aviation industry. One area in which they were widely accepted was in service to the airlines, but their image was often molded to conform to corporate ideas about women's roles. In "'Who Says It's a Man's World?': Women's Work and Travel in the First Decades of Flight," Suzanne L. Kolm dispels the notion that women were not part of commercial aviation until recent times. Kolm analyzes the ways in which women were integral to airline travel in the earliest days of its existence, especially in regard to the training of a professional corps of stewardesses. In "Experiment in the Cockpit: The Women Airforce Service Pilots of World War II," Katherine Sharp Landdeck investigates the degree to which the WASPs were effective pilots for the U.S. Army Air Forces and why the organi-

zation was disbanded over the objections of the military and argues that the
wartime women pilots left a distinctive legacy of inspiration for the women aviators of today.

From the earliest days of powered flight, the airplane was a powerful stim-
ulant to the creative imagination. For poets and intellectuals, the airplane represented the power of artistic creation, liberation, the conquest of spirit over matter, and personal transfiguration. In "'The Surly Bonds of Earth': Images of the
Landscape in the Work of Some Aviator/Authors, 1910–1969," Tom D. Crouch
explores the perceptions and feelings that flight aroused in pilots who also were
writers, especially Charles A. Lindbergh. In "The Airplane and American Literature," Laurence Goldstein argues that the airplane would "be humanity's
preferred emblem of uplifting hope, higher consciousness, and ecstatic revelation" but that it would also be "an ever-changing example of humanity's ability
to shrink time and space and link peoples and nations more efficiently." The airplane also has been an abundant source of inspiration for American artists. In
"'Our Future Is in the Air': Aviation and American Art," Gerald Silk argues
that it influenced American artists in matters of both form and content.

Aviation's relationship with military ideas is one area of the scholarship that
has been well defined. Unfortunately, the connection of those ideas to the technology of aviation, conceptions of national power and nationalism, the role of
popular culture in celebrating military aviation and its technology, and the institutional culture of military organizations that relate to aviation, and so on, is
less well defined. These areas are essential to understanding the cultural significance of aviation's role in war and preparation for war. In "Transforming Technology in the Army Air Corps, 1920–1940: Technology, Politics, and Culture for
Strategic Bombing," Timothy Moy analyzes how, out of a variety of possible
ways of making war, the Army Air Corps chose strategic bombing because it was
characteristic of a modern technology that seemed to suit its mission. Having
chosen a doctrine, the Air Corps sought the technology that would make the
doctrine a reality. In the post–World War II period, the airplane exerted important cultural influence through its ability to deliver nuclear weapons and because
of its pivotal role in the constant state of readiness for war in the 1950s and 1960s.
In "'Peace Is Our Profession': The Bombers Take Over," H. Bruce Franklin
traces the development of a foreboding mindset about nuclear weapons in the
Cold War to its origins in the late 1930s and World War II through Hollywood
films and published fiction. Central to the institutional identity of the U.S. Air
Force during the Cold War was the training and indoctrination of its pilot-
officers. In "Stick and Rudder University: Training and the Creation of the
Flight Suit Officer," John D. Sherwood demonstrates how military history and
social history can come together to provide new perspectives into the workings
of the armed forces. Sherwood contends that in the world of the flight suit offi-

cer, which was created during the Korean War, status among pilots is determined by piloting skills rather than by education or leadership ability.

Thus, *The Airplane in American Culture* exemplifies aspects of a significant twentieth-century technology as it comes in contact with the ebb and flow of cultural forces in American society. It is my hope that the book will serve as an entry into the social and cultural history of aviation, and that it will help to identify areas in which the airplane played a part in the cultural history of the United States. The areas outlined in this collection and other relevant ones could form the basis for a widescale reevaluation of the conceptual framework for the history of aviation. If the book succeeds as an initial attempt to delineate areas of interest for in-depth research in the social-cultural history of aviation, it will have fulfilled my fondest expectations for it.

Notes

1. The term *airplane* may be misleading. Leo Marx has observed that a bias operates in the use of the term *locomotive,* which, he says, was "probably the nineteenth century's leading image of progress," but which "did not adequately represent the manifold character or the complexity of the mechanic art of transporting persons and goods by steam-powered engines moving wagons over a far-flung network of iron rails." The same might be said of *airplane,* which, likewise, does not begin to describe the complex corporate nature of the aviation industry, its organization, people, and capital investment. See Leo Marx, "The Idea of 'Technology' and Postmodern Pessimism," in *Does Technology Drive History? The Dilemma of Technological Determinism,* ed. Merritt Roe Smith and Leo Marx (Cambridge, Mass.: MIT Press, 1995), 244.

2. David L. Lewis and Laurence Goldstein, eds., *The Automobile in American Culture* (Ann Arbor: University of Michigan Press, 1980).

3. James R. Hansen, "Aviation History in the Wider View," *Technology and Culture* (July 1989): 643. Hansen's article is the clearest statement of some of the most glaring deficiencies in the writing of the history of aviation.

4. Peter Novick, *That Noble Dream: "The Objectivity Question" and the American Historical Profession* (New York: Cambridge University Press, 1988), 16–17.

5. See "Introduction," *The U.S. Air Service in World War I,* vol. 1, *The Final Report and a Tactical History,* ed. Maurer Maurer (Maxwell AFB, Ala.: The Albert F. Simpson Historical Research Center, and Washington, D.C.: The Office of Air Force History, 1978), 1–14, for a detailed description of how "Gorrell's History" came to be compiled. Gorrell quoted in Maurer, ed., *U.S. Air Service,* 12.

6. The Jones Chronology is now in the collection of the National Air and Space Museum, Smithsonian Institution, Washington, D.C. Other aeronautical materials collected by Jones are located in the Prints and Photographs Division, Library of Congress, Washington, D.C.; Lauinger Library, Georgetown University, Washington, D.C.; Connecticut Aeronautical Historical Association, Inc., Windsor Locks, Conn., and Air Force Historical Research Agency Maxwell AFB, Ala.

7. "History of the Institute of the Aeronautical Sciences[:] Tenth Anniversary [,] 1939–1942," Organizational Files, Institute of the Aeronautical Sciences, National Air and Space Museum, Smithsonian Institution, Washington, D.C. The Institute of the Aeronautical Sciences (IAS) collection became a fundamental part of the documentary collection of the Smithsonian Institution's National Air and Space Museum. Part of the IAS collection (now called the American Institute of Aeronautics and Astronautics collection) was deposited in the Library of Congress. Other materials from the IAS collection were distributed to the Roswell

Museum and Art Center, Roswell, N.M., Connecticut Aeronautical Historical Association, Windsor Locks, Conn.; the Franklin Institute, Philadelphia, Pa.; and Nassau County Historical Museum, Long Island, N.Y.

8. Wesley Frank Craven and James Lea Cate, eds. *The Army Air Forces in World War II,* vol. I: *Plans and Early Operations, January 1939 to August 1942* (Chicago: University of Chicago Press, 1948), x; quoted in Craven and Cate, xvii; Craven and Cate, xvii.

9. Richard H. Kohn, "Foreword to the New Imprint," Wesley Frank Craven and James Lea Cate, *The Army Air Forces in World War II* (Washington, D.C.: Office of Air Force History, 1983), v–vi.

10. Quoted in Ronald Schaffer, *Wings of Judgment: American Bombing in World War II* (New York: Oxford University Press, 1985), 252–53.

11. Eugene M. Emme, "Space and the Historian," *Spaceflight* (November 1973), 412–13. See W. D. Kay, "Review Essay: NASA and Space History," *Technology and Culture* (January 1999), 120–27, for an assessment of the writing of NASA history.

12. Quotation from Melvin Kranzberg, "At the Start," *Technology and Culture* (winter 1959), 1. For an in-depth analysis of the content of *Technology and Culture,* see John M. Staudenmaier, S.J., *Technology's Storytellers: Reweaving the Human Fabric* (Cambridge, Mass.: MIT Press, 1989).

13. Hansen, 643. This is not to say that modest strides have not been made in writing the history of aviation. In 1978, the Federal Aviation Administration introduced a multivolume history of the FAA and its predecessors, which was lively in its treatment of the bureaucracy and of the ongoing and often bitter struggle between the agency and advocates of general aviation. The aforementioned NASA history program has recently sponsored the New Series in NASA History, published by Johns Hopkins University Press and edited by Roger D. Launius. In W. D. Kay's estimation, this series is not intended "to simply burnish its image in the historical record"; rather, its "range of views presented on topics such as human spaceflight, military space, and commercialization tends to be rather wide" (Kay, 126–27). The newly revised Smithsonian History of Aviation and Spaceflight Series (formerly Smithsonian History of Aviation Series) seeks to publish substantive works that will reshape our conceptions of how aviation and space flight have affected our conceptions of time and distance, our daily routines, and the conduct of exploration, business, and war. Finally, a glimpse at the titles of recent doctoral dissertations on the history of aviation and space flight (some of which are reflected in this volume) encourage one to believe that historical writing on the subject is getting better and better. Perhaps Hansen's call for "synthetic works taking a wider view and looking at social motives, aims, and second-order consequences of the aviation enterprise" will be answered.

14. Joseph J. Corn, *The Winged Gospel: America's Love Affair with the Airplane, 1900–1950* (New York: Oxford University Press, 1983), viii.

15. Corn, 135–36, 141–42.

16. William T. Larkins, "Introduction," *Journal of the American Aviation Historical Society* (spring 1956), 2. A glance at a recent issue of the *Journal* indicates that not much has changed over the lifetime of the organization; aircraft are still its exclusive focus.

17. Hansen, 649. This phenomenon can be attributed partly to the fascination that machines have held for Americans since the earliest days of the Republic. John F. Kasson, *Civilizing the Machine: Technology and Republican Values in America, 1776–1900* (New York: Grossman, 1976), 162, points out that public response to the Corliss engine at the 1876 Philadelphia Exposition had a great deal to do with its size and power: "fairgoers did not approach the engine as an immaculate work of engineering to be judged by its efficiency alone. Rather, in a way characteristic of popular reactions to powerful machinery in the nineteenth century, their descriptions frequently became incipient narratives in which, like some mythological creature, the Corliss engine was endowed with life and all its movements constructed as gestures. The machine emerged as a kind of fabulous automoton—part animal, part machine, part god." Like the Corliss engine, the airplane seems to have assumed a life of its own.

18. Hansen, 647.

19. Alex Roland, "The Impact of War upon Aeronautical Progress: The Experience of the NACA," in *Air Power and Warfare: the Proceedings of the 8th Military History Symposium, United States Air Force Academy, 18–20 October 1978,* ed. Alfred F. Hurley and Robert C. Ehrhart (Washington, D.C.: Office of Air Force History and U.S. Air Force Academy, 1979), 365. I. B. Holley, Jr., "Comment on a Scholar," in Hurley and Ehrhart, *Air Power and Warfare.* (Holley is commenting on Roland's paper and on Robert Perry's "The Interaction of Technology and Doctrine in the USAF," which also appears in the volume.)

20. Roland, 366.

21. John M. Staudenmaier, "Rationality Versus Contingency in the History of Technology," in *Does Technology Drive History? The Dilemma of Technological Determinism,* ed. Merritt Roe Smith and Leo Marx (Cambridge, Mass.: MIT Press, 1995), 265, 266–67, 269.

22. Steve Lubar, "Learning from Technological Things," in W. David Kingery, ed., *Learning from Things: Method and Theory of Material Culture Studies* (Washington, D.C.: Smithsonian Institution Press, 1996), 31.

The Airplane and the American Experience

Roger Bilstein

As one of the leading popular journalists of the early twentieth century, Mark Sullivan's long career also made him one of the most incisive observers of American thought and culture. Between 1927 and 1935, he completed a six-volume study entitled *Our Times: The United States, 1900–1925*. In his capstone volume, he looked back at the remarkable history of America in its first quarter century, and remarked that aviation had been the landmark event in America's cultural evolution. "Of all the agencies that influenced man's mind," Sullivan wrote, "that made the average man of 1925 intellectually different from him of 1900, by far the greatest was the sight of a human being in an airplane."[1]

As a newsman who had covered this tumultuous quarter century, Sullivan's encomium was singularly telling, because—like most of his fellow citizens—he had come reluctantly to accept flight as anything but humanly possible. During 1901, Sullivan responded to an invitation from Alexander Graham Bell to visit Bell's home in Nova Scotia. Bell had already achieved a towering reputation for his development of the electric light bulb and an impressive variety of other technological innovations. When the great man commented that piloted airplanes would someday fly around with cargoes as heavy as a thousand bricks, Sullivan remembered his own unspoken reaction of disbelief. Bell's invention of the telephone certainly qualified him to speak knowledgeably about unusual progress in the future; as an old man, Bell had a further latitude to speculate any way he chose. But to himself, Sullivan thought, "He is talking plain nonsense."[2]

The contrast of Sullivan's comments on human flight highlights the dichotomy of attitudes about aviation during its first quarter century. Despite considerable progress in gliding that pointed the way to human flight in powered aircraft, popular magazines like *McClure's* predicted—early in the twentieth century—that the idea of human flight was destined for about as much success as age-old mathematical attempts to square the circle. During 1903, when the secretary of the august Smithsonian Institution, Samuel Pierpont Langley, failed in two attempts to have his piloted *Aerodrome* fly from a houseboat moored in the Potomac River, the ridicule poured in from leading newspapers across the country. The diatribe included a typically sharp riposte from the iconoclastic Ambrose Bierce: "I don't know how much larger Professor Langley's machine is than his flying model was—about large enough, I think, to require an atmosphere a little denser than the intelligence of one scientist and not quite so dense as that of two."[3]

Even though magazines such as *Popular Science Monthly* (1904) and *Scientific American* (1906) reported on the Wrights' success, recognition came slowly, hindered in part by strong popular skepticism and in part by the reticence of the Wrights to surrender too much information until they felt they had perfected their airplane and flying technique. Recognition, when it came, still remained mixed. During 1907–8, the Wrights negotiated with governments in Europe and finally concluded an agreement to demonstrate their plane for the U.S. War Department. Also, in 1908, the brothers released their own account of how they had achieved powered flight, published as an article in *Century* magazine. The article captivated many young readers such as Charles Fayette Taylor. The fourteen-year-old Taylor pressed the story on his father, who stubbornly refused to accept the idea of human flight, despite the photos printed in the magazine. Just as stubbornly, young Charles remained fascinated by the notion of airplanes, and eventually became a highly respected figure in aeronautical engineering at the Massachusetts Institute of Technology. Nonetheless, the son's fascination in contrast to his father's skepticism characterized the ambivalence about flying machines for many Americans through World War I.[4]

Despite the War Department's interest in aeronautics, neither the Army nor the Navy placed orders large enough to keep pioneer builders such as the Wrights and Glenn Curtiss entirely solvent. Early revenues derived from aerial exhibitions, an activity that began to draw huge crowds to see if flying machines piloted by a daring aerial fraternity of "birdmen" (and women) could actually navigate the skies. Beckwith Havens, a prewar Curtiss exhibition flier, later recalled how such crowds reacted. "They thought you were a fake, you see. There wasn't anybody there who believed [an airplane] would really fly. In fact, they'd give odds. But when you flew, oh my, they'd carry you off the field. . . ." Mixed in with this adulation was a strong dose of morbid expectation to see a fatal crash. Henry H. (Hap) Arnold, as a young army lieutenant, attended the Belmont, New York, meet in 1910. He retained a strong memory of the ghoulish anticipation of many spectators. "The crowd . . . gaped at the wonders, the exhibits of planes from home and abroad, secure in the knowledge that nowhere on earth, between now and suppertime, was there such a good chance of seeing somebody break his neck."[5]

A growing roster of female pilots shared the adulation and dangers of prewar flying meets and long distance records. Harriet Quimby, a writer for *Leslie's Weekly,* became recognized as America's first aviatrix. In 1912, she won international acclaim as the first woman to pilot a plane across the English Channel. Katherine Stinson, Ruth Law, and others joined Quimby in capturing national headlines for daring aerial maneuvers and long-distance records. Although many women who flew in the aerial circuses of the time were genuinely interested in aeronautics and worked devotedly to perfect their flying skills, their presence at aerial events was a boon to promoters. Flying retained a daredevil reputation in popular opinion and feminine pilots heightened the interest, leading to fatter revenues at the ticket office. Stinson survived this flamboyant era; Quimby did not, falling to her death in an aerial demonstration in New York during 1912. Many newspapers and magazines ran critical cartoons and scathing editorials against risky exhibition flying, the lure of big prizes for dangerous flights, and the rising toll of fatalities. As the *Boston Transcript* declared in 1911, "Circus stunts . . . [must] be separated in the public mind from aviation proper, either as a sport or a business."[6]

Although the business of flying centered primarily on pilots of exhibition flights, a few others shared the experience. For a handful of these daring, articulate passengers, flight was truly an exhilarating event. The muckraking journalist Ida Tarbell agreed to an airplane ride in 1913, and gave readers a sense of the awe she experienced. After landing, she remained in her seat, "so overwhelmed was I at the wonder of the thing . . . so supremely superior to any other emotion that I had ever experienced." Through Tarbell's articles and other writing, a generation of twentieth-century Americans also came to view flight as a triumph of human aspirations. As one historian argued, flying machines came to symbolize the promise of twentieth-century technology, a shining promise of the machine age and exemplars of the "gospel of flight."[7]

This positive side of aeronautics found expression in a variety of elements representing aspects of mass, or popular, culture. Feature films with aviation themes flickered to life as early as 1913. Popular music represented an even longer genealogy, appearing as "Chanson sur le globe aerostatique," published in 1785 and featuring a cover illustration of the Montgolfier balloon. Winged planes were immortalized in the 1910 ballad "Come Josephine in My Flying Machine," one of numerous aerial ditties to appear in the prewar years. Although the first children's books began with eighteenth-century kite stories, the appearance of twentieth-century dime novels represented a growing tide of balloon and aviation sagas. The "Boy Aviator" series, launched by a Captain Wilbur Lawton, included a half-dozen titles that followed the young protagonists from the Antarctic to Africa and elsewhere, carried by their redoubtable flying machine, the *Golden Eagle,* "strong of wing and sound of engine." Young readers wanting to build model airplanes could join one of the flying-model clubs that formed in the era, purchase model kits, or follow plans and instructions from references such as the Century Book Company's *The Second Boy's Book of Model Airplanes.*[8]

All of this had a certain aura of innocence about it. A good deal of interest in aviation had to do with benign uses in flying for pleasure, to carry passengers, and to deliver cargo. As late as 1916, after two years of aerial warfare in Europe, the editor of *Flying* magazine praised airplanes as forces of "progress and enlightenment" rather than instruments of terror. As the carnage in Europe neared its end in 1918, Orville Wright wrote optimistically to a friend, "The Aeroplane has made war so terrible that I do not believe any country will again care to start a war."[9]

All the same, both European and American interests in applying aviation to military campaigns had early origins. Manned reconnaissance balloons appeared in the 1860s during the American Civil War and overseas during the Franco–Prussian War of 1870. After gaining confidence in their original machine, the Wrights themselves contacted the War Department about military contracts in 1904. Many of the early air meets included "bombing" demonstrations, and the U.S. Army organized its first aerial units in 1914. Following early wartime applications in reconnaissance and photography, airplanes in World War I evolved as deadly fighting machines in the form of single-seat fighters and large multiengine bombers that carried out attacks on military targets such as railroads in urban areas, the sort of campaign that brought indiscriminate terror to ordinary civilians who happened to be in the vicinity of such raids. The relative impersonality of these bombing campaigns by formations of many planes meant that fliers received little notoriety as individuals, although the strain of combat took its toll on crews. It was different, however, for fighter pilots. Even American schoolboys knew something about the exploits of Manfred von Richthofen, the "Red Baron" of Germany, whose string of eighty aerial victories made him a mythical figure by the time of his own death in the air in 1918. Americans had their own "ace of aces" by war's end—Eddie Rickenbacker, with twenty-five victories. The term "victory" was, of course, a euphemism that cloaked the more malign term, "kill." In this context, however, even the euphemistic term "victory" for the killing of some other flier marked the end of innocence involving Americans and the airplane.

There was another, subtle alteration in America's relationship with aviation during the war, and this had to do with mass production. In this case, headlines and cartoons promised a host of airplanes as a multitude of avenging angels to attack the dreaded Hun in Europe. Mass production was, after all, a fundamental principle of America's industrial strength. The Germans themselves thoroughly respected this manufacturing threat, and attempted to counter it with their own industrial scheme, christened, revealingly, as the "Amerikaprogram." The powerful image of aviation as technological avenger thus appeared in more than one guise, and became a part of the aeronautical mythology of the interwar years.[10]

The interwar era included this increasingly paradoxical attitude about aviation as both malign and benign factor in human life. The early postwar period witnessed several milestones in aviation developments. Air mail service, begun during the war as a means to train pilots and stimulate aircraft production, survived an uncertain start to become one of the marvels of its day. By 1924, with beacons to light the way over nighttime sections of air mail routes, fliers in open-cockpit biplanes carried mail between the Atlantic and Pacific coasts in twenty-four hours. This remarkable performance saved some two days in transcontinental mail deliveries, with immense benefits to banking, commerce, and communications generally. As a destroyer of time/distance barriers, airplanes had begun to reshape intercontinental concepts as well. In May 1919, the dogged crew of a U.S. Navy plane, the three-motored NC-4 flying boat, managed to fly the Atlantic in stages by reaching the Azores, continuing on to Portugal and then Britain. Flying a converted World War I bomber, an equally determined British crew made a nonstop, transatlantic flight the next month, crossing from New-foundland to Ireland. The Army Air Service organized a series of pioneering cross-country and transcontinental flights, with additional forays to Alaska and through the Caribbean. In 1924, a pair of Air Service planes completed the first aerial circumnavigation of the world. Achievements such as these, along with air mail service, gave substance to Louis Sullivan's remark about the significance of flight to the "average man" of 1925.[11]

Many others seemed to agree, including aviation journalists as well as professional engineers and writers in the popular press. Looking back on the past impact of transport technologies such as steamships and railroad, and considering the horrors of World War I, authors often felt that aviation would be a good thing. As the editor of *Aerial Age Weekly* noted in 1919, "the speed that we will realize by the aeroplane air route will bring that commingling of nations we are all striving for . . ." resulting in the eradication of antagonisms and warfare. Writing in the *Journal of the Society of Automotive Engineers,* another author declared national boundaries might well be eliminated by the airplane. "There will . . . be no east or west," he declared, "and with the new aerial age will come a new internationalism founded on speedy communication and good will toward all mankind." The same sentiment was echoed in popular journals such as *Living Age,* which ran an aggressively optimistic article, "Aviation and World Brotherhood," in 1919. In 1927, Charles Lindbergh's solo flight across the Atlantic solidified the sort of outlook expressed by Sullivan and others. In a singular affirmation printed in an American publication, J.J. Jusserand, French ambassador to the United States from 1902 to 1925, articulated the new spirit of international amity triggered by Lindbergh's flight. Writing for the *Review of Reviews,* Jusserand recalled some thoughts expressed in an essay by the chemist Pierre Marcelin Berthelot just before his death in 1907. Of all the inventions destined to make great changes in the world, Berthelot had written, surely one of the most significant was the airplane. In the mastery of the air, there would be no more frontiers to separate nations. Lindbergh, continued Jusserand, had demonstrated just that; the *Spirit of St. Louis* had inaugurated a new state of human relations.[12]

The decade of the 1920s witnessed remarkable growth in technological features such as the automobile, electricity, radio, motion pictures, and a cornucopia of domestic hardware and appliances. Some observers of the phenomenon considered aviation to be an embodiment of this collective progress. Indeed, to many people, the swift, high-flying airplane epitomized the promise of a technological age. Driving to the airfield to watch the preparations for the 1927 transatlantic flights, the essayist and literary critic Gilbert Seldes followed the highway through a gritty, bleak industrial area, succeeded, in turn, by the "tasteless monotony" of colonies of workers' homes. It left him depressed until suddenly he reached the flying field. An airplane, said Seldes, never failed to take hold of his imagination; his spirits lifted at the sight of a sky alive with aircraft. Each time one rose into the air he always wished he were a part of it. An airplane possessed fragility and grace—and dazzling speed to whisk it over the horizon. A dwindling speck, it turned; a polished surface of the wing reflected a waning ray of daylight like a window flaming in the setting sun. An aircraft embodied an anomaly of the prosaic notations of equations, wood, fabric, engine, and gasoline that produced the wonder and thrill of throwing off the bonds of earth. Even when reduced to the dollars-and-cents process of making a living, the nobility of aircraft in flight rose above the inanity and grossness of commercialism. "There is no ugliness, no monotony, no grasping," proclaimed Seldes. "They represent one of the ideals toward which commercialism and industry and mechanical progress can move; they are a triumph of applied science and a triumph of the human spirit at the same time. Watching them, you can forget mean streets and mean bickerings. Here is something better than machinery and better than man."[13]

Denying the charge that the machine age was eroding historic skills of the workman, Stuart Chase, a trenchant observer of the urban scene, reminded critics that, even though a certain number of trades were made obsolete, the advance of technology spawned new jobs as it proceeded. Moreover, Chase continued, the personal skills of the workman continued to find a place in the modern age. The aviation technology of the twenties, for example, put a high premium on the craftsman's intimate technique. Building an airplane required the time-honored vocations of cabinetmakers, tinsmiths, coppersmiths, and even seamstresses. The careful work they lavished on each "plane" imparted to it an individuality compounded of skilled craftsmanship, knowledge, and love. In a supreme compliment to these workmen of the machine age, Chase commented reflectively, "Somehow they put me in mind of the builders of Chartres." Then he admitted with regret, "It is sad to think of mass production hanging, like a sword of Damocles, above their heads."[14]

Even though the skills of the airplane workmen were doomed to give way to the spreading regimen of assembly-line technique, Chase hastened to reassure the pessimists that it was not wise to become too maudlin. In spite of the massive standardization of volume production, modern technology had the promise of producing a sound airplane that was practically priced and foolproof to boot. Moreover, "a standardized airplane need send no hostages to loveliness." The medium of the sky in which an aircraft functioned demanded the precision of a micrometer and the glossy finish of a buffing tool. It was possible that these machines could turn out a more appropriate and graceful ship than craftsmen ever could.[15] Individualism? It lived on in an age of power and the machine. The qualities of individualism had not been obliterated; they were recognized now in relation to the machine age. Charles Lindbergh, tending to a machine over three thousand miles of open sea, was so closely bound to his plane that he spoke to audiences not of himself alone but of "we." He felt a sense of kinship with his plane, said Chase, and people loved him the more for it. Nobody called Lindbergh a robot.[16] The social critic Lewis Mumford repeated an aspect of these sentiments in terms of aviation's relation to other fields of engineering. Although he commented that surface travel from outlying airfields to the city center consumed valuable time and worried about military aviation as an element of heightened international tensions,[17] aviation represented a positive facet of modernity. Aeronautical engineering set the standards for refined and exact engineering, ranging from bridges, to cranes, to the steel sinews of twentieth-century skyscrapers.[18]

Thus, most Americans seemed to accept the airplane as a symbol of technology, the result of the mating of two sciences, theoretical and applied, and also as a symbol that promised additional qualitative benefits. Lindbergh's flight could be interpreted as an aspect of the promise of the machine age while encompassing elements of the traditional concepts of the American heritage of individualism. Lindbergh epitomized the daring pioneer, striking out alone, an underdog challenging and conquering the hostile elements of nature and escaping the limitations of society. He was the self-sufficient individual who had settled the United States—the new technological citizen cast in the mold of the independent, moral Yankee character. Lindbergh's flight symbolized individual achievement within the framework of the age of technology. There were new frontiers to conquer in the contemporary world. The challenges of that world were met by society adapting itself to the technological discipline of the machine.[19] Lindbergh's conquest of the Atlantic became a metaphor for the mastery of the complexities of the twentieth century.[20]

During the 1930s, a new generation of modern airliners appeared. As low-

winged monoplanes became equipped with carefully cowled engines, retractable landing gear, and refined aerodynamic contours they became icons of
the decade. The Boeing 247, installed as a special exhibit for the 1933 Chicago
World's Fair, drew thousands of wide-eyed onlookers. This plane, along with
the Douglas DC-3, which entered airline service in 1936, delineated the standard
shape of virtually all stylized aircraft represented by illustrators and designers of
the 1930s and 1940s. Norman Bel Geddes, one of the era's leading industrial designers, unabashedly followed an aviation mode. "Keats wrote a few immortal
lines about a Grecian urn," Bel Geddes mused. "Had he known about it and felt
like it, he would have written them about an airplane." A fellow practitioner,
Walter Dorwin Teague, was even more explicit: "A Douglas Transport plane
presents a thrilling aspect of complete unification . . . yet in spite of this superb
unity there is no monotony whatever in its aspect." For many such observers and
social critics, modern aeronautics represented a positive image, symbolizing the
best of American ingenuity and technology in what has been called the "streamline era" of industrial design. Although the concept of streamlining seems to
have entered the realm of industrial design by way of aerodynamically shaped
railway engines, the airplane came to embody the best of the streamline style in
terms of lightness, economy of design, and use of modern materials such as aluminum. As the social critic Lewis Mumford noted in *Technics and Civilization*
(1934), aeronautical design set the standards for refined and exact engineering.
For Mumford, aircraft also represented a desirable aesthetic logic. In 1938, he
developed the script for *The City,* one of the landmark documentary films produced during the New Deal era. Toward the end of the film, narration and images urged the need for better urban planning and emphasized that a better life
was possible. In a cinematic climax, the camera focused on a DC-3 as it taxied
into position, accelerated, and soared majestically into the sky. Above the
crescendo of Aaron Copland's score, the narrator instructed the audience, "Science takes flight at last—for human goals." The plane represented an attainable
aspiration for modern urban environments, "molded to human wants as planes
are shaped for speed."[21]

   With greater frequency, airliners and the airline industry appeared as a positive icon in support of other consumer items. Implicit in such presentations was
the idea that if a product was used in the airline industry, which had high standards of quality and reliability, then the product was more than qualified for use
by ordinary folks in more pedestrian endeavors. During 1939 and 1940, for example, magazines such as the *Saturday Evening Post* carried a variety of ads for
automotive lubricants and spark plugs in which the vendor stressed the products' use in the aviation field as well. The cachet of aeronautical association was
carried into sales for a variety of other consumer products, from "Wings" brand
shirts, to raincoats chosen by airline crews, to special, lightweight typewriters de-

signed especially for air travelers, but obviously highly desirable for the average consumer who wanted only the best. For smokers, the fact that Lucky Strike cigarettes were endorsed by airline ground crews, traffic tower personnel, and pilots made it eminently clear that the rest of the public should choose the brand used by those who invariably purchased only the best products.[22]

By the early 1940s, air travel emerged as an acknowledged form of transportation, even for those who had not been aboard an airliner. In the final sequences from the classic film *Casablanca,* released in 1942, Humphrey Bogart and Ingrid Bergman played a dramatic farewell scene at a fog-shrouded airfield in Morocco. Customarily, stock cinematic farewells occurred at train stations or ship dockyards. The choice of an airfield underscored the increasingly recognizable symbol of aviation in contemporary life. There seemed to be a covert theme as well. The plot of the film included a strong sense of menace, related to the recent fall of France and the all-too-real threat of Nazi Germany. Air power had already been applied for tragic bombardment during the Spanish Civil War (1936–39) and used against historic European cities throughout the continent and across the English Channel into Britain. Ingrid Bergman's airline flight carried her to presumed safety; nonetheless, the appearance of the airplane in the context of warfare's maelstrom of urgency, danger, and personal loss hinted at aviation's new role as part of the madness of conflict.

For all the optimistic assumptions about aviation's role in promoting peace in the decades after World War I, the perceived needs of national security relentlessly drove the evolution of military aviation.

The role of aviation in national security received peacetime headlines during the bombing trials of 1921, when General Billy Mitchell led a flight of open-cockpit bombers that sank a variety of target ships, including the ex-German cruiser *Frankfort* and the battleship *Ostfriesland.* The dramatic sinking of the supposedly impregnable *Ostfriesland* sparked a lively debate in the press about the implications of aerial attack. Mitchell's subsequent book, *Winged Defense,* emphasized that air power had negated America's geographic isolation from Europe and Asia. To protect America's Atlantic and Pacific frontiers, the country needed to acquire aerial defense capability. Following Lindbergh's transatlantic crossing, even the normally dovish *New Republic* noted the significance of aviation in international power politics and endorsed a larger role for aeronautics in the interests of national security. Heywood Broun exemplified the often paradoxical hope and fear about aviation's role and world peace. The airplane could demolish national boundaries and geographic barriers on the way to assist the evolution of global amity. "The vision of a united world is no longer fantastic," he wrote in 1929. At the same time, the state of aeronautical application in the 1920s seemed to give it more of a warlike nature. "At the moment the score stands against the new invention," Broun muttered. "There is blood upon the fuselage."[23]

During the 1920s, the U.S. Navy built its first aircraft carriers and began the development of doctrine as well as specialized torpedo-bombers to conduct both offensive and defensive missions. The U.S. Army Air Service became the Air Corps and eventually the U.S. Army Air Force (June 1941) in a series of bureaucratic and equipment upgrades throughout the interwar years. During the mid-1930s, the air force launched development of very large, four-engine aircraft leading to the famous B-17 and B-24 long-range bombers of World War II; planning for the advanced B-29 bomber started in 1939. The theoretical paradoxes of the interwar years—aeronautical development as a positive global force while concurrently improving military capability for mass destruction—now became literal with the advent of World War II. Aviation could, indeed, bring nations closer and reduce tensions. On the other side of the coin, a hostile country could just as easily use aeronautical technology to attack nations whose geographical sanctity was now at risk because of the new reality of winged warfare.

The development of large bombers raised certain moral issues in terms of mass destruction of urban areas and the inevitable loss of civilian life. As a neutral in the early stages of World War II, Americans rationalized destructive aerial technology as a stark deterrent. In the summer of 1941, Frank Cunningham became the first magazine feature writer to inspect the Douglas XB-19, a true giant of the air that dwarfed both the B-17 and the latter's progenitor, the XB-15. Cunningham recalled his impression of the XB-19 as "this hell on wings, this mechanical bird of prey which hurls the defiance of American aviation at enemies which threaten our country." Destruction of enemy cities and populations could be accepted because the enemy deserved it. An early wartime poster, issued to encourage American aircraft production, showed a winsome young girl with her Raggedy Ann doll, looking skyward. The bold slogan above her read: "Please Keep the Bombs Away!" Indeed, this seemed to be a predominant theme throughout much of the war. American bombers, hitting hard at the enemy, would shorten the war, reducing Allied combat losses as well as massive civilian casualties.[24]

There was, nonetheless, debate on the issue. Early in 1944, the *New York Times* gave front-page coverage to a tract written by Vera Brittain, a British pacifist. She questioned claims that bombing German cities had shortened the war; in the meantime, innocent civilians suffered horribly. Subsequent letters to the editor included one from writer MacKinlay Kantor that bombing rightfully punished aggression and also served as a warning for future deterrents. Others advocated less bombing and more effective propaganda campaigns aimed at Germany. Most Americans seemed to agree with the liberal weekly *New Republic,* which deplored bombing simply for the sake of terror, but suggested that the issue was moot because, as the historian Michael Sherry phrased it, "there were no defenseless people in modern wars." By the end of the conflict, when the atomic bombs on Hiroshima and Nagasaki had ushered in the age of nuclear warfare, American views on bombing had taken on a more cautionary note. An editorial for the August 20, 1945, issue of *Life* magazine declared, "Every step in the bomber's progress since 1937 has been more cruel than the last. From the very concept of strategic bombing, all the developments—night, pattern, saturation, area, indiscriminate—have led straight to Hiroshima." Hanson Baldwin, the well-known military analyst for *Life* and the *New York Times,* worried that the U.S. Army Air Force had been so effective in its campaign of aerial warfare that the very name of America had "become a synonym for destruction."[25]

Even before the war had reached its conclusion, the significance of aeronautics seemed to stand out as a major technological phenomenon that would influence the postwar era. The role of military aviation had been dramatic; even though nobody wanted to see the devastation of conventional bombing repeated, it existed as a factor to be considered in the postwar years. After Hiroshima and Nagasaki, the threat of nuclear weapons made assessment of postwar air power even more compelling. In a different context, the role of global air transport held great promise, although aspects of national pride and competition raised prickly issues.

One of the first assessments of these realities appeared as early as 1941, when *Fortune* magazine dedicated its entire March issue to the overall theme of "Air Power as World Power." The editors ran articles that addressed aspects of combat aviation, including strategic bombing, but also noted the promise of revolutionized world travel via global air routes. Following Pearl Harbor, American armed forces increasingly relied on the Air Transport Command to provide such services for high-priority mail and high-level travelers involved in the war effort. Within a year, the Air Transport Command embraced all six continents, and its planes put any spot on the globe only sixty hours away from the United States. At one point during the war, one of its planes took off every thirteen minutes to cross the Atlantic. Given the new realities of air power and air travel, the public and educators alike became fascinated by what was called the "Air Age World." Within the Department of Commerce, the Assistant Secretary of Commerce for Air, Robert Hinckley, cooperated with the Institute of Aeronautical Sciences to develop a roster of appropriate books for use by teachers and high school students. Produced by the distinguished Macmillan publishing house, the "Air Age Education Series" ran to some twenty books and covered everything from math and weather to biology, geography, and literature. One of the titles, prepared by the editor, Professor N. L. Engelhardt of Teachers College of Columbia University, captured the flavor of the series in its didactic title, *Education for the Air Age.*[26]

Other wartime titles underscored an acknowledged impact of flight for the war as well as the postwar world. In 1944, the Brookings Institution published a

two-volume study, *America Faces the Air Age,* symbolic of the scholarly community's awareness of the subject. Leaders in the aviation community also acknowledged these issues. In the Thirty-Third Wilbur Wright Memorial Lecture, delivered in London on May 31, 1945, the Commerce Department's
Administrator for Aeronautics, Theodore P. Wright, entitled his remarks, "Aviation's Place in Civilization." Wright commented that the destructiveness of air
power could act as a deterrent to future conflicts, and expressed an optimistic
opinion that international conferences, facilitated by air travel, would greatly
contribute to world peace. Further scholarly interest in the impact of aviation
found expression in the postwar journal *Air Affairs,* beginning publication in
1946. In succeeding years, authors came from academe, upper echelons of the
federal bureaucracy, and leading international commentators; topics touched on
expanding aviation and airline activities, air warfare in the nuclear age, and the
political implications of a postwar world shrunk in time by long distance aircraft. The issues of postwar politics in the nuclear age continued to draw the attention of policy makers in Washington. In 1947, President Harry Truman
named a special Air Policy Commission, chaired by Thomas K. Finletter. The
Finletter Committee, as it became known, issued its final report in 1948. Its portentous title, *Survival in the Air Age,* made its concerns explicit, and it called for
increased aeronautical research as well as a bigger U.S. Air Force.[27]

At about the same time, an overhaul of the nation's military establishment
made the U.S. Army's aviation component into a separate service. Headed by a
Secretary of the Air Force, the new entity joined the Army Secretary and Navy
Secretary as an equal under the collective umbrella of the Department of Defense. The Cold War era brought expanded activities, with U.S. Air Force bases
located at strategic locations around the globe. During World War II, this dis-
persal of American military aviation had been logical. After 1945, the continua-
tion of a strong military presence in a peacetime situation—especially in areas
such as Europe and the Mediterranean, with major bases in Japan and elsewhere
in the Far East—represented a historic departure in the country's military pos-
ture. Much of this accentuated American commitments to the North Atlantic
Treaty Organization (NATO) and other postwar regional security agreements.

International tensions and the outbreak of limited wars often highlighted the
role of U.S. Air Force personnel and aircraft in the Cold War environment. A
number of motion pictures embodied a strong sense of patriotic sacrifice and
duty. *The Big Lift* (1950) portrayed the role of air transport in supporting the
blockaded city of Berlin during the 1948–49 winter when communist forces cut
off all surface access. Airlift was depicted in a crucial and benign role for delivering food, medicine, fuel, and clothing to the beleaguered city. With a plot based
on the Korean War, *The Bridges at Toko-Ri* (1954) combined combat sequences
with a sensitive portrayal of friendship and family ties under the pressure of

wartime traumas. *Strategic Air Command* (1955) captured impressive flight sequences of the operations of Strategic Air Command (SAC) and employed a
script that depicted the impact of Cold War military assignments on family ties.
A later Cold War film, *Apocalypse Now,* appeared as a strong indictment of the
Vietnam conflict. The destructive role of aviation in the war was embodied in
one sequence in which helicopters demonstrated the devastating effects of aerial onslaughts. Flying in over an azure sea, white surf, and tropical beaches, the
attacking choppers formed a malevolent wave of dark shapes. They appeared as
a presentiment of death, and the hollow beat of helicopter rotors was repeated in
a sinister counterpoint that frequently intruded into the film.

Apocalypse Now reflected the dark side of military aviation in the Cold War
era, a theme raised in several earlier films. The issue of a nuclear holocaust shad-
owed American society in the postwar era, a stark possibility in the case of misunderstanding or miscalculation on the part of superpower protagonists America and the former Soviet Union. In the context of air power, *Fail Safe* (1964)
portrayed a wrenching decision by the U.S. president to bomb New York City
to placate the Soviets after an American nuclear bomber, having surpassed all of
the "fail-safe" sequences to prevent such incidents, dropped an atomic bomb on
Moscow. At the end of the film, this chilling tit-for-tat scenario presumably
saved the world; in Stanley Kubrick's black comedy *Dr. Strangelove: Or How I
Learned to Stop Worrying and Love the Bomb* (1964), the world was not so lucky.
A nuclear bomber strike against the Soviet Union, engineered by a fanatical Air
Force officer, successfully escaped efforts by doomsday generals and crazed mil-
itary advisers to stop it.[28]

The haunting fear of such mistakes or the even more daunting specter of
massive nuclear strikes against the United States spurred efforts to prepare the
civilian population for this reality. Designated buildings throughout the country
bore large orange-and-black signs that identified them as nuclear bomb shelters.
A cottage industry developed in the printing and sale of plans for modern American families to build fallout shelters in their basements or backyards. Some
firms sold prefabricated shelters with built-in electrical appliances and filters to
cleanse atomically poisoned air. The pervasive orange signs and the reality of
family fallout shelters made cautionary novels and films seem all too real.[29]

By contrast, the air travel industry after 1945 mirrored a much more positive
image, especially in terms of the fascination about the rapidity of air travel and
the concomitant ability to visit distant places within the limits of ten-day or two-
week vacation periods that were increasingly common in the postwar era. The
pages of *Holiday* magazine carried more and more air travel ads, such as one
sponsored by the Glenn L. Martin Company in 1947. The ad copy stressed the
fact that airlines were in the business of selling time. At airports and travel agencies, "alert Americans [are] buying an hour, a day, a week," and these opportu-

nities enhanced the enjoyment of a weekend, permitted a longer vacation, or benefited a business trip. Some aviation ads solicited avid anglers to consider unique fishing adventures all over the world, not just close to home. The airlines also weighed in with travel ads inviting readers to escape the rigors of winter weather. American Air Lines encouraged people to board its "Sun Country" routes to the Gulf and to the Southwestern regions of the United States. Pan Am and others presented opportunities to book December flights in order to enjoy the paradox of "Summer!" in South America. TWA reminded travelers to consider its holiday routes such as the "Flight before Christmas" on its December connections across the United States or overseas to Europe.[30]

Increasingly, the film industry turned to air travel themes as a box-office draw. MGM's *Three Guys Named Mike* featured airliner crews as leading figures and included details of airline operations for the pilots and stewardesses alike. Jane Wyman, one of the leading actresses in the film, cooperated in promotional releases that praised the work of stewardesses for their poise and sophistication on the job. Even if the majority of Americans had not flown in an airliner during the 1950s, the idea obviously was judged to have a popular appeal for movie audiences and mirrored the way in which airline travel had become a recognized factor in modern life.[31]

Coach-class fares became commonplace on domestic U.S. routes during the late 1940s and appeared on oceanic routes during the 1950s. In 1951, domestic airline passengers exceeded railway Pullman travelers for the first time. By 1957, airline passenger miles surpassed those of both trains and busses, making airlines the nation's leading intercity passenger carrier. In 1956, more travelers between America and Europe went by air than traveled by sea. For international travel, traditional gateways such as New York and San Francisco were joined by a variety of inland cities such as Chicago and Houston, creating new travel markets for the airlines as well as exciting travel prospects for business and pleasure passengers.[32]

Nonetheless, for many years after the war, flying remained a comparatively expensive way to travel, even for coach-class passengers. A visit to major airports in the early postwar era revealed waiting areas and boarding gates crowded with well-dressed travelers. Airport restaurants, such as the Cloud Room at Houston's Hobby Airport, were regarded as upscale dining establishments—a place to see and be seen, a place to take visiting relatives to make an impression. Over time, the perceived glamour of air travel began to pale. Inexorably, the crush of air travelers had its impact on the Cloud Room and other high-toned establishments as the democratization of air travel changed the demography of airline clientele.[33]

Business activities and the relatively low costs of economy airfares drew thousands of Americans to domestic and foreign airline travel. The internationally acclaimed social critic Max Lerner referred to the new phenomenon in his book *America as a Civilization,* published in 1957. "The new Air Age, whose impact is just beginning to be felt, has further heightened the mobility of Americans," Lerner wrote. Airplanes would not replace cars, Lerner said, but planes would certainly change travel patterns, and create a greater democratization of travel. In Lerner's words, "What the Air Age has done has been to make the far-away vacation possible for the boss's secretary as well as for the boss."[34]

Democratization occurred on domestic as well as international routes, but it was the latter that produced some of the more striking patterns. Before the war, transoceanic leisure travel by steamship consumed many days of time. Only the wealthy elite could afford the expense or allocate the several weeks required to arrive in Europe, see the sights, and venture home again. Postwar transatlantic flights permitted a ten-day vacation to fit both the pocketbook and allotted vacation time for an astonishing cross-section of travelers. The international hotel magnate Conrad Hilton put it succinctly. "What used to be a month-long vacation trip is now almost a week-end possibility. . . . The airplane is here to stay." Economy fares, package tours, and resort hotels run by American companies offered white-collar and blue-collar travelers affordable and reassuringly modern American conveniences.[35]

The arrival of jets during the 1960s enlarged the range of affluent, footloose Yankees. Midwestern couples who might have summered in the Black Hills of South Dakota now jetted off to snorkel around the Seychelles in the Indian Ocean. By 1970, five million Americans made annual treks somewhere abroad, and only 3 percent went by sea. The historian Daniel Boorstin wrote that "the United States was the first nation in history so many of whose citizens could go so far simply in quest of fun and culture. The size of this phenomenon made international travel, for the first time, a major element in world trade."[36]

By the 1950s, the airplane had become an accepted feature of contemporary American life as well as an icon of its cultural heritage and its legacy to the world at large. Max Lerner's milestone study, *America as a Civilization,* acknowledged aviation's continuing aesthetic influence on the nation's physical psyche. "In contrast to the auto, the American airplane best illustrates the best in American design. Every element of it is shaped and built for speed, engineering, reliability, and safety. There are no frills or unnecessary gadgets," Lerner approvingly noted. "Yet—or perhaps therefore—the beauty of the airplane has scarcely been surpassed in the history of industrial design."[37]

Even if Americans did not interpret their physical world from Lerner's perspective, the image of aviation surfaced repeatedly in advertisements, motion pictures, and fiction. Aviation figured in the imagination of both young and old, as readers of daily newspapers followed the exploits of aerial heroes.

During the years prior to World War II, a series of aeronautical comic strips appeared, partly because of the era's penchant for escapism and partly because of the rapid evolution of aviation and its recognition by the American public. Zack Mosley's "Smilin' Jack" survived the Depression era and persevered well into the postwar decades. Mosley perfected a standard formula for his hero to best the machinations of sky pirates, outlast vicious storms, and skillfully bring a crippled airplane to a safe landing. Along the way, Mosley's strip passed along considerable aeronautical lore as well as subtle commentary on the practicality of aviation, primarily in the civil sector. Although the character of "Smilin' Jack" became involved with a variety of national security adventures during the war, other cartoon heroes made their mark in full-time military service. "Terry and the Pirates," by Milton Caniff, introduced its lead character as a somewhat desultory adventurer in China, eventually joining the Flying Tigers early in the war and finally gravitating into the regular U.S. Army Air Forces. Terry's adventures graphically paralleled wartime headlines, creating an audience appeal that made it a popular feature in both daily and Sunday newspapers. The U.S. Navy boasted a counterpart hero in Roy Crane's "Buzz Sawyer." During the 1930s, Crane's early strip, "Captain Easy," featured a character who operated as an aerial soldier-of-fortune; the evolution of Crane's and Caniff's strips mirrored a popular conception of aviation as an exotic, daring venture, one that naturally merged into the military experience. In 1946, Caniff turned over his original comic strip to a new illustrator and launched a new story, "Steve Canyon." The postwar era of Cold War confrontations involved both Steve Canyon and Buzz Sawyer (as military officers) in action and diplomatic adventures that often entailed propagandistic themes for the military services. Pentagon officials supported such messages and courted the cartoonists whose strips reached millions of readers every day. At one point after the war, "Steve Canyon" was carried by newspapers in over six hundred American cities as well as in seventeen countries overseas. Through such comic strips, the world of aviation took shape in the imaginations of uncounted individuals.[38]

Whether old or new, examples of the persistence of flight in the popular imagination continued to show up in American culture. These examples may vary, but military themes clearly play a strong role. In postwar literature, one such aspect appeared in James Thurber's wry short story "The Secret Life of Walter Mitty." A shy, postwar urbanite, the docile Walter Mitty indulges himself through a catalog of daydreams in which he plays heroic roles. One of his fantasy epics places Mitty in the cockpit of a World War II fighter, where he unerringly shoots down malevolent enemy aircraft while saving Western civilization. Thurber's image of the fighter pilot as a dashing hero has surfaced in a variety of American fictional devices, from cartoons (Snoopy as a World War I aerial knight) to films such as *Top Gun* (1986), which portrayed the demanding world of jet fighter pilots. The allure of aerial combat is embodied in commercial operations that put civilian hopefuls in the cockpits of actual planes; with an instructor in the rear seat, aspiring "aces" can square off against each other in mock dogfights. At the adventure's end, a debriefing completes the experience, and the fee of several hundred dollars includes an inflight video filmed from a gun-camera position. Walter Mitty lives on.[39]

The more routine world of civil aviation may not have inspired the avalanche of nostalgia that seems to attend military subjects, although the collectors of airline memorabilia continue to grow in number. The airlines themselves revived as a fascinating topic during the era of jet transport expansion from the 1960s onward. Arthur Hailey's novel *Airport* became a film—*Airport* (1970)—with a strong cast that included Burt Lancaster and Helen Hayes (whose performance won her an Oscar for best supporting actress). Although the plot centered on a potential disaster during attempts to land a damaged airliner in a snowstorm, this film (and others) reflected the public's fascination with the glamorous new air travel industry. The appeal of air travel also was reflected in the extremely popular Barbie dolls that figured in the childhood of thousands of young girls. During the 1960s and 1970s, Barbie doll characters progressed from stewardesses and airline personnel to pilots and astronauts. In 1995, the Smithsonian Institution's National Air and Space Museum acknowledged the Barbie phenomenon with an exhibit of Barbie dolls as related to the aviation and airline industry. The exhibit was as much a symbol of continuing adult fascination with the subject of flight as it was a reminder of youthful interest in dolls and make-believe.[40]

By way of myriad sources—print, illustration, film, cartoon, toys, radio, and personal travel—images of flight remain part and parcel of the American experience and its popular imagination.

Notes

1. Mark Sullivan, *Our Times: The United States, 1900–1925* (New York: C. Scribner's Sons, 1927), vol. II, 556–57. In preparing this synthetic essay, I have drawn material from some of my earlier books and articles. I wish to acknowledge permissions from editors at the University of Georgia Press, Johns Hopkins University Press, and the Smithsonian Institution Press.

2. Ibid., 558, note 1.

3. For a sampling of news accounts mentioning Langley, see Harold U. Faulkner, *The Quest for Social Justice, 1898–1914* (New York: Macmillan, 1931), 137–38; Mark Sullivan, *Our Times*, II, 562–67, which is the source of the Bierce quote.

4. Fred C. Kelly, *The Wright Brothers: A Biography Authorized by Orville Wright* (New York: Harcourt, Brace, 1943), 105–11, 117–19, 143–46; Charles Fayette Taylor, "Aircraft Propulsion: A Review of Powerplants," Smithsonian Institution, *Annual Report* (1962), 251. For a definitive history of the Wrights and aeronautics of the era, see Tom D. Crouch, *The Bishop's Boys: A Life of the Wright Brothers* (New York: W. W. Norton, 1989).

5. Interview of Beckwith Havens, housed in The Oral History Collection of Columbia University, New York City; Henry H. Arnold, *Global Mission* (New York: Harper & Brothers, 1941), 14.

6. Newspaper quote cited in "Immorality of Aviation," *Current Literature* 50 (February 1911), 126–27. For a colorful and informative survey of women in aviation, see Valerie Moolman, *Women Aloft* (Alexandria, Va.: Time-Life Books, 1981).

7. Ida M. Tarbell, "Flying—Dream Come True," *American Magazine* 76 (November 1913), 66. For a discourse on flight as inspiration, see Joseph J. Corn, *The Winged Gospel: America's Romance with Aviation, 1900–1950* (New York: Oxford University Press, 1983).

8. Wilbur Lawton, *The Boy Aviators' Treasure Quest* (New York: Hurst and Company, 1910), copy in author's collection; "How to Make a Model Airplane," *Scientific American* 105 (October 14, 1911), 334, 355. Musical themes can be analyzed in the Bella C. Landauer Collection, National Air and Space Museum, Smithsonian Institution. The museum also holds an extensive collection of juvenile books, as does the Ross-Barrett Historical Aeronautics Collection at the Denver, Colorado, Public Library.

9. O. Wright to Dr. Wallace C. Sabine (November 7, 1918), in Marvin McFarland, ed., *The Papers of Wilbur and Orville Wright* (New York, 1953), vol. II, 1104–5, 1121. See also Roger E. Bilstein, "Attitudes toward Aviation in the United States, 1910–1925" (M.A. thesis, Ohio State University, 1960).

10. Lee Kennett, *The First Air War, 1914–1918* (New York: Free Press, 1991), includes many relevant comments on popular responses, with remarks on combat fliers such as Richthofen. Dominick Pisano, et al., *Legend, Memory and the Great War in the Air* (Seattle: University of Washington Press, 1992), represents a wealth of information including aspects of attitudes on production.

11. For a survey and commentary on these and related events, see Roger E. Bilstein, *Flight Patterns: Trends of Aeronautical Development in the United States, 1918–1929* (Athens: University of Georgia Press, 1983).

12. G. Douglas Wardrop, "War Aviation in Retrospect: Commercial Aviation in Prospect," *Journal of the Engineers Club of Philadelphia and Affiliated Societies* (April 1919), 147–49; Evan John David, "Commercial Flying," *Journal of the Society of Automotive Engineers* 4 (March 1919), 200–202; *Living Age* 302 (September 6, 1919), 591–94; J.J. Jusserand, "Lindbergh in Paris," *Review of Reviews* 76 (July 1927), 35–36.

13. Gilbert Seldes, "Transatlantic," *New Republic* 51 (June 1, 1927), 47.

14. Stuart Chase, *Men and Machines* (New York: Macmillan, 1929), 178.

15. Ibid., 102.

16. Ibid., 144.

17. Lewis Mumford, *Technics and Civilization* (New York: Harcourt, Brace, 1934), 239, 266.

18. Ibid., 231; caption for commentary on plate XI. Although the book was published in 1934, Mumford had written the first draft in 1930.

19. John W. Ward, "The Meaning of Lindbergh's Flight," *American Quarterly* 10 (spring 1958), 14–16.

20. John Erskine, "Flight," *Century* 114 (September 1927), 514–15. This aspect of Lindbergh's flight also is discussed by Kenneth S. Davis in *The Hero: Charles A. Lindbergh and the American Dream* (New York: Doubleday, 1959), 243–44.

21. Quotes from Bel Geddes and Teague are found in Stephen Bayley, ed., *The Conran Directory of Design* (New York, 1985), 43, 46. This book includes considerable material on streamlining, but see also Sigfried Giedion, *Mechanization Takes Command: A Contribution to*

Anonymous History (New York: Oxford University Press, 1948), and Donald J. Bush, *The Streamlined Decade* (New York: G. Braziller, 1975). My comments from Mumford's script for *The City* are based on a film print catalogued by the Museum of Modern Art, New York.

22. Roger E. Bilstein, "Air Travel and the Traveling Public: The American Experience, 1920–1970," in *From Airships to Airbus: The History of Civil and Commercial Aviation,* International Conference on the History of Civil and Commercial Aviation (1992: Lucerne, Switzerland), vol. 2, *Pioneers and Operations,* ed. William F. Trimble (Washington, D.C.: Smithsonian Institution Press, 1995), 91–111. Cited hereafter as *From Airships to Airbus.*

23. Heywood Broun, "It Seems to Heywood Broun," *Nation* 129 (September 4, 1929), 241. Technical developments, as well as contemporaneous comments from the 1920s, are covered in Bilstein, *Flight Patterns.*

24. Frank Cunningham, *Sky Master: The Story of Donald Douglas* (Philadelphia: Dorrance and Co., 1951), 279; Michael S. Sherry, *The Rise of American Air Power: The Creation of Armageddon* (New Haven: Yale University Press, 1987), figure no. 13 following p. 146.

25. Sherry, *Air Power,* 140, 352. *Life* magazine and Baldwin quotes on p. 352.

26. *Fortune Magazine* 73 (March 1941); N. L. Engelhardt, *Education for the Air Age* (New York: Macmillan, 1943), exemplifies the style and content of the twenty volumes in the Air Age Education Series. See also Dominick A. Pisano, *To Fill the Skies with Pilots: The Civilian Pilot Training Program, 1939–46* (Champaign: University of Illinois Press, 1993), which provides many details on Hinckley and the air age phenomenon.

27. Roger E. Bilstein, *Flight in America: From the Wrights to the Astronauts* (Baltimore: Johns Hopkins University Press, 1994), 167–69; J. Parker Van Zandt, *America Faces the Air Age,* 2 vols. (Washington, D.C.: Brookings Institution, 1944); Thomas K. Finletter, *Survival in the Air Age* (Washington, D.C.: President's Air Policy Commission, 1948).

28. Among general film references, I frequently turned to Leslie Halliwell, *The Filmgoer's Companion* (New York: Hill and Wang, 1977). For an informative summary of civil and military aviation themes in films, see Stephen Pendo, *Aviation in the Cinema* (Metuchen, N.J.: Scarecrow Press, 1985).

29. A number of books on popular culture noted the public alarm relative to nuclear attack. See, for example, Jane and Michael Stern, *Sixties People* (New York: Knopf, 1990), 217–19; also John and Gordon Javna, *60s! A Catalog of Memories and Artifacts* (New York: St. Martin's Press, 1988), 69.

30. Bilstein, *From Airships to Airbus,* 99–100.

31. Author's notes from MGM promotional brochure, "Three Guys Named Mike," in a private collection.

32. Civil Aeronautics Board, *Handbook of Airline Statistics* (Washington, D.C.: U.S. Civil Aeronautics Board, 1964), 461, 530.

33. Information on the Cloud Room obtained in an interview with Gay Carter (Houston, Texas, 1992).

34. Max Lerner, *America as a Civilization: Life and Thought in the United States Today* (New York: Simon and Schuster, 1957), 97.

35. Quoted in Daniel J. Boorstin, *The Image: A Guide to Pseudo-Events in America* (New York: Harper and Row, 1964), 94–98.

36. Caskie Stinnett, "How Mombasa Became the New Place," *Saturday Review of Literature* (April 16, 1977), 11–14; Daniel J. Boorstin, *The Americans: The Democratic Experience* (New York: Vintage Books, 1974), 517.

37. Lerner, *America as a Civilization,* 868.

38. James Silke, "Aviation Comic Strips," *Air Progress/Aviation Review* (August 1980), 18–23, 68; Louis Kraar, "Funny-Paper Lobbyists Help Air Force, Navy Seek Funds, Recruits," *Wall Street Journal* (August 4, 1960). See also Al Flick, "Flying in the Funnies," *Aviation Quarterly* 8 (1985), 4–47, which supplies a fascinating sampling of strips from the 1920s through the 1940s.

39. The Walter Mitty short story appears in various anthologies, including *The Thurber Carnival*. Danny Kaye starred in a Hollywood version of the Mitty saga titled *The Secret Life of Walter Mitty* (1947). Film anthologies such as Jay Brown, *Rating the Movies* (New York: Beekman House, 1989), include a variety of aviation titles relating to the postwar era. Aspiring aces could inquire of firms such as Air Combat U.S.A., Inc., which charged a base fee of $695 and could arrange to stage your own aerial dogfight "at an airport near you!" See, for example, advertisement in *Air and Space Smithsonian* 10 (June/July 1995), 86.

40. There were a number of *Airport*-style successor films and similar pictures; see, for example, Brown, *Rating the Movies,* passim. The Barbie doll exhibit was described as "You've Come a Long Way, Barbie!" *Air and Space Smithsonian* 10 (June/July 1965), 16–17.

THE AIRPLANE

Public Perception

.

The Greatest Show Not on Earth

The Confrontation between Utility and Entertainment in Aviation

DOMINICK A. PISANO

> The life story of Ivan R. (Rubberneck) Gates should not be written on a type-writer; it should be played on a steam calliope, accompanied by a full, a very full, circus band. For Ivan (The Terrible) Gates is the Circus King of the Air. He was one of the first pilots to discover that aviation is a circus plentifully equipped with clowns, and that people would pay money to endure all manner of discomforts on a flying field . . . in the pious hope that something awful would happen and that they would see it.
>
> —CY CALDWELL, EDITORIAL WRITER, *AERO DIGEST*

> This wasn't an amusement park thing. . . .
>
> —WILLIAM P. MACCRACKEN, JR., ASST. SECY. OF COMMERCE FOR AVIATION[1]

In the contemporary era, the average person does not often think of the airplane as anything other than a machine to transport people and things to places around the world or as a weapon of war. It almost goes without saying that these are the principal uses of aviation. But, as Roland Barthes has pointed out, there is an ideological burden in assuming "what-goes-without-saying." Barthes maintains that we tend to attribute natural attributes to conditions that are culturally and socially constructed and that, by peeling away the layers of "nature," we uncover history. Like other culturally constructed phenomena, the history of how the airplane came to be used to carry passengers and cargo and wage war grew out of circumstances that reflect American society and its goals, purposes, and prejudices in interesting ways.[2]

This essay, which covers the period from the ballooning era to the present, will examine the origins of American aeronautics as entertainment and illuminate how culturally based biases helped to define a useful purpose for aviation. It also will show how changes in attitudes toward aviation's purpose reflected the broader cultural viewpoints of the period in which these changes took place.

The Ballooning Era

The legitimation of utility for American aeronautics grew out of a conflict that arose in the early twentieth century between those who espoused ballooning as

Aviation in the United States began as entertainment, but the industry promoters believed that this image was too reckless and soon moved to convince the public that flying had utility and was safe. As aviation became commercially viable, its value as entertainment became the province of the movies. Here, in a series of photographs, a wing walker performs typical barnstorming feats for an adoring movie audience. (Courtesy National Air and Space Museum, Smithsonian Institution [SI 84-566].)

entertainment for the masses and aristocrats who favored it as the more exclusive "sport of kings." Courtney G. Brooks, a historian who has analyzed American aeronautics as sport and spectacle, tells us that Jean Pierre Blanchard's balloon ascension from Philadelphia on January 9, 1793, the first in American history, "constituted the beginning of aeronautics in the United States, the first contact of the American people with actual air travel." Brooks also observes that Blanchard's flight "gave to aeronautics the character which it retained for about a century and a half—its appeal to crowds, its value as entertainment and recreation for great numbers of spectators. This was the primary role of the balloon, and it remained one important aspect of American aeronautics until the Second World War."[3]

As a recreational activity, however, ballooning had its less appealing side. Critics often compared promoters of ballooning spectaculars to confidence men. Brooks tells of "'the prevalence of unscrupulous, greedy promoters and aeronauts who entered the exhibition business in large numbers solely for the purpose of making money by whatever means at their disposal. This type pretended to offer more to the public than he actually delivered, and left town with the gate receipts before action could be taken by irate citizens.'" A noted and reputable balloonist, Carl E. Myers, Brooks says, "warned promoters and managers to beware of amateur and unknown aeronauts. Many evidently learned the hard way, when balloonists failed to perform as advertised." Other criticisms were leveled at balloonists who tried to legitimate their activities by affixing the title "professor" or "captain" before their names. The *New York Times,* for example, adopted a disapproving attitude toward daredevil balloonists who jeopardized their lives for the public's amusement. When its correspondents referred to ballooning or balloonists in print, they usually put the words *professional* or *professor* in quotation marks.[4]

Moreover, from its earliest days, ballooning attracted large, often boisterous crowds, which gave it a less than acceptable social aspect. Rock throwers, for example, damaged Blanchard's balloon while it was on public display. In 1819, Michel, a French aeronaut performing in Philadelphia, avoided serious injury but not damage to his balloon and theft of his gate receipts, when an angry crowd attacked an attendant who had overzealously dealt with a young boy he caught trying to sneak into the show. Incidents such as these were common at ballooning events. As time went on and audiences became blasé about ordinary balloon ascents, aeronauts were forced to expand their repertoire and add daring and novel innovations and showmanship. Tom D. Crouch, a historian of early flight in America, remarks that by the 1870s, showmanship had replaced expertise and skill in handling a balloon: "Daredevil acrobats who performed their stunts dangling from trapeze bars slung beneath primitive hot air balloons were thrilling crowds at local fairs and holiday celebrations. After 1882 the acrobats began to give way to the parachutists, for whom the balloon was nothing more than a means of attaining sufficient altitude from which to make a crowd-pleasing jump."[5]

Eventually, ballooning became indistinguishable from circus performance. In 1874, the great American circus impresario P. T. Barnum used the balloonist and trapeze performer Washington H. Donaldson to attract crowds to his Great Roman Hippodrome in New York. Donaldson, whom the *Chicago Tribune* characterized as "short and very square shouldered, with a gymnast's breadth of chest and big jointedness," was a show business natural, having worked as tightrope walker, magician, and ventriloquist. Attired in fleshtone tights, purple satin shirt, and blue kid boots, Donaldson would ascend to two or three thousand feet and begin a succession of vaults and somersaults that would leave the astonished crowd breathless. The act culminated dramatically in a fake fall, during which Donaldson would catch his foot in the trapeze and then fall again, this time securing himself by grasping a rope. One writer observed of Donaldson, "time and time again I have seen him do every difficult feat of trapeze work ever done above the certain security of a net."[6]

With increasing complexity of performance came the potential for accidents. Crouch recounts incident after incident in which falls or exploding balloons killed or seriously injured aerial performers. That newspaper accounts sensationalized these deaths, which horrified and fascinated the public, only added fuel to critics' arguments about the unappealing aspects of American ballooning. A typical example of lurid reporting is "Killed by a Fall from a Balloon," an account in the *New York Times* of the death of Annie Harkness, a young aeronaut who fell to her death while parachuting out of a balloon over an amusement park in Cincinnati:

> Faster and faster descended the parachute. More intense and terrible came the strain upon the madly excited crowd, as horror-stricken it stood waiting for the fearful end. Suddenly there struck upon the ears a dull sickening sound— the end had come. A life had gone out in the midst of pleasure. Quickly a sympathetic crowd gathered around the lifeless, mangled form of the poor girl as she lay in crushed mass upon the ground. Blood spattered her gaudy clothing and the wreck of the frail parachute that had borne her to her death, and fast running from her broken body, formed little pools about the spot where she lay, and the people shuddered, and stood back as they looked.[7]

Thus, after being associated with undesirable crowds, unscrupulous promoters, and daredevil aeronauts who misrepresented themselves, ballooning became identified with recklessness and death. George Dollar, writing in *Strand* magazine in 1898, roundly condemned what he called the "balloonatics." Dollar produced statistics that claimed to show that nine out of ten aeronauts met with accidents, that in 1897, forty-seven aeronauts were killed, and that in one week in 1898, seven parachute jumpers were injured, some even dying from their injuries. Dollar took the aeronauts to task for performing in front of spectators. "Considering ... the danger of it," he wrote, "ballooning may be counted a form of foolhardiness."[8]

To understand fully how balloons (and, later, aircraft) came to have such negative cultural connotations, we must look to American perceptions of sports and entertainment. (Sports is here characterized as competitive athletic activity, and entertainment as theatrical productions such as circuses and carnivals, pageants and parades, and popular entertainments such as music hall and variety shows, burlesque productions, nightclub shows, cabaret, and musical comedy and revue.) Negative public perceptions of the propriety of leisure-time activities can be traced back to its roots in the Puritan idea of faith and salvation. Whereas the Puritans believed that no one could be saved by good works alone, prayer, sacrifice, and a life free of embellishment were considered orthodox behavior. Merrymaking and gaiety were not purposeful to right living and thus were diversions from the path of piety.[9]

Nathaniel Hawthorne's sketch "The May-Pole of Merry Mount" amply illustrates this point. In the story, a fictionalized illustration of a conflict in cultural values, the light-hearted citizens of Merry Mount, a New England town with a reputation for gaiety and merrymaking, are confronted by the dour Puritan John Endicott and his lieutenants. Hawthorne based his story on a true incident that took place in Mount Wollaston (now Quincy, Massachusetts), a settlement of British fur traders. By 1627, Mount Wollaston had been taken over by the pleasure-loving Thomas Morton, an attorney and "adventurer." Morton changed the name of the colony to "Merry Mount," and, as James McIntosh describes it,

> set out to make it as high-living a place as he could in wilderness circumstances. He adopted the maypole, the traditional center for dancing on May Day in England, as the permanent symbol of his enterprise. The Merry Mounters decorated a forest tree with flowers and engaged in "revels and merriment after the old English custom" round about it. These pagan activities scandalized their neighbors, who several times invaded Morton's settlement.

Later, Morton was arrested for selling arms to the Indians and deported. John Endicott, governor of the emerging Massachusetts Bay Colony, went to Merry Mount, cut down the maypole, and warned the settlers to behave more properly.[10]

Negative perceptions of entertainment and leisure continued after the Puritan era had ended. As late as the mid–eighteenth century, the Massachusetts General Court prohibited "public stage-plays, interludes, and other theatrical entertainments" because they "occasion[ed] great and unnecessary expenses, and discouraged industry and frugality, but likewise tend[ed] generally to increase immorality, impiety, and a contempt for religion." Eventually, prohibitions against entertainment lost their religious connotations and instead became culturally based. Diversions that once had been outlawed for moral reasons now were forbidden or looked on with disfavor because they were a threat to society.[11]

In her book *Confidence Men and Painted Women,* Karen Halttunen argues that strictures against "confidence men," tricksters associated with the world of nineteenth-century entertainment, were couched in terms of "defense against enslavement by tyrants." As long as good citizens "practiced the republican virtues of industry, sobriety, frugality, and simplicity, their liberty was safe. Once they were corrupted by the poisonous love of luxury, their vigilant watch over their liberty would relax and they would be reduced to slavery." The American clergyman Henry Ward Beecher warned of the power of confidence men over young males. "We grade our streets, build our schools, support our municipal laws, and the young men are ours. . . ." This privilege of ownership over youth, however, was being usurped by a "whole race of men, whose camp is the Theatre, the Circus, the Turf, or the Gaming-table . . . a race whose instinct is destruction, who live to corrupt, and live off of the corruption which they make."[12]

In a secularized version of Puritanical criticism of leisure activity, Beecher was indicting common forms of nineteenth-century popular American entertainment and sport—theater, the circus, horse racing, gambling—things that twentieth-century Americans take for granted as wholesome, some even suitable for family participation. With its unsavory crowds, questionable promoters akin to Beecher's confidence men, fly-by-night aspect, and performance in the types of settings Beecher had warned against—fairs, circuses, and other celebrations—and especially danger and death, ballooning was an activity that had questionable value to the guardians of American culture and morals.[13]

In 1905, however, the formation of the Aero Club of America changed the emphasis of American aeronautics culturally from spectacle for the masses to sport and spectacle for the moneyed and wealthy. Made up of wealthy aviation enthusiasts and members of the Automobile Club of America, the club's primary objectives were "the promotion of a social organization or club composed in whole or in part of persons owning aeronautic inventions for personal or private use." According to Herbert A. Johnson, one of the Aero Club's chroniclers,

> common bloodlines, parallel interests in mercantile and industrial affairs, and records of achievement in a broad range of human enterprises and activities, united the Aero Club of America into a strong, coherent social organization. Men joined the Aero Club because it was fun; it was in keeping with their social status, and they enjoyed taking the risks of early sport ballooning in the company of close friends and like-minded acquaintances. When the Aero Club spoke through its officers it represented the views of a large and influential segment of America's men of affairs, people of substance who were able to influence public opinion not only by what they said, but by who they were.

In a short time, the Aero Club, with affiliates in Massachusetts, Connecticut, Ohio, Wisconsin, Missouri, Illinois, Colorado, California, and Washington, had created an influential network of aeronautical enthusiasts.[14]

More important than its significance in promoting a positive image for American aeronautics was that in 1905, the Aero Club, along with its European colleagues in Germany, Spain, Belgium, Britain, Italy, Switzerland, and France, helped to found the Fédération Aeronautique Internationale (FAI). FAI became the sanctioning body for aeronautical records and record attempts, a distinction that it holds to this day. For the first time in American history, aeronautics had an elite social group of advocates who banded together institutionally to promote it, and a network of affiliates that stretched from New York to New England, to the Midwest and West, and across the Atlantic to Europe. It also had legitimation—a means of measuring achievement and keeping official statistics and a method of choosing the highest achievement; that is, records and record-breaking attempts.[15]

In 1906, a year after the formation of the Aero Club of America, James Gordon Bennett, Jr., the wealthy playboy publisher of the *New York Herald* and sports enthusiast, put a stamp of approval on this cultural change when he sponsored the Gordon Bennett International Aeronautic Trophy for Free Balloons with $25,000 in prize money. Bennett thus became the "First Patron Saint of International Aeronautics." Four years later, Robert J. Collier, son of P. F. Collier, publisher of *Collier's Weekly,* and president of the Aero Club from 1911 to 1912, reinforced the high status of American aeronautics. Collier sponsored a trophy to be awarded yearly by the Aero Club "for the greatest achievement in aviation in America, the value of which has been thoroughly demonstrated by use during the preceding year." The Collier Trophy, as it has come to be known, was the most significant honor in aviation, and it remains so to this day. Many influential persons believed that, finally, aeronautics in America had shed its shabby carnival image for the more respectable ambience of the clubhouse.[16]

To understand how the Aero Club of America could take a disreputable activity such as ballooning and transform it into a gentlemanly pursuit, we must examine the change in cultural attitudes toward sport and recreation in America from the mid-nineteenth century to the early twentieth century. Courtney Brooks explains the shift as a loss of public interest. "In the 1890's," Brooks says,

> American ballooning reached a saturation point. . . . "The public had grown tired of the same type of performance year after year. As long as the parachute and the balloon retained an aura of mystery and novelty, the demand for exhibitions remained fairly constant, but in time the novelty of flight in a lighter-than-air craft vanished with the repetition of unvaried performances, and the daring and skill of the aeronaut became commonplace."[17]

Although this may be an accurate statement, it is also true that American attitudes toward sport changed considerably from about 1850 to the turn of the century. During this time, sports and recreation became legitimate activities, which as Elliott J. Gorn and Warren Goldstein point out in their *A Brief History of American Sports,* could be "viewed as a moral force, especially those sports that could lay claim to such virtues as self-discipline or bodily development or rural innocence." Unlike the colonial era and early nineteenth century, when recreational activities were condemned by the elite as the opiate and corrupter of the masses, this period was characterized by their legitimation in a way that protected the elite from "status anxiety" [Richard Hofstadter's term], in a society they perceived was slipping out of their control.[18]

Gorn and Goldstein also point out that people who could be considered in the same strata of society as the founders of the Aero Club of America shared "a heritage of leadership based on old family ties, education, and often wealth." These elite "took it as their common role to be intellectual leaders, cultural arbiters, and moral stewards. Respectable Americans looked to them and they to each other for social guidance." "Yet by mid-century," Gorn and Goldstein argue, "the old elite of clergy, intellectuals, and patricians found itself confronted with external and internal conflict. Democratic politics and new concentrations of economic and social power challenged the cultural legitimacy of the 'Brahmin caste,' as [Oliver Wendell] Holmes called men of his background."[19]

Increasingly, as the men of this caste felt themselves marginalized and weakened, they turned to manly, rigorous sports to justify their identities. "The same ideological constellation of the Protestant and bourgeois ethic that had led to an attack on sports, especially boisterous working-class and gentry sports, now increasingly came to the defense of reformed recreations. The spirit of improvement, hard work, and self-control could all be reinforced through the right sorts of sports and recreations, undermined by the wrong ones." "Wholesome sports and recreations," Gorn and Goldstein contend, "refreshed and uplifted the working class, replaced vicious amusements with moral ones, and inculcated new forms of discipline. Membership in sporting clubs and organizations offered group solidarity in anonymous cities, served as a clear sign of one's social status, and helped make new ideas such as competition and team work second nature."[20]

Another cultural influence in American aeronautics' transformation from lower-class spectacle to upper-class sport was its exclusivity. Expense was one restricting element; only the wealthy could afford to buy balloons and the equipment required to operate them. More important, ballooning made it possible for a person to move away from earthly cares, placing one a remove further from ordinary people. The comments of one early-twentieth-century sportsman balloonist illustrate this point. By 1906, Julian P. Thomas of New York had made twenty voyages in the *Nirvana,* a balloon he ordered from France. Thomas claimed that he had tried other sporting activities such as automobile racing but found none as exciting as ballooning. It gave him "a thrill that cannot be experienced on any other occasion. . . . Ballooning is the sport of sports. There is no other form of exploring that a man can start on from his city home and reach a mysterious world of new sensations and novel experiences after he has left his starting point." Regarding this phenomenon, George L. Mosse has commented that "the adventure of flying, the conquest of speed and space, the loneliness of the pilot, had all the makings of myth, and the conquest of the sky, where the gods lived and from which they descended to earth, had always held a vital place in human mythology."[21]

More important is what these cultural changes worked and how as a result American aeronautics was set on a course that it has deviated from little in the intervening years. The formation of the Aero Club of America and the Fédération Aeronautique Internationale brought about the institutionalization of aeronautics in the United States. Institutionalization led to gathering statistics, keeping records, and a self-regulating system of competition. Culturally, this phenomenon fits the historian Allen Guttmann's paradigm of how activities that begin as playful recreations acquire the trappings of modern sports.

Guttmann identifies seven characteristics (secularism, equality, bureaucratization, specialization, rationalization, quantification, and the obsession with records) that define contemporary sports. American aeronautics passed through some of these stages from its early ballooning days to the formation of the Aero Club and FAI, primarily in establishing an organized formal structure to administer aeronautics (bureaucratization), keeping statistics (quantification), and reaching for the highest achievement using statistics as the standard of excellence (obsession with records). Quantification and competition were the first steps in aviation's cultural development from sport to industry in the 1920s: assimilation into what Louis Galambos calls "a bureaucratic or corporate culture [which became] the dominant value system throughout middle-class America—on the farm and in the factory, behind the pulpit as well as on the drawing board."[22]

The Birdman Era

Although the Aero Club of America believed it was changing the image of American aeronautics, the organization did not reckon on the influence the invention of the airplane would have on the American public. Even after the arrival of heavier-than-air flight, the Aero Club was content to continue to be a group of aristocratic sportsmen. This sense of complacency among the old guard members of the club would lead to a series of power struggles out of which would come a new direction for aeronautics in the United States. The central conflict involved what the Aero Club would be and what American aeronautics would become. Some members such as Albert Triaca felt that the Aero Club should remain the domain of the sportsmen balloonists and not become captive to business interests. In 1908, Triaca broke away from the Aero Club and formed the Aeronautic Society of New York because he felt that the organization was not paying enough attention to promoting aeronautics in America. Triaca returned to the fold after he discovered that his partners in the Aeronautic Society of New York venture had tried, in his words, "to turn a popular association into a commercial enterprise, in which the word 'business' had a much more potent sway than the word 'sport.'"[23]

Much more than the balloon, the airplane represented a multitude of moneymaking possibilities. Once heavier-than-air flight was practicable, the question was: Should aeronautics remain a sport or become a business, and if it became a business, what kind of business would it be? The airplane had no practical purpose because it was so primitive technologically. There was, however, quick money to be made by using the airplane in stunt flying to entertain the multitudes, and that was an avenue that could not be ignored even if it did not have the sanction of the elitist Aero Club of America. As Bill Robie, author of an incisive book on the Aero Club-National Aeronautic Association points out, the Aero Club

> officially denounced this kind of flying, but it was powerless to control it. Many
> of the same pilots who had contributed ... to the genuine advancement of flight
> were unable to resist the lucrative exhibition business. Even the Wrights, per-
> haps the most conservative of all American aviators, fell under the spell of this
> unique trade, until the deaths of their two best pilots caused them to disband
> their own exhibition company.[24]

To take advantage of the public's fascination with the recently perfected flying machine, the Wright brothers and Glenn Curtiss formed aeronautical exhibition teams that toured the country. The Wright team, established in 1910, was under the direction of the aerial showman Roy Knabenshue. The Curtiss team, begun in the same year, was organized by Jerome S. Fanciulli, a reporter for the Associated Press and advertising manager for the Jamestown Exposition of 1907. Typical venues for the teams were circuses, county fairs, carnivals, and other entertainment attractions that might fetch a crowd and gate receipts. The exhibition company charged sponsoring organizations $5,000 for each aircraft used. Pilots, or "birdmen" as they were popularly known, were paid $50 for each flight and $20 a week plus living and travel expenses. Trophies and cash prizes were kept by the company. Despite the tawdry carnival atmosphere reminiscent of the ballooning era, touring was profitable. The Curtiss company grossed nearly a million dollars in 1911.[25]

The profits garnered by the aerial exhibition teams were tainted, however, by the constant specter of death and the perception of aviation as dangerous and foolhardy. The Wright team's so-called heavenly twins and most popular flyers, Arch Hoxsey and Ralph Johnstone, competed with each other time and time again at air meets, each trying to outdo the other's performance. Within a month of each other in late 1910, they and another famous exhibition pilot, John B. Moisant, were killed in crashes. In November, Ralph Johnstone died when the wing of his aircraft collapsed during a spiral glide at Overland Park in Denver,

Colorado. The following month, Johnstone's fellow pilot Arch Hoxsey was killed in Los Angeles during an attempt to beat his world altitude record of 11,474 feet, when he spun in from seven thousand feet. Moisant also died in December in New Orleans while he was competing for a world's record for the longest sustained flight of the year. By mid-1912, five of the nine pilots who had served on the Wright Exhibition Team had died in crashes.[26]

The fate of the flyers merely whetted the appetites of the thrill-seeking crowds, many of whom were drawn to the aerial exhibitions by death in the air, both actual and suggested. They also drew criticism from the guardians of propriety. In 1911, *Scientific American,* for example, in reference to "irresponsible aeroplane exhibitions, with their shocking list of fatalities," condemned what it called "the spirit of the coliseum" and linked the same appetite for bloody spectacle that attracted people to automobile races with air shows.

> Can it be possible that a touch of the savage desire to look upon mangled bodies and hear the sob of expiring life . . . is responsible for the vast crowds which gather at our modern race tracks to witness the criminally dangerous automobile race, or watch the aviator straining for a fall with Death? . . . The death of an aviator under such conditions comes very near to being homicide of the most atrocious character.[27]

In a *Harper's Weekly* magazine article titled "What's Wrong with Aviation?" published in 1912, Alberto S. Le Vino took flying to task for being overpublicized, impractical, and frivolous. "There seems to be a three-hundred-and-sixty-five-day-long silly season against which not even the sanest city editor appears immune." Moreover, Le Vino concluded, "the serious practical side of flying is an almost unknown quantity, because aviation has so far been mostly circus 'stunts.' Shorn of these features—and the end of exhibitions and meets is fortunately now in sight—the aeroplane will come into its own."[28]

World War I

World War I ushered in a new era in American aeronautics and with it another attempt to find some useful purpose for the airplane. The Wright brothers had successfully flown their revolutionary invention on December 17, 1903, but they had not unveiled it to the multitudes until 1908, when Orville showed the Military Flier to government officials at Fort Myer, near Washington, D.C. After the Fort Myer demonstration, spokesmen for the Aero Club of America began to clamor for making the airplane a part of America's military arsenal. In 1911, *Aeronautics,* one of the first journals devoted to aviation, printed chief of the U.S. Army Signal Corps Brig. Gen. James Allen's speech before the Aero Club of New York, in which he advocated a $125,000 budget for new military airplanes and training officer pilots. In the editorial pages of *Flying,* the official organ of the Aero Club, there were persistent calls for use of the airplane in American preparedness for war, formation of national guard aviation units, and training of military pilots.[29]

Herbert A. Johnson has observed that "the Aero Club of America and its affiliated groups in the aeronaut constituency, were of vital importance to the future growth of military and naval aviation in the United States." Its members were "well placed in the political, economic and social hierarchy of the United States," and especially forceful "in making Congress and the American people aware of Army aviation." In 1912, the Aero Club was instrumental in the passage of the Hardwick Bill, which proposed increasing the pay of military flyers. More important, the club supported the Hay Bill in 1914, which had provisions for flight pay and death benefits for military flyers and for creating the Aviation Section of the Signal Corps, the first step in institutionalizing military aviation in the United States. In 1915, the Aero Club took another step toward emphasizing military aviation in the United States with the creation of the National Aeroplane Fund (sometimes called the National Aeroplane Subscription). The fund's purpose was to use money raised by public subscription to provide aircraft, pilots, and mechanics to National Guard and militia units in states that wanted them and landing fields along the coast from which patrols could be flown. The pilots would be military reservists who would fly the mail to remote areas until called for military service. Another important function of the National Aeroplane Fund was to convince the press, the military, and politicians of the need for a strong aerial armada. With increasing awareness from influential people in Congress, the Aero Club hoped that appropriations for military aeronautics would increase, and they did. When Congress voted an emergency appropriation of $13,300,000 for modern aircraft in mid-1916, *Aerial Age Weekly* declared that "at last it may be said that the United States had taken up aviation ... the Aero Club of America is to be congratulated for this achievement."[30]

The institutionalization of military aviation in the United States and its development during World War I contributed culturally to the idea that the airplane was useful as a weapon of war. John Morrow has remarked that

> the airplane established its real significance in support of the army on the battlefield. Aircraft reconnaissance made it difficult for armies to achieve surprise and forced the movement of men and materiel behind the lines at night. ... Politicians and generals such as Churchill, Ludendorff, and Pétain recognized the importance of airpower. Control of the skies over the battlefield had become essential to victory in World War I, just as it would be 20 years later. Strategic aviation, if it had played little role in the 1914–18 conflict, seemed to offer the key to victory in future wars. ... In both strategy and tactics the air war of 1914–18 portended the larger struggle of 1939–45.[31]

Moreover, as Bill Robie has observed,

the advent of wartime aviation had made sporting flight in America seem a somewhat frivolous pastime and of course international competition was out of the question. The Aero Club continued to officiate at record attempts and competitions for trophies, but more often than not the competitors were no longer sportsmen in private aircraft, but military officers testing the limits of new war machines. Even the Aero Club's licensing program lost some of its impact. Pilots trained by the military and experienced in combat flying often saw no purpose in obtaining a sportsman's certificate that carried no "legal" weight.

There was dissension among Aero Club members about whether the purpose of American aeronautics should be purely sport or strictly utilitarian. This conflict would play out in the interwar years and determine the future course of American aviation.[32]

The Barnstorming Era

After World War I, American aeronautics underwent another transformation that coincided with larger currents in American culture. The conflict between those who insisted that aviation be utilitarian and those who saw it as purely entertainment continued. Stunt pilots, the "birdmen" of the prewar era, were now known as "barnstormers." This was a term borrowed from the theatrical world (in the early nineteenth century, theater groups followed the westward migration and played in barns), because the flyers toured from place to place giving flying exhibitions and taking passengers for rides. Barnstorming was flying for pure sport and entertainment with little organized competitiveness and even less remuneration, no rules or regulations, and more than a hint of foolhardiness and danger. It was an activity that fit appropriately into the frivolous spirit of the Roaring Twenties, a time of carefree nonsense, and often of life lived on the edge. Slats Rodgers, a barnstorming pilot from Texas, characterized the spirit of the breed. "I guess we were a strange lot," he wrote,

those of us who flew those old traps every Sunday at the field. Maybe we were a sort of mixture of the cowhand of the Old West, the hot-rod driver of today, and the real gypsy. We thought we were as free as the birds, when we got in the air, just the way the oldtime cowhand thought he was as free as a coyote. We deliberately missed death by inches just like the hot-rod driver of today. And we played the suckers wherever we could find them, which meant roaming the face of the earth like a gypsy.[33]

Soon, however, the improvisational nature of barnstorming changed, and groups of pilots directed by a promoter banded together to form "flying circuses," or touring exhibition teams, with corporate sponsorship. Ivan D. Gates, head of the Gates Flying Circus, one of the most famous and well-traveled of the aerial exhibition teams, struck a deal with the Texas Oil Company (Texaco) in which he obtained gasoline and oil free in exchange for advertising the distinctive green-and-red Texaco star trademark on the company's aircraft. The Gates Flying circus began operations in the western states in 1922, but by 1925 they had traveled as far east as Pennsylvania. In the words of one writer: "Tens of thousands of people jammed the improvised flying fields to see their complete shows and they were lugging first-time passengers into the air in droves. They spent from two to four days in every city or town they visited."[34]

In 1926, Ivan Gates estimated that from the time the Gates Flying Circus was formed, the company had put on 1,836 exhibitions in 1,042 cities and towns and had traveled throughout forty-one states. By the spring of 1926, attendance ranged from twenty to thirty thousand paid spectators at each performance. From 1922 to 1928, it is estimated that the Gates Flying Circus carried roughly 1.5 million passengers. Besides sponsorship by a major oil company, local newspapers editorialized in the company's behalf in exchange for the company's dropping newspapers with free tickets to their show. It was not surprising that the big-time flying exhibition companies such as Gates enjoyed such widespread popularity, and that they had such an effect in promoting the widely accepted daredevil image of aviation during the 1920s.[35]

Soon, the barnstorming spirit of recklessness and danger described by Slats Rodgers, which hearkened back to the carnival atmosphere of the balloon and prewar birdman eras of American aeronautics, was confronted by a reform movement that proposed to legitimate, rationalize, and organize aviation and have the government regulate it. This mood of reform was apparent in the postwar Aero Club, which seems to have been rife with dissension over whether the purpose of aviation should be sport or industry. The discord among club members finally led to the organization's demise, and the formation in 1922 of the National Aeronautic Association (NAA), its successor, a group whose goals were distinctly different from the Aero Club. Principal among them was "to aid and encourage the establishment and maintenance of a uniform and stable system of laws relating to the science of aeronautics and the art of aerial navigation and all allied and kindred sciences and arts." The NAA and other aviation groups such as the Guggenheim Fund for the Promotion of Aeronautics, led the crusade for government regulation that culminated in the 1926 Air Commerce Act. The legislation gave the federal government sweeping powers to regulate the issuance of licenses for pilots and the airworthiness of aircraft and spelled the end of the barnstorming era of aviation.[36]

The postwar Aero Club of America was divided on issues similar to those that in the earlier period had caused Albert Triaca to withdraw because he believed the club had been diverted from its goal of promoting sportsman aeronautics. Alan R. Hawley, sportsman balloonist, longtime member and president of the club, and Henry Woodhouse, a publisher of various aeronautical periodicals, were pitted against Howard E. Coffin, a Hudson Motor Car Company executive and former head of the government's Aircraft Production Board during World War I, and Courtland F. Bishop, a sportsman balloonist and longtime club member. The Coffin–Bishop faction was intent on remaking the Aero Club from a parochial group of wealthy sportsman pilots, to a national organization that would lobby congress to regulate American aviation and thereby bring into being a practical commercial aviation industry. To that end, in August 1920 Coffin and Bishop engineered a merger of the Aero Club with the American Flying Club, a group of military pilots and veteran flyers of World War I who had become disaffected with the old guard of the Aero Club. Then Coffin organized the First National Aero Congress, bringing aviation leaders from across the country together in Omaha in the fall of 1921. There the National Air Association was created in the hope that it could be merged with the Aero Club of America to forge a national organization to be called the National Aeronautic Association.[37]

Coffin was well qualified for the takeover of the Aero Club of America. An industrial engineer by profession, he was member of the Naval Consulting Board, headed the Aircraft Production Board, founded the Aircraft Manufacturers' Association (AMA), and was governor of the Aero Club of America. Coffin helped settle the dispute created by the patent infringement suits filed by the Wright brothers against Glenn Curtiss by negotiating a cross-licensing agreement among aviation industry firms in 1917. His efforts, along with those of the National Advisory Committee for Aeronautics (NACA), in ending the longstanding patent dispute, allowed wartime aircraft production to begin in earnest.[38]

Coffin's motives, however, were not entirely altruistic. As an executive of the automotive industry and engineer, he believed that through associationalism, the aircraft industry, in conjunction with the government and trade associations, could flourish in much the same way that the automobile industry had in affiliation with the Society of Automotive Engineers. Settling the patent dispute would allow automotive industry firms such as Ford, Willys-Overland, and Fisher Body, with their knowledge of mass production, to enter the aircraft industry and transform it from a loose conglomeration of workshop craftsmen to a monolithic federation of modern industrial giants. "There is no question whatever," Coffin asserted, "but on the whole development of the motor car art not only in an engineering line, but in a commercial way, is based absolutely on the work of the engineers." Similar solutions could work for the aviation industry, he said, for "the problems confronting the aircraft industry are wonderfully simple compared with those of the automobile industry."[39]

Coffin's optimism grew out of what the aviation industry historian Jacob

Vander Meulen sees as a belief in aviation's unlimited future. Aviation, Vander Meulen says,

> was and is perceived as a redemptive force, an agent for the preservation of institutions and values which seem threatened by modern society. Aeronautics as the creator of a new, unbounded frontier for the independent American inventor, entrepreneur, craftsman, adventurist, and warrior; as the harmonizer of the individual and the machine age; as the guarantor of international stability and peace—these elements of the faith in early aeronautics and the antagonism and blame that their disappointment produced shaped in key ways the political context in which the aircraft industry had to develop during its first decades.

Vander Meulen believes that "to Coffin and his associates, the aircraft industry seemed an ideal laboratory for this vision. Public and private officials would jointly and scientifically manage industrial change. Traditional rights of private enterprise and values of competition would be preserved but modified to encourage cooperation and technical advance." As an industrial engineer, Vander Meulen says, Coffin became "the leader of a national movement to standardize manufacture and eliminate waste and conflict through data collection, publicity and industrial self-regulation. He and his associates perceived aircraft manufacture as a great mass-production industry of the future . . . and thus a perfect forum for their crusade for efficiency and expert guided progress."[40]

To his chagrin, Coffin found out that he was wrong about the similarities between aviation and the automobile industry. His faith in mass-production of aircraft in World War I was woefully misplaced because of the state of the industry, the constant bickering between government and the manufacturers, the labyrinthine federal bureaucracy, and criticism from other quarters that there was a conspiracy led by the so-called aircraft trust to defraud the government. America's aircraft production effort was a decided failure, which led to investigations by Congress, the War Department, and the Department of Justice. The Justice Department's probe, headed by the former Supreme Court Justice Charles Evans Hughes, uncovered disorganization, lavish expenditures of government funds, and a lack of concern for conflict of interest, but neither corruption nor conspiracy. Coffin was criticized for his role in the production snafu. He complained bitterly to his superiors about the advisory nature of the Aircraft Production Board, which, he felt, hamstrung its effectiveness, the slowness of filling important positions, and the constant interference of what he called "discontented contractors . . . disgruntled members of the military establishment [and] brokers representing foreign interests . . . and aeronautical and patriotic organizations of private citizens bent upon criticism with no constructive intent." Nevertheless, the persistent disapproval seemed to steel his resolve to create an aircraft industry in the postwar period and to use the influence of the Aero Club of America to forge an association between industry and government.[41]

After the war, Coffin set about to establish an association that could provide the proper environment for a modern aircraft industry. He understood that three things were required if aviation were to become a profitable business venture: risk on investment had to be minimized; risk had to be managed by making aviation insurance available; insurance companies had to be convinced that they should underwrite air transportation by being able to predict accurately the extent of risk. As Bill Robie points out,

> the surest way to achieve all of these objectives would be to have the federal government regulate the aviation industry. Once the government had established and begun to enforce air traffic regulations, set standards for pilot certification and aircraft airworthiness, and developed a national system of airways and airports, the amount of risk involved in the industry could be predicted. Not surprisingly, the National Aeronautic Association's first efforts were concentrated on achieving exactly that sort of government intervention.[42]

As one of the first steps in the plan to form a national aviation organization, Coffin hired William P. MacCracken, Jr., a former military pilot and lawyer who had been involved in the American Bar Association's Special Committee on the Law of Aviation, to draw up the charter for the fledgling NAA. Coffin's ideas about automotive industry involvement in aircraft manufacturing had not changed, and it is no accident that the initial meetings that led to the formation of the NAA were held in Detroit, home of the automotive industry, in October 1922. In the company of august aviation personalities such as Orville Wright, Glenn Curtiss, chief of the Navy's Bureau of Aeronautics Adm. William A. Moffett, chief of the U.S. Air Service Gen. Mason M. Patrick, and his assistant Gen. William Mitchell, Coffin was elected first president of the NAA.[43]

Next, MacCracken helped draft legislation that would regulate aviation in the United States. MacCracken made alliances with those who, as he said, believed that "uniform regulation of aeronautics [was] not only desirable but absolutely indispensable to the effective development of aerial transportation as an instrumentality of interstate commerce." As a committee member of the Special Committee on the Law of Aviation, and later, as advisor to Howard Coffin and first head of the Aeronautics Branch of the Department of Commerce, he set out to reach that goal. MacCracken's knowledge of aviation law led him to the office of Congressman Samuel Winslow, chair of the House Committee on Interstate and Foreign Commerce. Winslow suggested that MacCracken work with Frederic P. Lee, a staff lawyer for the House Legislative Drafting Service, to write aviation regulatory legislation. The resulting Winslow Bill was not passed by Congress because it was far too exhaustive. Other bills, such as the ones proposed by

Senator James W. Wadsworth and Senator Hiram Bingham, also failed to pass. Among the issues to be resolved was the question of whether the individual states or the federal government should have control and whether power to enforce the legislation should reside in a federal department of aeronautics that would regulate civil and military aviation. MacCracken convinced Congressmen Schuyler Merritt and James S. Parker to sponsor a bill that came down hard on the side of federal regulation. The resulting Air Commerce Act, signed into law by President Calvin Coolidge on May 20, 1926, strongly reflected MacCracken's work. MacCracken's efforts on behalf of Coffin and the NAA had borne fruit.[44]

Although the originators of the NAA were sincere in their efforts to promote aviation, Bill Robie believes that the NAA's birth can be viewed "as a carefully orchestrated event intended to serve a specific role in strengthening the growing military/industrial complex." Whatever the reasons, the NAA did change the course of American aeronautics in the 1920s by removing it from the hands of wealthy sportsmen pilots, deemphasizing its entertainment aspects, emphasizing its industrial potential, promoting government regulation, and trying to give it a respectable image in contrast to its perceived recklessness. It is perhaps no accident that William P. MacCracken, Coffin's collaborator in creating the NAA and in helping to draft the federal regulation legislation, was named as assistant secretary of commerce for aeronautics, and that he created the Aeronautics Branch to carry out the mandate of the Air Commerce Act.[45]

Under MacCracken's leadership, the branch began, in his words, "to ride herd on . . . barnstorming going on around the country," which in his opinion and in the opinion of "almost everyone seriously committed to the future of aviation," was necessary to gain public confidence in and public acceptance of aviation. MacCracken believed that "the time had come for a new kind of aviation to emerge in this country, perhaps less colorful but certainly more responsible." Barnstormers and air show performers were seen as dangerous in the sense that aircraft accidents were caused largely by them, but, more important, because they were threatening to the image of aviation as a safe means of transportation. If this image was not maintained, investors would be frightened away, and the aviation industry could not develop in the way that its promoters had seen fit for it.[46]

Eventually, wingwalking, a stock-in-trade air show act, was banned or limited to an altitude of fifteen hundred feet, with a further requirement that the wingwalker wear a parachute. Air show companies were required to provide fences to contain spectators, their insurance increased drastically, and flying acts were moved away from the crowd, making it difficult to see what was happening. Jessie Woods, a woman pilot and veteran of the Flying Aces Flying Circus, recalled that the government regulators had so many rules, just choking us down. They got very nasty about us being there. Every time we did something a CAA [Civil Aeronautics Authority, successor to the Aeronautics Branch] inspector would jump into the cockpit to check and see what we were doing. They did not want air shows anymore, too sensational. All they wanted then was to educate the people to the safety of flight and encourage the growth of business aviation and the airlines. But what they did not realize was that there would not have been any airlines if there had not been people like us. We kept aviation before the eyes of the public and showed airplanes and flying to people all over the country who, otherwise, might not have even been aware that airplanes existed. We developed pilots and mechanics who later went on to the airlines and the military, and who know how many kids our air show influenced into becoming pilots.[47]

Although barnstormers may not have been entirely at fault for aviation's negative image in the 1920s, they were blamed. The *Aircraft Year Book,* published by the Aeronautical Chamber of Commerce of America, Inc., an aviation industry interest group, claimed that in 1923 reckless flying was the cause of 179 crashes that killed 85 people and injured 162; in 1924, the publication estimated that barnstormers caused 66 percent of fatal aircraft accidents. Other sources claim that from 1921 to 1923 barnstormers accounted for 419 accidents and 196 deaths. The accuracy of these statistics is not easily determined, but they were credible to the vast majority of people. The aviation press was especially disparaging. As in the ballooning and prewar birdman era, stunt flying was called "useless and foolhardy." *Aero Digest,* one of the leading aviation journals, said that "the so-called 'gypsy' flyers, such as can be seen at state fairs, usually thrill their rustic audiences by doing stunts in some old crate which should have been junked for lo, these many years. Such boobs frequently come to grief, much to the delectation of the onlookers who have been getting their tonsils sunburnt watching them in the hopes that 'something would happen.'" The *Chicago Tribune* was even more direct. It said that barnstormer aircraft were "potential death traps . . . hand-me-downs, many of them archaic survivors of war days." It called barnstorming pilots "irresponsible—men whose incompetence in other endeavors has induced them to seek riches in flying."[48]

To understand the change in aeronautics from primarily a sport and spectacle before World War I to primarily an industry in the 1920s, we must examine how the fluctuating cultural climate was reflected in the conflicting aims and purposes of the Aero Club of America, the organization that had controlled American aviation since the turn of the century. The Aero Club in the early 1920s represents in microcosm the forces that had been shaping American culture since the end of World War I. It was obvious that interest among club members in making aviation a business had won out over other considerations. This is no coincidence, because, with the election of Warren Harding in 1920, the Progressive movement, which had given birth to the notion of purposeful, manly, vigorous sports—a goal similar to the one stated in the Aero Club's original charter—came to an end. The Progressives, who had feared big business and tried to keep it in check, were gone, and the era of the corporation was at hand.

During that time, Geoffrey Perrett observes, "nearly 20 percent of the entire national wealth of the United States was shifted away from private ownership to corporate ownership," and there was a lack of competition "based on oligopoly, nonprice competition, the setting of prices for an entire industry by a single price leader (for example, US Steel), and by informal market sharing under the supervision of trade associations." "The result," Perrett says, "must have had a million dead Progressives spinning in their graves." Moreover, Perrett points out, business underwent scientific management "in selling, in budgeting, in research, in financing new ventures, in abolishing old ones, in hiring and firing." Schools of management were founded—Harvard Graduate School of Business Administration opened in 1924 with a gift from George Fisher Baker, president of First National Bank of New York, and the largest shareholder in AT&T and U.S. Steel. Business in the 1920s was given an exalted cultural importance.[49]

Moreover, the wartime profiteering of the aircraft industry increased emphasis on aviation as a potentially lucrative enterprise. The NAA was one of many trade associations that came into being under Secretary of Commerce Herbert Hoover that sought favors from government. Michael Parrish comments that "many businessmen saw them [trade associations] as a wonderful tool for fixing prices, allocating markets, and engaging in other practices forbidden by the antitrust laws—all with the official imprimatur of Hoover's department." Similarly, David Lee, who has analyzed Hoover's role in promoting commercial aviation, notes that the creation of the NAA "boosted aviation's stock with the government, especially Secretary of Commerce Herbert Hoover, who considered, constructive industrywide organizations crucial to economic progress. The NAA thus was an important step toward winning Hoover's support for a federal air law."[50]

Equally important is the cultural change that took place in the 1920s in spectator aviation from individual barnstormers working independently to companies with corporate sponsorship, such as the Gates Flying Circus, to the gradual disappearance of these forms of aviation as entertainment and their progression to spectacle-contests such as the National Air Races and to Hollywood-produced motion pictures. These changes were brought about because the nature of American popular entertainment was undergoing rapid transformation in the 1920s. Like the air show spectacles, huge productions such as circuses, mock naval and land battles, Wild West shows, automobile races, and airplane dogfights that ran at the five-thousand-seat New York Hippodrome, for example, had to give way to the movies for purely economic reasons. Such entertainments were so expensive that the only way producers could operate profitably was by keeping a show running for a whole year. Other changes in American entertainment patterns were taking place. Road show theater productions, for example, which had played in more than fifteen hundred theaters in 1915 declined to fewer than 675 by 1925, according to *Billboard* magazine. Vaudeville, a theatrical entertainment consisting of a variety of live acts and a staple of American entertainment for years, and similarly the circus, another form of live entertainment on which air shows had been modeled since the ballooning era, were being displaced by the movies. As Robert C. Toll has observed, "even the most elaborate stage productions could not portray action and spectacle as convincingly as crude, early movies." In an 1899 review of an extravagant New York stage production of *Ben Hur*, the critic Hilary Bell observed "in the play we see merely several horses galloping on a moving platform. They make no headway, and the moving scenery behind them does not delude the spectators into the belief that they are racing." Bell believed that only film could capture the excitement of the action in the scene.[51]

The Hollywood–Air Race Era

After the barnstorming era of the 1920s, aviation as entertainment emerged in two primary forms during the 1930s: feature-length films produced in Hollywood and air racing. With the resounding success of the Academy Award–winning *Wings* (1927) and *Hell's Angels* (1930), Hollywood had produced a formula of narrative and photography that would be imitated throughout the 1930s. Barnstorming and aerial exhibitions had their limitations in terms of satisfying their audiences—airplanes could only be seen from a distance, and after the Aeronautics Branch enforced restrictions on the height at which aerial maneuvers could take place, that distance increased. Movies, by contrast, had the opposite effect. Improved film technology and the advent of aerial cameras also helped to provide an intimacy that live production could not approximate, and, by the end of the 1930s, Hollywood was almost exclusively the main purveyor of aviation as entertainment. Aviation for amusement was thus channeled into another medium that was potentially more profitable and capable of reaching a far wider audience than other previous forms had been.

Because its European competitors were occupied with the war, the American film industry had grown to a position of prominence stylistically and economically during World War I. Between World War I and the end of the 1920s, Hollywood, as the handful of studios that represented the U.S. film industry became known, established three major aspects of the business: production, distribution, and exhibition in a vertically integrated structure. Vertical integration meant that the studio system established markets in which they owned produc-

tion facilities, distribution outlets, and theaters for exhibition. The studios therefore controlled every facet of the marketplace from production to exhibition. In
an attempt to regulate the expense of production, Hollywood created the genre
system, in which the studios established categories—westerns, war films, gangster films, melodramas, action-adventure films, and so on—for the films to be
made. This system of standardization cut down on risk because a proven genre
could be repeated with a reasonable assurance of success at the box office.[52]

From its earliest use in feature films to the end of the 1930s, aviation became
part of the action-adventure genre. It was no accident that Hollywood chose to
portray aviation according to the same formula of entertainment that had dominated the previous eras of its history—sensationalism, danger, and recklessness—and that kept audiences coming back for more. This formula was obviously what the public wanted and it was responsible for making the aviation film
subgenre successful during its heyday, which ran from 1927 to 1939. Like the
reckless impression of aviation that the birdmen and barnstormers had created,
the brash image perpetuated by Hollywood was enticing and attractive if handled prudently. However, it also was potentially damaging to the public perception of aviation's safety and respectability that the industry's image makers were
working hard to create.[53]

Skirmishes between the emerging image-conscious aviation industry and
Hollywood were infrequent until 1935, the year that Warner Brothers decided
to produce a film version of *Ceiling Zero,* a successful Broadway play scripted by
Frank W. "Spig" Wead, a former naval aviator who had been forced to retire because of injury. The studio was known, especially in the early 1930s, for its gritty,
realistic gangster films and social problem films and, later, for its prewar anti-
Nazi stance. Warners also had produced action-adventure films, so it was not
out of character for the studio to turn Wead's drama into a screenplay. Warners
had in fact already purchased the rights to *Ceiling Zero* when it was a Broadway
play.[54]

Because of the similarity in the locations of cities along the route of the drama's
fictitious Federal Air Lines with that of United Air Lines, the Broadway production of *Ceiling Zero* had caused much consternation in the aviation industry.
Another production problem was the portrayal of the lead character, Dizzy
Davis, whom *Literary Digest* called "an amorous, reckless magnifico of the air
. . . a menace to passengers, husbands, and American womanhood." "All he
knows," the *Literary Digest* continued, "is that a plane must be flown, and radio
beams, automatic pilots, two-way radiotelephony, icebreakers on wings and similar safety gadgets he brushes away." Dizzy simply did not fit the wholesome and
professional corporate air pilot image the industry was trying to promote to convince potential passengers of the safety and reliability of the airlines.[55]

Despite the potential trouble with the industry, Warners decided to proceed with the film. There were, however, some initial misgivings that the film would run afoul of the Production Code, a voluntary means of self-regulation of film content designed to avoid government censorship. In January 1935, Samuel Bischoff, a Warners "line" producer who reported to executive producer Hal Wallis, wrote to him to express his concerns about *Ceiling Zero*. Bischoff liked the play, saying that "the story has a lot of guts and is well-written and is good picture material," but was worried about "a sad ending in which the leading man is killed." Bischoff believed, however, that this was "the only logical way for the story to end as he [Dizzy Davis] is a no-good guy from the beginning to finish and his end is his regeneration." Bischoff also was worried about censorship problems with Joseph I. Breen of the Production Code Administration, the office set up by the Motion Picture Producers and Distributors of America (MPPDA) to enforce moral standards within the industry. "There is," Bischoff wrote, "some censorable material in this story as written, too, which—if eliminated—would hurt the story badly; namely the affairs with numerous women. . . . There is, also, a political angle in this, discussions etc., concerning the government and contracts to the airlines which would have to be taken out, but which would hurt the story." Despite the misgivings, Warner Brothers hired Howard Hawks to direct the film. James Cagney, one of the studio's most proven and popular stars, would play the lead. Cagney was to be teamed with Pat O'Brien, who would in later years become his familiar costar.[56]

After production had begun, Breen did voice some concern that Cagney's character, Dizzy, "was depicted too broadly as an habitual seducer who cheerfully deserted his victims," and that his objections to Cagney's character "would be calculated to put this story in a class objectionable to audiences" made up of "children and young people." Breen also pointed out "the necessity of avoiding any material which will reflect unfavorably upon, or cause objection from, the manufacturers of air planes, or any of the operating companies." "Most important," Breen wrote, "is the necessity of avoiding any material which will identify the characters of the story with any particular Company."[57]

Breen's concern about the industry's objections to the film were well founded. In May 1935, before production of *Ceiling Zero* had begun, Howard Mingos of the Aeronautical Chamber of Commerce of America, a trade organization devoted to the aircraft manufacturing industry, had written to Will H. Hays, head of the so-called Hays Office (the MPPDA), about Warner Brothers' intention to make a film of *Ceiling Zero*. Hays was no stranger to aviation, having been Postmaster General during the time the Post Office Department began operating the Air Mail Service. "The United Airlines," Mingos wrote, "has been very much troubled by the thought that the current play 'Ceiling Zero' in its present form reflects too strongly on United Air Lines by dealing with scenes along the United Air Lines route, and naming cities which are definitely in

United territory." Mingos sought Hays's help "in having any scenario of 'Ceiling Zero' altered enough to prevent an injustice being done to United Air Lines or any of the other operating companies." The industry, Mingos went on, felt "that the artistic quality of 'Ceiling Zero' would not be harmed in the slightest degree by shifting the scenes to localities which are not station stops for a regular transcontinental line." Mingos further suggested that "a motion picture of 'Ceiling Zero' " would be put back in time to, say about ten years ago, thereby implying that such conditions might have existed in the pioneer days, but do not exist today." Moreover, Mingos said, "the air lines today are not operated in the manner implied by 'Ceiling Zero' and they did "not employ pilots like the 'Dizzy' in the play." Mingos concluded by saying that

> the uninterrupted development of our air transport system is of the utmost importance to our national defense, we believe it reasonable to ask the producer of this motion picture to carry an introduction in the film stating that the air lines of the United States today are operated in a most business-like manner, with every regard to safety, and with the unexcelled discipline of personnel throughout the organizations, and that nothing in the dramatic version should be interpreted as an exposition of current conditions.[58]

A few days later, after having received a copy of Mingos's letter to Hays, Harry M. Warner, the New York–based president of Warner Brothers, wrote an assuring letter to Mingos saying that although "the picture rights for the play CEILING ZERO have not been sold to any motion picture company ... should we purchase the picture rights and produce the film, we will do everything we possibly can to prevent an injustice being done anyone, as that is not our method of doing business." Later in the year, after Mingos's requests had been agreed to by the studio bosses and granted by Howard Hawks, Don Black, a representative of United Air Lines, wrote to Hawks:

> Following our conference this morning ... in which you voiced the sincere intention of Warner Bros. to eliminate from the forthcoming production, "Ceiling Zero," most of the features found objectionable by the aviation industry in the stage play, this letter may be considered an expression of United Air Lines willingness to cooperate in making the picture. We are gratified to find an attitude on the part the producers sympathetic to air line problems. It is a further source of gratification to learn that the picture will be directed by you, Mr. Hawks. Your long and valued association with members and leaders of the aviation industry, your frequent patronage of the air lines, and the friendly prospective which this experience has provided you offer further assurances of fair treatment in the filming of this picture. The suggested device of definitely back-dating the story several years happily eliminates likelihood that the public will confuse that pioneering, experimental era with the high safety, comfort and speed of air trans-

port today. You will thus be enabled to employ logically the now obsolete single-engined mail planes for crash sequences instead of the multi-motored liners that now ply the skylanes. We feel that added emphasis to this backdating of the picture may be brought out appropriately in the screen introduction of opening sequences, as proposed by the Aeronautical Chamber of Commerce of the United States. We note with appreciation the care taken in the script to feature constructive angles, to present in detail the great technical advances made in radio, weather reporting, safety devices and facilities generally. In particular does United Air Lines appreciate the elimination of the play's veiled but pointed references to this company in disparagement of its route, equipment and personnel.[59]

These tactics may have amounted to blackmail, but they point up how sensitive the industry was to what it perceived as unfavorable portrayals in the movies, which had the potential of reaching audiences of millions and persuading them that flying was unsafe. In a sense, the aviation industry's insistence on changes to *Ceiling Zero* did not alter the spirit of the film, which is "barnstorming" in nature because it relies on thrills and crashes to excite its audience. These effects were heightened by the sound of the film. In a studio memo, Hal Wallis wrote to Warner Brothers chief sound engineer Nathan Levinson,

> This is a great picture and a big, important picture and we want as fine a job as it is possible to make it. Sound effects will play a large part in the finished product, especially in those scenes where they are trying to get TEXAS CLARK's plane down through the fog, and where he flys [*sic*] over the air port at different altitudes and where he finally comes gliding in and hits the high tension wires. This must be the most terrific sound job you have ever done, and it must absolutely lift the people right out of their seats.

Wallis's memo illustrates that even after the requested changes to the film were made, there were discrepancies between the studio's intentions and the aviation industry's expectations.[60]

Despite the studio's capitulation to the industry on the issue of the portrayal of contemporary aviation, Cagney's Dizzy is a man out of time, who, as the film critic Andrew Sarris points out, "lives according to the rules of an earlier era—war, pioneering, stunt flying, and danger for its own sake. When times change, he cannot change with them." Although it is only hinted at in the exchange of letters between Howard Mingos and Will Hays, it is probable that the Cagney character's undisciplined, womanizing behavior and his deception in persuading Texas Clark into taking his mail run under the pretense that he was ill with a heart ailment, offended the industry as much as the film's portrayal of aviation.[61]

Sarris further notes that [Pat] O'Brien, "Cagney's superior and erstwhile comrade-in-arms, accepts the more difficult and ultimately impossible task of reconciling the two ages of aviation." Like the O'Brien character, many real-life aviators made the transition without qualm that the era Sarris characterizes was passing out of existence. Charles A. Lindbergh, for example, a former barnstormer, arranged financial backing for his 1927 transatlantic flight through Harold Bixby, head of the St. Louis Chamber of Commerce, from businessmen in St. Louis. After the transatlantic crossing, he became associated with wealthy and powerful men such as Dwight Morrow, a J.P. Morgan partner and his future father-in-law, Harry Guggenheim, head of the Guggenheim Fund for the Promotion of Aeronautics, an organization that helped facilitate the passing of the barnstorming era, Henry Breckenridge, a Wall Street lawyer and Lindbergh's personal advisor, and Juan Trippe, head of Pan American Airways. Legitimacy for aviation meant that Lindbergh had to disavow all "illegitimate" purposes, in particular his barnstorming past, which would give flying a negative image and potentially jeopardize the growth of aviation as a business.[62]

The aviation industry's objections to *Ceiling Zero* served notice to Hollywood that commercial aviation could not be taken lightly. Thereafter, the few films that dealt with the airlines were respectful and noncontroversial. Paramount's *Thirteen Hours by Air* (1936), for example, was produced because of the studio's desire "to help commercial aviation." *Thirteen Hours* prominently featured the United Air Lines logo and the Boeing 247 airliner, manufactured solely for the airline. Again, Hollywood made concessions to the aviation industry when Paramount rewrote and reshot the ending of the film after United Air Lines officials objected to a fight between the airliner's pilot and the villain that took place on board the aircraft. The scene was shifted to the ground at no small expense to the studio.[63]

Through Hollywood, aviation had become part of the mass consumer culture during the 1930s. Americans who had little hope of seeing an airplane in person much less riding in one unless a barnstorming aerial circus came to their community could experience the thrill of flying vicariously through the movies. Like Hollywood, the National Air Races, the dominant live performance sport-entertainment-recreation showcase for aviation from 1929 to 1939, helped create a mass market for aviation as entertainment. Unlike Hollywood, which had no illusions about portraying aviation as anything but entertainment, the National Air Races' promoters tried to associate the event with aviation's legitimacy and utility by claiming that increased speed and improvements in technology came from a racing test-bed. The analogy between air racing and aviation technology was a borrowing from auto racing that recalled the other connections between automobiling and aeronautics.[64]

Undoubtedly, the National Air Races were the premier aviation spectacle of the 1930s and were as popular in their time as the Indianapolis 500 automobile race is in American culture today. The brainchild of the Henderson brothers, Clifford W. and Philip T., before 1929 the National Air Races were a loose assortment of closed-course and distance races, aerial stunt and aerobatic shows, with little organization and less effect on the public. The Hendersons, in the words of the aviation journalist Cy Caldwell, brought "sound management and superior showmanship to an affair sadly in need of both." By 1930, the National Air Races had been pared down to three races: the Bendix Trophy race, a transcontinental speed race across the United States; the Greve Trophy race, a closed-course event for aircraft with engines of less than 550-cubic-inch displacement; and the Thompson Trophy race, an unlimited class race. These primary events were supplemented by barnstorming stock-in-trade such as aerial stunting and aerobatics, parachuting, and flyovers by military and civilian aircraft. But it was the racing that attracted the crowds, and by the end of the 1930s, attendance for the Nationals had risen nearly threefold to more than 350,000 spectators over a three-day period.[65]

The relationship between the National Air Races and the aircraft industry, however, was at best tenuous. To some observers, air racing's image was incompatible with that of safety and assurance that the industry was laboring hard to promote. "Because of the high speeds involved," Courtney Brooks points out, "few Nationals were staged without some fatal accident during the series of races. Indeed, the story of the Thompson race was largely one of crashes and deaths." General Manager Clifford Henderson was sensitive about criticism: "Skeptics see in the annual air pageant only a circus ballyhoo event, a publicity parade for a few prominent pilots.... The doubters see in the audiences attending chiefly a mob of ghoulish-minded yokels out for thrills from the hair-raising nature of events by which they will be impressed with the Dangers of flying rather than its genuine offerings of Safety, Convenience and Speed." Moreover, Henderson described air racing as "the laboratory of the aeronautical industry" and cited the two main contributions of air racing as technological progress and public acceptance of aviation.[66]

Henderson must have known that no one was fooled by his rhetoric of utility. *Aviation* magazine, for example, stated unequivocally,

> We've never been particularly impressed ... by the claim that air racing, national or otherwise, makes great scientific contribution toward the advancement of the art of flying. Talk of "improving the breed" and "the great laboratory of the industry," and glib comparisons with the Kentucky Derby and the Indianapolis Classic [in regard to air racing's utility] seem to us to be the most specious form of twaddle.

In 1937, Henderson was troubled enough over repeated criticism of the National Air Races to accede to the wishes of Lester Gardner, head of the Institute of the Aeronautical Sciences, to include in the 1937 National Air Race program a seminar called "Engineering for Speed," a discussion of the benefits of air racing to the aeronautical engineering profession. Speakers from the industry were invited to present papers on topics ranging from aircraft design to fuels to engines and piloting. Two of the six speakers, Robert Insley of Pratt & Whitney, and Edmund T. Allen, a noted test pilot, saw little or no value in air racing, while others saw some distinct but esoteric value. *Aviation* lamented that "absent to a man were the plane builders and pilots taking part in the races ... for they definitely could have contributed much to the discussion."[67]

This example indicates how far apart the two aviation cultures were in their thinking. Comparisons of air racing with the Kentucky Derby and Indianapolis 500 in an attempt to correlate the National Air Races' utility to aviation may have been misleading at the time. In retrospect, however, these comparisons were perhaps true as a measure of the races' popularity with the public. The Kentucky Derby and Indianapolis 500 still exist and are still popular, while the National Air Races have long since disappeared, the victim of public disinterest, the attempt to provide utility where none existed, and, ultimately, shunning by an image-conscious industry. The National Air Race's demise was not helped by the defection of personalities such as James H. "Jimmy" Doolittle, winner of the Thompson Trophy in 1932 and a perennial air race drawing card. Doolittle abandoned air racing when accidents began to give the sport a bad name. "Air racing originally did promote safety in aviation through testing of materials used in construction of planes and engines," Doolittle said, but "lately it appears that the value received is not commensurate with the personal risk involved." Even the veteran air racer Roscoe Turner, three-time winner of the Thompson Trophy, who retired in 1939 after his third victory, admitted that "backers as well as pilots are out for glory ... their names in the headlines. There isn't much sport. Flying a racing job is not only dangerous, but it's uncomfortable. It's not relaxing. You fly on your nerve."[68]

World War II and After

World War II brought to a close the air racing era and with it the heyday of aviation as entertainment. On the one hand, tactical and strategic employment of the airplane during the war had helped further aviation's military utility. On the other, the dropping of atomic bombs on Hiroshima and Nagasaki in 1945 left no doubt of the martial purposes to which the airplane could be put. The war helped rationalize aviation even further, putting in place a massive aircraft industry that would capitalize on the gains it had made during the war to maintain its position during the Cold War. Moreover, the world air routes forged during the war became the basis for commercial routes in the postwar period, further consolidating the position of the commercial airline industry.

By the end of World War II, aviation's "serious" purpose and utility was even more rigidly impressed in the public consciousness, and aviation as entertainment and aviation as industry reached a tenuous accommodation in the years after the war.[69]

Although air racing and exhibition flying continued, performances were fewer than before the war. As one air race chronicler has pointed out,

> the National Air Races were resumed at Cleveland August 30 through September 2, 1946. But nothing was the same. The military came with its new jets, and the civilian unlimiteds were all WWII surplus fighter airplanes. The race course, which had previously measured ten miles around, was stretched to 30 miles per lap. Even the spectators were different. They, too, had been changed by the war. America had lost its charming naivete and nothing would ever look the same to us again. Those famous warplanes, those venerated weapons of freedom, familiar to everyone, did incite interest for what they were and what they had meant to the nation; but they really weren't racers.[70]

The National Air Races continued through 1949, but after Bill Odom's disastrous crash into a residential neighborhood in suburban Cleveland, the event was radically transformed. The celebrated National Air Races ceased to exist. In 1964, the National Championship Air Races were inaugurated in Reno, Nevada, where they have been held regularly ever since. The National Championship Air Races, however, have never attained the popularity of the National Air Races held in the 1930s.[71]

The decline of air racing and other forms of exhibition flying was a cause for concern among those who saw other roles for aviation beyond its commercial or military applications. The rules had changed. Recreational flying, which before the war had been dominated by the exhibition pilots and air racers, was now primarily the realm of the private pilot. Immediately after the war, the Civil Aeronautics Administration, expecting a boom in private flying that never came, changed the Civil Air Regulations in favor of the personal pilot, but even that was not enough to satisfy the Aircraft Owners and Pilots Association (AOPA), an interest group for private flyers. During the 1950s, constraints on private aviators became tighter and the struggle between the Federal Aviation Administration (FAA; the CAA's successor) and AOPA became more bitter. The FAA, in its concern for safety of the airways, tightened flight space restrictions, required expensive electronic equipment for navigation and communication, and a medical examination by a qualified doctor. In the early 1960s, the relationship between the private flier and the FAA improved, but there was still a great deal of tension over familiar issues during the remainder of the decade. In the 1970s, the question of general aviation's paying a fair share of the costs of the airspace was added to the controversy.[72]

During the last few decades, not much has changed; the adversarial relationship between the FAA and the AOPA continues. In an op-ed piece for *General Aviation News* & *Flyer* in 1994, Max Karant, a former high AOPA official and the FAA's longtime nemesis, accused the agency of having "taken upon itself to dictate every mandatory rule and regulation it can dream up, all 'in the interest of safety.'" Karant took the FAA to task for trumping up the issue of safety in aviation. "If the government is justified in spending nearly $10 billion each year for the FAA, and there is a total of 932 fatalities in both airline and general aviation (in 1992), why is it not acting this hysterically over the 43,500 citizens who were killed by motor vehicles in that same year?"[73]

Much of what Karant says is true. The FAA's hypersensitivity to aviation safety may in a cultural sense be the last vestiges of an institutionalized prejudice against aviation as recreation/entertainment that began in 1926 with the passage of the Air Commerce Act and the formation of the Aeronautics Branch of the Department of Commerce. It is also noteworthy culturally that the current-day aviation scene is drastically dissimilar to the pre–World War II period. That was a time when commercial and military aviation were still in their infancy and there seemed at least to be a rationale for limiting recreational aviation through federal regulation. Unlike the 1920s and 1930s, the airlines and the military have become dominating giants of the aerospace industry that have long since proven their utility and enjoy the full support of the government. Yet, the perceived unsafety of exhibition and private flying is still considered a threat to institutionalized flying. Although the safety of the airlines has been demonstrated beyond a doubt, instead of reduced regulation of recreational flying, there is increased regulation.

One way that people who want to fly but also want to avoid the FAA regulation of private flying have gotten around the restrictions is through the ultralight movement. At its most rudimentary level, an ultralight is a hang glider with an engine. It weighs less than 254 pounds, carries five U.S. gallons of fuel, and flies at fifty-five knots airspeed at full power. An ultralight is not required to meet the airworthiness certification standards usually specified for aircraft, nor does it need a certificate for airworthiness issued by the FAA. Operators of ultralights do not have to meet aeronautical knowledge, experience, or age requirements, nor do they have to have pilot licenses or medical certificates to fly them. Ultralights do not have to be registered or have markings of any type on them. Over the years the movement has been going on, the description of an ultralight has changed considerably. Microlights, which are considered ultralights, are rather more sophisticated craft, often heavier than the FAA standard, often two-place. The movement's popularity is summarized by the U.S. Ultralight Association's president John Ballantyne: the U.S. Ultralight Association (USUA), Ballantyne says, "simply reflects member enthusiasm for fun flying. To this organization higher and faster is less important than low and slow—we

take fun flying seriously." Yet it is entirely possible that the FAA will take a restrictive position against ultralights as it has in the past against other forms of
recreational flying.[74]

Despite the restrictions, flying as recreation and entertainment is as popular
for pilots and spectators as it was two centuries ago in the ballooning era. (Sport
ballooning has in fact had a resurgence of popularity in the last two decades.)
The highly popular Experimental Aircraft Association Fly-In at Oshkosh, Wisconsin, is a tribute to the founder Paul Poberezny's concern in the early 1950s
that the interests of recreational and sport flyers were being disregarded in favor
of commercial and military aviation. Each year in August, upward of three
quarters of a million people congregate at Oshkosh to see every kind of aircraft
imaginable: military aircraft of both World Wars; airliners from the 1930s; air
racers of all vintages; homebuilts of every type; ultralights. Also part of the festivities are airshows with the world's best performers—wing walkers, parachute
jumpers, solo aerobatic pilots, and teams of aerobatic aircraft. "Oshkosh," as it
has come to be known, has grown steadily in popularity during its forty-year history and is a testament to the public fascination with flying for fun.[75]

Oshkosh and the ultralight movement, along with other types of sport aviation such as aerobatic flying, are perhaps also indicative of a longing for the days
when aviation was in its fledgling period and the dream of flight, with all of its
romantic associations, was fresh in the public mind. This was an era that Joseph
Corn, a cultural historian, tells us ended in 1950 with the loss of faith in the
dream of mass private airplane ownership, but may actually have terminated in
1939 with the prewar National Air Races. Although times and cultural conditions have changed over the two hundred years of flight in the United States, one
thing appears certain: the confrontation between the airplane's utility and its entertainment value will continue. The public's fascination with flying as a source
of amusement and entertainment, thrills and fun, however, will also continue
because it corresponds with Lewis Mumford's belief that only sport provides
"the glorification of chance and the unexpected," the feeling of being truly alive.
That a machine such as the airplane can provide such a feeling in a technologically complex and increasingly mechanized and dehumanized world may be
ironic, but it is not likely to change.[76]

Notes

    1. Cy Caldwell, "Personairlities," *Aero Digest,* July 1932, 36–37; Michael Osborn and
Joseph Riggs, *"Mr. Mac": William P. MacCracken, Jr. on Aviation Law, Optometry* (Memphis,
Tenn.: Southern College of Optometry, 1970), 36. My sincerest gratitude goes to Heidi Munro
for her help in researching this essay. Heidi helped to ferret out much of the material for the
barnstorming and air racing sections as well as for the *Ceiling Zero* and postwar developments
segments.

2. Jonathan Culler, *Roland Barthes* (New York: Oxford, 1983), 33–34.

3. "The Sport of Kings" is taken from a chapter title in Tom D. Crouch, *The Eagle Aloft: Two Centuries of the Balloon in America* (Washington, D.C.: Smithsonian Institution Press, 1983), 531–60; Courtney G. Brooks, "American Aeronautics as Spectacle and Sport" (Ph.D. diss., Tulane University, 1969), 2, 10. Although it is true that Benjamin Franklin urged members of the American Philosophical Society in Philadelphia to pursue scientific investigations into ballooning, his entreaties were never taken very seriously. In fact, the society refused to sanction manned balloon flights in the United States. It was fearful that its affiliation with ballooning, which was then considered controversial largely because of its association with less than desirable elements of society, would tarnish its professional image. See Michael E. Connaughton, "'Ballomania,' The American Philosophical Society and Eighteenth-Century Science," *Journal of American Culture* (1984), vol. 7, 71–74.

4. Howard L. Scamehorn, *Balloons to Jets: A Century of Aeronautics in Illinois, 1855–1955* (Chicago: H. Regnery Co., 1957), 12, quoted in Brooks, 41.

5. Crouch, *The Eagle Aloft,* 465; Brooks, 11–12. So obstreperous were the throngs of people that attended the balloon ascensions of the period that promoters and aeronauts worried that these events were not a proper place for women. At Jean Pierre Blanchard's ascent in Philadelphia in 1793, Courtney Brooks tells us, "there was some concern that about the prison [Walnut Street Prison] as the site, fearing that the surroundings would offend the ladies. But Philadelphia women quickly assured Blanchard. In a letter to the aeronaut, printed in the Philadelphia General Advertiser, a number of ladies who had purchased tickets informed him that there was no cause for concern." This incident illustrates that critics of ballooning performances were rather more squeamish than the actual spectators. Brooks, 51.

6. Donald Dale Jackson, "The Last Flight of Professor Donaldson," *Air and Space Smithsonian* (October/November 1989), 92–93; quoted in Bill Robie, *For the Greatest Achievement: A History of the Aero Club of America and the National Aeronautics Association* (Washington, D.C.: Smithsonian Institution Press, 1993), 5.

7. *New York Times,* August 16, 1891, quoted in Crouch, *The Eagle Aloft,* 477–78.

8. George Dollar, "Foolhardy Feats," *Strand* (January 1898), 705, quoted in Brooks, 58.

9. See "Section 622. Theatre," *The New Encyclopaedia Britannica* (Chicago: Encyclopaedia Britannica, 1995), 234–36, for a suggested typology of the theater arts. See Nancy L. Struna, *People of Prowess: Sport, Leisure, and Labor in Early Anglo-America* (Urbana: University of Illinois Press, 1996), and Bruce Daniels, *Puritans at Play: Leisure and Recreation in Colonial New England* (New York: St. Martin's Press, 1995), for cogent analyses of the role of sport, leisure, and recreation in early America. Elliott J. Gorn and Warren Goldstein, *A Brief History of American Sports* (New York: Hill and Wang, 1993), contains a useful discussion of Puritan attitudes toward leisure activities.

10. Notes to "The May-Pole of Merry Mount," in *Nathaniel Hawthorne's Tales,* James McIntosh, ed. (New York: W. W. Norton, 1987), 88.

11. Donna R. Braden, *Leisure and Entertainment in America* (Dearborn, Mich.: Henry Ford Museum and Greenfield Village, 1988), 126.

12. Karen Halttunen, *Confidence Men and Painted Women: A Study of Middle Class Culture in America, 1830–1870* (New Haven: Yale University Press, 1982), 9; Beecher, quoted in Halttunen, 23.

13. This is a far cry from ballooning's present-day All-American image as exemplified by annual meets such as the Kodak Albuquerque International Balloon Fiesta in New Mexico.

14. Quoted in Herbert A. Johnson, "The Aero Club of America and Army Aviation," *New York History: Quarterly Journal of the New York State Historical Association* (October 1985), 376, 377; Robie, 55.

15. Robie, 9–10.

16. Julia Lamb, " 'The Commodore' Enjoyed Life—But N.Y. Society Winced," *Smithsonian* (November 1978), 139. "James Gordon Bennett/First Patron Saint of Aeronautics," unidentified clipping, James Gordon Bennett Biographical File, National Air and Space Museum, Smithsonian Institution, Washington, D.C.; Robie, 307.

17. Scamehorn, *Balloons to Jets,* 12, quoted in Brooks, 40.

18. Gorn and Goldstein, 84. See Richard Hofstadter, *The Age of Reform: From Bryan to F.D.R.* (New York: Vintage Books, 1955), 131–73, for an analysis of what he terms "The Status Revolution." Hofstadter says, "It is my thesis that men of this sort . . . were Progressives not because of economic deprivations but primarily because they were victims of an upheaval in status that took place in the United States during the closing decades of the nineteenth and the early years of the twentieth century. Progressivism, in short, was to a very considerable extent led by men who suffered from the events of their time not through a shrinkage in their means but through the changed pattern in the distribution of deference and power."

19. Gorn and Goldstein, 93.

20. Ibid., 86, 97.

21. Brooks, 83–84; George L. Mosse, *Fallen Soldiers: Reshaping the Memory of the World Wars* (New York: Oxford University Press, 1990), 119.

22. Allen Guttmann, *From Ritual to Record: The Nature of Modern Sports* (New York: Columbia University Press, 1978), 15–55. See also Allen Guttmann, *A Whole New Ballgame: An Interpretation of American Sports* (Chapel Hill: University of North Carolina Press, 1988), 5–6; Louis Galambos, *The Public Image of Big Business in America, 1880–1940: A Quantitative Study in Social Change* (Baltimore: Johns Hopkins University Press, 1975), 261.

23. Robie, 50–51.

24. Robie, 71–72.

25. Roger Bilstein, "The Public Attitude toward the Airplane in the United States, 1910–1925" (M.A. thesis, Ohio State University, 1960), 27–28; C. R. Roseberry, *Glenn Curtiss: Pioneer of Flight* (Syracuse, N.Y.: Syracuse University Press, 1991), 219.

26. Tom D. Crouch, *The Bishop's Boys: A Life of Wilbur and Orville Wright* (New York: W.W. Norton, 1989), 430, 434–35; Brooks, 120–21; Curtis Predergast, *The First Aviators* (Alexandria, Va.: Time-Life Books, 1980), 107.

27. *Aeronautics,* July 31, 1914, quoted in Brooks, 118; *Scientific American,* October 28, 1911, 382, quoted in Brooks, 124.

28. Quoted in Brooks, 136–37.

29. Johnson, "The Aero Club of America and Army Aviation," 384–85.

30. Ibid., 388, 389, 393; Robie, 89–90.

31. John H. Morrow, Jr., *The Great War in the Air: Military Aviation from 1909 to 1921* (Washington, D.C.: Smithsonian Institution Press, 1993), 365.

32. Robie, 97.

33. Russell Nye, *The Unembarrassed Muse: The Popular Arts in America* (New York: Dial Press, 1970), 194; Hart Stilwell and Slats Rogers, *Old Soggy No. 1: The Uninhibited Story of Slats Rogers* (New York: Julian Messner, 1954; New York: Arno Press, 1972), 130–31.

34. Bill Rhode, *Baling Wire, Chewing Gum, and Guts: The Story of the Gates Flying Circus* (Port Washington, N.Y.: Kennikat Press, 1970), 54.

35. Ibid., 86–89, 98–99.

36. Robie, 104.

37. Ibid., 96–99, 100–101.

38. By the terms of that agreement, members of the aircraft industry had to join the Manufacturers Aircraft Association (MAA), a trade organization, and paid MAA $200 for each air-

craft manufactured. Out of the $200, $135 and $40 would go to Wright-Martin and Curtiss-Burgess, the primary patent contestants, and $25 to the MAA for expenses. Payments to the primary contestants would end when their patents ran out, or in Curtiss-Burgess's case, when the royalty paid equaled what had been paid to Wright-Martin. See Jacob Vander Meulen, *The Politics of Aircraft: Building an American Military Industry* (Lawrence: University Press of Kansas, 1991), 20–26; Alex Roland, *Model Research: The National Advisory Committee for Aeronautics, 1915–1958,* vol. 1 (Washington, D.C.: National Aeronautics and Space Administration, 1985), 37–42.

39. Vander Meulen, 20; quoted in Roland, 35.

40. Vander Meulen, 15, 16.

41. Vander Meulen, 37; Howard Coffin to Newton D. Baker, Jan. 2, 1918, RG 18, Aircraft Board, Corresp. Files, 1917–1918, Box 5, Fd. 7, National Archives and Records Administration, Washington, D.C.; Coffin to Baker, Jan. 18, 1918, RG 18, Aircraft Board, Corresp. Files, 1917–1918, Box 7, Fd. 281; Coffin to W.S. Gifford, Jan. 18, 1918, RG 18, Aircraft Board, Corresp. Files, 1917–1918, Box 2, Fd. 72. Baker was Secretary of War. Gifford was the director of the Council of National Defense, the federal organization that had sponsored the War Production Board.

42. Robie, 105.

43. Robie, 103–4.

44. *Aero Digest,* November 1922, 139, quoted in Nick A. Komons, "William A. MacCracken, Jr., and the Regulation of Civil Aviation," in *Aviation's Golden Age: Portraits from the 1920s and 1930s,* ed. William M. Leary (Iowa City: University of Iowa Press, 1989), 35, 41, 43. On the Winslow Bill, see also Komons, *From Bonfires to Beacons: Federal Civil Aviation Policy under the Air Commerce Act, 1926–1938* (Washington, D.C.: Smithsonian Institution Press, 1989), 55–58, 61, 62–64.

45. Robie, 106–7.

46. Much of the discussion on the formation of the NAA is taken from Robie, *For the Greatest Achievement,* chapters 1 through 12. Quoted in Robie, 106–7; Osborn and Riggs, "Mr. Mac," 64. Interviewed later in his career by Charles Planck, MacCracken reiterated his belief that the industry "realized they were not going to get public acceptance until they generated public confidence and they had to get rid of a lot of this barnstorming that had been going on around the country." Interview, William P. MacCracken with Charles Planck. William P. MacCracken, Jr., Biographical File, National Air and Space Museum, Smithsonian Institution, Washington, D.C.

47. Thomas E. Lowe, "The Flying Aces Flying Circus," *American Aviation Historical Society Journal* (summer 1977), 118, 120.

48. Dominick A. Pisano, Foreword, *American Airport Designs* [reprint ed.] (Washington, D.C.: American Institute of Architects, 1990), v; *Aero Digest* (March 1926), 124; *Chicago Tribune* quoted in *Literary Digest,* October 27, 1928, 17.

49. Geoffrey Perrett, *America in the Twenties: A History* (New York: Touchstone, 1982), 336–37.

50. Michael E. Parrish, *Anxious Decades: America in Prosperity and Depression, 1920–1941* (New York: W.W. Norton, 1992), 21; David D. Lee, "William P. MacCracken, Jr.," *The Encyclopedia of American Business and Biography: The Airline Industry,* ed. William M. Leary (New York: Facts on File, 1992), 286. See also David D. Lee, "Herbert Hoover and the Golden Age of Aviation," in *Aviation's Golden Age,* 127–47.

51. Quoted in Robert C. Toll, *The Entertainment Machine: American Show Business in the Twentieth Century* (New York: Oxford, 1982), 13–14, 15, 20.

52. Nick Roddick, *A New Deal in Entertainment: Warner Brothers in the 1930s* (London:

British Film Institute, 1983), 3; Toll, 29; John Belton, *American Cinema/American Culture* (New York: McGraw-Hill, 1994), 64. Thomas Schatz, *Hollywood Genres: Formulas, Filmmaking, and the Studio System* (New York: McGraw-Hill, 1981), contains an excellent discussion of the genre system.

53. Paramount's *The Grim Game,* starring Harry Houdini, and Universal's *The Great Air Robbery,* 1919, and *The Skywayman,* 1920, starring stunt-pilot-turned-actor Ormer Locklear are two of the earliest aviation films produced by Hollywood. Information on Locklear and Houdini from James H. Farmer, *Celluloid Wings: The Impact of Movies on Aviation* (Blue Ridge Summit, Pa.: Tab Books, 1984), 18–24.

54. Wead's life was recreated on film by John Ford in the 1957 production *The Wings of Eagles;* "Broadway: 'The Dog' of Hollywood," *Literary Digest,* April 20, 1935, 20.

55. See Roddick, *A New Deal in Entertainment,* for an excellent history of Warner Brothers from its origins to the end of the 1930s; *Literary Digest,* April 20, 1935, 20.

56. Thomas Doherty, *Projections of War: Hollywood, American Culture, and World War II* (New York: Columbia University Press, 1993), 36–37; Samuel Bischoff to Hal Wallis, January 10, 1935, *Ceiling Zero* File, Box 3, Warner Brothers Archives, University of Southern California.

57. Joseph I. Breen to Jack L. Warner, October 11, 1935, *Ceiling Zero* File, Box 3, Warner Brothers Archives, University of Southern California.

58. Howard Mingos to Will H. Hays, May 17, 1935, *Ceiling Zero* File, Box 3, Warner Brothers Archives, University of Southern California.

59. Harry M. Warner to Howard Mingos, May 20, 1935; Don Black to Howard Hawks, September 21, 1935, *Ceiling Zero* File, Box 3, Warner Brothers Archives, University of Southern California.

60. Hal Wallis to Major [Nathan] Levinson, November 27, 1935, *Ceiling Zero* File, Warner Brothers Archives, University of Southern California.

61. Italics mine. Andrew Sarris, "The World of Howard Hawks," in *Focus on Howard Hawks,* ed. Joseph McBride (Englewood Cliffs, N.J.: Prentice Hall, 1972), 45.

62. Sarris, 45; on Lindbergh's connection to the wealthy and powerful, see Joyce Milton, *Loss of Eden: A Biography of Charles and Anne Morrow Lindbergh* (New York: Harper Collins, 1993), 132–48.

63. Farmer, 94–96.

64. Airplane racing also was prevalent in the 1920s; the dominant events were the Pulitzer Trophy and Schneider Cup races, but the enterprise was almost exclusively controlled by the military services. The National Air Races of the 1930s are thought of as the dominant form of American air racing. The association between automobiles and airplanes also is evident in the formation of the Aero Club of America from the membership of the Automobile Club of America and, later, in the involvement of the automotive industry in wartime aircraft production and the formation of the NAA.

65. Brooks, 158–59, 162, 161.

66. Clifford W. Henderson, "The Value of National Air Races," *Aero Digest* (July 1930), 70, quoted in Brooks, 163–64 (italics Henderson's).

67. The brochure for the 1937 National Air Races makes the emphasis on thrills and speed apparent, with descriptions such as "Thrilling Speed Contests," "Stirring and Fearless Stunt Flying," "Skywriting with Fire," "High-Speed Races for World's Records," and "Entirely New, Different and More Nerve-Gripping Attractions." In advertising the Nationals to the public, utility was the farthest thing from the promoters' minds. "Race Progress," *Aviation* (September 1937), 21. Despite the rhetoric of racing's role in aviation's utility and progress, by the mid-1930s the real technological innovations in aviation, particularly commercial aviation—structures, aerodynamics, propulsion, design—were coming from the industry and

government-sponsored research (the National Advisory Committee for Aeronautics, for example). The development of the Douglas DC-series commercial aircraft is a classic example of the roots of technological innovation in aviation.

68. Lowell Thomas and Edward Jablonski, *Doolittle: A Biography* (Garden City, N.Y.: Doubleday, 1976), 128; Roscoe Turner, "Air Racing Is Hell," *Popular Aviation* (September 1939), 11, quoted in Brooks, 161.

69. On the industry in the postwar period, see Wayne Biddle, *Barons of the Sky* (New York: Henry Holt, 1993), chapter 10, "Permanent Rearmament," 288–319; on the development of American commercial aviation in the immediate postwar world, see Henry Ladd Smith, *Airways Abroad: The Story of American World Air Routes* (Madison: University of Wisconsin Press, 1950).

70. Joe Christy, *Racing Planes & Pilots: Aircraft Competition, Past and Present!* (Blue Ridge Summit, Penn.: Tab Books, 1982), 137.

71. On the consequences of the Odom crash, see Dominick A. Pisano, "Collision Course [The Demise of the National Air Races]," *Air and Space Smithsonian* (April/May 1997), 28–35.

72. John R.M. Wilson, *Turbulence Aloft: The Civil Aeronautics Administration amid Wars and Rumors of Wars, 1938–1953* (Washington, D.C.: U.S. Dept. of Transportation, Federal Aviation Administration, 1979), 25–27, 134–36, 164–68; Stuart I. Rochester, *Takeoff at Mid-Century: Federal Civil Aviation Policy in the Eisenhower Years, 1953–1961* (Washington, D.C.: U.S. Dept. of Transportation, Federal Aviation Administration, 1976), 70–71, 176–77, 265–68, 270, 272; Richard J. Kent, Jr., *Safe, Separated, and Soaring: A History of Federal Civil Aviation Policy, 1961–1972* (Washington, D.C.: U.S. Dept. of Transportation, Federal Aviation Administration, 1980), 34–38, 114–16; Edmund Preston, *Troubled Passage: The Federal Aviation Administration during the Nixon-Ford Term, 1973–1977* (Washington, D.C.: U.S. Dept. of Transportation, Federal Aviation Administration, 1987), 61.

73. Max Karant, "The 'Big Three' Have Reasons for Keeping Aviation Mysterious," *General Aviation News & Flyer,* Second April Issue 1994, 23. Statistically, flying in private aircraft is four times as dangerous as driving an automobile, but from twice to four-and-a-half times as safe as walking or bicycling, and three times as safe as riding a motorcycle. See Susan A. Skolnick, *Book of Risks* (Bethesda, Md.: National Press, 1985), 41–50.

74. AIM/FAR 1994: Airmen's Information Manual/Federal Aviation Regulations (Blue Ridge Summit, Pa.: TAB Aero, 1994), 425; "Director's Memo," *Ultralight Flying* (January 1994), 18.

75. Tom D. Crouch, "Wingding at Oshkosh: The Annual Aircraft Fly-In," *National Geographic Traveler* (Summer 1985), 53, 57.

76. Quoted in John Rickards Betts, *America's Sporting Heritage: 1850–1950* (Reading, Mass.: Addison-Wesley, 1974), 320.

The Man Nobody Knows

Charles A. Lindbergh and the Culture of Celebrity

CHARLES L. PONCE DE LEON

In July 1930, Charles A. Lindbergh appeared before a select group of reporters to announce that he would no longer "cooperate" with five New York newspapers. These papers, he claimed, had repeatedly violated his privacy.[1] Lindbergh's decision marked the culmination of a bitter and well-publicized feud between the aviator and reporters for the tabloid press. To all intents and purposes, Lindbergh had ceased cooperating with the tabloids a year earlier, when he and Anne Morrow had wed in a secret ceremony and had eluded reporters for more than a week during their honeymoon. Therefore, no one was especially surprised by his announcement, which elicited a chorus of cheers among writers for "respectable" newspapers and magazines that shared his disgust for the tabloids' "contemptible" practices. Lindbergh's views on tabloid journalism, a writer for *The Nation* observed, "raise him still higher in our respect and admiration, something that we hardly felt possible in view of his great modesty, his dignity, and his refusal to let himself be ruined by the unparalleled publicity and popularity which have been his."[2]

Concerns about the tabloids were widespread in upper-middle-class and elite circles during the 1920s, uniting liberals and conservatives who could agree on little else. For many educated Americans, tabloid journalism was emblematic of a steep decline in public morals, the quintessential product of a society lacking dignity and good taste.[3] The critique often hinged on the issue of privacy. By directing attention to the private lives of prominent individuals, tabloid journalism had shattered conventions that had enabled such figures to keep their private affairs out of public view. But most writers who made this claim neglected to mention that "respectable" newspapers, even the august *New York Times,* were filled with gossip about the private affairs of celebrities—most of it planted by celebrities and their publicists. The real problem with the tabloids was not their fixation on gossip. It was their unwillingness to content themselves with press releases or authorized inside dope, and the lengths to which they were willing to go to get such unauthorized material. These practices not only threatened the right to privacy, but they undermined the ability of celebrities to control their representation in the press.

Lindbergh's celebrity was the product of the intersection of his 1927 transatlantic flight with mass communication—radio, sensational newspaper journalism, newsreel films. Lindbergh's fame after the transatlantic flight of 1927 offers a way of looking at the cult of celebrity in the United States during the twentieth century. On his return to the United States on the U.S.S. *Memphis* after the transatlantic flight, Lindbergh and the *Spirit of St. Louis* were greeted at the Washington Navy Yard in June 1927. The awarding of the Distinguished Flying Cross by President Coolidge was only one of the honors bestowed on Lindbergh as a result of the flight. (National Aeronautics and Space Administration (NASA), courtesy National Air and Space Museum, Smithsonian Institution [SI 97-15222].)

Lindbergh often had complained to friends about his depiction in newspapers. Considering the gulf between the image he sought to project and the one created by elements of the press, his frustration can be understood. In the immediate aftermath of his spectacular flight from New York to Paris in 1927, many papers had "misrepresented" him in order to make him appear more colorful to the public, stressing details about his personality and his experience in the air that he had consistently downplayed. Even before he took off from Roosevelt Field on Long Island, when he was but one of several fliers vying to be the first to cross the Atlantic, Lindbergh had begun to lose control over his media image. To his dismay, reporters dubbed him "Lucky Lindy" and the "Flying Fool," nicknames that were supposed to distinguish his expedition from the well-financed, meticulously organized, and relentlessly hyped expeditions of his rivals. In the "race" across the Atlantic, Lindbergh had been cast as the "dark horse." Someone had to play this role, and as the only aviator who planned to make the dangerous journey alone, Lindbergh was best suited for the part. Yet he believed this angle minimized the planning and expertise he and his backers had put into his flight, and he resented the press for employing it.[4]

After his triumphal return to the United States, Lindbergh was determined to correct these misperceptions and reassert control over his portrayal in the media. But this proved more difficult than he had imagined. Newspapers had published reams of hastily gathered and often inaccurate material on his family background, childhood, and early career as a barnstormer and air mail pilot. Lindbergh had become the property of the media, the latest product of a vast culture of celebrity that had blossomed during the 1920s. Much to his chagrin, editors and reporters would retain significant power over his public image, selecting the angles and contexts in which he would be placed. In this respect, Lindbergh was no different from other celebrities who were used by the mass media to personify newsworthy ideas and trends. But his celebrity also was peculiar. Unlike other public figures, Lindbergh was promoted as exceptional—an authentic hero who refused to allow himself to be "cheapened" or "spoiled" by his fame and fortune. This angle focused attention on an issue that was implicit in other celebrity discourse but explicit in discourse on Lindbergh: the moral corruption that could result when a person was elevated to celebrity status.

Media representations of Lindbergh directly addressed this issue, offering the public two distinct versions of the famous aviator. In the first version, which dominated media discourse between 1927 and the late 1930s, Lindbergh was depicted as a person who had successfully withstood the temptations and tribulations that confronted all celebrities. The second version emerged more slowly. It first appeared between the lines of wire-service reports and in newsreel footage when Lindbergh was still being lionized. Not until the late 1930s, when Lindbergh became an outspoken isolationist and lost support in the media, was it clearly articulated. This Lindbergh was a "swelled head," a man who had made no effort to resist the corrupting effects of celebrity, becoming a haughty recluse and a dangerous crank. This chapter will demonstrate that these versions of Lindbergh were opposite poles in a fascinating debate among journalists about the "price" of celebrity, a debate that reflected widespread anxieties about maintaining the integrity of the self in a society in which social relations were intrinsically theatrical.

Charles Lindbergh's greatest misfortune was performing a dramatic feat in an era obsessed with celebrity, when technological developments, economic imperatives, and cultural trends all conspired to direct an unprecedented amount of media attention on public figures. The roots of this culture of celebrity can be traced back to the 1830s. During this period, the penny press began publishing gossip and brief human-interest stories about various local and regional "notables." By the 1850s, the interview had become a regular feature of mass-circulation journalism, and in the latter half of the century it would become the primary vehicle through which the public became acquainted with famous politicians, businessmen, reformers, actors, and authors. In the 1880s, Joseph Pulitzer began to use famous individuals as the "angles" of stories about complex institutions or trends, a development that marked the advent of "personalized" news, one of several Pulitzer innovations that were initially criticized yet widely imitated in the years to come. Another was the biographical profile or sketch, which, accompanied by illustrations or photographs, first appeared in Pulitzer's Sunday supplements but then quickly spread to the new mass-circulation magazines of the 1890s. By the turn of the century, many public figures had become the subjects of elaborate, open-ended narratives that readers could follow in the press.[5]

These trends in journalistic practice were reinforced by other developments. Technological innovations in candid photography and moving pictures gave celebrity discourse a compelling new visual dimension. Efforts to reach working-class and immigrant readers, inaugurated by Pulitzer and accelerated by William Randolph Hearst and the tabloids, led many publishers to increase dramatically their emphasis on human-interest stories, including stories about celebrities. Cultural changes affecting the middle classes heightened their interest in such material, creating a huge pool of potential consumers. Finally, after 1900, New York emerged as the hub of a vast network of wire services and feature syndicates, and from here a regular stream of stories about the nation's most prominent public figures flowed out to provincial newspapers around the country. By the 1920s, celebrities had become highly visible, almost ubiquitous. Their names and faces appeared in news and human-interest stories, in syndicated gossip columns, in the rotogravure sections of the "respectable" press, in newsreels, and in advertisements, where they could be seen promoting a wide array of products.

In the 1920s, moreover, a wider range of figures was accorded celebrity status than ever before. Until World War I, most celebrity discourse was devoted to politicians, businessmen, and socialites. To be sure, certain actors, entertainers, and athletes also received attention, and in the Hearst press in particular this attention could sometimes surpass that of more conventional celebrities. But it was not until the 1920s and the enormous success of the tabloids that a rough parity between these two camps was achieved. The tabloids played a key role in expanding the definition of a celebrity by publicizing the activities of Hollywood stars, professional athletes, and underworld figures such as Al Capone. Unlike "respectable" papers, which sought to confine their gossip to "wholesome" or "serious" public figures, the tabloids showed little concern for the fact that some of their subjects were disreputable. Having decided that the public was sincerely interested in Capone, for example, they published as much as they could about him. Indeed, the tabloids publicized anyone who might be interesting to the public, hoping that the interest he or she aroused would result in increased circulation. Their inclusiveness had a significant impact on more "respectable" papers, forcing the latter to open their columns to celebrities they might have preferred to ignore.[6]

Most celebrity discourse was either planted by press agents and publicists or produced in cooperation with them. By the 1920s, publicists had become important players in the newspaper business. Their emergence was a direct response to the increasing power of the media to determine how celebrities would be portrayed, and a decisive step in a campaign by celebrities to regain some of the initiative. Press agents had first been employed by circuses and traveling theatrical companies. In the 1890s, they began to be hired by prominent actors and New York socialites who hoped to exploit the new vogue of "personalized" news. After the turn of the century, newspaper crusades against large corporations and powerful businessmen led former journalists to establish the new field of "public relations." Although public relations "counselors" such as Ivy L. Lee and Edward L. Bernays publicly disavowed the fakery of theatrical press agents, their techniques differed only slightly from the latter's. Both press agents and publicists were responsible for protecting the client's image and ensuring that press coverage was congruent with his or her wishes. This often required planting stories in the press as well as using their newspaper connections to suppress unflattering publicity. Over time, publicists developed an elaborate set of conventions for dealing with the press. These included regular interviews, press releases, and photo opportunities, all which were designed to provide newspapers with a regular diet of "inside dope" and forge bonds between clients and the reporters assigned to cover them. Although many clients objected to these techniques, there was no denying their effectiveness. Celebrities who developed good relations with the press were "protected" by reporters, and in some cases sympathetic journalists served as their unofficial flacks.[7]

Yet such cooperation was rarely as smooth as publicists might have wished. Although they gradually learned to accept the mediating role of publicists, many journalists were disturbed by their incorporation into the publicity machine, particularly when they found themselves engaged in egregious examples of fakery or self-censorship. In addition, personal loyalty to a celebrity often conflicted with institutional or ideological commitments, making unequivocal support impossible. This was especially true when celebrities acted in ways that contradicted their carefully crafted images. Such "misbehavior" made journalists look bad in front of readers, and usually inspired defections from a celebrity's circle of unofficial publicists. In short, celebrities were free agents. They had the power to upset the plans of their press agents and advisers, compelling their hirelings to leap to their defense. Charles Lindbergh was notorious in this regard. Not only did he refuse to employ a publicist for most of his career, but also he continually behaved in a manner that made things difficult for his supporters in the press.[8]

These problems were compounded by the appearance of the tabloids. Competition among these papers was fierce, and in their efforts to best their rivals, editors displayed an unprecedented insouciance toward the "rules" laid down by publicists. Driven to get exclusives, they began to publish unauthorized material, including nasty exposés. Publicists responded to such negative publicity by issuing a new round of authorized material: interviews with sympathetic journalists, rebuttals by well-connected insiders, explanations and carefully worded "confessions" that altered the terms of debate or placed acknowledged transgressions in the best possible light. These might appear in the offending tabloid, but they were more likely to appear in "respectable" newspapers and influential magazines such as *Collier's* or *The Saturday Evening Post*. With the appearance of the tabloids, celebrity discourse gained a greater complexity and assumed its modern shape: an elaborate cycle of exposure and inside dope. Questions raised by the tabloids or maverick journalists eager for a "scoop" were answered by a flood of authorized information meant to set the record straight. In time, however, new questions were raised, requiring another round of damage control. This seemingly endless process kept celebrities in the news and endowed them with an aura of mystery. Indeed, celebrity discourse revolved around questions of identity that, by the turn of the century, had come to pervade everyday life. Was he on the level? Was she the person she seemed to be? What was he *really* like?

The aim of celebrity discourse was to answer these questions, to provide a glimpse of the "real" selves of the nation's most prominent public figures. Like other forms of journalism, it was informed by a profound suspicion of appearances, by a nagging fear that people consciously misrepresented themselves not only in the harsh, competitive world of the market but also in personal relations. As Jean-Christophe Agnew has shown, concern about appearances was a result of the spread of a dynamic "market culture" that allowed for new forms of deceit and imposture. It was reinforced by urbanization, geographic mobility, and the proliferation of new trades and occupations. By the mid–nineteenth century, large numbers of American men were being encouraged to "make" their own success and identity. And in subsequent years, as increasing numbers of women were drawn into the urban labor market, they were given similar encouragement. The development of a consumer culture was crucial in this regard. It provided men and especially women with a highly accessible means of creating and displaying one's identity. Yet the very ease with which people could adopt and change identities, a freedom unique to modern capitalist societies, heightened anxieties about appearances and made revelation and exposure cultural obsessions.[9]

This obsession with the "real" was the defining trait of celebrity discourse, the feature that distinguished it from earlier discourses on fame and heroism. As America's most ostensibly "successful" individuals, celebrities usually were portrayed as exemplars of virtue. In so doing, their supporters drew on a venerable hagiographic tradition.[10] As early as the mid–nineteenth century, however, many Americans began to question whether public achievement and virtue were as compatible as the hagiographic tradition had assumed. And during the latter half of the century, as industrialization altered the landscape and gave rise to new social problems, such questions acquired a new urgency. To many observers, the most "successful" Americans appeared to be those who were the most ruthless and cunning.[11] These doubts about the efficacy of virtue also were fueled by new intellectual currents, particularly the new psychology. By the 1890s, it was widely assumed that humans were subject to unconscious impulses and desires, that lurking within the hearts of men were "animal passions" that could never be completely suppressed. Such views made belief in the unalloyed virtue of public figures even more problematic and dealt a severe blow to hagiography.[12]

To appease public skepticism, it became necessary for celebrities and their supporters to provide new kinds of material. Celebrities continued to be depicted as paragons of virtue, and elements of hagiography persisted in residual form. But now details about their hobbies, tastes, and personal life were included along with the usual summaries of their extraordinary talents and achievements, making them appear more "real" to the public. The inclusion of this "human-interest" material shifted the focus of celebrity discourse away from the explicit didacticism of hagiography. Unlike hagiography, which tended to highlight a famous person's divergence from the "ordinary" in order to accentuate his or her saintliness, celebrity discourse narrowed the gap between the two. Celebrities were portrayed as "human beings"—in some cases, flawed human beings—who just happened to be famous. This heralded a new emphasis. The major theme of celebrity discourse was not how famous people achieved "success" or lived a "moral" life but, rather, how they coped with life's vicissitudes and mastered the "art of living"—a theme that perfectly expressed the new secular, therapeutic orientation of the mass media during the early twentieth century.[13]

Lindbergh was not unaware of these conventions. Yet, compared to most public figures, he was quite uncomfortable with them. He knew, of course, that his flight would attract public attention, and that he would come to "personalize" the fledgling aviation industry. And he fully expected to parlay his fame into a respectable career as a consultant and spokesman for civilian aviation. Before he left New York, he signed endorsement contracts with several companies that had provided parts for his plane, and he anticipated making similar arrangements in the future. From the beginning of his celebrity, however, he stubbornly refused to answer reporters' questions about his private life, the kinds of questions that virtually every other celebrity—even the taciturn Calvin Coolidge—regularly answered. Lindbergh's lack of cooperation in this area might have been tolerable if he had been a more exciting spokesman for "airmindedness." But unlike other pilots, who played up the adventure of flying in interviews with the press, Lindbergh preferred to discuss technical matters. He believed that to successfully promote civilian aviation it was necessary to make air travel appear safe, and emphasizing adventure did not serve this purpose. Thus, in interviews he habitually referred to his record-setting, often dangerous flights of the late 1920s and early 1930s as scientific "experiments."[14]

Lindbergh's views were shared by a group of wealthy and influential players in the aviation industry. Harry Guggenheim, Harry Davison, Jr., Henry Breckinridge, and Dwight Morrow were Wall Street insiders who envisioned an industry dominated by large corporations. Guggenheim and his friends admired Lindbergh's seriousness, and after his return from Europe they sought to employ him as a spokesman for commercial aviation. Yet Lindbergh's triumph had created new dangers. Public interest in aviation had increased exponentially, and new investment money now filled the coffers of many firms. A considerable portion of this money was speculative, and the Guggenheim group feared that many investors would abruptly sell and incite a panic if they perceived a decline in the fortunes of the industry. Because Lindbergh was linked to aviation, damage to his reputation could imperil the entire industry's financial stability. They were particularly concerned about the possibility of Lindbergh's name being gradually cheapened through "overexposure": appearances in advertisements, motion pictures, and on the vaudeville circuit. By keeping him away from this course, they hoped to protect the fledgling industry from the taint of hucksterism and ensure that the public would not tire of its foremost public representative. There were legitimate reasons for the Guggenheim group to be concerned about this. Within days of his arrival in Paris, Lindbergh's press agents in New York, who had been assigned to him by his St. Louis backers, received endorsement and motion picture offers worth several million dollars. But Guggenheim and Breckinridge convinced Lindbergh to refuse these offers and put himself under their wing, arguing that such a course was in the best interest of aviation.[15]

Lindbergh's decision not to cash in on his celebrity was the pivotal moment in his career as a public figure. Had he accepted the endorsement and motion picture offers, he would have no doubt remained highly visible. And, more than likely, he also would have retained many admirers, because celebrities such as Babe Ruth, Jack Dempsey, and Al Jolson accepted these offers without suffering the "overexposure" feared by the Guggenheim group. Yet if Lindbergh had done so, he would not have been celebrated so widely or loudly by the media and by spokesmen for the dominant culture. Influential businessmen, politicians, ministers, educators, and newspaper editors praised Lindbergh's determination not to be "cheapened" by America's "tabloid culture," and their tributes to him betrayed a strong revulsion for the "personality advertising" of the era—a revulsion that pervaded elite circles during the 1920s and echoed the Guggenheim group's concerns about "overexposure." For these Americans, Lindbergh was a godsend, a popular idol who shared their professed disdain for publicity and the tawdry lures of the entertainment industry. From the moment he landed in Paris, they began to use him as a weapon in their campaign against what they perceived as the "excesses" of 1920s America. In their hands, he was transformed into a symbol of modesty, dignity, and youthful idealism—values that were antithetical to the avarice, ballyhoo, and cynicism of the "jazz age."

This required more than simply illuminating the man. It demanded a measure of exaggeration and fakery—the very practices that elites associated with "personality advertising" and the tabloids. While Lindbergh was not always happy with his saintly image, he played along out of loyalty to the cause of aviation. One can understand his embarrassment. The "Lindbergh" promoted by spokesmen for the dominant culture was too good to be true, an exemplar of "youthful earnestness" and "clean living." Poised and gracious, he accepted the praise heaped on him with a remarkable sense of dignity. Editors insisted that this ability to keep his head, "when flooded with flattery that would upset most men," was his most endearing and significant trait. It proved that Lindbergh had character, that he understood "the fundamental things in life." Unlike so many other public figures, who succumbed to the lures of "easy money" or the "cheap notoriety which many mistake for fame," Lindbergh eschewed money-chasing and self-promotion. According to President Calvin Coolidge, this "absence of self-acclaim" and "refusal to become commercialized" was the source of Lindbergh's enormous popularity. It had "endeared him to every one." Compared to the myriad "celebrities" who filled the pages of newspapers and magazines, Charles Evans Hughes asserted, Lindbergh was an authentic hero whose behavior provided the youth of America with "a stirring, inspiring vision of real manhood."[16]

The image of the saintly Lindbergh carried profound implications. By insisting that the primary reason for Lindbergh's enormous appeal was his refusal to commercialize himself, his champions were suggesting that the American public shared their disdain for commercialism and "personality advertising"— in effect, projecting views held by elites onto the country at large. And by linking Lindbergh's authenticity as a hero to his rejection of commercialism, editors and politicians were implicitly criticizing other celebrities, who were now associated with the despised culture of self-promotion. Although never mentioned by name, celebrities such as Jack Dempsey and Babe Ruth—Lindbergh's chief rivals as the most popular male public figures of the 1920s—were dismissed as greedy, cynical, and undignified. Compared to a real hero, they were products of hype and ballyhoo. Nor were they real men. By making Lindbergh's reserved, chaste brand of masculinity the national standard, Hughes and others denigrated the flamboyant, swaggering style of Dempsey and Ruth, a style derived from working-class culture. But Lindbergh's supporters went even further. They asserted that the values Lindbergh embodied—middlebrow WASP values—were "American" values, the foundation of the "national character." Commercialism and self-promotion were depicted as "alien" and linked to urban dwellers, immigrants, and the working class.

These associations were not made at random. They closely mirrored media efforts to legitimize corporate capitalism during the 1920s, a campaign that hinged on constructing a rogue's gallery of scapegoats. In venerating corporate executives and big business in general, the media sought to encourage the belief that large corporations stood for probity, efficiency, and public service. Meanwhile, traits such as greed, ruthlessness, and dishonesty were projected onto a host of "others." The most obvious and inviting of these scapegoats was "organized crime," but many legitimate businesses and industries dominated by immigrants and ethnics also were portrayed as corrupt. On the surface, the press was simply drawing on anti-immigrant stereotypes. Yet editors may well have had a more ambitious aim. Having lived through the Progressive era, when anti-corporate sentiment was widespread, they may have been preparing for another outbreak, hoping that when the backlash came it would be directed against immigrant and ethnic entrepreneurs, not corporate America.[17] Such fears were not baseless. By 1927, financial speculation had become a serious concern among Wall Street insiders, leading many to expect a costly "readjustment" that would revive populist outrage against corporate capitalism. Scandals had rocked the Republican Party and several large corporations, mocking the notion that big business was reformed. Prohibition also had proven to be a disastrous experiment, producing bitter divisions in elite circles as well as among ordinary Americans. Finally, immigrants and second-generation Americans had gained considerable economic and political power, often by going outside established channels and catering to their own communities.[18]

The burgeoning influence of immigrants and ethnics in politics, business, and popular culture was accompanied by heightened public interest in urban and ethnic cultural styles. Embodied by celebrities such as Dempsey, Ruth, Rudolph Valentino, Gloria Swanson, and Clara Bow, these styles had enormous appeal. Many immigrants, ethnics, and working-class Americans found them more familiar than the more austere styles associated with WASP paragons such as Mary Pickford, Will Rogers, or Henry Ford. But their appeal was not confined to these groups. As countless ministers, educators, and editors lamented, millions of middle-class WASPs were attracted to them as well. They appealed to such Americans for the same reasons that jazz, nightclubs, and tabloid newspapers did. The new styles were sensual, dramatic, expressive—perfect antidotes to the official morality preached by censorious ministers, teachers, and employers. They also satisfied yearnings for intense experience that had become an integral part of life in the new corporate economy. Widespread interest in the new styles made it impossible for the media to ignore them. Some papers and magazines, generally those catering to the lower classes, openly endorsed the new styles, while more "respectable" organs sought ways of dulling their edge. The most common strategy was to link them to "youth," an angle that allowed for extensive coverage yet also limited their impact. Associating the new styles with youth effaced their roots in ethnic and working-class culture and encouraged Americans to believe that interest in them should wane when people reached "maturity."[19]

The Lindbergh created in the wake of his flight was the antithesis of the new cultural styles. Commentators stressed that Lindbergh's refusal to "cheapen" himself was most unusual for a person so young, a sign of his maturity. It also was a sign of his devotion to "old-fashioned" values that had been swept aside amid the ballyhoo of the 1920s. At the same time, Lindbergh was associated with technology and scientific expertise, which gave him a decidedly modern aura.[20] But the Lindbergh persona was more than an amalgam of the pioneer spirit and veneration for the machine. He was crafted as an antidote to class and ethnic divisions that deeply perplexed many elites and middle-class Americans. Lindbergh's supporters in the press perceived that segments of the public were alienated from many of the values the media had promoted for the better part of a decade, and that even Americans who had embraced these values had grown weary of the hype that had accompanied their promotion. Accordingly, they made Lindbergh's most salient trait his principled detachment from the culture of the market, a culture in which the distinction between aggressive "salesmanship" and deceitful self-promotion had never been especially clear. Here we can see early signs of the revisionism that would blossom during the Depression. By the early 1930s, the "jazz age" would be reviled as a mindless, wasteful debauch, and spokesmen for the dominant culture would be hard at work trying to kindle public interest in national symbols that bore no trace of the booster spirit of the 1920s. Lindbergh was the first of such symbols. As constructed by his champions in editorial offices around the country, he symbolized an America purged of the unseemly traits of a "business civilization."[21]

Believing they had a "moral investment" in Lindbergh, many editors were determined to protect him against debunking. Yet their promotion of him as an authentic "hero" created new problems. As we have seen, heroes were out of vogue, and portraying Lindbergh in this fashion was certain to arouse the curiosity of the public. Satisfying this curiosity would require regular evidence of

Lindbergh's virtue. Unfortunately, the conventional means of providing such evidence was through the kinds of "human-interest" material that Lindbergh refused to provide and editors had implicitly linked to the disreputable practice of "personality advertising." Even worse, by harping on Lindbergh's modesty and refusal to capitalize on his fame, his supporters in the press directed public attention toward the possibility of his corruption. Before Lindbergh had even returned to the United States, reporters and columnists began speculating about his chances of withstanding the temptations that continually beset popular idols. A whole new series of questions was raised—questions that turned Lindbergh's great refusal into an epic drama. Would Lindbergh remain "unspoiled," the simple, down-to-earth flier who wanted nothing more than a chance to live a "normal" life? Or would public adulation cause him to develop a "swelled head" and become a selfish egomaniac? Would he be able to resist the offers from Hollywood and the advertisers and vaudeville promoters? Or would he finally succumb to their blandishments and cash in on his fame? Would he maintain his remarkable poise and self-control in the glare of the spotlight? Or would the pressure lead him to commit a disgraceful *faux pas* that would forever tarnish his reputation and quickly make him a "has-been"?[22]

Lindbergh was not the only public figure haunted by the specter of the "swelled head." It was a central theme of celebrity discourse, a theme based on one of the most pervasive assumptions in American culture: that wealth, power, and social prestige were morally corrosive. According to this view, the rewards of public achievement made people arrogant, self-absorbed, and contemptuous of the public. They became "spoiled." Arresting this process required vigilance and iron resolve. It was especially difficult for celebrities such as Lindbergh, who were the objects of continuous flattery and acclaim and thus more likely to "lose their heads." Those who were able to prevent this from occurring achieved "true success," a sublime happiness and peace of mind. To achieve true success, celebrities had to maintain their "balance." This meant remaining modest, down-to-earth, and accessible to family, friends, and the public. It also meant rejecting the license for self-indulgence that accompanied celebrity status. Truly successful celebrities conformed to "respectable," middle-class values—despite myriad opportunities to do otherwise.[23]

Over the years, critics and commentators have blithely dismissed such views as envy or sour grapes. By doing so, however, they overlook the fact that suspicion of wealth and power has deeper roots in American culture than the worship of material success. Concerns about "swelled heads" echoed ministers' warnings against the sins of pride and vanity. They also drew on republican critiques of dissolute "aristocrats" and the corrupting influence of power. They were derived as well from traditions of popular gossip, which the lower orders in preindustrial Europe and America had employed to question or mock the pretensions of elites.

These threads were gathered together by the publishers of the commercial press and woven into a secular discourse with widespread popular appeal. In its original form, this discourse was quintessentially petit-bourgeois, reflecting the common social backgrounds of publishers and the audience they hoped to reach. By the turn of the century, it continued to express a vaguely populist sensibility, although journalists no longer identified with lower-middle-class and working-class readers. For the press, promoting discourses with populist accents served economic and ideological ends. This was an essential marketing tool for winning the support of lower-class readers, the new frontier in newspaper publishing. This also was thought to be an effective device for recreating a unified public in an era when class and ethnic divisions threatened to tear the country apart. The discourse of the "swelled head" established a seemingly popular standard against which public figures could be measured, and could be used against virtually anyone who appeared to be putting on airs.[24]

Throughout his career, Lindbergh was especially susceptible to the "swelled head" charge. Hailed by editors as a sign of modesty, his refusal to discuss personal matters also could be viewed as a manifestation of haughtiness. Reporters came to resent his refusal to say more than a few words about the promise of civilian aviation, and their bitterness was exacerbated by the fact that Lindbergh played "favorites," providing a select group of aviation writers with more information than the rest, including exclusive interviews. These reporters maintained good relations with Lindbergh by studiously ignoring subjects he did not want to discuss and revealing very little about his personality and private life. As Lindbergh's relations with reporters became increasingly strained, many editors were careful to excise any subtle jabs that disgruntled reporters might try to include in their copy. More than a "moral investment" was at stake here. As one Washington daily learned in 1929, papers that ventured to criticize Lindbergh could expect a torrent of angry letters and canceled subscriptions. But perhaps the greatest danger that accompanied criticism of Lindbergh was the likelihood of angering Lindbergh's myriad supporters and admirers in influential business circles—the kinds of people who could impede the smooth flow of advertising revenue and exert tremendous financial pressure on a newspaper.[25]

Yet suppressing negative publicity about Lindbergh also threatened to undermine the print media's credibility with the public. This was because newsreel footage of Lindbergh's public appearances presented a very different view of him. In newsreels he appeared stern, arrogant, and contemptuous of the crowds that gathered to greet him. As ordinary Americans viewed the newsreels, they must have been surprised, even bewildered, by what they saw. This was the modest, down-to-earth Lindbergh? Anxious to avoid the impression of complicity, some editors began to back away from their commitment to him, reasoning that Lindbergh himself, by acting so gracelessly in front of newsreel cameras, had made it impossible to protect him. Not surprisingly, the tabloids were not only the first papers to break ranks but also the ones to go the furthest in pursuit of the "real" Lindbergh. They assigned platoons of reporters and photographers to the Lindbergh beat, giving them free rein to hound the aviator until he opened himself up to the press. The wise course, as many of Lindbergh's friends recognized, was to call a truce and give the tabloids a few exclusives, if only to get them off his back. But Lindbergh responded to this new intrusiveness by becoming even more uncooperative and elusive, the quarry in an elaborate game of hide-and-seek. His supporters attributed this to "stubbornness." To his growing legion of critics in the press, however, his sphinxlike reticence and determination to elude their gaze seemed calculated—part of a sophisticated plan to attract the very publicity he professed to despise.[26]

These suspicions were too explosive for publication in the "respectable" press, and the tabloids only hinted at them. It was left to *The New Yorker*, a new magazine that specialized in satire and chic cynicism, to air them in detail. The case against Lindbergh took the form of a two-part profile in the fall of 1930 by Morris Markey, a former reporter for several New York papers, including the *Daily News*, who had joined the magazine's staff at its inception in 1925. Markey's position as a staff writer—rather than a freelancer who worked for a newspaper—made him the perfect debunker of a celebrity who had powerful admirers in the upper echelons of metropolitan journalism. And *The New Yorker* was the perfect vehicle for debunking, a magazine that proudly expressed its contempt for popular sensibilities, announcing in its first issue that it was not written for "old ladies from Dubuque." *The New Yorker* could get away with debunking Lindbergh because debunking was what its affluent, urbane readership expected. Lindbergh also was the perfect subject for such a profile, as no other public figure of the era had been portrayed in such saccharine terms. From the perspective of Markey and his editor, Harold Ross, it was time to bring him down a few notches.[27]

Although Markey's portrait of Lindbergh was ambiguous, expressing admiration as well as contempt, it directly challenged both the image the aviator himself sought to project—the scientific Lindbergh—and the saintly image constructed by his supporters. Markey's Lindbergh was not a scientist but a stunt pilot, the "Barney Oldfield of aviation," whose often reckless escapades were of "extremely dubious value" to the industry. Far from avoiding publicity, his flights were "calculated to draw the attention of the crowd." His seeming detachment from the marketplace also was a ruse. Although Lindbergh had turned down endorsement and movie deals, he had found less ostentatious ways to line his pockets: royalties, consulting fees, and large blocs of stock in well-financed aviation ventures such as Pan American Airways and Transcontinental Air Transport, which later became TWA. From these he had amassed a con-

siderable fortune—a sum, given his "unwavering shrewdness," that was likely
to grow. Markey's Lindbergh hated the public and the rituals he was forced to
observe as a popular idol. This stemmed from his "utter contempt for the herd."
He was openly rude to reception committees, and he derived pleasure from ignoring and thumbing his nose at the fawning crowds that pursued him. According to Markey, Lindbergh was a man of "mystery" who carefully shielded
his private self from view, but the fragments he revealed were not especially attractive. As far as anyone could tell, the "real" Lindbergh was grim and humor-
less, a stubborn, irritable, puritanical fellow.[28]

Despite Markey's bravado, publication in *The New Yorker* was unlikely to do
serious damage to Lindbergh's reputation, for the magazine's readership was mi-
nuscule compared to those of the newspapers and magazines that protected him.
More important, clever cynicism was expected of *The New Yorker,* and in this respect his critique of Lindbergh did not carry as much weight as a critical piece in
a serious magazine such as *Collier's* or *The Saturday Evening Post* would have.
Nevertheless, there is evidence that Markey's profile irritated Lindbergh and his
advisers, who perhaps feared that its irreverence would establish a dangerous new
precedent and prompt similar critiques in the widely read tabloids. Less than a
month after its appearance, Lindbergh consented to be interviewed by a writer
for *Pictorial Review,* a popular women's magazine. And in the spring of 1931 he
agreed to allow *The Saturday Evening Post,* the premier mass-circulation magazine of the era, to publish a long feature story about him. The latter marked a watershed. Lindbergh not only discussed his private life, and authorized these details to be published, but he invited the author to spend the night at his home in
rural New Jersey, enabling him to sketch the kind of "human" portrait that had
never appeared in newspapers or magazines.[29]

One reason for Lindbergh's cooperation was that the writer assigned to the
story, Donald E. Keyhoe, was a man he could trust. In July 1927, Keyhoe, a former Marine pilot and Commerce Department publicist, had been assigned by
the Guggenheim Fund to accompany Lindbergh on his goodwill tour of the
United States, and during the three months they traveled together he and Lindbergh had become friends. Keyhoe was one of the first to recognize the public relations problems created by Lindbergh's reticence, and in early 1928, with the
full support of Lindbergh and the Guggenheim group, he published a book
about their travels, *Flying with Lindbergh.* Excerpted in *The Saturday Evening
Post,* Keyhoe's book was expressly designed to offset any negative impressions
that Lindbergh's behavior during the tour might have created. It was the first attempt to defuse potential criticism and provide the public with an intimate
glimpse of "the least understood of all public figures."[30]

Similar efforts to correct "misperceptions" of Lindbergh were made by
prominent aviation writers. Although devoid of the anecdotes and human-

interest material that filled *Flying with Lindbergh,* feature articles written by C. B. Allen, Lauren D. Lyman, or Russell Owen addressed the "myths" and "queer stories" that had begun to circulate about him. In a modest, seemingly authoritative way, they also provided readers with a view of the "real" Lindbergh that closely resembled his official persona. The fact that Lindbergh remained friendly with these men suggests that he must have approved of these articles, although it is unlikely they were written at his behest. One such piece, written by Owen, appeared on the front page of the *New York Times* in March 1928. Its aim was to explain to the public why Lindbergh seemed "weary of the limelight," and to reassure readers that any irritation he might have displayed was not a result of arrogance or contempt for his millions of admirers. Owen's article included no direct quotations from Lindbergh and few of the other rhetorical gambits that commonly accompanied authorized inside dope, yet it sought to perform the same functions: answering rumors, exploding myths, reassuring a potentially skeptical public.[31]

As Lindbergh's war with the tabloids escalated, a new kind of apologia began to appear in newspapers and especially in mass-circulation magazines— "think pieces" and commentaries analyzing the nature and causes of the conflict. The authors of these were usually newspaper editors, and they claimed to understand the views of both sides. But they were far more sympathetic to Lindbergh than they were to his adversaries. Ironically, it was in such articles that some of the "incidents" that threatened to tarnish Lindbergh's image were revealed in detail. For example, most Americans had probably failed to notice that during a ten-minute layover at Washington's Bolling Field in April 1929, Lindbergh had maliciously spattered mud on a crowd of reporters, photographers, and well-wishers, as the incident was barely mentioned in wire-service accounts of his brief stop in Washington. Several months later, however, thanks to extensive discussion of this incident and others like it in national magazines, it had become well known to the public and a *cause célèbre* among journalists. Of course, "think pieces" portrayed such incidents in a manner favorable to Lindbergh, offering lengthy, often belabored explanations for his behavior. Yet, by directing public attention to previously obscure events, their authors actually may have fueled public skepticism of him.[32]

His supporters conceded that the Lindbergh the public saw in parades, at large receptions, or in newsreel footage of such events was not the "real" man. It was a façade that obscured his private self. With old Army buddies, fellow pilots, or other chums, Russell Owen argued, Lindbergh was a "far different person from the celebrity one sees in a crowd." Donald Keyhoe agreed, noting that during their tour Lindbergh underwent "a lightning-like transformation" every time a reporter or a reception-committee member appeared, becoming the "serious-eyed youth" who was familiar to the public. When the interloper left, he reverted back to "Slim," Keyhoe's fun-loving companion. Yet even the public Lindbergh was not the haughty person he sometimes seemed to be. Keyhoe reported that Lindbergh was always courteous to reception committees, and sincerely grateful to the thousands of Americans who gathered at airports and along parade routes to see him. If he seemed less than appreciative, Keyhoe explained, it was because of concerns for the safety of onlookers, who often rushed his plane before he had turned off the propeller. Lindbergh's determination to remain on schedule, which would demonstrate the viability of aviation as a transportation medium, was another source of controversy. Keyhoe revealed that it was the tour's tight schedule—and not contempt for the public—that forced Lindbergh to turn down many requests for appearances and spend so much time attending to the condition of his plane.[33]

According to his supporters, Lindbergh maintained a serious façade for several reasons. First, out of propriety, because the stolid Midwesterner had been raised to regard it as appropriate public behavior. As one of his old Army buddies told Keyhoe, Lindbergh had always had a clear sense of "when and where to play." Moreover, he was not a naturally effusive person, and for him to have acted like one because it was expected of him would have been awkward and artificial. "If he had replaced his self-contained demeanor with a hail-fellow-well-met demeanor, or his simple, direct words with flowery phrases," Keyhoe contended, "he would no longer have been Lindbergh, but a man who had lost his head at the laudations of the world." Lindbergh's reticence, then, was "natural," one of the "basic elements" of his character, not a calculated pose designed to enshroud himself in mystery. It had been reinforced by his experience as a celebrity. Reporters, crowds, autograph hounds, well-meaning admirers, self-interested schemers, cranks—all pursued him relentlessly, and over time the pressures of such a life took their toll. As his supporters noted, Lindbergh could not go out in public without attracting a crowd, and eating in a restaurant or attending a movie was impossible. Given the "terrific penalties" he was forced to endure, it was only natural for him to want a little privacy.[34]

These burdens, journalists argued, were particularly hard on Lindbergh because he had not sought to become a celebrity. Celebrity had been thrust on him without his consent. As numerous writers observed, Lindbergh had severely underestimated the adulation his flight to Paris would spark. He had hoped to return to the United States and resume a "normal" life, and, as early as the fall of 1927, after his Guggenheim tour, he was "ready, even anxious, to step out of costume and settle down to the serious business of aviation." Yet, much to his dismay, the public would not let him. At the end of their cross-country tour, as Lindbergh reiterated his desire to resume a normal life, Keyhoe felt sorry for his companion, whose "hope of becoming once more just Charles A. Lindbergh was only a dream—destined not to be fulfilled." When Lindbergh came to realize the extent of his predicament, he resolved to carve out as much of a private life as possible, even at the price of public misunderstanding. Thus, Lindbergh's desire for privacy was motivated by sensible longings to escape from the public's gaze. Once beyond it, he could drop his façade and allow "Slim," his real self, to emerge. Implicit here was the assumption that Lindbergh's celebrity was alienating—that the demands it placed on him were not merely onerous but psychologically corrosive, compelling him to play the role of "serious young spokesman for aviation" nearly every waking hour.[35]

Although his supporters admitted that even they did not know him very well, they nonetheless presented their own version of the "real" Lindbergh. According to Keyhoe, he was not a "plaster saint" but a modest, sensible, fun-loving young man. Despite his fame, he did not expect to be treated like royalty, and his opinion of old friends "depended directly on their forgetting that he was other than a comrade." When Keyhoe visited Lindbergh three years later, he was pleased to discover that "Slim" had survived the ordeal of celebrity: "Never had I seen him so completely free of that tense, on-guard manner which had necessarily grown to be part of him on his 1927 tour . . . and which had remained with him long afterward. That night . . . I saw more of the old likable Slim in his infectious smile than I had observed for two years in public." In short, fame had not gone to Lindbergh's head. Deep down, beneath the façade he displayed in public, his real self remained unscathed. In fact, Keyhoe noted, the enormous pressures of the past four years had made him more considerate of the public and more sensitive to his responsibilities as a spokesman for the aviation industry, allowing him to tolerate "many things which formerly caused him a very natural irritation." Yet, although his tolerance for imposition had increased, he was still adamant about keeping his personal life out of the spotlight. This resolve, Keyhoe argued, was the main reason why Lindbergh had been able to cope so successfully with the burdens of fame. In rural New Jersey he and his wife and infant son enjoyed "a quiet, simple and happy home life," which prepared him emotionally for the moments when he re-entered the spotlight's glare.[36]

Keyhoe's piece in *The Saturday Evening Post* was supposed to end speculation about Lindbergh, and no doubt the aviator hoped that he and his family would now be left alone. Yet, on March 1, 1932, less than a year after Keyhoe's visit, the Lindberghs' son, Charles Jr., was kidnapped and eventually found murdered, and the grief-stricken couple became the subjects of a new round of media attention. Before the body was discovered, Lindbergh was unusually cooperative with the press, hoping to use them to make contact with the kidnappers and arrange the child's safe return. But after the boy's decomposed remains were located in a shallow grave a few miles from their home, the Lindberghs withdrew from public view, more determined than ever to guard their privacy. Although newspaper editorials expressed sorrow at their loss, the tragedy had increased public interest in them, preventing editors from taking reporters off the Lindbergh beat. Charles and Anne remained a focus of attention, and tabloid reporters continued to stalk them, particularly when another son, Jon, was born a few months after Charles Jr.'s murder. Lindbergh himself did not help matters when he chose to attend the trial of the accused killer, Bruno Richard Hauptmann. His presence in the courtroom made him fodder for the dozens of reporters and human-interest writers assigned to the case, and contributed to the trial's circus atmosphere. Finally, in December 1935, the Lindberghs secretly boarded a cargo ship bound for England, where they established a new home.[37]

On the eve of their departure, Lindbergh had summoned his old friend, Lauren D. Lyman of the *New York Times,* for a final interview in order to explain his reasons for becoming an expatriate. Lyman reported that the Lindberghs had been driven into exile not merely by the harassment of the tabloids but by a new series of threats against Jon. Adding to the long list of "terrible penalties" that the aviator had been forced to endure, Lyman revealed that Lindbergh had received countless threats during his years as a celebrity. Most were the work of harmless "cranks," and, until the kidnapping of Charles Jr., the Lindberghs had never paid much attention to them. They were not about to make this mistake again, especially as the threats against Jon had recently "increased both in number and virulence." Yet, if the tabloids were not the primary reason for the family's flight, they still bore a good deal of responsibility. Lyman noted that threats against the family had multiplied after bouts of unwanted publicity, and that overzealous tabloid reporters had added to the Lindberghs' fears. Only a few weeks before they decided to leave, the automobile driving Jon and his governess had been forced off the road by a car full of photographers, scaring the boy out of his wits. The Lindberghs had left the United States in search of "the tranquility and security which have been denied them in their own land."[38]

Lyman's exclusive, which won the Pulitzer Prize, signaled the end of a lengthy campaign. Since late 1927, when Lindbergh's public demeanor first began to raise eyebrows, his supporters in the media had made great efforts to allay suspicions of snobbery and ingratitude that could have been aroused by his behavior. From the outset, the main argument employed by his supporters was that it was Lindbergh's desire for privacy—a desire that was "natural" and understandable—that had led to his conflict with the press. But journalists insisted that it was not privacy alone that Lindbergh craved. Indeed, a desire for privacy could be a sign of elitism or aloofness. For Lindbergh, privacy was the foundation on which he and his wife could build the "normal" life they so ardently desired—the kind of life that would allow him to retain the identity of "Slim," the fun-loving, down-to-earth air mail pilot. It was this desire, Lyman observed, that had led the Lindberghs to move to rural New Jersey, and now this same desire

had compelled them leave the United States for England. By linking his desire
for privacy to the ideal of true success and a middle-class conception of "normalcy," Lyman and other writers confined the potentially disturbing implications of Lindbergh's public behavior and established a master narrative that res-
onated with the hopes, fears, and anxieties of many ordinary Americans.

Public interest in the Lindbergh saga—in his continuous struggle to resume
the "normal" life that would allow for the preservation of his "real" self—may
well have derived from the fact that many Americans understood the pressures
that social roles and conventions could place on individuals, not only at work but
also in one's personal life. The spotlight that shone on Lindbergh was but a more
powerful version of the one that shone on everyone. Success on the job, among
friends, or in the "marriage market," as Americans were constantly reminded,
required social skills that veered perilously close to the theatrical, placing everyone "on stage." It demanded that people suppress some of their emotions and
cultivate a pleasing façade, even at times when they would have preferred not
to. Moreover, the enormous emphasis that the dominant culture placed on social
mobility encouraged Americans to think of themselves as "projects," perenni-
ally in the process of "becoming" the people they hoped to be. Even as it enabled
some Americans to fulfill their dreams, this process could lead others away from
their roots and old identities, generating nostalgic yearnings for things left behind. Immigrants, first-generation Americans, and native-born newcomers to
the city were those most likely to feel this sense of loss. But it affected prosperous
and well-educated Americans as well. The ideal of true success, which lay at the
heart of the Lindbergh narrative, spoke directly to these yearnings. It posited a
self that was "real" and "natural," an inner core that could be protected from the
corrosive pressures that social relations placed on the self.[39]

Lyman's explanation of the Lindberghs' departure had the desired effect,
prompting an epidemic of hand-wringing among editorial writers. Most
blamed their exile on the lawlessness of "gangster-ridden America," but many
journalists also excoriated the "yellow press," whose "Peeping Tom tactics" had
made Lindbergh's life "intolerable." No one criticized Lindbergh for rejecting
his homeland and the millions of people who revered him, the scenario that
Lyman's article was implicitly designed to refute.[40] If Lindbergh had remained
in relative seclusion during his years abroad, he might have continued to ride this
wave of journalistic goodwill. Instead, he became involved in a new controversy
that would tarnish his reputation in the eyes of the press and lead to a profound
transformation of his media image.

His troubles began in 1938, when he and Anne paid their third visit in three
years to Nazi Germany. Since moving to Europe, Lindbergh had become very interested in military aviation, and in the course of his travels he had visited aviation
facilities in several countries, including the USSR. From these trips, Lindbergh

had concluded that the Nazis possessed an insurmountable advantage in air-power over Britain, France, and the Soviet Union, and that a war between Germany and Britain would be a disaster for all concerned. At first, Lindbergh shared his views with a select group of British and American officials and did not make them widely known. In the aftermath of the Munich crisis, however, they were leaked to the British press, which accused Lindbergh and the aristocratic "Cliveden Set" of influencing Prime Minister Chamberlain's decision to appease Hitler. Less than two months later, at a dinner hosted by the American ambassador, Lindbergh received a medal from Luftwaffe chief Hermann Goering, ostensibly for his "contributions to aviation" in 1927. For antifascist elements of the British press, this was proof of Lindbergh's complicity in the Munich sell-out, and they proceeded to vilify him as a crypto-Nazi. Reaction in the United States was less dramatic. Newspapers duly reported Goering's gift to Lindbergh without comment. It was the Roosevelt administration that seized on the incident and widely publicized it, particularly after the brutal anti-Semitic pogroms of November 1938 made the Nazis appear all the more sinister.[41]

Lindbergh's problems mounted when he returned to the United States and elected to make public his controversial views. On September 15, 1939, as German tanks rolled through Poland, he delivered the first of several radio addresses that he hoped would galvanize public opinion against the interventionist leanings of the Roosevelt administration. He also began writing articles, making speeches, and appearing at isolationist rallies, and in early 1941 he officially joined the America First Committee, becoming its leading spokesman. Drawing on a large supply of venerable American themes, Lindbergh's message was not very different from other isolationist fare. Yet the areas where it diverged were significant, and his detractors focused on these in their efforts to undermine his public appeal and discredit the cause of isolationism.[42] One of the most problematic was his seeming sympathy for Nazi Germany; another was his unabashed racism, which tainted many of his articles and speeches. But Lindbergh virtually handed his opponents his head in September 1941, when he made anti-Semitic remarks at an America First rally in Des Moines, Iowa. By this time, criticism of isolationists had ceased to be a monopoly of the Roosevelt administration, and much of the press joined in the orgy of Lindbergh-bashing. The syndicated columnist Dorothy Thompson, a rabid antifascist since the mid-1930s, led the assault with a vicious piece suggesting that Lindbergh desired to be an American Hitler. Even Lindbergh's friends in America First felt compelled to distance themselves from him.[43]

In the early stages of the controversy Lindbergh's unofficial flacks were quick to leap to his defense. Both Russell Owen and C. B. Allen published lengthy "explanations" of their friend's behavior. They noted that Lindbergh had accepted the medal from Goering in order to avoid offending his German hosts and embarrassing the U.S. ambassador. They also insisted that Lindbergh's trips to Germany and other countries were done at the behest of U.S. military officials. Lindbergh was "a completely loyal American" who felt no bitterness toward his homeland, Owen reported. Writing in the spring of 1940, Allen went considerably further, revealing that the Roosevelt administration had tried to bribe Lindbergh to cease criticizing U.S. efforts to aid Britain. "Had he strung along with the Administration he would have continued to be extolled in official circles as the oracle of American aviation, and undoubtedly would have been given an important post in the aerial-development program ahead." But Lindbergh had refused to sacrifice his principles, believing that "the United States should not become involved in Old World power politics." Allen noted that Lindbergh was "no reactionary or economic royalist." In fact, his views on both foreign and domestic affairs were quite moderate, the product of extensive thought and deliberation. In Allen's account, Lindbergh emerged as the victim of a vicious smear campaign by the administration and its allies, who feared his opposition would erode public support for their interventionist policies.[44]

But as the United States moved closer toward intervention, and the media lined up behind the Roosevelt administration, voices such as Owen's and Allen's were replaced with new ones that presented a strikingly different portrait of Lindbergh. These writers professed to be "impartial" and "objective," and they were careful to distance themselves from Lindbergh's attackers and apologists. Yet, although they rejected the claim that Lindbergh was a traitorous "fifth columnist" with dictatorial ambitions, they concluded that America's most famous isolationist was a dangerous crank. The most charitable explanation was that Lindbergh was a naive eccentric who had been duped by the Nazis into serving as their unwitting propaganda tool.[45] More disturbing were accounts suggesting that the murder of his son had turned Lindbergh into a bitter paranoiac who admired Germany's "order," "discipline," and "efficiency."[46] But the most devastating criticisms of Lindbergh were those that attributed his "strange ideas" to his experience as a celebrity. From the moment he became a popular idol, one writer noted, Lindbergh had displayed "an overwhelming desire to get away from the public which had given him his fame and his riches and to seek sanctuary among those people who, he believed, were rich enough and powerful enough to give him the privacy which he now considered essential to his happiness." For a few years, wealthy patrons such as the Guggenheims and the Morrows had been able to do this, but by the mid-1930s Lindbergh realized that only a country run along the lines of Nazi Germany could protect people like himself from the "common herd."[47]

Such criticism reversed the estimate his supporters had labored for so long to create. But it did not shatter the terms of debate that had always structured the Lindbergh narrative. Indeed, his critics simply turned the conventional wisdom on its head, drawing exactly the opposite conclusion. Lindbergh had been warped by his celebrity. It had gone to his head, contributing to his "inability to orient himself to the democratic way of life."[48] His obsession with privacy was now depicted as a manifestation of his elitism—an elitism that was implicitly antidemocratic and un-American. Rather than an exemplar of "true success," Lindbergh was recast as a tragic failure, a man who had cut himself off from his roots and the great American mainstream. This revision of the Lindbergh narrative was only partly a result of Lindbergh's decision to air his views on international relations. His most judicious biographers agree that the views he expressed publicly on the eve of World War II were consistent with those he had expressed privately since the early 1920s. Like most Americans of his background, Lindbergh had always been something of an elitist and a racist.[49]

It was the media that had changed. When he first became a celebrity, it had purposely obscured these dimensions of Lindbergh, constructing a hero who combined "respectability" with a kind of populist simplicity. As we have seen, this version of Lindbergh was a promotional weapon in a campaign to impede the spread of values that seemed to threaten the cultural and political hegemony of WASP elites. In the late 1930s, after the Depression and the rise of fascism had produced a very different intellectual milieu, the press publicized many of the same traits it previously had suppressed in an effort to make Lindbergh the personification of a movement it opposed and sought to portray as inherently un-American. Although Lindbergh contributed to his own downfall with some of his ill-considered remarks, it was the media that sealed his fate. Instead of ignoring or playing down these *faux pas,* it exploited them to create a new, sinister version of him.

Lindbergh's career as a public figure is a vivid illustration of the power of the media to set agendas and use individuals to suit their own purposes. Throughout his career, Lindbergh, too, had specific aims, but these were realized only with the cooperation of the press. When the media ceased to support him, he once again became a character in a script over which he had little control—not "Lucky Lindy," but the elitist with "strange ideas" who seemed indifferent to Hitler.

Notes

Originally published in a slightly different form in *Prospects: An Annual of American Cultural Studies* 21 (1996): 347–72. Reprinted with the permission of Cambridge University Press.

1. *New York Times,* July 26, 1930, 14. See also Marlen Pew, "Shop Talk at Thirty," *Editor and Publisher* 63 (July 26, 1930), 60, for a complete discussion of Lindbergh's decision, including an interview with the aviator. The newspapers Lindbergh severed relations with were the *New York Post;* the *New York Daily News;* and the three New York Hearst papers, the *American,* the

Evening Journal, and the *Daily Mirror.* This information comes from Joyce Milton, *Loss of Eden: A Biography of Charles and Anne Morrow Lindbergh* (New York: HarperCollins, 1993), 495.

2. "Fame and Privacy," *The Nation* 131 (August 20, 1930), 195.

3. For a summary of these views, see Aben Kandel, "A Tabloid a Day," *The Forum* 77 (March 1927), 378–84; and "Are Tabloid Newspapers a Menace?" *The Forum* 77 (April 1927), 485–501. More insightful, although no less contemptuous, is Silas Bent, *Ballyhoo: The Voice of the Press* (New York: Boni and Liveright, 1927). See also Walter Lippmann, "Blazing Publicity," *Vanity Fair* 29 (September 1927), 47, 110; and Lippmann, *The Phantom Public* (New York: Harcourt, Brace, 1925).

4. For an authoritative account of Lindbergh's view, I have relied primarily on Milton, *Loss of Eden,* and Walter S. Ross, *The Last Hero: Charles A. Lindbergh* (New York: Harper and Row, 1968). For a suggestive discussion of the ways in which reporters "cast" Lindbergh, see Kenneth S. Davis, *The Hero: Charles A. Lindbergh and the American Dream* (Garden City, N.Y.: Doubleday and Co., 1959), 174–75. Davis's book, a brilliant effort to connect Lindbergh to the larger processes of hero-worship and celebrity-making, has strongly influenced my own essay.

5. For an account of the evolution of celebrity discourse during the eighteenth and nineteenth centuries, see Charles L. Ponce de Leon, *Self-Exposure: Human-Interest Journalism and the Emergence of Celebrity in America, 1890–1940* (Chapel Hill: University of North Carolina Press, 2002), 11–105. For a more impressionist account that concentrates on the early twentieth century, see Richard Schickel, *Intimate Strangers: The Culture of Celebrity* (Garden City, N.Y.: Doubleday and Co., 1985).

6. On the tabloids, see Simon Michael Bessie, *Jazz Journalism: The Story of the Tabloids* (New York: E. P. Dutton, 1938); James E. Murphy, "Tabloids as an Urban Response," in Catherine L. Covert and John D. Stevens, eds., *Mass Media Between the Wars: Perceptions of Cultural Tensions, 1918–1941* (Syracuse: Syracuse University Press, 1984), 55–69; and John D. Stevens, *Sensationalism and the New York Press* (New York: Columbia University Press, 1991).

7. On press agentry and the emergence of the public relations industry, see Stuart Ewen, *PR! A Social History of Spin* (New York: Basic Books, 1996); Richard S. Tedlow, *Keeping the Corporate Image* (Greenwich, Conn.: JAI Press, 1979); Ray Eldon Hiebert, *Courtier to the Crowd: The Story of Ivy Lee and the Development of Public Relations* (Ames: Iowa State University Press, 1966). For contemporary accounts of PR practice, see Charles Washburn, *Press Agentry* (New York: National Library Press, 1937); and Stanley Walker, *City Editor* (New York: Frederick A. Stokes, 1934), 134–51.

8. See Ponce de Leon, 11–105.

9. On "market culture" and the problem of appearances, see Jean-Christophe Agnew, *Worlds Apart: The Market and the Theater in Anglo-American Thought, 1550–1750* (New York: Cambridge University Press, 1986); and Karen Haltunnen, *Confidence Men and Painted Women: A Study of Middle-Class Culture in America, 1830–1870* (New Haven: Yale University Press, 1982). For a modern account of its influence on social life, see Erving Goffmann, *The Presentation of Self in Everyday Life* (Garden City, N.Y.: Doubleday Anchor, 1959). See also Thomas L. Haskell and Richard F. Teichgraeber III, eds., *The Culture of the Market: Historical Essays* (New York: Cambridge University Press, 1993).

10. See Leo Braudy, *The Frenzy of Renown: Fame and Its History* (New York: Oxford University Press, 1986); Catherine N. Parke, *Biography: Writing Lives* (New York: Twayne, 1996); Reed Whittemore, *Pure Lives: The Early Biographers* (Baltimore: Johns Hopkins University Press, 1988); and Ira Bruce Nadel, *Biography: Fiction, Fact, and Form* (New York: St. Martin's Press, 1984).

11. On the misgivings about virtue and success in the late nineteenth century, see Richard Weiss, *The American Myth of Success: From Horatio Alger to Norman Vincent Peale* (New York: Basic Books, 1969).

12. The new psychology is discussed in Nathan G. Hale, *Freud and the Americans: The Beginnings of Psychoanalysis in the United States, 1876–1917* (New York: Oxford University Press, 1971); and John M. O'Donnell, *The Origins of Behaviorism: American Psychology, 1870–1920* (New York: New York University Press, 1985). See also Robert C. Bannister, *Social Darwinism: Science and Myth in Anglo-American Social Thought* (Philadelphia: Temple University Press, 1979).

13. On the therapeutic ethos and its links to consumerism, see T. J. Jackson Lears, "From Salvation to Self-Realization: Advertising and the Therapeutic Roots of the Consumer Culture, 1880–1930," in Richard W. Fox and T. J. Jackson Lears, eds., *The Culture of Consumption: Critical Essays in American History, 1880–1980* (New York: Pantheon, 1983), 3–38; and Roland Marchand, *Advertising the American Dream: Making Way for Modernity, 1920–1940* (Berkeley and Los Angeles: University of California Press, 1985).

14. There is no better example of the sobriety of Lindbergh's approach to aviation than the autobiography he wrote in the weeks after his New York-to-Paris flight, *We* (New York: G. P. Putnam's Sons, 1927). For a discussion of "airmindedness" as an American cultural obsession during the first half of the nineteenth century, see Joseph J. Corn, *The Winged Gospel: America's Romance with Aviation, 1900–1950* (New York: Oxford University Press, 1983). As Corn's fascinating book makes clear, Lindbergh's views on aviation represented only one side of the coin—the utopian promise of technology the new industry embodied. They ran against the other side, a romantic conception of flight that was inextricably linked to daring and adventure.

15. For information about the Guggenheim group and their fears for the industry, I am indebted to Milton, *Loss of Eden,* 132–38. See also Richard Hallion, *Legacy of Flight: The Guggenheim Contribution to Aviation* (Seattle and London: University of Washington Press, 1977); and Harry Guggenheim, *The Seven Skies* (New York: G. P. Putnam's Sons, 1930), 73–91. After Lindbergh's elevation to celebrity status, Guggenheim, Breckinridge, and Davison became his closest friends and Morrow served as his financial adviser, and in 1929 he cemented his ties to their milieu by marrying Morrow's daughter.

16. "Lindbergh the Exemplar," *Literary Digest* 94 (July 9, 1927), 29; "Why the World Makes Lindbergh Its Hero," *Literary Digest* 93 (June 25, 1927), 6.

17. My analysis here is greatly indebted to the work of Michael P. Rogin. See his essays, "Political Repression in the United States" and "American Political Demonology: A Retrospective," in *Ronald Reagan, the Movie and Other Episodes in American Political Demonology* (Berkeley: University of California Press, 1987). For theoretical background, see Peter Stallybrass and Allon White, *The Politics and Poetics of Transgression* (Ithaca: Cornell University Press, 1986), 1–26. On the image of large corporations during the 1920s, see Roland Marchand, *Creating the Corporate Soul: The Rise of Public Relations and Corporate Imagery in American Big Business* (Berkeley: University of California Press, 1998); Louis Galambos, *The Public Image of Big Business in America, 1880-1940* (Baltimore: Johns Hopkins University Press, 1975); and Jan Cohn, *Creating America: George Horace Lorimer and The Saturday Evening Post* (Pittsburgh: University of Pittsburgh Press, 1989).

18. See Lynn Dumenil, *The Modern Temper: American Culture and Society in the 1920s* (New York: Hill and Wang, 1995); Ellis W. Hawley, *The Great War and the Search for a Modern Order* (New York: St. Martin's Press, 1979); Paul A. Carter, *Another Part of the Twenties* (New York: Columbia University Press, 1977); and Roderick Nash, *The Nervous Generation: American Thought, 1917–1930* (Chicago: Rand McNally, 1970).

19. On the new cultural styles and their widespread appeal, see Ann Douglas, *Terrible Honesty: Mongrel Manhattan in the 1920s* (New York: Farrar, Straus, and Giroux, 1995); Robert Sklar, "Introduction," Sklar, ed., *The Plastic Age, 1917–1930* (New York: George Braziller, 1970); and Lewis A. Erenberg, *Steppin' Out: New York Nightlife and the Transformation of American Culture, 1890–1930* (Westport, Conn.: Greenwood Press, 1981).

20. These contradictions are explored in John William Ward's seminal essay, "The Meaning of Lindbergh's Flight," *American Quarterly* 10 (spring 1958), 3–16. Ward's essay is confined to the cultural significance of the 1927 New York-to-Paris flight and does not address the significance of Lindbergh's celebrity.

21. On efforts to disentangle "American" values from the booster spirit of the 1920s, see Warren I. Susman, *Culture as History: The Transformation of American Society in the Twentieth Century* (New York: Pantheon, 1984). The definitive revisionist text is Frederick Lewis Allen, *Only Yesterday: An Informal History of the 1920s* (New York: Harper and Brothers, 1931).

22. For the term "moral investment," I am indebted to Kenneth S. Davis. Although he applies it to the entire country, I confine my use of it to the editors who constructed the "heroic" Lindbergh. See Davis, *The Hero,* 220.

23. I have borrowed the concept of "true success" from John G. Cawelti, who employs it in his analysis of contemporary "social melodrama." See Cawelti, *Adventure, Mystery, Romance: Formula Stories as Art and Popular Culture* (Chicago and London: University of Chicago Press, 1976), 260–84.

24. The literature on religious and republican critiques of wealth and power is enormous. On the relationship between these critiques and success literature, see Weiss, *The American Myth of Success.* On gossip and the roots of the petit-bourgeois attack on aristocracy, see Robert Darnton, *The Literary Underground of the Old Regime* (Cambridge, Mass.: Harvard University Press, 1982). The role of the penny press as arbiter of the common good is covered in Dan Schiller, *Objectivity and the News: The Public and the Rise of Commercial Journalism* (Philadelphia: University of Pennsylvania Press, 1981).

25. On Lindbergh's estrangement from reporters, see Davis, *The Hero,* 263–72. On his relations with his "favorites," see Milton, *Loss of Eden,* 167–68. These writers included C. B. Allen of the *New York World* and Lauren D. Lyman and Russell Owen of the *New York Times.* Both Allen and Lyman later went on to serve as important figures in the aviation industry—Allen with the Civilian Aeronautics Board and Lyman with United Aircraft Corporation, a leading manufacturer, for which Lindbergh also worked as a consultant.

26. Even his supporters conceded the problems created by the newsreels. See John S. Gregory, "What's Wrong with Lindbergh," *Outlook and Independent* 156 (December 3, 1930), 532. For a general discussion of the Lindbergh "mystery," see John Lardner, "The Lindbergh Legends," in Isabel Leighton, ed., *The Aspirin Age, 1919–1941* (New York: Simon and Schuster, 1947), 190–213.

27. See George H. Douglas, *The Smart Magazines: Fifty Years of Literary Revelry and High Jinks at Vanity Fair, The New Yorker, Life, Esquire, and The Smart Set* (Hamden, Conn.: Archon Books, 1991); and John Tebbel and Mary Ellen Zuckerman, *The Magazine in America, 1741–1990* (New York: Oxford University Press, 1991).

28. Morris Markey, "Young Man of Affairs—II," *The New Yorker* 6 (September 27, 1930), 33, 32, 30, 31. See also Markey, "Young Man of Affairs," *The New Yorker* 6 (September 20, 1930), 26–29.

29. See *Pictorial Review* 32 (November 1930), 14–15; and Donald E. Keyhoe, "Lindbergh Four Years After," *Saturday Evening Post* 203 (May 30, 1931), 21, 46–53.

30. Donald E. Keyhoe, *Flying with Lindbergh* (New York: G. P. Putnam's Sons, 1928), quote on 250. See *Saturday Evening Post* 200 (May 19, June 2, June 23, 1928) and *Saturday Evening*

Post 201 (July 21, 1928). Portions of this book also appeared in *National Geographic* 53 (January 1928), 1–46. See also Keyhoe, "Has Fame Made Lindy High Hat?" *Popular Science Monthly* 115 (July 1929), 32–40, 142–44.

31. *New York Times,* March 25, 1928, 1, 27.

32. See, for example, Constance Lindsay Skinner, "Feet of Clay—Eyes of Envy?" *North American Review* 228 (July 1929), 41–46; Julian S. Mason, "Lindbergh and the Press," *Saturday Evening Post* 202 (August 3, 1929), 5, 98–102; and Gregory, "What's Wrong with Lindbergh."

33. *New York Times,* March 25, 1928, 1; Keyhoe, *Flying with Lindbergh,* 20.

34. Keyhoe, *Flying with Lindbergh,* 86, 208; Mason, "Lindbergh and the Press," 101.

35. Gregory, "What's Wrong with Lindbergh," 534; Keyhoe, *Flying with Lindbergh,* 296.

36. Keyhoe, *Flying with Lindbergh,* 279, 104; Keyhoe, "Lindbergh Four Years After," 48, 53.

37. See George Waller, *Kidnap: The Story of the Lindbergh Case* (New York: Dial Press, 1961).

38. *New York Times* (December 23, 1935), 1.

39. See Susman, *Culture as History,* 271–90.

40. For a sample of editorial reaction to the Lindberghs' exile, see the *New York Times,* December 24, 1935, 2. Quotes are from editorials in the *New York Daily Mirror,* the *Dallas News,* and the *New York Herald-Tribune,* all of which were reprinted in the article cited above.

41. See Wayne S. Cole, *Charles A. Lindbergh and the Battle Against American Intervention in World War II* (New York: Harcourt Brace Jovanovich, 1974).

42. On this issue, see Cole, *Charles A. Lindbergh.* Lindbergh's writings include "Aviation, Geography, and Race," *Reader's Digest* 35 (November 1939), 64–67; "What Substitute for War?" *Atlantic Monthly* 165 (March 1940), 304–8; and "A Letter to Americans," *Collier's* 107 (March 29, 1941), 75–77.

43. Lindbergh's seeming sympathy for Germany and racism are especially apparent in "Aviation, Geography, and Race." For a vivid example of his demonization, see the pamphlet produced by the New York group Friends of Democracy entitled "Is Lindbergh a Nazi?," which juxtaposed Lindbergh's views with those of Hitler, Goebbels, and assorted American fascists. See also Dorothy Thompson, "What Lindbergh *Really* Wants," *Look* 8 (November 18, 1941), 13–15.

44. Russell Owen, "What's the Matter with Lindbergh?" *American Magazine* 127 (April 1939), 66; C. B. Allen, "The Facts About Lindbergh," *Saturday Evening Post* 213 (December 28, 1940), 53.

45. See, for example, Frederic Sondern, Jr., "Lindbergh Walks Alone," *Life* 6 (April 3, 1939), 64–75.

46. See Roger Butterfield, "Lindbergh: A Stubborn Young Man of Strange Ideas Becomes a Leader of Wartime Opposition," *Life* 11 (August 11, 1941), 64–75.

47. See the series by Frederick L. Collins, "Why Lindbergh Acts That Way," *Liberty* 18 (June 7, 1941), 16–17, 46–47; ibid. (June 14, 1941), 18–19, 46–47; ibid. (June 21, 1941), 18–19, 41–42; ibid. (June 28, 1941), 34–36. See also Harry Bruno and Lowell Thomas, "What's the Matter with Lindbergh?" *American Magazine* 132 (August 1941), 106–9. Quote from Collins, "Why Lindbergh Acts That Way" (June 28, 1941), 36.

48. Collins, "Why Lindbergh Acts That Way," ibid. (June 21, 1941), 42.

49. Despite her sympathy for the Lindberghs, Milton is frank on this issue. See *Loss of Eden,* 384–85, 441. For a thorough discussion of Lindbergh's comparatively reactionary views, see Cole, *Charles A. Lindbergh.*

THE AIRPLANE
Race and Gender

"Great Shadow in the Sky"

The Airplane in the Tulsa Race Riot of 1921 and the Development of African American Visions of Aviation, 1921–1926

JILL D. SNIDER

Soon after daybreak on Wednesday, June 1, 1921, a shrill whistle pierced the morning air hanging like a damp curtain over Tulsa, Oklahoma. The sharp, sudden blast shot fear through the hearts of Tulsa's black citizens, who, after enduring a night of racial violence, felt they were hearing the call-to-arms of the enemy. Moments later, their worst imaginings materializing before their eyes, residents spotted fires engulfing the southern rim of Greenwood, their segregated quarter tucked into the city's northeastern corner. Huge orange-blue flames snapped and lurched erratically as billows of thick, dark smoke roiled upward, choking the air, and snakelike strands of fire curled toward Greenwood's residential area, forcing people to flee for their lives. Panicked men and women, some leading frightened children or supporting feeble parents, began pouring into the streets and alleys of Greenwood.[1]

What they met as they abandoned their threatened homes made their blood run cold. All around them sang bullets delivered from the staccato firing of a machine gun mounted on a hilltop overlooking "Little Africa," as whites referred to the segregated section. Tulsa policemen, aided by over five hundred newly sworn white deputies, many volunteers from a lynch mob that had gathered the night before, herded black citizens into small groups. Waving guns in their faces, they ordered their captives to march, some only partially clad, to makeshift detention centers (formerly a baseball park and a convention hall), while overhead, to the horror of many, six airplanes dove and looped in large circles above Greenwood. It was as if, one fleeing woman observed, they were "great birds of prey watching for a victim."[2]

This early morning invasion of Greenwood, which witnessed the airplane's first known appearance in a racially motivated attack on American soil, had been sparked early on the previous evening by a thwarted lynching. When close to forty armed Greenwood residents had arrived at the County Courthouse to defend a black teenager against a white mob of nearly fifteen hundred, the stage was set for what would later be remembered by many as the "Tulsa Race War of 1921." The riot that ensued raged out of control for over six hours, and it con-

Fédération Aéronautique Internationale

FRANCE

. Ious soussignés pouvoir sportif
reconnu par la Fédération
Aéronautique Internationale
pour la France certifions que:

Mme Bessie Coleman
né à *Atlanta, Texas*
le *20 Janvier 1896*
ayant rempli toutes les conditions
imposées par la F.A.I. a été breveté

Pilote-Aviateur
à la date du *15 Juin 1921*
Commission Sportive Aéronautique
Le Président:

Signature du Titulaire
Bessie Coleman

N° du Brevet *18.310.*

African Americans viewed aviation through two lenses after the Tulsa riot of 1921. Integrationists thought that if blacks could prove their equality through flying, whites would reform, and the new age would be reached in America. African redemptionists, convinced that whites were incapable of being reformed, viewed the airplane in part as a doomsday technology, which ultimately would spell the end of white supremacy. Integrationist Bessie Coleman, a well-known African American aviator of the 1920s, was the shining example to many of her race who aspired to become aviators. (Courtesy National Air and Space Museum, Smithsonian Institution [SI 99-15416].)

cluded with as many as seventy-five Tulsans, two thirds of them black, dead, and more than one thousand black homes and Greenwood's business district smoldering in ashes. It had begun as a scuffle at the courthouse when a white man in the crowd, incensed that one of the Greenwood group, a World War I veteran, was carrying an army-issue revolver, tried to take the gun away from him. When he refused to yield it, shots were exchanged and, before the group could retreat, by various accounts, between three and twelve men, a majority of them black, lay dead.[3] The would-be lynchers, enraged at what they perceived as black impudence, rapidly lost interest in the original target of their anger and, seeking revenge, fell in hot pursuit of those fleeing back toward Greenwood. Joined along the way by gangs of white men and boys, many of whom were reacting to rumors that blacks had launched an attack on the crowd at the courthouse, they ransacked local hardware stores and pawnshops, stripping their shelves of all available firearms. With focused excitement and fury, they headed for Greenwood, their sights having shifted from a lynching to a larger offensive against blacks in the city.

As Greenwood's populace became aware of the danger looming outside its borders, a number of men volunteered as reinforcements for those retreating from the courthouse, and dug in their heels along the railroad tracks separating black from white Tulsa to ward off the impending invasion. Snipers took up defensive positions in the tower of the recently constructed Mt. Zion Baptist Church, while others perched atop nearby buildings where they could shoot at whites trying to cross the tracks into Greenwood. Throughout the night, the district's defenders held the mob at bay. As the long hours passed, however, the mob's fury flamed higher, stoked by black resistance and fear. Rumors traveled rapidly through the streets that blacks were killing white women and children and that they were marshalling forces from nearby towns to carry out a massive assault on white Tulsa. Even Guardsmen from the local battalion of the Oklahoma 3d Infantry, called out to control the riot, fell prey to the war mentality of the swelling horde. Near midnight, Lt. Col. L. J. F. Rooney, the 3d Infantry's commander, heard reports that blacks were attempting to "take the City" and, at approximately 2:30 A.M., he ordered his men to meet a train from Muskogee on which he had been led to believe five hundred black residents of that town were arriving to join their compatriots in Tulsa. Although the train was empty, Guard officers continued to fret over a possible black offensive.[4]

Despite the failure of rumored black aggression to appear, the mob had by early morning hours, according to Associated Press reports, openly proclaimed its intention to destroy Greenwood completely, and law enforcement, blaming the violence on the men who had confronted the lynch mob, focused on ferreting out these and other perceived black troublemakers rather than protecting the lives and property of Greenwood citizens. By daybreak, armed whites, some of them recruited for the purpose by Guardsmen, had encircled Greenwood, setting up a blockade with automobiles. Soldiers from the 3d Infantry mounted a machine gun atop Standpipe Hill overlooking the northwest side of Greenwood and, according to at least one claim, a white policeman, Van Hurley, later confessed that prominent city officials held a conference with local pilots to plan an aerial assault. Part of this plan, Hurley reportedly stated (his affidavit, although cited in newspaper accounts, has not been found), was to drop nitroglycerin on buildings to set them on fire. Hurley maintained that police captain George Blaine rode in one of the planes. His superiors, Hurley asserted, instructed him and his fellow officers that "if the niggers wanted to start anything," to "kill every d— son of a b— they could find." No one waited, however, to determine the motives of black Tulsans, and at the sound of the whistle blowing near 5:30 A.M., the onslaught began, with the city's police force and many of the five hundred newly sworn deputies on the front lines, and airplanes reputedly dropping "white fire" from above.[5]

The riot left black America reeling. The scale of the destruction in Greenwood and the specter of modern technologies such as the machine gun and airplane being turned on private citizens stunned the black public, despite the fact that they had been witnessing an escalation in racial violence since World War I. In 1917, in the midst of the war, blacks had suffered a terrible riot in East St. Louis, Illinois, which had left by most conservative estimates fifty people dead. Following the war, rioting had increased dramatically, with 1919 emerging as the bloodiest year. In the last six months alone of that year, approximately twenty-five riots had broken out. The "Red Summer," as National Association for the Advancement of Colored People (NAACP) head James Weldon Johnson dubbed the months between May and August 1919, resulted in bloody conflicts in seven major cities, including Washington, D.C., Chicago, and Charleston, and in a number of smaller municipalities. The most destructive of these, in Chicago, lasted thirteen days and deprived close to forty individuals of their lives and over one thousand families of their homes. In these earlier conflicts, however, the destruction had come from torches, bottles, stones, and rifles. Now whites had added machine guns and airplanes to their arsenals, and black Americans found themselves forced to struggle with the implications of this ominous development.[6]

Who had been flying over the destruction transpiring that morning in Tulsa, and their exact role in it, remains in part a mystery. In his 1982 study of the riot, Scott Ellsworth noted that city police used privately owned airplanes to survey the riot scene and to keep a check on the fires. The aviators they engaged to pilot them most likely worked for the Curtiss-Southwest Airplane Company, an airfreight carrier only recently established on Tulsa's northern outskirts. Curtiss-Southwest owned fourteen airplanes, and an eyewitness reported seeing armed men taking off from the company's airfield during the riot. At least one of these planes, argues the historian Richard Warner, belonged to the Sinclair Oil Company, which supplied fuel to Curtiss-Southwest. Ellsworth and other historians of the riot also have documented that police officers flew with local pilots to observe the mob and to look for refugees. In addition, panicked by rumors of retribution from blacks living in outlying towns such as Muskogee, Boley, Red Bird, Taft, and Wybark, police monitored the activities of their residents by air as well.[7]

Eyewitnesses to the riot, however, went much further in their claims, contending that the pilots of the planes flying over the city were themselves active participants in the attack. The statements of many riot victims supported the assertion that an aerial force had organized to invade Greenwood. Mary E. Jones Parrish, a young schoolteacher, after having seen planes flying over her home, described how she had spotted a number of men at the Curtiss-Southwest field as she fled Greenwood, and she observed that they were loading high-powered rifles into their cockpits as they prepared to take off. Another Tulsa school-teacher, a former Baltimore resident referred to simply as J.B.C., informed that city's *Afro-American* two weeks after the riot that airplanes had actually dropped "bombs" on Greenwood. This woman's allegation was corroborated by Buck Franklin, an attorney who claimed the planes overhead "dropped explosives," and by W. I. Brown, a railroad porter who arrived in Tulsa aboard a train on the Kansas and Texas Railroad. Brown stated that he watched from his car window as two airplanes "would every few seconds drop something and every time they did there was a loud explosion and the sky would be filled with flying debris." Another eyewitness described the bombings in a poem penned after the riot. A.J. Smitherman, editor of the *Tulsa Star,* who was forced to flee the city, soon after wrote:

> At the signal from the whistle
> Aeroplanes were seen to fly,
> Dropping bombs and high explosives,
> Hell was falling from the sky!

What is more likely to have been dropped from the planes than explosive de-vices was gasoline or turpentine. Several sources reported witnessing liquids being poured from planes that led to huge convulsions in the fires already burn-ing below. The *Washington Bee* alleged that aviators had spilled "scorching white fire" onto the heads of those fighting to defend Greenwood.[8]

Other accounts assert that whites in airplanes shot at blacks as they fled their homes. A Mrs. Williams, who eventually made her way to safety among rela-tives in Chicago, told a National Urban League representative there that pilots dipped so low over Greenwood that she could clearly see them, and that they had fired shots at those attempting to escape. A Tulsa physician noted that, while still inside his home, he heard the cry of a woman outside warning others to "Look out for the aeroplanes, they are shooting at us," and another Greenwood resi-dent, in describing her attempts to get her invalid mother to a hospital, claimed that an aviator shot down a man directly in their path. In a similar vein, a drug-gist and his wife who had escaped Greenwood related a story of having been forced to spend all day hiding in a creek outside Muskogee to avoid the bullets fired at them by white men chasing them by air.[9]

Events such as these elicited cries of outrage from the black press, the most crucial forum black Americans had for discussing the riot. Journalists, in their condemnation of the airplane's use, castigated white aviators for their arrogance and for their viciousness in attacking helpless victims. A reporter for the *Chicago Defender,* for example, fumed that the flyers who had dropped nitroglycerin on the burning Mt. Zion Baptist Church had later boasted of how they had "killed bunches of niggers," and a writer for the black nationalist *Negro World,* in a story headlined, "Home Guards Set Fire to Buildings While Airplanes Dropped Bombs on Homes in Negro District in Tulsa," deplored the aviators as "air murderers." Expressing shock and dismay at the airplane's deployment against civilians, an editorialist for the socialist *Crusader* magazine joined many others in deriding white rioters for dropping incendiary bombs on "defenceless women and children, and helpless aged and sick, bedridden people." (In the same issue, the *Crusader* expressed a newfound appreciation of the airplane's power, listing it as one of The Seven New Wonders of the World.)[10]

The airplane's presence for many exposed the hypocrisy of the country's still resonant war rhetoric to "make the world safe for democracy." Justifying entry into the European conflict on the premise that America had a Christian duty to protect the rights of Europe's weaker populations from German despotism, President Wilson and members of his administration had claimed for the country a particularly exalted place in world affairs. After the war, they proposed that the Allied powers, led by the United States, act as a world police, enforcing the rights of all people to self-determination. As a politician shaped by a long-standing myth that Americans were a people with a world mission, Wilson drew on political and religious ideas central to American identity since the Revolution. American patriots, in their efforts to forge a new nation, had defined themselves as the truest defenders of liberty, claiming they had been called by God to lead the world out of political tyranny. In forming the nineteenth-century doctrine of Manifest Destiny, which posited the divine right of Americans to expand their nation outward to spread democracy, this idea eventually found a central place in the rhetoric of Wilson, who stated that America had always been "a spiritual enterprise" and that it, from its beginnings, had had "the high and honorable hope that it might in all that it was and did show mankind the way to liberty." Americans possessed, he believed, a Christian covenant to defeat tyranny and usher in a new age of democratic peace.[11]

After the riot, the black nationalist poet Ethel Trew Dunlap of Chicago pointed to the shame aviators flying over Greenwood had brought to such a high-minded ideal, lamenting that when

Hands that wave the flag
Dropped bombs down on the race
From airplanes that night,
Columbia hid her face.

Others joined in Dunlap's refrain. J.C. Cunningham, a frequent contributor to the *Washington Bee,* turned Wilson's rhetoric on its head, suggesting that the decision of white Americans to employ airplanes against black citizens showed them to be more corrupt than the German tyrants they had proposed to defeat. In a letter to the *Bee,* he stated that when the Germans had bombed Paris during the war, "A mighty cry of 'shame' was heard in this country." But, he offered for consideration, "We wonder what the Germans thought when the Associated Press informed them of the Americans flying over Tulsa, Okla., killing innocent women and children from their planes, piloted by ruffians in Christian (?) America!" "Perhaps," he mused, "they . . . said, 'As mean as we are, we have never stooped so low as to throw bombs from airplanes on our own loyal citizens!'" The extreme irony of white Americans, purporting to be the Christian defenders of freedom abroad, turning deadly airplanes on their own neighbors at home, was not lost on black journalists. A *St. Louis Argus* editorial crystallized the sense of betrayal many felt at white American duplicity. Criticizing the U.S. government's willingness to intervene militarily on behalf of the Cubans against Spain, while it ignored the pleas of black Tulsans, the *Argus* charged, "where is an Uncle Sam that will hear the cries of the innocent women and children at Tulsa? We are told their cries rose above the roaring of guns and the buzzing of the airplanes. Where is an Uncle Sam that will say to American mobs 'stop'!" In its lament, the *Argus* bewailed the failure of America's mission at home.[12]

Besides outrage and betrayal, the airplane's appearance on the horizon over "Little Africa" evoked deep anxiety among black journalists who, only shortly before the riot, had begun to ponder the potential dangers of aviation in the hands of white racists. Part of a public fed on grisly war stories, which depicted the killing of innocent civilians by Zeppelin attacks and bombings from warplanes, journalists could imagine all too well the ramifications of air power turned against them. In an eerie foreshadowing, the Associated Negro Press (ANP) had voiced this apprehension in a release it sent out to newspapers only two weeks before the riot, in which it claimed that the U.S. Army Air Service was being taken over by the Ku Klux Klan. The release reported the formation of a fraternal organization by seven hundred former members of the country's air corps to be known as the "Knights of the Air." The Knights allegedly had invited William J. Simmons, imperial wizard of the Klan, to serve as their titular head. On a national level, the ANP worried, the airplane could serve as the tool of an organization whose philosophies were dedicated to the ultimate subjection of black Americans. The attack on Greenwood, with its frightening aerial display, had realized their worst fears.[13]

The fears of racial warfare apparent in the ANP's press release found full-blown expression in journalists' descriptions of Tulsa, as they turned repeatedly to the metaphor of war to describe the riot. No word other than "war" seemed capable of conveying the horror and devastation wrought in Greenwood, and its choice flowed naturally from an experience that had included the presence of military troops and modern weaponry. As James Weldon Johnson explained in a public statement on the riot, he chose "the word warfare advisably as press reports inform us that airplanes, automobiles, and guns have been used by the combatants." In the weeks following the conflict, reporters recreated the battle scenes of Tulsa for their readers in horrific detail on the front pages of the country's most widely read black weeklies, including Chicago's *Defender,* Baltimore's *Afro-American,* Norfolk's *Journal and Guide,* New York's *Age,* and New York's *Negro World.* These papers, counting subscribers from across the country, including the Deep South, saturated their audiences with news of "pitched battles," "armies," and "refugees," and offered up a steady diet of editorials and letters to the editor condemning the use of machine guns and airplanes against Greenwood. Other more regionally based papers such as the *St. Louis Argus, California Eagle, Denver Statesman, Houston Informer,* and *Washington Bee* adopted martial language as well in their descriptions of the "race war."[14]

Riot coverage in newspapers reflected the still vivid memory of World War I. Journalists, regardless of their location or the size of the papers for which they wrote, were quick to draw the parallel between events in Tulsa and those on the battlefields of Europe. The early coverage of the *St. Louis Argus* was typical. Several days after the riot, it claimed that Tulsa was "recovering from a most brutal war." "Nothing," it asserted, "surpasses it, even Belgium or in France during the world's war." James Weldon Johnson claimed in the *New York Age* that "there was no more hellish passion loosed against the Germans in the late war than was loosed by these white citizens of Tulsa against their colored fellow citizens." Crystallizing this sentiment, the *Chicago Defender* referred to the riot as the "'Belgianizing' of Tulsa."[15]

Oklahoma City's *Black Dispatch* was only one of many newspapers to inject a territorial twist into the war theme, taking the position that the use of aerial bombs, guns, and other weapons in the assault on blacks constituted a war to take their land. Citing as evidence attempts prior to the riot by white railroad officials to obtain much of the property in Greenwood for use as a station, the newspaper asserted that the race war raging in Tulsa was little more than a battle for blacks' property. This idea gained credibility when it was reported after the riot that Tulsa's city commissioners had passed a fire ordinance forbidding the construction of wooden buildings in the burnt-over district, making it impossible for Greenwood residents to rebuild their homes. The white commissioners proposed, in recompense, to trade black landowners less valuable lots on the edge of the city.[16]

The war metaphor seen in response to Tulsa, of course, was not an entirely new phenomenon. Militaristic language had for some time appeared in newspaper coverage of riots, even prior to World War I. In Tulsa itself, a full decade before the 1921 riot, a racial disturbance there had been referred to by the NAACP's *Crisis* magazine as a "race war." Moreover, journalists had often cast the wartime and postwar violence in cities such as East St. Louis and Chicago in the mold of the European conflict. As a *New York Age* writer charged after the vicious attack on blacks in East St. Louis, the riot "will go down in history alongside the atrocities committed in Brussels and Rheims."[17]

The discussion of the 1921 riot, however, escalated the martial metaphor to new heights and, significantly, it emphasized one facet of war absent in the coverage of previous riots. World War I's technological character had changed forever how people would think of war. The advent of the airplane, aerial bombs, machine guns, torpedoes, and mustard gas made fighting, once contained to the battlefront, no longer a limited affair. Now civilians as readily as soldiers were targets of the enemy, as the airplane, especially, extended the reach of military arms. In addition, the incredible effectiveness of the new instruments of death left little possibility for self-defense, creating a paralyzing sense of horror among the public. The presence of the latest machines of war in Greenwood brought this aspect of war alive for black Tulsans. Thus, the disturbance evoked not simply the image of war, as earlier riots had done, but its more unnerving twentieth-century counterpart, "modern" war. A *California Eagle* contributor recognized this distinction clearly, stating, "We look at the burning of the homes of our people, the dropping of bombs from aeroplanes, [and] the throwing of hand grenades from passing automobiles as acts of modern warfare." NAACP Assistant Secretary Walter F. White concurred. After citing the use of airplanes in Tulsa, White claimed that "all that was lacking to make the scene a replica of modern 'Christian' warfare was poison gas."[18]

The specter of modern racial warfare brought to the surface for black journalists not only fears for the race's well-being but also for its very existence. Two weeks after the riot, a *Chicago Defender* artist expressed the thought that no black American could escape having cross his or her mind in the face of Tulsa. In a biting political cartoon, Leslie Rogers depicted an Allied soldier smiling as he surrendered to his captor, confident that the German would not kill an unarmed man. In Rogers's second frame, white American men, grinning evilly, shot down black citizens, while an airplane swooped overhead dropping blasts of destruction. The caption read:

In times of war, when an allied soldier dropped his weapons and raised his hands as a sign of surrender, the barbarous Germans spared his life. In Tulsa, Oklahoma, however, defenseless men, women, and children were murdered without a chance for their lives.

Comparing white rioters unfavorably to the so recently hated "Hun" of Germany, Rogers suggested that the riot had gone beyond warfare; it had bordered on extermination. In war, Rogers implied, certain rules of fairness, based on the martial respect of one soldier for another, applied. In Tulsa, however, white rioters showed no acknowledgment of the humanity of their victims. Whites were engaged, not in a battle of equals, but in a bloodbath to erase blacks' presence. A veteran who had fought with New York's all-black 15th Infantry during World War I agreed, averring, "It is safer on the battle-field than in such places as Oklahoma, for on the battle-field you get a man's chance to defend yourself."[19]

The theme of racial extermination also had appeared in the *Defender*'s earlier coverage of the riot. A June 4 story compared the violence perpetrated in the riot to the early Indian massacres, juxtaposing the decimation of America's native populations to the murder of blacks in the streets of Tulsa. The author left little doubt about his or her perception that the war whites were fighting was not one between equals. Airplanes and machine guns, they claimed, had been aimed at blacks to "wipe them out." The fear of extermination ran deep in the psyches of a people whose existence was despised by most white Americans. Now, in the face of technologies that just might make it possible, they could not avoid the implications of America's scientific advancements.[20]

This held especially true for the airplane. Although all the symbols of war appearing in Tulsa had frightened and angered blacks, it had been the presence of airplanes that had elicited the deepest terror and greatest outrage. The young schoolteacher Mary Parrish expressed in vivid and poignant detail the fear the airplane in the hands of white rioters could engender. She wrote that, on hearing a loud buzzing in the air, she and her neighbors ran to their doors to look out, and when they looked up, she declared:

> the sights our eyes beheld made our poor hearts stand still for a moment. There was a great shadow in the sky and upon a second look we discerned that this cloud was caused by fast approaching aeroplanes. It then dawned upon us that the enemy had organized in the night and was invading our district the same as the Germans invaded France and Belgium. . . . People were seen to flee from their burning homes, some with babes in their arms. . . . Yet, seemingly, I could not leave. I walked as one in a horrible dream.

Immobilized by fear and shock, Mary Parrish saw her own ordeal as little different from that of the victims of Germany's air raids. For her, it was the "great shadow in the sky" that represented modern warfare.[21]

The airplane's prominence in Tulsa and the fears of extermination it spawned underscored dramatically the racial technology divide the ANP's press release had addressed, as well as its potential consequences. In the face of the riot, the threat to black life that this widening differential posed could not easily be ignored. In fact, technological disparity between the races would figure as a central theme in the visions of aviation formulated by journalists and other air-minded black Americans after Tulsa, profoundly influencing how they came to see the airplane. And, not surprisingly, the specter of modern race war loomed large over black views of flight. Although the reporters, editors, pilots, and others who helped shape popular attitudes toward flying in the early 1920s often arrived at conflicting conclusions concerning the role of aeronautics in the race's future, they all were compelled to grapple with the implications of the airplane as a white-controlled technology in a world defined by race.

In the shadow of Tulsa, two competing philosophies of aviation, reflecting deeper political and social divisions within black communities, emerged. One, the product of black nationalist thinkers active in what frequently was called the Garvey Movement (after its founder Marcus Garvey), focused primarily on the military menace of the airplane. The rhetoric of Garveyites often adopted apocalyptic tones, encouraging blacks to secure airplanes in preparation for a great coming race war. Prophesying a future Armageddon that would determine which races survived and which suffered extinction, black nationalists deemed the procurement of modern technologies such as the airplane to be essential. Should blacks fail to arm themselves with these new weapons of war, already possessed in large numbers by whites, they threatened, the consequences could be dire, and the race could be inviting its own demise. Tulsa would not remain an isolated incident but instead would become the norm, and blacks would inevitably turn out the losers in a battle for racial survival.

A second vision, more loosely articulated by writers for the popular black press, represented by papers such as the nationally circulated *Chicago Defender, Pittsburgh Courier, New York Age,* and *Baltimore Afro-American,* chose to downplay the airplane's physical threat. These journalists emphasized instead the economic opportunity offered by the nascent aviation industry, and the need for blacks to learn to fly to ready themselves for the new air age in America. They also touted the possibilities for social change offered by the technology, claiming that black Americans, by becoming able pilots, could dispel white stereotypes of themselves as incompetent, easily frightened, lacking in ambition, and unintelligent. By learning to fly, they believed, blacks could help pave the way for true democracy in America.

Differing greatly on the surface, these visions nonetheless shared many ideas, assumptions, and values in common. Nationalists exhorted blacks to pursue the growing economic opportunities of aviation within America as vigorously as anyone, and sometimes, too, hoped to use the airplane to impress on whites their equality. And popular journalists, in their high hopes for flight, could not escape the sinister threat the flying machine posed. Beneath their optimism ran a steady current of doubt, for at the core of their vision, as at that of Garveyites, stood

Tulsa's legacy—that aviation was power and if blacks allowed whites to monopolize that power, the results could be devastating.

Black nationalist ideas concerning aviation formulated in the years after the riot can best be viewed through the philosophical lens of Marcus Garvey, whose rhetoric often reflected and sometimes shaped the beliefs of his adherents. Born in St. Ann's Bay, Jamaica, in 1887, the son of a bricklayer, Garvey as a young man apprenticed himself in the printing trade. Drawing on this experience, between 1909 and 1912 he edited and published two short-lived newspapers. Garvey was not content with editorializing on the racial and class injustices he saw around him, however, and soon turned his attention to political activism.[22]

In 1914, Garvey established in Kingston the Universal Negro Improvement Association (UNIA), an uplift organization that sought to foster racial solidarity and the social and economic betterment of blacks worldwide. Dissatisfied with the limited support he received for the UNIA in Kingston, the young leader in 1917 decided to move its headquarters to the United States. There, along with thirteen others, in May of that year he founded the Association's first American division in Harlem. Despite its humble beginnings, the UNIA grew phenomenally in the racially volatile atmosphere of postwar America. By the early 1920s, membership had swollen to impressive numbers (some estimate a membership of over one million), making it the largest black political organization in the country's history. By 1920, the UNIA's official organ, the *Negro World,* enjoyed a circulation of fifty thousand, and, reflecting the growth of a racial consciousness among blacks not only in America but worldwide, the UNIA soon boasted more than eight hundred chapters across the country, in the West Indies, Latin America, South America, Europe, and Africa.[23]

At the heart of Garvey's vision for racial advancement was the goal of black nationhood. The black race, the UNIA leader argued, constituted a once-great people scattered in exile from Africa. It was the duty of black Westerners, especially those in America, to help reunite the race and build up an independent nation on the African continent. Claiming blacks could never achieve self-determination or safety from white violence without a country of their own, he encouraged his fellow race members to dedicate themselves to the realization of an African homeland. "Young men and women, awake!" he exhorted *Negro World* readers in April 1919. "Be ready for the day when Africa shall declare for her independence." The nation Garvey envisioned, once developed and fortified, would be open to blacks anywhere who wished to emigrate, and would offer its protection to blacks around the world, regardless of where they chose to reside. The race would make of Africa, he claimed, "a strong and powerful Republic to lend protection to the success we make in foreign lands."[24]

Garvey's orations in support of a black nation frequently appealed to the fears of race war and extermination so vividly documented in the popular press's response to Tulsa. In November 1918, just after the signing of the Armistice to end World War I, Garvey declared future racial warfare unavoidable, predicting a "new war that is to be wagered—the war of the races." Initially, Garvey imagined this conflict as a battle between Asians and Europeans, and he advised the world's black peoples to cast their lot with whichever side was willing to offer them justice. Blacks could, by serving as the balance of power between the other races, he hoped, gain leverage for their demands. As the rioting in America reached its bloody height in the summer of 1919, however, Garvey became increasingly disillusioned with this possibility, and began to embrace more fully the need for an African nation strong enough to strike for its own freedom. He reconfigured the coming race war as one that would be fought on an African battlefield to redeem Africa from white colonial rule, and counseled blacks to steel themselves for this future revolution. "I am now asking the Negro peoples of the world to prepare themselves for such a war to free Africa from the thraldom of the white man," he wrote in June 1919. If blacks in America did not assume their duty to redeem Africa, he warned, they could suffer the same fate as America's native peoples. Telling a Carnegie Hall audience in August 1919 that the "African question" was "one that every negro must understand now or never," he encouraged them to "remember what the white man did to the North American Indian."[25]

Garvey regularly resorted to the threat of racial extinction to prod his listeners to action but, simultaneously, he expressed an unwavering faith that eventually the race would restore Africa to its past greatness and guarantee itself a glorious future. At times, he invested the envisioned African nation with a transcendent purpose similar to that claimed for America. In November 1919, for example, he told UNIA members in Newport News, Virginia, "There will be no democracy in the world until the Negro rules." Drawing on the idea, deeply rooted in the nationalist intellectual tradition, that the black race had a world destiny, Garvey came to believe in an African calling to spread democracy through the world. This notion of an African mission paralleled and, some have argued, in part grew out of, the myth of an American world mission, which, too, had its genesis in racial thought. White Americans during the Revolution had seldom separated the idea of an American and an Anglo-Saxon cause in their rhetoric, and the nineteenth-century doctrine of Manifest Destiny often had equated "America" with the Anglo-Saxon race. Garvey felt, however, that Anglo-Saxon Americans had forsaken their mission. "The white man has shown himself an unfit subject to rule," he told his audience in Newport News. Now it would fall to Africa to usher in the new age of peace. "[The future] portends a leadership of Negroes that will draw man nearer to God," Garvey exclaimed, "because in the Negroes' rule there will be mercy, love, and charity to all." To achieve these noble aims, Garvey argued, blacks would have to prove their mettle on the African battlefield, where the great war of the races would be played out.[26]

The program Garvey proposed blacks undertake to prepare themselves for the coming race war, and for the role of moral leader at its conclusion, stressed the need to achieve economic and military power. Insisting that a weak race could not succeed in world affairs, Garvey preached with vigor the ideas of an independent black commerce and an autonomous military, ideas that found an enthusiastic response among black Americans weary of economic exploitation, lynching, and rioting. In pursuit of these goals, the UNIA, in June 1919, incorporated the Black Star Line, a steamship company proposed to connect black producers and consumers around the world, thus providing a solid economic underpinning for the race. Its ships also were to provide transportation for those who chose to go to Africa. Garvey at times exalted the Black Star Line as one means of reaching the envisioned new age. On the launching of the line's first steamship, the *Yarmouth,* in October 1919, he proclaimed it a sign of "the dawning of a new day, the ushering in of a new era for the Negro race."[27]

In 1919, the UNIA also took concrete steps toward providing its members military training, establishing the paramilitary Universal African Legion. An all-male auxiliary, the Legion offered its recruits training in the fundamentals of precision drilling and weapons use. Legion members often provided security for meetings and acted as bodyguards for UNIA officials. In addition, at least one historian has claimed, they on occasion gave blacks protection against Ku Klux Klan and other racist violence. Developed alongside the African Legion were two women's auxiliaries, the Universal Motor Corps and the Black Cross Nurses. The Motor Corps encouraged women to learn to drive so that they could operate ambulances and other emergency vehicles in the event of a race war, and the nurses, as Garvey explained, would perform "the work of a Florence Nightingale," tending the Legion's soldiers on the African battlefield.[28]

In the UNIA's martial preparations, Garvey did not call for blacks to confront whites on American soil, despite the apparent willingness of some to do so. Cognizant of the race's small numbers in relation to whites, he realized the futility of risking a race war before they were properly prepared. Rather, they would build their power slowly in cooperation with native Africans, then seek their safety in the newly established homeland. Once this new nation proved itself in the battle of the races, it would undertake its mission, and blacks anywhere in the world could call on its forces to protect them.[29]

Modern military technologies were viewed as a vital part of Garvey's plans for building a black nation. Exhorting UNIA members to obtain weapons for Africa's benefit, he and his followers asserted that the coming race war would be fought along modern technological lines. "Only by mastering modern science, modern machinery and all modern and naval forces," claimed William Ferris, editor of the *Negro World,* in July 1920, could blacks redeem Africa from the grip of Anglo-Saxons. It would be the race that adopted most fully "scientific principles" in its inventions of war, Garvey claimed in 1922, that would rule the world.[30]

Before the Tulsa riot, however, Garvey's attention focused almost exclusively on naval technology. His speeches and writings between 1919 and mid-1921, often crafted in support of the Black Star Line, regularly stated the need for blacks to obtain sea power. "The command has gone forth," he wrote in September 1920, for "'ships and more ships.'" Garvey's call for ships most often emphasized the need to establish a strong merchant marine to ensure the economic basis for African power. Much of his interest in ships, however, also derived from the postwar rhetoric of men such as U.S. Secretary of the Navy Josephus Daniels, whose well-publicized plea for "ships, ships, and more ships" Garvey had paraphrased. Daniels considered naval power "the determining factor in war," and he encouraged the government, after the war, to build ships for the purpose of carrying out the country's peacetime mission of protecting democracy.[31]

The ship also possessed emotional significance for Garvey and his followers. It had been in ships that African slaves had first been brought to the Americas, and the symbolic pull they thus exerted proved strong. Wilford H. Smith, counselor general of the UNIA, drew on the image of the slave ship in April 1921 as he spoke before an audience in Liberty Hall, the UNIA's meeting place in Harlem. He prompted applause from the crowd when he exclaimed, "[W]e came in the ships of the white man. We came as slaves. We are going to return freemen, and in ships of our own." The psychological sense of closure offered in returning by the means their ancestors had arrived, but now under their own power, held the imagination of many, because it symbolized a completion of the incredible journey from slavery to freedom. As a *Negro World* editorial put it in 1925, "None of those who came over here on the free ship [the *Mayflower*] and the slave ship . . . could have dreamed that the descendants of those who came over on the slave ship would own and operate a steamship of their own." The airplane, while it held a fascination as an awe-inspiring invention, did not speak as directly to the historical black past.[32]

With this emphasis on ships, references to airplanes in UNIA rhetoric were rare before Tulsa's outbreak. In September 1920, Garvey told an audience in Washington, D.C., that they would have to have "the latest battleships, the latest cruisers, the latest submarines, [and] the latest airships," if they were to have any protection. This remark, however, is the only encouragement to his followers to obtain airplanes found in a survey of Garvey's published papers and extant copies of the *Negro World* prior to the riot, and in this case his mention of the airplane seems to have been more an afterthought on a weapons wishlist than a serious call for black Americans to take up aviation.[33]

In fact, on several occasions, Garvey appeared to find the airplane inferior for the purpose of developing Africa. Discussing his proposal for black Americans to emigrate to Liberia in July 1920, he claimed that that country would need skilled mechanics and craftsmen, but that airplanes could not transport them to Africa. Proof of the airplane's long-distance capabilities still lay years in the future. Garvey repeated this drawback of the airplane several months later when soliciting stock sales for the Black Star Line, claiming, "We cannot fly to Africa at present in airships.... The only way we can get there is through ships."[34]

Although the airplane had proven itself a useful military machine in World War I, it had not yet become a major concern for members of the UNIA. Thus, *Negro World* editor William Ferris in 1920 could both acknowledge a place for aviation in the African nation's battle plan, claiming that the redemption of Africa would come about only after black men obtained machine guns, tanks, aeroplanes, and battleships and, in the same speech, criticize the airplane as an impractical luxury, equating it with wasteful daydreaming. "While you soar in your ethereal dreams and soar in your aeroplanes," he chided, "all men must have at least two square meals." The ship, conversely, promised commercial gain and military protection.[35]

The events of June 1, however, instilled in Garveyites a new awareness of air technology. While the riot did not remove the emphasis Garvey had always placed on ships, nonetheless it engendered a new appreciation of the airplane's role in race relations. Serving as a clarion call for the organization, Tulsa awakened its members to the dangers of white air power. After the riot, Garveyites across the country began to encourage aviation's development for self-protection and empowerment. At the beginning of July, the *California Eagle,* whose editors headed the UNIA chapter in Los Angeles, published alongside riot coverage an editorial entitled, "Airplanes? Yes!," in which it called the need for black Americans to seek flight instruction "timely and imperative." "[G]ain knowledge [of the air]," the editorial claimed, "and its synonym is power." Even before the *Eagle*'s urgings, however, a number of Los Angeles citizens had already decided to organize, forming an aviation club dedicated to training black youth to fly. Headed by Mrs. Kate Hendershott, the group soon attracted 175 avowed supporters. Unfortunately, the fate of this group is unknown.[36]

Others spoke more directly to the airplane's role in Africa's future. In Montreal, a speaker before the UNIA division there told his audience after the riot that airplanes were essential to speed up the necessary redemption of Africa, where blacks could find safety. Bemoaning the slow results of political organizing, he counseled, "The Negro has been organizing during the last 300 years." "An airplane," he offered, "is organized in nine days and soars o'er the earth." Seemingly having taken this advice to heart, a group of UNIA members at the organization's annual convention the following month carried a banner in the opening-day parade proclaiming, "The Negro will build aeroplanes."[37]

Following the convention, Garvey began to address aviation with growing frequency in his calls for the development of an African military. In a September speech in Liberty Hall, he included—as he had earlier—airplanes in his list of technologies necessary for blacks to force whites to "come to terms." The following month, in a front-page *Negro World* editorial, he stated the need for blacks to enter aviation more directly, exhorting his followers, "You will have to build your aeroplanes, you will have to give the world your latest inventions and develop your military skill . . . and not until then will the world call a halt to the outrage of the Negro." By January 1922, Garvey had taken a confrontational tone, informing the enemies of the race that the "present day Negro" knew how to use the machine gun and the airplane.[38]

Several months later, Garvey extrapolated the lesson of Tulsa to a larger world context. When the white colonial government in South Africa used airplanes to bomb the Bondelzwarts people, who were resisting colonization of their homelands, Garvey bemoaned the employment by the Bondelzwarts (whom he referred to as Hottentots) of sticks, stones, and spears to repel their enemy. The Hottentots, he lamented, "have no aeroplanes and because of that the Boers and the British can bomb them out of their huts and ultimately subdue them." Garvey proposed as a remedy that black flyers from America go to Africa to build planes for the Hottentots. Rethinking the disadvantages of the flying machine, he acknowledged, "It is true that we cannot get our aeroplanes from America to Africa; but after all, we can build aeroplanes anywhere for that matter, even in South West Africa."[39]

Already thinking along similar lines, air-minded members of the Brooklyn division had begun making plans after the August 1921 convention to purchase an airplane for the African Legion. That winter, they brought their idea before the New York local, explaining that the plane would be used by Capt. Edison C. McVey, an attaché in the Universal African Royal Guards, a Legion division. McVey, according to one contemporary, had served with the U.S. Army Air Service's 95th Pursuit Squadron as a mechanic during World War I. He also had learned to fly, although it is unclear where he had obtained lessons or for how long. Despite the objections of E.C. Gaines, the UNIA's Minister of Legions, who supported the plane's purchase but remained unconvinced of McVey's aeronautical abilities, the New York local enthusiastically approved the idea and set fundraising efforts in motion.[40]

While Brooklynites were heading the drive to purchase an airplane for Capt. McVey in New York, a twenty-four-year-old Trinidadian, who briefly would rise, along with McVey, as a hero among the ranks of the UNIA, was arriving in Cleveland, Ohio. Hubert F. Julian had discovered flying as his life's ambition at the age of twelve, through the unlikely event of having witnessed an aviator die in a plane crash in his birthplace of Port-au-Spain. Since that time, he had made flying, as he remembered fondly in his autobiography, "The one abiding love of my life." After emigrating to Montreal, Canada, in 1914, Julian began work on designing a mechanism intended to slow the fall of a disabled plane. By May 1921, he had succeeded in obtaining a U.S. patent for his "Airplane Safety appliance," a device that resembled a large parachute attachable to an airplane.[41]

Julian first encountered the Garvey movement in March 1921 when he made a trip to the United States to apply for a patent. On his way back to Montreal, he stopped over for a week in New York to visit family friends from his native Trinidad. Julian later wrote in his autobiography that he met Marcus Garvey on this trip, although this is an impossibility, as Garvey was lecturing in the West Indies from February to late July 1921. Julian more likely learned of the UNIA from his New York acquaintances (West Indians heavily populated the Brooklyn and New York divisions), or from the soapbox orators, named for the wooden soap crates on which they stood to address their audiences, who regularly appeared on the street corners of Harlem. Regardless of the source of his introduction, however, Garvey's organization appealed strongly to Julian, who, on moving to Cleveland in January 1922, joined that city's UNIA division.[42]

Julian spent several months in Cleveland trying to convince white-owned aviation concerns there, including the Glenn Martin Company, to manufacture his invention. Rebuffed by Martin and others, he had almost given in to discouragement when, by a stroke of luck, he was elected a delegate to the UNIA's annual convention to be held that summer in New York. At the August gathering, Julian met other men and women of his race whose newly found interest in aviation paralleled his own. Enthusiasm for flying had been building steadily among Garveyites in the year since the riot, and the arrival of Julian in New York spurred their hopes for the new technology.[43]

On the convention's opening day, Julian rented a plane and placed on its sides several large placards bearing UNIA slogans. He then flew over the organization's massive inaugural parade that blanketed Harlem's streets below and, passing over the city, dropped circulars to advertise a mass meeting planned to kick off the convention. As evidence discussed later indicates, Julian's claim that he was flying the plane above the parade is doubtful. The machine's appearance over the festivities nonetheless stirred great excitement, as paraders trained their eyes upward to make out who was above them. Their initial response was a telling one; the *Negro World* reported that "the enemy" was the first thought of those assembled. Once assured that the plane belonged to "a recent addition to the forces fighting for Africa's redemption," however, the spectators looked on admiringly. That evening, as Garvey took the podium at Madison Square Garden to greet the convention, he gave Julian a hero's welcome and introduced him to the cheering crowd of ten thousand.[44]

To at least one UNIA spokesman, Julian offered a glimpse of the possibilities aviation promised for the new age. The Rev. J. C. Austin of Pittsburgh, a popular speaker at the convention, promised his audience that this "ship of the air manned by a blackman was a prophetic declaration of what the world may expect of us in the activities of the new day." Julian augured proof for Austin of the role blacks would fulfill in the new era they hoped to usher in. Expressing their admiration for Julian, the UNIA announced that he would head an aeronautics division being planned by the Association, which would devote itself to developing aviation among the race.[45]

Several days later, on August 22, interest in aeronautics received another boost when a young woman named Bessie Coleman, the first black American to earn a license from the prestigious Fédération Aéronautique Internationale, appeared before the convention to publicize an upcoming exhibition. Coleman, who had recently returned from a trip to Europe, where she had learned to stunt fly, had come to New York to perform at the city's famed Curtiss Field. The excitement Coleman's Liberty Hall appearance created, coupled with that already sparked by Julian's flying over the convention's parade, undoubtedly contributed to the Association's warm embracing of aviation. The week after Coleman's appearance, the convention announced that $1,500 had been donated by individuals to establish its aviation program, and it formally established a "bureau of aeronautics," the immediate purpose of which was to found a flying school.[46]

The UNIA's emphasis on both military and economic strength surfaced in discussions of aviation during the convention. In a Resolution on Aeronautics passed by the body on September 2, the UNIA codified its conviction that learning to fly was necessary, claiming that it was pursuing flying because the world was "at present centered on aviation as a subject of ever increasing importance." It had been demonstrated clearly during the proceedings that flight's "increasing importance" was, in part, its military potential. In the speech he delivered after introducing Julian to the crowd on the convention's opening day, Garvey spoke to the airplane's military significance reminding his audience that during the year, when native Kenyans (like the Hottentots) had staged a revolt against their colonizers, their wooden spears and leather shields had proven useless against bombings from airplanes, and that they had been forced to accept alien rule. Five days later, William F. Sherrill of Ohio, the UNIA's assistant president general, elaborated on the need for blacks to empower themselves with technologies such as the airplane. In his speech, Sherrill deflected criticisms that the UNIA would never be able to free Africa from white colonial powers, by pointing out the dismal failures of integrationist strategies and claiming that those supporting integration would never be able to collect the debt owed black Americans by the country. Concluding that it would be a separate black nation protected by its military strength that would save the race, he proclaimed that the UNIA would "lay mines and build our submarines and construct aero-planes ... we are going to train an army of 10 or 15 million black soldiers, and if there is anybody anywhere that owes black men anything they will have to pay off." Given the failure of traditional tactics, illustrated so clearly by the stepped-up racial violence of the postwar period, Sherrill saw little recourse other than military arms, including the airplane, to protect the rights of the world's black citizens.[47]

The convention's Resolution on Aeronautics also explained that all nations were developing the science of aeronautics "as a potent factor in their commercial lives." One such application appeared in a report made later in the day by the UNIA committee appointed to study the development of Liberia, a possible locus of the black nation Garvey envisioned. Among the committee's six recommendations was the development of transportation in Liberia, including the use of airplanes and hydroplanes. Commercial possibilities closer to home were demonstrated by Bessie Coleman as she took to the air the day after the convention ended to fly before a paying crowd of between two and three thousand. Both Julian and Edison McVey appeared at Coleman's exhibition, Julian thrilling the crowd with his first recorded parachute jump from fifteen hundred feet over the field, and McVey, dressed in his African Legion uniform, officially greeting Coleman at the end of her flight with a bouquet of flowers.[48]

After the convention, interest in aviation remained high, spurred on by events on the African continent. Increasingly after 1922, European powers used the airplane against native Africans to enforce colonial rule, and these events fueled Garveyites' already growing awareness of the airplane as an indispensable weapon. The *Negro World* frequently commented on the airplane's deployment to subdue black populations in Africa and elsewhere, condemning the Italians for bombing Arabs in Southwest Africa in 1924, the British for bombing delinquent taxpayers in Mesopotamia in 1924, and the French for using airplanes between 1922 and 1925 to turn the tide in their war with the Riffians of Morocco and for attacking poorly defended Syrian villages in 1925 and 1926. Writers for the paper made much of the fact that the French were employing airplanes to kill unarmed women and children in the Riffian region of northwestern coastal Morocco. It stepped up its criticisms when a group of white American aviators, who had fought for France during World War I in the highly lauded Lafayette Escadrille, volunteered their services to help fight against the Riffians. Calling these American mercenaries cowards, the *Negro World* condemned them for their lack of manliness and sense of fair play.[49]

In their attacks on European colonialism, Garvey and writers for the *Negro World* drew stark comparisons between technologically advanced Europeans and helpless Africans. Garvey, for example, in 1922, proclaimed the barbarity of the British decision to bomb the natives of Southwest Africa "when they had nothing else than sticks and stones to fight with." Urging the race to claim for themselves the power necessary to prevent such outrages, he proclaimed, "the age of sticks and stones is past, and the age of scientific combat is here." "If you want to meet the other fellow and he has his aeroplane, get one," he encouraged *Negro World* readers. To his urgings Garvey also added a warning. Criticizing black Americans for not pursuing opportunities for obtaining modern technologies, he recalled for them the "great plan that is laid out for the extermination of the weaker peoples and races of the world."[50]

The *Negro World* continued throughout the early 1920s to coax black Americans to take up aviation, threatening them with stories bearing such titles as "Yellow and White Races Prepare for Future Armageddon—Mr. Blackman, What About You?" and urging them forward with queries of "Where Is Your Airplane, Mr. Blackman?" Editorials appearing in the paper often turned to the rhetoric of white supremacists to convince readers of the importance of aviation. Quoting white writer Arthur Brisbane, who warned whites, "When you . . . realize that any average human being can be taught to run a flying machine in eight hours, you wonder how long 'white supremacy' will last," a 1925 *Negro World* editorial called on its readers to "read, reread, and seriously consider" Brisbane's statement.[51]

In his own pleas for the race to take up aviation, Garvey often stressed that in international conflict, it was "might" that made right. Illustrating his point in 1924, the UNIA leader explained to a Liberty Hall audience that France could dare to break the particulars of her peace agreement with Germany because other world powers knew "that France is well-equipped with many thousands of airplanes and that she can [ho]ver over their cities and drop certain [thi]ngs not pleasant to their populations." "There is no justice but power," he concluded, "[The]re is no right but strength." Encouraging his followers to take a lesson from France, Garvey asserted that vainly hoped for legislation to protect blacks would not be needed if the race obtained physical power. "Your aeroplanes hovering over cities," he asserted, "will talk for you." Eschewing domestic politics, Garvey encouraged his followers to concentrate instead on strengthening the race militarily in an African location, and arming it with airplanes.[52]

As awareness of the airplane grew, sparked by the Tulsa riot, and fueled by the conflicts in Africa, aviation came to occupy a more central position in the apocalyptic visions of some Garveyites. The Rev. James Morris Webb of Seattle, for instance, prophesied in a sermon delivered at Liberty Hall in September 1924, that Garvey was on a mission to prepare Africa for a universal black king, whom the Bible, he claimed, had foretold would come to rule the world. When this king descended from Heaven, Webb exclaimed, he would "fill the air with airplanes." And, he thundered, "Battleships will go down and submarines be destroyed." In Webb's vision, aeronautical replaced naval power as the dominant technology of the new age.[53]

While visions of an Armageddon where blacks emerged triumphant in the air sustained some nationalists, others placed greater emphasis on the more immediate successes of the UNIA's own aviators. After the 1922 convention, Garveyites followed with interest the careers of Hubert Julian and Edison McVey. In November, Julian returned to Curtiss Field, the site of Bessie Coleman's exhibition two months earlier, to make a second jump, this time leaping during an American Legion Flying Circus from a plane flown by white pilot Clarence Chamberlin. Chamberlin, who operated an airfield in Hasbrouck Heights, New Jersey, would serve frequently as Julian's pilot over the following months. He later wrote that en route to and from Julian's engagements he occasionally gave him impromptu flying lessons, and that the young stuntman had proven an apt student.[54]

For the time being, however, it was as a parachutist that Julian was known. He gained national attention in late April when he made a daring descent over Harlem, becoming the first person to parachute over the city limits. Julian's leap from near three thousand feet thrilled Harlem residents, especially his fellow West Indians, and earned him accolades from black journalists across the country. The crowd that witnessed his feat was estimated by the *Chicago Defender* at fifty thousand and, on his landing on a tenement rooftop, close to six thousand people pressed forward to see him, in their eagerness breaking a shop window, knocking over a shoeshine stand, and collapsing an iron railing. Attesting to his popularity among the UNIA, Julian was carried on the shoulders of the crowd to Liberty Hall, where he was called on to speak.[55]

Stating as one purpose of the jump to draw attention to the imminent closing of the black-owned A.I. Hart Department Store in Harlem, Julian urged the crowd to patronize Hart's business. This strong nationalist concern with independent black economic endeavors also appeared in the *Negro World*'s coverage of Julian's leap. Calling Julian an "asset to the Negro race," H.J. Saltus, business manager of the paper, suggested that blacks around the country would eagerly pay to see Julian perform, and he encouraged race men to help send Julian on a national tour. It would be, he claimed, "a paying proposition." Such a commercial venture could, Saltus promised, eventually serve a greater purpose. He urged black businessmen to "nurse him until the time presents itself when he can put his abilities to practical use."[56]

By the summer of 1923, Edison McVey had joined Julian, and the two formed a stunt team, with McVey flying and Julian performing parachute jumps. They made their debut together in an air circus at Hasbrouck Heights in June, during which they unveiled to the public a Curtiss "Canuck" training plane recently purchased for their use by the black movie producer Peter Jones.

Jones had for some time been interested in filming an aviation picture for black audiences. The previous fall he had signed Bessie Coleman to perform in such a film, but when Coleman withdrew from the project following a dispute with its director, he abandoned his efforts. According to Chamberlin, Jones now had fresh plans to star Julian and McVey in a "super thriller of the clouds," and had bought the Canuck for that purpose.[57]

To open the exhibition, Mrs. Sadie Warren, publisher of the *New York Amsterdam News,* christened the Canuck the *Bonita La Primera* (The First Beauty). Praising Julian and McVey as pioneers for the race, she claimed that in naming the plane she was doing so "with the feeling that future generations of the race need not despair." Her words still ringing in the air, McVey roared off into the sky. When he had reached thirty-five hundred feet, Julian made his jump and, to the crowd's delight, pulled out a saxophone as he wafted downward and played "Runnin' Wild," a popular jazz tune.[58]

For a time, Mrs. Warren's hopes seemed well placed in Julian and McVey. The pair continued to please crowds and garner praise from the press during July. On July 4, Julian jumped and McVey competed in a stunt-flying contest at an Independence Day Jubilee and Aviation Carnival held at Hasbrouck Heights. Near mid-month, the *Baltimore Afro-American* reported, they traveled to Atlantic City, New Jersey, to make plans for an upcoming exhibition they had contracted to perform for the Colored Young Men's Republican Club. With bright prospects for the future, by late July they had signed a contract to appear as a feature with the Michaels Brothers' Carnival, which was booked to travel on the Negro agricultural fair circuit in the fall. The duo was fast becoming what the *Pittsburgh Courier* had once called Julian, "the talk of aeronautical circles."[59]

By the end of July, however, the dreams invested in these young airmen came crashing abruptly down, when McVey took off during a trial flight at Hasbrouck Heights with Clarence Chamberlin as his passenger. The two were going up to test the worthiness of the Canuck for its flight to Atlantic City when the plane stalled at one hundred feet in its climb. Too close to the ground to parachute, McVey and Chamberlin braced themselves for the fall. Astonishingly, Chamberlin, thrown clear of the wreckage, walked away with only minor wounds. Less fortunate, McVey sustained a broken jaw, two broken legs, a broken arm, and a number of internal injuries. Despite the gloomy prognosis of doctors at the nearby Hackensack Hospital, however, who announced he would not live, McVey fought back against all odds. According to at least one source, the courageous aviator had returned to the airshow circuit within the year. Evidence also indicates that he began to travel for the UNIA as a lecturer on aviation.[60]

After losing his partner, Julian's career faltered, but he displayed none of the recuperative powers of McVey in attempting to resuscitate it. Mostly because of his own intemperate actions, Julian's reputation suffered considerably in the following months. In August, he was arrested for assaulting Simon Bernard, a former associate, who claimed Julian had failed to pay him for a parachute. Then, in October, word reached black newspapers that Julian's wife, whom he had left behind in Montreal, was suing for divorce, listing abandonment, adultery, and physical abuse as grounds. The scandal quickly became headline news in the national black press, with the often sensation-seeking *Chicago Defender* even publishing a personal letter of Julian's confessing an extramarital affair. The legitimacy Julian had enjoyed while touring with McVey suddenly eroded as reporters began to scrutinize the parachutist's past more closely. Investigating claims by Julian's wife that he made his living primarily as a swindler, reporters soon uncovered a number of individuals in Cleveland and New York who claimed to have been misused by Julian. The *Pittsburgh Courier,* in a front-page story, published a list of their charges, which ranged from complaints of unpaid loans to no-shows for planned exhibitions to frequent misrepresentations of himself as a licensed aviator, a war hero, and an unmarried man.[61]

Julian was in fact guilty of many of the charges made against him. Prone to exaggeration, he claimed on his arrival in the United States that he had been a medical student at McGill University, an assertion not borne out by the school's enrollment records. Julian also stated on many occasions that he had flown as a lieutenant with the Canadian air services during World War I, an unlikely boast. Canadian pilots flew for Britain's Royal Flying Corps, Royal Naval Air Service, or Royal Air Force (there was no Royal Canadian Air Force until 1924), and the British required all pilots to be officers, a status they restricted by race. Julian also at times asserted he had flown during the war with a regiment raised from the British West Indies, a statement he later contradicted in his autobiography, in which he described his father's successful maneuverings to keep him out of the West Indian outfit. Despite his presentation of himself as a military aviator, no evidence appears to indicate that the unlicensed Julian could fly when he came to America. Although he had proven himself an able parachutist, the public would not witness him at the controls of an airplane until 1924.[62]

Julian's overstatement of his war experience and flying ability might have been received more kindly had it not been coupled with a flamboyant personal style journalists often found irksome. On his first leap over Harlem, the daring parachutist had worn a bright red devil suit, complete with horns and tail, and he frequently donned the uniform of a British officer in the streets of Harlem. Many during Julian's first few months in the spotlight were willing to pass off his self-aggrandizement and attention-grabbing garb as simply the idiosyncrasies of a performer. It was the nature of an entertainer to dazzle and surprise. But, by late 1923, Julian's panache had become an embarrassment for some, especially as it increasingly caught the eye of white journalists. The *New York Times* and other white papers frequently made Julian a target of their humor, publishing numerous articles parodying him as a Negro buffoon attempting to master a white man's technology. Much like the master showman P. T. Barnum, however, Julian sought out this type of publicity because it enhanced his livelihood. As Barnum had discovered in the nineteenth century, publicity, be it good or bad, was the lifeblood of a performer's career. Julian's decision to seek attention regardless of its nature, while good for business, did not make him popular among a growing number of editors across the country, who objected to what they considered harmful and degrading pandering to white stereotypes.

Julian's precipitous fall from grace in the popular black press, however, cannot be attributed entirely to his personal failings or his flamboyance. In 1923, as a highly visible member of the UNIA, the budding aviator became something of a lightning rod for more general animosities felt toward Garveyites. Since 1920, the UNIA had fallen under escalating attack from a number of prominent journalists, politicians, and ministers. The most severe criticisms were aimed at fundraising efforts for the Black Star Line. UNIA leaders regularly traveled across the country to sell stock in the line and raise monies for other Association projects, and although the steamship company in its first year had purchased three ships, by 1922, fraud and price gouging by the ships' original owners and Garvey's lack of business experience had combined to result in fairly consistent losses. Distrustful of Garvey's financial acumen and doubtful of his sincerity, many opposed his continued solicitations.

Adding to the Black Star Line's financial problems was legal harassment from the U.S. government. In January 1922, postal officials had Garvey arrested on charges of mail fraud, claiming advertisements he mailed to potential stockholders were intentionally misleading. Soon after, the Line was forced temporarily to shut down operations. While Garvey's trial was pending, criticism of him reached a peak. During the UNIA's 1922 convention, a number of his critics cooperated to stage a "Garvey Must Go" campaign, holding anti-Garvey meetings not far from Liberty Hall.

The attacks on Garvey delivered by those involved in the "Garvey Must Go" campaign, as well as by other critics, while ostensibly about UNIA finances, oftentimes assumed a more personal nature. Journalists and others mocked the leader's donning of academic robes and military uniforms at the UNIA's conventions, his conferring of royal titles on organization members, and his often bombastic rhetoric. Deriding what they perceived as Garvey's ostentation and regal pretensions, they characterized him as a buffoon seeking personal aggrandizement at the expense of his race.

By January 1923, many had come to believe that Garvey was also dangerous. Prompted by the assassination of the Rev. J. W. H. Eason, a former UNIA official and vocal opponent of Garvey, a group of journalists and business leaders petitioned the U.S government to expedite its charges against Garvey. Among those signing the petition were Robert Abbott, editor of the *Chicago Defender,* and George Harris, editor of the *New York News,* both longtime Garvey adversaries. By May, the group had received its request, and Garvey's trial for mail fraud had begun. Convicted in June, Garvey was released on bail in September when he appealed the case. By early 1925, however, after having his court battle drag on for over a year, Garvey had lost the appeal, and began serving a five-year sentence in the Atlanta Federal Penitentiary.[63]

The objections journalists raised toward Julian often paralleled closely those directed toward the UNIA leader. No event demonstrates this better than the flyer's 1924 proposed around-the-world flight. In the spring of 1924, Julian announced he would pilot a plane alone from New York to Liberia. By April, he had expanded his plans, claiming he would circle the globe. Setting the Fourth of July as his takeoff date and New York as his point of departure, he stated his trip would take him down the Atlantic Coast to Florida, through Cuba and the West Indies, south to Venezuela, across the Atlantic Ocean to Liberia, and then northward through Europe and Iceland and westward to Canada, then, finally, back to New York. Although the route Julian had mapped out was actually a double transatlantic crossing, he undoubtedly dubbed his journey an "around-the-world" flight to gain benefit from the publicity then being given to an attempt by eight U.S. Army Air Service pilots to fly together around the world.

In April, Julian began to lecture and make parachute jumps in major East Coast cities, including Boston, New York, Norfolk, and Baltimore, to raise money for a rebuilt Boeing seaplane he had arranged to purchase from Clarence Chamberlin. It was clear to journalists, however, who had just watched the experienced Army pilots take off in specially equipped military planes, that Julian's plans to undertake an arduous transatlantic crossing alone in a reconditioned seaplane were wildly impractical. One of the four Army aircraft had already flown into an Alaskan mountainside during a snowstorm, and the public held out little hope of the others completing their trip. Thus, most newspapers reported Julian's endeavors to raise money for the flight with a smirking tone, and others directly questioned his claims and his aeronautical ability. In early May, the *Afro-American,* for example, criticized Julian's failure to make a promised Easter Sunday leap from atop the chute-the-chute at Wonderland Park, a Baltimore amusement park catering to blacks. The paper laughed that Julian had entertained the crowd with a soapbox rather than a parachute after the aviator addressed park patrons requesting money to pay back an advance he had already received for the stunt. Later in the month the *Afro-American* attacked Julian more harshly, publishing reports from New York papers that he was a fake who could not fly. In Pittsburgh, the *Courier* also circulated rumors of Julian's inability to fly, noting that the Boulin Detective Agency of New York had uncovered evidence that he was not a pilot. *The Courier* did, however, report that Julian had actually produced a plane for the flight and that its procurement should quiet criticism temporarily. The fledgling flyer himself responded by claiming he would prove his abilities, offering to take up any reporter who would go for a plane ride.[64]

Even the UNIA, recognizing the liability Julian represented, attempted to distance itself from him. When Julian requested that his flight be endorsed by the organization, the *Negro World* columnist Norton Thomas, along with the paper's business manager, made a trip to Hasbrouck Heights to view the plane in which Julian proposed to make his flight. Unimpressed both with the craft and with Chamberlin, whom Julian identified as his technical advisor, they refused to lend their name to the project, placing notices in the *Negro World* requesting UNIA divisions to ignore Julian's solicitations. Thomas, in his column, expressed doubt that Julian really intended to make the flight. "This writer does not believe Julian will do any such thing," he asserted. "And why?" he asked. Because Julian, he claimed, "daring as he undoubtedly is, knows too much about the inexorable law of gravity."[65]

The UNIA could not, however, prohibit Julian from using nationalist rhetoric. Dubbing his plane the *Ethiopia I,* he decorated its tail with the red, black, and green tricolors of the Association and painted on its sides the statement, "This Plane Is the Property of the Negro Race, Donated by Them for Their Future Advancement in Aviation." He put the plane on display at the corner of 139th Street and Lennox Avenue in Harlem. Julian's promotion of the flight as a nationalist project drew him much support, especially from West Indians in the city, among whom he remained popular. It appealed to others as well, as the comments of W. J. Wheaton of the *California Eagle* indicate. The *Eagle,* earlier a black nationalist publication, had by this time shifted its politics in the direction of socialism, but its editors and writers remained sympathetic to nationalist goals. Wheaton, who penned his weekly offerings in a column for the paper, proudly acknowledged Julian's plane as "the property of the Colored people," and he encouraged his readers to follow Julian's example, pleading, "We have a few aviators, but have we enough? Don't we want to see some of our young men skimming like a bird through the ether ... making our bid to keep abreast of the march of progress." Even Norton Thomas of the *Negro World* could not stay angry at Julian long. Lamenting in early July that the flyer spent more time on promotion than serious preparation, he nonetheless praised him as "young, ambitious, and daring" and wished him well.[66]

The disappointing failure of Julian's flight, however, downed the hopes of even the most optimistic. As he readied himself for takeoff from the Harlem River on the morning of the Fourth of July, an almost endless series of complications arose to stymie his plans. First, Chamberlin, not having yet received full payment for his plane, insisted that Julian pay the remaining balance before he would allow him to take off. In response, West Indian friends of Julian's made their way through the holiday crowd of over ten thousand and, after several hours, collected the money owed. Receiving the go-ahead, Julian attempted to maneuver the craft into takeoff position, but the tide, having receded during the delay, had left the ship's pontoons stuck in the mud. It took several men in the crowd to push the plane into deeper water. Once there, however, its motor developed trouble, and by the time it could be repaired, the pontoons were striking against rocks as the receding tide continued to lower the water level.[67]

The wisest choice at this point would have been to abort the flight, as precious hours of daylight were slipping away. Pressure from the impatient crowd, however, and from a government postal inspector, who for several weeks had been warning Julian that if he did not take off he would be prosecuted for raising funds under false pretenses (and who now stood in the crowd ready to carry out his threats), led the nervous flyer to risk having the plane towed through the rocks into the nearby East River, where the water was deeper. At 5:30 P.M., four hours after his estimated takeoff time, Julian finally fired up its engines, and the *Ethiopia I* cleared the water's surface, evoking cheers from the crowd below. Their cheers soon turned to groans, however, as minutes later they watched a pontoon, damaged in the towing, fall from the plane. Flipping over, the craft landed in nearby Flushing Bay. Julian, suffering from internal injuries after the fall, was rescued by a police boat and taken to Flushing Hospital.[68]

The popular black press was not kind to Julian after his crash. The major weeklies derided the young aviator in much the same tone they had Garvey, mocking his penchant for military uniforms and his boastful claims. Some papers, such as the *New York Age* and the *Norfolk Journal and Guide,* expressed their distaste by simply ignoring Julian, refusing to cover the story of his flight. Others took the opportunity to ridicule his pretensions. The *Chicago Defender,* for instance, ran a cutline beneath a picture of Julian's plane jeering, "Lieut. Hubert Julian's around the world and to Africa plane ... 'hopped off' for four miles and then 'flopped' right down into Flushing [B]ay, New York." At the end of its story on the flight, the paper recalled for its readers the earlier scandals in which Julian had been involved.[69]

By the time of his 1924 flight, Julian in many respects had become merged in the public mind with Garvey. This phenomenon can be seen clearly in the discussion of the flight by William Pickens, field secretary of the NAACP and a leader in the anti-Garvey movement. In an article written for the *Afro-American,* Pickens laughed "From Harlem River to Flushing Bay! The President of Africa is determined to take us over,—if not on the water, then thru the air." Equating Julian's with Garvey's aims, he stated that he was not opposed to Garvey's disseminating a Back-to-Africa vision to the public, "But," he added, "we are opposed to his carrying money out of their pockets into Flushing Bay." Despite the UNIA's clear attempts to distance itself from Julian, Pickens considered the young flyer's actions as inseparable from those of Garvey. Criticizing what he saw as the impracticality of both the Black Star Line and an around-the-world airplane trip, he declared, "No old boat and no defective airplane will ever take them to Africa—or to Flushing Bay." Pickens, unconvinced that Garvey, or Julian, offered to the black American public any real means of reaching the goals they had set out, judged the pleas of both for financial support as little more than calculated scams.[70]

Embarrassed by Garvey and critical of the unfulfilled promises of his rhetoric, writers such as Pickens, who earlier had been supportive of the UNIA, could no longer see a viable way to achieve a separate black nation. Thus, they turned to the closer question of how to live in America and, rejecting Garvey as a legitimate leader, sought out solutions in other quarters. As Pickens wrote in 1922, "The best thing is to see how best the whites and blacks here can get along together."[71]

Writers such as Pickens, whether they were civil rights activists, socialists, or conservatives, found in the pages of the popular black press a welcome home for their thoughts. Few of the country's major black papers had ever embraced Garvey wholeheartedly, and many, such as the *Chicago Defender* and the *Baltimore Afro-American,* often had actively opposed the UNIA leader and his programs. In the 1920s, these newssheets spoke with an increasingly powerful voice. Before World War I, few black newspapers had achieved wide circulation. However, as migrants increasingly left the South to take wartime jobs and to escape segregation and economic exploitation, they swelled the populations of urban black communities in the North, Midwest, and West, making it possible for the first time to support newspapers as moneymaking ventures. The larger papers that resulted, in contrast to their predecessors, reached homes and businesses across the country, including the South, where they were often carried by railroad porters. A few, such as the *Chicago Defender,* were read by as many as 180,000 paying subscribers and by numerous others who passed the papers from hand to hand. These nationally circulated weeklies, along with regionally strong papers such as the *California Eagle* and *Houston Informer,* gained an unprecedented influence over black public opinion in the early 1920s.[72]

Black entrepreneurship and a strong reform ethic informed the bulk of the writing in the popular press. Invariably the major weeklies touted the idea of separate black business, encouraging blacks to buy from other race members and to pursue businesses of their own. Their commitment to "economic nationalism," however, did not extend to the social realm. Viewing integration as a better hope for racial progress, they encouraged their readers to engage actively in politics, working to change discriminatory segregation laws and to gain federal aid in ending vigilante violence. Deeming the ideal of building a black nation impractical at best, they sought to reform American society instead.[73]

The popular press reflected the mood prevalent among many urban black Americans, which author Ralph Ellison later described as "an optimism . . . a sense of possibility, which, despite our awareness of limitations (dramatized so brutally in the Tulsa race riot of 1921), transcended all of this." Black editors and journalists, members of a rising middle class that benefited enormously from the separate economies made possible by growing urban black ghettos, viewed the world through the spectacles of personal success. Robert Abbott, the editor of the *Chicago Defender,* had even reached the pinnacle of the rags-to-riches myth, becoming a millionaire in the 1920s. His triumph reinforced the notion that the American Dream could be achieved by black Americans. Although the majority of editors and writers remained considerably less well remunerated for their work (many were forced to take second jobs to supplement their income), they nonetheless shared Abbott's fervent belief in America's promise.[74]

The business values and social reform philosophy articulated in the popular press in the years after the Tulsa riot led to a view of aviation sharply at odds with Garvey's. Like Garveyites, journalists writing for mainstream audiences remained cognizant of Tulsa. Several months before his attack on Julian's flight in 1924, William Pickens himself had, in a letter to the *New York Age,* reminded readers of white Tulsans' aerial assault on Greenwood. In the vision of aviation integration-minded writers offered their readers, however, they chose to downplay the airplane's threat as a weapon controlled by white racists, and to emphasize instead its economic promise and its potential for creating positive images of the race. Hoping to avert future racial conflict, they saw aviation as holding greater opportunity than danger.[75]

Just as Hubert Julian had come for many to symbolize Garvey's philosophy, Bessie Coleman, the young flyer who had appeared at the UNIA's convention in 1922, emerged as a representative of popular journalists' more optimistic strategy. A poor Texas native, Coleman had migrated to Chicago around 1914, and soon after came to the attention of the *Chicago Defender.* The paper in 1917 lauded her pioneering spirit in becoming one of the first women to work as a manicurist in the formerly all-male realm of the barbershop. Coleman's initiative in this area again garnered praise in 1918 when the *Defender* deemed her as "a progressive up-to-date young woman." "Up-to-date" must have been how she appeared to *Defender* editor Robert Abbott when, three years later, in 1920, Coleman approached him with an unusual request—to help her finance a trip abroad to learn to fly. Abbott readily agreed.[76]

With the newsman's help, Coleman sailed for Le Crotoy, France, where she earned her license from the prestigious École d'Aviation des Frères Caudron in June 1921, just two weeks after the Tulsa riot. On her return home, Coleman decided she wanted to open her own flying school for black youth and, in order to prepare herself, she made a second European trip to learn to stunt fly. This time she traveled not only to France but also to England, Germany, and Holland as well. The young flyer arrived home in the summer of 1922 with a plan to barnstorm across the country. With support from Abbott, who sponsored her Curtiss Field exhibition, she hoped to raise money through her performances to start her school.

Coleman, who toured extensively between 1922 and 1926, employed many strategies for persuading blacks to take up aviation. Not far removed from Tulsa's shadow, she initially appealed in her rhetoric in 1921 to some of the same fears Garvey had addressed. Expressing dismay that blacks in America "were so far behind the white men" in aeronautical experience, and that the "darker races" worldwide remained behind the lighter ones, she echoed Garvey's mistrust of the growing technological power of whites. Warning *Defender* readers in October that the formidable Goliath airplane she had seen in France was being developed as a fighting machine, she pleaded, "We must have aviators if we are to keep pace with the times."[77]

Coleman's appeals for blacks to embrace flying, however, soon moved away from this strategy as she began to pursue aviation as a business. As an entrepreneur, the young aviator began to stress aviation's more practical applications. According to one of her flying students, Coleman often claimed that aeronautics represented the way to future job security for blacks. In 1923, Robert Paul Sachs told readers of the *California Eagle* that Coleman thought blacks would someday, because of their good performance as chauffeurs, comprise a majority of skilled pilots. Recognizing the future need for trained aviators, he stated, Coleman hoped to persuade young men and women to prepare to enter the field.[78]

Popular journalists shared Coleman's enthusiasm for aviation's economic promise. Roscoe Simmons, a *Defender* columnist, urged blacks that they had made good chauffeurs, and now they should "Go a step higher and make it read 'pilot.'" W. J. Wheaton, the *Eagle* columnist who had coaxed blacks to take up flying in response to Julian's 1924 flight, regularly exhorted black youth to take up flying. "Chauffeurs will soon be as obsolete as the stage driver," he told his readers. E. L. Dorsey, another *Eagle* writer, agreed, stating, "Air pilots will be in demand, as chauffeurs are today[,] and there will be a place for our boys who are able to qualify and make the grade." Dorsey had no doubt that America would provide a place for blacks if they proved themselves deserving.[79]

Journalists also quickly recognized in Coleman a figure with the potential to disprove white stereotypes of the race. In 1925, when the young pilot flew an exhibition in Houston, a reporter from that city's *Informer* remarked, after she took over seventy-five black spectators for rides, that their ascension had "disprove[d] the assertion that the Negro is afraid to fly." A year later, after Coleman's death in a crash in 1926, an *Eagle* editorialist made a similar claim, writing, "It can never be said that as a race we have failed along any line of effort and the sacrifice of Bessie Coleman is the answer to the part the race has played in aviation." At times journalists expressed broader hopes for Coleman, presenting her as a symbol of the race's uplift. In 1921, for example, *Defender* artist Leslie Rogers, in an editorial cartoon, depicted a biplane flying high above the city draping a large sign that read, "Miss Bessie Coleman—The Race's First Aviatrix." The caption asserted, "They Can't Keep Us Down." In this image, the flyer's achievement came to serve as a collective act. Her rise equaled that of her race, and was interpreted not simply as a brave deed but also one intended as the group's challenge to its oppressors. This tendency to merge individual success with group advancement was not a new development in racial reform thinking. As early as 1912, the *New York Age* had, in an editorial describing the feats of aviator Lucean Headen, one of the first black Americans known to have taken to the air, rejoiced that Headen's accomplishment had proven that "it is impossible to keep the Negro down."[80]

Journalists who embraced aviation as a technology through which they could destroy stereotypes and challenge oppression strove to place before the public positive images of black flyers, commenting proudly on the achievements of Coleman and other budding aviators. Their praise extended as well to blacks involved in aviation in minor capacities. For instance, in August 1922, the *Pittsburgh Courier* published a story praising John Gainey, a clerk in the Railway Mail Service, for flying to New York in the company of several other Post Office officials to inspect mail planes. Newspapers even gave attention to blacks who took rides in airplanes. Typical was a story printed by the *Denver Statesman* in September 1921, reporting that Carroll Hardwick, a Tennessee restaurant owner, had hired a plane to fly him to Atlanta to attend a meeting of the National Negro Business League.[81]

Convinced of their ability to impress their equality on whites, writers for the popular press expressed a far more optimistic view of America's aeronautical power than Garveyites. Intensely patriotic, the large weeklies regularly portrayed the airplane as a tool of American democracy. In June 1922, for example, Robert Abbott hired an airplane to fly over the ceremonies to dedicate Chicago's Giles Avenue, newly renamed for a black World War I hero. As Chicago mayor William Thompson spoke, a *Defender* reporter later noted, the plane "hove into sight, bringing with it grim reminiscences of the struggle for democracy." In its recital of the affair, the *Defender* described the response of those below to the plane, exalting,

> Hearts strained with a thrill when the great *Chicago Defender* airplane, especially secured for the occasion, purred its majestic way into a position above the ceremony. Not a soldier but thought of "over there." Not a civilian but thought of how grand, how filled with an inspiring awe was this symbol of the heavens.

A thing celestial, the airplane emerged in the *Defender* as a symbol of American patriotic fervor.[82]

In its discussion of American military aviation, the *Defender* expressed faith in the ultimate triumph of the democratic spirit in the country. It did not, however, plan to leave it to whites to bring about change. The paper criticized severely the color line drawn by the U.S. Army Air Service, and lobbied to gain inclusion for blacks. "Let Us Fly" the paper demanded of the U.S. government in a May 1922 editorial.[83]

The *Defender,* despite its hopes for America, could not ignore the continued exclusion of blacks from what remained essentially a white-controlled technology. It also could not escape the shadow of Tulsa, for a number of events after 1921 kept the specter of airplanes in the hands of white racists alive. Just one year after the riot, in August 1922, Klansmen in Oklahoma City flew over black sections of the city on the day before a tightly contested gubernatorial race and dropped leaflets bearing the picture of a hooded Knight and a warning to black voters not to try to cast their ballots unless they were registered and could vote for "clean law enforcement." The mild message scarcely masked the intended threat, and the *Defender*'s headline, "Ku Klux 'Bomb' City From Air," interpreted the Klansmen's actions in the familiar metaphorical context of war.[84]

The potential of the airplane to be deployed against blacks also extended beyond instances of social conflict. As an occurrence in 1926 demonstrated, the airplane could serve as a weapon of random, capricious violence as well. In late October, two military pilots on maneuvers from Maxwell Air Base decided to seek amusement in "buzzing" black farm workers picking cotton in a field near Montgomery, Alabama. Chasing a woman and her three sons out of the field and back to their home, the plane then turned and flew toward two men, one the white owner of the farm and the other a black laborer. The plane knocked both over with its wing, killing the farm's owner and critically injuring the other man. The *Defender* scored the action of the pilots, sarcastically remarking that the "South's latest form of amusing itself is by airplane hunting." Calling the craft a "vampire plane," the paper claimed that the pilots had intended to kill the woman and her children and that they had been surprised to find a white man in the field. The writer went on to criticize the police, asserting that only the death of a wealthy white man had prompted them to seek out the culprits.[85]

The *Defender*'s reference to airplane hunting showed a clear awareness of the tendency of whites to view blacks as subhuman beings, who could be "hunted" without remorse. James Weldon Johnson had used almost the *Defender*'s very words less than two weeks after the Tulsa riot when he claimed concerning the use of airplanes to chase blacks in the riot, "Negro hunting had long been a sport in the South." In a reversal of this perception, the *Defender* reporter characterized the pilots' actions as "one of the most brutal and inhuman ever recorded in this district." In a melding of man and machine, he then suggested what the pilots and plane may have been instead of human—vampires. The vampire plane, one could assume, was a technology controlled by murderous racists, who fed off black victims to live.[86]

Responding to events such as these, integration-minded journalists, recognizing the vulnerability of blacks to white air supremacy, joined nationalists in urgent appeals to their race to learn to fly. In January 1925, William N. Jones, an *Afro-American* columnist, encouraged his readers to work toward gaining entry for black youth in the U.S. Army Air Corps (formerly the U.S. Air Service) as a means for them to obtain knowledge of the air. Their experience, he warned, might be necessary in case of a "mighty cataclysm." Until the world became a safer place for blacks, he claimed, "the Negro must learn to use every modern impliment [implement] of defense." Several months later, Jones again urged blacks to take up aviation, arguing "Some of our youth must learn to fly. Not some of them but thousands of them." Pleading that blacks not "trail in the big undertakings of the world," he counseled the race's young men to start saving to purchase their own planes so that they might be among "the nation's flyers." Not completely convinced of the all-white Air Corps' willingness to share the skies with them, however, he added, "and perhaps sometimes to serve your own group in an important crisis."[87]

The fears so close to the surface in Jones's comments were articulated with greater emotional force by the *New York News*. The paper exhorted its readers in an editorial on the anniversary of Coleman's death in a plane crash in 1926, pleading,

> How can the race ever compete without knowing how to fly? What protection will our progress, our communities, our countries ever have if all these can be wiped out with impunity by one fell swoop of a hostile airplane? How can we ever compete in the great coming commercial industry of aviation if we cannot fly?

Just as Garveyites long had, the anti-Garvey *News* recognized the danger inherent in a white monopoly of air power.[88]

Still, writers for the popular press maintained their hopes for America, asserting that black success, especially in the economic realm, would eventually lead to reform. For some, the race's triumphs in aviation even signified the coming of the new age promised in the rhetoric of American statesmen such as Woodrow Wilson. When Joel Foreman, a Californian, took to the sky for an exhibition flight in Los Angeles in 1925, an *Eagle* reporter proclaimed,

> For many it simply meant a Negro had flown. But the event had truly a deeper significance. The dawn of a new era was at hand and the race through its repre-

sentative was paving the way for qualifying in the commercial part the airplane is to play in the near future.

In contrast to Garvey, popular journalists embraced the rhetoric of American rather than African exceptionalism, expressing a belief in their ultimate ability to avert disaster by participating fully in the country's commercial affairs. By achieving in the field of aviation, they claimed, they might help America fulfill its promise and reach the "new age."[89]

Underpinning the philosophies of aviation that emerged after Tulsa were two very different ways of looking at the world. The premise of integrationist strategies for racial uplift was that if blacks could prove their equality through flying, whites would reform, and the new age would be reached in America. African redemptionists, by contrast, saw aviation more as a means to physical rather than persuasive power. Convinced of the unreformability of whites, they viewed the airplane in part as a doomsday technology, which ultimately would spell the end of white supremacy. Beneath both visions, however, ran the lesson of Tulsa. Aviation was power, and to achieve their goals the race would have to obtain that power. The great shadow in the sky had cast a long trajectory.

Notes

1. Several sources note that a loud whistle blew that marked the subsequent invasion of Greenwood. See, for example, interviews with James T. A. West, Dr. R. T. Bridgewater, and J. C. Latimer in Richard Halliburton, Jr., *The Tulsa Race War of 1921* (San Francisco: R & E Research Associates, 1975), app. III, 55, 61, 70. See also "Police Aided Tulsa Rioters, Armed White Ruffians Who Begged for Guns to Help Murder," *Chicago Defender,* June 11, 1921, city ed., 3.

2. Mary E. Jones Parrish, "Events of the Tulsa Disaster," Halliburton, app. II, 46.

3. In his 1982 study of the Tulsa riot, the historian Scott Ellsworth estimated that at least seventy-five people died. See Scott Ellsworth, *Death in a Promised Land: The Tulsa Race Riot of 1921* (Baton Rouge: Louisiana State University Press, 1982), 66, 70–72. A more recent study, carried out by the forensic anthropologist Clyde Snow, has produced a similar estimate. Snow confirmed the death of thirty-nine individuals (twenty-six African Americans and thirteen whites) through death certificates, funeral home records, and other documentary sources, and he listed an additional thirty-four deaths mentioned in hospital and detention camp reports, in newspapers, and in published and unpublished memoirs. Snow points out that in the confusion of the riot's aftermath numerous other victims may have gone unnoted in the historical record. See Clyde Collins Snow, "Confirmed Deaths: A Preliminary Report," in Oklahoma Commission to Study the Tulsa Race Riot of 1921, *Tulsa Race Riot: A Report by the Oklahoma Commission to Study the Tulsa Race Riot of 1921,* February 2001, 109–22, available at <http://www.okhistory.mus.ok.us/trrc/freport.html>. Halliburton and Ellsworth give similar accounts of the genesis of the fight at the Courthouse. Halliburton, however, estimates only three men killed in the initial clash. Ellsworth puts the number at twelve. Contemporary accounts gave death tolls falling between these two figures.

4. L. J. F. Rooney and Charles W. Daley to the Adjutant General, letter, June 3, 1921, Halliburton, app. IV, 72, 73; Major C. W. Daley to Lt. Col. L. J. F. Rooney, "Information on activ-

ities during Negro Uprising May 31, 1921," memorandum, July 6, 1921, Halliburton, app. IV, 85–87.

5. "Series of Fierce Combats; Angered Whites Surround Negro Quarter and Set It on Fire," *New York Times,* June 2, 1921, n.p. *Tuskegee News Clipping File* (hereafter TNCF), reel 14, frame 807; Major C.W. Daley to Lt. Col. L.J.F. Rooney, 86–87; Halliburton, 14 (Halliburton notes that pilots from the Southwestern Curtiss Company were engaged by city officials to observe looters and fires and to search for refugees.); "Ex-Police Bares Plot of Tulsans," *Chicago Defender,* October 15, 1921, city ed., 1; "Tulsa Riot Intrigue Is Uncovered, Former Policeman, In Affidavit, Tells Story of How High Officials Planned Death and Destruction Through Raid of Airplanes," *Norfolk Journal and Guide,* October 22, 1921, 1; "Tulsa Riot Intrigue Uncovered," *Indianapolis Freeman,* October 29, 1921, n.p., *Hampton Newspaper Clipping File* (hereafter cited as HNCF), item 462, no. 82; For accounts of the participation of police, Guardsmen, and deputies in the riot, see "White Man Says Police Burned Tulsa," *California Eagle,* June 24, 1921, 1, reprint from *Wichita Eagle.*

6. Elliott M. Rudwick, *Race Riot at East St. Louis, July 2, 1917* (Carbondale: Southern Illinois University Press, 1964), 50; John Hope Franklin, *From Slavery to Freedom: A History of Negro Americans* (New York: Alfred A. Knopf, 1988), 307; Franklin, 313; Franklin, 315.

7. Ellsworth, 63, 78; Halliburton, 14, 16; Richard S. Warner, "Airplanes and the Riot," in Oklahoma Commission to Study the Tulsa Race Riot of 1921, *Tulsa Race Riot: A Report by the Oklahoma Commission to Study the Tulsa Race Riot of 1921,* February 2001, 104.

8. Parrish, "Events of the Tulsa Disaster," 45; J.B.C., "Former Morgan Teacher Tells of Tulsa Riot," *Baltimore Afro-American,* June 17, 1921, nat. ed., edit. p.; "Home Guards Set Fire to Buildings While Airplanes Dropped Bombs on Homes in Negro District in Tulsa," *Negro World,* June 18, 1921, 1; John Hope Franklin and John Whittington Franklin, eds., *My Life and an Era: The Autobiography of Buck Colbert Franklin* (Baton Rouge: Louisiana State University Press, 1997), 197; A.J. Smitherman, "The Tulsa Riot and Massacre (ca. January 1922)," in A.J. Smitherman File, NAACP Papers, Library of Congress, Washington, D.C., quoted in Alfred Brophy, *Reconstructing the Dreamland: The Tulsa Race Riot of 1921, Race, Reparations, and Reconciliation* (New York: Oxford University Press, 2002), 44; see, for example, Tulsa citizen, letter, *New York Age,* July 16, 1921, 7 and "Police Aided Tulsa Rioters," 3; "Roland Not A Tulsa Native," *Washington Bee,* June 25, 1921, 2.

9. "Tulsa Refugee Tells Story of Bloody Rioting," *Chicago Defender,* June 11, 1921, city ed., 3; R.T. Bridgewater, interview, Halliburton, app. III, 61; Carrie Kinlaw, interview, Halliburton, app. III, 65–66; Roscoe Dunjee, "Editor Black Dispatch Places Riot Loss at $4,000,000—Authorities Coveting Land to Rebuild Negro Section Far Out," *Oklahoma City Black Dispatch,* June ?, 1921, n.p., HNCF, item 462, no. 5; "Home Guards Set Fire to Buildings While Airplanes Dropped Bombs on Homes in Negro District in Tulsa," 1.

10. "Police Aided Tulsa Rioters, Shield Rioters; Hunt Citizens as Criminals," *Chicago Defender,* June 11, 1921, city ed., 1; "Home Guards Set Fire to Buildings While Airplanes Dropped Bombs on Homes in Negro District in Tulsa," 1; "The Tulsa Riot," *Crusader,* July 1921, 5; untitled, *Crusader,* July 1921, 30.

11. Catherine Albanese, *Sons of the Fathers: The Civil Religion of the Founding Fathers* (Philadelphia: Temple University Press, 1976), 28–29; Woodrow Wilson, "Democracy No Longer An Experiment," speech, Washington, D.C., September 28, 1915, Woodrow Wilson, *Selected Literary and Political Papers and Addresses of Woodrow Wilson,* vol. II (New York: Grossett & Dunlap, 1927), 126; Woodrow Wilson, "Essential Terms of Peace in Europe," speech, U.S. Senate, Washington, D.C., January 22, 1917, Wilson, vol. II, 219; Woodrow Wilson, "Success Means Self-Sacrifice," speech, Conference on Americanization, Washington, D.C., July 13, 1916, Wilson, vol. II, 189.

12. Ethel Trew Dunlap, "The Tulsa Fire," *Negro World,* July 2, 1921, 5; J.C. Cunningham, letter, *Washington Bee,* June 18, 1921, 6; "A Night of Blood and Orgy," *St. Louis Argus,* June 3, 1921, n.p., TNCF, reel 14, frame 799.

13. See the release's appearance, for example, in "Current Events," *Chicago Defender,* June 4, 1921, nat. ed., 2; "Simmons of Ku Klux Heads New Order," *Norfolk Journal and Guide,* May 21, 1921, 8; "Simmons Heads Air Service," *Baltimore Afro-American,* May 13, 1921, nat. ed., n.p.

14. James Weldon Johnson, quoted in "Real Truth About the Tulsa Riot," *Norfolk Journal and Guide,* June 11, 1921, 4; The National Urban League's *Opportunity* magazine in 1924 listed the *Chicago Defender, Baltimore Afro-American, Norfolk Journal and Guide,* and *Pittsburgh Courier* as the four top-ranking black newspapers in the country, and named the *Negro World* and *New York Age* as among the top twelve. Unfortunately, issues for 1921 are not available for the *Courier,* and the remaining six papers ranked (not mentioned by name here) are no longer extant. See Eugene F. Gordon, "Outstanding Negro Newspapers," *Opportunity: A Journal of Negro Life,* December 1924, 366. Exact circulation figures are difficult to determine for these and other black newspapers because circulation records were rarely kept. By estimates, however, the *Defender* had by 1915 reached a circulation of nearly 230,000, and it maintained a postwar level at approximately 180,000 (Roland Wolseley, *The Black Press, U.S.A.,* 2d ed. [Ames: Iowa State University Press, 1989], 54). The *Courier's* circulation was near 12,000 in 1919, but the paper grew rapidly in the 1920s, and by 1935 its circulation had reached 250,000 (Andrew Buni, *Robert L. Vann of the Pittsburgh Courier: Politics and Black Journalism* [Pittsburgh, Penn.: University of Pittsburgh Press, 1974], 119, 222).

15. "Tulsa, Okla. Is Quiet After the Race War," *St. Louis Argus,* June 10, 1921, n.p., TNCF, reel 14, frames 759–760; James Weldon Johnson, "Views and Reviews; A Roman Holiday in Tulsa," *New York Age,* June 11, 1921, 4; "The 'Belgianizing of Tulsa,'" *Chicago Defender,* June 18, 1921, city ed., 3.

16. Dunjee, "Editor Dispatch Places Riot Loss at $4,000,000," n.p.; Ellsworth, 85; "Tulsa Whites Seek Now to Placate Colored Citizens," *New York Age,* August 13, 1921, 1.

17. "Along the Color Line," *Crisis: A Record of the Darker Races,* December 1911, 56; "Country Applauds Roosevelt; Riot Pictured by Eye-Witness," *New York Age,* July 12, 1917, 1.

18. An Ex-Soldier, letter, *California Eagle,* July 2, 1921, 1; Walter F. White, "The Eruption of Tulsa," *The Nation,* June 29, 1921, 909.

19. "In War and Peace," editorial cartoon, *Chicago Defender,* June 18, 1921, nat. ed., edit. p.; Lester A. Walton, letter, *New York World,* June 6, 1921, n.p., TNCF, reel 14, frame 768.

20. "Tulsa Aflame; 85 Dead in Riot, Bombs Hurled from Aeroplanes in Order to Stop Attacks on the Whites," *Chicago Defender,* June 4, 1921, nat. ed., 2.

21. Parrish, "Events of the Tulsa Disaster," 44.

22. Robert A. Hill, ed., *The Marcus Garvey and Universal Negro Improvement Association Papers,* vol. I (Los Angeles: University of California Press, 1983), 36–37.

23. Theodore Vincent, *Black Power and the Garvey Movement* (Berkeley, Calif.: Ramparts Press, 1973), 13; "Black Star Line Vindicated By White American Jury," *Negro World,* June 19, 1920, n.p., Hill, vol. II, 352.

24. "Enthusiastic Convention of 3,000 American, Canadian, West-Indian, African, So. & Central American Negroes Denounced Dr. W. E. B. Du Bois Characterized as Reactionary Under Pay of White Men—Resolution Carried Unanimously," *Negro World,* April 5, 1919, n.p., Hill, vol. I, 397; Marcus Garvey, editorial letter, *Negro World,* November 1, 1919, n.p., Hill, vol. II, 122.

25. Marcus Garvey, "Race Discrimination Must Go," editorial, *Negro World,* November 30, 1918, n.p., Hill, vol. I, 304; see, for example, "A New Radical Organization," *Baltimore Afro-*

American, December 13, 1918, n.p., Hill, vol. I, 321. For similar claims made by another UNIA official, see Elizier Cadet, letter, to H. Dorsinville, January 13, 1919, Hill, vol. I, 360; Marcus Garvey, "Message to Negro People of the World, President-General of Universal Negro Improvement Association Writes," *Negro World,* June 24, 1919, n.p., Hill, vol. I, 445; Marcus Garvey, speech, Carnegie Hall, New York, New York, August 25, 1919, Hill, vol. I, 503.

26. "Stirring Speech Delivered by Hon. Marcus Garvey in the South," *Negro World,* November 1, 1919, n.p., Hill, vol. II, 116; At least one historian has claimed that the belief blacks as a people possessed a divinely ordained mission on earth is the defining characteristic of black nationalism. See Wilson Jeremiah Moses, *The Wings of Ethiopia: Studies in African-American Life and Letters* (Ames: Iowa State University Press, 1990), 35–36; Wilson Jeremiah Moses, *Black Messiahs and Uncle Toms: Social and Literary Manipulations of a Religious Myth* (University Park: Pennsylvania State University Press, 1982), 14; Reginald Horsman, *Race and Manifest Destiny: The Origins of American Racial Anglo-Saxonism* (Cambridge, Mass.: Harvard University Press, 1981), 81–97; "Stirring Speech Delivered by Hon. Marcus Garvey in the South," 118.

27. Marcus Garvey, "All Negroes Should Get Ready to Protect Themselves in the Future, Universal Movement Getting Stronger All Over the World," *Negro World,* July 18, 1919, n.p., Hill, vol. I, 461; Marcus Garvey, letter to Black Star Line stockholders, February 27, 1920, Hill, vol. II, 225; Marcus Garvey, speech, reprinted in "Greatest Meeting in History of the Universal Negro Improvement Ass'n Held in Liberty Hall," *Negro World,* October 11, 1919, n.p., Hill, vol. II, 68–69.

28. Rupert Lewis, *Marcus Garvey, Anti-Colonial Champion* (Trenton, N.J.: Africa World Press, 1988), 68; "Thousands Pack Liberty Hall to Hear Messages of Inspiration and Hope," *Negro World,* July 17, 1920, n.p., Hill, vol. II, 416.

29. "Garvey Urges Organization, Radical New Yorker Says Time Has Come for Colored Soldiers to Fight for Themselves," *Baltimore Afro-American,* February 28, 1919, n.p., Hill, vol. I, 377.

30. "Near Approach of Great Convention Draws Record Crowd at Liberty Hall," *Negro World,* July 31, 1920, n.p., Hill, vol. II, 441; "Public Mass Meeting at 71st Armory of Third Annual International Convention of Negroes, Thronged with Notables and Friends of the U.N.I.A.," *Negro World,* August 5, 1922, 4.

31. Marcus Garvey, editorial letter, *Negro World,* September 11, 1920, n.p., Hill, vol. III, 10; Josephus Daniels, "Ships the Prime Need," Message to Shipbuilders, September 19, 1918, Josephus Daniels, *The Navy and the Nation: War Time Addresses of Josephus Daniels* (New York: George H. Doran Co., 1919), 346; Josephus Daniels, "Comrades of the Seas," speech, December 8, 1918, Daniels, 292.

32. "Enthusiastic Crowd Packs Liberty Hall at Regular Sunday Night Meeting of Universal Negro Improvement Association," *Negro World,* April 23, 1921, 3; "The Free Ship and the Slave Ship and Our Ship," *Negro World,* February 7, 1925, 4.

33. Marcus Garvey, speech, Washington, D.C., September 1920, Hill, vol. III, 28.

34. Marcus Garvey, editorial letter, *Negro World,* July 31, 1920, n.p., Hill, vol. II, 467; Marcus Garvey, editorial, *Negro World,* October 11, 1920, n.p., Hill, vol. III, 50.

35. "Liberty Hall, New York Crowded to Doors: Great Marcus Garvey on Return from Boston," *Negro World,* March 13, 1920, n.p., Hill, vol. II, 243–44.

36. "Airplanes? Yes!," *California Eagle,* July 2, 1921, 4; *Los Angeles News Age,* June 24, 1921, 1, 6 (cited in James de T. Abajian, comp., *Blacks in Selected Newspapers, Censuses and Other Sources,* vol. 1 [Boston: G. K. Hall, 1977], 2); "League to Promote Colored Aeroplane Field," *Washington Bee,* July 16, 1921, 6.

37. Charles H. D. Este, "Montreal Notes," *Negro World,* July 2, 1921, 8; "Convention Parade of the UNIA," Hill, vol. III, 568.

38. Marcus Garvey, speech, September 1921, Hill, vol. IV, 38; Marcus Garvey, "The Negro Has Travelled Across the Deserts and Prairies of Human Prejudice," *Negro World,* October 22, 1921, 1; "Prepared Statement by Marcus Garvey and Speech by Marcus Garvey on His Arrest," *Negro World,* January 21, 1922, n.p., Hill, vol. IV, 351.

39. The Bondelzwarts of South Africa's Warmbad District were a people of mixed European and Hottentot ancestry. See Franz DeWaldt, ed., *Native Uprisings in Southwest Africa* (Salisbury, N.C.: Documentary Publications, 1976), i; Marcus Garvey, "Christian Boers of South Africa Use Aeroplanes to Bomb Hottentots," *Negro World,* June 17, 1922, 1. For discussion of the Bondelzwarts' resistance movement, see Hill, vol. IV, 676–77. n. 1.

40. "Brooklyn U.N.I.A.," *Negro World,* July 2, 1921, 5; for information on the Brooklyn division's plan to buy an airplane, see Benjamin A. Osborne, "Negro Aviator Convinces Optimistic Public," letter, *Negro World,* July 7, 1923, 3; for information on McVey's position in the UNIA, see "Captain Edison McVey, Negro Aviator, Is Now at Home Convalescing," *Negro World,* October 6, 1923, 4; "Negro Aviator Convinces Optimistic Public," 3; Osborne indicated that Gaines had published several articles attacking McVey's credentials in the spring of 1922. The issues of the *Negro World* in which Gaines voiced his uncertainty, unfortunately, are no longer extant.

41. Hubert Julian, as told to John Bulloch, *Black Eagle* (London: The Adventurers Club, 1965), 25; Julian, 33; Julian obtained patent No. 1,379,264. See U.S. Patent Office, *Official Gazette* 286 (May 24, 1921), 732.

42. Julian was listed in January as a contributor from the Cleveland division in the *Negro World.* See "African Redemption Fund," *Negro World,* January 28, 1922, 8.

43. The official list of convention delegates names Julian as a representative of the Montreal division; however, the actual proceedings identify him as representing Cleveland. See "Delegates to the 1922 Convention Listed by Divisions," Hill, vol. IV, app. III, 1075; "Summarized Report, Second Week of Convention," *Negro World,* August 19, 1922, 6; "Garvey Flays His Critics—Taking Them to Task, One by One, Deals Them Severe Body Blows—Tremendous Sunday Night Audience at Liberty Hall Hears Great Leader Excoriate His Opponents," *Negro World,* August 19, 1922, 11.

44. "Liberty Hall Jammed At First Sunday Night Meeting of Third Annual International Convention of Negroes of the World—U.N.I.A. Riding on Wave of Unprecedented Popularity, Sweeping Everything Before It," *Negro World,* August 12, 1922, 2; "Negro Aviator Electrifies Convention Parade," *Negro World,* August 5, 1922, 3.

45. Junius Caesar Austin, speech, Liberty Hall, New York, New York, August 3, 1922, quoted in Randall K. Burkett, *Black Redemption: Churchmen Speak for the Garvey Movement* (Philadelphia: Temple University Press, 1978), 117.

46. "Miss Coleman, Colored Aviatrix, Visits Harlem," *Negro World,* August 26, 1922, 7.

47. "Third Mammoth International Convention Comes to a Successful Close," *Negro World,* September 9, 1922, 6; "Public Mass Meeting at 71st Regiment Armory, Of Third Annual International Convention of Negroes, Thronged with Notables and Friends of the U.N.I.A," *Negro World,* August 5, 1922, 4; William F. Sherrill, quoted in "Liberty Hall Jammed at First Sunday Night Meeting of Third Annual Convention of Negroes of the World," 3.

48. "Third Mammoth International Convention Comes to a Successful Close," *Negro World,* September 9, 1922, 7; "Negress Pilots Airplane," *New York Times,* September 4, 1922, 9; "Only Colored Aviatrix Gives Exhibition at Curtis[s] Field," *Norfolk Journal and Guide,* September 9, 1922, 1; untitled clipping, *Schomburg Center Clipping File* (hereafter SCCF), fiche 386–1.

49. See, for example, "Italian Aviators Bomb African Arab Village," *Negro World,* November 8, 1924, 3; "Britain's Labor Government Halts British 'Civilized' Methods of Tax-

Collecting in Mesopotamia," *Negro World,* February 9, 1924, 2; "Why Abd-El-Krim Is Fighting France, French Airplanes Kill Fifty Women and Children to One Riffian; Reprisals to Come," *Negro World,* June 13, 1925, 2; "French Airmen Bomb Civilians in Damascus," *Negro World,* October 31, 1925, 2; "Why Abd-El-Krim Is Fighting France," 2; "American Hessians Will Leave Morocco," *Negro World,* October 24, 1925, 4; "Conscience Is Dead Where Africa Is Concerned," *Negro World,* October 31, 1925, 10; "Abd-El-Krim Tells Own Story of the Methods of the Enemy," *Negro World,* November 7, 1925, 5.

50. Marcus Garvey, speech, Liberty Hall, New York, New York, September 17, 1922, Hill, vol. V, 22; Marcus Garvey, "Christian Boers of South Africa Use Airplanes to Bomb Hottentots," *Negro World,* June 17, 1922, 1.

51. "Yellow and White Races Prepare for Future Armageddon—Mr. Blackman, What About You?" *Negro World,* July 4, 1925, 7; "Where Is Your Airplane, Mr. Blackman?" *Negro World,* April 25, 1925, 7; "When Black Men Conquer Distance by Ships and Aeroplanes, What Then?" *Negro World,* June 27, 1925, 7.

52. Marcus Garvey, speech, Washington, D.C., January 15, 1924, Hill, vol. V, 528–29; Marcus Garvey, speech, Liberty Hall, New York, New York, Hill, vol. V, 519.

53. "Says a Black King Will Rule World," *New York Times,* September 15, 1924: n.p., Hill, vol. VI, 13.

54. "He Jumped a Mile," *Baltimore Afro-American,* November 24, 1922, 1; Clarence Chamberlin, *Record Flights* (Philadelphia: Dorrance and Company, Inc., 1928), 233.

55. See, for example, "Julian Jumps From Plane 3,000 Feet Up," *New York Amsterdam News,* May 2, 1923, 1; "Aviator Thrills Harlem by Descent to Roof Top," *New York Age,* May 5, 1923, 1; "Crowd Sees Lieut. Julian in Daring Parachute Jump," *Chicago Defender,* May 5, 1923, nat. ed., 5; "Sentenced to Six Months' Probation for 'Chute Jump,'" *St. Paul Appeal,* May 12, 1923, 1; "Aviator on Probation," *Baltimore Afro-American,* May 11, 1923, nat. ed., 1. Although black newspapers claimed McVey was at the controls during Julian's jump over Harlem, Chamberlin describes taking Julian up for the leap in his autobiography. See Chamberlin, 239; "Crowd Sees Lieut. Julian in Daring Parachute Jump," 5; "Aviator Thrills Harlem by Descent to Roof of House," 1.

56. "Harlem Sees Daredevil Drop From the Sky," *New York Times,* April 30, 1923, 3; "All New York Thrilled When Negro Aviator Descends in Parachute," *Negro World,* May 12, 1923, 2.

57. Chamberlin, 244.

58. "Julian 'Runs Wild' 3500 Feet in Air," *New York Amsterdam News,* June 13, 1923, sect. 2, 7.

59. "The Independence Day Jubilee and Aviation Carnival," *Negro World,* June 16, 1923, 3; "Flyers at Seashore," *Baltimore Afro-American,* July 20, 1923, 10; James A. Jackson, "Here and There Among the Folks," *Billboard: A Weekly Digest and Review of the Show World,* August 11, 1923, 53; "Daredevil," *Pittsburgh Courier,* June 9, 1923, 14.

60. "Extra! Capt. McVey Hurt in Crash," *New York Amsterdam News,* August 1, 1923, 1; "Aviator and Passenger Hurt When Plane Falls," *Chicago Defender,* August 4, 1923, nat. ed., pt. 2, 1; Doris L. Rich, *Queen Bess, Daredevil Aviator* (Washington, D.C.: Smithsonian Institution Press, 1993), 50; Lottie V. M. Wagoner, letter, *Negro World,* February 7, 1925, 9. Wagoner reported having attended a talk on aviation by McVey at a school assembly in Hillsboro, Texas.

61. "Aviator in Court on Assault Charge," *St. Paul Appeal,* August 25, 1923, 1; "Dare-Devil Drops Out of Court," *New York Amsterdam News,* August 29, 1923, 5; "In Again—Out Again!" *Pittsburgh Courier,* September 29, 1923, 3; "Lieut. Julian an Imposter, Says Wife,"

Chicago Defender, October 13, 1923, nat. ed., 1; "Daredevil Painted as Love-Thief," *Pittsburgh Courier,* October 13, 1923, 1.

62.   *Calendar,* McGill University (Montreal: Gazette Printing Company Ltd., 1913–1923). The Calendar does not list Julian as registered in any field of study between 1914 and 1922; S. F. Wise, *Canadian Airmen and the First World War: The Official History of the Royal Canadian Air Force,* vol. 1 (Toronto: University of Toronto Press, 1980), 31, 576; S. F. Wise to J. D. Snider, personal letter, March 8, 1994; O. A. Cooke, Chief Historical Archivist, National Defence Headquarters, Ottawa, Canada, to J. D. Snider, personal letter, April 8, 1994; Julian, 33; Julian's assertion in his autobiography that he learned to fly from Canadian war ace William Bishop is also unlikely. Bishop was not a flight instructor in Montreal after the war as Julian claimed, but traveled instead on the lecture circuit and then moved to Toronto in early 1919. See William Arthur Bishop, *The Courage of the Early Morning: A Son's Biography of a Famous Father* (Toronto: McClelland and Stewart Ltd., 1965), 166–67.

63.   "Report by Special Agent James E. Amos," Hill, vol. V, 182–87; David E. Cronon, *Black Moses: The Story of Marcus Garvey* (Madison: University of Wisconsin Press, 1968), 103–37.

64.   "Explains 'Round World Flight,'" *Baltimore Afro-American,* April 18, 1924, extra ed., 1; "Julian Brings $8,000 Airplane to Harlem," *Pittsburgh Courier,* June 21, 1924, 13; "The Horizon," *Crisis,* May 1924, 24; Chamberlin, 241; Alvin M. Josephy, Jr., ed., *The American Heritage History of Flight* (Washington, D.C.: American Heritage Publishing, 1962), 221; "Julian Disappoints Wonderland Crowd," *Baltimore Afro-American,* May 2, 1924, city ed., 8; "Lt. Julian Is Called A Fake," *Baltimore Afro-American,* May 16, 1924, city ed., 5; "Julian Brings $8,000 Airplane to Harlem," 13; "Julian Says He Will Prove He Can Fly," *Baltimore Afro-American,* May 23, 1924, city ed., 1.

65.   "Mr. Julian's Proposed Airplane Flight Around the World Was Never Endorsed by the Universal Negro Improvement Association," *Negro World,* May 24, 1924, 2; Norton Thomas, "The Spotlight," *Negro World,* May 24, 1924, 2.

66.   Untitled clipping, July ?, 1924, SCCF, fiche 386–1; Julian, 52; W. J. Wheaton, "Comments," *California Eagle,* July 25, 1924, 1; Norton Thomas, "The Spotlight," *Negro World,* July 5, 1924, 2.

67.   "Lieut. Julian's Plane Falls Into Bay and Pilot Goes to Hospital," *Chicago Defender,* July 12, 1924, nat. ed., 1; Chamberlin, 242.

68.   John Peer Nugent, *The Black Eagle* (New York: Stein and Day, 1971), 42, 45; Chamberlin, 241; Floyd Calvin, "Aviator Hurt When Plane Falls," *Pittsburgh Courier,* July 12, 1924, 1; "Julian's Round World Flight Ends Suddenly," *Baltimore Afro-American,* July 11, 1924, city ed., 1.

69.   "The Ill-Fated Airplane," *Chicago Defender,* July 12, 1924, nat. ed., 1.

70.   William Pickens, "Pickens Talks on Farce of Aviation and World Tours," *Baltimore Afro-American,* August 1, 1924, city ed., n.p.

71.   William Pickens, quoted in Vincent, 73.

72.   Wolseley, 54.

73.   John Bracey, August Meier, and Elliott Rudwick, eds., *Black Nationalism in America* (Indianapolis: Bobbs-Merrill, 1970), 4.

74.   Ralph Ellison, quoted in Ellsworth, 107.

75.   William Pickens, letter, *New York Age,* September 15, 1923, 4.

76.   "[The] Cream of Chicago Manicurists, Young Ladies Who Have Put [the City's Tonsorial Parlors] on a Plane with the [Best in the World], Part 1 of 2," *Chicago Defender,* March 3, 1917, city ed., 2; "Miss Bessie Coleman among the First to Clamp on 'Flu' Lid," *Chicago Defender,* November 2, 1918, city ed., 12.

77. "Aviatrix Must Sign Away Life to Learn Trade," *Chicago Defender,* October 8, 1921, nat. ed., 2.

78. Robert Paul Sachs, letter, *California Eagle,* March 4, 1923, 1.

79. Roscoe Simmons, "The Week," *Chicago Defender,* September 26, 1925, nat. ed., 1; W.J. Wheaton, "Comments," *California Eagle,* September 4, 1925, 1; W.J. Wheaton, "Comments," *California Eagle,* March 27, 1925, 1; E.L. Dorsey, "Negro Aviator Makes Good," *California Eagle,* August 28, 1925, 1.

80. "Flying Circus Unusual Event to Be Repeated," *Houston Informer,* June 27, 1925, 1; "Bessie Coleman Makes Supreme Sacrifice for Promotion of Science of Aviation," *California Eagle,* May 14, 1926, 6; Leslie Rogers, "Bessie Coleman—First Race Aviatrix," editorial cartoon, *Chicago Defender,* October 8, 1921, nat. ed., edit. p.; untitled, editorial, *New York Age,* January 18, 1912, 4.

81. "Race Man, Chief Railway Clerk, Will Fly to N.Y.," *Pittsburgh Courier,* August 18, 1923, 12; "Made Airplane Trip to Business League Meeting," *Denver Statesman,* September 10, 1921, 1.

82. "Paying Tribute to Heroes of 8th Regiment," *Chicago Defender,* June 10, 1922, nat. ed., 2; "Giles Avenue Dedicated with Solemn Tribute," *Chicago Defender,* June 10, 1922, nat. ed., 3.

83. "Let Us Fly," editorial, *Chicago Defender,* May 20, 1922, nat. ed., edit. p.

84. "Ku Klux 'Bomb' City From Air, Klan Drops Warning Over Town," *Chicago Defender,* August 5, 1922, nat. ed., 1.

85. "Airplane Chases Alabama Cotton Pickers, Man Killed by Airplane in Cotton Field," *Chicago Defender,* October 30, 1926, nat. ed., 1.

86. "Views and Reviews; A Roman Holiday in Tulsa," 4; "Airplane Chases Alabama Cotton Pickers," 1.

87. William N. Jones, "Day by Day, Air Service and Negroes," *Baltimore Afro-American,* January 3, 1925, 2nd ed., 16; William N. Jones, "Day by Day, Airplanes and the Ford Program," *Baltimore Afro-American,* March 7, 1925, city ed., 3.

88. "The Monument to Bessie Coleman," *New York News,* July 30, 1927, n.p., SCCF, fiche 386–1.

89. E.L. Dorsey, "Negro Aviator Makes Good," *California Eagle,* August 28, 1925, 1.

"Who Says It's a Man's World?"

Women's Work and Travel in the First Decades of Flight

Suzanne L. Kolm

W ho says 'It's a Man's World?'" asked an advertisement in 1954: "Not the woman who flies TWA." Appearing in *Time, Look,* and the *Saturday Evening Post,* the full-page spread depicted a sharp-looking stewardess bidding goodbye to two women as they stepped out the door of an aircraft. The advertisement included a map at the bottom of the page showing the destinations across the globe that the airline served, destinations that women might visit now that commercial flight allowed them "new freedom and greater opportunity."[1] This advertisement was one of many attempts to bring women aloft by major airlines in the United States during the first thirty years of air travel, and it was one of many representations of flight in these years that treated the cabin members as dignified and competent. Only later, in the jet age, especially the late 1960s and early 1970s, did some airlines forget that women were a significant portion of their market, and only later, in these years, did some airlines exploit their female flight attendants' sexuality to help sell seats. This later period, brief as it was, has left among many people the mistaken impression that only in the last couple of decades, since deregulation in 1978, have airlines treated female passengers and employees with respect. This is not to say that the first three decades of air travel were a "golden age" of equality. Discriminatory hiring practices meant that only a fraction of American women could apply for airline work, and those who were hired suffered far more than did their counterparts later from restrictive employment policies. Exclusive, too, was access to tickets; the passengers that airlines carried were generally of some means. But those women who did get hired in the first three decades of air travel, and those who could afford a ticket, found that the airline industry brought benefits that had special value and meaning to them. To these women, commercial aviation was not a man's world.

Working women had a place in aviation thanks to the vision and courage of the first generation of stewardesses. The occupation was invented by a graduate nurse named Ellen Church who had been intrigued by aviation ever since she saw the famous barnstormer Ruth Law perform at a county fair. In 1930, Church visited the San Francisco airport hoping to find a job piloting one of

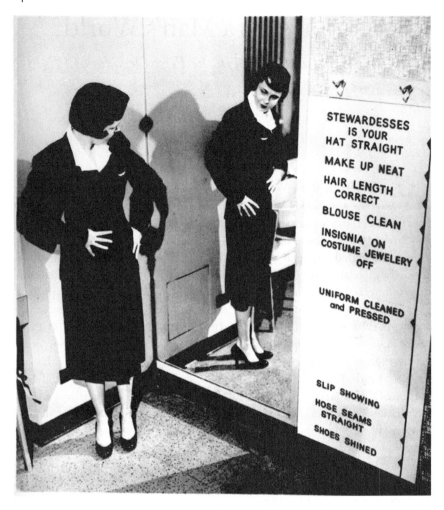

By the era of airline deregulation, beginning in 1978, stewardesses had succeeded in redefining themselves as safety professionals and their formal title was now "flight attendants." The reference to safety laid claim to being skilled workers, worthy of respect, and the emphasis on professionalism made clear that their friendliness was paid and impersonal. This 1951 United Air Lines attendant had many preflight responsibilities, including a grooming check. (Courtesy National Air and Space Museum, Smithsonian Institution [SI 88-18946].)

Boeing Air Transport's small aircraft that carried mail and a few passengers between Chicago and western cities. When the traffic manager at the airport, Steve Stimpson, refused to consider Church as a pilot, she suggested that her nursing training could be useful in the cabin. Stimpson was aware that a couple of other airlines employed young white men as "stewards" or "couriers," but the idea of hiring women such as Ellen Church seemed even better. The airline agreed that nurses were ideal for the job, not because their medical training might be needed in an emergency, but because, as a vice president said, "hospital routine instills discipline and a keen sense of responsibility." In addition, he noted that a background in nursing taught women how to "handle people of all kinds with tact" and "courteous firmness."[2] The gender of the nurses also was valued by airlines because they hoped the presence of women would tame the image of flight. A stewardess explained that women's "home-making instincts" brought aloft "familiar aspects to which travelers may cling."[3] The feminine presence helped highlight the masculine competence of the cockpit crew, just as the white skin of the cabin crew helped distinguish air travel from the rival Pullman service that employed black men. One popular account noted the difference by pointing out that stewardesses did not accept tips: "Airline heads decided at the very beginning to let George, the Pullman porter, collect the quarters and half dollars."[4] The decision to put white women in the cabins also may have been influenced by the example of the Fred Harvey Corporation, which ran a chain of restaurants at railroad depots on the Santa Fe line. Since the 1880s, this chain had hired only white women as waitresses, calling them Harvey Girls.[5] Boeing Air Transport's choice for cabin attendants was adopted by most of the other airlines in the United States during the formative years of air travel. American Airways hired stewardesses in 1933, and Transcontinental and Western Air (TWA) conformed to the industry's emerging pattern in 1935.

Stewardesses exercised their "home-making instincts" by greeting passengers and conversing with them, serving coffee and meals, as well as helping with tickets and arranging for hotels or railroad tickets if a flight was canceled or grounded by a storm. For the work, stewardesses earned about $100 to $125 a month, and they also received paid vacations, free passes for air travel, and moderate funds for expenses. The wages were comparable to other service jobs in this era; stewardesses received about as much as teachers, librarians, and hospital nurses, and slightly more than clerical workers and department store saleswomen.[6] Jobs such as these were becoming increasingly common in the 1930s as the national economy shifted away from heavy industry and manufacturing. Many observers recognized, as Ellen Church must have, that this shift could provide new jobs for women. The *Independent Woman,* created by the National Federation of Business and Professional Women's Clubs, recognized that airline cabin service was one of the new areas in which a woman could "commercialize" her "hostess sense."[7] Although describing airline work as homemaking or hostessing reinforced sometimes restrictive gender distinctions, this rhetorical strategy was common during the Great Depression. Working women faced competition from men for new jobs, and they also faced hostility from those who feared women were taking jobs from men. In response, many women workers, and their advocates, reserved and protected some of the new service and retail positions by claiming the jobs required special feminine qualities or experiences.[8] In this way, references to stewardesses' "home-making instincts" and "hostess sense" helped win cabin service for women workers. With a sense of victory and relief, the *Independent Woman* announced "aviation has a future" for women.[9]

The work that stewardesses performed was difficult and sometimes dangerous, especially in the early 1930s when aircraft designs were only slowly becoming sufficiently aerodynamic to lift metal off the ground. One of the original eight stewardesses on Boeing Air Transport, Harriet Fry Iden, recounted why a flight she was on "set down" unexpectedly in Nebraska: some of the "planes were all canvas on the outside, and the wings were wrapped in linen and they were glued down by something called 'dope.' Every so often, this would start coming loose."[10] Jessie Carter Bronson had similar experiences flying the route between Oakland and Chicago. The trip was "supposed to take eighteen hours," she reported, but it usually took "more like twenty-four hours. If the weather got bad, we would land in a field for a while, and wait for the storm to clear up." Once a stabilizer on the plane broke and the pilots made an emergency landing on the shores of Salt Lake, and another time the aircraft ran out of gas short of Cheyenne.[11] Even the flights that stayed in the air presented challenges to the cabin crew. The unpressurized aircraft flew low through, rather than above, all sorts of weather. Stewardesses passed out chewing gum to relieve the pain of pressure changes, and supplied cotton for passengers' ears to block out the droning engines and rattling fuselage. The cabins often were cold and drafty and smelled of oil and exhaust. Airsickness cups were always within reach. The twelve-passenger all-metal Boeing Trimotor, often used in the early years, had wire cross bracings that sometimes shrieked in the wind, or popped loose, causing hysterics in the cabin. Stewardesses held hands, reclined seats, and sometimes administered sedatives, often drawing on the skills they learned in nursing to help calm people and explain unfamiliar sensations and surroundings. The very first stewardesses drew on another part of their backgrounds in nursing as well—they moved on when conditions proved unsatisfactory, displaying the same selectivity, the same discriminating mobility, that moved many service workers from restaurant to restaurant, hospital to hospital, or bedside to bedside. Bronson quit after three months because she was fatigued and her ears hurt. The same problems sent Iden seeking a better position after eighteen months, and Church after twenty. The women who took their places, and many more who filled the new openings as air travel grew in the 1930s, were well aware the work was dangerous. One vocational writer frankly warned women about "harrowing experiences or accidents that incapacitate flyers from earning a living."[12] Every so often, a stewardess was incapacitated or worse; crashes on United Air Lines alone between 1930 and 1942 killed eleven stewardesses.

Stewardesses in the 1930s did not have to rely only on their nursing backgrounds to handle the many challenges of air travel because the airline companies provided training, although it was extremely informal for the first few years. When United Airways hired Mary O'Connor in 1933, for example, the company sent her to Kansas City for two weeks to be trained. Her actual instruction for the job, however, lasted only an hour because it was left to a couple of copilots who grumbled that they would rather be playing golf than showing her the paperwork and the methods for serving coffee. Soon, however, companies replaced what O'Connor called the "old independent procedure, the learn-as-you-go method," with formal training programs that prepared women to work on the more sophisticated and comfortable aircraft that companies put into service as the decade progressed.[13] A former stewardess who had been promoted to instructor often taught the programs, which usually lasted several weeks. At mid-decade, she might have trained women to work on the Trimotors, or on the ten-passenger Boeing 247 that flew coast to coast with only seven stops. When American Airlines instituted its six-week training sessions at a hotel in Chicago in 1936, the stewardesses would have trained to serve on the new aerodynamic, twenty-one-passenger DC-3 with its comfortable cabins, its galleys for food preparation, and on the sleeper version, its berths. When United Airlines opened its training program at the Chicago Airport in 1939, the DC-3 had become the industry workhorse, carrying 75 percent of air travelers. United's classroom contained a mockup of the DC-3 interior, allowing recruits to practice serving food and making up berths. Stewardesses also received instructions on paperwork and procedures, and were briefed on aerodynamics, flight controls, radio communications, and meteorology to prepare for questions from passengers. Also during training, stewardesses were fitted for their uniforms. Most uniforms for both cockpit and cabin crews included tailored jackets, sometimes with stripes on the sleeves or brass buttons, because the look of airline clothing derived from the same source that lent to aviation the titles "steward" and "stewardess": the maritime tradition.

When airline managers praised nurses for their training in handling the public for their "courteous firmness," they may have been referring in part to their ability to handle gender relations aloft, which were similar in many ways to a hospital. Like nurses, stewardesses worked closely with their male superiors, requiring them to maintain amiable relations at the same time they showed deference. Like doctors, the pilots sometimes maintained the hierarchy with hazing, teasing, and touching, which served, in the words of a reporter, "to keep the air hostesses in their place."[14] And, as in a hospital, women workers were in a position superior to the consumers of the service. Just as nurses were in charge on a hospital floor, stewardesses controlled the aircraft cabin. They had the authority to remove passengers for drunkenness, for disorderliness, or for refusing to obey commands, and they initiated, controlled, and terminated contact. Just as nurses knew more than most patients about medical conditions and procedures, stewardesses had superior knowledge about aviation technology. These gender reversals could make men uncomfortable, and one element of the popular images of nurses in this era expressed this discomfort—it transformed male patients' desires for enhanced control into fantasies of nurses' sexual availability. One stewardess overheard a passenger whisper to another: "I wonder why the airlines select registered nurses for its stewardesses. I never regarded a nurse very high morally."[15] But if this stereotype followed the nurses aloft, so did the professionalism that protected them. "Profession" has meant an occupation that selects, monitors, and evaluates it own members, and it also has been used to distinguish activities performed for money rather than love. Many women have used the second meaning of the word to describe the measure of impersonality they have used to maintain distance, to remain aloof, to communicate they were not personally interested in the men they met in the course of making a living. The journalist Ellen Tarry, for example, decided in this era that to fend off unwanted amorous attention she needed to become "strictly professional."[16] Being strictly professional was a strategy that served stewardesses well. Harriet Fry Iden explained: "Men tried to get fresh. That was an occupational hazard. We could handle that."[17] And they could. Dressed in their sharp-looking uniforms, confident in conditions that terrified passengers, familiar and comfortable with complicated machinery, stewardesses exuded what one reporter called a "cool, professional air."[18] If necessary, the women backed up their authority with force. Iden slapped a professor when he chased her around the cabin, and Mary O'Connor struck a passenger who grabbed her. Neither received a reprimand; Iden's supervisor told her the man must have had it coming. This professional protection, supported by the airline companies, was one of the rewards of the job that had special value to women. It allowed them to perform their duties, earn their living, and travel around the country with minimal harassment.

In addition to the presence of stewardesses aloft, aviation in the early years was not only a man's world because of the strategy airlines chose to help sell seats. In the first years of the decade, most companies organized large sales departments with representatives in cities across the nation. They used national and local advertising in newspapers and magazines, initially aimed at the industry's best potential market: businessmen. Soon, however, salespeople had heard so many men claim that their wives vetoed flying that one aviation promoter announced that "Airline Enemy No. 1" was a woman. To win over number one, companies represented flight in terms they thought would sell to women. Marketing departments were advised by a trade journal to show a woman, first, that air travel was safe, and, second, that it meant "her loved ones will be home sooner, that fewer days will be consumed in travel and that family reunions can be enjoyed without loss of working days."[19] By mid-decade, a couple of companies created special advertising campaigns directed to women, and, by the middle of the decade, a couple of the companies had separate woman's bureaus or traffic departments that encouraged women to allow their male relatives to fly and also to travel on the airways themselves. Drawing on a network of women's organizations, companies sent representatives, sometimes stewardesses, to clubs or to charity events to promote flying. Airlines made use of women's professional ties as well. United Air Lines sent the director of its Women's Traffic Division to a luncheon of women in advertising. She coached the listeners to tell women "how comfortable they'd be, how delicious their meals are, how capable the stewardesses are, how luxurious their surroundings will be."[20] Another company offered free tickets or half-priced fares for wives to join their husbands on board. Such efforts paid off. Women accounted for only 10 percent of air travelers in 1930 but, by 1936, according to one report, women comprised 34 percent of travelers by air.[21]

Women's place in aviation was secured during and after World War II because, amid growth in the industry, airlines needed stewardesses more than ever. In 1940, the industry transported three million people a year, and this figure more than doubled to seven million in 1945, and then doubled again to nineteen million in 1950. While in the past, as one trade writer pointed out, "keeping customers happy was a problem far secondary to getting customers," now the priorities had changed.[22] Keeping passengers happy became increasingly important after 1940, when the government began regulating fares and, in response, companies began competing for market share on the basis of their schedules, connections, reputations, and especially their service. "The personal attention factor," pointed out a pair of trade writers in the late 1940s, had become "an important competitive part of the airline product."[23] To deliver this product to the growing number of passengers, airlines hired more women. Domestic scheduled airlines employed about one thousand cabin attendants in 1940, who were mostly stewardesses, but a few were pursers and stewards. This figure was just over two thousand in 1945 and nearly six thousand ten years later in 1955. These women were not nurses; the wartime shortage of medical personnel forced companies to permanently drop the nursing requirement. Companies could no longer rely on hospital training to instill discipline, just as delivering personal attention was growing ever more difficult. A passenger described the problem at the close of the war, pointing out that in the earliest aircraft, a stewardess "soon became acquainted with everybody," but on the DC-3s in the middle of the 1930s, "the personal attention became a little more difficult to dispense." And, by 1946, with loads up to forty-four passengers on the DC-4s, the stewardess's "attempts to anticipate and meet each individual need for comfort and convenience are further diluted—even with another stewardess to help her."[24] The problem only grew worse in the 1940s and 1950s on the large aircraft such as the Convair 220, the DC-6, and the DC-7, which could hold forty, sixty, and one hundred passengers, respectively. The increasing numbers of passengers compounded the problem; air travel had become a mass market.

To help keep customers happy in the emerging mass market, airlines relied on their training programs to teach, in the words of one trainee, about "pleasing our passengers and making them feel at home."[25] Women learned how to make conversation, how to seat a variety of passengers from the blind to the belligerent, how to prepare and serve meals, and how to keep their faces pleasant and carefree, even in turbulence. The emphasis on the comportment and grooming women needed to be a gracious hostess made airline training similar to a charm school, and at least one modeling agency branched into training airline recruits.[26] Companies used training to introduce their extensive appearance codes, which helped create visual uniformity in their stewardess corps. Some elements of the codes were not new; a consultant to the industry explained in the 1930s that "first because of weight and second because of standardization, all cabin attendants are required to be within certain weight limits."[27] But in the 1940s and 1950s, the standardization became more extreme. A few airlines narrowed their hiring qualifications even further—for a period National Airlines hired only blondes and Delta Airlines only petite women. And all of the companies regulated not only uniforms, hosiery, and shoes but also nail polish, perfume, jewelry, and hair length. As in a modeling class or charm school, airline training also spent considerable time in training on makeup, weight, and fashionable clothes and styles. One woman who was trained during this era explained why the blonde who sat next to her in class one day disappeared: "TWA found out she bleached her hair."[28] Strict control over matters such as hair helped airlines establish discipline among the stewardesses in the same way that institutions of all sorts, from the military to sororities, have used clothing and grooming to influence behavior. In such settings, institutional authority over intimate bodily regions has helped to sever former habits and preferences and make way for new behavioral ideals. Airlines shared this management technique with hospitals and restaurants. The Harvey operation, for example, also established its corporate image with employees who showed "little or no personal variation from person to person or place to place."[29] But this management technique was more important to airline corporations than to most other service operations. Like many service workers, stewardesses had the most contact with the customers, yet they were unique in that they performed their duties far away from supervision. They worked thousands of feet in the sky, monitored only by occasional "check riders" who observed the women at work. The "isolation from control" of stewardesses, as one trade writer called this distance, made the abundant appearance codes of the airlines especially rigid and their investments in training especially worthwhile.[30] American Airlines, for example, built a new million-dollar "Stewardess College" near Dallas in 1957. The big flagstone school building housed classrooms, a dining hall, and about 120 women, and it was located on twenty-two wooded acres that included tennis courts and a swimming pool. Although the company did not pay women for the five and a half weeks they spent in training, it absorbed the costs, which it estimated to be about $500 from a recruit's first interview to her first flight. The curriculum covered topics in aviation, from meteorology to first aid, and topics in grooming, from cosmetics to posture and weight. But the most important lessons, in the words of a reporter, taught "the psychology of serving passengers."[31] Like other airlines' training programs, the session concluded with a graduation ceremony in which the women received diplomas.

Some of the appearance regulations and comportment requirements that companies enforced in the late 1950s and early 1960s became ruses for racial discrimination. Northwest Airlines, whose president confessed he felt "the time is not yet ripe to integrate Negroes into stewardess positions," eliminated a black applicant named Marlene White with a hiring checklist that covered many areas from conversational abilities, to femininity, to refinement, to taste in clothing. The checklist stated that White's clothes were rumpled and, little wonder, she was "lacking" in humor and "somewhat" impatient.[32] Capital Airlines, which was the nation's fifth largest carrier in the late 1950s, disqualified Patricia Banks because its hiring routine found a "defect" in an upper right molar.[33] Pressure for change came first from the Urban League in the 1950s, and soon the pressure became formal complaints. The New York State Commission Against Discrimination, for example, had before it seventeen cases concerning airlines' hiring practices by the end of the 1950s. As it did in many other cases of racial and gender discrimination, the Cold War added urgency to these complaints because the United States government was anxious to prove itself egalitarian to the emerging Third World nations it wished to bring into the "free world." In 1957, the State Department had been embarrassed to admit to a group of Asian and African visitors that the Soviet newspaper *Pravda* had not lied "when it declared that bigotry barred Negro girls from one of the most coveted careers open to women in this country."[34] Shortly after this incident, New York successfully persuaded Mohawk Airlines to hire Ruth Taylor, the industry's first African-American flight attendant. New York also forced Capital Airlines to hire Patricia Banks. Following the lead was TWA, which, after Michigan investigated its hiring practices, brought aboard Margaret Grant, and, soon after, Mary Tiller.

As *Pravda* mentioned, this career was indeed coveted among many American women; in 1951, for example, American Airlines received 20,000 applications to fill 347 openings.[35] Ligea McCracken Painter, who worked for Continental Airlines during World War II, explained one reason why the job was so attractive, recalling that the life she led as a stewardess was "respected and glamorous."[36] Air travel was one situation in which the skills, efforts, and practice women devoted to making people comfortable earned respect. In some situations, this work has been dismissed or invisible; nursing, for example, has sometimes appeared as if it came naturally to women, requiring "little education and few special skills."[37] In contrast, airline managers often recognized the skills and work stewardesses exercised aloft. A supervisor who evaluated Carla Knurr in 1951, for example, urged her to "try to develop more warmth in your contacts" with passengers, adding that the task wasn't easy: "if you work on it, it will come with experience."[38] Airline companies and popular sources often gave the titles that referred to prestigious jobs usually held by men, such as "intimate ambassador" or "diplomat in skirts."[39] Far from suggesting the qualities they sought were common to all women, airline companies publicized the enormous number of applications they reviewed to find suitable candidates. Airlines also recognized and rewarded the work stewardesses devoted to perfecting and maintaining their appearances. Sometimes discounted as vain or trivial, this work was very important to many American women as courtship and other social relations became more urban and anonymous in the twentieth century, requiring that women learn and monitor the messages sent through grooming and clothing. The first impression women made at a dance hall or social club told potential suitors a lot about their backgrounds, their class, and their ethnicity. But, although many women performed this work, few employers other than airlines paid for it, considered it worthy of extensive training, even attendance at a "college," and rewarded it with a diploma. The women who worked on airlines in the first three decades of air travel valued the acknowledgment. Juanita Musty, who began a long flying career on Western Airlines in 1953, said that she liked most "being a 'stewardess' in an adventurous age of aviation and being respected by other employees and management."[40] Kay Park Haney, of United Airlines, said she "enjoyed the high regard that was accorded stewardesses."[41]

Working as an airline stewardess did have negative aspects, but these were outweighed by the positive. During and after World War II, when most industries were lifting restrictions on married women, many airlines were maintaining or newly imposing these prohibitions, as well as creating policies that required women to retire when they reached the age of thirty-two or thirty-five. Initially in this era, the pay was another negative feature of the job because it did not keep pace with other kinds of service work. In 1946, the base pay at United Airlines, for example, was $125 a month and had not changed since the early 1930s, in part because of wartime wage and price controls. Yet, even with these controls in place, most wages and prices did rise during the war, and a stewardess named Ada Brown noticed that her employer was not keeping up. Brown joined United Airlines in 1940 and over a period of three years she rose to chief stewardess. In 1944, she returned to the ranks to form a union. She was aided by the flurry of women's unionizing activity at the close of the war, by the pilots' union, and by the sense of community, the "sorority of the skies," that was especially strong because stewardesses frequently saved on expenses by sharing living quarters.[42] United Airlines recognized the Air Line Stewardesses Association in 1945, and in the following years the union joined with the Air Line Pilots Association and organized stewardesses on other airlines. By 1950, these efforts had raised the average salary to $170 a month to start, reaching $350 a month depending on seniority, hours, and the types of aircraft flown.[43] The paycheck was similar to that earned by an office worker, but as a benefit, the work did not impose an office routine. The bidding system that determined a stewardess's schedule gave women with the most seniority first choice of schedules, which rarely made for a nine-to-five workday and often allowed considerable flexibility. Also distinguishing the job from office work was the chance to travel. The expansion of airline's routes during and after World War II meant that the women's choices in destinations extended far beyond Boeing's Air Transport's old Oakland-to-Cheyenne run, for example, and included points all over the continent, sometimes all over the globe. Even a woman who worked for an airline with relatively limited service could take advantage of passes and discounts on other airlines for travel in the United States and abroad. According to one stewardess, women especially valued this benefit. She pointed out that flying offered "one of the few opportunities a girl has for adventure, such as a boy taking a tramp steamer to Europe, or hitchhiking around the world." This opportunity was the main reason she took the job, she said: "the airlines give a girl a chance to get around."[44]

This was a chance that airlines offered women passengers as well, and they devoted a portion of their advertising in the postwar years to bringing women aloft. The ratio of women passengers declined during World War II when airlines, under orders from the State Department, gave priority for boarding to those people flying for the purpose of national defense. But, after the war, companies redoubled their efforts to sell to women, especially the growing ranks of working women. As an aviation trade journal noted, this market was growing: in 1940 only 13.8 million women were working, and in 1956 this figure had grown to 21.2 million.[45] TWA's efforts included the "Who Says It's a Man's World" advertisement as well as a magazine advertising campaign featuring a fictional character named Mary Gordon. Mary Gordon offered tips on traveling and assured women they did not need the company of men to enjoy traveling. An advertisement in *Ladies Home Journal,* for example, promoted the airline's group tours by asking: "Wondering if you'll find excitement and adventure traveling alone?" The copy continued: "Of course you will if you always go the friendly, fun-packed TWA way."[46] The campaign offered free brochures, such as "How to Stretch Your Travel Dollar," which emphasized that even women on limited budgets could afford international vacations. The advertisements also invited groups and businesses to request personal appearances by Mary Gordon, resulting in so many invitations that the company employed five women to pose as the helpful travel planner. The five women fanned out across the nation, visiting clubs and meetings, offices and factories, speaking on radio and television, urging women to travel by air. Like TWA, many airlines attempted to convince single working women to fly by suggesting that traveling by air was fun, economical, and safe. American Airlines assured women they could "Travel Alone and Love It," with an illustration of a young woman taking a moment from writing postcards to gaze out the aircraft window. Her ability to relax in the cabin, forget her surroundings, and enjoy the view suggested that no longer did travel involve awkward or threatening situations. No longer, the text stated, did a woman have to share a table with strangers in the dining car of a train, or negotiate the etiquette of requesting services and giving tips. "Delicious, delightfully served meals *come to you,*" the advertisement emphasized, "friendly stewardesses *cater to you.*"[47] This astute advertisement made clear that aspects of flight that might have been inconvenient or annoying to some men—the confined spaces, for example, or the lack of personal mobility—could protect a woman traveling alone from the encroachment of strangers. Aided by increases in the numbers of vacation and leisure travelers that typically included more women, airlines' efforts to sell to women in the period after the war were as successful as the earlier campaigns in the 1930s had been. Although companies did not always have precise data, many airlines noted increases in the number of women travelers during these years. TWA, for example, found in 1957 that women accounted for about 44 percent of its domestic passengers.[48]

In the first three decades of air travel, aviation was not a man's world, not for passengers and not for stewardesses. But for a brief period in the late 1960s and early 1970s, some airlines used women's sexuality to sell seats rather than trying to sell seats to women. The new approach was part of a larger movement on Madison Avenue in which the "gray-flannel anonymity" of postwar advertising "gave way to personal expression."[49] This change especially appealed to airlines' marketing departments after aircraft such as the Boeing 707, the Boeing 727, the DC-8, and the DC-9 opened up jet service to smaller cities and decreased flight times, making air travel irresistible to business travelers. Airline advertisers feared flight had become boring and routine to these travelers. Mary Wells, an advertising account executive who helped create the new campaign at Braniff Airlines, said her efforts were to spare the passenger "the terrible Kafka-like monotony of flying."[50] For a period in the late 1960s and early 1970s, airline companies tried to make air travel more exciting; their strategy was part of a tradition in aviation that associated flight with sex and thrill, and it also was part of the 1960s "sexual revolution."[51] One face of the sexual revolution was a utopian vision of equality and freedom for women and men, but another side was more libertine and commercial, a side in which "raw sex was posed as the oasis in an arid society."[52] Airline advertisements expressed this latter side. Mary Wells explained, as though the airline was advancing a freedom, "When a tired businessman gets on an airplane, we think he ought to be allowed to look at a pretty girl."[53] To accommodate the tired businessman, Braniff Airlines introduced "The Air Strip" in 1965 that featured stewardesses removing pieces of their new, layered uniforms at intervals during the flight.[54] The campaign also included a new paint scheme in which each airplane was painted one of seven different solid colors meant to accentuate the structure of the aircraft, in the words of the company president, "to give it a masculinity, a feeling of being solid and sound and so forth."[55] In the same period, TWA created "foreign accent flights" that clad the stewardesses in costumes representing countries the airline served, and in another campaign the company advertised its cabin crews as "mini harems," composed of "lovely lassies catering to every wish."[56] Beginning in 1972, National Airlines spent nearly $10 million a year on a campaign that featured a closeup photograph of the face of a smiling stewardess who beckoned in bold-faced copy: "Fly Me, I'm Cheryl." Using this line with a host of women's names and faces, this campaign ran for four years in magazines and newspapers, billboards and buses. The image of the sexy stewardess seeped into books such as the famous *Coffee Tea or Me* series and into pornographic movies such as "The Swinging Stewardesses."[57] These popular images expressed the same discomfort with women's control as had the stereotypes of nurses' availability, as one stewardess in this era explained that people felt discomfort, even anger, because the women were on their own. "We could have sexual affairs if we wanted to," she said, "That's the issue. That we have a choice."[58] In the earlier years, the airline companies helped defend stewardesses from passengers' invasions, but now some of their own advertising suggested stewardesses were fair game.

Cheryl and her ilk helped preserve the exhilaration of flight by representing to some an element of sexual thrill, but at the cost of airlines' previous appeals to women and also at the cost of many stewardesses' approval. Some worked to change the image of the occupation, such as Stewardesses for Women's Rights, which was founded in 1972 by two women at Eastern Airlines, Sandra Jarrell and Jan Fulsom. The one thousand or so women who joined the group were just a tiny portion of cabin attendants in these years. Although cabin attendants numbered about eight thousand in 1957, the tremendous growth of the industry that accompanied jets such as the Boeing 707 and DC-8 brought their numbers to thirty-five thousand in 1970. But the organization was able to garner media attention far out of proportion to its membership. Airline companies had long capitalized on the public's interest in stewardesses to promote air travel; airlines had frequently received free publicity by showing off stewardesses in new uniforms or inviting reporters to visit training sessions. Now some stewardesses used this high profile to publicize that they were neither sex slaves nor glamorized waitresses but, instead, were professionals, trained and responsible for safety in the cabin. With members of National Organization of Women (NOW), the group staged protests against National Airlines' "Fly Me" campaign, and also voiced complaints about advertisements for Continental Airlines and Southwest Airlines. Their voices received coverage in magazines from *Newsweek* to *Ladies Home Journal* to *Advertising Age*.[59] Stewardesses for Women's Rights also won attention by tapping into the public's perennial fears of flying by declaring that the sexy advertisements and skimpy uniforms hampered the cabin crew's performance of safety functions. The group created a "countercommercial," stating that the popular representations of the job were "a threat to your flying safety."[60]

The emphasis on safety dovetailed with efforts by the unions. Unlike an increasing portion of workers in these years, most stewardesses were unionized. They belonged to the original union started by Ada Brown, or to an affiliate of the Transport Union Workers. Stewardesses gained power in their unions as their tenure on the job increased; in a string of legal challenges and contracts beginning in the mid-1960s, stewardesses won the right to stay on the job as they aged, wed, and bore children. By 1974, the average tenure was close to five and a half years and still climbing.[61] And they gained power as the 747s and the other wide-bodied aircraft that entered service in the middle of the 1970s required more cabin attendants in the industry while the number of pilots grew more slowly. In addition, their solidarity grew from working together in larger numbers on aircraft that could now seat three and four hundred passengers.[62] As new, independent bodies, or as strengthened segments of existing unions, the cabin attendants' organizations addressed the changing conditions of the work, including the faster pace and the bigger crowds. They also contributed to increasing the women's wages, which in this era surpassed those in factory work, sales work, and clerical work, and also helped redefine the job itself. The unions for many years had held safety forums at their national meetings, recommended safety features and equipment to the aircraft manufacturers, and countered the carriers' tendency to avoid raising the matter of accidents. Reinforcing the unions' efforts was the federal government's intensified interest in cabin safety, which resulted in stiffer regulations covering training on safety and emergencies. The presence of men in the cabin as attendants, more frequent after 1971 when a court decided companies must consider male applicants, also helped change the image of the occupation.

By the era of airline deregulation, beginning in 1978, stewardesses had succeeded in redefining themselves as safety professionals and their formal title was now "flight attendants."[63] The reference to safety laid claim to being skilled workers, worthy of respect, and the emphasis on professionalism made clear that their friendliness was paid and impersonal. With this new designation, the women recaptured some of the dignity and control that cabin crews had enjoyed in the first three decades of air travel. But a few problems have remained. Their employers' advertisements punctured a hole in the protection they had once enjoyed as professionals, and it has been slow to mend. The many recent incidents of "air rage" directed at flight attendants, whatever the mitigating factors such as cramped space and overbooking, show that some passengers do not give the cabin crew the respect they received in the first decades of air travel.[64]

Notes

1. Advertisement in *The Saturday Evening Post,* May 15, 1954, n.p., from the D'Arcy Collection of the Communications Library of the University of Illinois at Urbana-Champaign, Urbana, Illinois.

2. E. P. Lott, in Joan Thomas, "What About That Hostess Job?" *Popular Aviation,* May 1933, 290. Ellen Church, in Sally Knapp, *New Wings for Women* (New York: Thomas Y. Crowell Co., 1946), 78.

3. Olette Hasle, in W. B. Courtney, "High-Flying Ladies," *Collier's,* August 20, 1932, 30.

4. Ben B. Follett, *Careers in Aviation* (Boston: Waverly House, 1942), 101. See also Charles Gilbert Hall and Rudolph A. Merkle, *The Sky's the Limit: Jobs in Commercial Aviation and How to Get Them* (New York: Funk & Wagnalls, 1943), 143.

5. Lesley Poling-Kempes, *The Harvey Girls: Women Who Opened the West* (New York: Paragon House, 1989), 55. The aviation historian Donna Corbet suggested the connection to me between Harvey Girls and stewardesses in a personal communication in September 1990.

6. Wages for these occupations are shown in Robert W. Hambrook, "Airline Hostesses," *Air Commerce Bulletin* 11 (August 15, 1939), 33; Mary Elizabeth Pidgeon, *Women in the Economy of the United States of America* (Washington, D.C.: United States Department of Labor, Women's Bureau, 1937), 125–28; and Susan Porter Benson, *Counter Cultures: Saleswomen, Managers, and Customers in American Department Stores, 1890–1940* (Urbana: University of Illinois Press, 1991), 49–50.

7. Marie Elwell Onions, "Welcoming the Nation," *Independent Woman,* February 1938, 60.

8. Lois Scharf, *To Work and To Wed: Female Employment, Feminism, and the Great Depression* (Westport, Conn.: Greenwood Press, 1980), 96.

9. Julietta K. Arthur, "Airways to Earning," *Independent Woman,* February 1940, 56.

10. Harriet Fry Iden, in George Vecsey and George C. Dade, *Getting Off the Ground* (New York: E. P. Dutton, 1979), 272.

11. Jessie Carter Bronson, in Gwen Neblesick Mahler, *Legacy of the Friendly Skies: A Pictorial History of United Airlines Stewardesses and Flight Attendants* (Marceline, Mo.: Walsworth Publishing Co., 1991), 68.

12. Mary Rebecca Lingenfelter and Harry Dexter Kitson, *Vocations for Girls* (New York: Harcourt, Brace and Co., 1939), 232–33.

13. Mary O'Connor, *Flying Mary O'Connor* (New York: Rand McNally, 1961), 59.

14. Leo Freedman, "Duties of an Air Hostess," *Popular Aviation,* February 1933, 125.

15. Jeanette Lea, "We *Don't* Fly for Love," *Popular Aviation,* September 1938, 26.

16. Ellen Tarry, *The Third Door: The Autobiography of an American Negro Woman* (New York: David McKay Co., 1955), 111.

17. Iden, in Vescey and Dade, *Getting Off the Ground,* 275.

18. Joan Thomas, "What About That Hostess Job?" *Popular Aviation,* May 1933, 290.

19. Harold Holmes, "AD-venture in Air Transportation," *Aero Digest* 33 (July 1938), 62.

20. "Gives Ad Theme for Air Travel," *New York Times,* September 29, 1937, p. 3.

21. Alice Rogers Hager, "More Women Take to Air," *New York Times,* July 11, 1937, sec. 6, p. 6.

22. George P. Saunders, "The Airlines . . . And the Public," part 1, *Air Transport* 4 (December 1946), 46.

23. Frederick W. Gill and Gilbert L. Bates, *Airline Competition: A Study of the Effects of Competition on the Quality and Price of Airline Service and the Self-Sufficiency of the United States Domestic Airlines* (Boston: Harvard University Press, 1949), 147.

24. "Nurses Aren't Necessary," *Collier's,* May 25, 1946, 33.

25. Madelyn Mecklem, in Gwen Nebelsick Mahler, Mary Lou Axcell Finch, and Marie B. O'Connor Trainer, eds., *Wings of Pride: TWA Cabin Attendants, A Pictorial History 1935–1985* (Marceline, Mo.: Walsworth Publishing, 1985), 106.

26. For a period in the late 1940s, Zell McConnell, who ran a string of modeling schools, set up classes to train recruits for Continental Airlines, Northwest Airlines, and TWA. See "McConnell Schools Training Stewardesses for 3 Airlines," *American Aviation* 10 (November 15, 1946), 48.

27. A. E. Blomquist, *Outline of Air Transport Practice* (New York: Pitman Publishing, 1941), 271.

28. June Cranston, in Mahler, Finch, and Trainer, eds., *Wings of Pride,* 33.

29. Lesley Poling-Kempes, *The Harvey Girls,* 55. Hospitals used uniforms to create "institutional personalities" according to Susan Reverby in "The Search for the Hospital Yardstick: Nursing and the Rationalization of Hospital Work," in Susan Reverby and David Rosner, eds., *Health Care in America: Essays in Social History* (Philadelphia: Temple University Press, 1979), 213. Dorothy Sue Cobble discussed appearance codes in restaurants in *Dishing It Out: Waitresses and Their Unions in the Twentieth Century* (Urbana: University of Illinois Press, 1991), 47.

30. Blomquist, *Outline of Air Transport Practice,* 276.

31. "Glamor Girls of the Air," *Life,* August 25, 1958, 73. See also Craig Lewis, "New School Expected to Enhance American's Bid for Stewardesses," *Aviation Week* 67 (December 2, 1957), 46.

32. Donald Nyrop and "Stewardess Appraisal Sheet," in Michigan Fair Employment Practices Commission, "Marlene White v. Northwest Airlines, Inc.," *Race Relations Law Reporter* 7 (summer 1962), 619–20.

33. "Patricia Banks v. Capital Airlines," *Race Relations Law Reporter* 5 (spring 1960), 271.

34. James Rorty, "The First Colored Air Hostess," *The Crisis,* June–July 1958, 339. Some of the early prodding by the Urban League was reported in "US Seeks to End Transit Job Bias," *New York Times,* September 21, 1955, 1, and the complaints are mentioned in Richard Witkin, "Aviation: Stewardess," *New York Times,* December 29, 1957, sec. 2, p. 25. Cynthia Harrison described the influence of the Cold War on efforts to win racial and sexual equality in *On Account of Sex: The Politics of Women's Issues, 1945–1968* (Berkeley: University of California Press, 1988), xi.

35. "Aviation News and Notes," *New York Times,* December 24, 1951, 25.

36. Ligea McCracken Painter, in Helen E. McLaughlin, *Walking on Air: An Informal History of Inflight Service of Seven U.S. Airlines* (Denver: State of the Art, Ltd., 1986), 164.

37. Janet Muff, "Of Images and Ideals: A Look at Socialization and Sexism in Nursing,"

in Anne Hudson Jones, eds., *Images of Nurses: Perspectives from History, Art and Literature* (Philadelphia: University of Pennsylvania Press, 1988), 208.

38. "Stewardess Flight Observation Report," in Gwendolyn Nebelsick Mahler, *Wings of Excellence: American Airlines Flight Attendants, A Pictorial History 1933–1993* (Marceline, Mo.: Walsworth Publishing Company, n.d.), 114.

39. Joseph Kastner, "Joan Waltermire: Air Stewardess," *Life,* April 28, 1941, 102; and Morris B. Baker, *Airline Traffic and Operations* (New York: McGraw-Hill, 1947), 141. Sometimes, as in these cases, the qualifiers attached diminished the terms.

40. Juanita Musty, in Janis Fraser Bauer, *Western Airlines: Pictorial History of In-flight* (n.p., 1986), 110.

41. Kay Park Haney, in McLaughlin, *Walking on Air,* 78.

42. Mary F. Murray, *Skygirl: A Career Handbook for the Airline Stewardess,* with an introduction by Ellen E. Church (New York: Duell, Sloan and Pearce, 1951), 40.

43. For this history, see Georgia Panter Nielsen, *From Sky Girl to Flight Attendant: Women and the Making of a Union,* introduction by Alice H. Cook (Ithaca: Cornell University, New York State School of Industrial and Labor Relations, ILR Press, 1982), 30.

44. Pat Brown [pseud.] in Paul E. Deutschman, "Hostess on Flight 408," *Holiday,* June 1958, 185.

45. Glenn Garrison, "More Women Travelling—Airlines Increase Promotions to Ladies," *Aviation Week* 67 (July 15, 1957), 41.

46. Advertisement in the *Ladies Home Journal,* August 1953, n.p., from the D'Arcy Collection of the Communications Library of the University of Illinois at Urbana-Champaign, Urbana, Illinois.

47. Advertisement in the *Ladies Home Journal,* December 1949, n.p., from the D'Arcy Collection of the Communications Library of the University of Illinois at Urbana-Champaign, Urbana, Illinois.

48. Garrison, "More Women Travelling—Airlines Increase Promotions to Ladies," 41.

49. Stephen Fox, *The Mirror Makers: A History of American Advertising and Its Creators* (New York: William Morrow and Co., 1984), 218.

50. Mary Wells, in "More Blue in Braniff's Yonder," *Business Week,* January 21, 1967, 106.

51. Linda Grant, *Sexing the Millennium: Women and the Sexual Revolution* (New York: Grove Press, 1994), 154. Roger Rawlings discusses the traditional association between flight and sex in *The Last Airmen: Exploring My Father's World* (New York: Harper and Row, 1989), 87–89.

52. Todd Gitlin, *The Sixties: Years of Hope, Days of Rage* (New York: Bantam Books, 1987), 30.

53. Wells, in "More Blue in Braniff's Yonder," 106.

54. Advertisement in the *Dallas Times,* December 5, 1965, n.p., from the D'Arcy Collection of the Communications Library of the University of Illinois at Urbana-Champaign, Urbana, Illinois.

55. Harding Lawrence, in "Lawrence: Marketing at Braniff," *Airline Management and Marketing* 1 (October 1967), 16.

56. Advertisement in the *Los Angeles Times,* June 14, 1968, n.p; advertisement in the *Los Angeles Times,* June 20, 1968, n.p.; advertisement in the *Chicago Tribune,* April 3, 1968, n.p., and advertisement in *Air Travel,* January 1968, n.p., in the D'Arcy Collection of the Communications Library of the University of Illinois at Urbana-Champaign, Urbana, Illinois.

57. The movie title was mentioned in Lindsy Van Gelder, "Coffee, Tea or Fly Me," *Ms.,* January 1973, 87; Trudy Baker and Rachel Jones, *Coffee, Tea or Me? The Uninhibited Memoirs of Two Airline Stewardesses* (New York: Bartholomew House, 1967); Trudy Baker and Rachel Jones, *The Coffee, Tea, or Me Girls' 'Round the World Diary* (New York: Grosset and Dunlap,

1970); Trudy Baker and Rachel Jones, *The Coffee, Tea or Me Girls Lay It on the Line* (New York: Grosset and Dunlap, 1972); Trudy Baker and Rachel Jones, *The Coffee Tea or Me Girls Get Away from It All* (New York: Grosset and Dunlap, 1974). The series credited two stewardesses with authorship, but many people believe the books came from a publicity man at American Airlines. See, for example, Paula Kane, *Sex Objects in the Sky*, 104. I believe Cornelius Wohl, the coauthor of *Fly Me*, wrote the series because of similarities in style and because the notes about the authors in *Fly Me* identified Wohl as "the ghost author of many bestsellers." *Fly Me* took off on the National Airlines advertising campaign. It was a collection of cartoons and jokes suitable for *Playboy* magazine, featuring buxom women in tight uniforms who provided the kind of service that National's campaign was meant to bring to mind. Bill Wenzel and Cornelius Wohl, *Fly Me* (Greenwich, Conn.: Fawcett Publications, 1974).

58. Barbara, in Roberta Lessor, "Unanticipated Longevity in Women's Work: The Career Development of Airline Flight Attendants" (Ph.D. dissertation, University of California, San Francisco, 1982), 132. Emphasis in Lessor removed.

59. "In a Stew," *Newsweek*, March 18, 1974, 100–102; Letty Cottin Pogrebin, "The Working Woman," *Ladies Home Journal*, November 1976, 86; "Stewardess Group Sets Counter to 'Sexist' Ads," *Advertising Age* 45 (September 23, 1974), 62.

60. As quoted in "Stewardess Group Sets Counter to 'Sexist' Ads," 62.

61. Rosalind K. Ellingsworth, "Flight Attendants Flexing Labor Muscle," *Aviation Week and Space Technology* 100 (June 3, 1974), 30.

62. Frieda S. Rozen, "Technological Advances and Increasing Militance: Flight Attendant Unions in the Jet Age," in Barbara Drygulski Wright et al., eds., *Women, Work, and Technology* (Ann Arbor: University of Michigan Press, 1987), 220–38.

63. Louise Kapp Howe, "No More Stewardesses—We're Flight Attendants," *Redbook Magazine*, January 1979, 65–75.

64. "Flying Wildly Out of Control," *Newsweek*, November 29, 1999, 42.

Experiment in the Cockpit

The Women Airforce Service Pilots of World War II

KATHERINE SHARP LANDDECK

While practicing landings with her student in Honolulu, Cornelia Fort was forced to maneuver violently to avoid hitting an incoming aircraft. When she looked back to see the other plane she spotted the bright red balls on top of its wings and saw formations of more fighters coming toward her. Fort watched, helpless and with heart breaking, as Pearl Harbor was bombed. She and her student landed safely, but not everyone escaped harm that day.[1] As the news of Pearl Harbor raced across the United States, few people could have predicted the changes the nation would face over the next four years. Technology advanced and the roles of men and women were altered. As men went to war, American women stepped forward to fill the jobs they had vacated and the new jobs the massive war machine demanded. Some women stayed home and tried to make do with rationing and missing husbands, while other women themselves went into the military in a variety of positions, including as pilots of military aircraft.

Some women's military organizations such as the Women's Army Corps (WAC) or the Navy's Women Accepted for Voluntary Emergency Service (WAVES) struggled to recruit their quotas of women. The civilian program of women pilots who flew for the Army Air Forces (AAF) had fourteen times more women apply to the program than were accepted. Women had been a part of aviation since its inception. From Katherine Wright, a strong supporter of her brothers' efforts, to early aviators Harriet Quimby and Bessie Coleman, to the legendary Amelia Earhart, women played an active role in early aviation. By 1941, these women had influenced other women to look to the sky, and with war, to be airminded about their wartime efforts. The historian Dean Jaros argues that the first women aviators left no legacy.[2] It is quite clear that they did leave a legacy, part of which was to inspire the women who would fly for the AAF during World War II. As will be shown, it is also clear that the women pilots of World War II left a legacy of their own—one of inspiration for the women aviators of today. The World War II–era women pilots earned their place in history by aiding their country when it needed them most.

By the fall of 1942 it was apparent that the AAF was in trouble. The AAF's

Members of the Women's Airforce Service Pilots (WASPs) capably flew all varieties of military aircraft during World War II, but they were unable to obtain benefits as members of the military nor able to obtain employment in flying careers after the war was over. Here four WASPs are shown leaving their Boeing B-17 at the four-engine school at Lockbourne, Kansas, in mid-1944. *(From left to right):* Frances Green, Peg Kirshner, Ann Waldner, Blanch Osborne. (U.S. Air Force, courtesy National Air and Space Museum, Smithsonian Institution [SI 91-1471].)

Ferrying Division, or FERD, was experiencing a serious shortage of pilots. The FERD was responsible for ferrying AAF planes from the factories to training bases or points of debarkation. Because of the large number of new planes being built, the pace of ferrying planes was furious. The FERD desperately needed pilots, and it turned to women as an experimental answer to its problem. In early September, Nancy Love, a Vassar-educated commercial pilot with many hours flying, was appointed Director of Women Pilots, and began recruiting women to fly for the FERD. These women were required to be highly experienced pilots, and after a short training period, became civilian pilots for the FERD. The women pilots were designated Women's Auxiliary Ferrying Squadron, or WAFS.

As the WAFS began to fly with the FERD, Jacqueline Cochran, a prominent pilot and businesswoman, claimed her spot as leader of women pilots. On September 15, 1942, Cochran began organizing the Women's Flying Training Detachment, or WFTD, with the blessing of the AAF chief, General Henry "Hap" Arnold. The WFTD was created to train women pilots who had some experience, but were not qualified to join the WAFS directly. The women moved through army-style training identical to that of male cadets with the exception of combat aerobatics.[3] Primarily for the sake of simplification of policy making, in early August 1943, the WAFS and WFTD were consolidated by the AAF into the Women Airforce Service Pilots, or WASPs, with Cochran at its head and Nancy Love as the Executive of Women Pilots in the Air Transport Command (ATC). (For the remainder of this study, unless specifically referring to the WAFS, all of the women pilots will be referred to as the WASPs, despite the fact the name was not used until August 1943.) By December 1944, only sixteen months after they were brought together, the experiment of women flying for the Army Air Force was ended. The WASPs were disbanded and the women were sent home. Some of the reasons for their demise were directly related to the general push to remove women from the workforce as the war came to a close.

Several historians have looked at the role American women played during World War II as volunteers, workers, and members of the military. Others have noted the changes in attitudes about women in these roles in the postwar years. In *The American Woman: Her Changing Social, Economic and Political Roles, 1920–1979,* William Chafe argues that the war was a watershed for women and that it permanently expanded the role women, particularly married women, were able to play in the workforce.[4] Some historians have since contradicted Chafe's conclusion. Leila J. Rupp, author of *Mobilizing Women for War: German and American Propaganda, 1939–1945,* contends that the increased role of women in the workforce was not permanent. She argues that "it is clear that the wartime changes expanded the options of women in a way intended by the propagandists as temporary." More important, Rupp explains that the acceptable public image of women expanded during the war only because it was necessary, but that "the wartime range of options would contract once again in peacetime."[5] Other historians support Rupp's conclusions that the acceptable public image of women was not permanently changed by the war.

D'Ann Campbell, for instance, supports Rupp's arguments in her book *Women at War with America.* Campbell maintains that the American government had to use massive propaganda to get women into the military and factories, and that despite these efforts, they were still short of their goals. According to Campbell, the shortages were caused in part by the fact that American society did not or could not accept the dramatic changes in women's roles.[6] Following Campbell's line of thinking, the fact that the WASPs had thousands more women apply to the program than there were positions available suggests that the idea of women as pilots was not such an unreasonable assumption for many Americans. Maureen Honey analyzes wartime fiction, advertising, and propaganda in her book *Creating Rosie the Riveter: Class, Gender and Propaganda during World War II.* Honey wanted to discover why women shifted from the strong Rosie the Riveter model to the "naïve, dependent, childlike, self-abnegating model of femininity in the late forties and 1950s."[7] She analyzes the various tactics the government used and their effectiveness in recruiting women to work, as well as their success in the drive to get women back into the home after the war.

According to Honey, the government used propaganda throughout the war to emphasize the nuclear family. She argues that the nuclear family was presented, and seen, as representative of "the survival of decency and humanity in a world rent by suffering." This image grew stronger as the war began drawing to a close, and women were "idealized as healers who would salve men's wounds while nurturing the generation that would harvest the rich fruit of postwar prosperity." Honey's contentions agree with both Rupp's and Campbell's suggestions that American women, particularly married women, were never intended to hold jobs permanently once the crisis of war had passed.[8]

Doris Weatherford extensively discusses the role women played during the war in her book, *American Women and World War II.* Weatherford discusses the fears of another economic depression as the war began to wind to a close, and cites titles of magazine articles such as "Getting Rid of the Women," "Watch Out for the Women," and "Give Back the Jobs," as representative of attitudes of the times.[9] All of the historians agree that thousands of American women were mobilized to participate in the war effort through massive propaganda campaigns and an appeal to patriotism. Although not as obvious, propaganda campaigns also pushed for the women to return home as the war came to a close. This propaganda, and fears of postwar depression, were a significant part of the reasons for the disbandment of the WASPs.

Although there have been a number of general works on the WASPs, the best of which is Sally Van Wagenen Keil's *Those Wonderful Women in Their Flying Machines,* very little academic work has been done on them. Molly Merryman's *Clipped Wings* is among the first, and it deals primarily with the end of the WASP program. Although Merryman is solid in her presentation of the media outburst against the WASPs, which supports Weatherford's arguments, she falls a bit short in her overall analysis. As will be discussed later, the ending of the WASPs program was a complex event encompassing not only the general push to return women to the home and return jobs to men but also incorporating members of Congress, Jacqueline Cochran, General Henry "Hap" Arnold, and the shift in the war itself. Another factor was the fact that the program was always intended to be a "test" to see if women could fly. Before the significance of the WASPs' disbandment can be appreciated, it is useful to analyze the women's effectiveness as pilots.[10]

The major sources utilized for this study include oral histories with surviving WASPs and questionnaires completed by surviving WASPs. Two official histories, one from the AAF, and the second from the ATC (of which the FERD was a part), were analyzed as well. Corroborating evidence has been cited whenever possible.[11]

Throughout their existence, from September 1942 to December 1944, the WASPs fulfilled a number of duties for the AAF. The women towed targets behind everything from the North American AT-6 Texan, an advanced trainer, to the four-engine bomber, the Boeing B-17 Flying Fortress. They performed engineering test flights on new or newly repaired aircraft. They did administrative flying and trained bombardiers and navigators. This study examines only one role of the women, as ferry pilots for the FERD in the ATC.

There are two major reasons to focus on the WASPs within the FERD. First, the women were initially brought into flying military planes for the sole purpose of ferrying aircraft for the FERD. The FERD utilized the women as pilots before any other part of the AAF and fought the hardest to keep them when they were disbanded in December 1944, arguing that they were desperately needed. Second, the women who were initially admitted to the FERD, the original WAFS, acted as guinea pigs for the AAF's experiment of utilizing women as pilots, proving that women were indeed physically and emotionally capable of flying military aircraft.

The WAFS were initially limited to flying light trainers. They slowly proved themselves and on April 17, 1943, the ATC decreed that the women could fly any aircraft they were capable of flying. This was a major turning point in the women's role as pilots. The safe flying of the WAFS, while unquestionably a major reason for the ATC and FERD change of heart, was not the only factor that encouraged policy changes. In the spring of 1943, the FERD became part of the AAF training system. The AAF utilized the FERD as part of the more advanced stages of training its combat pilots. The male pilots would first ferry light planes and then more advanced planes to gain experience with the aircraft, particularly vital cross-country experience, before entering combat. As the number of pilots needed for combat increased, any slowdown in their training would be detrimental to the Allied cause. If women were restricted to ferrying only trainers and other light aircraft, the number of planes available for men to fly would be limited and there would be a blockage in the training cycle. By allowing the women to progress to the most advanced aircraft they were able to fly, there would be no blockage, the combat pilots would be trained, and the planes would be delivered.

With the removal of limitations, the women advanced to flying operational aircraft, which became more vital as the war progressed, and the women's program expanded. On April 24, the first class of WFTDs, class 43-1, graduated and joined the original WAFS in the FERD. The success of the WAFS in the FERD eased the way for the new women. From April 1943 to their disbandment in December 1944, the women progressed into advanced pursuit aircraft and, despite some controversy, proved that women could fly military aircraft. This study investigates the degree to which the WASPs were effective pilots for the AAF, and why they were disbanded while the war was still in full force.

The qualifications for the original WAFS were very high. The women had to be high school graduates, between twenty-one and thirty-five years old, hold a commercial pilot's license, have at least five hundred flight hours, and hold a certificate showing that they were capable of flying planes with two hundred horsepower engines. In addition, the women had to supply two letters of recommendation and proof of their flight time. The men who were hired by the FERD of the ATC as civilian pilots had lower qualifications. The civilian men had to be between nineteen and forty-five years old, were required to have finished three years of high school, and have at least two hundred flight hours. The head of the WAFS, Nancy Love, apparently made the women's qualifications tougher because she "recognized that her pilots would be scrutinized" as they were considered for militarization.[12] Love herself was a highly qualified commercial pilot and envisioned an elite group of women pilots aiding in the war effort. She proposed that the women be paid a salary of $250 per month, $130 less than the men civilian pilots, apparently because the women would be flying only trainer and liaison-type aircraft. Love's later actions to expand the types of aircraft the women could fly indicate that she believed these to be "foot-in-the-door," temporary measures. The fact that Love accepted the inequalities indicates that the women believed this was their best opportunity to prove themselves as capable pilots. It must be remembered that, only a few years before the WAFS began, women were considered "too high strung for war-time flying."[13] The WAFS had a great deal to prove, and they were fully aware of their responsibility to other women pilots.

On arriving at the 2nd Ferrying Group in Wilmington, Delaware, in early September 1942, Teresa James said a short prayer, "whereas, they have decided to let us try, be it resolved that come hell, high water, and insulting criticism, we will not let Washington down. Amen."[14] Cornelia Fort recognized the pressure as well. "All of us realized the spot we were in. We had to deliver the goods—or else," she said, "or else there wouldn't ever be another chance for women pilots in any part of the service."[15] In keeping with their experimental status, after the initial announcement of the creation of the WAFS by Secretary of War Henry Stimson, all publicity on the WAFS ceased as the women began ferrying planes across the nation.[16] The lack of publicity can be explained as a safety mechanism for the AAF. If the women failed, the bad publicity would not be as severe. By December 1942, the twenty-five original WAFS were actively ferrying for the

FERD. The average flight time of the first thirteen women was over twelve hundred hours.[17] These highly experienced pilots carefully flew the trainers and liaison aircraft with the weight of the future of all women pilots on their shoulders. The women kept busy flying the light aircraft and following the rules, hoping to prove their abilities.

As the WAFS began flying for the FERD, Jacqueline Cochran was beginning her flight school to train additional women pilots for the AAF, the WFTD. On November 16, 1942, the first class, 43-1, arrived in Houston to begin training. The qualifications for this first group were much lower than for the WAFS, but the women were still experienced pilots. They had an average of 350 flight hours, well over the two-hundred-hour requirement.[18] While the WFTDs were learning to fly the army way, the WAFS began expanding their role within the FERD.

It is evident that even fairly early in the experiment the AAF commanders saw the WAFS as capable pilots. Originally the WAFS worked out of only one base, the 2nd Ferrying Group in Wilmington, Delaware. By December 1942, the WAFS were moved to other bases to be available to ferry aircraft where they were most needed. WAFS joined the 6th Ferrying Group in Long Beach, California; the 5th Ferrying Group in Dallas, Texas; and the 3rd Ferrying Group in Romulus (Wayne County), Michigan. According to the *Army Air Force Historical Study No. 55,* "Mrs. Love and some of the other women were dissatisfied because they were restricted at Wilmington to ferrying elementary types of planes."[19] Although no evidence has been found to support this conclusion, the experience level of these women was sufficient enough to assume that they quite easily could have become bored and frustrated flying only simple trainer aircraft. This reinforces the idea that although Love agreed to the limitations originally placed on the women, she fully expected them to be upgraded to more sophisticated aircraft once they had proven their abilities. Love left Wilmington in January 1943, to join the new WAFS squadron at Dallas. The women were still limited to flying light primary trainers, but in her first month at Dallas, Love flew an AT-6, an advanced trainer, and was soon followed by other WAFS in more basic and eventually advanced, trainers. The opportunities to upgrade to flying more advanced planes were yet another sign of the growing confidence the FERD had in its women pilots.

In February 1943, Love got the opportunity to fly a North American P-51, one of the newest and hottest pursuit aircraft of the time, capable of flying 440 miles per hour. Other WAFS ferried a Douglas C-47, known domestically as the DC-3, a twin-engine cargo plane, and Betty Gillies, second-in-command in the WAFS, flew a Republic P-47, another high-performance pursuit aircraft. Love transferred to the Long Beach, California, base in March and checked out in sixteen different types of aircraft within one month of her arrival. She was quickly followed by other WAFS because, as Sally Van Wagenen Keil points out, "the Sixth Ferrying Group saw women simply as pilots, much needed to fly the vast number of airplanes produced by the manufacturers it served."[20] Although the commanders at the different bases could and did make a difference in how much the WAFS were able to fly, the workload of each base differed. The Long Beach base was surrounded by aircraft factories and was responsible for getting those planes to points of debarkation as quickly as possible. The commanding officers needed competent pilots and they very obviously were not particular about their pilot's gender. The WAFS continued to prove themselves with an outstanding safety and delivery record, but they still faced discrimination on some bases.

Despite their successes, on March 25, 1943, the commander of the 3rd Ferrying Group at Romulus, Michigan, ordered that WAFS from that base could only fly light trainer aircraft. The directive stated that the women "were not to be assigned as co-pilots on ferrying missions or to transition on any high-powered single-engine plane or on twin-engine aircraft." Also, supposedly to protect their morals, the young women, "were to be assigned missions in individual flights and, so far as possible, deliveries on alternate days with male pilots. If at all possible they were to be sent in a different direction from any male flights."[21]

Why 3rd Ferrying Division commanders felt compelled to make such restrictive orders is not clear. The logistics of following such a directive would have been a nightmare and would undoubtedly have led to a further limit on the number of hours the women assigned to Romulus were able to fly, removing an important pool of pilots from active duty. As for the likelihood of the directive's being aimed at the women because of prejudice against women pilots, rumors that the women were not treated as well at Romulus as at other bases do exist, but no specific examples have been found for this study. In her book *Sisters in the Sky, Volume I–The WAFS,* Adela Riek Scharr, a WAF herself, only conveyed that the WAFS were welcomed by some and ignored by most when they arrived at Rom-ulus. Scharr explained that Sis Bernheim, also a WAF, told her years after the war that they were the "darlings of the enlisted men. They'd do anything for us, not like some of those beardless lieutenants who thought we were in the service only to look for husbands."[22] This statement indicates that there may have been some animosity from the male pilots and officers.

Louise Bowden Brown (43-4), who was one of the first graduates of the WFTD to be based at Romulus, explained: "I don't remember any resentment from male pilots, but I do remember many who were proud of us, also officers and C.O.'s."[23] The final report on the WASPs at Romulus was filled with critical comments that clearly indicated a substantial bias against women pilots in general. The commanding officers at Romulus may have hoped to ground their women pilots by issuing the directive cited above, but the ATC and FERD moved quickly to overrule them.

On a copy of the Romulus directive held in the Ferrying Division files is the comment, penciled in by Colonel George D. Campbell, the Director of Operations, stating, "Mrs. Love objected to this directive."[24] Love did more than simply object. Between the Romulus directive and the FERD's new limits on the times of the month women could fly (the male commanders were concerned about the effect of the menstrual cycle on flying ability), the women's flight activities were being severely restricted. Love made a personal appeal to ATC headquarters and used the women's excellent flight record and her own and others' successful upgrade to more sophisticated aircraft as evidence of the women's abilities. The ATC apparently agreed with Love and, on April 17, the Chief of Staff (no name available in source) sent a letter to the FERD describing the new policies to be taken concerning the WAFS. Part of the letter stated:

> It is the desire of this Command that all pilots, regardless of sex, be privileged to advance to the extent of their ability in keeping with the progress of aircraft development. Will you please ensure that the terms of this policy are carried out insofar as it applies to ferrying of aircraft within the continental U.S.A.[25]

The FERD responded to the letter by rescinding its earlier directives and issuing a letter of new rules concerning the WAFS. The letter stated that "WAFS will be transitioned upon multi-engine aircraft or high-powered single-engine aircraft under the same standards of individual experience and ability as apply to any other pilot." The WAFS were still restricted from flying with male pilots "except during training," but delivery flights could be considered training flights when deemed as such prior to takeoff. The failure of the Romulus directive is further evidence that the women were proving their abilities as effective and capable pilots.[26]

The decisions concerning the WAFS were made just as the first class of the WFTD was about to graduate. If the original WAFS had not had a safe and efficient flight record when the decision time arrived, there is little doubt that the experiment of women pilots would have been ended. No one was about to risk the training of male combat pilots simply so women could ferry trainers. The FERD decision in April 1943 to expand the duties of the WAFS to ferry more advanced planes was a major turning point in the experiment of women flying for the AAF. The WAFS proved that women were capable of safely flying military aircraft and helped to open the door for the women who had completed military training and were ready to prove they could fly too.

On April 24, 1943, WFTD class 43-1 finally graduated. After the graduation ceremony, the women received a short leave and then joined the WAFS who were already flying for the FERD. In June, the second class graduated, and in July, with a flurry of media attention, Jacqueline Cochran was officially named Director of Women Pilots. Nancy Love, who had directed the WAFS since the

previous September, was relegated to the less influential position of Executive of
Women Pilots in the ATC. The ambiguity underlying Cochran's appointment
was evident in the title of a *Newsweek* article, "Coup for Cochran," in which the
reporter revealed that "the ATC maintained that Miss Cochran's job was merely
advisory and not superior to Mrs. Love's executive post." Officials at the AAF
headquarters disagreed, insisting that Cochran had "highest authority" over the
women pilots and that "if the Air Transport Command is not already aware of
this, they will have to be made aware of it."[27] Any controversy was ended when
the WAFS and the WFTD were brought together as the Women Airforce Service Pilots (WASPs) on August 5, with Cochran as its chief.

The question about Cochran's authority over Love suggested that the ATC
preferred to work with Love rather than Cochran. Jacqueline Cochran and
Nancy Love were different from each other. Although both were highly successful and experienced pilots, and were both committed to the war effort, that
is where the similarities end. Love attended Vassar College and lived a relatively
privileged life. She was determined to lead a small group of elite women pilots
in flying for the United States in its time of need. Love cooperated with the Air
Transport Command and the Ferrying Division and flew a great deal during
the war, using a solid flying record to expand the role the women played. Her
primary goal for the WAFS appears to have been to help the war effort in any
way possible.[28]

Jacqueline Cochran grew up in poverty in Florida. She was on her own at
the age of ten and fought her way to success, eventually creating a cosmetics
business, marrying the multimillionaire Floyd Odlum, and breaking air records
across the nation. Cochran was determined to have women release men from all
continental flying, and she was equally determined to accomplish her goal *her*
way. Cochran's goals for the WASPs included helping the war effort and as an
experiment to determine whether women could fly military aircraft.[29] Martha
Wagenseil, a WASP from class 43-2, described the differences between Love and
Cochran succinctly:

> Everyone loved Nancy, I in particular. She was beautiful, she was sweet, she was
> skilled, she was accomplished, she was everything I would have liked to be.
> Jacqueline Cochran was everything Nancy was not. She was tough, she was
> hard, she was shrewd, and she was political. We needed Jackie to fight our bat-
> tles and win for us. We needed them both.[30]

Although many of the women who became WASPs declare loyalty to Cochran
and firmly believe that they would have never been given the opportunity to fly
if she had not been so determined to achieve her goals, her frequently abrasive
personality and unwillingness to compromise may have had a role in the disbandment of the WASPs. Regardless of their different personalities and goals,

both Love and Cochran were vital to the success of the experiment of women military pilots.

The duties of WASPs within the FERD were slowly expanded as the demands of the war called for more aircraft, particularly advanced aircraft, to be delivered quickly and efficiently. By November 1944, the majority of WASPs within the FERD were flying twin-engine cargo and transport planes or pursuits. In addition to their ferrying duties, the women pilots were, on occasion, used to convince the men pilots that a particular aircraft was safe. The idea was that if a woman could fly a type of plane safely, then the men should be able to as well; it was a play to the male ego. In mid-1943, the male ferry pilots at Romulus were having difficulties flying the new Bell P-39 Airacobra, a sensitive pursuit airplane. Unfortunately, a number of the men had not followed the manufacturer's technical orders closely enough on takeoff and landing, and several of them had been killed in crashes. The other male pilots began calling the P-39 a "flying coffin" and refused to fly it. Then a WAF convinced her commanding officer to give her a chance to fly the P-39. After carefully following the technical orders she safely checked out in the plane, with two more WAFS following shortly afterward. Once the women began successfully delivering the planes, the men learned what they had been doing wrong, and began to fly the planes safely.[31] WASPs in other divisions of the AAF were used to prove the safety of various aircraft and to shame male pilots into flying them. Women were trained to fly the Martin B-26 Marauder and the gigantic Boeing B-29 Superfortress, among others. The FERD utilized women in this role when they were able.

In August 1943, the head of the domestic wing of the FERD, Colonel William Tunner, was having problems with the vital B-17 Flying Fortress. Male pilots were very nervous about flying the massive, four-engine bomber across the Atlantic Ocean to Great Britain, where it was desperately needed. Nancy Love and Betty Gillies were the answer to Tunner's problem. The women trained and were checked out on the aircraft, which for tiny Gillies meant cushions behind and under her. On September 2, the women and a carefully selected flight crew headed for Prestwick, Scotland, via Goose Bay in Greenland. Because of bad weather, the trip to Goose Bay took three days, but on September 5, the women were ready to make the final jump to Scotland. Unfortunately for the pilots, AAF Commanding General Henry Arnold, who was in London at the time, heard of the flight and canceled it, issuing orders that "no women fly transoceanic planes until I have time to study and approve."[32]

Love, Gillies, and much of the ATC and FERD staff believed that Jacqueline Cochran wanted to be the only woman to fly a military plane across the Atlantic (which she had done a few years earlier, although the male crew did not let her take off or land) and that she had the flight stopped. The official *History of the Air Transport Command* insisted that Cochran was wrongly accused and that the sequence of events proved that she had nothing to do with it. However, to this day, Gillies believes that Cochran maliciously stopped the flight.[33]

As the WAFS and the WFTDs were being consolidated into the WASPs and Love and Gillies were attempting to fly across the Atlantic, the new WASPs were being kept busy. The war was intensifying and demand for aircraft was high. The new WASPs were welcomed into the FERD and put to work almost immediately. When Margaret Ray Ringenberg (43-5) arrived in Wilmington, she was quickly sent out to ferry airplanes that were backlogged at a nearby aircraft factory.[34] Tex Brown Meachem (43-7) was transferred to Wilmington, and declared that she was so busy she did not remember spending more than one overnight at the base at a time. "When we came back in, snafu, train, or however we came back, there would be orders on the bulletin board. And when you checked in they would find out what planes you had been checked out in and they would pull it off the bulletin board and put your name on it, and the next day you were out."[35]

Cornelia Fort described the experience of the typical ferry pilot for an article in the July 1943 *Woman's Home Companion*. She expressed dismay at the misguided attitude many nonfliers held toward pilots.

> They chatter about the glamor of flying. Well, any pilot can tell you how glamorous it is. We get up in the cold dark in order to get to the airport by daylight. We wear heavy, cumbersome flying clothes and a 30-pound parachute. We are either cold or hot. Lipstick wears off, and hair gets straighter and straighter. We look forward all afternoon to a bath and steak; we get the bath, but seldom the steak. Sometimes we are too tired to eat and fall wearily into bed.[36]

Fort went on to explain why she flew, despite the obvious hardships. The experiences she described of discomfort and a very unglamorous lifestyle were familiar to every pilot who flew for the ferry command, male or female. The duties and experiences of WASPs in the FERD are clear, but how they were evaluated by others, namely the FERD and the AAF, is important in determining the degree to which the women were effective pilots.

The first indication of concern about the women pilots came with the utilization of the first class of WFTD graduates in April 1943. By mid-May, the various ferrying groups reported to the FERD Command that the new women pilots were highly qualified and doing a good job. While they praised the early class, officers from at least one base voiced concern about the possible quality of future graduates, citing their lack of flight experience.[37] The dilemma for the FERD, and a key source of Colonel Tunner's arguments with Cochran, was that the FERD believed the women should be required to have three hundred flight hours on joining the organization, the same as the male civilian pilots. Cochran and the AAF disagreed, citing the fact that the women went through identical military flight training as the male AAF cadets, with the exception of aerial combat and formation flying training, and were well qualified to ferry aircraft across the United States. This primary conflict of opinion about minimum qualifications for ferry pilots would continue throughout the life of the WASP experiment.

By the fall of 1943, tangible concerns about the WASPs emerged from FERD headquarters. In August, Colonel Tunner reported that there were "an excessive number of accidents and mishaps among women pilots, all of which since April involved graduates of the Women's Flying Training Detachment."[38] Tunner and the FERD became increasingly concerned over whether these women could safely upgrade to pursuit aircraft. In September 1943, the FERD Headquarters sent a letter to ATC headquarters that included the following observations: "It is felt that many recent graduates are so-called 'airport pilots' and have neither the training nor the qualifications to assume the responsibility of completing a ferrying flight distant from the home base without close personal supervision." The letter continued to recommend changes be made in the women's training to make them more suitable for ferrying duties. The official history of the ATC contends that, for ten months, "the two most important themes were that graduates of WFTD were less capable than those first received, and that it was difficult to fit them into the pursuit program." But, the report continued, "as to the first complaint, it appears to have been leveled against a minority of new WASPs rather than against them as a whole."[39]

These allegations against the WASPs deserve analysis. The decrease in required minimum flight time (the admission requirement had been dropped from two hundred hours to eventually only thirty-five hours) was a sore spot with Colonel Tunner from the beginning of the women's training program, but Tunner was not unreasonable in his requests for experienced pilots. He was responsible for making certain the planes were ferried quickly and safely to their destinations. He could not, in wartime, be concerned with unqualified pilots. It is possible that his bias against lower-time pilots may have prevented him from recognizing that the training the women received was directly relevant to the type of flying and the types of planes they would be ferrying with the FERD, making them more qualified than the average civilian pilot. However, Tunner's concern over the lower flight time is valid in that less experience could logically lead to a lower level of learned abilities. With the grave importance of his responsibilities and the increase in the number of accidents, it is understandable why Tunner and the FERD were concerned.

The WASP accident rate did increase as the program progressed. In the first six months of 1943, the WASP accident rate per thousand aircraft hours flown was a low .38. The male pilot accident rate for the same period was 1.27 per thousand hours flown. The second half of 1943 saw the WASP rate nearly double to

.87, while the male rate dropped to .78. The rise in the WASP rate can be attributed to the increase in the number of women pilots, namely those that Tunner expressed concern about with less flight experience. For all of 1944 the WASP rate was again higher at 1.38 accidents per thousand hours flown. The male rate for the same period was only .58 accidents. The increase in the women's accident rate for 1944 can be directly tied to the increased number of pursuit aircraft flown. Of the 6,922 deliveries made by WASPs in 1944, 3,677, or 53 percent, were of pursuit aircraft.[40]

The significance of the high percentage of pursuit aircraft flown by the WASPs is that more pursuit planes were involved in accidents in the FERD, for all pilots, than other types of aircraft. Although only 20 percent of the FERD ferrying movements involved pursuit aircraft, 37 percent of all accidents involved pursuits. The *History of the Air Transport Command* stated that, "for the continental Air Forces in 1944, the accident rate for heavy bombers was 0.29, for single engine pursuits it was 1.34, and for a single notorious type, the P-39, it was 2.88." The report continued,

> the most interesting conclusion to which these considerations lead is that throughout their career the women ferry pilots, for a variety of reasons, concentrated on types of ferrying essentially more hazardous than done by their male colleagues. So far as is known, there was no tendency among them to complain about this; if anything, as least in the pursuit period, it was a matter of pride.[41]

Although the WASPs' overall accident rate within the FERD equaled 1.11 per thousand flight hours while the men's overall rate equaled only .78 per thousand hours, the numbers are not directly comparable. The official history of the ATC revealed that during the same period while the women were flying increasing numbers of pursuit aircraft, the men were flying heavier aircraft, particularly bombers that had sophisticated instruments and navigators aboard. The women always flew solo, often without working instruments, and because of the light fuel load on board the aircraft, made more takeoffs and landings, the most dangerous part of flying. In an April 1944 confidential AAF letter in response to a media request for the WASPs' safety data, Lt. Col. Murl Estes, Deputy Chief of Flying Safety, explained the WASPs' record. "In the one operation where activities of men pilots and WASPs are very comparable, the fatal accident rate is identical. Though wide differences in activities, there is no reason to believe that there should be wide discrepancies between the accident rate for women pilots and men pilots." So although the overall accident rate of the women was somewhat higher than the men's rate, the AAF believed that the types of duties the women carried out explained the difference, and that the women pilots were equal to the men.[42]

Perhaps partially in response to Colonel Tunner's and the FERD's concerns about the less experienced pilots, the WASP training program did become longer and more complex as it went on. The later graduates were required to receive 560 hours of ground school and 210 of flight training, in contrast to the substantially lower requirements of the first class, 180 hours of ground school and only 115 hours of flight training. The later classes spent more time training for cross-country flying and trained in more advanced planes, including the AT-6.[43] These changes in training may have helped eliminate some of Tunner's concerns. The transfer, in July 1944, of 123 women out of the FERD and into the AAF's Training Command apparently eased tensions as well. The women transferred out of the FERD "consisted of the least experienced, plus some whose ability was doubted, and others who signified that they did not wish to fly fighters."[44] The last group included three of the original WAFS. As is evident from the high percentage of pursuit aircraft the women flew, being able to qualify to fly pursuit aircraft was essential to the needs of the FERD.

According to Jacqueline Cochran, "considerable criticism and resentment [had] been directed at WASP personnel who ferry the higher class aircraft." The criticism was apparently from male pilots who saw the WASPs flying aircraft they were not yet qualified to fly.[45] Marion Hodgson (43-5) supported Cochran's comment: "some men resented us. They were insecure types who thought we were taking something away from them. So we knew we had to fly better and gripe less than the men."[46] The Air Transport Command admitted that some resentment against the women existed among some of the male pilots. "Allegations that women were favored in transition training and in desirable assignments were made," the official history noted, "but seem to have been entirely unfounded. Undoubtedly it was galling to some young men to see a woman fly a plane which they were not yet qualified to handle." According to the history, the resentment "was always confined to a minority."[47]

Several of the WASPs corroborate ATC's contention that it was the minority of men who showed resentment toward the women. While Marion Hodgson supported Cochran, she also explained that "male pilots were mostly friendly and admiring."[48] Margaret Chamberlain Tamplin (44-3) believes she was fortunate because she "never felt discriminated against by the male pilots." Tamplin maintained that the men "treated me with respect and as an equal in so far as flying."[49] Mary Edith Engle (43-4) described the mixed response the women received. "Many [of the men] would just walk by and ignore us while others were friendly and accepted us as one of them." Engle stated that the men's "reactions didn't bother me as I was happy doing what I loved to do—FLY."[50] Lillian Epsberg Goodman (43-5) supported Engle's view, saying, "I was so young and happy to be flying that if there was any animosity toward us, I never noticed."[51]

There is no evidence that male resentment could have been a motivation for the transfer of some of the women. On the contrary, there is evidence that the

FERD highly valued the women they kept, as will be seen in the analysis of the WASPs' disbandment. According to the official ATC history, once the women the FERD deemed not qualified to fly pursuits were transferred out, the division "had a fairly stable women's auxiliary which concentrated largely on ferrying fighters, thereby rendering a very valuable service." Moreover, the division "was well satisfied with the group which remained."[52] A lack of further complaint about the women, not to mention the FERD's struggle to retain its women pilots on the WASPs' disbandment, supports the official history's conclusion.

On the WASPs' disbandment in December 1944, the ATC called for evaluation reports from each of the bases that had utilized the WASPs. This information was used in part to create the official ATC history that has been referred to throughout this study. Fortunately, the appendix of the history included the reports as they were submitted to the ATC. As a result, a direct analysis of the WASP evaluations is possible. The bases sent ATC Historical Officer Captain Walter Marx letters answering specific questions about the utilization of the WASPs on their bases. The women participated in pursuit school at a variety of bases and the overall evaluation is discussed below.

The WASP performance in pursuit school was, overall, quite good. Of the first fifteen WASPs to attend pursuit school in late 1943, fourteen graduated. The fifteenth woman, Dorothy Scott, was killed while on final approach by a male piloting a P-39. The P-39 collided with Scott's BC-1 from above and behind. The accident was deemed to have been entirely the fault of the male pilot and the tower. Of the fourteen women who graduated, five were from the original WAFS and the remaining nine were WFTD graduates. Although exact figures are unavailable, at least 113 women became pursuit qualified, with anecdotal evidence suggesting that the actual number was much higher.[53]

The evaluations of the WASPs did reveal some problems. The most common report was that the women did not share the same level of mechanical aptitude as the men who attended pursuit school. This lack of aptitude is understood to indicate a lack of experience and/or education in working with mechanical equipment. Part of the WASP ground school curriculum included mechanical courses on engines, and the time required in the courses was increased as the training program developed. To compensate for their lack of knowledge and experience with hydraulic and electrical systems, the women simply reported to pursuit classes at the Operational Training Units five days earlier than the men. The extra time appears to have been enough for the women to successfully complete that part of the program.

The postdisbandment evaluations also revealed other problems or deficiencies the bases found or perceived in the WASPs. Half of the FERD bases that returned reports on the WASPs mentioned a lack of physical strength in the women as compared to men. The question was whether the women would be strong enough to handle specific aircraft, particularly four-engine planes, in times of emergency.[54] Considering the massiveness of the four-engine bombers, it is not difficult to understand the division's qualms, but the women themselves proved these concerns to be unnecessary. In reference to the training of Love and Gillies in the B-17, Sally Van Wagenen Keil reported that "the men in the ferrying division transition crew marveled at the skill and stamina of the two women pilots, especially…Gillies who, with cushions behind and under her, could hold the bomber level on a three-engine procedure like any AAF officer twice her size."[55] Other WASPs, not in the FERD, flew four-engine bombers within the United States with great success, proving that the worries of the FERD commanders were unfounded. No other major complaints concerning the WASPs arose from the evaluations.

Positive comments about the WASPs' excellent stamina, vital in a ferry pilot who is often required to fly long distances solo, were consistent throughout the base evaluations of the WASPs. All the reporting bases declared that the personal conduct of the WASPs was excellent. It should be remembered that before the WASP experiment, the military was not certain if women were emotionally grounded enough to fly military aircraft, and the early restrictions of the women's movements were designed to limit their contact with male personnel. These evaluations about the women's conduct prove that these concerns were unnecessary.

Although the WASPs' safety record has already been compared to the men's, it is interesting to note that several of the bases reported that the women's record was comparable to that of men who performed the same duties. These reports support Lt. Col. Estes's argument that the overall accident rates may have contained discrepancies as compared to men, but that this could be accounted for by the different types of aircraft, namely pursuits, that the women flew. One of the final questions addressed by each of the base reports dealt with whether the WASPs could be effectively utilized as pilots in a time of national emergency. The 5th Ferrying Group in Dallas was concerned about the continued flying proficiency of the women after the war, and so questioned the practicality of using them in a time of emergency, but all other bases who reported were very positive about the future utilization of the WASPs. The 552nd AAF Base Unit (2nd Ferrying Group) in Wilmington, Delaware, declared:

> It is the considered opinion of this Headquarters that the WASPs have demonstrated beyond question, the fact that they can be counted upon to successfully complete domestic flying missions during national emergency. Their splendid record and untiring efforts have made them invaluable to this Command.[56]

A consistent theme that ran through all of the base evaluations was that the WASPs should have been militarized, and if utilized again they should immediately be brought into the military. The reasons for militarization included everything from elimination of duplication of authority to increased discipline, improved morale, and government insurance. It is apparent that the bases where the WASPs were stationed believed that the women had fulfilled their duties as ferry pilots safely and efficiently.

In January 1944, the public began to learn of the WASPs' efficiency when several articles appeared that discussed the WASPs in a positive manner. One *New York Times* piece described General Arnold's commendation of the WASPs for doing an "effective job of delivering aircraft in the United States." On the same page an article titled, "Wasps to Be 600 Strong This Month, Hope Soon to be Members of the Army Air Forces," brought to light the desire of the WASP organization to become an official part of the military.[57] Congressional action toward the goal got under way on February 17, 1944, when Representative John Costello of California proposed H.R. 4219, which called for militarization of the WASPs. But controversy surrounded the bill because of two announcements that had been made the previous month.

On January 15, the Civil Aeronautics Administration (CAA) announced that its War Training Service (WTS) program was being eliminated and the AAF announced that the training of pilots by WTS program civilian instructors would be ended on June 30. Apparently losses of airmen in the European theater had been lower than expected, thus new pilots were no longer in high demand. The announcements put thousands of male civilian pilots who had been serving as flight instructors for the CAA and AAF out of work, and ended their deferment from the draft. On February 24, just one week after Costello proposed the WASP bill, another bill was submitted to the House that proposed to commission the out-of-work CAA-WTS pilots. That same day, Representative Robert Ramspeck (Georgia), head of the Civil Service Investigating Committee, began his investigation of the WASPs, prompted by members of the House and Senate and supporters of the male pilots. The issues of the unemployed male pilots and the fate of the WASPs became hopelessly intertwined, and the issues surrounding both became clouded by politics. The WASPs' losing battle for militarization and their eventual disbandment in December 1944, despite a successful record, place them among thousands of American women who were removed from their jobs in favor of men.

In order to understand the battle over the WASPs' militarization and the failure of the attempt to militarize the organization, it is important to understand first who made up the differing sides of the militarization bill and their reasons for supporting or opposing the WASPs. Representative Costello proposed the bill and gained the support of at least 169 fellow Congressmen who voted in favor of the bill's passage. Many undoubtedly supported the bill because the AAF, including General Arnold and Colonel Tunner, strongly supported the WASPs' being brought into the AAF. Originally Tunner envisioned the women working as civilians for a ninety-day trial period, and then being commissioned into the WAC. Problems concerning the women pilots joining the WAC arose with the legislation that created the organization, namely the lack of provisions for flight pay and some discrepancies in admission requirements. The problems prompted Nancy Love to push for acceptance of the women as civilians until something could be worked out at a later date. Love recognized the need for pilots, and wanted the women to have a chance to prove themselves. Jacqueline Cochran agreed that the women pilots should prove themselves useful to the AAF before there was any attempt to militarize them. As a result of this decision, the WASPs' militarization was postponed until 1944. The AAF wanted the women to be made an official part of the service for reasons of discipline and morale, and so the women would receive government insurance and hospitalization benefits.[58]

The WASPs themselves supported militarization for the previously named reasons but also for the respect that came with being a member of the USAAF. Although some women preferred flying as civilians, according to a survey completed by Cochran in early 1944, 94.7 percent of the women wanted to be an official part of the military. Among those who opposed militarization were some women who had children and feared they would be forced to resign, and a few who simply preferred the flexibility of civilian status.[59] The WASPs wore uniforms, received demerits for poor behavior, and lived in barracks. Their lives were everything one envisions when imagining military life. And yet the women had no government insurance in case of injury or death. Of the thirty-eight WASPs who were killed flying for their nation, only Cornelia Fort's family received any benefits; she was the first woman to die, and no policy concerning the women had yet been established.

At some of the bases, friends of the deceased WASPs donated money to ship the women's bodies home to their families. At others, the base commanders sent the bodies home to their families with a WASP escort. These varying practices reveal to what extent the women were at the mercy of the whims of the commanding officers of the bases where they were assigned, a situation that would have been somewhat alleviated with militarization. The women were civilians, and so they were not entitled to the benefits militarization would provide, although they lived the lives and endured the risks of military pilots. For all of the reasons listed above, Jacqueline Cochran pushed hard for WASPs' militarization, and her opponents accused her of desperately wanting to be the highest-ranking woman in the army, particularly over Colonel Oveta Culp Hobby, head of the WAC.[60]

The opponents of WASPs' militarization were many, including at least 128 congressmen who voted against the WASPs bill. The congressmen were pressured to vote against the bill by the unemployed CAA-WTS pilots. On losing their jobs, the male civilian pilots lost their draft deferments, and there was no guarantee that their absorption into the AAF would be automatic. With the invasion of Europe and a planned later invasion of Japan, the likelihood of the healthy men of the group being drafted into the army was high. The argument that these men were skilled pilots and that it was a waste of taxpayer money to train more women as military pilots when they were available had some merit, although the total dissolution of the women's program wasted taxpayer money, too. The CAA-WTS pilots recruited the American Legion and much of the press to promote their cause.

It is clear that the male pilots opposed militarization of the WASPs because of their own unemployment and possible induction into the army, and the congressmen were likely influenced by the intense lobbying of the men and their supporters. The shift of the press from lauding the role of the WASPs in the war effort to accusing them of stealing men's jobs can be tied to the exaggerated claims made in the House against the WASPs and the general trend that was beginning in the nation to push American women out of nontraditional jobs and back into the home. The battle for passage of the Costello bill to militarize the WASPs may have been one of the first signs of the struggle American women would face to retain the progress they had made during the war.

The battle for militarization of the WASPs began on March 22, 1944. General Henry Arnold, who advocated bringing the WASPs into the AAF, was the only witness to testify before the House Committee on Military Affairs, which conducted hearings concerning the WASP bill. Arnold began his statement to the committee with the observation that "right at this moment the Army is short over 200,000 men. . . ." He continued to discuss the manpower shortage and how utilizing women was the best way to relieve the problem. Arnold explained what duties the WASPs were carrying out and boasted about their abilities as pilots. He went on to describe why the WASPs could not be a part of the already established WAC. Many of the WASPs were younger than the WAC entrance requirement of twenty years old (the WASP minimum age requirement had been lowered to eighteen), and several of the pilots violated the WAC regulation against having children under the age of fourteen. Arnold declared the women needed to be admitted to the AAF because as civilians the women did not have the insurance and death benefits that were their due.[61]

The remainder of the hearing was devoted to Arnold's explanation of why the male former CAA instructors were not being automatically admitted into the AAF. Arnold described how the men who were qualified were being accepted as pilots, bombardiers, navigators, or as ferry pilots in the ATC.

> If they cannot qualify according to our standards in one of these capacities then we offer them other training in the Army Air Forces. We cannot lower our

standards because a man has had a few hours in the air. They must meet our standards.[62]

The majority of men Arnold said the AAF was trying to find jobs for were a part of the AAF Reserve. As for the other men, Arnold bluntly stated, "we don't consider we owe them anything because they were offered a chance to join the Reserve and did not take advantage of it. And now when they see they are likely to be drafted they want to come in and it is too late."[63] General Arnold's obvious disgust reveals his attitude toward the former civilian instructors who, as he saw it, were not willing to make any commitment to the AAF when they had nothing to gain for it, and then, in order to avoid being drafted into the army, pleaded to become a part of the AAF. He had not been supportive of the CAA-WTS program while it was active, and he certainly did not support the civilian instructors after they had become unemployed. In response to the male CAA pilots' accusations that the women's qualifications were lower than the men's qualifications, the Military Affairs Committee asked Arnold questions concerning the WASPs' standards and training as compared to those of male pilots. Satisfied with Arnold's explanation of the equality of requirements, the Committee voted to recommend the passage of the WASP bill, H.R. 4219.

Jacqueline Cochran silently sat next to General Arnold during his testimony to the Military Affairs Committee. She did not speak out in support of the WASPs and ordered the women to refrain from writing their congressmen and from landing their planes in Washington to avoid publicity. Cochran believed that with only the respected and admired General Arnold speaking out in favor of the WASPs' militarization, the women would not appear "pushy," thus reflecting attitudes about women in the 1940s.[64] A group of women asking for what they wanted and rightly deserved could have easily been perceived as too aggressive and unfeminine, and Cochran hoped to avoid that image.

Although the WASPs themselves did not write to their congressmen on their own behalf, some did encourage their families to write. The FERD was not vocal in expressing its need for the women pilots either, based on a War Department decision to halt all publicity concerning the WASPs because of the misrepresentation of the women's actions by the out-of-work male pilots and their supporters. Also at the time the WASPs' advocate Colonel William Tunner was commanding the airlift over the Himalayas when the WASPs disbandment was announced and was thus unable to defend the women.[65] The decision to have the WASPs' militarization depend entirely on the prestige of General Arnold, who up to this point had not been refused any requests from Congress, was fatal for the WASP bill.

On March 25, the *New York Times* reported that Representative Charles Halleck of Indiana had raised the question of whether the women even wanted to join the AAF. He pointed out that none of the women themselves had come be-fore the House declaring their desire to do so.[66] This question was undoubtedly also on the minds of other congressmen, and the WASPs' silence did not ease their doubts. The congressional proponents of the bill did not organize as they could have and probably would have if support for the bill had been louder and more demanding. The cautious approach was a sign of the times concerning women in a traditionally male role; it was a continuous thread throughout the experiment of women pilots. In early May, Secretary of War Stimson came out in favor of the WASPs and defended their work by declaring that "neither the existence nor the militarization of the Wasp will keep out of the Army Air Forces a single instructor or partially trained civilian pilot who desires to become a ser-vice pilot or cadet and can meet the applicable standards of the Army Air Forces."[67] Despite Stimson's assurances, the WASPs' opponents seized on the bill and utilized the sympathies of the press and the traditional bias against women in nontraditional roles and quashed the AAF's plans for the WASPs' militarization.

The male CAA pilots intensified their fight for their own utilization as pilots and against the WASPs in April 1944. The disgruntled pilots inundated their congressmen with letters and visits protesting their loss of deferment status and especially objecting to the use of women pilots when the men were available. The congressmen responded to the male pilots' pleas, many fervently supporting the men at the expense of the WASPs. Throughout the months of April, May, and June 1944, several members of Congress publicly questioned the necessity and quality of the women pilots. The question of the authorization for the money spent on the WASP program also was a sore point for a Congress, whose author-ity had been weakened by strong presidential leadership during a depression and a world war. Several congressmen extended their comments against the WASPs in the appendices to the *Congressional Record,* with some even including negative comments from the press. Some of the comments put forth legitimate concerns, while others were thinly veiled or openly biased attacks.

On April 25, Representative James Morrison of Louisiana showed concern for the unemployed male pilots and for the potential cost of training more women. "Why release male pilots who have been trained at great cost and with great expenditure in time and effort from pilot duties," he asked, "just so women can be trained, while receiving salaries of $150 per month, to replace them?" Morrison continued by quoting an article in the February 1944 issue of *American Aviation,* stating that although it was understandable that the women wanted to fly, they simply were not as "suitable" for the job as men and that everyone, in-cluding the AAF, knew it.[68] As has been shown, these accusations against the women's abilities as compared to men's were unfounded and untrue. The atti-tude that the women could not possibly be as capable in the cockpit of military aircraft as were men was prevalent in many of the WASPs' opponents' comments.

Some of the articles submitted to the appendices of the *Congressional Record* were vicious in their degradation of the WASPs. A May 1944 article in the *Idaho Statesman* speculated that the women were allowed to fly because of the "sentimental softness of American men in regard to their women." The article crassly continued, "in colleges the smooth, good-looking gals can get A's without a lick of work; and in the armed services it may be that dimples have a devastating effect even on the generals."[69] Insults of this type continued in Congress and the media throughout the battle for militarization. In early June, Austine Cassini wrote an article in the *Washington Times-Herald* entitled "These Charming People." Describing Cochran as a "shapely pilot" and "an attractive composition of wind-blown bob, smiling eyes and outdoor skin," Cassini accused General Arnold of gazing into Cochran's eyes and taking "her cause celebre very much 'to heart.'" Cassini snidely concluded,

> It's whispered he's battling like a knight of olde, or olde knight, for "the faire Cochran." So the announcement can be expected any day that Jackie's commission has been approved, if the captivated general is victorious in his tournaments.[70]

These articles are only a few examples of the biased and often vicious attacks the WASPs faced in their struggle to be recognized by Congress as part of the AAF.

The negative image the WASPs' opponents were using to portray the women was consistent with the conflicting images for women of the period. "Rosie the Riveter" was hailed as a heroine early in the war, but the shift in advertisements and articles toward pushing the women back into the home and a return to femininity and family, mentioned earlier in discussion of Maureen Honey's work, had already begun by the time of the WASPs' struggle. WASPs themselves presented conflicting images. Cornelia Fort has already been cited as having been frustrated by the contradictions between the notions that, while the women were performing a glamorous job, they were expected to keep their image nonthreatening. Jacqueline Cochran, even when she was competing in air races, would always pause to fix her hair and reapply her lipstick before climbing out of the cockpit to greet reporters. She expected her WASPs to be ladies at all times. The July 19, 1943, issue of *Life* magazine had WASP Shirley Slade on its cover, braided pigtails and all.[71] The image of these "girl" pilots was one of young adventurers, playing in a man's world, rather than as serious pilots doing a serious job. With attitudes such as these already prominent, it was easier for the uneducated or blatantly biased to attack the women as unnecessary, wasteful, and underqualified for the "man's job" of military pilot.

Not only did the WASPs face negative press and the false image as glamorous adventurers. On June 5, 1944, the Ramspeck Committee released the report they had been working on since the previous February. The Ramspeck Committee, formally the House Committee on the Civil Service, was utilized to help Civil Service agencies make the most of their funding and to find any abuses within the agencies. The committee made clear early in the report that its investigation of the WASPs was "not a question of the utilization of male or female personnel, but it is a question of the utilization of experience and capabilities before resorting to the use of inexperience and costly training."[72] In other words, the committee did not intend the report to be an attack against the women but, rather, an attack against wasteful spending and an argument for the most efficient utilization of personnel.

Despite the reassurance, the overall theme of the report was negative in nature. Early on, it declared:

> The implication contained in the proposal [the WASP bill], that it is now either necessary or desirable to recruit stenographers, clerks, school teachers, housewives, factory workers, and other inexperienced personnel for training at great outlay of public funds as pilots for the military planes of this Government, particularly when there already exists a surplus of personnel to perform these identical duties, is as startling as it is invalid.[73]

The reference to the "surplus of personnel" is only one of the many references to the unemployed male pilots who had been flooding Congress with letters describing their plight. The report speculated about the problems of the probable postwar surplus of pilots and noted that any additional training of pilots would only "add another surplus to this recognized post-war surplus." That the committee would even address such a concern is evidence that attitudes were shifting toward postwar worries as the Allies pushed toward Berlin.[74]

The Ramspeck report addressed the high cost of training the women and pointed out what the committee saw as questionable authorization for the original training program, namely, no specific authorization from Congress for the expense of the women's training program. The War Department justified its authority for the experiment of women pilots as part of a 1943 act allowing expenditures for the training of civilian employees. The complaints concerning proper authorization for money spent on the women's program may have added to the negative feelings already generated in Congress about the WASPs. For most of the 1930s and early 1940s, the Congress had allowed its authority to be diminished by the president and the military as a result of the back-to-back emergencies of the Great Depression and World War II. By mid-1944, Congress was beginning to reassert itself and its role in the government. The fact that the AAF had not specifically asked for funding for its experiment with the women placed additional doubt on the legitimacy of their claim for military status.

The Ramspeck report briefly described the cost of training the women and compared the fatality and accident rate of male and female pilots. The remainder of the report was dedicated to the male civilian instructors and whether they were being treated unfairly and how they could be effectively utilized. The committee completed the report with some basic conclusions and recommendations. They argued that there was no justification for the expansion of the WASP program and suggested that further recruitment and training be ended. Significantly, they recommended that "the use of the WASPs already trained and in training be continued and provision be made for hospitalization and insurance." Finally, they turned again to the surplus male pilots and proposed that they be immediately utilized.[75]

Although the opponents of the WASP bill embraced the Ramspeck report, the WASPs' supporters struggled to disprove it. Representative Costello, the author of the bill, tried to refute the report just days after its release in a speech to the House. "The most astounding part of this report," Costello responded, "is the assumption that there does exist a vast pool of well-trained pilots ready to serve the Army Air Forces at a moment's notice. This is an error which I would like to correct now." Costello addressed the Ramspeck report's concerns about the unemployed male pilots and revealed that many of the men were unable to pass the AAF class 2 physical examination, as required of male ferry pilots. He then disproved the WASPs' opponents' contentions that the women were not physically qualified to fly military aircraft and that the male pilots were being discriminated against in favor of the women. "If there has been any discrimination at all it, in my opinion, has certainly been discrimination in favor of these pilot instructors," Costello insisted. "It is apparently not understood that every girl trainee must pass a physical examination in every way equal to that of a combat pilot."[76]

Finally, Costello cited the eleven thousand aircraft that had been used in the invasion in Europe on D-Day less than a week earlier. He admitted that he did not know how many replacements would be needed as a result of the air war over Europe, but asserted his certainty that the men in charge were more qualified in determining the need for pilots than were members of Congress. He concluded his arguments with a reminder that the head of the AAF, General Arnold himself, had requested the passage of the WASP bill. Despite Costello's and a few others' efforts, the WASPs' official inclusion into the AAF was not to be. On June 21, 1944, after extensive debate on the House floor, the enacting clause of the WASP bill was stricken by a roll call vote of 188 to 169, with 73 members abstaining. The failure of H.R. 4219 meant that the training program would be ended, although those already in training would graduate, and the women already on active duty would remain so.[77]

This is the point at which this study's analysis of the end of the WASP program diverges from Molly Merryman's *Clipped Wings*. Merryman approaches the disbandment by intersecting her study with "theories of feminist history to reveal a pattern in which cultural gender constructions were forcefully maintained because of erosions that were occurring as women substantially increased their roles in the work force and the military."[78] By utilizing this method, Merryman takes one aspect of the WASPs' disbandment, that is, the prejudice and fear generated by women fulfilling traditional men's roles and the drive to return women to the home, and excludes other important factors. Although her arguments about the gender-biased views of American society are for the most part accurate, she misses or dismisses pivotal factors that complete the picture.

To some extent, Jacqueline Cochran, Director of the WASPs, can be held responsible for the dissolution of the women's program. Cochran's determination to have events go her way or not at all had already gained her some enemies. Cochran knew what she did and did not want for her women pilots. Her thoughts on the WASPs being made a part of the WAC, an idea considered by the FERD and AAF both before and after the failure of the WASP bill, were very clear. Cochran strongly disliked Colonel Oveta Culp Hobby, the head of the WAC, and refused to even consider the WASPs becoming a part of that organization. Some have accused Cochran of being jealous of Hobby's position and of not being willing to be subordinate to another woman, and they may not be completely mistaken. In her autobiography, Cochran described her confrontation with Hobby when General Arnold first suggested that the WASPs become part of the WAC. She wrote that "if she [Hobby] didn't understand airplanes or the kind of women who flew them, then she had no business being their commanding officer. It was my job and I wanted to keep it. I just couldn't see throwing my girls in with that bunch." Cochran explained the failure of the WASP bill as follows:

> I lost the battle for militarization of the WASPs in Congress in the summer of 1944 and I believe I lost because of *Mrs.* Hobby [Cochran's italics] and her powers. But, looking back at the outcry of telegrams from congressmen who voted against us, I don't think they all knew what they were voting away.[79]

Cochran's apparent unwillingness to work with Colonel Hobby as her immediate superior is not the only evidence suggesting she played a part in the WASPs' disbandment. Cochran's personality was such that if she could not have complete charge of a situation, she simply turned against it. The ATC, apparently convinced that this was true, stated in one memorandum that she [Cochran] was "determined to take the WASP program down with her if she is turned down in her efforts to militarize the WASPs."[80] Support for this theory concerning Cochran's character is evidenced by events later in her life, particularly Cochran's dealings with the women's astronaut program in the early 1960s.

As Margaret Weitekamp argues in a forthcoming study of the women astronaut trainees of 1959 to 1963, "in aerospace, as in aviation, Jackie would help to advance women, but never at the expense of her own recognition." She continues,

> Cochran's actions also illustrate one way that a powerful woman negotiated the masculine world of aviation. Susan Ware has written about Amelia Earhart, Cochran's friend and contemporary, as an early feminist. Cochran does not fit that mold. One could almost say that Jackie Cochran aspired to be a good old boy. She excelled at using personal, professional, and financial connections to create her opportunities.[81]

Weitekamp's analysis of Cochran some fifteen years after the end of the WASP program supports the suggestion that personal ambition was a motivator, and that Cochran must be considered when evaluating why the WASPs were disbanded. Even with Cochran's potential role in the WASPs' disbandment, there were other factors at work.

The AAF's decision to terminate the WASP program in December 1944 appears to be a total reversal of its position earlier in the year. While advocating the WASPs' militarization, General Arnold contended that he desperately needed more women pilots and yet, by October 3, 1944, he announced that the WASPs would be disbanded in December. One major factor that influenced the decision to end the WASP experiment was the apparent shift in the tide of the war. In August 1944, Paris was liberated, and by October American B-29s were bombing Japan. The Battle of the Bulge had not yet begun, and the level of emergency that had existed when Arnold had gone before the House Committee on Military Affairs the previous March no longer seemed as intense. The projected losses of men in Europe had not occurred and so the need for women to replace male pilots to release them for other duties no longer made sense.

In his book *Global Mission,* written shortly after the war, Arnold said, "the WASPs did a magnificent job for the Army Air Forces in every way." He explained the disbandment as a result of a movement in Congress, "obviously backed by male pilot organizations." Despite his obvious support for the WASPs, Arnold does seem to be sidestepping responsibility here. When the prospect of a second battle for the WASPs arose in the Senate in the fall of 1944, Arnold was not willing to stand up and fight for the WASPs again. A letter from Arnold to Cochran, dated October 1, 1944, reveals why his support for the WASPs' militarization had waned. Arnold begins the letter by explaining that "the reduction in the flying training program and the changing war situation's bearing on the availability of pilots make it evident that the WASP will soon become pilot material in excess of needs." He continues by praising the women for their valuable performance of duties but reminds Cochran that the women "are serving, however, to release male pilots for other work and not to replace them," and announces "the time has arrived to plan the program's deactivation." This letter is strong evidence that the shift in the tide of the war in favor of the Allies was an important factor in the WASPs' disbandment. It also supports the contention that women's wartime roles were always considered to be temporary, at least by those who were in charge of delegating those responsibilities.[82]

Earlier, in August 1944, Jacqueline Cochran submitted a report to General Arnold as the WASPs neared their second anniversary. She reviewed the purposes of the WASPs, explained the training program, and described the duties the women were carrying out and their effectiveness at carrying out those duties. Cochran also revealed her surprising view on the permanence of women in the AAF, writing, "certain it is that the WASPs will have no useful place with the AAF when the male pilots who wish to remain in service are sufficient in number to perform all the duties." In addition to this revelation that she did not believe women should retain a permanent role as pilots in the AAF, the final point in Cochran's report was considered by some as an ultimatum on militarization. Cochran declared that "serious consideration should be given to inactivation if militarization is not soon authorized. If such action should be taken, an effort should be made to obtain military status, if only for one day, and resulting veterans' recognition of all who have served commendably."[83]

There is no evidence to suggest that Cochran was insincere in her efforts to gain military status for the WASPs. In addition to her personality traits as discussed earlier, her apparently conflicting positions concerning women replacing men were consistent with the times and the propaganda of the period to encourage women back into the home once the emergency of the war had ended. While fears of a postwar depression gnawed at the American public, government and business responded with propaganda campaigns calling for male war veterans to return to work. In addition, federal agencies and corporations released women from jobs to make room for the returning men. The thought that women were *replacing* male pilots, rather than *releasing* them for more important duties, was as unacceptable as the idea of women retaining their positions in factories while men remained unemployed. The WASPs were among the first of tens of thousands of American women who were thanked for a job well done, given a paternalistic pat on the head, and sent home.

One final factor in why the AAF did not follow the advice of the Ramspeck report and retain the women who had already been trained is hinted at in a May 1944 letter cited from General Arnold's office. The letter, addressed to Congressman Andrew J. May of Kentucky, Chairman of the House Committee on

Military Affairs, explains the goals of the WASP program and the AAF's desire to have the WASPs militarized. One of the primary reasons the program was created, in addition to releasing men for combat duty, was to "determine the manner and extent that women pilots can be effectively used in the Army Air Forces," for any future need. The fact that the WASP program was an experiment was not hidden and is of no surprise. Of great importance in this document is the AAF's second point: "If we are going to test the project completely and fully we must have enough WASP so that the groups allocated to various phases of non-combat service will be large enough for us to reach definite conclusions. Without the enlargement of the present WASP training program, we will have the numbers necessary early in 1945."[84] The WASPs were disbanded on December 20, 1944. Could the main reason for the end of their program have been simply because the AAF had enough data to analyze the experiment of women military pilots? It is probable that this was just one of many factors in the decision to terminate the program, but it cannot be entirely dismissed.

On the announcement that the WASPs were to be disbanded, the FERD began to take steps to hire the women on an individual basis, just as they did male civilian pilots. The official history explains this by maintaining that "the Ferrying Division did not want to lose a corps of pilots who were rendering an extremely useful service." The FERD was still busy ferrying aircraft and could not afford to lose pilots, particularly those qualified to fly pursuit aircraft, regardless of their sex. Arnold quickly quashed the FERD attempt to hire the women individually by declaring that "there will be no repeat no women pilots in any capacity in the Air Force after December twenty." Despite his assertion that the women were effective pilots, and despite the intensity of the Battle of the Bulge that had begun in December, General Arnold refused to allow the FERD to retain the WASPs in any capacity. Men were available to take the WASPs' positions, aircraft production had slowed somewhat, and public opinion called for women to return home.[85]

Even Cochran did not advocate retaining the women. In her final report, Cochran explained her belief that "all WASP should either stay or, to avoid preference as between commands or individual WASPs, go out of the service altogether." Her detractors would be quick to point out that if the WASPs had been retained in the FERD, Cochran would have had no authority over them. First, the FERD wanted to hire the women as civilians, just as it did men pilots, thereby having the women answer directly to the FERD commanders. Second, Jacqueline Cochran was Director of Women Pilots, but Nancy Love was the Executive of Women Pilots in the ATC. If the women had retained some sort of organization while flying for the FERD, a part of the ATC, they would have had to answer to Love. Cochran would have been completely out of power. Whether this was a factor in her decision to advocate the end to women flying for the AAF is pure conjecture. Such a hypothesis, however, does support Margaret Weit-ekamp's argument that Cochran would not support women in aviation if she could not be recognized, and it is worth considering.[86]

Cochran confirmed that the WASPs should be inactivated following her late summer 1944 inspection trip to more than fifty bases where the WASPs were on duty. With the loss of the women in December 1944, the FERD was forced to borrow 161 pilots from other branches of the Air Force to make up for their ab-sence. The majority of the men were not qualified to fly pursuits and had to be trained, creating a backlog of aircraft at the factories. Many of the women saw the problems the FERD would face on their dismissal and a number of them volunteered their services on a dollar-a-year basis until they were no longer needed. Their offer was refused.[87] Their disappointment is well represented by one of the WASPs from the 6th Ferrying Group who wrote to the command at her base that

> It is unfortunate that a group so highly trained and skilled can no longer use that skill for the benefit of the Air Forces. With the war still far from over and a very apparent need for trained pilots I personally feel guilty about returning to civil-ian life where my training can be of no further use in helping to win the war.[88]

Despite the continuing need for the women in the FERD, the WASPs were officially disbanded on December 20, 1944. Cochran reacted to the disbandment in a businesslike manner, writing a fifty-three-page report for General Arnold, analyzing the great experiment of women pilots. At the December 7, 1944, grad-uation of the "lost last class," class 44-10, General Arnold spoke favorably of the WASPs. Only thirteen days before their deactivation, Arnold reassured the women that thanks to their efforts the experiment had been a success, and he de-clared the AAF's debt to them.[89] It is clear that Arnold was right, the experiment was a success.

By flying for the AAF, the women released more than one thousand men for duty elsewhere in the war effort. In addition to releasing men, the duties the WASPs carried out were significant in themselves. Within the FERD the WASPs delivered 12,652 aircraft, flying a distance of some 9,227,261 miles, and they flew more than 89,000 hours.[90] The WASPs in other parts of the AAF also carried out important responsibilities. The short-term accomplishments of re-lieving men for duty and of efficiently ferrying and training men for a variety of roles prove that the WASPs were effective pilots and important to the war ef-fort.

The WASPs also had more long-term significance. One of the original pur-poses of the women's pilot program was to discover if women could be effec-tively used as pilots in case of national emergency. The WASPs vigorously proved that they could be counted on. Their accident rate was comparable to male pilots doing the same types of flying, and their training proved that women were not too soft or too high-strung to be successfully trained in a military environment. The WASPs proved that women were capable of flying the heaviest, fastest, and most sophisticated aircraft of the day. They were aware of the precedent they were setting and were serious about doing the job professionally.

Also, the WASPs realized that they were breaking ground and that their efforts would one day be looked on as evidence of women's ability or inability to fly military aircraft. Dean Jaros is correct that today's women earned their places on their own, without direct benefit from the earlier women pilots, but that does not mean they have not learned from their predecessors nor that their forerunners did not leave a legacy.[91] Despite the delay in recognizing the WASPs' accomplishments, the fact that both modern women pilots and the WASPs recognize the link is enough to prove that the earlier women were significant. In 1978, Congress acknowledged the significance of the WASPs by finally recognizing them as veterans and granting them limited benefits. Today the women of the WASPs talk about their wartime exploits and grin, happy to have done their part for the war effort and to have carried out a successful experiment.

Notes

1. Cornelia Fort, "At Twilight's Last Gleaming," *The 99 News,* November 1985, 13. Originally published in *Woman's Home Companion,* July 1943, 19.

2. Dean Jaros, *Heroes Without Legacy: American Airwomen, 1912–1944* (Niwot: University Press of Colorado, 1993).

3. The women were organized by class, designated by the year they were to graduate and the order in which they would graduate. For example, the first class was 43-W-1 because they were the first class to graduate in 1943. The "W" designates that they were women. It will be left out in this study, as this is obvious.

4. William Henry Chafe, *The American Woman: Her Changing Social, Economic and Political Roles, 1920–1979* (New York: Oxford University Press, 1972), 176.

5. Leila Rupp, *Mobilizing Women for War: German and American Propaganda, 1939–1945* (Princeton: Princeton University Press, 1978), 175.

6. D'Ann Campbell, *Women at War with America: Private Lives in a Patriotic Era* (Cambridge, Mass.: Harvard University Press, 1984), 14.

7. Maureen Honey, *Creating Rosie the Riveter: Class, Gender, and Propaganda during World War II* (Amherst: University of Massachusetts Press, 1984), 2.

8. Ibid., 216.

9. Doris Weatherford, *American Women and World War II* (New York: Facts on File, 1991), 16.

10. Sally VanWagenen Keil, *Those Wonderful Women in Their Flying Machines: The Unknown Heroines of World War II* (New York: Four Directions Press, 1979); Molly Merryman, *Clipped Wings: The Rise and Fall of the Women Airforce Service Pilots (WASPs) of World War II* (New York: New York University Press, 1998).

11. CWO J. Merton England, AAF Historical Office, Headquarters, *Army Air Forces,*

Army Air Forces Historical Studies, No. 55: Women Pilots With the AAF, 1941–1944 (publisher unknown, 1946); Captain Walter J. Marx, Ferrying Division Historical Officer, Historical Branch, Intelligence and Security Division, Headquarters, Air Transport Command, *History of the Air Transport Command: Women Pilots in the Air Transport Command* (publisher unknown, March 1945), Yvonne Pateman Collection, United States Air Force Academy, MS 31, Microfilm roll no. 8, A3003.

12. Deborah Douglas, *United States Women in Aviation, 1940–1985* (Washington, D.C.: Smithsonian Institution Press, 1991), 42.

13. Keil, *Those Wonderful Women,* 51.

14. Jan Churchill, *On Wings to War: Teresa James, Aviator* (Manhattan, Kans.: Sunflower University Press, 1992), 44.

15. Fort, "Twilight," 13.

16. Telegram on August 12, 1943, from Headquarters, FERD, ATC to 2nd Ferrying Group, Newcastle AAB, Delaware, directing a blackout on publicity on women pilots.

17. Marx, *ATC History,* 30–31.

18. Keil, *Those Wonderful Women,* 45.

19. England, AAF No. 55, 39.

20. Ibid., 39; Keil, *Those Wonderful Women,* 242.

21. Marx, *ATC History,* 74.

22. Adela Riek Scharr, *Sisters in the Sky: Volume I—The WAFS* (St. Louis, Mo.: The Patrice Press, 1986), 349.

23. Louise Bowden Brown, questionnaire, June 23, 1996, in author's possession.

24. England, AAF No. 55, 40.

25. Marx, *ATC History,* 85–86.

26. Ibid., 86.

27. "Coup for Cochran," *Newsweek,* July 19, 1943, 40–42.

28. Douglas, *United States Women,* 28.

29. Jacqueline Cochran Odlum, *The Stars at Noon* (Boston: Little, Brown, 1954).

30. Martha Wagenseil, Oral history. Texas Woman's University's WASP Collection, Denton, Texas. MSS 265, Box 10, Byrd Granger Collection.

31. Keil, *Those Wonderful Women,* 245–46.

32. Marx, *ATC History,* 158.

33. Ibid., 159; Rob Simbeck, author of *The Daughter of the Air: The Short Soaring Life of Cornelia Fort* (New York: Atlantic Monthly Press, 1999), telephone interview with author, January 29, 1997.

34. Margaret Ray Ringenberg, WASP Class 43-5, interview with author, July 20, 1996, Dayton, Ohio, tape recording.

35. Tex Brown Meachem, WASP Class 43-7, interview with author, October 3, 1996, Anaheim, California, tape recording.

36. Fort, "Twilight," 13.

37. Marx, *ATC History,* 120.

38. Ibid., 126.

39. Ibid., 128–29.

40. Ibid., appendix 1, 13; ibid., appendix 1, 17–18.

41. Ibid., 157.

42. Ibid., appendix 1, 13; ibid., 155; Lt. Col. Murl Estes, Deputy Chief of Flying Safety. Confidential letter dated April 15, 1944, National Archives, Record Group 18, Entry 54 A, Box 25.

43. Gabrielle Marie Everett, *The Women Airforce Service Pilots: A Comparative Analysis of Class 43-W-1 and 44-W-10* (Master's thesis, Arkansas State University, 1995), 43, 45, 69, 71.

44. Marx, *ATC History*, 147.

45. Jacqueline Cochran, Report on Women Airforce Service Pilots, August 1, 1944.

46. "Typist Flew to Our Defense," *Ft. Worth Star Telegram*, August 9, 1988, part 2, section 1.

47. Marx, *ATC History*, 125.

48. Marion Hodgson, WASP class 43-5, questionnaire, November 5, 1996, in author's possession.

49. Margaret Chamberlain Tamplin, WASP class 44-3, questionnaire, October 10, 1996, in author's possession.

50. Mary Edith Engle, WASP class 43-4, questionnaire, August 25, 1996, in author's possession.

51. Lillian Epsberg Goodman, WASP class 43-5, questionnaire, June 1996, in author's possession.

52. Marx, *ATC History*, 143–44.

53. Ibid., 146.

54. Ibid., appendix 2, 170.

55. Keil, *Those Wonderful Women*, 246.

56. Marx, *ATC History*, appendix 2, 170.

57. "Arnold Hails WAC on Air Force Duty," and "WASPs to Be 600 Strong This Month, Hope Soon to Be Members of the Army Air Forces," *New York Times*, January 4, 1944, 14.

58. Deborah Douglas, "WASPs of War," Texas Woman's University's WASP Collection, Denton, Texas, WASP Bio-Files; Cochran, *Final Report*, 45.

59. Keil, *Those Wonderful Women*, 300.

60. U.S. Congress. House. *Appendix to the Congressional Record*, 78th Congress, 2nd Session, 1944 (Washington, D.C.: U.S. Government Printing Office, 1944), 3561.

61. U.S. Congress. House. *Hearings Before the Committee On Military Affairs;* on H.R. 4219, 78th Congress, 2nd Session, March 22, 1944 (Washington, D.C.: U.S. Government Printing Office, 1944), 2–4.

62. Ibid., 5.

63. Ibid., 8.

64. Keil, *Those Wonderful Women*, 300.

65. "WASP Special to Couple," *Panorama*, July 9, 1978, 15.

66. "WASP Bill Strikes a Committee Snag," *New York Times*, March 25, 1944, 19.

67. "Wasp Militarization Favored by Stimson," *New York Times*, May 5, 1944, 2.

68. House, *Appendix*, 1970–71.

69. Ibid., 2879.

70. Ibid., 3093.

71. "Girl Pilots," *Life*, July 19, 1943, 73–81.

72. House, *Appendix*, 3059.

73. Ibid., 3058.

74. Ibid., 3059.

75. Ibid., 2937.

76. Ibid., 2937–38.

77. Ibid., 2938.

78. Merryman, *Clipped Wings*, 174.

79. Jacqueline Cochran and Maryann Bucknum Brinley, *Jackie Cochran: The Autobiography of the Greatest Woman Pilot in Aviation History* (Toronto: Bantam Books, 1987), 207, 214.

80. Deborah Douglas, "WASPs of War," *Aviation History,* January 1999.

81. Margaret Weitekamp, "The Aviatrix and the 'Astronauttes': Jacqueline Cochran and the First Lady Astronaut Trainees," paper presented at the National Aerospace Conference, Dayton, Ohio. The title of Weitekamp's dissertation is "The Right Stuff, The Wrong Sex: The Science, Politics and Culture of the First Lady Astronaut Trainees, 1959–1963," for the Cornell History Department, under the direction of Richard Polenberg.

82. Henry "Hap" Arnold, *Global Mission* (New York: Harper Bros., 1949), 358; Gen. H. H. Arnold, letter to Jacqueline Cochrane, Director of Women Pilots, October 1, 1944, Arnold Papers, Library of Congress, Manuscript Division, Container 294, Reel 205.

83. Jacqueline Cochran, "Report on Women Airforce Service Pilots," August 1, 1944, 10–11.

84. AAF letter to Honorable Andrew J. May, House of Representatives, May 2, 1944. At National Archives, Record Group 18, Entry 54A, Box 25. Declassified: NND 770089.

85. Marx, *ATC History,* 167.

86. Jacqueline Cochran, *Final Report on Women Pilot Program,* 1945, 48, located in Byrd Granger Collection, Box 4, WASP Collection, Texas Woman's University, Denton, Texas.

87. Marx, *ATC History,* 169.

88. Ibid., 170.

89. General Henry "Hap" Arnold, "Address to Last WASP Class 44/10," December 7, 1944.

90. Marx, *ATC History,* appendix 1–2, 3, 4.

91. Jaros, *Heroes Without Legacy,* 217.

THE AIRPLANE
Perceptions of the Landscape, Literature, and Art

"The Surly Bonds of Earth"

Images of the Landscape in the Work of Some Aviator/Authors, 1910–1969

Tom D. Crouch

At precisely 5:52 on the afternoon of July 2, 1939, Charles Augustus Lindbergh lifted a U.S. Army Air Corps P-36A off a runway at Denver, Colorado, and headed west toward Salt Lake City. He had returned to America from an extended stay in Europe on April 14. Four days later he had accepted General Henry H. "Hap" Arnold's invitation to go on active duty as a colonel in the Air Corps. Since that time, his military duties, and his consulting work for the National Advisory Committee for Aeronautics and the Guggenheim and Rockefeller Foundations, had kept him constantly on the move.

Over the past two and a half months he had repeatedly driven, taken the train, or flown to Washington from his home on Long Island. He had flown to Dayton twice, and made round-trip solo flights to Buffalo, Indianapolis, and Kansas City. Between May 1 and May 13, he made a solo, coast-to-coast flight with stops in Dayton; St. Louis; Marshall, Kansas; Albuquerque; Winslow, Arizona; March Field, California; San Diego; Los Angeles; Tucson; Roswell, New Mexico; Midland, Texas; and Charlotte, North Carolina.

Climbing away from the Denver airport on that July afternoon, Lindbergh was setting out on the sixth leg of yet another transcontinental solo flight. He had a great deal on his mind. At each stop he had encountered "the usual press nuisance." Newsmen had been an inescapable and unwelcome presence in his life since he had soloed the Atlantic in May 1927. Angered by the constant harassment of reporters and photographers during the long months of horror following the kidnapping and murder of his son in 1932, he had moved his family to Europe in 1936, following the execution of Richard Bruno Hauptmann for the crime.

Since his return, however, he had begun to make use of the press to publicize his opinions on the international situation. He had seen German military might at first hand, and had been impressed. Convinced that "British and Jewish interests" would attempt to draw the United States into any future conflict with the fascist powers, Lindbergh was increasingly determined to do what he could to maintain American neutrality. It would not, he knew, be an easy fight.

Aviation dramatically changed perceptions of the landscape, and flying high above it often gave pilots a view of the earth that was unique. Charles Lindbergh, for example, made archaeological ex-
plorations from the air. "Under certain angles of light," he explained, "old ruins can be seen from
an airplane, but you might walk across them on the ground without knowing they existed. Walls,
rain-washed to the level of the earth, may appear as criss-cross lines to the aviators eye, and
changed shades of vegetation show where people dug pits and dumped their refuse a thousand
years ago." Here, for the time, is a rare view of Antarctica taken on one of Richard Byrd's aerial expeditions of the South Pole. (Courtesy National Air and Space Museum, Smithsonian Institution
[SI 76-17139].)

As always, however, he left those problems behind him as he climbed into
the sky. "The high peaks are so close to Denver," he would report in his diary
that evening, "that I had to climb the plane almost at its maximum rate to get
over them without circling."

> I climbed . . . and rode on top like a god—the cloud strewn sky, the white-capped
> peaks, the rain-filled valleys, mine. I owned the world that hour I rode over it,
> cutting through my sky, laughing proudly down on my mountains, so small, so
> beautiful, so formidable, I could dive at a peak; I could touch a cloud; I could
> climb far above them all.

In the air, Charles Lindbergh was free. Yet he knew that flight represented nothing more than a breathing space, a temporary respite from the troubles of the world. He had no desire for a complete escape.

> This hour was mine, free of the earth, free of the mountains, free of the clouds—yet how inseparably I was bound to them, how void my space would be if they were gone. Everything—life, love, happiness—all depended on their being there when I returned. Everything depended on their being there to receive me when I glided back down into those valleys, to take my place among the great mountains, to be covered coolly by those mists of rain. This hour I rode the sky like a god, but after it was over, how glad I would be to go back to earth and live among men, to feel the soil under my feet and to be smaller than the mountains and the trees.[1]

Charles Lindbergh was by no means the only pilot who came to be admired for his prose style as well as for his skill in the cockpit. From the time of the Wright brothers, airplane pilots have proven to be an extraordinarily articulate breed. The first genuine aviator/authors appeared before 1914, when pilots like Jean Conneau and Claude Grahame-White captured the imagination of arm-chair airmen with their thrilling personal accounts of flight. "Flying and literature," the historian Robert Wohl has remarked, "were more compatible than anyone could have imagined."[2]

The fighter pilots of World War I seem to have produced a greater number of combat memoirs than the generals who commanded the armies. The best of those books set a high standard for the scores of memorable air combat memoirs that would flow from a century of aerial warfare. Because their principal focus is on the personal experience of war in the air, however, autobiographical books by combat pilots are often more akin to military memoirs than to the accounts of flight by the classic aviator/authors. Nor do the purely fictional narratives of novelists who fly, like Ernest Gann or William Faulkner, fit the autobiographical pattern of pilot/authors who focus on the experience of flying.

More than any other individual, Antoine de Saint-Exupéry established a successful pattern for other aviator/authors who sought to communicate a sense of what it was like to fly. Saint-Exupéry emerged as an acknowledged literary master in two languages during the years between the wars, producing four best-selling autobiographical novels and one of the most popular children's books of the century.[3]

Anne Morrow Lindbergh, who knew and admired Saint-Exupéry, also emerged as a leading aviator/author during the years between the wars, as did Francis Chichester and Harold Penrose. Charles Lindbergh and Beryl Markham joined the ranks of much admired writers when they described their prewar aerial adventures in postwar books. Writers such as Richard Bach and the astronaut Michael Collins have carried the tradition of the aviator as littera-teur into the age of jet aircraft and space travel.

How is it that a relatively large number of individuals were able to combine a life in aviation with a successful literary career? Why were so many pilots anx-ious to commit their experiences to paper, and why were so many readers will-ing to invest in books by aviators? What did the aviator/authors have to say, and what impact did they have on their readers and their world?

Perhaps the most intriguing theme explored in the work of these articulate aviators is the tension between the euphoria of flight engendered by a sense of power and escape and a fascination with the ever-changing landscape that was constantly unrolling beneath their feet. While all pilots savored the transcendent personal experience of breaking free of earthly restraint to soar aloft, they were always conscious of the panorama below and appreciative of the extent to which their unique aerial perspective had enabled them to see and understand the past, present, and future of the landscape in new and different ways. Any attempt to understand this tension between the ethereal and the earthly in the lives and work of the classic aviator/authors must begin with an appreciation for the ex-traordinary psychological impact and symbolic meaning of the airplane.

For nineteenth-century Americans, the locomotive had represented the power, speed, and efficiency of the machine age. It was a relentless instrument of change, and a symbol of the blind power of technology. The fact that there was a human hand on the throttle of the rushing engine was a matter of no symbolic importance. The image that counted was that of the locomotive moving relent-lessly across the landscape. While small boys might admire the locomotive engi-neer, the only members of that profession who made a lasting impression on popular culture were usually the victims of merciless technology, men such as Casey Jones, and the man with his hand on the throttle of "Old '97," who was "scalded to death by the steam."[4]

For the children and grandchildren of those nineteenth-century Americans, the airplane represented the power of technology to set an individual human being free. Far from being constrained by rails, the flying machine was com-pletely responsive to the will and the skill of the pilot. A human being was al-ways in command of the machine and of his or her own fate. The airplane rep-resented the liberating power of technology. It was a machine that not only conquered time and distance but also satisfied our deepest human aspirations.

At the very time the airplane first appeared, pioneer students of the mind were exploring the symbolic meaning of flight. Sigmund Freud, Carl Jung, and Alfred Adler were fascinated by the fact that dreams of flight and falling were experienced by so many of their patients. Modern studies confirm that these are the most common themes encountered in dreams. It should come as no surprise to discover that Freud linked such dreams to infantile sexuality.

When we consider that inquisitive children are told that babies are brought by a large bird, such as the stork; when we find that the ancients represented the phallus as having wings; that the commonest expression in German for male sexual activity is "voglen" ['to bird': 'Vogel' is the German for 'bird']; that the male organ is actually called l'ucello ['the bird'] in Italian—all of these are only small fragments from a mass of connected ideas, from which we learn that in dreams the wish to be able to fly is to be understood as nothing else than a longing to be capable of sexual performance.[5]

Freud's notion that our penchant for nocturnal aerial voyaging is a function of infantile sexual aspiration was long ago rejected by psychiatrists. Whatever its root, however, there cannot be much doubt that flight is, quite literally, our oldest dream and one of the most potent of human symbols. To fly is to achieve mastery and control over the environment, to taste ultimate freedom, to escape restraint. In short, flight symbolizes our deepest and most personal aspirations for power, freedom, self-determination, and control of our destiny.

Small wonder that the aviator emerged as great heroic figure of the new century. Here were individuals for whom the ultimate risk was a small price to pay in order to taste absolute freedom through the mastery of a new technology. Their courage, physical prowess, strength of will, and intellect enabled them to soar above the world and the mere mortals that inhabited it. Some enthusiasts went so far as to suggest that aviators were superior individuals who might one day form the basis for a new and improved race of human beings.

One does not have to read too deeply in the work of the author/aviators of the 1920s and 1930s to discover that many of them regarded flight as a mystical, even religious, experience. Certainly the best-known statement of what the historian Joseph Corn has called the "Winged Gospel" came from John Gillispie Magee, Jr. The son of a missionary who became chaplain of Yale, Magee enlisted in the RCAF in 1940, at the age of eighteen, joined 412 Squadron as a Spitfire pilot, and died in a midair collision five days after Pearl Harbor. While the great mass of Americans may have lost their taste for poetry, a great many Americans who fly, and a good many who cannot, are able to recite key sections of Magee's "High Flight" from memory.[6]

> Oh, I have slipped the surly bonds of Earth
> And danced the skies on laughter-silvered wings;
> Sunward I've climbed,
>   and joined the tumbling mirth
> Of sun-split clouds—and done a hundred things
> You have not dreamed of—
>   wheeled and soared and swung

High in the sunlit silence.
Hov'ring there,
I've chased the shouting wind along, and flung
My eager craft through footless halls of air.
Up, up the long, delirious burning blue
I've topped the wind-swept heights with easy grace,
Where never lark or eagle flew;
And, while with silent, lifting mind I've trod
The high untrespassed sanctity of space,
Put out my hand, and touched the face of God.[7]

Not many aviators would admit to having touched the face of God, but any number have remarked on the extent to which flying makes them feel godlike. British test pilot and author Harold Penrose first experienced that sensation flying in an open cockpit biplane just after World War I. "Far below, groups of people stood, watching us," he recalled many years later. "I looked down in triumph at the scores of upturned faces. I was a god; the world a plaything." Penrose made no bones about it. The ability to fly set him apart from less venturesome mortals.

> Whilst we were still very high, the bewitchment of extreme altitude passed, and the earth took on reality.... I could remember that men and women lived down there. I could sigh because the spark of their divinity was subdued by endless regimentation to which they tacitly subscribed, even though the whole world was theirs. In my aeroplane, I could dream I was of their race, yet free of human bondage. In unfettered flight lay a sweet illusion of immortality that could forget the ticking of the clock.[8]

Francis Chichester, the British sailor/aviator, in his classic, *Alone over the Tasman Sea,* expressed a similar pity for the human beings whom he left behind on the ground.

> Inconceivable that I should have become concerned about paltry things. How people down below do worry about trivialities! When they should let themselves respond to the thrill of life. Ha! ha! ha! Flying through space, devouring distance like gods.... By heavens! what an intensity of living! Poor wretches below that had never touched the heart of living.[9]

"There were times in an airplane," Charles Lindbergh once remarked, "when it seemed I had partially escaped mortality, to look down on earth like a god." "I began to feel that I lived on a higher plane than the skeptics on the ground," he wrote.

> In flying, I tasted a wine of the gods, of which they could know nothing. Who valued life more highly, the aviators who spent it on the art they loved, or those

misers who doled it out like pennies through their antlike days. I decided that if I could fly ten years before I was killed in a crash, it would be a worthwhile trade for an ordinary lifetime.[10]

For pilots such as Lindbergh, the exhilaration of flight was felt most keenly when separation from the earth was most complete. Flying on a clear day, with the landscape spread beneath him, "a pilot may drink the wine of the gods, but it has an earthy taste; he's a god of the earth, like those Grecian deities who lived on worldly mountains and descended for intercourse with men." Flying at night above a heavy cloud cover, however,

> all sense of the planet may disappear. . . . And if at times you renounce experience and the mind's heavy logic, it seems that the world has rushed along on its orbit, leaving you alone, flying . . . somewhere in the solitude of interstellar space.[11]

To land is to return to the world of mere mortals. "Without my airplane," Richard Bach tells us,

> I am an ordinary man, and a useless one—a trainer without a horse, a sculptor without marble, a priest without a god. Without an airplane I am a lonely consumer of hamburgers, the fellow in the line at a cash register, shopping cart laden with oranges and cereal and quarts of milk. A brown-haired fellow who is struggling against pitiless odds to master the guitar.[12]

And how does a pilot react to the loss of power and control that comes with the return to earth? Obviously, it varies with the individual, and with his or her state of mind at any particular moment. Following that flight over the Rocky Mountains in 1939, Charles Lindbergh, at the peak of his career both as an aviator and a public figure, relished the opportunity to resume his mortality. Writing almost four decades later, having experienced the horrors of war and the loss of his once complete faith in technological advance as a measure of human progress, his attitude was very different. "I always felt that I escaped from a city into the expanse of the sky," he wrote, "and then sank back to submersion in degenerating human life."[13]

Like it or not, Charles Lindbergh, John Magee, Harold Penrose, and every pilot since Orville Wright has had to return to the ground, one way or another. Short of flying into space, slipping the surly bonds of earth was simply not a possibility. A careful reading of the work of aviator/authors reveals an extraordinary awareness of the landscape below. It is perhaps not overstating the case to argue that the extent to which these writers are able to help their readers share a new aerial perspective on the landscape represents their most important cultural contribution.

The notion that a pilot would pay much attention to the ground is not so difficult to understand. Since the beginning of the air age, the wise pilot has always been very much aware of the landscape below. That was especially true during the pioneering decades. In an era of balky, temperamental power plants, an aviator was never really comfortable without a potential emergency landing field in sight. Prior to the development of the first radio direction finders, the principal system of aerial navigation was known as pilotage. It was simple enough. The pilot kept one eye on the compass, and the other on prominent landmarks, towns, highways, railroads, and other navigational checkpoints on the ground.

Charles Lindbergh described his use of the process during the first transcontinental flight with the *Spirit of St. Louis* in May 1927:

> About forty minutes ago, in early dawn, I crossed a fairly large river. If I haven't drifted off my route, it must have been the Arkansas. . . . Finding my position will be a matter of elimination. For the moment, I can eliminate all railroads which don't run northwest and southeast. There's another roadbed that enters my field of vision from east of north, converging with the first on the same little city. I try to find a line of ink that corresponds to it. And there's a third railroad, with straight miles of track coming in from the east and bending sharply southwest. Such straight lines and definite angles should be distinctive even in the state of Kansas. But I see no printer's counterpart in the area where I think I ought to be.[14]

As early as the 1920s, it had become obvious that the unique vantage point of the airplane, high above the landscape, and its ability to cover great distances at high speeds, could be put to a good many useful and completely earthbound purposes. Over the next two decades, aircraft would be used to explore the ends of the earth. The world's highest waterfall and the top of Mount Everest were both seen for the first time from the cockpit of an airplane. By 1940, aviators had removed the last blank spots from the geographer's maps.

Aerial cameras and photogrammetric equipment and techniques, pioneered during World War I, revolutionized cartography. Aerial mapping expeditions criss-crossed Alaska and the Canadian Arctic, the jungles of South America, and the desolate highlands of Central Asia. The leaders of the U.S. Air Service, anxious to demonstrate the peacetime utility of military airpower, and to attract favorable publicity that might be translated into increased federal spending on their programs, led the way in aerial mapping. Army aviators also demonstrated crop dusting for the first time, and established the first aerial forest fire patrols.

Quite beyond this rather impressive list of practical contributions to an improved understanding of the earth resulting from the invention of the airplane, the aviators themselves were startled by the fundamentally different way in which the landscape was perceived from above. Appropriately enough, Wilbur Wright was among the first to point out the difference.

Once above the treetops, the narrow roads no longer arbitrarily fix the course. The earth is spread out before the eye with a richness of color and beauty of pattern never imagined by those who have gazed at the landscape edgewise only. The rich brown of freshly turned earth, the lighter shades of dry ground, the still lighter browns and yellows of ripening crops, the almost innumerable shades of green produced by grasses and forests, together present a sight whose beauty has been confined to balloonists in the past.[15]

Like Wilbur Wright, almost all new pilots were captivated by the appearance of the earth as seen from on high. Most were also fascinated by the ways in which flight altered their perception of familiar things. Harold Penrose understood "why the gods were omnipotent," when he "learned . . . the trick of height which dwarfs a river and turns a mountain to a molehill."[16]

Having grown up in East Africa, Beryl Markham had seen a good many elephants in the wild, but none quite like those she encountered while flying Baron von Blixen across country in an Avro Avian in the early 1930s. "A herd of elephants, seen from a plane," she wrote, "has the quality of an hallucination."

> The proportions are all wrong—they are like those of a child's drawing of a field mouse in which the whole landscape, complete with barns and windmills, is dwarfed beneath the whiskers of the mighty rodent who looks both able and willing to devour everything, including the thumb-tack that holds the work against the schoolroom wall.[17]

The ground was lovely when seen from the air, and familiar things often looked strange, but there was more to it than that. Quite simply, from an altitude of several thousand feet, you saw the forest, not the trees. Aviators discovered that they could perceive patterns on the ground, patterns that were hidden from those who, as Wilbur Wright put it, "gazed at the landscape edgewise only."[18]

Antoine de Saint-Exupéry remarked that "the airplane has unveiled for us the true face of the world," explaining what he meant with a fable.

> For centuries, highways had been deceiving us. We were like that Queen who determined to move among her subjects so that she might learn for herself whether or not they rejoiced in her reign. Her courtiers took advantage of her innocence to garland the road she traveled and set dancers in her path. Led forward on their halter, she saw nothing of her kingdom and could not know that over the countryside the famished were cursing her.[19]

Referring to North Africa, where he flew the mail for a time, Saint-Exupéry remarked that the roads led from oasis to oasis, and were lined with "well-watered lands, so many orchards, so many meadows," that the area seemed "merciful and fruitful." The depth of the deception was apparent from the air. "And then only, from the height of our rectilinear trajectories, do we discover the essential foundation, the fundament of rock and sand and salt in which here and there from time to time life like a little moss in the crevices of ruins, has risked its precarious existence."[20]

For Harold Penrose, a flight over the gentle and well-cultivated landscape of England became a lesson in geology. "Again and again," he wrote, "I watched with enchantment England take form." No map could "hint at the miracle of seeing this island with a comprehension that a hundred years of traveling on foot could not give. With each successive flight the individual characteristics of every county became more recognizable, until they were patently related to the geological structure of the land."

> I began to see the countryside not merely as a cameo of exquisite beauty, but as the expression of the gigantic forces of expansion and contraction unleashed on the world as it grew from elemental form. Its later history was there to read as well: old boundaries of the sea, newer incursions, dried river valleys.[21]

Penrose could also see the marks that two thousand years of history had left on the land. Remnants of the past that were invisible to someone standing on top of them—the ring forts and mounds of the earliest Britons, vanished Roman roads, medieval fields, and long-forgotten villages—could be seen quite clearly from the air. It was an astonishing discovery, and one that archaeologists were quick to exploit.

Charles Lindbergh, flying the mail over the American Middle West during the 1920s, had seen hundreds of prehistoric burial mounds and curious geometric earthworks spread out on the ground below. A decade later, he took part in a series of aerial archaeological surveys of Mexico, Central America, and the Southwestern United States sponsored by the Carnegie Institution. "Under certain angles of light," he explained, "old ruins can be seen from an airplane, but you might walk across them on the ground without knowing they existed. Walls, rain-washed to the level of the earth, may appear as criss-cross lines to the aviators eye, and changed shades of vegetation show where people dug pits and dumped their refuse a thousand years ago."[22]

Guiding his open-cockpit Curtiss Falcon along a line of Arizona cliffs one day in 1929, Lindbergh discovered a new pueblo, larger than any he had seen before. Banking the aircraft to take photographs, questions flooded into his mind. He wondered, "what enemies had forced those ancient people to a place so high and far from water? How could attacking warriors have escaped through a neck so narrow, or scaled walls so sheer? What had caused the abandonment of a large, well-fortified city? Was it disease? Starvation? A battle line that did not hold?"[23]

Surveys such as those conducted by Lindbergh provided archaeologists with some entirely new approaches to answering those questions. Prior to 1920, attention had focused on the detailed study of individual sites. Attempts to map the geographic extent of a particular cultural group rested on a detailed comparison of the artifacts, building styles, decorative motifs, burials, and other social patterns found at different sites.

Suddenly, archaeologists were presented with the big picture. Aerial photographs revealed unsuspected large-scale features—previously undiscovered towns, villages, and fields, along with the roads, walls, trails, and canals that linked them together. The ability to map archaeological features over an entire geographic region enabled students of the past to study broad patterns of settlement and land use against the background of the natural landscape for the first time. It was an essential first step toward an understanding of the way in which the environment that shaped a civilization was, in turn, exploited and reshaped by human activity.

The aviators of the 1920s and 1930s had a bird's-eye view of the current state of the relationship between civilization and the landscape. On a single flight, Harold Penrose could see the past, the present, and, he feared, the future of his nation written on the face of the land.

> Its . . . history was there to read. . . . turf-disguised mounds and marks of early man; Norman roads and Saxon paths; castles of conquerors uncertain of their hold, side by side with gracious dwellings of a more peaceful age, and the staring council houses of today's planned state. I saw too the grimness of industrial centres set like scars on the fair face of England, their smoke and fog covering a third of the countryside upon which the sun once shone unveiled through uncontaminated air.[24]

But of all the men and women who flew during those years, no one seems to have paid more attention to the landscape, or to have been more affected by the changes that he saw taking place, than Charles Lindbergh. For most Americans during the years between the wars, he personified aviation. Flyers were the great public heroes of the era, but none of the others—Amelia Earhart, Wiley Post, Ruth Nichols, Clarence Chamberlin, Richard Byrd, Jacqueline Cochran, Jimmy Doolittle, Howard Hughes—rivaled Lindbergh's fame.

It is safe to assume that no American pilot logged more hours in the air than Lindbergh during the 1920s and 1930s. He returned to America following the Atlantic crossing in 1927, and immediately set out on an aerial tour of the nation, sponsored by the Daniel and Florence Guggenheim Fund for the Promotion of Aeronautics. Next, he was off on a similar tour of Central America and the Caribbean. He met his future wife, Anne Morrow Lindbergh, daughter of the ambassador to Mexico, Dwight Morrow, during the course of that trip.

After their marriage, the Lindberghs always seemed to be preparing for the next flight, or returning from the last one. Together, they undertook an around-the-world tour in their own Lockheed Sirius, scouting potential commercial air routes to the far corners of the globe. They flew the rim of the Atlantic, publicizing air travel and preparing the way for the airliners that would follow their path in the not-too-distant future. As a consultant with Pan American, Lindbergh made repeated flights around the Caribbean and through Central and South America. After their move to Europe, Charles and Anne Lindbergh crisscrossed that continent, just as they had North America, roving ambassadors of the air age.

But it was the landscape of his own nation that Lindbergh knew and loved the best. He had flown over most of the Middle West, and occasionally into the South, as a barnstormer and air mail pilot before 1927. The flight from San Diego to St. Louis and on to New York with the *Spirit of St. Louis* that spring was his first opportunity to see a narrow swatch of the country from coast to coast. The Guggenheim tour after his return took him into every corner of the United States.

Nothing on this scale had ever been attempted before. In 95 days (July 20–October 23, 1927), Lindbergh flew 22,350 miles and spent 260 hours in the air. He landed in eighty-two cities, and spent at least one night in each of the forty-eight states. The Guggenheim tour served its purpose, to publicize aviation and encourage the development of local airports across the nation. It also introduced Lindbergh to the length and breadth of America. "That tour," he recalled years later, "let me know my country as no man had ever known it before."

> When I returned to New York in October, the United States was represented by a new image in my mind. Instead of outlines on a paper map, I saw New England's valleys, dotted by white villages, the crystal waters of Michigan's Great Lakes, Arizona's pastel deserts, Georgia's red cotton fields, the cascades and deep forest of the Oregon northwest. I saw three great mountain ranges running north and south: the Appalachians, the Rockies, the Sierras—walls of a continent, holding rivers, warning off oceans. I saw waves foaming on the rocks of Maine, cloud layers pressing against Washington's Olympics. I saw California's "Golden Gate," Louisiana's delta, Florida's wide sand beaches hundreds of miles long.[25]

He saw it all, from Death Valley, where the hot sands swept by ten feet below his wheels, to "a skiff-filled harbor in New Hampshire, with fishermen standing at their nets and looking up." On this trip, and the others that would follow over the next decade, he was struck by the extraordinary richness and diversity of the nation—particularly when compared to other parts of the world that he had seen from the air. There was the Mississippi Valley, with its "dairy barns, silos, pastures, quarter sections of corn and hay."

More than a dozen Yangtze peasant huts would fit into a single barn. One American farmer owned enough land to cut across hundreds of Asia's rice paddies. Over China we had looked down on young and old hoeing the earth, or hand-nursing blades of rice. Over the United States we saw machines pulled by tractors—gang plows, harrows, binders, combines. A Chinese peasant could work a lifetime without earning enough money to buy parts for an Illinois farmer's combine.[26]

He liked the regularity of the Middle West as seen from the air. There was a sense of order and purpose in the neat quarter sections, squared off "with the taut lines of roads and fences . . . extending north, south, east, and west beyond the horizons we could see." He was fascinated by the system of "highways, wires, and railroads," binding the thriving towns and villages, and found comfort in the fact that there was, down there, a schoolhouse within the reach of every child. He saw a very different pattern superimposed on the wrinkled landscape of eastern Pennsylvania. Here, "the power that modern organization can give to man" was spread out below him, "in the railroad entering a cliff, in the filling stations where concrete highways crossed, in the towers and electric lines that went slashing out through forests."[27]

New England was very different. "How these Northeastern states are crowded together!" He had first noticed the difference flying out over New England on his way to Paris in 1927.

> I look down on small fields spread out in stream-fed valleys and slopping toward heavily wooded hills . . . so unlike the farms of my own Mississippi Valley, with their straight miles of fence lines, "square with the world." Here, there's no direction, no sense of north, south, east, and west. The tumbled down stone walls run every which way, with hardly a right-angle corner in sight. . . . Highways and villages are everywhere. I can't keep count of them on the map. And the railroads are too close together to make good check points—it's hard to tell one from another. The engines leave long trails of smoke that hang motionless in the air. . . . Columns of factory smoke spread out lazily in whatever direction they desire, as undisciplined as the stone walls of the fields.[28]

In view of his love of the wide-open spaces of the sky, it is not too surprising to discover that Lindbergh came to prefer the southwestern landscape. "I love to fly over the southwestern deserts in the early morning," he wrote in 1939. "The faded and changing shades of color, the weird rock formations, and the vastness and loneliness of it all give me an understanding of why religion owes so much to the desert."[29]

Nor should it be too surprising to discover that he abhorred cities, New York most of all. Approaching New York for the first time with the *Spirit of St. Louis* in 1927, he found himself both "repulsed by its bigness, luxury, and artificial life," and "fascinated by the stupendous forces it commanded and by its influence in the material accomplishments of man." As a businessman and aviation consultant, he would live within easy driving distance of New York for most of his life, yet he was never able to overcome his basic distaste for the place. In later years, when piloting an airplane toward the city, he would sometimes "bank and let a wing blot out the expanse of buildings below while I looked westward to the mountains or eastward to the sea." Each time he flew back to New York, he once remarked, "I always felt I was leaving a better life behind."[30]

Of course, the diverse patterns that Lindbergh recognized in the American landscape of 1927 were not fixed. Over the years he watched them change, almost never, he thought, for the better. "In the decades that I spent flying civil and military aircraft, I saw tremendous changes taking place on the earth's surface," he wrote. "Trees disappeared from mountains and valleys. Erosion turned clear rivers yellow. Power lines and highways stretched out beyond horizons."[31]

He could scarcely miss the changes in the landscape of Texas and Oklahoma during the mid-1930s. Most Americans could only read about the Dust Bowl. Lindbergh saw it from the air. "Hundreds of thousands of tons of topsoil had been stripped from the fields. Prairies were washed with streaks of earth as though a gigantic paintbrush had been swept across them."[32]

The process of change, as reflected in the altered landscape seen from above, accelerated during the postwar years. When John A. Macready and Oakley G. Kelly of the U.S. Army Air Service made the first nonstop transcontinental flight in 1924, the nation seemed very large and empty. "The strongest impression of the United States obtained from the panorama of this transcontinental non-stop flight was the immensity of the lonely, isolated territory which passed beneath us," Macready remarked. "Travelers and tourists follow the auto roads and railroads, and the population stays close to them, but the area seen from the air is practically without human life."[33]

That was the way Lindbergh had seen the nation from the cockpit of his mail plane, but the America of the 1950s seemed a very different place. "To me," he wrote, "the most spectacular change came in the myriad sprinkling of lights that I saw when flying over the United States on a clear night. Huge areas that once lay black when I was a young pilot now glowed with electrification."[34]

The enormous growth of Los Angeles symbolized a fundamental change in America.

> On my first visit as a boy in 1916 . . . it seemed a lovely place, basking in clear air and sunlight, surrounded by orchards and little farms, framed by the ocean and a distant semicircle of mountains. When I flew over it in a Pan American jet transport fifty years later, the orchards and farms had vanished. The city itself had expanded to the distant mountains and spilled over into valleys beyond. Smoky haze screened off the sunlight that once bathed farm yards and streets.[35]

It was the same everywhere he went. On his first trip to the Philippines, shortly after World War II, he had been "enthralled by the beauty of the is-lands—the sea-dashed coasts, the horizon-pushing jungles." Returning a decade later, he was "shocked by the slashes in the jungle I looked down on, caused by lumber companies," and depressed to see "mountains denuded, their stream beds dry, their rice paddies useless."[36]

Lindbergh had no doubt as to the nature of the forces of change. "Within a fraction of my lifetime," he remarked, "I have seen New York parking spaces disappear, the waters of Long Island Sound become polluted, and the coasts of Maine and Florida packed to the shoreline with houses and motels. The distant howl of a superhighway and the thunder of jet aircraft in the sky broke into the tranquility of my . . . home. Rampant pressures of improved technology . . . were rapidly destroying what . . . I considered freedom."[37]

He devoted the last years of his life to the preservation of the environment, working tirelessly on behalf of the World Wildlife Fund, the International Union for the Conservation of Nature, the Nature Conservancy, the President's Citizens Committee on Environmental Quality, and a variety of other conser-vation organizations around the world. He used his prestige to urge the presi-dent of Peru to ban whaling, to convince the president of the Philippines to pro-tect endangered species, and to promote the creation of parks and preserves in the Amazon basin.

Convinced that "science has become the victim of its technologists, just as re-ligion became the victim of its fanatics," even flight technology lost its hold on him. When in the United States, Lindbergh usually flew aboard the commer-cial airliners he had worked to create. "In the cabin of these transports one is in-sulated from the elements," he wrote. "And it is the very contact it used to have with the elements that made flying in those early planes such an attraction for me. Riding in a modern transport plane is strangely like riding the train in a sub-way. In an aisle seat you see and feel about as much in the one as in the other."[38]

Lindbergh had spent most of his lifetime working to put aviation to work for the benefit of his fellow beings. "The development of transport air-craft . . . seemed to me a wonderful way to increase human freedom and to bring the peoples of the world together in understanding and peace." He was no longer sure that was the case. If the airplane had brought improved communi-cation, it also had opened the wilderness to civilization, and brought a stan-dardization that made the world a less interesting place. On a global scale, civi-lization had followed the airplane, just as it had pursued the locomotive across the face of nineteenth-century America.[39]

The profound shift in Lindbergh's thinking was primarily a result of his hav-ing had a bird's-eye view of the pattern of change taking place on the landscape over a period of half a century. Through the books that he produced, from *Of*

Flight and Life in 1948, to the posthumously published *Autobiography of Values,* he attempted to communicate something of what he had seen from on high, and warn his fellow citizens of the fragility of the natural world in an age of runaway technological growth.

By the end of his life, the man who had found freedom and exhilaration in the power of a technology that carried him away from the earth, came to recognize the extent to which flight had played a role in creating the changes that made him so uncomfortable. He could no longer regard technological advance as either the answer to the problems of the world, or as an adequate measure of human progress. Charles Lindbergh, the pilot who had pioneered commercial air routes around the globe, ended his long career as a vocal opponent of federal funding for an American supersonic transport aircraft on environmental grounds.

But Lindbergh was never to completely abandon his faith in the potential of technology as a force for positive change. He was fascinated by space flight. During the 1930s, he had played an important role in funding the work of the American rocket pioneer Robert Hutchings Goddard. He followed Goddard's work with interest, paying repeated visits to his laboratory and launch facility near Roswell, New Mexico. He maintained that early interest, following the U.S. space program with enthusiasm, attending a number of major launches as NASA's honored guest, and befriending astronauts and space agency officials.

Lindbergh could not have foreseen the extent to which the advent of space flight would focus attention on the problems of the earth. The patterns of deforestation, air and water pollution, and urban sprawl that had been apparent to a young pilot flying relatively low and slow over the landscape of the 1930s were revealed to the entire world in spectacular images produced by orbiting satellites. Within a decade after the launch of Sputnik I in 1957, robot spacecraft equipped with sophisticated cameras and sensors had revolutionized environmental science, measuring and monitoring the condition of earth, air, and water around the globe. Images from Landsat, and from manned orbital missions, had an enormous impact on the general public as well. One picture in *Time* magazine of an oil spill spreading along the California coast as seen from orbit was worth ten thousand words from the most persuasive environmental advocate.

But it was the image of the whole earth as seen from space that had the most profound effect on public environmental consciousness. A single photograph taken by the astronauts of Apollo 8, the first crew to circle the moon, came to symbolize a new era of concern for the ultimate fate of the home planet. Michael Collins, a friend of Lindbergh's who served as Command Module Pilot on the Apollo 11 lunar landing mission, described his own feelings when confronted with the sight of the earth suspended in space.

To begin with, it looks tiny, the size of your thumbnail held at arms length. It is mostly ocean and clouds, the blue and white dominating the brownish green of jungles, mountains, and plains. The only land mass that really stands out is the North African desert, especially the oxide-rich, reddish Atlas Mountains. And does the earth glisten in the sunlight! We think a full moon is very bright, but it's a dullard by comparison . . . . From a lifetime of prowling its surface, I know the earth is a huge, rugged place, but from my window now it looks fragile somehow, smooth as a billiard ball, but delicate as a Christmas ornament. I wish I had some way of protecting it, of keeping it pristine. It looks so clean and yet it is so dirty, in places at least. The boundary line between a blue and white planet and one that is gray and tan, is fragile. Is the riverbank a delight or an obscenity, a place for diving ducks, or greasy truck tires? I cry that the technology that produced this marvelous machine we call Columbia leaves in its wake the detritus of a century of industrial abuse. It need not be that way. We can use technology to cleanse, to repair, to maintain—even as we build, as we spiral out into the universe.[40]

Charles Lindbergh and his companions, the men and women who had first looked down on the landscape from above, could not have said it better.

Notes

1. Charles A. Lindbergh, *The Wartime Journals of Charles A. Lindbergh* (New York: Harcourt Brace Jovanovich, 1970), 222.

2. Jean Conneau, *Mes trois grandes courses* (Paris: Hachette et Cie, 1912); Claude Grahame-White, *The Story of the Aeroplane* (Boston: Small, Maynard, and Col, 1911); Robert Wohl, *A Passion for Wings: Aviation and the Western Imagination* (New Haven: Yale University Press, 1994), 270.

3. Antoine Marie Roger de Saint-Exupéry was the first of the aviator/authors to emerge as a literary figure of international reputation. His major books include: *Southern Mail* (1929), *Night Flight* (1931), *Wind, Sand and Stars* (1939), *Flight to Arras* (1942), and *The Little Prince* (1943), almost certainly the most successful and bestselling children's story of the twentieth century. Saint-Exupéry is perhaps the only aviator/author whose portrait, together with a portrait of one of his most famous characters (*Le Petit Prince*), appears on one of his nation's bank notes.

4. Leo Marx, *The Machine in the Garden: Technology and the Pastoral Ideal in America* (New York: Oxford University Press, 1964), offers the fullest and most perceptive treatment of the image of the locomotive in nineteenth-century American art and literature.

5. Sigmund Freud, *Leonardo da Vinci and a Memory of His Childhood* (New York: W. W. Norton, 1964), 75–76.

6. Tony French, an English scholar, has indicated that Magee lifted some of his most memorable lines (including "on laughter-silvered wings," "untrespassed sanctity of space," and "and touched the face of God") from other poems published in *Icarus: An Anthology of the Poetry of Flight* (1938). See "The Lowdown on High Flight," *Air & Space Smithsonian* (April-May 1997), 7.

7. John Gillispie Magee, *High Flight,* <http://www.du.edu/^wdoddpoetry.html>.

8. Harold Penrose, *No Echo in the Sky* (New York: Arno Press, 1972), 76.

9. Francis Chichester, *Alone over the Tasman Sea* (London: George Allyn & Unwin Ltd., 1945), 133.

10. Charles A. Lindbergh, *An Autobiography of Values* (New York: Harcourt Brace Jovanovich, 1977), 64.

11. Charles A. Lindbergh, *The Spirit of St. Louis* (New York: Charles Scribner's Sons, 1953), 262.

12. Richard Bach, *Stranger to the Ground* (New York: Harper and Row, 1963), 28.

13. Lindbergh, *Autobiography of Values,* 33.

14. Lindbergh, *Spirit of St. Louis,* 142–43.

15. Wilbur Wright, "Flying as a Sport—Its Possibilities," *Scientific American* 98 (February 28, 1908), 139.

16. Penrose, *No Echo in the Sky,* 15.

17. Beryl Markham, *West with the Night* (San Francisco: North Point Press, 1983), 206.

18. Wright, "Flying as a Sport—Its Possibilities," 139.

19. Antoine de Saint-Exupéry, *Airman's Odyssey* (New York: Harcourt, Brace and Co., 1939), 58.

20. Ibid.

21. Penrose, *No Echo in the Sky,* 34.

22. Lindbergh, *Autobiography of Values,* 204.

23. Ibid.

24. Penrose, *No Echo in the Sky,* 34.

25. Lindbergh, *Autobiography of Values,* 81.

26. Ibid., 258.

27. Ibid., 259.

28. Lindbergh, *Spirit of St. Louis,* 195.

29. Lindbergh, *Wartime Journals,* 198.

30. Lindbergh, *Autobiography of Values,* 259.

31. Ibid., 32.

32. Ibid., 257.

33. John A. Macready, "The Non-Stop Flight Across America," *National Geographic Magazine* 46, no. 1 (July 1924), 77.

34. Lindbergh, *Autobiography of Values,* 32.

35. Ibid., 33.

36. Ibid., 34.

37. Ibid., 40.

38. Lindbergh, *Wartime Journals,* 484–85.

39. Lindbergh, *Autobiography of Values,* 41.

40. Michael Collins, *Liftoff: The Story of America's Adventure in Space* (New York: Grove Press, 1988), 12.

The Airplane and American Literature

LAURENCE GOLDSTEIN

A merican writers have been fascinated by the airplane ever since it first rose from the ground at Kitty Hawk on December 17, 1903. They appreciated at once that the flying machine was a realization of myths of ascent in the folklore and premodern literature of many different cultures. If the early inventors of aviation looked back to pioneers such as Maxim, Lilienthal, Chanute, and Langley as guides for their experiments, so authors looked back to imaginative texts that articulated the means and ends of airflight by human beings. Some of the commonly cited texts in the tradition include the notebooks of Leonardo da Vinci, the narratives of gods, angels, and demons in works such as John Milton's *Paradise Lost* and J.W. Goethe's *Faust,* the fantasies of winged humanoids in Robert Paltock's novel *Peter Wilkins* and Restif de la Bretonne's *La Découverte Australe par un Homme-volant,* and the science fiction of H. G. Wells, Jules Verne, and many others, which envisioned futuristic aeronautical achievements in the decade before the Wright brothers lifted their Flyer into the sky.

Most of these writers did not regard the human desire for ascent favorably. In the scheme of the Creation, as they saw it, man was given the earth and the sky was given to the birds; the "heavens" beyond were the domain of the gods or God. Those who aspired beyond their station courted retributive punishment, for example, Icarus, whose fall into a watery grave became the proverbial example of overreaching by those who wanted wings. A popular American poem of the late nineteenth century, "Darius Green and His Flying Machine," by John Townsend Trowbridge, lampooned the efforts of one inventor to fly like a bird:

> he's goin' to fly
> Away he goes! Jiminy! what a jump!
> Flop-flop—an' plump
> To the ground with a thump!
> Flutt'rin' an' flound'rin', all'n a lump![1]

Darius Green's comic lapse haunted the early inventors no less than Edgar Allan Poe's send-up in 1844 of popular enthusiasm for aerial wonders. Poe as-

The American novelist John Dos Passos chronicled the titanic historical forces transforming American culture into a dynamic modern civilization. Thomas Edison, Charles Steinmetz, Henry Ford, Frederick Winslow Taylor—these and other Promethean makers of twentieth-century industrial society take their place in the pantheon of powerful figures whose inventions affect every person in the nation. The Wright brothers belong in this company because they, too, were "practical," to cite Dos Passos's constant term of praise. This mural, painted by David C. Hutchinson in the Yonkers, New York, Public Library, depicts the Wrights (at far left) among the pantheon of nineteenth- and twentieth-century inventors. (Courtesy Yonkers Public Library via National Air and Space Museum, Smithsonian Institution [SI A-525].)

tounded readers of the *New York Sun* by reporting a transatlantic balloon flight. The reporter who describes the event in Poe's sketch, afterward known as "The Balloon Hoax," calls the flight "unquestionably the most stupendous, the most interesting, and the most important undertaking ever accomplished or even attempted by man."[2] This kind of inflated rhetoric, used here in mockery, presented a challenge to authors who after 1903 wanted to write about aviation in a language appropriate to its epoch-making implications for society. What tone was proper if one wanted to pay homage to the astounding fact of heavier-than-air flight, and yet also measure the negative consequences of this sudden and impious access to unprecedented technological power?

American writers saw clearly that, for the twentieth century, the airplane embodied the desire for spiritual elevation represented in the literature of divine beings, on the one hand, and symbolic birds like Shelley's skylark and Keats's nightingale, on the other. The airplane would henceforth be humanity's preferred emblem of uplifting hope, higher consciousness, and ecstatic revelation. It would be an ever-changing example of humanity's ability to shrink time and space and link peoples and nations more efficiently. Just as Walt Whitman proclaimed the locomotive a "Type of the Modern" in the 1870s, so the airplane would become the dominant "Type" or myth for the twentieth century, and all men, women, and children, especially in America, would learn to look at it with the reverence and fear exacted by a supreme symbol of speed and power. Whitman's tone when he regarded new inventions was always celebratory, and the majority of writers would follow his lead when they wrote about the Flyer or *The Spirit of St. Louis* or "miracles" of civil aviation such as the Douglas DC-3 and the Boeing 247.

At the same time it offered mankind the opportunity for new thrills and the voluptuous comforts of commercial passenger service, the airplane became a dangerous agent of ever more destructive warfare. The "war birds" caused many writers to change their language of praise to a prophetic tone of denunciation. Was the airplane a fulfillment of God's covenant with his chosen people in the new Israel, America? Or was it a scourge for punishing mankind for whoring after strange gods, machines rather than things of the spirit? Each decade added more layers of meaning as the airplane evolved historically, constantly changing its relation to its inventors, pilots, crews, passengers, and earthbound spectators. The airplane became an American icon as complex as any myth in the history of literature, continually challenging authors to reimagine its identity as they looked backward into the literary tradition and forward into a future to be shaped in large part by aerial technology itself. The result has been a series of texts central to our understanding of what it meant to be an American in the twentieth century.

The Matter of Kitty Hawk

The poet Robert Frost was a personal friend of Orville Wright, and all his life he defended the claim of the Wright brothers to be the legitimate inventors of the first heavier-than-air flying machine. He blamed journalists who overlooked the Wright brothers' career when they covered new developments in aviation, and encyclopedias that slighted the achievements of the Wrights in favor of more glamorous machines and pilots of the postwar period. "When all this thing is written," he told a friend in 1932, "that about Lindbergh and all, there will still remain only the Wright boys, the Columbuses of the air."[3] In 1936, Frost wrote a punning epigram to make their claims memorable and canonical:

> THE WRIGHTS' BIPLANE
> This biplane is the shape of human flight.
> Its name might better be First Motor Kite.
> Its makers' name—Time cannot get that wrong,
> For it was writ in heaven doubly Wright.[4]

Behind the whimsical tone is an iron determination to accord to the great inventors the honor of being original. "Time," or written history, must not get that fact wrong because the destiny of an aeronautical civilization such as our own depends on indisputably attributing the foundations of flight to the "right" citizens. In this poem, and especially in his later long poem "Kitty Hawk," Frost is representative of many American authors who focus on those epic events at Cape Hatteras as a means of establishing a sacred history of the century's most significant technological innovation.

The Wright brothers themselves had understood that a sacred history required an agreed-upon moment of Creation, when human names, for the first time, were "writ in heaven." Wilbur constantly insisted on "the real truth" of origins. "The world owed this invention to us, and to no one else," he remarked of the crucial system of control, and elsewhere, "It must always be remembered that today [1911] when everyone knows the Wright invention, and the world has assigned certain words to describe it, those words now produce a mental picture which they did not and could not produce when men knew nothing of this method of control."[5] He calls attention to the verbal, one might even say literary, component of their mechanical achievement, for according to patent law precise description is an essential part of originality. Wilbur conscripts writers to speak for and with him as to the uniqueness of his invention. By this logic, the admiring journalistic articles that followed soon after the first flight at Kitty Hawk, and grew in volume as new versions of the Flyer proceeded from triumph to triumph, count as the first literary testaments in our literature about the airplane. These articles are often filled with hyperbolical rhetoric of a kind that irritated the Wright brothers, but more often they spoke with technical specificity about the nuts and bolts of the new machine. Precise terminology was the essence of their achievement, the Wrights insisted, and this was a message not lost on authors who returned to these founding fathers in order to trace and retrace the design and significance of their apocalyptic invention.

Before eminent poets and novelists got around to the subject, however, a multitude of popular writers adapted the Wright brothers' lives and work as models for success stories aimed at children and adults alike. In many juvenile books, patterned after the Horatio Alger stories, we find a formulaic cast of characters and narrative line. Hard work on a new invention, often a flying machine, leads to frustration as experiments end in crash-landings or mechanical failures, but then a breakthrough offers the opportunity for adventure and virtuous triumph over some antagonist, followed by business contacts and the hand of a rich man's daughter. Sinclair Lewis published a novel in this genre in 1915, *The Trail of the Hawk*. In series such as The Boy Aviators, The Aeroplane Boys, Tom Swift, and Frank Reade, youthful tinkerers are likewise rewarded by universal respect for their mechanical aptitude. Such books initiated young readers into the challenges of the machine age, not least by reminding them of the necessity of learning through trial and error how to build, fly, and repair the variety of gliders, monoplanes, biplanes, and airships increasingly visible at air shows around the country. In such books, the Wright brothers are constantly summoned as models for boys to emulate in their own mechanics.

It is no surprise, then, that when John Dos Passos devoted one of his biographical interludes in *U.S.A.* to "The Campers at Kitty Hawk" he employed the factual style appropriate to his subjects. In this trilogy of novels covering the period from 1896 to the mid-1930s, Dos Passos chronicles the titanic historical forces transforming American culture into a dynamic modern civilization. Thomas Edison, Charles Steinmetz, Henry Ford, Frederick Winslow Taylor— these and other Promethean makers of twentieth-century industrial society take their place in the pantheon of powerful figures whose inventions affect every person in the nation. The Wright brothers belong in this company because they too were "practical," to cite Dos Passos's constant term of praise. When he writes about them, he uses no stylistic flourishes, no adornments of metaphor, but instead the dry notation of data that characterizes their own reports and journals:

> There with a glider made of two planes and a tail in which they lay flat on their bellies and controlled the warp of the planes by shimmying their hips, taking off again and again all day from a big dune named Kill Devil Hill, they learned to fly

> Once they'd managed to hover for a few seconds and soar ever so slightly on the rising aircurrent, they decided the time had come to put a motor in their biplane.[6]

Literary language cannot be made plainer. When the Wrights' invention enters the fictional narrative, in the career of Charley Anderson, a flier most likely modeled after Charles Lindbergh, Dos Passos returns to a more intense and imaginative style for his tale of Charley's Icarian fall into the degrading world of "the big money." But Wilbur and Orville stand outside the tragic and the melodramatic stories of *U.S.A.* Even as Dos Passos describes the honors heaped on them by Alfonso of Spain, King Edward, the Czar, and the King of Italy, he bends his vignettes back toward the memory of the first flight, and ends his biography with a last nostalgic view of the young Daedaluses as they "soar into the air / above the dunes and the wide beach / at Kitty Hawk."

Dos Passos writes his biography in a prose broken typographically into verse units. It is an odd fact that these two sober-minded engineers inspired more poets than fiction writers in the decades after 1903. Fiction writers took more interest in the air battles of both world wars, in the romance and perils of barnstorming, and in the use of the airplane for commercial purposes. Because poets have a special interest in origins and in archetypal figures, they returned again and again to Kitty Hawk as a way of measuring the impact of the flying machine. By doing so, they modernized the subject matter of verse itself and rescued poetry from its reputation as genteel and effete, the medium of moonlight, daffodils, and nightingales. Twentieth-century poets who accepted Whitman's admonition that "sacred industry" and "practical invention" must fill modern poems increasingly turned to topics like the Wright brothers in order to enhance their prestige as knowledgeable bards of their ever-changing culture.

Hart Crane took up the subject of the airplane in the section of his book-length poem *The Bridge* (1930) called "Cape Hatteras." *The Bridge* begins with Columbus's discovery of America and proceeds, section by section, from the pioneers and the dominion of sailing vessels to Crane's own time in which the Twentieth Century Limited, the radio, the cinema, the subway, and other dynamic forces have conquered space and time so as to bring people and places into more immediate contact. Crane insists that, instead of creating the utopia Whitman imagined, these new inventions have brought confusion and despair to the first generation of the new century. He looks to the Brooklyn Bridge as a symbol of stability, continuity, and spirituality, a link between the country and the city, between past and present, between America and the rest of the world. In his assessment of value to modern inventions, the airplane emerges as the most complex case study, for the flying machine has all the positive poetic associations of the angel and the Romantic bird, but also has negative associations as a figure of sublime power threatening to the earthbound. In the mythic history of the poem, the moment of ascent at Kitty Hawk becomes a crossroads of American culture, an annunciation of profound spiritual opportunities and dangers for an industrial civilization.

Having said all this, the surprise of "Cape Hatteras" is the scant treatment accorded the inventors who made the landscape of the poem world-renowned. The few lines given to the events at Kitty Hawk are really only one sentence, which ends in a question-exclamation:

> There, from Kill Devils Hill at Kitty Hawk
> Two brothers in their twinship left the dune;
> Warping the gale, the Wright windwrestlers veered
> Capeward, then blading the wind's flank, banked and spun
> What ciphers risen from prophetic script,
> What marathons new-set between the stars?

The answer is a pessimistic reading of the nativity:

> The soul, by naphtha fledged into new reaches
> Already knows the closer clasp of Mars,—
> New latitudes, unknotting, soon give place
> To what fierce schedules, rife of doom apace![7]

Crane's collapsing of the triumph at Kitty Hawk into the Great War is justified in part by the slight lapse of time dividing those two events, and also by the fact that from the moment the heavier-than-air machine was conceived in the new century it was linked to military use, not least by the Wright brothers. Crane regarded this deformation of the creative spirit as similar in kind to the corruption of America by materialist and militarist values he deplores elsewhere in the poem.

Here Crane confronts the paradox of the Whitmanian gospel essential to his myth-history. Just as Whitman could affirm after the Civil War that the smash-up of his dream of brotherhood would give way to even greater democratic vistas, so Crane wanted to affirm that the world war recently past would lead to some kind of spiritual renewal. He therefore attributes to the predatory pilot the powers of a creative demiurge:

> Remember, Falcon-Ace
> Thou hast there in thy wrist a Sanskrit charge
> To conjugate infinity's dim marge—
> Anew . . .

Hit by a shell, the pilot falls "into mashed and shapeless debris . . . /By Hatteras bunched the beached heap of high bravery!" The bad magic of the Wright brothers' science returns back on their own landscape, where it must remain until Whitman, summoned in the lines immediately following, appears to resurrect the airplane by his noble wizardry in "Easters of speeding light." As Whitman and Crane advance onward, the future of America is seemingly secured by the covenant of "the rainbow's arch" above the Cape. It is the Bridge-form and not the airplane's that finally glorifies Kill Devil Hill.

The allusiveness and experimental quality of Crane's style indicate how seriously he wanted to be a rival to the Wright brothers, putting his workmanship in competition with theirs in hopes that the poetic tradition would win out in the battle for the hearts and minds of the American people. Most poets, however, continued to defer to the inventors rather than challenge them. Muriel Rukeyser, for example, in *Theory of Flight,* the Yale Series of Younger Poets award-winning volume of 1935, took it as axiomatic that theories of flight beginning with the Wright brothers have permanently and profoundly altered American culture in ways that poets were obligated to analyze. The flying machine becomes the chief metaphor in her Depression-era poem for a perfectly functioning social machine. "Distinguish the metaphor most chromium clear," she advises. And to do so, she roots it in the Old World renaissance when a great inventor tried and failed to cobble together a flying machine that worked:

> Leonardo's tomb
> not in Italian earth
> but in a fuselage
> designed
> in the historic mind
> time's instrument
> blue-print of birth[8]

Here Rukeyser confronts the same problem that bedeviled Crane. "Leonardo's tomb" contains the seeds of the airplane but, by analogy to Jesus' tomb, it also reminds her of the defeat of the spirit as well. The "blue-print of birth" calls for a new energy to be crucified in history before attaining transfiguration. By 1935, the airplane already had a history as long as Jesus' if one took the flight in 1903 as the true nativity. And that history had a trajectory as familiar and inflexible as the ballistic curve of a rocket. Hardly have we entered the poem when "Icarus' phoenix flight" becomes the commanding figure, with its associations of defeat for the aspiring spirit. The confident section called "The Gyroscope" gives way to "The Lynchings of Jesus":

> Kitty Hawk is a Caesar among monuments;
> the stiff bland soldiers predestined to their death
> the bombs piled neatly like children's marbles piled
> sperm to breed corpses eugenically by youth
> out of seductive death

Rukeyser's critique of warfare and social injustice in the modern period has the effect of tarnishing the chromium-clear distinction of her metaphor. The flying machine is first derived from Leonardo, thence to Icarus (not Daedalus), thence by analogy to the doomed Jesus, and from Jesus to figures who have been victimized in Rukeyser's own time by merciless warmongers and oppressors. Thus, the lengthy sections devoted to the Scottsboro Boys, the coal miners suffering from poverty and silicosis, and various other social problems, darken the central metaphor into a final obscurity. And her conclusions become foregone and pessimistic, for if the test of the flying machine's viability as a cultural symbol is the Scottsboro Boys, then the special characteristics of ascent and transcendence are canceled out. The airplane loses its identity as a "new special product of mortality." Despite Rukeyser's considerable research for the poem, including ground school instruction, she has not provided a historical scheme capacious enough to isolate the airplane in character and function.

When Rukeyser begins the section on the Wright brothers with the passage quoted above, her approach is deferential but wary. She keeps the description of their achievement factual for many lines in the notebook style the Wright brothers shared with their admired Leonardo:

> "To work intelligently" (Orville and Wilbur Wright)
> "one needs to know the effects of variations
> incorporated in the surfaces... The pressures on squares
> are different from those on rectangles, circles, triangles, or ellipses...
> The shape of the edge also makes a difference."

This is the enabling terminology of flight and Rukeyser's willingness to mimic it in her poetry, as Dos Passos did in his novel, represents a recurring mode of tribute to the great inventors. The Wrights were remarkable for the methodical observation and testing on thousands of occasions of each detail pertinent to their machines. They are perfect examples of "the instinct of workmanship" praised by Thorstein Veblen as the fundamental ingredient of the national character. Their journals and letters contain almost nothing but research data, and even their accounts of the first flight eschew sublimity of phrasing for rigorous documentation. Imaginative writers found such material intransigent, for the Wrights had not just been silent—which would have permitted their admirers to speak for them—but had insisted on the privileges of scientific speech. Others must defer to its authenticity, as Rukeyser did, or speak in a different tongue and thereby violate the spirit of their hard-won achievements.

One example of the dilemma is Selden Rodman's book-length poem, *The Airmen* (1941), which offers lengthy accounts of Daedalus and Icarus, and Leonardo da Vinci, before taking up the Wright brothers. A fourth section is devoted to Lauro de Bossis, a young Italian poet who dropped anti-Fascist pamphlets on Rome in 1931. "The Brothers" is the longest narrative of the poem (forty pages) and the longest verse passage ever written on the subject. Several sections are devoted to a chronicle of experiments by the Montgolfiers, Cayley, Pilcher, Maxim, Lilienthal, and Langley. As in so much American writing about the airplane, this obsessive recapitulation of the honored tradition, the naming of ancestors and the ritual recording of their achievements, serves a biblical function, like the counting of generations in Chronicles. It is reminiscent of the many prose histories of flight published in the 1930s. Once again, the industrial muse fails to provide satisfactory wings to the poet, however. Rodman clearly feels constrained by the diaries and letters of the Wright brothers, as well as the testimony he gathered while researching the book. The poem sinks into the documentary style the author conceives to be the truest wedding of form to content:

Encasing all surfaces and crossbars in a covering of muslin,
All wires tightened simply by foreshortening two,
They shift the frame's main cross-piece to the cutting edge;
Run after it in the wind, warping the wings by rope; find the response true.

If the glider balks on the beach, at Kill Devil Hill
Two volunteers from the Life Saving Station will get under the tips.
It floats on the up-currents. It slides in the eddy of the slopes,
Wilbur maneuvering the wingtips from the cradle with his hips.[9]

Rhyme heightens the awkwardness of the passage, calling attention to the prosaic language by a noticeable poetic device. By deferring so entirely to the authority of fact, Rodman yields up his own prerogative as an inventor. He imagines himself to be joining hands in brotherhood with his fellow technicians, but they have usurped his power of making by his consent.

These authors believed that the damaged social machine of American industrial society could only be fixed by following the lead of the founding fathers of aerial technology who knew how to put complicated things in working order. The airplane became the chief metaphor of the period before World War II because it was a visible success up there in the sky where everyone could appreciate its evolution year by year. Likewise, when America entered the war in 1941, the airplane served as a metaphor for the overpowering force of sophisticated weaponry, as we shall see. After the war, Robert Frost, among others, returned to the subject of the Wright brothers as a way of guiding America into the space age. His poem of 1953, "Kitty Hawk," is the most important literary work to consider the implications of the Wright brothers' flight in the second half of the twentieth century.

Having lost the western frontier in the 1890s after centuries of pioneering, the American people confronted another vast tract of open space in the postwar world. Like the continent they had settled, outer space offered an exhilarating sense of sublime mystery, as well as opportunities for commercial and political exploitation. Unlike the land, however, access to this new world required a form of as yet undeveloped technology, one that existed plentifully in the literary imagination but had no working physical model. While engineers set their minds to the technical problems of rocketry, some intellectuals, uneasy with the costs and results of the first cycle of Manifest Destiny, posed ethical questions as well. Not could a spaceship be invented, but *should* it be invented? Wasn't it time to put by the obsession to occupy open space as an embarrassment to human morality?

If there is such a thing as a representative American answer to that question, Frost's lines in "Kitty Hawk" qualify better than most:

Pulpiteers will censure
Our instinctive venture
Into what they call
The material
When we took that fall
From the apple tree.
But God's own descent
Into flesh was meant
As a demonstration
That the supreme merit
Lay in risking spirit
In substantiation.
Westerners inherit
A design for living

Deeper into matter—
Not without due patter
Of a great misgiving.
All the science zest
To materialize
By on-penetration
Into earth and skies
(Don't forget the latter
Is but further matter)
Has been West-Northwest.[10]

The expansion of the human spirit, in Frost's view, can be charted geographi-
cally, West–Northwest, from the cradle of civilization in the Middle East
through Greece and Italy to Western Europe and then to North America.
Christ's descent into matter necessarily became the central myth of a restless,
wandering people who looked on external nature as essentially dead until infused with human presence and purpose. In lines immediately following those
quoted above, Frost contrasts the Western movement with the "long stagnation / In mere meditation" of the East. Frost's chief metaphor throughout
"Kitty Hawk" is the footrace; here the East hurries "to catch up with us" in the
enjoyment of material advantages, which Western science has fashioned in its
acceleration.

Frost selects the Wright brothers' success at Kitty Hawk as a moral demonstration of his West–Northwest thesis. The progress of spirit cannot go further
West—it would then sink into the East—so it must advance vertically, toward
the open sky and empty planets. Even before President Kennedy proclaimed the
moon landing a high priority of his New Frontier administration, Frost had
pleaded in "Kitty Hawk" for no waste of time. "Matter mustn't curd, / Separate
and settle," he warned. "Action is the word."

Frost realized that Kitty Hawk could be made most appealing to a postwar
generation if it were approached from the nineteenth-century's vantage point.
Frost himself (born 1875) incarnated the previous century's pride in the new
birth, and he felt the goading of parental responsibility for its defense. The events
of 1903 seemed to need defending a half-century later. If some poets sighted
Kitty Hawk through the blood-colored filter of World War I and World War II,
Frost would admonish them that the flying machine must never lose the enduring promise of cultural benefits celebrated by its first enthusiasts. Despite the
seizure of the flying machine by the advocates of air power after World War II,
Kitty Hawk remained for Frost a place of covenant that the congregation of be-
lievers could revisit in order to renew their faith in progress. In the late 1940s,
the development of rocket technology impressed him as such a perfect analogy

for the inventions in the first decade of the century that the Matter of Kitty Hawk seemed more pertinent than ever.

In the first part of the poem, Frost recalls how as a lovelorn adolescent he had wandered over the same field which the Wright brothers would use a decade later as a runway. That's when he should have written a prophetic poem about airflight, he says, but it never occurred to him then that such a transformative event in American culture was destined to occur at that very place. "Kitty Hawk" is a belated penance that Frost offers to share with his reading public. Poets and poetry readers alike lack the true understanding of historical events, he acknowledges, because they have been insufficiently trained in the quotidian coping ("Action is the word") of a frontier people. In Frederick Jackson Turner's classic definition, the "composite nationality" is a "practical, inventive turn of mind, quick to find expedients . . . a masterful grasp of material things, lacking in artistic but powerful to effect great ends."[11] Meditative it is not (Frost delights in the rhyme of meditation and stagnation); Americans more often seek to know the spiritual meaning of an event long after it has passed into history. History is an unending process, however, and even the poetic reconsideration remains of practical use. "Kitty Hawk" is a warning to the nation that stands in 1953 on the brink of penetration into the heavens. Frost endorses the aims of the space program and asserts that the enterprising spirit of the Wright brothers can refresh the national will by establishing new goals, new horizons. New frontiers must constantly be located and settled.

As if John F. Kennedy had taken "Kitty Hawk" to heart—and perhaps he did—one theme of his election campaign became the necessity of occupying outer space. The conjunction of Frost and Kennedy on Inauguration Day 1961 seemed to endorse the notion of American destiny as Frost had defined it in that poem. Frost's panegyric to the nation's new leader, "For John F. Kennedy His Inauguration" brings further pressure on the new president to realize his promises. Frost once again cites the Wright brothers as models of national achievement, and calls on Kennedy for a kindred spirit of high endeavor. It should have come as no surprise, then, that on May 25, 1961, Kennedy, departing from the custom of addressing Congress only once a year, convened an extraordinary session to present a proposal for, his phrase, "mastery of space." The president made the specific recommendation that the nation commit itself to the goal of landing a man on the moon before the end of the decade. Since NASA had not yet put a man into space the notion of a moon landing seemed even to poets a vainglorious effort doomed to failure. And yet it happened. On July 20, 1969, Neil Armstrong, who carried with him a piece of the original linen wing fabric from the Flyer of 1903, helped Edwin Aldrin unfurl the Stars and Stripes on the lunar surface.

Writing "Kitty Hawk" at the end of his career, Frost, his nation's unofficial poet laureate, argued that science can best play the heroic role that fate has given the superior in spirit. "Some people worry because science doesn't know where it's going," Frost said in an interview of 1961. "It doesn't need to know. It's none of its business. I like anything that penetrates the mysteries. And it if penetrates straight to hell, then that's all right, too."[12] In "Kitty Hawk," Frost bows to the flying machine and its first inventors, who did forge a new relation between earth and heaven and a sense of optimism about American leadership in the new century. "God of the machine," he prays at the conclusion, "Thanks to you and thanks / To the brothers Wright." Those aptly-named mechanics on Kill Devil Hill did win a race against the poet, and against poetry itself, but by saying so in 1953 Frost at least outran the astronauts, planting the literary imagination's soiled flag in advance.

The Legacy of Lindbergh

As we have seen, American writers attended very closely to the history of aviation while they formed their own myths of airflight. Fact and fancy cooperated to a considerable extent because actual events provided authors with all the astonishing material they needed in order to create an imaginative literature full of wizards, heroes, tragic conflicts, and newly forged community values. For example, the coming of World War I so soon after the invention of the airplane permitted authors to adopt at least two persistent literary conventions from the days of yore: they could write popular tales of dashing aviators and exciting dogfights, or they could emphasize instead the harrowing and soul-destroying lives and deaths of young men doomed to a form of crucifixion by their respective national governments. There was ample precedent in literary tradition for both kinds of stories.

The heroic version runs something like this: The airplane had scarcely entered the teen years of its life before being pressed into service for significant tasks in the Great War. Its rickety structure guaranteed a high fatality rate so that only the bravest warriors would defy the low life expectancy to rise into aerial battle with antagonists. Those who saw the war as a Great Crusade could therefore apotheosize the aviators and their machines as throwbacks to the highest form of human nobility, as literature had defined it. "Every flight is a romance; every report is an epic," proclaimed the British prime minister David Lloyd George. "They are the knighthood of the war, without fear and without reproach. They recall the old legends of chivalry, not merely the daring of their exploits, but by the nobility of their spirit, and, amongst the multitudes of heroes, let us think of the chivalry of the air."[13] It hardly needs demonstrating that this viewpoint became a powerful element of our modern memory of the war. Almost every biography and memoir about aerial adventure in the war makes some use of glamorous association with the stories of King Arthur or the Crusades. W. H. Auden was not the only writer to believe that the closest equivalent in modern times to the Homeric hero was the air ace. This figure filled popular magazine fiction, films, and advertisements, all the way down to send-ups of the myth in Snoopy's feverish fantasies, dressed in scarf and flier's goggles, of being the Red Baron.

If we scrutinize the myth closely, of course, we see something more complex. Air aces were usually not chivalric but predatory and cold-blooded, and there was nothing glamorous about most of the fiery deaths of new recruits. Also, the myth was better suited to European literature because of its insistent echoes of aristocratic privilege and *noblesse oblige*. The essence of America, according to most nineteenth-century writers, was the rejection of heroes in the hierarchical mode of romance and epic. Walt Whitman had denounced the stories of the Trojan War and the Round Table as outdated rubbish in his "Song of the Exposition," and Mark Twain had done likewise in *A Connecticut Yankee in King Arthur's Court*. America required new legends relevant to a progressive democratic civilization, and the more European writers talked about the knighthood of the air, the more American writers emphasized the human cost of these dangerous illusions. Less committed to the war in any case, American writers persistently communicated their resentment at being dragged into the national enmities and militant folklore of Europe. Disillusionment and disenchantment became the dominant literary modes of representing the flying machine during and after the 1914–18 conflict.

In the decade stretching from the end of the war to Charles Lindbergh's transatlantic flight, we find American writers trying to pry loose the affections of their readers from the seductive image of the dashing flyer standing next to his Sopwith Camel or Nieuport 11. Authors do this by dramatizing the corrosive effects of daily air battles and the aftereffects of the war on surviving aviators. John Monk Saunders, Elliott White Springs, and James Warner Bellah are fiction writers who produced influential accounts of the air war and its melancholy aftermath. But the most important author on this subject is William Faulkner, who trained as a pilot, although he never earned his wings or saw action in Europe. In short stories and especially in two novels he wrote during the 1920s, *Soldiers' Pay* and *Sartoris,* Faulkner described the almost posthumous life of young men returning from the air war, traumatized by the deaths they had witnessed and totally unable to reenter the normal society of their home communities. Bayard Sartoris, especially, has become the model for all subsequent narratives about the veteran flier adrift in postwar society, down to his self-chosen death as the pilot of a prototype aircraft he knows to be unsafe. Faulkner mortifies his readers' romance with the flying machine by showing how it extends its deadly reach for years, even decades, after its service in a Great Crusade.

Readers of the 1920s, then, were treated to many scenes of aerial warfare in the imaginative literature of the time, and also to a fair amount of imagery of barnstorming pilots—themselves usually veterans of the Great War. These are not positive depictions of the flying machine, however. What was needed to re-deem the vision of the airplane represented by the Wright brothers' amazing ac-complishment was some genuine and specifically American knight of the air who would give the public a wholly different image of pilot and airplane alike. This is the signal contribution of Charles Lindbergh and *The Spirit of St. Louis* to the literary tradition, for Lindbergh's flight in 1927 entirely transformed the airplane into a redemptive symbol of hope for the future. Rather than having to imagine the airplane in the act of mortal combat, as in Springs's novel *War Birds* or Faulkner's *Sartoris,* readers could now be treated to the positive image of the airplane as a medium of peaceful communication and bonding between the Old and New World, between the past and the present, and the present and the fu-ture. The rainbow trajectory of Lindbergh's flight established a covenant for a new heaven and new earth arising from the chaos and bloodshed of the war.

Lindbergh himself helped to forge this new definition in his autobiography "WE" written immediately after the flight. The title asserts that he and his ma-chine were cooperating parts of a new entity, a unity of man and machine created for a single purpose. Lindbergh's factual exposition of his apprenticeship and his famous flight recalled the Wright brothers' scientific treatment of their labors to invent the flying machine. And, like the Wrights, Lindbergh advertised the prac-tical uses of airplanes for a nation eager to establish closer commercial and politi-cal ties with the rest of the world. Lindbergh saw clearly just how useful a sym-bol he could be and gladly extended his influence over admiring readers by laying out "trails" for the future that would require more pilots like himself as leaders and entrepreneurs. His young readers, especially, would have been prompted by "WE" to forget about what Faulkner called "all the old bunk about knights of the air and the romance of battle" and turn their eyes to the glorious future.[14]

After Lindbergh's flight, thousands of poems were submitted to a national contest to honor the event. The best entries were published in a book called *The Spirit of St. Louis,* and these poems tell us much about how poets preferred to imagine the event.[15] They did not, for the most part, follow Lindbergh's lead and write about oil consumption, motor design, and the necessity of new air-ports. Rather, they chose to glorify him according to the very models of heroic derring-do that he condemned as outworn conventions of literary discourse. (The astronauts would receive the same treatment, and feel just as resentful of it.) "You are America, Lindbergh," one poet proclaims, and another adds that the aviator is "the embodiment of all / We've prayed America might be." The poets compare Lindbergh to a multitude of gods and heroes in the Western tradition. He is Jehovah and Christ, Apollo, Prometheus, Hermes, Bellerophon, David, Moses, Roland, Lancelot, Adam, Columbus, Ulysses, Beowulf, Marco Polo, Galahad, and Lohengrin, to name a few. And his beloved plane is compared frequently to Pegasus, the legendary flying horse. The machine is his "dear monster," in Babette Deutsch's phrase, something nonhuman, all-powerful, and perhaps a bit frightening like Dr. Frankenstein's monster, the demonic model for human invention in the literature of technology. Although Lindbergh disdained all this mythologizing, it nevertheless contributed to making his flight a boundary break in the history of Western thinking about the flying machine, for it set a standard by which all future pilots and machines would be measured, and usually found wanting.

The most positive and important reading of Lindbergh's flight can be found in children's and juvenile literature, for it is in these texts that the heroic version of airflight as a fulfillment of American destiny was made attractive to readers who would fly in the European and Pacific theaters during the next war. A good example is *The Red Eagle: A Tale for Young Aviators* (1930), by Alexander Key, an expensively produced book aimed at fourth- to sixth-grade pupils. The story opens with two boys, Ned and Richard, awaiting the arrival of Uncle Jim, who visits them occasionally in his monoplane *The Red Eagle*. A former "ace in the Argonne" with a scar on his face, he flies a plane raised to exalted status by its associations with the already legendary figures of flight: "The ship was powered with a Wright Whirlwind Motor, one of the same type that took Charles Lindbergh across the Atlantic."[16] They accompany Uncle Jim on a race at the flying club; he unexpectedly passes out during a thunderstorm because of a recurrence of shell-shock suffered during the war, and the boys pilot *The Red Eagle* to first place while he lies paralyzed in the cabin. Clearly an allegory of sorts is at work. The aviator's secret wound, of which the scar is an outward sign, represents the mixed effect of the war on the air tradition. If the conflict enabled the pilot to master his wings it also made an inward lesion that sets limits on his performance. He is redeemed by the children of promise, who inherit his powers. He and their father present them with a plane of their own, *The Red Eagle II,* as a reward and sign of confidence in their future as pilots.

The poets who celebrated Lindbergh insisted that he and his Pegasus represented a higher evolutionary state of being, more divine than mortal, and that his proper sphere of action was not the mortal coils of earth but the heavens. And clearly Lindbergh must be given credit for a transcendental strain in the literature of aviation that followed his flight. Frank Ernest Hill, who later collaborated with Allen Nevins on the first major biography of Henry Ford, published in 1928 a volume of poems called *Stone Dust* that praised the airplane as a means of masculine escape from the bonds of Mother Earth. As he puts it in the sestet of one sonnet:

Yet we shall brood upon this haunt of wings
When love, like perfume washed away in rain,
Dies on the years. Still we shall come again,
Seeking the clouds as we have sought the sea,
Asking the peace of these immortal things
That will not mix with our mortality.[17]

Here there is no reference to the return to earth that concludes every description of flight. The reader remains in the clouds, above the domesticity and mutability of the fallen world. Such poems remind us of the powerful strain of individualism in the American character, often manifested in the rejection of social obligations. In another poem, Hill asserts that "Earth is our yesterday" and that "Air is today." The progress of the species, he asserts, lies in its refinement of the means of participation with the higher things, the cloudy refuges and cosmic retreats. Likewise, the avant-garde author and editor Eugene Jolas issued several manifestoes in the 1930s calling for a new religion he called "Verticalism" based on the opportunities for ecstatic experience offered by the airplane.[18]

So often, when reading the poetry and fiction of this period, one feels that the author has Lindbergh in mind when some young, stalwart, and technically adept pilot is being described. The rhetorical assumptions derive directly from "WE" and nowhere more so than when the pilot is seen as one with his Pegasus, an artist of flight who makes amazing discoveries in his exalted views of the Creation. In her poem "Aviators' Eyes," Mina Loy asserts that "Aviators' eyes / never efface their far focus. . . / on arrow excursion / into profusion of distance / beyond our residence."[19] Harold Rosenberg, in a poem of 1935, "The Aeroplane Eye," provides a cinematic montage of airflight:

A trance of force, the
Steel
Within a hurrying of wires
              Spins
The plane
Slices the landscape
High
In backward folds. . .

The pilot sees the landscape as a god sees, or a Cubist artist. The airplane has given to man the immense advantage of new perspectives, and new responsibilities, but it has alienated him from the obligations of the earthbound. Rosenberg's poem turns dark as he considers the pilot further:

Who are these pilots
Wagering history
On the turn of one idea

Whose crackling geometrics wake
Far birds of sorrow round
The tolling angels of the inland ways?[20]

Like Hart Crane and Muriel Rukeyser, Rosenberg worries that a fractured vision of earth and an addiction to ascent above the multitude will diminish the sense of duty pilots ought to feel toward their humanistic origins and their native beliefs. Some writings cite Lindbergh's quick absorption into the corridors of power, as businessman and political pundit, as a cautionary lesson about the disadvantages of habitually cutting one's ties to ordinary people and their unglamorous experience. When James Thurber, in "The Greatest Man in the World," dared to imagine a famous aviator exploiting and abusing the hero-worship of his admirers, nobody had to ask the author which public figure inspired the short story.

In his play *Airways, Inc.* (1928), John Dos Passos likewise presents a disenchanted interpretation of the way new Horatio Algers had wedded themselves to machinery on the model of Lindbergh's "WE." Like Charley Anderson in *U.S.A.*, the play's young aviator hopes to cash in on the burgeoning airline industry and gradually suffers a loss of moral integrity because of his devotion to getting rich. Fascination with new machinery, Dos Passos suggests, has a way of transforming people into machines. "We must become steel automatons," says one of the characters.[21] This transformation changes everything in turn: the father-son relation that becomes competitive and embittered, the social contract that becomes more and more mercenary, and the environment which is gradually degraded by new industry as land values around factories and airports climb. "There's money in it…in the air," the young man says; his grasping materialism represents the antithesis of what Lindbergh's flight had meant to the poets, who saw his ascent as an escape from materialism and commercialism into a purer world of the spirit.

A more complex view of the Lindbergh legacy is offered by William Faulkner in his novel *Pylon* (1935). Through the eyes of a reporter who remains outside the main action, Faulkner tells the story of a team of air-racers who enjoy a bohemian life full of risks and the thrill of speed, of "blind furious motion." These are not ordinary people, the narrator tells his editor: "Because they ain't human like us; they couldn't turn those pylons like they do if they had human blood and senses and they wouldn't dare to if they just had human brains. . . . It ain't even human blood when you haul him out [after a crash]: it's cylinder oil the same as in the crankcase."[22] These daredevils have become mythic creatures; they have blended into the alien reality of the flying machine; and the reporter, who stands in for all of his readers, feels both envious of their unusual life and grateful for his difference from them. The airplanes, he believes, are "fatal animals," and his suspicion is confirmed when the chief pilot crashes after racing a defective plane because he needs the prize money for his pregnant wife.

In a book review of the period, Faulkner had called for "a new folklore of the air," one based on "this whole new business of speed."[23] He desired a literature that responded to the airplane as a mode of transportation, not a glorified tool of aggression. Faulkner himself could not create a new folklore because he was so intent on demolishing the old folklore, the old lies about the knighthood of the air. But other writers were more optimistic about discovering an ideal equilibrium between man, machine, and nature, and about how all of society could benefit not only from a perception of flight as a means of self-perfection but from a fervent endorsement of the future of aviation as a model for the conduct of nations in a time of crisis. In France, Antoine de St. Exupéry was popularizing this ideal of flight in books such as *Southern Mail, Night Flight,* and *Wind, Sand and Stars,* all very popular in the United States during the 1930s. These books argued that civil aviation not only allowed pilots a personal ecstasy and sense of purpose but also created greater solidarity between people and nations by means of mail routes, passenger service, and—ultimately—the example of a smoothly functioning worldwide network of services that bypassed national interests to forge a global consciousness.

In America, the figure closest to Saint-Exupéry was Anne Morrow Lindbergh, who accompanied her aviator-husband on many flights around the world, and recorded her experiences in poetry, fiction, and nonfiction throughout her life. Especially in early works such as *North to the Orient, The Steep Ascent,* and *Listen, the Wind,* she emphasized the moral and spiritual uplift that comes with dutiful attention to the needs and potentialities of the airplane. As with the Wrights and Charles Lindbergh, her language is precise, practical, and rational, eschewing the romanticism of the poets and the polemical skepticism of fiction writers such as Dos Passos and Faulkner. Although she did not have a feminist program, her assumption that women can be skilled aviators, knowledgeable about the mechanical intricacies of their airplanes and influential in forging new routes across boundaries to other nations, anticipated the full entry of women into positions of authority in the world of aviation. Like Beryl Markham, the remarkable East African aviatrix whose memoir *West with the Night* (1942) is a modern classic, Anne Morrow Lindbergh pioneered in both the experience and the literature of flight.

In *North to the Orient,* the two Lindberghs fly their Lockheed Sirius over the fabled Northwest Passage, enjoying the new visual reality afforded by a machine she compares to a "glass-bottomed bucket with which to look through the ruffled surface of life far down to that still permanent world below."[24] A kind of dialogue is established between the fliers and the earth, a paradigm, we are to understand, of the ideal social and political hierarchy. Their mastery as technicians, a central element in her novel *The Steep Ascent,* endows on them responsibilities for the preservation of the natural order and the leadership of the human community. Implicit in this placement of aviators atop the moral order of the species is an imperial politics that matched the sense of destiny shared by powerful industrial nations just before World War II. Mrs. Lindbergh would develop this point of view in her controversial monograph of 1940, *The Wave of the Future,* which seemed to many readers, especially because of her husband's activity in isolationist causes, too reminiscent of profascist writings in Europe. Nevertheless, her narratives of flight familiarized the general public, the more so because of her celebrity status, with the pleasures and profits of building an international network for aviation.

Wartime and After

World War II darkened the luster of the flying machine in much the same way as the first. But, whereas the dirigibles and fixed-winged aircraft of 1914–18 were limited in their ability to inflict casualties, the new bombers, so much more powerful and precise in their targeting, loomed in the public imagination as monsters from the nightmares of fantasy literature. In England, George Orwell, Vita Sackville-West, W. H. Auden, Stephen Spender, and Graham Greene had written eloquently about the human cost of aerial bombardment, especially in the context of the Spanish Civil War. That war seemed even in the late 1930s to be a dress rehearsal for the world war waiting in the wings. And in the testimony of the most famous American novelist of the era, Franco's assault on the Spanish Republic made immoral use of flying machines to enforce his fascist will on the citizenry. In *For Whom the Bell Tolls* (1940), Ernest Hemingway established the convention for all later writers of identifying the airplane as an icon of total destruction:

> They stood in the mouth of the cave and watched them. The bombers were high now in fast, ugly, arrow-heads beating the sky apart with the noise of their motors. They are shaped like sharks, Robert Jordan thought, the wide-finned, sharp-nosed sharks of the Gulf Stream. But these, wide-finned in silver, roaring, the light mist of their propellers in the sun, these do not move like sharks. They move like no thing there has ever been. They move like mechanized doom.[25]

Like no thing there has ever been. In the novel's most famous passage of combat, these same Heinkel bombers annihilate the hilltop defense of the valiant Spanish partisan El Sordo and his compatriots. There and elsewhere, the image of the air fleet "hammering the sky apart as they went over" fixed in the mind of the American reading public the awesome power of these new machines.

Whatever one's politics, the sense of the airplane as preeminently an agent of mass destruction entered the American psyche. For Alexander de Seversky, in his alarmist tract of 1942, *Victory through Air Power,* the airplane provided America's only chance to resist being overwhelmed by massive bombardment of the nation by the fascists. In order to argue for air power on our side, however, he had to create a compelling and frightening picture of the danger from abroad. His description of a punishing bombardment of the United States in the opening chapter of his bestselling book haunted the public imagination throughout the war and the Cold War that followed. Seversky creates an apocalyptic scenario by recourse to nightmare imagery from the literary tradition. As the nation sleeps, "the invading aerial giants strike at the nerve centers and jugular veins of a great nation." Here the vampire myth is combined with the fantasy of the giant to render the helplessness of the victim. "[The naval force] can now do nothing, literally nothing, against the locust swarms of giant airplanes," Seversky continues.[26] Walt Disney translated Seversky's images into animated form in a propaganda film, with such horrifying results that the Disney studios withdrew the film after a first showing. Nevertheless, book and movie alike enforced Seversky's conviction that in order to survive in the nightmare world of mid-century, "Every American—man, woman, and child—must be an airman in his heart."

America's entry into the war after Pearl Harbor led to an immediate and salutary revision of the flying machine as a popular icon. Now the devastating firepower of the bomber could be imagined not as aimed against helpless humanity, in America or elsewhere, but as an agent of Allied determination to repel the forces of totalitarianism. The airplane regained much of its heroic identity as an irresistible force of good in the world. Lindbergh's own conversion from isolationist to working member of the military team, designing and piloting new aircraft in the Pacific theater, symbolized the restoration of the Daedalean myth in the wartime generation. Once again, flying machines showed up in films and children's books, as in all popular literature, as a figure for American ingenuity and American muscle, a sign of the enlightened community cooperating to preserve its humanistic heritage.

A good example of these sentiments in action is John Steinbeck's nonfiction account, *Bombs Away: The Story of a Bombing Team* (1942). As the title suggests, Steinbeck's purpose in what is candidly a propaganda work is to call attention to the necessity for cooperation in the flying of a successful bombing mission. The book is not about combat but about the stages of training that precede combat. The members of the team learn about the resources of the plane, and most important, they learn how to work together toward a common goal. Steinbeck argues that Americans are predisposed to cooperate in this manner because of their upbringing in democratic institutions. Here, as so often in the literature of war, sports provides the author with a convenient metaphor:

This is the kind of organization that Americans above all others are best capable of maintaining. The bomber team is truly a democratic organization. No single man can give all the orders to make a bomber effective. The effectiveness of its mission rests on the initiative and judgment of each one of its members. Not everyone on a football team insists on being quarterback. He plays the position he is best fitted to play. The best football team is one where every member plays his own particular game as a part of the team. The best bomber team is the one where each man plays for the success of the mission.[27]

Steinbeck uses baseball metaphors for the same purpose. Here the airplane is being presented as a microcosm of the American experience, so different from the fascist model of the charismatic leader and his mass of idolaters. The pilot is no longer appreciated as a "Knight of the Air" as in the first war, nor as "Master of the Empyrean," as Lindbergh was called by his poet-admirers. Rather, the pilot is one among equals in an organization of specialized talents.

The bomber, then, becomes a symbol of America itself, a container of diverse and virtuous lives working together, not without tension and prejudice, toward the salvation of civilization. In Steinbeck's account, as in many novels about bombing crews that followed, we learn about the backgrounds and personal dreams of the crewmembers. The pilot was an athlete who liked to tinker with a Ford jalopy; the navigator had a mathematical bent; the gunners enjoyed hunting in the woods; the radioman was fascinated with modern electronics. They form a geographical cross-section of the nation, with homes in South Carolina, Idaho, California, and Indiana, but now they have the tremendous responsibility of working together for the good of the whole society they symbolize. This communitarian ideal can be found in much war literature, of course, but the flying machine offers the more persuasive metaphor because when airborne it is less subject to the will of a leader than is an army platoon or naval vessel on the move.

Novels featuring sailing vessels did explore the same psychic and social territory in the nineteenth century. Above all, Herman Melville's *Moby-Dick* (1851) casts a shadow over the fiction of modern warfare. The temptation to create a mad captain and a restless crew can be seen in postwar novels about the navy such as Herman Wouk's *The Caine Mutiny,* and in novels like John Hersey's *The War Lover* (1959), in which a pilot named Buzz Marrow at first fascinates the crew of a bomber by his verbal flair and his knightly code, and then is revealed during a crisis to be a hollowed-out egotist who endangers the mission. The crew is saved by the skills of the narrator and copilot, Charles Bowman, who like the reader is shaken out of his hero-worship when he discovers that the plane's survival depends on unromantic personality traits such as steadiness, kindness, loyalty, and respect for one's fellow workers. When Hersey's novel appeared, it was widely cited as a dramatic illustration of William H. Whyte's *The Organization Man,* a social science text of the postwar period that described and in some cases critiqued the conversion of American business from the model of the independent titan who shapes the organization in his image—Ford, Rockefeller, Edison—to that of the facilitator and team player in a democratic enterprise. Hersey used the airplane to cast his vote against the Ahabs of American society and in favor of a more egalitarian model of "crew integrity," in the military phrase.

And yet the pilot never loses the Romantic or heroic aura derived from the early years of flight. When James Dickey looks back on wartime experience from the vantage of twenty years, in his dramatic monologue "The Firebombing" (1964), he shows an ex-pilot exulting in retrospect over "the greatest sense of power in one's life" that he once wielded in sorties over Japan.[28] In his lyrical recreation of a bombing run, he imagines himself as part of the airplane, imposing his will on the enemy. Because he is guided by "Old Testament light" toward his destination, he feels as if he and his airplane are agents of God's will, redeeming the promised land by subjecting the "enemy rivers and trees" to "all / American fire." Dickey opens up the poem typographically to give the sense of "sailing artistically over" a landscape at night, and mimics the air turbulence by his lineation. No other person appears in the poem, only "some technical-minded stranger with my hands," the speaker's younger self, who undertook such a glorious crusade before falling into the postwar doldrums of the suburbs, just as Faulkner's pilots descended in their Icarian fall into unsatisfying experiences back home.

Dickey's novel *Alnilam* (1987) is another investigation into the essential nature of the flying machine and the experience of flight. Like James Gould Cozzens's novel *Guard of Honor* (1948), and William Faulkner's novel *A Fable* (1954), it is set at an Army Air Corps base where crews are being trained for combat. The time is 1943, and the main character, Frank Cahill, has come to the base to learn more about the accidental death of his son, a pilot of such precocious skills that his commander compares him to Lindbergh. Cahill is instructed as the novel proceeds in the living qualities of the flying machine. "An airplane is not like a car," he is told by one of the instructors. "It's a lot more like an animal of some kind, a bird, a big on.... You're ... you're ridin' in it, and it feels everything that's in the thing it's in, the air, and you feel it through the plane."[29] Knowledge of aerodynamics and celestial navigation is essential, he is told, but more important is instinct, natural grace, "the whole-air feeling" that gives the pilot a sense of absolute control and unlimited power. When he has this feeling, the pilot can make contact with the deepest secrets of the cosmos, as Cahill's son was trying to define in his semimystical teachings to a band of disciples. As his initials suggest, Joel Cahill's life and death are meant to take on the parabolic character of a religious allegory. The airplane is not only his means of transcendence but his Cross as well, and the secret society called Alnilam founded after his crash-landing presages a religion of flight for the next millennium.

It must not be thought, however, that this ecclesiastical version of the sacred calling has dominated postwar literature. It was inevitable that a heretical, iconoclastic countertradition would arise to challenge the iconography of Kitty Hawk, Lindbergh, and the sanctified bombing crew. The work of American literature that exploded the pieties of military aviation especially, and transformed the image of the airplane-as-microcosm into something less sublime than ridiculous, was Joseph Heller's novel of 1961, *Catch-22*. This satire of a B-25 squadron stationed on a Mediterranean island during World War II, along with the film *Dr. Strangelove* (1963), enforced on a younger generation a sense of the rituals of aviation as absurd and destructive. The countercultural implications of *Catch-22* extended beyond aviation and nourished the movement to undermine established authority throughout the 1960s and afterward.

Joseph Heller had served as a wing bombardier in the Army Air Corps during World War II, and flew sixty combat missions. The novel's protagonist, Yossarian, is a bombardier who in 1944, after some forty missions, discerns with numbing clarity how unsafe he is. Yossarian is a survivalist; he sits over the escape hatch in the bombing runs thinking only of how many more missions he must endure before being allowed to go home. His fellows in the plane are not Steinbeck's or Hersey's team of responsible citizens but incompetents and cowards like himself. His superiors in rank are more dangerous than the enemy, especially as epitomized by Colonel Cathcart, who keeps raising the number of missions required before a flier can be released from service. And the enemy is after him, too. Yossarian's chief goal, then, is to make it through the day: "His only mission each time he went up was to come down alive."[30]

The airplane, in this book, is not a means of escaping the problem of mortality, as in the Romantic version of flight; it is the problem. The only character who benefits from the modern airplane's powers is the entrepreneurial genius Milo Minderbinder, who sends the air force around the world to collect delicacies and sell them at immense profits, and even contracts with the Germans to bomb his own squadron. In this scathing parody of the teamwork/leadership theme of so much fiction about military aviation, Milo's ability to engineer a thriving international business points up what Heller sees as the demonic destiny of the airplane. The flying machine is an emblem of an elitist capitalism triumphant over the proclaimed democratic values of flight. Ordinary people are fated forever to be shot down or bombed in wars made necessary by global business interests in search of new markets.

This paranoid vision made a perfect fit with the protests against the Vietnam War that began shortly after *Catch-22* was published. It was easy to see the aerial bombardment in Vietnam as brutal and senseless, and the loss of American life as pointless and absurd. *Catch-22* became a classic in part because it spoke to the suspicion of Americans about the wisdom and honesty of their leaders and the moral and political justifications for undertaking combat in places such as Korea and Vietnam. The protest poetry of Robert Bly, Galway Kinnell, and Denise Levertov; fiction such as Norman Mailer's *Why Are We in Vietnam?* (1967)—an allegorical novel about hunting bears from a helicopter in Alaska— and films such as *Apocalypse Now* (1979), with its terrifying imagery of aerial bombardment, presented the airplane in ever-darker tones in the manner of Hemingway. The comedy of Heller's novel gave way to nightmare fantasies about an insane culture of violence. The literature of Vietnam marks the nadir of the airplane's reputation in the twentieth century.

Conclusion: Nostalgia and Renewal

In 1969, in the midst of social and political turmoil in the United States, the astronauts of Apollo 11 became the first human beings to walk on the surface of the moon. The amazing accomplishment of this event, the subsequent Apollo missions, the Viking missions, the Space Shuttle, the Hubble telescope, and the space program in general overshadowed in significance the history of aviation, in public discourse as in literature. If poetry and fiction can be trusted as an index of public attitudes, the achievements of NASA had a dual effect on the status of the airplane during the period after 1969. First, the space program stole the glamour from mere aircraft. The sublime associations of flight now belonged almost totally to astronauts and rockets, as science fiction and speculative fantasy usurped other literary modes in popularity among the younger generation. But because the origins of space travel lie in aeronautics, the glory of "the high frontier" was reflected back to the history of aviation, which became subject to nostalgic recuperation as visionary writers and readers reminded themselves of the dreams that lifted the wings of aircraft before Saturn-Apollo.

Because poetry has always privileged the solo lyrical voice and the expression of intense and concentrated feeling, the renewal of enthusiasm for the flying machine is most visible in poems of the 1970s, 1980s, and 1990s. One thinks of Philip Levine returning in fancy to Kitty Hawk in the opening poem of *One for the Rose* (1981):

> I would be
> the original pilot, thirty-one, bare-headed,
> my curly brown hair cut short and tinged
> with blood from a wounded left hand
> that must be attended to. Only an hour
> before it was a usual summer morning,
> warm and calm, in North Carolina,
> and the two hectic brothers had laid aside

their bicycles and were busily assembling
the struts, wires, strings, and cranking
over the tiny engine. I faced the wind,
a cigarette in one hand, a map of creation
in the other. Silently, I watch my hand
disappear into the white gauze the lady
turns and turns. I am the first to fly.[31]

I am the first to fly. As writers look back into aviation history, they indulge themselves in the fantasy of being pioneers, of inventing a new machine as complex and powerful as the big machine of America itself, a nation originally constructed by the founding fathers at the height of the Enlightenment and advancing at cyberspeed in the twenty-first century. As spaceflight nourished the confidence of Americans that gravity of all kinds could be defied by technical ingenuity, the various "firsts" of aviation became more and more appealing as metaphors for the rebirth of national confidence and national purpose following the Vietnam era.

Of special interest to writers in recent decades is the succession of women aviators from the early period of flight to the present. No doubt, the feminist movement has influenced the attention being paid to independent-minded pilots such as Amelia Earhart, the first woman to fly the Atlantic Ocean alone, five years to the day after Lindbergh, and the first to fly across the United States alone in both directions. One hears the contemporary note in a dramatic monologue given to Earhart by Donald Everett Axinn:

Up there I am free of the ground, apart from men
who say, "You're a woman, you can't handle
danger, you don't understand engines and can't cope with
mechanical requirements. And your navigation . . . ?"
I say to all of you that women are as good
as men; we do not need male strength or braggadocio.

. . . .
Our nerves are as steady, we are certainly
as alert; and women have endurance that men do not.[32]

Pamela Alexander pays tribute to Earhart also, in her poem "Flight":

she renews
herself, like the engine, for
one thing. Flight
above the wine-dark shining flood
is order, makes the squares
come and go, makes the plane
a tiny gear that turns the world.[33]

The "squares" are the portions of land she takes into her consciousness in the act of flying. As in the rapturous books of Saint-Exupéry, Earhart's experience of flight permits her intimate participation with the whole of the cosmos, the stars above and the earth below. S. Ben-Tov's three poems on Earhart transform the aviatrix into a symbol of mobility, of the movement not only from place to place but from the self to the transcendent, otherworldly realm:

> To travel light! To make travel
> my self, my body, both more and less than these,
> my smoke plume a slight roughening on the sky,
> the engine cowl's sheen, the throttle's surge,
> these small events the stars
> in a constellation of pure travel.[34]

"Pure travel" is a phrase that takes us back to the romances of nineteenth-century American literature in which the restless movement of independent spirits across the frontier represented the dream of occupying a privileged place in the New World, shedding the roles and burdens of a moribund Old World culture. Natty Bumppo in James Fenimore Cooper's novels, Ishmael in Melville's *Moby-Dick,* and Huckleberry Finn in Mark Twain's masterpiece are the clearest literary ancestors of this desire for absolute freedom from social constraints. The nostalgia for the American dream of redemptive travel articulated by these authors appeals especially to female writers who see their task as a recuperation of the visionary experience bequeathed by writers earlier in our history. (Pamela Alexander also has written a book-length poem about John James Audubon.) Earhart's mysterious disappearance during an attempted round-the-world flight in 1937 makes her even more of a cultic figure, as if she had flown into some divine realm of being. One thinks of the African American folklore of flight, especially as Toni Morrison adapts it in her novel *Song of Solomon* (1977), and Robert Hayden in his poem "O Daedalus, Fly Away Home," in which select individuals are given the power of flying to the paradise denied them in their sordid everyday experience.

As the century came to an end, then, it was no surprise that one of the most popular novels ever written about aviation concerned Amelia Earhart and the "paradise" she discovers after her plane crash-lands on a remote atoll in the South Pacific. *I Was Amelia Earhart* (1996) by Jane Mendelsohn sold hundreds of thousands of copies, thanks in large part to a media blitz initiated by a New York talk-show host. The novel imagines Earhart as a complex figure, both a "great heroine" wedded to her Lockheed Electra with all the fervent practicality of a Lindbergh, and also a dreamy and sensual woman with a Romantic death wish who conducts a steamy sexual affair with her copilot Noonan after she disappears from the world's ken:

When I wake up, when the tide is out, when Noonan is asleep, I go and sit in the cockpit whose every inch I know by heart. I sit under the light of a starry sky, illegible to me but sparkling so clearly it seems a different sky than the ones I've known before, written in an intricately beautiful foreign language, and the flights I have made in the past retain their original magic when I reenact them in my mind.[35]

Mendelsohn's novel successfully revived the Romantic iconography of airplane and pilot not by focusing on a contemporary figure but by returning to a glamorous prewar era in which the apocalyptic promise of the flying machine attracted women as well as men to try their wings and rise on currents of instinctual desire to the heavens.

A reader looking for signs of renewal, then, would find them first in the retrospective texts of the last few decades. World War II is the setting not only of James Dickey's *Alnilam* but of Jim Shepard's novel *Paper Doll* (1986), which reprises the theme of crew teamwork on a B-17 bomber headed for its target. Tom Wolfe's *The Right Stuff* (1979) is a debunking account of the Mercury astronauts, but it treats reverently the development of the supersonic jets at Edwards Air Force Base, and casts Chuck Yeager, the first man to break the sound barrier, in 1947, as an authentic hero, the heir to the mantle of glory bequeathed by Lindbergh. Even when the setting of the narrative is not an earlier era but a contemporary theater of conflict, the storytelling conventions recall earlier novels so vividly that the reader seems to be returning in spirit to a historical period when the sense of a just crusade permeated the society. In Stephen Coonts's novel of 1986 about Vietnam, *Flight of the Intruder,* one feels constantly the presence of famous earlier tales of aerial combat and aerial exploration, such as those by Ernest K. Gann, or the James Michener of *The Bridges of Toko-Ri.* Coonts himself flew A-6 Intruders for the U.S. Navy during the Vietnam conflict, and his descriptions of the exhilaration of battle, and the harrowing doubts and fears of his fliers have the ring of authenticity. Coonts's book is filled with "the facts of aerial life"; perhaps no fiction about the airplane has been so technical in its vocabulary:

> Jake Grafton was relaxed. He kept his position about 300 feet aft and to the right of the skipper's plane without conscious effort. Each plane carried sixteen Mark 82 500-pound bombs beneath its wings, plus the usual 2000-pound fuel tank hung on the centerline—or belly—station. . . . The controller passed the flight to a forward air controller, a FAC, who would be flying a light plane with the call sign "Covey" somewhere up ahead. Greve toggled the radio to the assigned frequency, and Grafton keyed the mike twice.[36]

As with so much literature of flight, the language here appeals to the American fascination with the minute particulars of mechanical systems. The novel eschews the poet's lyrical voice for the obsessive precision and detail of actual operations. Coonts is sensitive to moral and emotional issues as well in the novel, but he is faithful above all to the procedures of flight, the technical accomplishment, in the spirit of aviators like the Wright brothers, Lindbergh, and the chroniclers of World War II. Indeed, to the extent that Ronald Reagan appealed for a return in spirit to the glorious and triumphant American past as a keystone of his presidency, war stories such as Coonts's that reprised the conventions of earlier novels fit neatly into the "top gun" mentality of the decade.

Indeed, the emergence of America as the lone superpower following the end of the Cold War, the Gulf War, and the aerial bombardment of Kosovo and Serbia in 1999 has created a market for imagery of aerial dominance throughout the mass media. As television and movies, especially, constantly recirculate documentary and recreated footage of the airplane's evolution toward its present high-tech incarnations, the American public has become increasingly fascinated with the fine points of this ever-changing machine on which the viability of American leadership depends. The prestige of computer technology has helped to revive the positive associations of mechanical inventions in general, and popularize literary accounts of aerial procedures in particular. Like the information superhighway, the airplane carries its nation of travelers into a global future designed on the imperial model of American systems, but unlike the software enjoyed in the cozy spaces of office and home the airplane continues to offer postmodern tourists in cyberspace the possibility of authentic physical movement to the familiar, stable sites of American experience.

Coonts's book *The Cannibal Queen: An Aerial Odyssey across America* (1992) offers readers a nostalgic vision of this kind. *The Cannibal Queen* is another in the genre of the flier's memoir, beginning with bestselling accounts of the air war by veterans of World War I. But, unlike militaristic memoirs, *The Cannibal Queen* and works like it celebrate the peaceful uses of the flying machine as a means of solidarity between fellow citizens. Coonts refurbished a 1942 Stearman open-cockpit biplane, and with his fourteen-year-old son wended his way across America toward Disney World. On the way, he stops in small towns similar to the one in which he grew up, and measures the changes in American society between his own boyhood and the 1990s. His report is a positive one; he becomes a messenger of good news not only from town to town but from the American past to the American future. His mobility allows him a special vision of the opportunities of American life and the native resourcefulness of the American people. One senses, as always, that the airplane has permitted Coonts to speak about renewal and redemption with special authority—the authority given him by piloting a wonderful invention that sponsors a sense of childlike wonder in one exemplary father-and-son team. Likewise, Jim Shepard's novel of a boy's fascination with and furtive theft of an airplane, *Flights* (1983), and Diane Ackerman's prose account of learning to fly, *On Extended Wings* (1985), dramatize the desire of young people to join the visionary company of fliers. It may well be that the development of ultralight aircraft, with its promise of solo flight for no purpose but the pleasure of ascent and birdlike maneuvering, will inspire renewed enthusiasm for the act of putting on wings like that of Coonts, Shepard, and Ackerman.

Unlike horizontal engines of movement such as cars and trains, the airplane holds the promise for every generation of vertical ascent with metaphorical affinities to the spirit's liberation from captivity in the body and on the earth. Writers who represent the airplane continue to see it as an instrument of our successful negotiations with the constraints of time and space, and as a means of achieving extraordinary vitality and power. We triumph over obstacles in the liftoff and glide of the flying machine, and return to the conditions of mortal life as the plane sets down again on the runway. This pattern of ascent and descent reflects a fundamental emotional and intellectual contour of our lives, akin to sexual performance, professional accomplishment, the tides of battle, the rise and decline of generations and nations. The airplane remains one of the most powerful metaphors yet devised for our whole experience as human beings. It was the indispensable symbol of American life in the twentieth century and will undoubtedly keep its elevated position in the public imagination throughout the present century.

Notes

1. A convenient reprinting of Trowbridge's poem is in Joseph B. Roberts and Paul L. Briand, eds., *The Sound of Wings: Readings for the Air Age* (New York: Henry Holt, 1957), 48–55.

2. Stuart and Susan Levine, *The Short Fiction of Edgar Allan Poe* (Indianapolis: Bobbs-Merrill, 1976), 557.

3. Cited in Louis Mertins, *Robert Frost: Life and Talks-Walking* (Norman: University of Oklahoma Press, 1965), 195.

4. *Complete Poems of Robert Frost* (New York: Holt, Rinehart, and Winston, 1964), 407.

5. *The Papers of Wilbur and Orville Wright,* ed. Marvin W. McFarland (New York: McGraw-Hill, 1953), II, 1042, 979, 1019 (italics added).

6. John Dos Passos, *U.S.A.* (Boston: Houghton, Mifflin, 1946), 250–55.

7. *The Poems of Hart Crane,* ed. Marc Simon (New York: Liveright, 1986), 79.

8. *The Collected Poems of Muriel Rukeyser* (New York: McGraw-Hill, 1982), 22.

9. Selden Rodman, *The Airmen: A Poem in Four Parts* (New York: Random House, 1941), 89. Another book-length poem of the period that honored the Wright brothers by an excess of technical and historical data is John William Andrews, *Prelude to "Icaros"* (New York: Farrar and Rinehart, 1936).

10. Robert Frost, *In the Clearing* (New York: Holt, Rinehart, and Winston, 1962), 48–49.

11. Frederick Jackson Turner, *The Frontier in American History* (New York: Henry Holt and Co., 1920), 22, 37.

12. *Interviews with Robert Frost,* ed. Edward Connery Lathem (New York: Holt, Rinehart, and Winston, 1974), 266.

13. David Lloyd George, *The Great Crusade: Extracts from Speeches Delivered during the War* (New York: George H. Doran, 1918), 212.

14. William Faulkner, *Soldiers' Pay* (New York: Liveright, 1926), 41.

15. Charles Vale, ed., *The Spirit of St. Louis* (New York: Doran, 1927).

16. Alexander Key, *The Red Eagle: Being the Adventurous Tale of Two Young Fliers* (New York: The Wise-Parslow Co., 1930), 11.

17. Frank Ernest Hill, *Stone Dust* (New York: Longmans, Green, 1928), 21. The most widely reprinted example of this neo-Romantic sentiment is the sonnet by John Gillespie Magee, Jr., titled "High Flight." "Oh, I have slipped the surly bonds of earth," it begins, and concludes, "I've trod / The high untrespassed sanctity of space, / Put out my hand, and touched the face of God." Magee was killed serving with the Royal Canadian Air Force (RCAF) during the early years of World War II. His poem can be found in Roberts and Briand, *The Sound of Wings,* 171.

18. See, for example, his commentary in the anthology he edited, *Vertical: A Yearbook for Romantic-Mystic Ascensions* (New York: Gotham Bookmart Press, 1941). A like-minded predecessor is Bruce Gould, *Sky-Larking: The Romantic Adventures of Flying* (New York: Liveright, 1929).

19. Mina Loy, *The Last Lunar Baedeker* (Highlands, N.C.: The Jargon Society, 1982), 215.

20. *Poetry,* XLV, no. VI (March 1935), 325.

21. John Dos Passos, *Airways, Inc.* (New York: Macaulay Co., 1928), 141–42. The following quotation is on page 77.

22. William Faulkner, *Pylon* (1935; New York: Random House, 1967), 45.

23. William Faulkner, "Folklore of the Air," *The American Mercury,* XXXVI (November 1935), 370–72.

24. Anne Morrow Lindbergh, *North to the Orient* (New York: Harcourt, Brace, 1935), 244.

25. Ernest Hemingway, *For Whom the Bell Tolls* (New York: Scribner's, 1940), 87.

26. Alexander P. de Seversky, *Victory Through Air Power* (New York: Simon and Schuster, 1942), 8, 10. The following quotation is on page 329.

27. John Steinbeck, *Bombs Away: The Story of a Bomber Team* (New York: Viking, 1942), 23. A good analysis of this book and its tradition can be found in Richard Taylor Dillon's Ph.D. dissertation, "The Sound of Wings: Aviation in Twentieth-Century Literature" (University of California, Berkeley, 1970).

28. James Dickey, *Poems 1957–1967* (Middletown, Conn.: Wesleyan University Press, 1967), 181–88. Dickey's pilot can usefully be compared to the soul-searching aviator-hero in Jeremy Ingalls's epic poem, *Tahl* (New York: Alfred A. Knopf, 1945). Tahl considers the bombardment of Spanish cities, especially Guernica, as an outrage against humanity, and seeks with passionate intensity for some transcendent meaning in all the violence of his era.

29. James Dickey, *Alnilam* (New York: Doubleday, 1987), 138. "I doubt if Lindbergh was any better [than your son]," the instructor tells Cahill. "I doubt if he was as good" (162).

30. Joseph Heller, *Catch-22* (New York: Simon and Schuster, 1961), 30.

31. Philip Levine, *One for the Rose* (New York: Atheneum, 1981), 3.

32. Donald Everett Axinn, *Dawn Patrol* (New York: Cross-Cultural Communications, 1992), 24.

33. Pamela Alexander, *Navigable Waterways* (New Haven, Conn.: Yale University Press, 1985), 4.

34. S. Ben-Tov, *During Ceasefire* (New York: Harper & Row, 1985), 81.

35. Jane Mendelsohn, *I Was Amelia Earhart* (New York: Alfred A. Knopf, 1996), 76–77.

36. Stephen Coonts, *Flight of the Intruder* (Annapolis: Naval Institute Press, 1986), 78–79.

"Our Future Is in the Air"

Aviation and American Art

Gerald Silk

T he relationship between aviation and American art presents two problems. The first involves defining the precise nature of this relationship. The inclusion of an aeronautical image in a work of visual art is the most obvious connection, and *selected* examples of these will be the main focus of this chapter. (I emphasize the word "selected," because space constraints force the omission of many provocative images of aviation in art.) But the airplane affected not just the content of art but also its form, and I shall explore how sensibilities changed by flight surfaced in the visual arts. In addition, principles believed to be associated with aeronautics—streamlining perhaps the most important—influenced twentieth-century art and design; for the most part, I shall not touch on this link.

The second problem involves the relative dearth of images of airplanes in American art, particularly by important artists in the early part of the century. Although this might be attributed to an alleged antipathy between art and technology, some facts militate against this interpretation. Certain contemporaneous European movements and artists enthusiastically embraced this theme (although its treatment is hardly widespread), and several American artists incorporated other technological motifs into their art. Considering that America was the birthplace of heavier-than-air vehicles, and had its share of pioneering aeronautical achievements, the paucity of aviation iconography in early-twentieth-century American art may seem even more surprising.

I shall deal with this second problem by devoting the introductory part of this chapter to European developments, as they establish themes crucial to the understanding of the role of the airplane in art, no matter what the geography. After that, I shall offer reasons, admittedly speculative, as to why American artists in the early part of the century, for the most part, neglected this subject.

Italian Futurism

The European art movement most enamored with the motif of flight was Italian Futurism, and its approach to aeronautical phenomena lays the groundwork for any study of the relationship between aviation and art. Founded in 1909 by the poet Filippo Tommaso Marinetti—shortly after Wilbur Wright's European flight demonstrations and several months prior to Marinetti's own initial flying experience—Futurism was the first major art movement to declare that modern technology provided suitable aesthetic subject matter. In the christening broadside of the movement—"The Founding and Manifesto of Futurism"— Marinetti makes two references to flight: one ancient, one modern. In the first instance, he invokes the famous classical masterpiece, the winged Nike of Samothrace, which to him represented an old, outmoded canon of beauty that was being surpassed by a new, more contemporary sensibility—"the beauty of speed." But the Nike is a sympathetic foil: it is one of the earliest and most evocative attempts in art to suggest movement, flight, even speed, and to signify victory or conquering, all components central to Futurist aesthetics and ideology.

Marinetti had a particular passion for images of flight.[1] They figure prominently in his writings before the birth of Futurism and continue as a leitmotif throughout the history of the movement. His aerial imagery offers ideal examples of changes in the treatment of this theme at the time when the modern airplane was invented, when the fantasy of flight became reality.[2] In his early work, Marinetti, very much a Symbolist poet, used flight as a metaphor for freedom and liberation, poetic imagination, and, in a revival of the neo-Platonic notion of ascent, transcendence from the material and corporeal world. By 1905, however, Marinetti's journey of the soul became a union of man and machine battling the forces of nature, expressed in a poem variously titled "To My Pegasus," and "To My Automobile," which mixes symbolist analogy, anarchic violence, and proto-Futurist technological exaltation. Invented two years after Orville Wright's first brief flight, and one year after Jules Verne's visionary fabrication of a hybrid motorcar, airplane, and submarine in his *Master of the World,* Marinetti's "Pegasus-car" flies "intoxicatingly, into the liberating Infinite! / Hurrah! No longer contact with the impure earth!" In adopting technology as a vehicular muse that surpassed the dreams of mythology, Marinetti did not abandon the association between flying and liberation, but used an image from modern reality to express escape from reality.

For Marinetti, and for many twentieth-century artists, this was a critical change in emphasis. Man's power, and the artist's source of inspiration, no longer lay in yearning and imagination, but in science and technology, no longer in dreams, but in actuality. Suddenly, man could fly like the angels. He appeared capable of invention and discovery that rivaled God's creations and was filled with a sense of awesome power. And, in the era of Nietzsche's proclamation, "God is Dead," technology would, for many, become something of a new "religion."

In 1909, Marinetti announced the birth of Italian Futurism in his "The Founding and Manifesto of Futurism."[3] In it, he urged artists to address a variety of modern subjects, among them "the gliding flight of planes whose pro-

Mark Tansey, *Picasso and Braque* (1992), oil on canvas, 80 × 108 in. Based on a photograph of the Wright brothers' maiden flight, Tansey's painting addresses the interaction between aviation and art and the European fascination with the achievements of the Wright brothers. Tansey relocates these trailblazing modernist artists from Paris to Kitty Hawk, replacing the Wright brothers with the team of Picasso in the plane and Braque running alongside. The Wrights' original biplane Flyer is instead a painted version of an early-twentieth-century cubist collage of a violin. Braque and Picasso had themselves adopted variations on the names Orville and Wilbur, perhaps imagining their aesthetic innovations as akin to the invention of flight. (Courtesy Los Angeles County Museum of Art, Modern and Contemporary Art Council Fund, photograph © 2003 Museum Associates/LACMA; and courtesy of the Gagosian Gallery, New York.)

peller flaps in the wind like a flag and seems to clap like an enthusiastic crowd."[4] The main feature of this document, however, is a "joy-ride" in a motorcar, and especially during the first phases of Futurism, the car was a more popular technological icon than the airplane. (The modern city and its dynamic activities, such as entertainment and labor, also were favored Futurist motifs.) The car's impact on daily life was direct, immediate, and widespread, and the experiences of auto travel, both as passenger and driver, were far more accessible than those of air travel. Then, as now, contact with the static ground was close, causing certain sensations created by the car, especially speed, to seem more dramatic than those of flying. Automobiles were a more integral part of the city; airplanes hovered above, remaining physically and psychologically aloft and aloof, and thus were a less logical symbol for the Futurist credo of intense involvement in life.[5] When the founding manifesto was written in 1909, Marinetti had already driven, ridden in and had an accident in (!) a car.[6] His first plane flight did not come until several months later.[7]

Nonetheless, Marinetti now had to confront how fantasy had become fact, as airplanes engaged in warfare, provided new points of view, simultaneously expanded and shrunk space, and widened experiences. Moreover, the airplane became a machine with which man could achieve an intoxicating union, as Marinetti exclaimed in the first manifesto: "We're about to witness the centaur's birth and before long we shall see the flight of angels."[8] Culling ideas from Bergson, Jarry, Nietzsche, Sorel, science fiction, and Lamarck's evolutionary theories (to mention but a few sources), Marinetti forecasts the cyborg or, as he called it, the "non-human-type." "Wings are asleep in the flesh of man ... [and he] will reign sovereign over Space and tame time," Marinetti wrote.[9] To him, science and technology were now producing inventions to rival the creations of mythology and God alike.

Several Futurist artists responded to Marinetti's exhortations and addressed aviation phenomena in their art. In the early years of the movement, aerial imagery often is allied to war (generally World War I), as in Gino Severini's *War* (1915) and *Flying over Rheims* (1915?), Marinetti's *Air Bombardment* (1915–16), Gerardo Dottori's *Wings over the Trenches* of circa 1916–18, and several pieces from Carlo Carrà's 1915 series entitled *Warpicture,* to mention but a few. The Futurist nexus between airplanes and battle is hardly surprising since Italy was the first to use airplanes militarily (which Marinetti observed firsthand in Libya in 1911), and as the Futurists were enthusiastic about war as a reassertion of Italian nationalism, an opportunity to destroy the old and implement the new, and a multisensory spectacle.[10]

Certainly Futurist military aeronautical depictions were politically motivated—supportive of the Allies and critical of the Central Powers—but haunting many of these images was recognition of the destructiveness of the war and the increasingly devastating role of aircraft. Severini's *Flying over Rheims* (1915?), a "plane's-eye" pictorialization of a poem titled "The Cathedral of Rheims" by his father-in-law Paul Fort, denounced the German bombing of the famous French church.[11] Within but also outside of the Futurist orbit, artists ranging from the Italian Mario Sironi to the German Otto Dix focused on military aircraft as an instrument of mass destruction, and its fundamental transformation of the practice of war and terrifying threat to previously inaccessible civilian locales and populations. This is the archetypal double-edged sword of modern technology: it could be harnessed beneficently or destructively. As one of a host of new technologies appearing around the turn of the twentieth century, the modern airplane, as reality and symbol, held forth the promise of either a century of hope and good, or despair and terror.[12]

On a formal level, Severini's *War* is noteworthy because its central image—a representation of a propeller—also functions as an organizing compositional force that generates a gentle centrifugal movement around which rotates a variety of images related to military conflict. Use of the propeller as both image and producer of pictorial dynamism and coherence probably derives from the French Cubist (although his distinctive brand of Cubism has been labeled "Orphism") Robert Delaunay's various depictions of the feats of the pioneering aviator Louis Blériot and his related abstractions consisting of slices of juxtaposed color meant to suggest a more universal dynamism.

The propeller motif appears in the art of several Futurists. Marinetti himself addressed this subject in *The Propeller* (1915–16?), a "words-in-freedom," his innovative literary form that he attributed to aerial (and also military) experiences. "Looking at objects from a new point of view, no longer head on or from behind, but straight down, that is foreshortened, I was able to break the old logical shackles and the plumb lines of ancient comprehension," he declared in his 1912 "The Technical Manifesto of Futurist Literature." He continued: "In the airplane, sitting on the gas tank, my stomach warmed by the pilot's head, I sensed the ridiculous inanity of the old syntax inherited from Homer. A burning need to liberate words, to pull them out from the prison of the Latin period."[13] Marinetti emancipated letters and words from pure literary functions. He transformed them into visual shapes, frequently combining them with numbers and mathematical symbols, and exploited alliteration and onomatopoeia to produce imagistic, expressive, and acoustic verbal-visual arrangements. "Words-in-freedom," like poetry in general, was meant to be spoken, albeit pugnaciously, rather than read. Some also operated as a radical form of war correspondence: multisensory, and visually and verbally chaotic, like battle itself. Some were published in an unusual format, meant to be unfolded like a letter, map, or a written military order; as one opened the page, he or she set the words free, giving them flight, so to speak.[14]

The Futurist Carlo Carrà's 1914 collage—*Free-Word Painting—Patriotic Festival*—may also be indebted compositionally to the image of a spinning propeller. Although questions remain as to the precise meaning of this piece, in regard to the issue of flight, some points can be made with reasonable certainty.[15] Designated a "painting-in-freedom," Carrà's collage is related to Marinetti's flight and war inspired "words-in-freedom." Carrà's use of collage and the mixing of visual and verbal signs, bringing together discrete, often fragmented, materials in a single, unified composition, recalls Marinetti's words: "Aerial speed has multiplied our knowledge of the world. . . . The whirling propeller told me, while I was speeding along at two hundred meters . . . [that] there is *an ever-vaster gradation of analogies,* there are ever-deeper and firmer connections, however remote. Analogy is none other than the deep love that connects distant, seemingly diverse and hostile things."[16]

The major compositional rhythms of the piece—spinning spokes of form that link the helix to Futurist notions of universal dynamism—derive, at least in part, from propeller movements. Filled with onomatopoeic references, many to machine sounds, the collage may present not just the configuration and energy of a propeller, but the noise produced by it and the motors of an airplane.

The perspective in this piece may well be from above, from a circling, spiraling aircraft, causing the mélange of data and stimuli below to appear vertiginous and whirling.[17] The view is of a piazza in which a flag-waving "interventionist demonstration" is underway, reestablishing the analogies in the first "Futurist Manifesto" between planes, propellers, fluttering flags, and cheering crowds. (Spiraling swirls of propagandistic leaflets—textually political bombs, so to speak—dropped from aircraft, also influenced Carrà's composition.)[18] Other allusions may include the rays of a central sun, and perhaps those of the recently invented electric light, invoking the generative associations of natural and artificial illumination, which may in turn imply the dawning of a new age of energy and the century of the machine. In a composition suggestive of a graphical representation of radio waves, the artist may be alluding to the "wireless," or "TSF"—"telegrafo senza fili" or "telegraphy without wires or strings"—perfected by the Italian Guglielmo Marconi.[19] Intriguingly, Marinetti envisioned that the next literary step beyond "words-in-freedom" would be "l'immaginazione senza fili" ["the imagination without strings"]. He states that "Futurism is grounded in the complete renewal of human sensibility brought about by the effects of great scientific discoveries," and includes the telegraph and the airplane among the list of the inventions that have "exerted decisive influence on [man's] psyche."[20] Aviation itself is tied to wireless telegraphy, as ground-to-air communication became essential to flying in general, and to military aviation in particular. Of course, both airwaves and airplanes travel through the air in an effort to vanquish space and time.

Fusing the sun-electric light-wireless references, Carrà in some of the text in the work (snipped from his own 1913 prose-poem entitled "Bilancio" or "Balance"), implies that Futurism is like a newborn star, the incandescence of which is recognized worldwide by other sensitized, perceptive "astronomer-avant-gardists." The composition then can be understood as like a sun sending out concentric waves of light and energy or like a wireless transmitter tower emitting radio waves of vanguard information, and both are metaphors for a central, generative, Futurist orb of ideas spreading and echoing throughout the world.[21] In the new aesthetic technique of collage, Futurism is represented as the new cultural/technological beacon of a new cultural/technological age. The rapid, far-reaching effects of Futurism are also implied through the use of a plane's-eye view that brings distant things into the same visual field (and promotes feelings of omnipotence and establishes affinities with potentially dehumanizing aerial reconnaissance and bombardment), and of the airplane as one of several new technologies that encouraged a totalizing globalism, expansionism, and ultimately imperialism: militarily, economically, politically, socially, as well as aesthetically (see note 12).

The abiding interest in aviation in the early stages of Futurism turned into something of an obsession when, in 1929, Marinetti announced the birth of a new phase of the movement called Futurist Aeropainting. By this time, Futurism was a far less notorious and influential movement than it had been in the teens, but it is worth mentioning this development because it is a modern art movement that made aerial phenomena its guiding principle. Many reasons can be offered as to why it emerged when it did: suffice it to say Marinetti launched Aeropainting just two years after Lindbergh's successful transatlantic journey, and, in the midst of Benito Mussolini's Fascist regime, aviation was propagandized as a key tool in establishing and controlling an expanding modern empire, embodied in a series of Italian long-distance flights and mass squadron crossings, especially those by the Fascist leader Italo Balbo. In addition, Mussolini, himself a reasonably accomplished flyer, is frequently portrayed as a heroic leader-pilot, personifying initially the fusion of the civilian and the military, later the fusion of Empire and aviation. The picturing of Mussolini in aviator's garb, sometimes at the controls of an airplane, bearing captions such as "The First Pilot," and "Pilot of the New Italy," refers not only to Mussolini as leader of both the government and the military but also to an individual equipped with the daring and intelligence to commandeer new technologies such as the airplane, needed as well to commandeer Italy toward a modern imperial future.[22] Mussolini also exploited the venerable fusion of flight and ascent, implying, somewhat metaphorically, that, like the skillful and courageous aviator, he would take Italy to a "higher level" in all spheres of life—historically, militarily, economically, but also morally and spiritually.[23] It is hardly surprising that Marinetti once described Futurist Aeropainting as the "daughter of Fascist aviation and Italian Futurism."[24]

The manifestos of Aeropainting urged artists to address "the immense visionary and sensory drama of flight," emphasizing the new points of view aviation offers, as if to say a changing world requires a new perspective from which it should be observed and which demands and inspires novel expressive means.[25] Moreover, this perspective puts the viewer in constant motion, having no fixed vantage point, and it encourages a suppression of detail and promotes a synthesis and transformation that brings forth universals. To put it another way, the altered observation of outer reality that the airplane allows provides clues to understanding a deeper, more profound reality. All will result in "a new extraterrestrial plastic spirituality," which suggests a mystical, spiritual component of Futurist Aeropainting, placing it within a larger Surrealist context, while revealing its Symbolist roots. In the ambitious, all-embracing spirit of Futurism, a movement claiming to be as committed to changing life as it was to changing art, the "aero" sensibility spread to other media, including aeropoetry, aerosculpture, aerophotography, aeromusic, aerodance, aerofood, aerial theater, aerial architecture, aerial set-design, and aero-radio-television theater. Marinetti went so far as to speak of the "aerolife."

Other Early European Modernists

In their fascination with the "aerolife," the Futurists were not alone among European artists. France, though beat out by the Wrights in the quest for heavier-than-air flight, liked to think of itself as the nation most devoted to aviation, especially because of its early successes in ballooning. The French artist Robert Delaunay (who had a synergistic but also rivalrous and combative relationship with the Futurists)[26] was a fan of French flying feats, and he appositely celebrated native aviation achievements, in particular Louis Blériot's 1909 solo flight across the English Channel. Although Blériot could be erratic and impulsive both personally and mechanically, he was a determined, aggressive, and daring pilot. Although Wilbur Wright's deeds in France captivated the French, the nation now had in Blériot a Frenchman who could fit the bill of native heroic aviator. Transchannel flight was rife with social meaning, and Blériot was instantly catapulted into popular fame.

In *Homage to Blériot* of 1914, and in related depictions, Delaunay chauvinistically chronicled a range of images illustrative of French (and also global) energy, centennialism, and modernity. These included Blériot's plane, dirigibles, the Eiffel Tower (and such images commingled in the popular mind, as the Tower was a beacon for aeronautical events), the "Astra" airplane company, the Ferris wheel, leaping soccer players, soaring birds, and the sun, what Delaunay called "the poetry of modern life."[27] The style of these works distinguish a brand of Cubism sometimes called "Orphism," and are characterized by the use of "simultaneous contrasts of colors," in which segmented, interpenetrating, often concentric discs of differing hue produce an abstract pictorial dynamism that unifies an anthology of energetic emblems. Although Delaunay would continue to explore aviation themes throughout his career, culminating in his monumental series on flight for the "Air Pavilion" at the 1937 World's Fair in Paris (on which his wife Sonia collaborated), what is most remarkable are his apparently pure abstractions beginning in 1913. In these, the "simultaneous contrast of colors" used to evoke the energy and power of flight, other modern inventions and activities, and celestial bodies, now signifies a more abstract and universal or cosmic dynamism. These forms, however, frequently seem tethered in some fashion to representational sources, such as the sun and moon, and they also may have origins in the helical "aerofoil effects" of swirling propellers that Delaunay may have learned about on his visits to the workshops of the French airplane manufacturer, Emile Borel, and to Blériot's airfield.[28] Delaunay's roots in neo-Impressionism and its belief that an artist could achieve certain optical and emotional effects by "constructing" a work based on the arrangement of color and composition, reverberates in Delaunay's art of the early 1910s: He "builds" a painting like an engineer makes an airplane, indicated by phrases on *Homage to Blériot* that pair his "solar disk-simultaneous form" technique with the "great constructor Blériot." Ultimately, flight functions as a symbol of freedom paralleling Delaunay's working abstractly, in which art is liberated from the representational restraints of the material world.

Like Delaunay, the Russian Suprematist artist Kasimir Malevich found flight an impetus toward abstraction, both literally and metaphorically. In some instances, Malevich's abstractions hardly seem non-representational: a composition consisting solely of a criss-crossing black-and-red rectangle floating slightly askew on a white ground might suggest a soaring airplane, a hammer, or a new cross, in which pure transcendental feeling replaces traditional religious sentiment. In his 1927 book *The Non-Objective World* (the publication of which might have partly propelled Marinetti to launch Aeropainting), two sections of photographs, one labeled "Environmental Inspirations of Futurism," the other "Environmental Inspirations of Suprematism," emphasize aircraft, often planes soaring in space, and views from above, sometimes reminiscent of the forms in Suprematist art. In the accompanying text, he wrote that "the environment corresponding to this new culture has been produced by the latest achievements of technology, and especially of aviation, so that one could also refer to Suprematism as 'aeronautical.'"[29] His 1915 *Suprematist Composition: Airplane Flying* makes this nexus explicit, and based on the similarity between this work and other Suprematist pieces by Malevich, it is safe to assume that some carry aeronautical associations. It is not surprising to learn that by 1917 such art was even called "Aerial Suprematism," and that in 1919, conflating communism and aeronautics, he referred to himself and other Suprematists as "comrade-aviators."

Before leaving Europe, it should be mentioned that perhaps the two most significant and radical stylistic developments of early Modernism, Cubism and collage, if not directly affected by aviation, introduced innovative ways of looking at the world that parallel the new perspectives made available by plane flight. (As discussed earlier, Marinetti explicitly compared collage and the experiences of flying.) One acknowledgment of this bond may be embedded in three Pablo Picasso 1912 still-lifes, which include fragments of the phrase "Our Future Is in the Air," combined with the image of the French tricolor flag. The words, a popular slogan at the time, and the flag come from the cover of a jingoistic 1912 brochure that urged greater aggressiveness in France's use of military aeronautics (and it should be mentioned that Blériot manufactured armaments for military aircraft).[30]

Furthermore, Wilbur Wright astounded France with record-breaking flights made there in 1908, and one newspaper account of his feats sits directly below a review of the work of the other major cubist artist, Georges Braque. In this review, the term *Cubism* was born, and the critic seems to place Braque's pictorial exploration in a league with Wright's achievements, calling the artist "a strongly audacious young man."[31] Picasso himself likened the "scaffoldings" of Braque's collages, particularly his paper sculptures, to Wright's biplanes.[32] Both shared a fascination with flight, visiting airfields at Issy-les-Moulineaux and perhaps crafting model airplanes. That these two pioneers of Cubism may have thought of their aesthetic discoveries as analogous to the invention of the airplane is revealed in Picasso's application of the nickname of "Wilbourg" or "Vilbour" (for Wilbur) given to Braque by flyers at the airfield. (Although the evidence is less definitive, Braque, in return, may have dubbed Picasso "Orville.") "Our Future Is in the Air" thus takes on further meaning beyond the military: it may commemorate Wilbur Wright, who died in 1912; suggest Cubism's influence as "in the air" and its uncertain fortunes as "up in the air"; and allude to a characterization of Cubist form as floating and suspended.[33] Gertrude Stein sensed this art-aviation nexus when she wrote:

> One must not forget that the earth seen from an airplane is more splendid than the earth seen from an automobile. . . . So the twentieth century is not the same as the nineteenth century and it is very interesting knowing that Picasso had never seen the earth from an airplane, that being twentieth century he inevitably knew that the earth is not the same as in the nineteenth century, he knew it, he made it inevitably he made it different and what he made was a thing now that the world can see.[34]

Stein's ideas embrace more than Picasso; the invention of new pictorial (and also literary), often abstract languages, corresponds, in part, not simply to efforts to portray the world from above but also to changes in sensibility wrought by modern innovations, the airplane key among them.[35]

Early Modern American Art

How curious it is that two European artists—a Frenchman and a Spaniard, both working in Paris—would compare the American Wright brothers' exploration of technological space (as it might be called) and the changed consciousness this wrought, with their own radical probe of pictorial space and rupture with traditional aesthetic sensibilities. Meanwhile, most American artists, especially the major ones, mainly ignored the native aerial revolution that occurred at Kitty Hawk, North Carolina. This may be in part because of a general skepticism and lack of both awareness and understanding of the magnitude of the Wright brothers' achievements; for example, the U.S. Army turned down their initial offer to sell it their Flyer. Consequently, they explored other paths and Wilbur traveled to France, where the public, cynical at first, was won over by his exploits.[36] Yet, despite their success, the Wrights lacked a certain charisma. Their doggedness, laconism, and ultimate cautiousness, hardly fit the bill of daredevil excitement that most wanted to ascribe to the new breed of aviator, and American artists may have found them unlikely subjects for heroic portrayal.

Furthermore, there seems to have been a succession of artistic events that conspired to exclude the airplane from American art in the early years of the century. Because the artists associated with the Ashcan School, the American movement that chronologically coincided with the Wright brothers' invention of the airplane, were not hostile to dealing with modern subjects, one might expect that they would deem the plane a worthy motif. For them, however, modernity consisted of the burgeoning American metropolis as the site of human activity, often its drama and folly. Machines were regarded as not enhancing and perhaps even obstructing such intercourse; consequently, technological subject matter played a minor role in most Ashcan art. When modern inventions do appear, they are those associated with the cityscape, such as motorcars, streetcars, and els. They function as but one component of a total urban carnival, most often subordinate players in a welter of human interactions. As the Ashcan denomination implies, these artists trained their eyes on the ground, not the skies; the physical and psychological remoteness of the airplane from daily life made it among the least likely of modern subjects these artists might address.

In the mid- and late 1910s, there emerged a second generation of American artists, more modernist in approach, who were intrigued with urban and mechanical themes. Often influenced by Italian Futurism and French Cubism, these American artists were mesmerized most by the overall dynamics of the city. To their eyes, gigantic and distinctive American artifacts such as the bridge and the skyscraper functioned as symbols aptly evocative of the grander energies of the modern metropolis. When they looked up, it was to gaze at the tops of tall buildings, the very height of which had begun to block views of the sky. In occasional instances of views from above, such as John Marin's *Lower Manhattan* of 1922, the dramatic perch is not the cockpit of an airplane but the observation deck of a towering skyscraper—the Woolworth Building.

Images of planes by major early-twentieth-century American modernist artists are relatively rare. There are well-known photographs of the Wright brothers' initial experiments; the most famous documents their maiden voyage on December 17, 1903. Intriguingly, Orville himself set up the camera equipment, aiming it at the point where he anticipated the airplane would lift off, entrusting the snapping of the shutter to another.[37] The plane that he pilots is barely off the ground as Wilbur runs along its side, and simple tools are scattered about. The brothers thus engineered two successes that day: the first powered flight, and its well-executed photographic record, in which the event itself provides all the necessary visual excitement.

In his 1910 photograph titled *The Aeroplane,* Alfred Stieglitz, the important American photographer, gallery owner, and advocate of vanguardism in all the arts, shows how visual drama can derive from the acute sensibility of the astute artist. *The Aeroplane* is one of several images dealing with the modern city and with themes of transport, such as the dirigible, the car, the train, the ferry, and the ocean liner (and in several, the role of the sky is significant, foreshadowing his later provocative photographs of simply sky and clouds, called "Equivalents"). By this time, Stieglitz had supposedly rejected the suffused and atmospheric approach of an earlier style dubbed Pictorialism in favor of unmanipulated, sharply focused photos of scenes containing strong formal elements, labeled straight photography. But *The Aeroplane* has a poetic moodiness all its own: a thin strip of bright in a mostly gloomy sky backlights the dark, silhouetted image of an upward-tilting biplane, viewed from the distance and from the ground below. A scallop of treetops at the lower left establishes the diagonal thrust of the piece. Rhymed by the orientation of the airplane and the sliver of light sky, the trees indicate the proximity of aircraft to earth, suggesting the humbling struggle between gravity and flight that characterizes so many man-made efforts to fly. Still, in having the plane ascend above as well as come toward the viewer, Stieglitz seems to imply the beginning of a new era, making the brightness surrounding the plane appear like a ray of hope for the future.

Of the few examples of early modern American aviation art, most have strong ties to Europe. The American artist Marsden Hartley made *The Aero* in 1914 while in Berlin. Like most of his series of war-related pictures done at this time, *The Aero* consists of brightly colored abutting and overlapping emblematic images derived from German military life, placed in a shallow, indefinable space. Influenced by a host of modern European developments from Fauvism and the Blue Rider to collage and Delaunay's Orphic Cubism, these pieces appear to approach pure abstraction. But their basis in military symbolism suggests the use of trappings and insignia, abstract and otherwise, to rouse patriotic sentiments. Although this work has been affiliated with dirigibles, *The Aero* expresses the "soul state" of an airplane, according to Hartley,[38] who began the painting soon after he encountered Delaunay's impressive *Homage to Blériot.*

Like Picasso and Braque—two European artists living in France who displayed their captivation with the achievements of Orville and Wilbur, the "First

Birdmen"—the Aero Club of France later expressed its affection for Wilbur in a monument to the aviator that included a relief commissioned in 1920 from John Storrs, an American sculptor then living in France. Because Storrs had established a reputation for amalgamating subjects of heroism, creativity, and flight, he seemed an appropriate choice to honor Wilbur Wright, who had set dazzling aviation records in France in 1908. For example, in the artist's 1919 relief of Joan of Arc, quasi-mechanistic, streamlined waves of her hair suggest wings, exploiting flight's associations with heroic freedom. As early as 1914 Storrs created works devoted to Walt Whitman, the American poet much admired in Europe. Between 1917 and 1923, he made designs for a monument to Whitman, further inspired in 1919 by a centennial celebration in Paris of the poet's birth. Several of Storrs's sculptures depict a stylized male or female figure riding a winged Pegasus, in which this symbol of flight evokes the poet's creative imagination and his themes of transcendence, globalism, and technological progress. Storrs's sculptural style, influenced by Cubism, had a streamlined and mechanistically architectural quality that looked ahead to Art Deco. His contribution to the Wright monument, erected in 1922 in Le Mans where the aviator made his French flights, conflated flight and Americanness in the image of a proud, almost defiant American eagle (aviators were dubbed "birdmen," or even "eagles," and Wilbur's profile struck many as avian). In this shallow relief, the bird's stylized and geometricized body parts, such as wings and feathers, seem formed more by a lathe than by nature.

Europe continued to influence American artistic attitudes toward aeronautics in Stanton MacDonald-Wright's 1920 painting, *Aeroplane: Synchromy in Yellow-Orange,* which resembles contemporaneous European modernist treatments of aviation iconography. True to his essay "Influence of Aviation on Art," written one year earlier, MacDonald-Wright tried to "mak[e] concrete . . . [the] cosmic rhythm[ic] . . . forces" of nature. Through flight man now "enters *physically* the realm of Cause where before, only the mind . . . has been able to penetrate," which ultimately "justif[ies] the modern artist's abstraction."[39] With fellow American artist Morgan Russell, MacDonald-Wright founded the movement Synchromism while in Europe in 1913. A painting was generally titled a "synchromy" (along with the major color chords of the composition), meaning "with color" and rhyming loosely with "symphony." Combining Cubist fragmentation with luminous hues, the Synchromists looked synaesthetically to music as one model for an endemically abstract art, which in visual terms could be achieved through arrangements of color rather than sound. Part of a widespread international exploration of abstraction in modernism in the early 1910s, which for our purposes included Delaunay and the Futurists, Synchromism was about as European as an American art movement could get. Although living in California when he painted *Aeroplane: Synchromy in Yellow-Orange* (the ethereal qualities of the piece may reflect, in part, the powerful yet even-tempered light of the West Coast), MacDonald-Wright still seems to have Delaunay's *Homage to Blériot* in mind. Despite his rhetoric, MacDonald-Wright leavens an abstract vision with unmistakable imagery. A propeller-driven airplane moves diagonally upward from right to left and from background to foreground, with the tops of houses indicated below; the motor of its propeller is defined by concentric circles of varying hue and the blades by echoed shapes of different colors; and other parts of the plane consist of repeated or intersecting wedges, rectangles, circles, and other geometries. Colors, often translucent, seem to pulsate from the objects under scrutiny, producing a sense of volume, motion, and energy, which Mac-Donald-Wright probably hoped would border on, if not achieve, the transcendental.

Horace Pippin, the Airplane, and the War

In America, as in Europe, such transcendent portrayals of flight, aptly expressed through a pure or quasi-abstract pictorial syntax, are counterbalanced by a grimmer reality of aircraft and warfare done in more bluntly representational styles. The African-American artist Horace Pippin, who served in a black infantry unit in World War I (he received a Purple Heart retroactively in 1945), makes this clear in the sketch "Airplane over Trees," from his *War Diary Notebooks* (1917–18). A soaring Allied plane scores a hit on a Central Power craft that catches fire and falls, an event he describes at the bottom of the page: "as he got over the strip of seder [cedars?] he open[s] up on the German[']s plain [*sic*] and all at once, he were [sic] a fair [afire?] and came down, to rise no more" Although Pippin said that the war "brought out all the art in me,"[40] it resulted in a sniper shot to his right arm that made painting an arduous procedure.

His first true painting, the 1930 *The End of the War: Starting Home,* is based on a recollection of the war. As in most of his pictorial records of World War I, including *Gas Alarm Outpost: Argonne* (1931), *Shell Holes and Observation Balloon: Champagne Sector* (1931), and *Dog Fight over Trenches* (1935), Pippin treats the new technologies that made the Great War so devastating, in which aircraft figure prominently. In *The End of the War,* the sky is punctuated by planes: some drop bombs on soldiers in trenches; another is aflame and dives earthward; yet another has already plummeted into a tangle of trees. In a startlingly troubling yet almost whimsical device, Pippin attached his own carved wooden images of warfare onto its frame, as helmets, bayonets, rifles, grenades, bombs, and tanks replace the often ornate whorling patterns of more traditional borders.[41]

Pippin's memories of battle, rekindled during World War II, figure significantly in what is often regarded as his most famous painting series, *The Holy Mountain.* Pippin's three versions, done in 1944–45, owe a debt to the American

Quaker artist Edward Hicks's well-known work, *The Peaceable Kingdom* (c. 1833), which in turn derives from other visual models. All take the Old Testament book of Isaiah as their ultimate source, which contains the prophecy of a paradisiacal peace in which all strife is eliminated and harmony reigns. As in Hicks's rendition, Pippin's features the pacific coexistence of tame animals and mankind, true to Isaiah's forecast that couples wolves with lambs, leopards with kids, calves with lions, and suckling babies with snakes. Unlike Hicks's painting, all is not peaceable in Pippin's paintings: in the forest that defines the background lurk tiny images of conflict, including soldiers with helmets and bayonet rifles, grave markers, and airplanes unloading bombs. Pippin described them as little "ghost-like memor[ies] of World War I" and life in the segregated South,[42] but it is unclear whether these images of war and hostility are meant as a foil for the peace to come or the fear that evil will never truly disappear.

Precisionism

Another response to aviation in American art beginning in the late 1910s and early 1920s was part of a worldwide development called the "machine aesthetic." On one level, this new sensibility was a reaction against what was felt to be the unbridled subjectivity, and nearly chaotic and anarchistic art of the early 1910s, an explosiveness that some related to the madness of World War I. As the war progressed, various artists and theorists began issuing a "call to order," urging adoption of more controlled, classicized styles. The sensational enthusiasm for all things technological, including war, that groups such as the Futurists espoused, was much to blame for this change in attitude. After the horrors of the war, greatly a result of innovations in destructive weaponry, technology could no longer be blindly embraced; instead, it should be harnessed in a careful and rational fashion for beneficent not pernicious purposes. Control of technology paralleled pictorial control in the arts, exemplified in more rigorously geometric and restrained styles that some described as a new or modern classicism. Interestingly, the machine was not displaced as a model, but its efficient operation and stripped-down and unornamented functionalism replaced sensational phenomena as inspirations. In America, the artists who embraced this sensibility have been classified as Immaculatists or Precisionists. Once again the airplane is not their predominant icon, as factories, grain silos, storage tanks, and cogs and gears joined the skyscraper and bridge as subject matter.

Of the few Precisionist aviation images, Elsie Driggs's 1928 *The Aeroplane* is among the most straightforward. Two trips in her life inform this picture. One was to Italy in the early 1920s, where she saw the work of the Renaissance painter Piero della Francesca and found in his classicized ideal geometries a dignified and orderly style as appropriate to the depiction of America's great industrial artifacts as that of a more modernist aesthetic. The second was her maiden airplane voyage in 1928 in a Ford trimotor, which sparked a passion for aviation that resulted in several aeronautical sketches and in the painting *The Aeroplane,* a view of a plane in the sky seen through the struts of the neighboring craft in which she rides.

Charles Sheeler, as the premier practitioner of Precisionism from the late 1910s until the late 1950s, depicted an airplane in 1939 as part of the series *Power* for an issue of *Fortune* magazine published the following year.[43] *Yankee Clipper,* named for the plane it depicts, fits the apparent criteria that Sheeler used for selecting the images for this series. He most often chose the mechanism that provides or issues the power from important technological icons: a turbine from the world's largest steam plant; radio transmission wires in front of the world's greatest dam; colossal turbine propellers from a mammoth hydroelectric plant; wheels, shafts, and pistons of a mighty locomotive; and the Wright Double Cyclone radial engine and propeller of the *Yankee Clipper,* the latest, fastest, and most powerful of Boeing's speed and distance record–setting Pan American "Clipper" passenger planes.

As a whole, *Power* was intended to demonstrate America's technological superiority, a literal and figurative engine to power America out of the Depression, to be enlisted in times of war, and ultimately to provide for a glorious democratic future. In this spirit, the series forged a link with American nineteenth-century images of an aggrandized, idealized, awe-inspiring, and even sublime landscape, all symbolic of her greatness. Except Sheeler's "landscape" was a mechanical one, replacing the American myth of the wilderness with that of technological prowess. In other words, Manifest Destiny was fulfilled in industrial terms. Wedding America's mechanical hegemony with Manifest Destiny imbued the notion of technological progress with possibly divine sanction. As in Futurism, technology became the new secular religion, what Henry Ford implied when he proclaimed "Machinery is the New Messiah."

In *Yankee Clipper,* Sheeler, an accomplished photographer, followed his frequent practice of modeling his painting on one of his own photographs, because he thought of the camera—a machine like those he depicted—as an emotionless transmitter of information. Foreshadowing the cool, mechanical approach of the Photorealists of the late 1960s and early 1970s, several of whom would make aircraft a motif, Sheeler not only worked from photos because he believed they ensured an objective factualness but also strove to simulate their look. Sheeler's static, tightly cropped presentation of the airplane's potent engine and propeller and a sliced-off portion of the wing and body create a sense of extraordinary anticipation. The restrained, immobile, and almost eerily silent rendering, viewed from below and pointed diagonally upward, ultimately amplifies its potential power. The copy accompanying the reproduction of Sheeler's painting in *Fortune* emphasizes flight's association with liberating and limitless possibilities, as it provides "the people of the U.S. [with] their latest and greatest freedom through the use of power." The article continues:

> It has given them a new and highly personal freedom. . . . It allows man to go where he pleases. . . . Forest and hills are no longer barriers. He pulls back on the stick and floats over them. He loses old realities and gains new ones. The internal combustion engine has suddenly expanded his adventure in space. Sheeler has expressed the new portent in this poised and infinitely precise propeller, aimed at the sky.[44]

The painting captivates not simply because of its latent might and its sense of technological potentiality, but because of its pristine and laconic formal beauty and elegance, as the *Fortune* article pronounced: "The airplane is the highest art of the engineer." It brings to mind a famous exchange among the European artists Fernand Léger, Constantin Brancusi, and Marcel Duchamp during a visit to the 1912 exhibition of aerial locomotion at the Grand Palais in Paris. Duchamp exclaimed to his artist companions: "Painting has come to end. . . . Who can do anything better than this propeller. Can you?" Léger added that "I still remember the bearing[s] of those great propellers. Good God. What a miracle!"[45] If Sheeler's image can be thought of as elegant, it is icily so, aptly evocative of the chill of power but perhaps also the chill of fear. Considering the historical events of Sheeler's lifetime—World War I, the Great Depression, and the beginning of World War II, to mention a few—these images suggest that, as Edmund Burke initially posited, the awe of the sublime derives from terror.

In its attachment to Russian constructivism (especially the "Proun" works of El Lissitzky), Precisionist Louis Lozowick's *The Aeroplane* (1925–27), part of the *Machine Ornament* series, demonstrates the internationalism of the machine aesthetic. For the politically leftist Lozowick, machines visually held formal beauty and ideologically embodied the belief in a technologically optimistic future. Lozowick's plane has been converted into a series of alternating black-and-white geometries, in which its isolation on the page simultaneously suggests an autonomous abstract power and a craft flying in the sky.

Changes in Lozowick's art from the 1920s to the 1930s signaled a shift in attitude toward technology, especially with the onset of the Great Depression. Conspicuously absent from most Precisionist depictions of technology was its relationship to man, in particular the worker. The crash of 1929 and its consequent economic woes sobered optimistic faith in technology and encouraged many artists to examine technology's true effects on society. Lozowick, who in the 1920s paired other industrial objects with the plane in settings essentially devoid of people (e.g., *Tanks* and *Hudson Bridge,* both of 1929), introduced into his 1931 lithograph, bluntly but cleverly titled *Mid-Air,* a brawny construction worker, whose muscles have a geometric power akin to the mechanisms Lozowick often illustrated. This laborer dangles expertly from the pulley he grapples near the girders of a skyscraper, at an altitude so high that planes appear to be flying below him. (This device of coupling planes with tall buildings was used, as well, by other artists; its purpose seems less to demonstrate the power of flight than the extraordinary heights that present and future skyscrapers might attain.)[46]

Aeronautical Murals

The relationship between man and machine in the art of the 1930s manifested itself in several ways, best summarized by the categories of manufacturing and murals. Because the production of airplanes must by necessity deal with the labor force of a factory, it became a popular way to probe how man and machine interacted. Moreover, during the Depression, the government supported artists through the Federal Art Project. Murals for public buildings were commonly funded, which by bringing art directly to a wide audience, demonstrated that New Deal projects benefited all the people.

Two of the most famous muralists of the day working in the United States—the Mexican Diego Rivera and the American Thomas Hart Benton—addressed aeronautical subjects in their art. Politically, they have generally been considered far apart: Rivera was an avowed communist and thus an internationalist, and Benton was a conservative isolationist who exalted traditional American democratic values and was considered the major exponent of the Regionalist wing of American scene painting.[47] But, in the early 1930s, as evidenced in respective mural cycles containing aviation motifs, they seem closer than might be imagined. Interestingly, both artists began their careers as modernists—Rivera was a Cubist, Benton a Synchromist—styles that later they each would reject vehemently. Both believed that during times of economic deprivation and social upheaval the apparent inaccessibility of abstraction was arrogant and elitist. They felt that representational art, especially when used in the more public-friendly mural arena, had a legibility that best communicated messages to the masses. Both looked back to earlier eras for inspiration, especially to the great frescos of the Italian Renaissance.

As part of his famous murals of *Detroit Industry* devoted largely to automobile manufacture at Henry Ford's mammoth River Rouge plant (Sheeler, at the behest of the Ford Motor Company, also made this the subject of photos and paintings), Rivera included the operations of Ford's Airplane Division, which assembled aircraft at the Stout Engineering Building in Dearborn, Michigan. Commissioned by and for the Detroit Institute of Arts in 1931 and completed in 1933, these epic murals covering four walls were controversial in their time and remain provocative today. Complex and turbulent, they have as a major focus the activity of the assembly line, especially the interactions between worker and machine. Rivera saw modern technology as symbolic of the "New America," comparable to the magnificent achievements of pre-conquest "Old America." "Industrial buildings, machine design, and engineering [are] the greatest expression of the plastic genius of the New World," he observed. "Your engineers are your great artists," he went on, calling modern technology "the most beautiful thing . . . in your country. In all constructions of man's past—pyramids, Roman roads and aqueducts, cathedrals and palaces, there is nothing to equal these. Out of them and the machine will issue the style of tomorrow."[48]

A major message of the murals is the split between the constructive and destructive potential of modern technology. Because of (or perhaps despite) his communist affiliation, Rivera saw assembly-line production as a prime example of collectivism, which when properly harnessed could benefit mankind. Throughout the fresco cycle, he compares apparently good and evil images. On the west wall, aeronautical scenes appear in a mural called *The Conquest of Air*. Its left side shows the manufacture of passenger planes, below which is an image of a dove; the right illustrates war planes (being built or used), joined below by the image of a hawk. To complicate matters, Rivera used a self-portrait for the image of a worker placed on the fresco's good side (holding a hammer and wearing a glove imprinted with a red star, which raised the specter of communism, but was in fact the logo of a local glove company), which he contrasted with a conflated image of Henry Ford and Thomas Edison as boss and magnate on the bad side.

Benton included airplane imagery in several works, most notably in his vast 1930–31 mural series initially located at the New School of Social Research in New York City (presently situated in the Sixth Avenue AXA headquarters in Manhattan), which chronicles the activities of *America Today,* as the cycle is titled. There is some confusion as to Benton's true political leanings at the time of its execution.[49] His statement that "the mechanical contrivances of buildings, the new airplanes, the blimps, the dredges, the ships of the [naval] base, because they were so interesting in themselves" impelled him to reject his earlier "play with colored cubes and classic attenuations, from esthetic drivelings and morbid self-concern,"[50] suggests that while he eschewed aesthetic modernism in the late 1910s and early 1920s, he was mesmerized by modern artifacts. This fascination continued in *America Today,* implying that Benton did not become a politically conservative Regionalist until later in the decade. Executed before the full and lengthy impact of the Depression was understood, Benton's murals are both optimistic and liberally reformist. Intriguingly, the murals address themes similar to those in Rivera's *Detroit Industry*: the role of the worker and the hegemony of American technology, the latter also figuring significantly in Sheeler's 1939 *Power* series. In *America Today,* aircraft imagery operates first as a source of pictorial dynamism. In addition, an airplane, seeming to surge forward, propeller blades blurring as they spin, is part of an anthology of symbols of technological innovation and power in the aptly titled centerpiece of the cycle—

Instruments of Power. The planes in *The Changing West* panel reassert the theme of aircraft as key to America's progress and potency. Stylistically, the murals are characterized by the almost caricaturish writhing and swirling activity common to Benton's work, although here he uses curving and zigzagging pictorial dividers (in the *Instruments of Power* these shapes are echoed by lightning-bolt forms, evocative of pure energy), suggestive of the streamlined vitalism of Art Deco.

Aircraft became tools of destruction, however, in Benton's huge ten-painting series, *The Year of Peril,* done in 1941 in direct response to the attack on Pearl Harbor. Airplanes—diving, bombing, and aflame—appear in one corner of the painting *Exterminate,* in which anonymous Allied soldiers assault the colossal and grotesque figures of Hitler and Tojo, personifications of international totalitarianism and terror. Comparing Axis aggression with the crucifixion, the moralistically titled *Again* features an image of Christ on the cross whose stigmata is produced by both a piercing lance thrust by Nazis, Japanese, and Fascists (the new Romans?) and an airplane above firing into the wound. The propagandistic value of Benton's *The Year of Peril* series was instantly recognized and its widespread reproduction may have numbered near fifty-five million!

In contrast to the more typically didactic and legibly representational murals of the 1930s, illustrated by Rivera and Benton, Arshile Gorky produced a more avant-garde aviation cycle. Under the auspices of the Works Progress Administration (WPA) Federal Art Project, Gorky executed a ten-panel piece for Newark Airport, entitled *Aviation: Evolution of Forms under Aerodynamic Limitations,* which was divided into four walls labeled *Activities on the Field, Early Aviation, Modern Aviation,* and *Mechanics of Flying.*[51] Initially intended for Floyd Bennett Airfield in New York under the title *Mechanical Aspects of Airplane Construction,* the cycle was to consist of photographs of aeronautical subjects by Wyatt Davis (the brother of artist Stuart Davis) intermixed with Gorky's paintings. When the project was shifted to Newark, considered in the early 1930s to be one of the most advanced centers of American aviation, the collaboration terminated, and Gorky and Wyatt Davis were assigned different spaces for decoration. Completed in 1935–36 and installed in 1937, the panels were painted over in the early 1940s, resulting in their near total destruction. Written off as completely buried, the two panels from the *Mechanics of Flying* wall—titled *The Mechanics of Flying* and *Aerial Map*—survived, and they were unearthed and restored in the mid-1970s. Gorky's largest and most elaborate series of paintings, the entire ensemble has been reconstructed based on extant drawings, photographic records, and the artist's own written accounts.

The cycle can be divided into two major styles. The first style, exemplified in the first and largest two panels of the series, *Activities on the Field,* consists of a laterally spreading field of mostly flat, brightly colored stylized shapes, although some shapes are modeled and deeper spatial pockets occasionally open up. According to the artist, the first panel represents "the airplane ... dissected ... into its constituent parts. ... composed of a variety of shapes us[ing] such elemental forms as a rudder, a wing, a wheel and a searchlight to invent ... plastic symbols of aviation." He went on:

> These symbols, these forms, I have used in paralyzing disproportions in order to impress upon the spectator the miraculous new vision of our time. To add to the aggressiveness of these shapes, I have used such local colors as are to be seen on the aviation field—red, blue, yellow, black, gray, brown—because these colors were used originally to sharpen the objects so that they could be seen clearly and quickly.

In the second panel, these shapes signify "objects commonly used around a hangar, such as a ladder, a fire extinguisher, a gasoline truck, and scales. These objects I have dissected and reorganized in a homogenous organization comparable to the previous panel."

Gorky, sometimes called the last of the Surrealists or the first of the Abstract Expressionists, was an artist whose style and sensibility bridged a serious, fundamentally romantic European commitment to abstract modernism with a more personal, brash, and unbridled emergent American expressionism. In the Newark panels, European influences prevail. The panels of "homogenous organization" recall the art of Fernand Léger, the European artist (close to Delaunay throughout his career) zealously interested at varying points in his career in the mural mode, dynamic abstract form and color, and contemporary technology, including the airplane (see note 45).

The second style, found in the remaining eight smaller panels, is less field-like, often has a central image or focus, and employs predominantly floating biomorphic shapes. Transforming the mechanical into the organic is implied in Gorky's remarks: "The first three panels of 'Modern Aviation' contain the anatomical parts of autogyros in the process of soaring into space, and yet with the immobility of suspension. The fourth panel is a modern airplane simplified to its essential shape and so spaced as to give a sense of flight." Existing studies demonstrate how Gorky took images of actual craft and boiled them down, made them less hard and angular and more pneumatic and curvilinear, and placed them on relatively amorphous grounds to suggest a sense of floating in air. In describing the coloration of the panels, he again emphasized whimsy and fantasy: "I have used arbitrary colors and shapes; the wing is black, the rudder yellow, so as to convey the sense that these modern gigantic implements of man are decorated with the same fanciful yet utilitarian sense of play that children use in coloring their kites."

Gorky is even more explicit in his discussion of the two surviving panels of *Mechanics of Flying*. "I have used morphic shapes," he wrote. "The objects portrayed, a thermometer, hygrometer, anemometer, an airline map of the United States, all have definitely important usage in aviation, and to emphasize this I have given them importance by detaching them from their environment." This "detachment" is displayed in the conversion of observed phenomena into colored, floating, abstracted, and mostly curvilinear shapes, making the composition essentially Surrealist in appearance. In *Mechanics of Flying* a dark mustard-colored ground plays host to a variety of syncopated forms in russet, blue, black, white, and gray, specifically derived from the mechanical devices Gorky describes. In *Aerial Map,* which implies a plane's-eye perspective, another mustard-colored ground supports a series of organic shapes colored like those of *Mechanics of Flying,* highlighted by the somewhat abstracted image of a white map of the United States hovering at the center, dotted with black lines and reddish circles signifying plane routes, and departure and destination points. In their association with contemporary international Surrealism, these panels correspond to work being done by the Futurist Aeropainters, who understood how fantasy, spirit, and imagination tied Surrealism to flight. The artists whose work comes closest to Gorky's are those associated with the cosmic or spiritual wing of Aeropainting, such as Fillia, Pippo Oriani, and especially Enrico Prampolini.

The two disparate styles in Gorky's Newark murals are conjoined nonetheless not simply by aeronautical iconography but, in a parallel to jazz, by a buoyant and lyrical compositional tempo, like that found in the art of his friend and contemporary Stuart Davis.[52] Many saw Gorky's art as purely abstract, even though he relied on things seen, which he transformed into stylized, often biomorphic forms. Much of his list of items in the mural are fairly easy to spot, and some have been traced to specific photographs taken by Wyatt Davis and by Leo Seltzer for the original Floyd Bennett Field project. For instance, the right-hand side of the first part of *Activities in the Field* derives from a Beech Model 17 Staggerwing; sources for the *Modern Aviation* panels include a Waco F for the modern plane and a Kellett for the autogyros.[53] Nonetheless, the abstractness of the murals, installed in June 1937, baffled contemporary audiences. A headline of one critical article published in *The Newark Ledger* on June 10, 1937, read: "'Plane, an Airplane, A Plane, Is It?'—Gertrude Stein," invoking an apparent quotation from the art patroness and writer, whose own work oscillated between the obvious and the obscure, and who herself (as mentioned earlier) had earlier wedded Picasso and planes. Gorky later readdressed aviation themes in the now lost Marine Building murals called *Man's Conquest of the Air* for the 1939 New York's World Fair.

A fate similar to that accorded Gorky's Newark paintings initially met James Brooks's WPA-sponsored murals, called *Flight,* installed in 1942 at the Marine Air Terminal of New York's LaGuardia Airport. One of the last great murals of the Federal Art Project (FAP), this huge work, covered over in 1955, was restored in 1980. The restoration reveals an imposing vision of flight, powerfully colored in a wide range of blues punctuated by brilliant reds and other hues and stocked with monumental, chiseled, and aerodynamically streamlined figures. Like Gorky, Brooks addressed the history of aviation in his cycle, but Brooks was even more ambitious, taking its origins back to mythology, while Gorky began his saga with ballooning. Whereas Gorky abstracted from mechanical forms throughout the murals, creating syncopated fields or floating biomorphic compositions, Brooks said he tried "to combine the abstract—the work that I liked—with Renaissance use of figures."[54] He admitted that this mix of abstract passages and representational forms, especially the huge, heroically stylized figures, produced problematic compositional tensions. But it is probable that Brooks, like most WPA muralists, was given specific thematic and even stylistic instructions. The history of flight was a standard subject of WPA-backed airport art and, in many instances, accessible, representational approaches were recommended. This was, as the WPA boasted, an "art for the millions." Although principally interested in abstraction, Brooks must have realized that to tell epic tales in the LaGuardia cycle—sweeping from Daedalus and Icarus through Leonardo to the Wright brothers in a tripartite arrangement labeled *Imagined Flight, Release,* and *Flight Accomplished*—a more realistic style, like that of most FAP murals, seemed apposite.

Other Art of the 1930s and 1940s

Aviation iconography in the 1930s and 1940s was not limited to large mural paintings. The American sculptor Theodore Roszak, who taught aeronautical engineering and built planes for the Brewster Aircraft Company, combined aesthetic ideas from the Bauhaus, Constructivism, and streamlined Art Deco, and mixed modern materials such as aluminum, metal, steel, and plastic along with copper, brass, and wood to produce pieces that oscillate between purely abstract sculpture, visionary architecture, and resemblances to aircraft, their parts, and related tools and instruments.[55] His *Airport Structure* (1932) reads like an arrangement of shiny, aerodynamically curved, tiered forms suggestive of airplane parts; *Trajectories* (1938) alludes to patterns and movements of flight and perhaps of stars and planets; and *Ascension* (1939) evokes an abstract, upward-soaring motion, powerful enough to reach the heavens, recalling the sense of pure flight and elegant upward thrust in Brancusi's *Bird in Space* series (see note 45).

The horrors of World War II, especially the nuclear bombings of Hiroshima and Nagasaki and the fire-bombing of Dresden, chastened Roszak's positivist sculptural vision. Rejecting his sleek, streamlined style of the 1930s, he adopted a highly expressionist approach, characterized by asymmetrical, thorny, thin-membered, scabrous-surfaced, steel sculptures mottled with other metals. Beginning in the forties, Roszak's aerial art addressed technology's dark rather than bright side. In his *Spectre of Kitty Hawk* of 1946–47, the title announces that the initial fears that the Wright brothers' invention might wreak terrible destruction in the future have now been realized. Made of steel hammered and brazed with bronze and brass, this spiky, tentacular piece with a scaly, repellent surface suggests a terrifying primitive beast, as alleged progress becomes atavism. Because of "the destructive way . . . aircraft has been used" Roszak remarked, he likened the sculpture to "the superior dominance of the pterodactyl that at one time was also the scourge of the air and the earth."[56] Roszak's trepidation toward military aviation recalls that found in one of the most famous paintings of the twentieth century—Pablo Picasso's *Guernica* of 1937. Although European rather than American and chronicling the Spanish Civil War rather than World War II (Philip Guston's 1937–38 *Bombardment* is an American example depicting Spanish Civil War air raids),[57] *Guernica* remains one of the most potent expressions of the horrors of aerial bombings of civilian populations and most enduring universal condemnations of brutality and war.

While avant-garde artists such as Roszak ultimately railed against warplanes as symbolic of the destructive potential of modern technology, more academic artists, such as Guy Wiggins, adopted a pragmatically patriotic attitude. Wiggins, working as a mechanic on army and navy gliders during the war, was commissioned by the manufacturer, the Pratt Read Company, to paint a twelve-work series devoted to its warplane production. These forthright yet glowingly colored paintings, done in 1943, are as workmanlike as the laborers building aircraft pictured in them. In most of the pieces (e.g., *The 02; Plant D, Assembly Line; Rolling Them Out; Assembly Line;* and *Plant D*) men methodically labor on orderly rows of planes in and around hangars that prominently and proudly display the American flag.

Dichotomous attitudes toward the airplane, manifest within Roszak's own sculptural career, is part of a continuing love-hate relationship with modern technology. On the one hand, the optimistic allusions to extraordinary ascension in Roszak's 1930s sculptures adumbrates the missiles and rockets of the future, recycling the venerable bonds between flight, progress, and transcendence. This art of sculptural augury coupled with the emphasis by American muralists on the history of flight suggests that something is "in the air" in the 1930s and 1940s: an assertion of the importance of American technology in the history of flight; a belief in the saving powers of this technology in the history of democratic capitalism, especially in the face of depression and war; and the recognition that since what was once imaginary has become reality, the current fantasizing of future feats of flight should not be considered unrealizable. On the other hand, Roszak's expressionist sculptures of the 1940s display an anxiety toward aviation, because the promise of Kitty Hawk had been transmogrified into the terror of sophisticated aerial weaponry. This sense of promise tinged with fear remains a potent force in much post–World War II aeronautical iconography.[58]

Post–World War II

Much aviation imagery from the 1950s on often reprises and amplifies earlier motifs. But, as plane flight became more ordinary and space travel became less visionary, the expression of more extraordinary means of flying emerged in a mix of American and European art that does not always refer specifically to aircraft. To mention a few: Jody Pinto's *The Henri Drawings* (1983), in which the leaping and soaring abilities of a circus performer are tied to the miracles of flying saints and angels; the use of Superman iconography in the work of several Pop artists; and in the tradition of Leonardo da Vinci and Vladimir Tatlin, the wedding of art and engineering in the production of sculptures evoking the imaginative and real potential of flight, such as that by the contemporary artists, the Belgian Panamarenko (named after the now-defunct Pan American Airways) and the Canadian Murray Favro, who also has made paintings and scaled down sculptural replicas of planes, which he displays as works of art.

One of the most famous postwar aerial images is Yves Klein's 1960 photographic self-portrayal titled *The Painter of Space Hurls Himself into the Void,* featuring the French artist apparently in the midst of a brief flight. Made three years after the Soviet launching of Sputnik but a year before Yuri Gagarin became the first man in space, Klein's image expresses both a dream of flying that harks back to mythology (and the Nike sculpture) and the aspiration to be a spiritually or imaginatively powered cosmonaut.[59] The success of the Russian and eventually the American space programs may have led to a spate of works that takes the entire world as its theme: to mention several, the Italian Piero Manzoni's *Base of the World* (1961); the Swiss Jean Tinguely's *Study for the End of the World* (performed first in Denmark in 1961 and then at a U.S. nuclear testing site in 1962); and Americans Edward Kienholz's *The World* (1964) and Claes Oldenburg's *Proposed Monument for the Intersection of Canal and Broadway, NYC: Block of Concrete, Inscribed with the Names of War Heroes* (1965).[60] Although these works may not refer specifically to aviation, the changed sensibility produced by space travel encouraged these artists to imagine the world as a more graspable entity, the "global village" and "spaceship earth," of which Marshall McLuhan and Buckminster Fuller spoke.

Some of these pieces seize the earth as a graspable entity in part to demonstrate its fragility: the same technologies that produced the understanding of the globe as a small hunk of roughly spherical matter hurtling through space could also bring this world to an end. In addition to the Oldenburg and Tinguely, Adolph Gottlieb's various *Blast* or *Burst* paintings of the 1950s and 1960s may allude to nuclear explosion, and Robert Morriss's "Techno-Catastrophe" series of the late 1970s and early 1980s envisions a world engulfed in "Firestorms," that fuse nuclear holocaust, biblical apocalypse, and Leonardo's cataclysm drawings.

Pop Art

In addition to these more universal and perhaps tangential approaches toward flight, there are several post–World War II works that address aerial subjects in conventional but often expanded ways. As the impact of aviation became commonplace and as artists became interested in an even wider range of subject matter—modern technology and popular culture among them—aeronautical images became more frequent. Such motifs occur often in the art of Roy Lichtenstein, a major American Pop artist, best known for work that borrows techniques and sometimes themes associated with comic strips. With the exception of some early pieces derived from better-known comics, his favorite strips are essentially anonymous ones, dealing with "true romance," "war," and "adventure." Intrigued by how a cartoon's graphic style produces powerful visual statements meant to illustrate profound emotions, such as intoxicating love or crazed violence, Lichtenstein also reveals how this standardized, formulaic syntax converted these sensations into the homogeneous, banal, and saccharine.

Aeronautical themes occur throughout his career and in various media including the simple flying passenger plane in *Airplane* (1961); the military plane dramatically tilted sideways in the sculpture *Airplane* (1990); the air force soldier in *Mr. Bellamy* (1961); the firing, dueling, and exploding planes in *Tex* (1962), *Live Ammo* (1962), *Blam* (1962), *Whaam!* (1963), and *As I Opened Fire* (1964); the mushroom cloud of *Atomic Explosion* (1966); the isolated explosions in *Varoom!*, and the *Explosion* series (all of 1965); the reference to postal delivery in *Salute to Airmail* (1968); the Art Deco based anthology of aeronautical motifs in *Aviation* (1967), *Little Aviation* (1968), and *Salute to Aviation* (1968); and the pilots in cockpits in the midst of air battle in *Jet Pilot* (1962), *Brattata* (1962), *Bratatat* (1963), and *Okay Hot-Shot* (1963).

Okay Hot-Shot demonstrates that Lichtenstein's interests do not lie solely in exploiting and exposing the pictorial and sensational cliched "oomph" of comic strips. The pilot pictured here, his contorted and demonic face smack against the picture plane, abruptly sliced by the painting's edge, screams "Okay Hot-Shot, Okay! I'm Pouring!" His words refer not only to his literal pouring of firepower on his enemy but also perhaps to the intramural subject of Jackson Pollock (and by extension Abstract Expressionism as a whole) furiously pouring paint on

large canvases placed on the floor of his studio. *Okay Hot-Shot* thus contains a little art history lesson of the story of the rejection and deflation of the intense subjectivism, emotionalism, gesturalism, macho heroism, and abstraction of America's most famous prior art movement in favor of a new art willing to deal with
crass, representational subjects in an impersonal, emotionless, and mechanical
way.

Among the alterations Lichtenstein made to the comic strip images from
which *Okay Hot-Shot* is derived is a critical change in headgear. In the original
cartoon, the pilot sports a typical World War II helmet; for the painting, Lichtenstein updated it to one that a cosmonaut, astronaut, or more contemporary
air force pilot might wear. Such a change, as minor as it may seem, hints that
Lichtenstein, despite his disavowal of politics in his art, is situating this image
(and that of the majority of his aerial combat motifs) in the midst of the 1960s revived Cold War hostilities and growing military involvement in the Vietnam
War. Was he implying that the heroics that defined the fighting in World War
II and became the stock-in-trade of comic books like *G. I. Combat* and *All-American Men of War,* the main sources for *Okay Hot-Shot,* were no longer applicable
to Cold War wars, despite the government's efforts to stir similar sentiments?[61]

It is in this historical context that the most famous and controversial Pop depiction of the airplane—James Rosenquist's painting *F-111* (1965)—should be
placed.[62] *F-111* is a huge, wraparound, fifty-one piece, four-wall panel, which
has the billboardlike appearance characteristic of Rosenquist's work, filled with
large, broadly defined, sharply colored depictions of people, food, consumer
products, and modern technology, disorientingly arranged in fragmented,
abutted, and inverted leaps of scale and space. In its approximation of a mural
and its ultimate condemnatory, antiwar stance, this ten by eighty-six foot ex-
travaganza recalls in general, the Mexican mural tradition, and more specifically
Picasso's 1937 *Guernica,* as it also addresses the subject of brutal aerial bombing.

In *F-111,* ostensibly innocent and innocuous images become adulterated
through juxtaposition with more menacing subjects. The portrayal of a smiling
young girl seems sunny enough, but she is capped by a disturbingly shiny, near ballistic, chrome salon-style hair dryer that suggests a fighter pilot's helmet or a type
of headgear for possible protection against the nearby formally echoing representation of an atomic explosion. Another visual rhyme with the mushroom cloud occurs in the spatially proximate sea diver's aqualung and its burst of aquamarine
water bubbles signifying "the breath of the atomic bomb. . . . the 'gulp!' of the explosion," as Rosenquist put it.[63] The visually coupled angel food cake and automobile tire with treads prominently displayed seem commonplace enough, but
Rosenquist once likened these circular forms with holes in their centers to a sunken
missile site. The piles of swirling spaghetti awash in orange-red sauce are what the
artist called archetypal "no-images," such that "if you paint Franco-American

spaghetti, they won't make a crucifixion out of it."[64] But the placement of one of the pasta mounds atop the explosion, and another overlaid by the nose cone of the jet fighter, makes it hard not to think of viscera exposed because weaponry has ripped open flesh. Even the floral-patterned wallpaper does not escape tainting: for Rosenquist, it is like a radioactive veil suspended in the atmosphere.

The most explicitly threatening images are the exploding atomic bomb and the mammoth eponymous F-111 fighter plane. Branded "a horrible killer" by the artist, the aircraft stretches the length of the painting, and its hard metal surfaces are evoked through occasional use of aluminum panels.[65] An open, primary-colored beach umbrella superimposed over this mushroom cloud suggests not simply a visual match but perhaps a ludicrously ineffectual form of protection against the fallout of an exploding nuclear sun. As the Bob Dylan song about nuclear devastation goes: "A hard rain's a-gonna' fall."

Started on the heels of the Tonkin Gulf resolution that served to justify U.S. military intervention in Vietnam throughout the history of the conflict, *F-111* refers to the financing and building of this technologically advanced, supersonic fighter-bomber (and in an interview about the piece Rosenquist refers directly to "bombers in Vietnam"). Touted as the airplane of the future and intended for use in the bombing of Southeast Asia, the F-111 project, fueled by millions of tax dollars and plagued by graft, cost overruns, and defects, became the personification of misguided government priorities and the chilling power of the American "military-industrial" complex. Its supersonic speed and wing design made it almost impervious to anti-aircraft detection and fire, and when used as part of the intensive bombing campaign called "Rolling Thunder," its nearly silent flight earned it the nickname "Whispering Death" among the North Vietnamese.

This mammoth four-wall work uses its sheer size not simply to surround and aggressively assault viewers but also to compete with the enormity of this artifact and problem: "You couldn't shut it out," Rosenquist announced. Like most Pop artists, Rosenquist strove for neutrality and detachment in his work, generally denying it political importance. But *F-111* is an exception, and the artist acknowledged that "the prime force behind this thing [the government project] has been to keep people working, an economic tool; but behind it, this is a war machine." This statement thus clarifies the imagistic minglings and the formal occlusions of the piece in which categories of innocence and malevolence are intentionally blurred and their interconnectedness in American society ultimately revealed: consumer products mixed with military hardware, the soft with the hard, the organic with the geometric.

The Vietnam War

A news report on the horrors of the Vietnam War by a photographer on helicopter missions was one impetus behind Rosenquist's *F-111*. Undoubtedly one of the most notorious antiwar artworks of the 1960s, Rosenquist's *F-111* is nonetheless more rarity than norm. Despite the political activism of the 1960s and the left and liberal leanings of many avant-garde artists, they tended to keep their art and politics separate. No single reason can be given as to why the visual arts was such a calm eye in a stormy decade, but certainly the strong reaction against the intense subjectivism of Abstract Expressionism by artists of various aesthetic stripes in the 1960s promoted an art of coolness and detachment. (As well, there is little about Abstract Expressionism that seems explicitly political, although it was coopted during the Cold War to exemplify American "freedom.")[66] Also, the stranglehold that "formalist" theory held during this decade encouraged artists to work abstractly and to divest their art of any references to nonaesthetic issues. Moreover, the 1960s continued to debate a problem that probably was first addressed in the 1910s in the Dada movement: what is the most efficacious type of political art? Some felt that representational work dealing directly with sociopolitical problems was the answer; others felt that realism was ineffective because its visual language had become debased because the dominant societal ideologies used it to propagandize false ideals, control information, and deter discourse. Art instead should be abstract, it was argued, because it suggested an "other" that would inspire imagining the idea of an "other" structure for government and society. And even if abstraction did not promote conjuring up a world unlike that which existed, at least it was honest in its devotion to allegedly fundamental truths about the nature of its media. As well, the artist remained ethically and morally pure by not dirtying his or her hands in the mess of politics.[67]

Certainly, the decade produced some political art and the Vietnam War was a major factor. As in all the wars of the twentieth century, aviation played a role. The artist Nancy Spero said: "I viewed the helicopter as *the* symbol of this war." She noted, "the omnipresent image of the chopper hovering, transporting soldiers, napalming villages, gunning fleeing peasants or picking up wounded and dead US soldiers,"[68] and its iconic position may have been best captured in the Wagnerian procession in Francis Ford Coppola's 1979 film *Apocalypse Now*. Even before its association with Vietnam, helicopter imagery was employed by Robert Rauschenberg in works such as *Bicycle, Dry Cell, Kite,* and *Transom* of 1963, and *Choke* and *Tracer* of 1964, possibly implicating its use in a host of U.S. military incursions and as an instrument of suppression or protection of civil rights actions, antigovernment demonstrations, and inner city riots.[69] In relation to the Vietnam War, the copter appears in a slew of works, many done after the 1960s when art and politics became less strange bedfellows.[70]

Spero's *Bombs and Helicopters* (1966) and *War Series* (1966–69) may be the most "angry . . . manifestos against a senseless obscene war," as the artist herself described it.[71] In these interrelated groups of vitriolic gouache and ink drawings—that she called "erectile, explosive, exaggerated symbols, mostly male obscene metaphors of power and force"[72]—she combined her feminist and pacifist concerns in images of victimization. Helicopters are the protagonists in most of these devastatingly and explicitly drawn and titled works such as *Helicopter Eating Victims and Shitting Remains* (1966); *Helicopter and Victims Killed* (1966); *Yellow Helicopter, Lynched Victims* (1966); *Helicopter and Victims* (1967); *Clown and Helicopter* (1967); *Search and Destroy* (1967); *Helicopter and Victims in a River of Blood* (1968); *Super Pacification* (1968); *Vietcong Prisoners* (1968); and *Pilot, Rape, and Gunship* (1968). An excerpt from a 1967 description of Spero's series by her husband, Leon Golub, himself a producer of potent political art, verbally parallels her visual venom. He wrote:

> Planes and helicopters are . . . anthropophagous, pitiless, gluttonous. Whirlybirds are bug-like or machined in luminous insect colors or lurid gold and aluminum. Monstrous or antiseptic, they go about their destruction, gorging and eating indiscriminately. The helicopter ingests its victims, regurgitates and shits out blood and entrails, drags and smashes bodies. The planes, elegant and silver winged, are often emblazoned with the mottoes or moral injunctions, e.g. K.I.L.L., F.U.C.K. or L.O.V.E.
>
> The whirlybird becomes the Beast of the Apocalypse, the machine becomes the technological equivalent for metaphysical nightmare. Victims are slaughtered in the terrible technological intimacy of the machine as it hovers over the ground. . . . Destruction is literally in our living room. All drops away, time, distance, the unthinkable.
>
> The malign fantasy and virtually insane imaginings of the paintings—the grotesqueries which form the delusions of the psychopathological—are given body by Hiroshima, by napalm.
>
> The art is terse and savage—a spewing out of metaphor analogical to the spewing of blood and spume in the images. This is an art of extraordinary and brutal fastidiousness, precariousness and contingent. Control seemingly sporadic, frantic or inchoate is spare and minimal—a very great simplicity contours the strained range of image. This art is promiscuously obscene, intemperate, spastic and irrefragable.[73]

Any further description of the series would most likely pale by comparison, but a few points should be added. Done on rice paper (obviously an allusion to Vietnam and Asia), the pieces meld an apparitional delicacy with fury, in which extraordinary brutality is wrenched from an economy of means. Some of the choppers, outlined in a skeletal metallic gray, seem to glow radioactively or fade into vapors, and others transmogrify into predatory, shiny bugs that incarcerate or feast on their victims, harking back, in their rapacious monstrousness, to Roszak's correspondences between airplanes and dinosaurs. For example, in *Helicopter and Victims* (1967), a whirling copter-animal with a leering, hungry smile and tail marked "KILL" excretes its prey, a conflation of turds, bombs, and severed, fiery, pain-stricken heads, blood spurting from open mouths. Obscene sex, scatology, and sadism become Spero's visual weapons.

Photorealism

More typical of the attitude toward planes and modern technology at this time is that expressed by the American Photorealists. Inspired by Pop Art's working from media representations and by the sense of detachment such a procedure putatively promotes, several artists in the late 1960s and early 1970s began painting from photographs, retaining in the final oils the qualities of the original photo source. Despite the Photorealists' claim that they were uninterested in social commentary and more concerned with the formal challenges that photographically derived compositions produced, there is a striking unanimity of subject matter: nearly vacant urban streets and storefronts, suburban housing complexes, malls and strips, and parking lots. Cars, trucks, and motorcycles often populate these scenes that lack human habitation.

With some exceptions (Don Eddy's 1969 *Departure: DC 8* series, Richard Estes's 1967 *Astrojet* and Ralph Goings's 1970 "Airport" pieces), the airplane appears infrequently, most likely because it plays such a minor part in this new standardized suburban environment that so intrigued these artists. To remedy this, Stuart M. Speiser, a New York lawyer and aviation buff, commissioned several Photorealists in 1973 to do works that incorporated aeronautical imagery, which he eventually donated to the National Air and Space Museum. For the most part, these paintings do little to amplify our understanding of these artists or aviation: for instance, Charles Bell, in *Untitled,* simply substitutes a toy hydroplane in a bathtub for one of his typical juvenilia; Tom Blackwell in *White Lightning* sought the same visual pyrotechnics he found in motorcycles, with less stunning results; Ralph Goings gained little by trading pickup trucks in parking lots for a small plane outside a small hangar in *Cessna.* For Jerry Ott, model planes simply become props for his typical nudes, and for Mel Ramos, the propeller of a plane becomes but another mechanical phallic symbol for one of his "Playboy-type" women to caress.

Some works in the series, however, add new dimensions to the artist's oeuvre. Audrey Flack, in *Spitfire Mk-1a* replaces her usual feminine domestic modern Vanitas images with a group of airplane model kits (although some women's jewelry lies amid the kits), bringing into sharp relief the issues of gender critical to her role as a rare female Photorealist. In *Betty,* Arne Besser, by posing one of his typical prostitutes in front of a store window in which a replica of a plane is perched, seems to pun on themes of sex, flight, adventure, dreams, and fantasy. Ron Kleeman, in *Mustang Sally Forth,* produced such a dynamic image of a plane that it appears to outshine the pictorial dazzle and outstrip the symbolic speed and power of the race cars he commonly depicts.

The NASA Art Program

One of the most significant developments in recent aviation art history is the establishment of the National Aeronautics and Space Administration (NASA) Art Program. Begun in 1962 and continuing today, it commissions "some of the nation's outstanding artists ... to experience the realm of rocketry and astronauts and to produce from their impressions an artistic record of the United States Space program in all its diversity and historical importance," according to Robert Schulman, a past director of the program. For NASA, "art [i]s a means of documenting not only the sights of the Space Age, but its spirit as well."[74] In the program statement inviting artists to participate, space travel is called "a worthy theme for the artist," because "it started in the imagination of the artist," a reference, most likely, to the historical theme of flight in mythology, literature, and to the visionary aeronautical designs of Leonardo. "NASA is commissioning your imagination," artists are told. "What is important is that the artist gives us his personal and sincere interpretation."[75] In justifying the program, much attention is paid to the alleged advantages the artist has over the photographer or filmmaker, the camera accused of being a mere eye, while art involves "imagination, understanding, emotions, and memory" in which one can "edit, interpret, emphasize, omit, and invent."[76]

These arguable assumptions aside, the NASA art program has produced an array of work by a variety of artists; among the better known are Peter Hurd, Lowell Nesbitt, Robert Rauschenberg, and James Wyeth.[77] For the most part, the work is representational and, although there are the expected dramatic depictions of rocket launches, the agency encouraged freedom of choice of motif. As a result, the range of subjects is wide, including the landscape, equipment, and interiors and exteriors of buildings in and around the launch site; the assembling and testing of equipment; the press and sightseers observing blastoffs; the activity at Mission Control; astronauts in all phases of training, testing, and flight; reentry, especially views from aircraft carriers during the initial water landings; satellites and shuttles in space; and, of course, the moon landing.

The moon landing, seen by many as the beginning of an era of space exploration, also signaled the end of an age. Norman Mailer in his 1969 book *Of a Fire on the Moon* weaves an elaborate personal and universal symbology in relation to Neil Armstrong's "one small step for a man, one giant leap for mankind." Around the beginning of the century, the Futurists and artists such as Delaunay and Malevich used solar symbolism, joined with icons of new technology, to announce a century of energy. Marinetti, in particular, rejected his initial Symbolist association of flight with dreams and reveries and thus with the moon. After the moon landing, Mailer and friends perform a eulogy for the internal combustion age. They bury a car around Labor Day, marking the death of an era at the season of the waning of the sun, while resurrecting the allure of the moon. On one level, Mailer, invoking technologies that once brought discovery but have been supplanted and surpassed—the *Mayflower,* for instance—senses that new technologies shall continue to replace the old, as missile power temporarily makes the engines that once reigned seem outmoded. On another level, he recognizes, as do the organizers of the NASA Art Program, that dreams and imagination are not opposed to technological progress, as what once seemed fantasy has come true and as imaginative leaps have sparked invention and discovery.

Other Recent Developments

To complete this highly selective survey, there remains a brief consideration of a quartet of artists whose work from the 1950s through the turn of the twenty-first century demonstrates continuing and often idiosyncratic approaches to aviation. The first is Georgia O'Keeffe, perhaps the most famous American woman artist. O'Keeffe's career dates to the beginning of the twentieth century: in the 1910s she produced radical nature-oriented abstractions and in the 1920s she began to depict Precisionist-related New York cityscapes. Aerial imagery made its appearance in her work in the late 1950s. Attracted throughout her career to unusual and dramatic perspectives, especially those that encouraged abstract patterning, O'Keeffe took advantage of the views that flight offered, despite a fear of flying. Struck by the sight from above "of deserts and wonderful rivers . . . [that] actually seem to come up and hit you in the eye,"[78] she did a series of charcoal drawings of this motif in 1959, as well as several oils, including *Only One* (1959), *It Was Red and Pink* (1959), *It Was Blue and Green* (1960), and *It Was Yellow and Pink* (1960).

Her most extraordinary airscapes depict clouds seen from above. "One day when I was flying back to New Mexico," she said, "the sky was a most beautiful solid white. It looked so secure that I thought I could walk right out on it to the horizon if the door opened. The sky beyond was a clear light blue. It was so wonderful that I couldn't wait to be home to paint it."[79] The result was her *Sky Above White Clouds* series, begun in 1962. The last in the series completed in 1965, number IV, was her most ambitious. At age seventy-eight, she completed this eight by twenty-four foot canvas. In the best tradition of O'Keeffe, this vast image of blue, white, and pink sky above irregularly oval and neatly lined up rows of receding white clouds on a bed of blue hovers between representation and abstraction and between reality and fantasy. "When you fly," she remarked, "you see such marvelous things, such incredible colors that you actually begin to believe your dreams,"[80] suggesting that her sensibility could dovetail with Surrealism.

Like that of O'Keeffe, the aerial art of Robert Smithson involves a plane's-eye perspective. Until his death in a 1973 plane crash while surveying one of his works, Smithson was a leading practitioner of earthworks. Forsaking the confines of the gallery and museum in favor of working directly in the land, earth artists commonly produce large-scale art, often in remote places, sometimes attuned to the ecology of its site. Intriguingly, Smithson's temporary participation in plans for art for the Dallas–Fort Worth Airport beginning in 1966 ultimately led him to imagine the earth as the arena for monumental art. Smithson thought of the project (which he invited other like-minded artists to join) as viewed from above, explaining in his 1969 essay "Aerial Art": "The world seen from the air is abstract and illusive."[81] He realized that his contribution had to contend with a landscape that "look[s] more like a three-dimensional map rather than a rustic garden." He focused on the periphery of the airport as the spot for "earthworks," as these "aerial sites would not only be visible from arriving and departing aircraft, but they would also define the terminal's man-made perimeters in terms of landscaping." Although his project demanded grand scale—his final conception was "a progression of triangular concrete pavements that would result in a spiral effect . . . built as large as the site would allow"—he recognized its ultimate humility. "This airport," he wrote, "is but a dot in the vast infinity of universes, an imperceptible point in a cosmic immensity, a speck of impenetrable nowhere." "Aerial art reflects to a degree this vastness," Smithson concluded.[82]

His ideas for an airport-earthwork art best taken in from above also led him to new conceptions of flight and aircraft. He sensed that as aircraft ascended to higher and deeper space, the principles of aerodynamic streamlining that affected earlier aeronautical designs were becoming obsolete. Curiously, he saw a similar obsolescence operating in the practice of art, as both fields would be forced to throw off "the rationalism that supposes truths." The new paradigm for flight, Smithson argued, lies in crystallography: "the stream-lines of *space* are replaced by the crystalline structure of time."[83] His 1966 sculpture titled *Terminal* incorporates these principles and thus functions as a model for what future spacecraft might look like.

If Smithson's project for the Dallas–Fort Worth Airport was designed to be viewed from above, then air-artist Steve Poleskie developed an aeronautical art initially intended for viewing from below. Beginning in 1969, the year of the moon landing, Poleskie, an artist-pilot, abandoned his more conventional paintings of aeronautical experiences and took to the air to make his art. "I attempt to surround the viewers with a highly charged environment of movement and sound," Poleskie wrote. "Drawing, sculpture, and dance are all absorbed into the act of flying itself."[84] He elevated skywriting and aerobatics to an art form: his decorated plane, trailed by colored smoke, became an instrument for drawing in space, a vessel for performing terpsichorean movements, and its motors, sometimes accompanied by music, part of a more total aesthetic experience. He often tried to incorporate natural elements into his work by choosing certain weather conditions for his performances so that wind, sky, and clouds play roles.

Because he felt that experiencing his art from the ground was at times inadequate, he developed Apogee Airway flights, in which his plane became a soaring art gallery and his passengers experienced "art . . . elevated to a dimension quantitatively and qualitatively superior: it escapes . . . the exhibition room to conquer nature, its infinite and elemental spaces."[85] His art is not exclusively visual, and, like Malevich, it challenged traditional notions of space and perspective, even as its more perceptual residues dissolved into thin air, so to speak. Also, his interest in the fourth dimension harks back to the art of the early 1910s, when modern science and technology encouraged artists to imagine how this and further dimensions might be incorporated into art.

Poleskie freely admitted his debt to the Futurist idea of "Aerial Theater." In 1919, the Futurist pilot, photographer, artist, and performer Fedele Azari authored the manifesto "Futurist Aerial Theater," which first appeared as a rain of pages dropped from his plane in flight to the ground below. Azari's broadside explained his efforts to create what might be called aero-choreography, an idea initially and most spectacularly demonstrated in 1918 in the skies over an airfield at Busto Arsizio, near Milan. He performed daredevil aerial acrobatics, doing loops, spins, rolls, tilts, and dives, the sky his stage, he and his plane the dancer.

As the subtitle of his manifesto—"Flight as an artistic expression of states of mind"—explains, Azari sought a novel means of exploring and representing states of mind, attempting to establish correspondences between aerobatics and emotion. In a technological variation on theories associating color, geometry, and the orientation of line with emotional and psychological states, he explained that "looping denotes gaiety, the barrel-roll impatience or irritation, while repeated side-slips to the right and to the left indicate 'carefreeness,' and long free-falling descents give a sense of weariness and nostalgia." Intending to enhance the multisensory aspects of Aerial Theater, he suggested that the motors of the plane be tuned "to regulate sonority," and that exhaust should "discharge . . . colored and perfumed" matter, amplifying the visuals of and incorporating smell into the performance. He called his exploits "a new form of art . . . analogous, but infinitely superior, to dance," in which "all the infinite variety of maneuvers . . . gives the spectator an *immediate* and *clear* understanding of what you are trying to represent and declaim with your airplane."[86]

The Futurists brought this concept down to earth in aerial dances, in which performers, sometimes costumed like planes with silver wings and whirling mock propellers, performed choreography designed to evoke flight. Establishing analogies between dance and aviation has a compelling logic. More so than most contemporary technologies, the airplane has a maneuverability and operates in an environment that allows for a range of movement like that in dance. Certain characteristics of dance—leaps and jumps, in particular—suggest the desire to be free of the earth's bounds, a longing that plane flight fulfills. Futurist photographer and theorist Anton Giulio Bragaglia called this aspiration "Aerodance," "a lyrical attempt to flee the earthbound," that likened the "aerodancer" to "the butterfly" and the traditional dancer to "the poor simple caterpillar." "Aerodance," he continued, "is, above all, exaltation of flight. . . . it is a lyrical flight, a flight of the spirit . . . its movement is beautiful like that of Icarus."[87]

It seems fitting to conclude this chapter with the work of Mark Tansey. At first glance, his art has the look of the down-to-earth, although it can conceptually climb to the height of a tower—not the early modern towers used to mark the ascent of pioneering aviation—but the proverbial "ivory tower" of academe and its rarefied atmosphere of art history and critical theory. Often his works seems to be dunked in a kind of "Old Master brown sauce" or weathered and faded into the sepias or blue-grays of an old photograph, and shot through with a tinge of 1940s illustrations. Tansey's art becomes an art historical game of postmodernist, historicist quotation. For our purposes, Tansey developed his own brand of aviation iconography. In *Halls of Montezuma (Study after Church's "Heart of the Andes")* of 1986, he took a famous Frederic Church nineteenth-century painting and subjected it to a series of incursions, several of them aeronautical. A modern helicopter dramatically appears from behind a clump of trees and a jet soars against the mountain backdrop. These, along with other contemporary intrusions—a radar or satellite dish strapped to a tree stump, modernized buildings, figures running, and the suggestion of a military encampment—produce an equivalence between pictorial and military invasion. Invoking Montezuma, Tansey addresses a history of colonialism and imperialism, enlisting, as did other contemporary artists, the helicopter as symbol of the American response to an impolitic world: "send in the Marines." Tansey's allusion to military invasion and exploitation is concretized in the painting itself, as the artist, in the spirit of postmodernism, appropriates Church's paintings for his own clever usage.

In *Action Painting II* (1984), he locates several artists of both sexes and of various ages, dress, and eras at their easels observing and painting a space shuttle lift-off. Punning on the term used to describe the gestural wing of Abstract Expressionism, Tansey provides this art class, or members of an art movement (who, like the artists of various movements of the past, sometimes worked together in front of the same motif), with "real" action. Their traditional, studied manner of working totally contradicts the freewheeling choreographic spontaneity of the original action painters.[88] The scene itself also suggests the possible working procedures of those in NASA's Art Program.

One of Tansey's most provocative aeronautical raids on the past occurs in his 1992 oil *Picasso and Braque* (page 252). He relocates these trailblazing modern artists from Paris to Kitty Hawk, replacing the engineering Wright brothers

with the team of Picasso in a plane and Braque running alongside. For his painting, Tansey appropriated the imagery from the photo mentioned earlier that the
brothers set up nearly nine decades earlier: how strange that only minor adjust-
ments convert the inventors' original tools cast about the ground into the accou-
trements of artists! Tansey maintains historical accuracy in casting Braque as
Wilbur, and Picasso as pilot Orville (his possible nickname-sake), as the latter
artist in the pair popularly gets most of the credit for launching vanguard aesthetic innovations. He soars aloft in what might be mistaken for the Wrights'
original biplane Flyer, but is instead a painted version of a collage like those of
Braque or Picasso from the early 1910s: a Cubist violin, partly drawn and partly
made from pasted newspaper, floats in the sky. Tansey recycles and reaffirms the
affinities and mythologies between modern art and modern flight: Picasso and
Braque using Wilbur and Orville as monikers, indicating identification of their
joint pictorial feats with aeronautical innovations; Picasso's specific correspondence between Braque's paper sculptures and the Wrights' biplanes; the common art-critical analysis of cubist space as holding objects that seem to levitate or
be suspended; the multivalent readings that Cubist art promotes; and the story
that Picasso occasionally wore an "aviator's outfit" when he worked. Tansey re-
evokes this last notion in the painting *The Triumph of the New York School* (1984),
in which Picasso wears World War I military garb for the French "surrender"
to the American Abstract Expressionists. "Our Future Is in the Air," Picasso announced in three 1912 works. As we have seen, a varied group of artists followed
his lead.

Epilogue

Because of the production schedule of this volume, it was impossible to incorporate into this essay any detailed discussion of the impact of 9/11 on aviation
iconography in the visual arts. Fears expressed in earlier art—that aviation
placed civilian population in increased danger of attack—intensified after 9/11
as terrorism made commercial planes as potentially ominous as military craft.
Images populating earlier art that paired airplane and skyscraper as testimony to
man's multipronged challenge to gravity and height also took on sinister meaning. After 9/11, an airplane flying seemingly too close to any tall structure caused
anxiety and trepidation.

Artistic responses to 9/11 have been widespread and varied, but could any
image match the power of the films that showed commercial jetliners filled with
civilian passengers exploding into fireballs as they flew into the World Trade
Center towers in New York City? After the attack, the skies became eerily quiet
as flights were grounded. As planes slowly took to the skies days later, their
drone or roar, generally not considered a comforting sound, produced not only

dread but also a sense of relief that the world was returning to normal, even though everyone knew that things would never be the same again.

Notes

I wish to thank several institutions and individuals for assistance during the preparation of this essay. They include: an Ailsa Bruce Mellon Senior Fellowship at the Center for Advanced Study in the Visual Arts at the National Gallery of Art in Washington; a Temple University Summer Research Grant; a National Endowment for the Humanities Summer Stipend; and a Temple University Study Leave. I am grateful to others who kindly provided assistance throughout this project, including Jessica Altholz, Greta Berman, Robin Biel, Stephen Brown, Jennifer Brushaber Calder, Contessa Maria Fede Caproni-Armani, Paolo Colombo, Joanne Gernstein London, hallie harrisburg, Mary Henderson, Marisa Incelli, Dominick Pisano, the late Steve Poleskie, Albert Reischuk, Renata Rossani, Charles Schmidt, Nancy Spero, Renee Williams, and Barbara Zabel.

1. For more on the relationship of Marinetti, Futurism, and flight, see Cinzia Sartini Blum, *The Other Modernism: F. T. Marinetti's Futurist Fiction of Power* (Berkeley: University of California Press, 1996); Bruno Mantura, *Futurism in Flight: "Aeropittura" Paintings and Sculptures of Man's Conquest of Space,* exh. cat. (London and Rome: Accademia Italiana delle Arti e delle Arti Applicate and De Luca Edizioni Arte, 1990); Jeffrey T. Schnapp, "Propeller Talk," *Modernism/Modernity* (September 1994), 153–78; Gerald Silk, "*Aeropittura* and Italian Futurism," in *1998 National Aerospace Conference Proceedings* (Dayton, Oh.: Wright State University, 1999), 46–55; Silk, "Flight; Futurism; *Aeropittura,*" in *Futurism Aeropittura* (Rome: Stilgraf, 1989), n.p.; Barbara Spackman, *Fascist Virilities: Rhetoric, Ideology, and Social Fantasy in Italy* (Minneapolis: University of Minnesota Press, 1996); and Robert Wohl, *A Passion for Wings: Aviation and the Western Imagination, 1908–1918* (New Haven, Conn., and London: Yale University Press, 1994).

2. In this instance, I am referring to the invention in 1903 by the Wright brothers of a successful heavier-than-air vehicle, the first modern airplane. Lighter-than-air vehicles, or balloons, date to the late eighteenth century, and beginning at that time, they appear as images in art, most often in illustrations.

3. In addition, Marinetti dealt with the theme of flight in the 1910 novel *Mafarka the Futurist,* in the 1912 prose-poem, *The Pope's Monoplane* (in part, inspired by André Beaumont's [né Jean Conneaut] 1911 flight over the Vatican), and he dedicated his 1909 play *The Electric Puppets* to the Wright brothers. Interestingly, Marinetti's greatest cultural rival, the flamboyant international celebrity. Gabriele d'Annunzio, although best known for his archaistic and sensuous poetry, announced after his first plane flight in 1909 that he would address contemporary heroes, "the ultra-modern figures of Wilbur Wright, Blériot, Farman, and Latham," all pioneering aviators. *Poesia* (August–October 1909), 38–39; quoted in Pär Bergman, "*Modernolatria*" et "*Simultaneità*" (Uppsala: Scandinavian University Books, 1962), 231. The heroes of D'Annunzio's *Maybe Yes, Maybe No,* published in 1910, were aviators and race-car drivers, and the novel invokes the myth of Icarus, a common motif in his poetry even from before the turn of the century. Much like the Futurists, D'Annunzio regarded speed and technology as enhancing sexuality, youthfulness, and the thrill of danger and possible death. Marinetti, however, regarded D'Annunzio's treatment of modern themes as reactionary.

D'Annunzio would eventually become an ace pilot, and was dubbed the "poet-soldier." His most famous mission occurred in 1918 during World War I, when he was well past the age of fifty. He dropped pamphlets bearing the Italian colors over the unfortified city of Vienna, which required flying for a great distance over enemy territory. One set of pamphlets contained the message, "We are flying over Vienna, we could drop bombs in tons. We are only sending you a greeting in three colours: the three colours of liberty." Quoted in Philippe Jullian, *D'Annunzio* (New York: The Viking Press, 1972), 266. For more on D'Annunzio, and for an excellent account of the impact of aviation on early modern European culture in general, see Wohl, *A Passion for Wings.*

4. F. T. Marinetti, "The Founding and Manifesto of Futurism," first published in *Le Figaro,* February 20, 1909. Unless otherwise noted, all translations are my own, taken from the Italian versions published in Luciano De Maria, *Teoria e Invenzione Futurista* (Milan: Arnaldo Mondadori Editore, 1968); De Maria, *Marinetti e il Futurismo* (Milan: Arnaldo Mondadori Editore, 1973); and Luigi Scrivo, *Sintesi del Futurismo: Scrivi e Documenti* (Rome: Mario Bulzone Editore, 1968).

5. See Gerald Silk, "The Image of the Automobile in Futurism," *Artsmagazine* 51 (December 1977), 93–97. Also, Silk, *Automobile and Culture* (New York and Los Angeles: Harry N. Abrams and The Museum of Contemporary Art, 1984), esp. 57–71.

6. For more on this accident, see Jeffrey T. Schnapp, "Crash (Speed as Engine of Individuation)," *Modernism/Modernity* 6:1 (January 1999), 1–49.

7. For more on the significance of that flight, see Schnapp, "Propeller Talk."

8. F. T. Marinetti, "The Founding and Manifesto of Futurism" (1912).

9. Marinetti, "Multiplied Man and the Reign of the Machine," from *War, the World's Only Hygiene* (1911–15).

10. From balloons through dirigibles to heavier-than-air-vehicles, aircraft were immediately put to military service. The airplane, first used extensively in World War I, brought about enormous changes in the conduct of warfare.

11. See Marianne W. Martin, *Futurist Art and Theory: 1900–1915* (New York: Hacker Art Books, 1978), 198, n. 4. Severini had thoughts of becoming a pilot, which he abandoned. For a further discussion of Severini and aviation, see Martin, "Carissimo Marinetti: Letters from Severini to the Futurist Chief," *Art Journal* 41 (winter 1981), 306.

12. A major criticism of Futurism has been its aestheticization of violence. The most famous analysis of this phenomenon is Walter Benjamin's "The Work of Art in the Age of Mechanical Reproduction," written in 1936, and which can be found in Benjamin, *Illuminations* (New York: Schocken Books, 1969), 217–52. Although Futurism is not his focus, Alan Sekula addresses the problematic connection between reconnaissance and "art" photography. See his "The Instrumental Image: Steichen at War," *Artforum* (January 1975), 26–35.

13. Marinetti, "Technical Manifesto of Futurist Literature" (May 11, 1912). See also Schnapp, "Propeller Talk."

14. See Christine Poggi, *In Defiance of Painting: Cubism. Futurism. and the Invention of Collage* (New Haven: Yale University Press, 1992), 234; also, Linda Landis, "Futurists at War," in *The Futurist Imagination,* exh. cat., ed. Anne Coffin Hanson (New Haven: Yale University Art Gallery, 1983), 60–75. Hugo Ball, an important figure in Zurich Dada, commented in a diary entry in 1915 after Marinetti sent him examples of "words-in-freedom": "You can roll up such poems like a map." See Hugo Ball, *Flight Out of Time: A Diary,* trans. Ann Raimes (New York: Viking Press, 1974), 25. The diary was first published in 1927.

15. In addition to discussions of this work in some of the basic Futurist texts, including Martin, *Futurist Art and Theory;* Joshua Taylor, *Futurism,* exh. cat. (New York: Museum of Modern Art, 1961); and Caroline Tisdall and Angelo Bozzolla, *Futurism* (New York and Toronto: Thames and Hudson, 1978), there are several specialized treatments of the collage. These include: Willard Bohn, "The Futurist Experience," in *The Aesthetics of Visual Poetry, 1914–1928* (Cambridge: Cambridge University Press, 1986), 29–45; Max Kozloff, "Paintings, Sounds and

Words," in *Cubism/Futurism* (New York: Icon Editions, 1974), 207–13; Lewis Kachur, "Carlo Carrà: Interventionist Demonstration," in *The Mattioli Collection: Masterpieces of the Avant-Garde,* ed. Flavio Fergonzi (Milan: Skira, 2003), 204–15; Landis, "Futurists at War"; Marjorie Perloff, *The Futurist Moment* (Chicago: University of Chicago Press, 1986), 61–64; Poggi, *In Defiance of Painting,* 221–25; Laura Mattioli Rossi and Emily Braun, "Carlo Carrà: Interventionist Demonstration," in *Masterpieces from the Gianni Mattioli Collection* (Venice and Milan: Peggy Guggenheim Collection, Solomon R. Guggenheim Foundation, and Electa, 1997), 66; Silk, "*Aeropittura* and Italian Futurism"; John J. White, *Literary Futurism: Aspects of the First Avant-Garde* (Oxford: Clarendon Press, 1990), 87–99; Alan Windsor, "Apollinaire, Marinetti, and Carrà's *Dipinto Parolibero,*" *Gazette des Beaux Arts* 89 (April 1977), 145–52; and Wohl, *A Passion for Wings,* 199–200.

16. Marinetti, "Technical Manifesto of Futurist Literature."

17. For a fascinating discussion of the "view from above" in art, see Kirk Varnedoe, "Overview: The Flight of the Mind," in *A Fine Disregard: What Makes Modern Art Modern* (New York: Harry N. Abrams, 1990), 216–77.

18. See Mattioli Rossi and Braun, "Carlo Carrà: Interventionist Demonstration." Futurist manifestoes themselves were later dropped from planes. See the discussion of Fedele Azari later in this chapter.

19. A source for Carrà's collage, Guillaume Apollinaire's 1914 calligramme titled "Lettre-Océan," makes mention of the TSF. The TSF figures explicitly in Carrà's 1914 *Aerial Reconnaissance Sea Moon - 2 Machine Guns +1 Northwest Wind,* which also has helical compositional rhythms and a "plane's-eye" perspective. It was published in his 1915 *Guerrapittura [Warpicture],* a collection of "words/paintings in-freedom," which intertwine aeronautics and militarism.

20. F. T. Marinetti, "Destruction of Syntax—Imagination without Strings—Words-in-Freedom" (May 11, 1913).

21. Carrà clarifies this "enlightenment" by including the words "concentriche echi echi echi" [concentric echoes echoes echoes], which are snipped from his "Bilancio." As Lewis Kachur observed in his excellent unpublished paper of 1979, "The Collages of Carlo Carrà," the entire phrase from "Bilancio" reads "azioni nostre propagarsi ondate concentriche echi echi echi . . . " [our actions to propagate concentric waves echoes echoes echoes . . .], followed by the pairing of the word "echi" with a list of cities, including Paris, Berlin, New York, Vladivostok, Tokyo, and others. In *Interventionist Demonstration,* "Tokio" is sandwiched between two "echi," and "Parigi" "London," and "Belgium" also appear. ("Austria" and "Hungary" can be found as well, but their inclusion applies more to enemies to be conquered militarily than to cities and countries to be converted culturally and aesthetically, although military conquest could be understood as a stage preceding ultimate cultural transformation.) Echoing, as visual and acoustic principles, operates throughout the piece, from sounds reverberating throughout a piazza during this "interventionist demonstration" to rhyming visual forms, many resulting from the concentric design of the piece. See Kachur.

22. Guido Mattioli, in his propagandistic tract titled *Mussolini Aviatore* written in 1937, observed: "The pilot truly knows what it means 'to govern.' . . . This is the symbol of Aviator Mussolini . . . . He commands the airplane with the same calm strength with which he leads the people." Mattioli, *Mussolini Aviatore [Aviator Mussolini]* (Editrice L'Aviazione, 1937), 2, 18. For more on the subject of Mussolini and aviation imagery see Giorgio Di Genova, ed., "*Uomo della provvidenza": iconografia del Duce 1923–1945,* exh. cat. (Seravezza: Palazzo Mediceo, 1997). Also see Silk, "Fascist Modernism and the Photo-Collages of Bruno Munari," in *Cummer Studies: Cultural and Artistic Upheavals in Modern Europe. 1848–1945,* vol. 1, ed. Sally Metzler and Elizabeth Lovett Colledge (Jacksonville, Fla.: Cummer Museum of Art, 1996), 41–76; and Silk, "*Il Primo Pilota:* Mussolini, Fascist Aeronautical Symbolism, and Imperial Rome," in *Donatello*

among the Blackshirts: History and Modernity in the Visual Culture of Fascist Italy, ed. Roger J. Crum and Claudia Lazzaro (Ithaca: Cornell University Press, forthcoming).

23. This theme recurs throughout Mattioli's *Aviator Mussolini.*

24. From the catalogue of the XXI Venice Biennale, 1938. Quoted in Lawrence Alloway, *The Venice Biennale, 1895–1968* (Greenwich, Conn.: New York Graphic Society, 1968), 110.

25. Marinetti and the Futurists Balla, Benedetta, Depero, Dottori, Fillia, Prampolini, Somenzi, Tato, "Manifesto of Futurist Aeropainting," first published in *La Gazzetta del Popolo,* September 22, 1929. For more on Futurist Aeropainting, see Enrico Crispolti, *Aeropittura futurista Aeropittori,* exh. cat. (Modena: Galleria Fonte d'Abisso, 1985); Massimo Duranti, *Dottori e l'aeropittura: aeropittori e aeroscultori futuristi* (Seravezza: Palazzo Mediceo, 1996); Mantura, *Futurism and Flight;* Claudia Salaris, *Aero: futurismo e mito del volo* (Rome: Parole Gelate, 1985); and Silk, "Flight; Futurism; Aeropittura."

26. When Delaunay's *Homage à Blériot* was exhibited at the Salon des Independents in March of 1914, the French poet and critic Guillaume Apollinaire, writing in *L'Intransigient,* called it "rotating Futurism." The day after this review appeared, Delaunay issued the rebuke: "I am not and I never was a Futurist." Quoted in Gustav Vriesen and Max Imdahl, *Robert Delaunay: Light and Color* (New York: Harry N. Abrams, 1967), 65.

27. From Robert Delaunay, *Du Cubisme a l'art abstrait,* ed. Pierre Francastal (Paris, 1957), 129; quoted in Vriesen and Imdahl, *Robert Delaunay,* 68. The entire quotation reads: "Sky over the cities, balloons, towers, airplanes. All the poetry of modern life: that is my art."

28. See Pascal Rousseau, "La constructions du simultané: Robert Delaunay et l'aéronautique," *Revue de l'art* 113: 3 (1996), 19–31. Also, Jean-Paul Ameline and Pascal Rousseau, *Robert Delaunay. 1906–1915: De l'impressionisme à l'abstraction,* exh. cat. (Paris: Centre Georges Pompidou), 1999, esp. 226–35.

29. From Howard Dearstyne's translation of *The Non-Objective World* (Chicago: Theobald, 1959); quoted in Herschel Chipp, ed., *Theories of Modern Art* (Berkeley and London: University of California Press, 1968), 338. For a good discussion of Suprematism and aerial phenomena see John E. Bowlt, "Beyond the Horizon," in *Kasimir Malewitsch zum 100. Gerburtstag,* exh. cat. (Cologne: Galerie Gmurzynska, 1978), 232–52. Also see Wohl, *A Passion for Wings,* 145–53, 157–79, for more on the flight impulse in Malevich's work, and its role among Russian futurist writers, especially in the poetry of Vasya Kamensky.

Between 1929 and 1931 the Russian avant-garde artist Vladimir Tatlin, in the spirit of Leonardo da Vinci's designs for flying machines, built his *Letatlin,* a "bicycleglider" intended for flight. Tatlin's invention, based on bird flight and close in conception to the idea of the ornithopter, differs from modern, motorized, heavier-than-air vehicles. It is more bicycle than airplane, a personal form of transportation, available to all and capable of instant flight at the whim of its rider. Being nonmotorized, it is meant to be quiet and nonpolluting. In design, it is organic, not geometric, and as much aesthetic as utilitarian.

30. See Ameline and Rousseau, *Robert Delaunay,* 228.

31. The review of Braque's work followed by the notice on Wright appeared in the French journal *Gil Blas* on November 14, 1908. The article on Wright reads: "The conquest of the air. . . . Wilbur Wright has won the prize for height."

32. See William Rubin, *Picasso and Braque: Pioneering Cubism,* exh. cat. (New York: Museum of Modern Art and Harry N. Abrams, 1989), 32–34. Also, Wohl, *A Passion for Wings,* 272.

33. The three *Our Future in the Air* works are all oval in shape, a format Picasso used for what some consider to be his first collage, the famous 1912 *Still-life with Chair Caning.* These works were done around the same time as *Still-life with Chair Caning,* and, like this piece, one substitutes a rope for a frame. One of the three, known as *The Scallop Shell,* uses ripolin enamel

paint (to depict the cover of the pamphlet), which makes this area almost seem to be collaged. This image of the scallop shell in one piece from the group also might suggest a parachute, and the use of a rope border in another could evoke a chute's ripcord. (Picasso and Braque have also been described as like two mountaineers lashed together in their ascent of the peaks of Cubism. Of course, a rope would connect them, and if it were to break, both might fall.)

34.   Quoted, without source, in "Conquest of the Air," *Art News* (February 1, 1944), 16–17.

35.   Kirk Varnedoe's remarks about the Russian artist El Lissitzky could apply to much of early modernist art affected by aviation: "The images do have something to do with flight, but they involve more than mere mimicry of aerial views: they demand a symbolic rethinking of the basic processes of conceiving a picture in relation to a viewer." Varnedoe, *A Fine Disregard,* 254.

36.   See Roger E. Bilstein, *Flight in America, 1900–1983: From the Wrights to the Astronauts* (Baltimore, Md.: Johns Hopkins University Press, 1984), esp. 8–39. As Robert Wohl described it: "Wright had come to France a 'marchand de bicyclettes' whom many suspected of being a charlatan and a fraud. After August 8 [1908], he became a hero lavished with praise, feted at ceremonial dinners, by those who had earlier denounced him, and the recipient of numerous medals, prizes, and distinctions, including the Legion of Honor." Wohl, *A Passion for Wings,* 23.

37.   The camera was a key adjunct to their endeavors: not only did the brothers recognize the importance of documenting their efforts for the sake of history, they also used photos as research tools in analyzing their experiments with flight. (They generally alternated roles: while one piloted, the other photographed, and vice versa.) Wilbur characterized the time in the photographic darkroom "as thrilling as any in the field, when the image begins to appear on the plate and it is yet an open question whether we have a picture of a flying machine, or merely a patch of open sky." Quoted in Russell Freedman, *The Wright Brothers: How They Invented the Airplane* (New York: Holiday House, 1991), 129.

38.   Marsden Hartley to Alfred Stieglitz; undated letter in Hartley Archive, Yale Collection of American Literature, Bienecke Rare Book and Manuscript Library. Quoted in Gail R. Scott, *Marsden Hartley* (New York: Abbeville Press, 1988), 49. The dirigible theory appears in Gail Levin, "Hidden Symbolism in Marsden Hartley's Military Pictures," *Artsmagazine* 54 (October 1979) 154–58.

39.   Stanton MacDonald-Wright, "Influence of Aviation on Art: The Accentuation of Individuality," *Ace: The Aviation Magazine of the West* 1: 2 (September 1919), 11–12.

40.   Undated letter from Horace Pippin, Horace Pippin War Memoirs, Letters, and Photographs Archives of American Art, Smithsonian Institution, Washington, D.C. Quoted in Judith E. Stein, "An American Original," in *I Tell My Heart: The Art of Horace Pippin,* exh. cat. (Philadelphia and New York: Pennsylvania Academy of the Fine Arts and Universe Books, 1994), 3.

41.   For a further discussion of Pippin's war imagery, see Judith Wilson, "Scenes of War," in *I Tell My Heart,* 56–69.

42.   Letter from Horace Pippin to Robert Carlen reprinted in Selden Rodman, *Horace Pippin: A Negro Painter in America* (New York: Quadrangle Press, 1947), 20. Quoted in Richard J. Powell, "Biblical and Spiritual Motifs," in *I Tell My Heart,* 132.

43.   A fine discussion of this series can be found in Carol Troyen and Erica E. Hirshler, *Charles Sheeler: Paintings and Drawings,* exh. cat. (Boston: Museum of Fine Arts and Little, Brown and Company, 1987).

44.   "Power: A Portfolio by Charles Sheeler," *Fortune* 22: 9 (December 1940), 83.

45.   Quoted in K. G. Pontus Hulten, *The Machine, as Seen at the End of the Mechanical Age,* exh. cat. (New York: Museum of Modern Art, 1968), 140. All three artists produced work apparently inspired by aeronautics. On a day at an airfield arranged by the famous French aviator

Henri Farman, Duchamp in the spring of 1912 saw planes take off, fly, and land. A month or so later and several months before visiting the aeronautics exhibition, he made a drawing titled *Aeroplane*. Moreover, Duchamp's radical "readymades"—in which he selected everyday, already made objects, and rechristened and recontextualized them as works of art—may have been inspired partly by his recognizing the stunningly sheer beauty of a manufactured functional propeller. Léger made the painting *Propellers* in 1918. In a 1924 essay titled "The Machine Aesthetic: The Manufactured Object, the Artisan, and the Artist," he wrote: "I will always remember that one year, showing at the Salon d'Automne, I had the advantage of being next to the Aviation show.... Never had such a stark contrast assailed my eyes. I left vast surfaces, dismal and gray, pretentious in their frames, for beautiful, metallic objects, hard, permanent, and useful, in pure local colors; infinite varieties of steel surfaces at play next to vermillions and blues. The power of geometric forms dominated it all." From *Bulletin de l'Effort Moderne* (Paris, 1924); quoted in Léger, *Functions of Painting,* trans. Alexandra Anderson (New York: Viking Press, 1973), 60. Between 1923 and 1952, Brancusi did several sculptures called *Bird in Space* which may owe something to the sensation of powered flight, to the associated principle of streamlining, and perhaps to the blade of a propeller itself. Describing these works Brancusi said: "It is not the bird that I wish to express, but its ... flight." In Claire Gilles Guilbaut, "Propos de Brancusi (1876–1957)," *Prisme des arts* 12 (December 1957), 7. Elsewhere, the artist explained: "All my life I've been looking for one thing, the essence of flight.... What a marvelous thing flight is." In Carola Giedion-Weicker, *Constantin Brancusi,* trans. Maria Jolas and Anne Leroy (New York: George Braziller, 1959), 13. As well, for Brancusi, flight was as much spiritual as it was aeronautical.

46.   Examples include Hugh Ferriss's drawing *Overhead Traffic-Ways* (1929), Leopold De Postels's drawing *Buildings Still in Blue-Print May Be Obsolete* (c. 1931), and Frank Hultzberg's oil *Fantasy New York* (1935). As mentioned in the text, Delaunay and Marinetti also coupled airplanes and architecture, in part because certain prominent towering landmarks were sites for aviation activity.

47.   Their differences were spelled out by Benton in response to an outcry, especially among left-wing intellectuals, to the removal of Rivera's 1933 mural form the RCA building in New York City because of the Mexican's refusal to eliminate an image of Nikolai Lenin. Benton did not come to Rivera's defense, "because," he said, "I do not feel, in view of the seriously decadent condition of our own art, that what happens to a Mexican artist is of great importance. I respect Rivera as an artist, but I have no time to enter into affairs concerning him, because I am intensely interested in the development of an art which is of, and adequately represents, the United States—my own art." Quoted in Henry Adams, *Thomas Hart Benton: An American Original* (New York: Alfred A. Knopf, 1989), 227. Nonetheless, certain scholars argue that Benton remained politically liberal into the early 1930s; see Emily Braun and Thomas Branchick, *Thomas Hart Benton: The America Today Murals,* exh. cat. (Williamstown, Mass. and New York: Williams College Museum of Art and The Equitable, 1985).

48.   Quoted in Bertram D. Wolfe, *The Fabulous Life of Diego Rivera* (New York: Stein and Day, 1963), 277.

49.   An excellent discussion of Benton's politics in relation to *America Today* can be found in Braun, "Thomas Hart Benton and Progressive Liberalism: An Interpretation of the New School Murals," in Braun and Branchick, *Thomas Hart Benton: The America Today Murals,* 10–38.

50.   Quoted in Matthew Baigell, *Thomas Hart Benton* (New York: Harry N. Abrams, 1974), 33. A stint in the navy led Benton to this assessment, and several watercolors from this time, including *The Observation Balloon, The Hydroplane,* and *Impressions, Camouflage WWI* (all of 1918), contain aeronautical imagery. Although he considered these works examples of his rejection of modernism, contemporary reviewers noted their "modernity" and "cubis[m]." In his

1919 essay "The Influence of Aviation on Art," Stanton MacDonald-Wright, Benton's close friend and to some extent early mentor, ranked Benton, along with Delaunay, as the only artists producing aeronautical art of any abstract interest (see note 39).

51. I have relied on Ruth Bowman's excellent catalogue *Murals without Walls: Arshile Gorky's Aviation Murals Rediscovered,* exh. cat. (Newark, N.J.: The Newark Museum), 1978, including her own essay and those by Francis V. O'Connor and Jim M. Jordan. The catalogue also reprints Frederick T. Kiesler's important 1936 essay, "Murals without Walls: Relating to Gorky's Newark Project," and Gorky's own "My Murals for the Newark Airport." All quotations by Gorky are taken from this essay.

52. Much of Stuart Davis's oeuvre indicates his interest in modern invention, urbanism, technology, and vernacular culture. Some pieces have been linked with flight, such as his 1916 painting *Airview,* its title and composition implying an aerial viewpoint. It was done at a time when Davis was first exposed to and when he experimented with the innovative styles of Modernism, including Cubism, Orphism, Futurism, and Synchromism. His 1963–64 *Blips and Ifs* refers to activity on a radar screen. Also, the spatial disorientation and its all-over field effects of some of his art have connected with Abstract Expressionism, especially to Jackson Pollock's work, and these qualities have sometimes been thought of as related to celestial or aerial phenomena.

53. See Jim M. Jordan, "The Place of the Newark Murals in Gorky's Art," in Bowman, 27–64. Also see Jordan and Robert Goldwater, *The Paintings of Arshile Gorky: A Critical Catalogue* (New York and London: New York University Press, 1982), esp. 56–65.

54. Greta Berman, "Does Flight Have a Future?" *Art in America* (September–October, 1976), 97. This article provides a fine discussion of the murals.

55. See Joan Marter, "Theodore Roszak," in *Abstract Painting and Sculpture in America, 1927–1944,* exh. cat., ed. John R. Lane and Susan C. Larsen (Pittsburgh and New York: Museum of Art, Carnegie Institute and Harry N. Abrams, 1983), 211–13.

56. Interview with Roszak by James Elliott, in Theodore Roszak Papers, Archives of American Art, Smithsonian Institution, Washington, D.C., 36. Quoted in Joan Marter, *Theodore Roszak: The Drawings* (New York: The Drawing Society, 1992), 21.

57. The Mexican muralists provided inspiration for Guston to paint murals. Furthermore, aviation motifs figure in some of Guston's early work, including navigation instructional murals he designed in the early 1940s for the War Art Workshop at the State University of Iowa, established to make a patriotic contribution to the American war effort. Like Sheeler, Guston produced illustrations for articles for *Fortune,* which appeared in 1943 and 1944. His military drawings constituted his first solo show at the University of Iowa Student Union in 1944, and several were included in his first one-person show in New York at the Midtown Galleries. See Michael Edward Shapiro, "Philip Guston: The War Years," *Print Collector's Newsletter* 35 (1994), 127–30.

58. One of the richest troves of World War II aviation imagery can be found in war correspondents' photography. Probably the most intriguing issues circulate around Margaret Bourke-White, the first woman to be accredited and uniformed as a war correspondent by the Pentagon. Working for *Life* magazine, she was assigned to an air force base, and in 1943 she eventually received permission to fly on a bombing raid, having been initially excluded because of her gender. Interestingly, the copilot of her maiden mission would later pilot the plane that dropped the first atom bomb on Hiroshima. She took photos on many fronts throughout the war: some from planes, some from the ground, and some dealing with aerial bombardment. There are many accounts of Bourke-White's activities; one useful study is Jonathan Silverman, ed., *For the World to See: The Life of Margaret Bourke-White* (New York: Viking Press, 1983).

59. Klein did his own version of the *Victory of Samothrace* in 1962, in a blue hue of his in-

vention, partly inspired by the color of the sky. He also had a particular penchant for the theme of flight, releasing balloons into the air as sculpture as early as 1957, and painting his *Planetary Reliefs* in 1961 after Gagarin remarked on the beautiful blue color of the earth as seen from outer space. Klein had earlier signed the back of the blue sky as his work of art, made a blue sculptural globe in 1957, and had himself photographed in 1960 as if levitating this globe, displaying his magical and godlike aesthetic powers over earthly matters. Several works from his *Living Brush* and *Anthropometry* series, such as *People Begin to Fly* and *Architecture of the Air* (both c. 1961), are related to flight. He refers to the atom bomb in the anthropometry painting *Hiroshima* (c. 1961). In *Man in Space* or *The Impossible Man,* from 1960, the Greek kinetic sculptor Takis rigged two magnets that he hoped would keep a poet placed between them aloft, who shouted, "I am a sculpture"; instead, the poet promptly fell to the protective netting below.

60. Foretelling earthworks, the 1947 *Sculpture to Be Seen from Mars* by the American Isamu Noguchi (who, because of his Japanese roots, was interned at a relocation camp during World War II), was a proposed colossal image of a human head meant to be viewed from outer space. The piece was inspired in part by Indian mounds, in which the image could only be understood from a vast distance (and the design of these mounds have been linked by some to alien life). *Sculpture to Be Seen from Mars* was originally called *Memorial to Man,* done in response to the 1945 dropping of the atomic bomb (which undoubtedly had even more complex meanings for an artist of Japanese origins). Noguchi also periodically made pieces relating to the moon; some predate space flight, but others owe a debt to astronautics. (He was an assistant to Brancusi, who, as discussed, had an interest in flight [see note 45], and as dance and flight have parallels, his frequent work with choreographers is worth noting.) Lee Bontecou, for whom planes were a frequent inspiration, did a series of Sputnik-inspired works, including her soot drawings that she called "worldscapes," and her 1958–59 "Untitled" boxes containing spheres. Bontecou is best known for her large wall constructions, which, on one level, express her lingering anger over the horrors of World War II. They contain menacing, often spiky and zippered holes and openings, which can suggest jet-engine intakes or exhausts; bomb craters; the barrels of cannons; and windows opening onto vast space. They also can evoke body orifices that have the potential to sever and maim: a zippered or slicing mouth referring to issues of silence, lying, and truth, and a castrating "vagina dentata," attacking the fused notion of militarism and machismo (which look ahead to Nancy Spero's twin attacks on virility and violence). Some of these works literally incorporate war surplus, both American and German, as well as portions of American bombers. For more on these facets of Bontecou's work, see Mona Hadler, "Lee Bontecou's 'Warnings,'" *Art Journal* (winter 1994), 56–61.

61. A useful discussion of this work can be found in the chapter "Comics," in Kirk Varnedoe and Adam Gopnik, *High & Low: Modern Art and Popular Culture,* exh. cat. (New York: Museum of Modern Art and Harry N. Abrams, 1991), esp. 202–8.

62. A good discussion of the piece can be found in Judith Goldman, *James Rosenquist* (New York: Viking Penguin, 1985), esp. 40–44. Emphasis on its political and antiwar context appears in Joan Seeman Robinson, "*Whispering Death*: James Rosenquist's F-111 as History Painting," in *1998 National Aerospace Conference Proceedings* (Dayton, Oh.: Wright State University, 1999), 41–45.

63. Quoted in G. R. Swenson, "The F-111: An Interview with James Rosenquist," *Partisan Review* 32: 4 (fall 1965), 599.

64. Quoted in G. R. Swenson, "What Is Pop Art" (part II), *Art News* 62 (February 1964), 41.

65. Swenson, "The F-111," 598. This and the following quotations from Rosenquist come from Swenson's "F-111" interview.

66. This is not to say that Abstract Expressionism was removed from politics; in fact,

there is much literature that argues that this development became a symbol of American freedom and liberation and a tool to establish American cultural hegemony during the Cold War.
The best discussion of this idea remains Francis Frascina, ed., *Pollock and After: The Critical Debate* (New York: Icon Editions, Harper and Row, 2000).

67.   Other responses include the tying of aesthetic principles to the production of objects,
thus allegedly bettering the world by turning it into a beautiful work of art. Some have argued
that abandoning art for direct political action is the only real solution. Of course, it is frequently
said that art itself has (or should have) nothing to do with politics, although it could be claimed
that ignoring politics in art is in itself a political position, and thus all art is political.

68.   Nancy Spero, "The War Series" (1993), in Jon Bird et al., *Nancy Spero* (London:
Phaidon, 1996), 124.

69.   See Sidra Stich, *Made in USA,* exh. cat. (Berkeley: University Art Museum, and University of California Press, 1987), 52.

70.   For art about the Vietnam War, see Lucy R. Lippard, *A Different War: Vietnam in Art,*
exh. cat. (Bellingham and Seattle, Wash.: Whatcom Museum of History and Art and The Real
Comet Press, 1990), and Eve Sinaiko, ed., *Vietnam: Reflexes and Reflections: the National Vietnam
Veterans Art Museum* (New York: Harry N. Abrams, 1998).

71.   Nancy Spero, "Creation and Pro-creation (1993)" in Bird, *Nancy Spero,* 119.

72.   Dominique Nahas, *Nancy Spero: Works since 1950,* exh. cat. (Syracuse, N.Y.: Everson
Museum of Art, 1987), 20.

73.   Leon Golub, "Bombs and Helicopters: The Art of Nancy Spero," *Caterpillar* 1 (1967).
Quoted in Nahas, *Nancy Spero,* 39.

74.   Robert Schulman, "The NASA Art Program," in *Reaching into Space: Selected Works
from the NASA Art Program,* exh. cat. (Sarasota, Fla.: Ringling School of Art and Design, 1991),
n.p. In addition, "unmanned" photographs—unrelated to the art program—of the earth, space,
the moon, and other phenomena taken from satellites have been included occasionally as works
of art in contemporary exhibitions.

75.   Quoted in Hereward Lester Cooke with James D. Dean, *Eyewitness to Space* (New
York: Harry N. Abrams, 1976), 11.

76.   Cooke and Dean, *Eyewitness to Space,* 13.

77.   Rauschenberg was greatly enchanted by space exploration. In the summer of 1969,
NASA invited him to the Kennedy Space Center for the Apollo 11 launch, which took the first
men to the moon. In response, the artist, in 1969 and 1970, made a thirty-three-part lithograph
series, punningly titled *Stoned Moon,* using visuals furnished by NASA, and that presents a
sweeping saga of the history of flight. As mentioned, Rauschenberg incorporated the helicopter
motif into several pieces in the early 1960s, which may possibly be construed as "antimilitary"
statements. During the turbulent late 1960s—amid the Vietnam War, antiwar protests, assassi-
nations, and urban riots—his incorporation of astronautic imagery may have represented, however, a positive flip side to the flight coin, marveling that "the whole project [Apollo 11] seemed
one of the only things at that time that was not concerned with war and destruction." Quoted in
Calvin Tomkins, *Off the Wall: Robert Rauschenberg and the Art World of Our Time* (New York:
Penguin Books, 1980), 288. This aerial fascination, especially with space exploration, is manifested in works throughout his career, including *Airplane* (1958), several pieces from his "Dante's
Inferno" series (1960), *Glider* (1962), *Barge* (1963), *Junction* (1963), *Quote* (1964), *Retroactive*
(1964), *Skyway* (1964), and *Trapeze* (1964). In *Autobiography* of 1968, the artist included a photo of
himself in the 1963 performance "Pelican," in which he wears a parachute. The event was dedicated to the Wright brothers, and Rauschenberg may be invoking the now venerable association
between heroic artist and inventor. He may also be making reference to his ongoing faith in collaboration (epitomized by the NASA space program), exemplified in his work with dancers, Ex-

periments in Art and Technology, and groundbreaking efforts in lithography, to mention a few. For more on Rauschenberg and astronautic themes, see Anne Collins, "Robert Rauschenberg's Space-Age Allegory, 1959–1970," in *1998 National Aerospace Conference Proceedings* (Dayton, Ohio: Wright State University, 1999), 82–91.

78. Quoted in Katherine Kuh, *The Artist's Voice* (New York: Harper and Row, 1962), 200. For more on the view from above, see Margret Dreikausen, *The Earth as Seen from Aircraft and Spacecraft and Its Influence on Contemporary Art* (Philadelphia: The Art Alliance Press, 1984).

79. Quoted in Charles C. Eldredge, *Georgia O'Keeffe* (New York: Harry N. Abrams, 1991), 150. Arthur Dove, whose work has at times been grouped with that of O'Keeffe, made pieces with unusual and disorienting perspectives. Some may be cloudscapes, and others, such as *Flight and Sand and Sea*, suggest views from a plane: Dove himself was a pilot. See William C. Agee, "New Directions: The Late Work, 1938–1946," in *Arthur Dove: A Retrospective*, ed. Debra Bricken Balkan (Andover, Mass., and Cambridge, Mass.: Addison Gallery, Phillips Academy, and MIT Press, 1998), 133–53. Beginning in the late 1940s and continuing periodically through-out his career, the American artist Sam Francis, also a pilot, made abstract paintings relating to flight, sky and clouds, and aerial views. Interestingly, Malevich's art had an impact on some these images, and Francis thought of the concept of floating and ascent not simply in aesthetic but also spiritual terms.

80. Kuh, *The Artist's Voice*, 202.

81. Robert Smithson, "Aerial Art," *Studio International* 177 (April 1969), 180–81; quoted in Nancy Holt, ed., *The Writings of Robert Smithson: Essays with Illustrations* (New York: New York University Press, 1979), 92. Smithson's ideas on aerial art are laid out in this essay and in "Towards the Development of an Air Terminal Site," *Artforum* 4 (June 1967), 36–40.

82. All of the above Smithson quotations come from "Aerial Art"; quoted in Holt, *The Writings of Robert Smithson*, 92–93. Another provocative and very different approach to the air-port as subject in art occurs in Martha Rosler's photo-text and video installation *In the Place of the Public: Airport Series* (1983–84). The images and texts evoke the strange and disorienting world of air travel; Rosler's ideas are dense and sophisticated, exploring "space [as] commodity and so-cial idea." Her analysis of the environment associated with air travel (especially terminals and runways) emphasizes its containment, control, alienation, and surveillance, interpreting it as a microcosm for society as a whole. She expands on her ideas in Martha Rosler et al., *In the Place of the Public* (Ostifildern, Germany: Cantz Verlag, 1998).

83. Smithson, "Towards the Development of an Air Terminal Site"; quoted in Holt, 41–42.

84. Steve Poleskie, "Art and Flight: Historical Origins to Contemporary Work," *Leonardo* 18: 2 (1985), 76.

85. Quoted in "Profile: Steve Poleskie/Apogee Airway," *Gallery Guide* (New York, May 1986), 23.

86. Azari issued the manifesto as a pamphlet dropped from a plane he piloted in Milan on April 11, 1919. Its publisher is *Direzione del Movimento Futurista* [Futurist Movement Editor], Rome. A typographic reproduction of the pamphlet appears in Salaris, 66–67.

87. Anton Giulio Bragaglia, "Aerodanza," *L'Ala d'Italia* (January 1933), 49–50.

88. *Action Painting I* of 1981 shows a lone female painter at an easel dispassionately and accurately painting a car that crashes before her eyes, pointing again to a painting with genuine action in it but also to Abstract Expressionist machismo and perhaps Jackson Pollock's death in a car crash.

The Airplane and the Culture of War

Transforming Technology in the Army Air Corps, 1920–1940

Technology, Politics, and Culture for Strategic Bombing

TIMOTHY MOY

For most of its existence, aerial bombardment has been the heart and soul of the U.S. Air Force. Based on an image carefully created and cultivated during World War II, the Air Force has identified itself as the military service with both the ability and the responsibility to bring down devastation from the sky, and to do so accurately and irresistibly. Whether the vehicle of destruction was a high-altitude heavy bomber with a human crew or an inertially guided intercontinental ballistic missile, and whether the instrument of destruction was a high-explosive dumb bomb, a precision-guided smart bomb, or thermonuclear warhead—the Air Force very deliberately created and embraced a bomber culture that has profoundly shaped the evolution of that service, of the U.S. military as a whole, and of the entire American aviation community.

How did this happen? Precision strategic bombing was hardly the only possible mission for the youngest branch of the military services of the United States; even a brief look at the evolution of the air forces of other nations during the twentieth century shows that, technologically and organizationally, strategic bombing was only one of several possible ways of war that the Air Force could have embraced.

The historical relationship between the Air Force and strategic bombing was far from preordained. It resulted instead from a confluence of contingent forces that, in the decades prior to World War II, combined to make high-altitude precision bombing against logistical centers the most attractive mission to Air Corps leaders.[1]

The first of these forces was a set of severe bureaucratic stresses threatening the political welfare of the Air Corps during the 1920s and 1930s. At a time when Americans largely turned away from Wilsonian globalism, and military budgets concurrently declined, Air Corps leaders realized that the well-being of their agency depended on their ability to articulate and promote a distinct and well-defined mission for the Air Corps—one that would be simultaneously attractive enough to justify congressional appropriations but also specialized enough to keep it within the Air Corps' purview.

During the 1930s, the U.S. Army Air Corps' hopes for the success of its pinpoint precision bombing doctrine depended on the Norden bombsight, which went on to become one of the United
States' most celebrated pieces of technology during World War II. The mystique surrounding the
bombsight, carefully cultivated by the Norden Company, fit wonderfully with the Air Corps' high-
tech self-perception. The bombsight was "top secret" and it was supposed to be able to put a
bomb in a pickle barrel from twenty thousand feet. Here, Carl Norden, the bombsight's inventor,
poses beside an unidentified aircraft, circa 1920. (Courtesy National Air and Space Museum,
Smithsonian Institution [SI 90-3721].)

It was a difficult balance. In order to patch together any kind of political con-
sensus, the Air Corps, as one element of the U.S. military (and as part of the U.S.
Army at the time), would have to find a mission that was reasonably well integrated into the rest of military thinking. At the same time, that mission would
have to be somehow dedicated to the Air Corps' assets to prevent some other
agency (like, for example, naval aviation) from stealing it away. This was a
thorny bureaucratic problem, and one that strategic bombing would later alle-
viate unusually well.

A note on the term *bureaucratic:* Sociologists and political scientists have long
noted that institutions behave like organisms. In finite environments, both are
driven by their innate penchant for self-preservation to interact competitively
with one another. The precise form of that competition, however, can vary enor-

mously. Organisms have many ways to compete for scarce resources. An organism's survival strategies might include killing its rivals, cooperating with them, stretching higher to gather more sunlight, or finding the underside of a slimy (but life-sustaining) rock that somehow went unnoticed by its competitors.

Institutions also compete in different ways. The venue of that competition can be a marketplace, a board meeting, or an appropriations hearing. The form of the competition can be a zero-sum confrontation in which a victor triumphs only at the expense of the vanquished, or it can be a remote interaction in which one or both agencies find new institutional niches in which to live and thrive. Throughout this chapter, the term *bureaucratic* will refer to this sort of institutional stress and competition. In no way should it be read pejoratively; it is exactly analogous to the terms *adaptive* or *selective* for organisms.

The second set of forces that helped wed the Air Corps to strategic bombing was the congruence between the image of strategic bombing and the institutional culture developing in the Air Corps in the decades following World War I. Despite the atrocious casualty rates and generally gruesome deaths that accompanied air combat, the air war in Europe had probably been the only arena of war to emerge untouched by the deromanticizing effects of contemporaneous technology. Although the war in the trenches was almost universally regarded as dehumanizing and ignoble, the air warriors had been able to maintain faith in an almost chivalric image, where professional, elite knights of the sky engaged in a form of single combat where courage and prowess still carried the day.[2] After the Armistice, returning airmen continued to regard the Air Corps and air war itself as the most professional form of military service, especially compared to the indiscriminate slaughter of the trenches.

During the interwar decades, the Air Corps' self-image was shaped additionally by a growing sense that the airplane itself represented the future of warfare. Especially as doped canvas aircraft surfaces gave way to sleek, shiny metal in the 1930s, the Air Corps began to regard itself as the most futuristic, even "high-tech," of the military services—a combination of the knights-of-the-sky image with that of Buck Rogers. Here, too, the seemingly precise, advanced, and professional nature of strategic bombing would become very attractive to Air Corps leaders.

Finally, the Air Corps became attached to strategic bombing during the interwar years because of several crucial technologies that made, or appeared to make, the strategic bombing vision technically feasible. Largely after the bureaucratic front had been stabilized, Air Corps leaders carefully encouraged the development of those elements of the bomb delivery system—consisting of aircraft, ordnance, bombsight, and crew—that could make strategic bombing possible.

The various forces that wedded the Air Corps to strategic bombing interacted profoundly with one another during the interwar decades. The Air Corps' bureaucratic difficulties deeply influenced the articulation of the strategic bombing vision, for example, just as that vision greatly shaped the Air Corps' technological demands. Nor, of course, were these forces inexorable. Air Corps leaders made generally self-conscious and well-informed choices that served to identify their service with strategic bombing—a fact that is clearly illustrated by the other possibilities that they considered and rejected in favor of bombing. After casting about for a well-defined and technologically feasible mission during the 1920s and early 1930s, Air Corps leaders found that the Corps' bureaucratic difficulties, its articulation of a strategic bombing vision, and new technological prospects made daylight precision bombing appear the most profitable and natural course to pursue.

The Stifled Promise of World War I

On the one hand, the pilots' experience of World War I had been one of the only bright spots in an otherwise horrifying and dehumanizing endeavor. War in the air appeared more gallant, more noble, than the indiscriminate slaughter of the ground war; it was seen as a form of combat, perhaps the only, that still rewarded courage and prowess, and in which chivalrous veterans saluted frightened novices whose guns had jammed, and flew off into the sunset.

On the other hand, World War I was an extremely frustrating enterprise for American air power enthusiasts. While German, British, and French air forces conducted daring bombing raids deep into their respective enemy's territory, the American Army Air Service entered the war too late to compile a comparable record. For the entirety of its war, the Americans dropped only 138 tons of bombs (the British had delivered 543 tons in the summer of 1918 alone), an amount so meager that it was often converted in service histories into 276,000 pounds. Plans for large American bombing raids were literally cut short by the Armistice.[3]

While British aviators were honored in 1918 with the elevation of their service from the Royal Naval Air Service and the Royal Flying Corps to a totally new and independent Royal Air Force (RAF), the Americans had to be satisfied with a shuffle from one part of the Army to another.[4] The RAF's bureaucratic emancipation brought with it the privilege of independent planning and operations. In contrast, the Army Air Service muddled through the war distributed piecemeal among the various ground units and employed mainly in support of ground operations: as reconnaissance for the infantry, spotting for the artillery, and, when necessary, preventing enemy planes from harassing the troops.

The Air Service's ability to bring large numbers of American airplanes to bear was also unimpressive. Although the Service enlarged its inventory from several hundred to over 6,200 airplanes by war's end, approximately 4,800 of those planes had been produced in France. American industry contributed only 1,216 airplanes, and almost all of these were of foreign design.[5]

The experience led many air officers to the understanding that their fortunes within the Army were much dimmer than their weapon warranted. The airplane, many of them felt, held out the promise of an entirely new form of warfare, and thus merited its own military branch.

It was precisely this belief—that the Army had not appreciated the prospects for aviation revealed during World War I—that led people such as Billy Mitchell to conclude that military aviation deserved and required an independent service organization on par with the Army or Navy. Before the war, then-Captain Mitchell (along with First Lieutenants H. H. Arnold and Benjamin D. Foulois) had told the House Committee on Military Affairs that "it would be a mistake to start a separate corps" for military aviation, because, as Mitchell argued, the Air Service's position within the Signal Corps provided everything that airmen wanted at the time. Moreover, Mitchell noted, "The offensive value of this thing has not yet been proved."[6] After the war, however, Mitchell reversed positions completely, with the war itself providing the proof he needed.

> One flight over the lines gave me a much clearer impression of how the armies were laid out than any amount of traveling around on the ground. A very significant thing to me was that we could cross the lines of these contending armies in a few minutes in our airplane, whereas the armies had been locked in the struggle, immovable, powerless to advance, for three years. To even stick one's head over the top of the trench invited death. This whole area over which the Germans and French battled was not more than sixty miles across. It was as though they kept knocking their heads against a stone wall, until their brains were dashed out. They got nowhere, as far as ending the war was concerned.
>
> It looked as though the war would keep up indefinitely until either the airplanes brought an end to the war or the contending nations dropped from sheer exhaustion.[7]

Although the war ended far more from exhaustion than air power, Mitchell had converted to the belief that military aviation had come of age.

> The air force has ceased to remain a mere auxiliary service for the purpose of assisting an army or navy in the execution of its task. The air force rises into the air in great masses of airplanes. Future contests will see hundreds of them in one formation. They fight in line, they have their own weapons and their own way of using them, special means of communications, signaling, and of attacking.[8]

Mitchell was particularly critical of the way air units had been organized during the war—as accessories of the infantry. Such organization, Mitchell realized, cemented the airplane's subservience to ground forces and therefore kept it from realizing its true potential as an independent weapon. He concluded that the only hope for American air power, and hence the nation itself, was for the Air Service to gain its independence from the Army.[9]

It was a tall order. The Air Service entered the return to normalcy very much a part of the Army. Through most of the 1920s, the Chiefs of Air Service had begun their careers as Army ground officers; most were not pilots when they assumed the office. The selection of Air Service leadership, coupled with the distribution of air units throughout the ground Army, led Mitchell and his followers to view their Air Service as being run by outsiders, especially from the infantry, which they considered to be a conservative and short-sighted bureaucracy unwilling or unable to appreciate the military value of this wondrous new technology. Airmen came to see their Service as the unwanted stepchild of the War Department, whose most fruitful recourse might be to run away from home.

Looking for a Job

Historical accounts of Mitchell's public relations exploits on behalf of an independent air force are well known, and need not be repeated here.[10] Like all proponents of air power, Mitchell realized that the bureaucratic well-being of military aviation turned on its ability to articulate its mission; without a well-defined job, no bureaucratic entity can expect to survive. But Mitchell wanted bureaucratic independence from the Army, and this required not only a well-articulated mission but also one that was as removed from the Army's traditional missions as possible.[11]

Through the early 1920s, Mitchell and his followers suggested several aerial duties as reason enough for independence. In the mid-1920s, Mitchell argued for a Department of Aeronautics by pointing to the great benefits of airborne communications, supply lines, transport, and the vulnerability of ships to attack by enemy aircraft.[12] To prove the point, Mitchell had staged several highly publicized demonstrations of airplanes' abilities to sink old warships, sending the *Ostfriesland* to the bottom and enveloping the *Alabama* in a shroud of flaming phosphorus.

After his court-martial and resignation, however, the direction of Mitchell's thinking changed. In a preface to his memoirs of World War I, Mitchell tried a new argument for an independent air force.

> War itself is a continuance by physical means of an altercation between nations, and its object is to impress one's will upon the enemy. This can only be done by seizing, controlling or paralyzing his vital centers, that is, his great cities and the sources of raw materials, his manufactories, his food, his production, his means of transportation and his railways and steamship lines.

... Air power can attack the vital centers of the opposing country directly, completely destroying and paralyzing them. Very little of a great nation's strength has to be expended in conducting air operations. A few men and comparatively few dollars can be used for bringing about the most terrific effect ever known against opposing vital centers.

The power of airplane bombs, and the use of chemical weapons will unquestionably decide a future war.[13]

In the four-page preface, Mitchell used the term "vital centers" or "nerve centers" seven times.

Rather than promote an air force for its value in communication, supply, or even attacking ships, Mitchell now proposed an air force whose primary mission was to attack logistical hubs far behind enemy lines. Massive attacks on these vital centers would so panic the population and impede industrial activity as to completely strip the enemy nation of its ability to wage war, and thus provide a quick and relatively inexpensive (both in lives and dollars) victory to whoever had the aerial resources to strike first.

The image of the crippling bolt from the blue was not original to Mitchell. The first expressions of the idea in military thinking had come from across the Atlantic. One source of inspiration was Hugh Trenchard, a RAF general who greatly shaped the bombing arm of the RAF in the years after the war; he was nicknamed "Boom." Mitchell had met Boom Trenchard during the war, and greatly respected him and his ideas on aerial warfare. He was particularly taken with Trenchard's conviction that airplanes were inherently offensive weapons, and that the bomber in particular could exert a psychological, or "moral effect" that was "out of all proportion to the [physical] damage which it can inflict."[14]

Mitchell's other source was the Italian air force proponent and agitator Giulio Douhet, whose 1921 *Command of the Air* portrayed naval and ground forces as essentially defensive factors in any future war, with all offensive operations assumed by the air force. Bombers, Douhet argued, would be certain to reach their targets—he, too, called them "vital centers"—and certain to cause such widespread destruction among enemy forces and cities that victory could come in a matter of days, well before opposing ground forces got even within striking distance of one another.[15]

Mitchell corresponded with both Trenchard and Douhet, and, by 1927, the three had arrived together at a vision of air warfare that would greatly affect their respective military services. For Mitchell, the court-martial and resignation served to radicalize him and his followers, and lend his emerging ideas on strategic bombing the credence of a martyr's testament. To his disciples, Mitchell became an icon, a holy symbol of everything air power could be but had not yet achieved. According to Mitchell disciple and future Air Force Chief of Staff Henry H. (Hap) Arnold,

> There were three Billy Mitchells: there was the man they court-martialed, not personally known to the public, who wouldn't rest until he became a martyr; there was Mitchell the air prophet, not in the sense of popular but of highly scientific forecasts. And then there was the third Mitchell, who included the first two, but added something. This was the Billy the public loved, and whom the Air Corps loved. . . . After he had gone too far, for a man in uniform, and his superiors had crushed him, the public and the Air Corps still loved him, and Billy, in civs, went right on fighting.[16]

The Bomber School

Mitchell's martyrdom and his increasingly radical ideas about bombing had a profound effect on the development of official Air Corps doctrine. The focal point of that influence was the Air Corps Tactical School (ACTS).

The school began in 1920 at Langley Field, Virginia, as the Air Service School, one of several service schools created as gateways for mid-career officers to enter the ranks of higher staff work and command of larger units. As the coursework and personnel of the school evolved, the name was changed to the Air Service Field Officers' School (in 1920), then to the Air Service Tactical School (1922), and finally to the Air Corps Tactical School (when the Air Service became the Air Corps in 1926).[17]

During the 1920s, the ACTS became the place where Air Corps leaders (many of them part of Mitchell's circle) worked out the intricacies of their new form of warfare, and then spread the word among those officers passing through the school as students. Unsurprisingly, the ACTS curriculum clearly reflected the thinking of the Mitchell camp, and how that thinking changed over time.

Through the mid-1920s, Mitchell believed that the primary mission of an air force was to maintain aerial supremacy through the use of fighter (pursuit) aircraft to control the contested airspace, thus allowing friendly observation and transport operations while denying those same operations to the enemy. "Pursuit aviation," he explained in 1920, "is the basis of an air force, just as infantry is the base on which an army rests."[18] During that same time, the primary texts at the ACTS likewise identified the maintenance of aerial supremacy as the principal job of the Air Service. The texts in the course on bombardment, for example, emphasized that strategic bombing "must not take precedence over the support of ground operations," and even questioned the morality of targeting civilian population centers.[19]

But as Mitchell's thoughts turned to the image of an enemy country laid waste by massive bombing attacks against its vital centers, and his martyrdom captured even greater devotion from young air power enthusiasts, his vision of strategic bombing and its central role in the Air Corps' identity gradually dominated thinking at the ACTS. By the summer of 1925 (after Mitchell had been "exiled" to Texas), the spirit of the school was already moving away from the idea of aerial supremacy and toward an image of strategic bombing as the Air Corps' primary mission. The school's conception of bombing vital centers, however, differed slightly from that of Mitchell, Douhet, and Trenchard. Rather than emphasizing the terrorizing effects of bombing, ACTS officers gradually made the doctrine more palatable to American audiences by arguing that future bombardment would be accurate enough to make the material effects—the actual destruction of enemy factories, railways, and so on—its principal military value. In July, the school's commandant, Major Oscar Westover, objected to one text's assertion that the psychological effect of bombing industrial centers was far greater than its physical effect—an assertion that Trenchard made often.[20] Westover optimistically argued,

> This is an old saying completely out of date. While it may have been true during the war, the school holds that it is no longer true. Bombing has developed to the point where it is accurate and destructive.[21]

The following year, the school's "Combined Air Force" text drew Air Corps thinking further away from the aerial superiority mission, and at the same time laid down what would become another fundamental tenet of American bombing doctrine. Whereas aerial superiority had made pursuit aviation the core of the Air Force, the 1926 text stated that advancing bomber technology would soon make it impossible for pursuit aircraft to stop a concerted bombing attack; once they were in the air, at least some bombers would always get through. The only way to "defend" against enemy bombers, the text argued, was to destroy them on the ground, presumably by preemptive bombing.[22] Gradually, bombardment aviation was becoming the central component of aerial warfare.

During the next several years, these two principles—that the bomber will always get through and that it has the ability to destroy materially an enemy's ability to wage war—became central to Air Corps bombing doctrine, just as bombing became central to the Air Corps' quest for bureaucratic independence. By 1930, for example, ACTS students were learning that "bombardment aviation, under the circumstances anticipated in a major war, is the basic arm of the Air Force," and that control of bombing units should be vested within the traditional Army hierarchy but in the Air Corps' own General Headquarters.[23] The school also made clear that the proper use of bombing was strategic rather than tactical. Although situations might arise that required bombers to attack ground units close to the front, the ACTS regarded enemy ground forces as unsuitable targets, too "tactical" to yield the maximum benefits of bombardment.[24] Tactical school doctrine increasingly held vital centers far behind enemy lines to be the only legitimate target for air force bombing.

During the early 1930s, shortly after the school's move from Langley, Virginia, to Maxwell, Alabama, its Bombardment Section further fleshed out a doctrine for strategic bombing. As bombing proponents at the ACTS gradually convinced themselves that bombing should be strategic in scope, of great material effect, and the primary mission of the Air Corps, one young instructor, First Lieutenant Kenneth N. Walker, worked out one final bombing axiom. Since the early 1920s, strategic bombing had been envisioned as a nighttime operation. For attacks on industrial targets deep within enemy territory, the cover of darkness would provide the bombers with protection from enemy fighters and anti-aircraft artillery. As late as 1931, most bombardment training at the school emphasized night operations; the bombardment text from that year stated that almost all raids would occur at night.[25]

But the darkness worked both ways. In 1932, reemphasizing the material results of bombing over its possible psychological consequences, Walker and others at the ACTS began to assert that bombing missions must succeed in placing their bombs precisely on specific industrial structures, a task impossible in the dark.

> To state that targets located at a considerable distance in hostile territory will usually be bombed at night is not a correct statement. Precision targets, which require accurate bombing will normally be engaged during daylight hours.[26]

By 1933, this concept of daylight, precision bombing from high altitude had become the warfare of choice for the doctrine-makers at the ACTS. The bombardment course that year synthesized all of the developments of the previous seven years: bombardment was the basic arm of the air force; its primary use was against strategic targets deep within enemy territory; centralized command was crucial; the bomber would always get through; and bombing was accurate and destructive enough to strip the enemy of its war-making capacity.[27] Walker summed up the idea in what would become a credo for bomber enthusiasts: "A well-organized, well-planned, and well-flown air force attack will constitute an offensive that cannot be stopped."[28]

It is not hard to see how this image of an inexorable, devastating, and precise assault from the sky proved popular for Air Corps theorists. In addition to vindicating the vision of the martyred Mitchell, as well as providing an independent and identifiable raison d'être for the Air Corps, daylight precision bombing also harmonized very nicely with the Air Corps' developing self-perception. Like the Air Corps itself, this form of strategic bombing was futuristic and high-tech. Like the Air Corps, it was precise, elegant, efficient, and even humane (for it could end war with a single, shattering bolt from the blue). And like the Air

Corps, it held out the hope of recovering the military professionalism that appeared so threatened after the indiscriminate killing of World War I; only highly skilled and technically proficient officers and crews, after all, would be able to operate the complex of technologies that comprised this intricate weapon.

It is important to note that this vision of warfare was not the only possible mission for the Air Corps to embrace as its own; the ACTS's extended consideration of the defensive aerial superiority mission clearly demonstrates that other missions were viable. Neither was this vision of strategic bombing the only one possible. Both Mitchell's early articulation and the bombing doctrine eventually adopted by the British were very different from the ACTS's precision bombing; Mitchell's terror bombing and the RAF's area bombing were a far cry from the notion of bombing not only certain parts of cities but also individual buildings within industrial complexes. The vision of the Air Corps, which was a direct response to political and cultural demands, demanded a level of technical precision that a different air force working from a different conception of bombing would find superfluous.

The primary difficulty, of course, was that the Air Corps' conception was, as of the early 1930s, technically impossible.

Technical Difficulties

In order for the strategic bombing vision to perform its military and bureaucratic functions, the Air Corps had to make it technologically feasible. This meant designing, developing, and producing a delivery system—a technological system that would accurately and reliably place bombs on target despite vigorous enemy defenses. Until World War II, the delivery system hardware consisted of a relatively fast, high-altitude airplane, and an extremely precise optical bombsight.

During the interwar decades, the Air Corps gradually acquired a diverse network of organizations that formed the nucleus of what would later become a military-industrial-academic complex. Although technical expertise (and the concomitant authority to set the research and development agenda) was distributed among the Air Corps, civilian government agencies, private industry, and educational institutions, the Air Corps itself provided much of the direction for aeronautical research and development (R&D).

Materiel Division

The Materiel Division (earlier known as the Engineering Division and ultimately headquartered at Wright Field, Ohio) was the heart of the Air Corps' in-house R&D apparatus. Established by the War Department during World War I, the Materiel Division housed impressive aeronautical laboratories; the forty-six-hundred-acre facility eventually included several large wind tunnels, the world's largest propeller test bed, enormous electric generators, and numerous small labs and staffs devoted to all aspects of military aviation—aircraft and engine design, cooling systems, superchargers, propellers, flight equipment, and production.[29] Private aircraft companies found these facilities so impressive that the division had to fight off legislation authorizing Wright Field to perform aircraft and equipment tests for the private sector; although the technical experience would have been valuable, the Materiel Division staff would have been overwhelmed.[30]

Perhaps even more important than its physical plant were the Materiel Division's project offices. The project offices were the central points of contact between the Air Corps and private contractors, and the lines of communication were open and casual. According to one member of the division's staff, the offices permitted a contractor easily to see or phone the project engineers at Wright to discuss technical matters, or, if necessary, consult directly with the Chief of Air Corps. Conversely, lieutenants and junior engineers had relatively open access to aircraft company presidents. The informality of communication greatly facilitated engineering decisions; for simple technical problems, it might take only a few hours from idea to implementation.[31]

By 1939, the staff at Wright had grown to about two thousand (over seventeen hundred of whom were civilians). Moreover, several key bomber proponents had served on the division's staff, including eventual Air Corps chiefs Benjamin Foulois and Hap Arnold, and future 8th Air Force commander Carl Spaatz.

National Advisory Committee for Aeronautics

Since its creation in 1915, the National Advisory Committee for Aeronautics (NACA) had served as the basic research arm of Army and Navy aviation.[32] Although NACA was charged with advising and coordinating aeronautical research for all of the federal government, its ties to the Air Corps and the Navy's Bureau of Aeronautics were particularly close. Of the seven permanent seats on NACA's twelve-person Executive Committee, four were held by representatives of the military; the Chief of Air Corps and Chief of the Materiel Division were always members.[33] Air Corps and Bureau of Aeronautics personnel served on all NACA technical committees, and the military aviation branches maintained close technical contact with NACA and each other through constant and vigorous exchange of reports and data.[34]

Throughout the 1920s and 1930s, NACA's Executive Committee made a habit of formally asking the Air Corps for prioritized lists of proposed research topics, and the Air Corps was happy to provide them. Sometimes, the Air Corps would transfer funds to NACA for the service, but usually not. In this way, the Air Corps benefited from NACA research on virtually every element of power plant design, like the effect of certain fuels on spark plug insulation, or the aerodynamic characteristics of the engine nacelles. NACA performed research on such diverse topics as spot welding techniques, the development of new instruments, the pattern of ice formation on the wings and fuselage, the theoretical and empirical relationship between propeller tip speed and efficiency. From NACA wind tunnels the Air Corps also received crucial flight characteristic data on the large bombers of the middle 1930s.[35]

To no surprise, the Air Corps lobbied vigorously and successfully to help NACA muddle through its own bureaucratic adversities during the interwar years. In 1925 and 1937, Congress considered legislation to absorb NACA into the Department of Commerce; in 1932, lame-duck President Hoover tried to reduce it to a branch of the Bureau of Standards. In all cases, the Chief of Air Corps drafted letters of opposition, sometimes following with remarkable precision arguments already drafted by NACA Secretary John F. Victory.[36] Also in all cases, the proposals were defeated; the Air Corps was hardly willing to let go what it practically considered to be a basic research branch of the Materiel Division.

Private Industry

Since its inception, the American aviation industry has enjoyed and suffered a symbiotic relationship with military aviation. While private aircraft corporations came to rely on the military as one of their largest and most reliable customers, the Air Corps came to rely on the industry for a reliable supply of technically advanced aeronautical materiel (from individual components to entire airplanes). By the early 1930s, the Materiel Division, though still central to the Army's aviation technology apparatus, had relinquished the aircraft design business to private industry while continuing to serve as a development clearinghouse.

The depth of this symbiotic relationship is best illustrated by the Air Corps' conduct regarding its primary tension with the industry: private companies exist to make money, and profit can come from having a large number of paying customers. The Air Corps, by contrast, was not always at liberty to spend money, yet it never wanted any of its overseas rivals to have airplanes as good as its own. After 1924, when the War Department discovered that Curtiss Aircraft had sold several engines to the British without notifying the Air Service, all contracts for sales abroad required War Department approval. Eventually, the Air Corps adopted a policy of not permitting any foreign sale of aircraft that represented the state of the art; that is, aircraft that had been in production for less than one year.[37]

But, during the commercially lean years of the late 1920s and early 1930s, the aircraft industry's financial situation became dire. With both the Air Corps and the Navy cutting back on new purchases, several companies sought approval to sell state-of-the-art aircraft abroad. How the Air Corps handled these requests reveals much about how it valued the well-being of the industry.

In the spring of 1934, after having lost on a competitive bid to produce a line of bombers for the Air Corps, Glenn Martin asked for permission to sell its bombers to Brazil, China, and the "U.S. Soviet of Russia" [sic]. Without the sale, Martin pleaded, the company faced bankruptcy.[38]

Under both the letter and spirit of the Air Corps' policy, the requested relief was impossible. The bomber in question, Martin's B-10, was then still a service test model, and had been in production for less than a year. It was, according to Chief of Air Corps Foulois, "by far the most efficient airplane of its type in existence today."[39] Remarkably, Foulois nevertheless recommended that the War and State Departments approve the sale.

> The shortage of aircraft in the Army Air Corps is fast becoming critical. This is particularly true with respect to bombardment aircraft. With no further business in sight, The Glenn L. Martin Company is faced with a shut-down on completion of its present contract with the Army Air Corps. This shut-down would throw approximately two thousand aircraft workers out of employment and remove one of the most important aircraft manufacturers from the field.
>
> Though I am loathe to recommend it, . . . in justice to the Glenn L. Martin Company and to keep these facilities available for national emergency permission should be given them to sell their bomber to any other customer, foreign or domestic, who desires to purchase it, and all government restrictions as to its sale abroad should be removed.[40]

The sale was eventually approved. A similar request, from Lockheed for foreign sale of its Electra transport, was approved a short time later, despite evidence that the company had been dealing secretly with German airplane magnate Anthony Fokker to convert the Electra into a light bomber.[41]

The Air Corps' nurturing of the industry is as revealing as it was full of foresight. Foulois and other Air Corps leaders apparently believed that the military threat of state-of-the-art aircraft in the hands of potential enemies was less grave than the threat of losing any of the large aircraft companies to economic ruin. They were probably right.

Academe

As the locus of innovation for aeronautical technology gradually moved from the workbench to the laboratory, the American aviation enterprise gradually demanded more academically oriented aeronautical engineers—people who could discuss things such as fluid dynamics and mechanical stresses in precise terms. The Air Corps was no exception.

Aeronautical engineering, however, was a very new endeavor in the 1920s, and had found little room in the academy. In 1922, only five universities offered any courses in aeronautical engineering; only two granted degrees.[42] Created in

1926, the Daniel Guggenheim Fund for the Promotion of Aeronautics deliberately set out to change that. With $2.8 million in hand, the fund endowed seven major schools for aeronautics in four years: at Stanford, Caltech, the University of Michigan, the Massachusetts Institute of Technology (MIT), the University of Washington, the Georgia School (later Institute) of Technology, and the University of Akron. All of the Guggenheim schools but the last (which focused on lighter-than-air flight) were very successful, and formed an educational establishment that remained central to American aeronautics through World War II. Caltech's Theodore von Kármán—brought to Caltech with Guggenheim funding—and his group played major roles in the development of several of Douglas Aircraft's large transports. Stanford's propeller research became a centerpiece for NACA's reports on the subject. The school at the University of Washington developed close ties to Boeing in nearby Seattle; practically every Boeing model underwent some wind-tunnel testing at the school. MIT and Michigan concentrated on producing engineers for consumption by industry and government. By 1942, a majority of senior aeronautical researchers were Guggenheim graduates; NACA's Langley Laboratory alone employed fifteen MIT alumni.[43]

The Materiel Division, of course, kept in close touch with the work at Caltech, Stanford, and MIT. Air Corps officers reported regularly on academic research projects of interest, and the Chiefs of Air Corps and the Materiel Division were often invited to visit the facilities personally.[44] Beginning in 1937, the Air Corps sent regular Army officers to these schools for graduate training; between 1937 and 1939, thirty officers took courses in aeronautical engineering, meteorology, and mathematics at Caltech, the University of Michigan, Stanford, and MIT.[45]

The aeronautical research performed at colleges and universities during the 1920s and 1930s was probably not critical to the development of bombardment aviation in the Army Air Corps; the very basic research typical of peacetime academe had a less-immediate impact than the development work performed by the aircraft companies, and the most relevant basic work could as easily have been done by NACA. However, the academic production of aeronautical engineers was vital to the Air Corps, and was beyond the capabilities of the Materiel Division, NACA, or the industry. Without the universities and the help from Guggenheim, the military and the industry would not have had the engineers it needed. And, without the engineers, the enterprise literally would not have gotten off the ground.

The Network

The decentralized character of Air Corps R&D during this period makes it extremely difficult to identify any unified, coherent research policy. With so many actors, it is impossible to distinguish a single research program, or even perhaps a clear research establishment. This difficulty, coupled with the low funding levels compared to expenditures in World War II, have left the impression that research and development for military aviation was practically nonexistent before Pearl Harbor.

The schematic diagram, however, tends to conceal the interaction between seemingly disparate parts. The primary factor promoting close communication was the simple fact that the administrators of these various entities—the Materiel Division, NACA, the aircraft companies, the universities—were often the same people. The Chief of Air Corps and the Chief of the Materiel Division were always members of NACA's Executive Committee, as were prominent members of the industry. The Assistant Secretary of War responsible for aviation, F. Trubee Davison, was one of the Guggenheim Fund trustees for the duration of the fund's existence.

This constant exchange of information meant that Air Corps leaders were always aware of the latest technical possibilities, and NACA, the universities, and industry were ever mindful of Air Corps needs. Certain bomber proponents, such as Hap Arnold, also were extremely interested in technical matters, and made every effort to enhance the Air Corps' technical capabilities by increasing engineering staffs and promoting new ideas themselves.[46]

So, despite the organizationally disjointed nature of the Air Corps' R&D establishment, it was possible to promote coherent, and sometimes detailed, research programs. As strategic bombing became the justification for the Air Corps' existence, it also became the priority for just about everyone else in the business.

The Bomber

Strategic bombing's novelty, while one of its greatest bureaucratic advantages, was also one of its greatest technological problems. Strategic bombing had no precedents; there were no proven rules by which to decide precisely what technical capabilities were required. Nor was there any a priori method by which such parameters could be calculated. Aside from the obvious requirement that bombers carry a large payload of bombs at high speed and high altitude to distant targets, the aspiring bomber designer had little to go on.

Designers were further confounded by the fact that, as in all engineering, designing the optimal machine entails a series of tradeoffs. Increasing carrying capacity tends to decrease speed and range, for example, and vice versa. And without a clear idea of how bombing would be done, it was impossible to know confidently which compromises would be advantageous and which would be disastrous.

In the face of such unknowns, the Air Corps' Materiel Division staff at Wright Field adopted what would become a classic research strategy: work on those areas that will be likely to help no matter how doctrine evolves later. General improvements, such as increasing aircraft speed, range, load, and other performance characteristics could be derived in several ways.

One method for increasing speed was to reduce drag on the airframe. The most immediate way of reducing drag was to reduce or remove protuberances or structures that interrupt the airstream. Most aircraft from World War I were externally braced biplanes; the struts and wires that supported the wings were prime sources of drag. A considerable amount of development effort during the 1920s thus went toward removing the external braces by supporting the weight of the wings internally by cantilever construction. Further general improvements came with the conversion from biplanes to monoplanes; the additional speed more than compensated for the reduction in lift. By the mid-1930s, drag was cut enormously by installing retractable landing gear, despite the newer gear's greater production and maintenance costs.

Another way to increase speed was to improve engine performance. At the beginning of World War I, the most powerful engine in general use was about eighty horsepower. At war's end, the best practical engines put out about four hundred horsepower. Over the next ten years, engine power rose to five hundred or six hundred horsepower, with higher energies on the way.[47]

High altitudes are another place to go for better aircraft performance. As the air gets thinner, drag decreases; an airplane gains about 1 percent in speed per one thousand feet in altitude. In military matters, being able to fly several thousand feet higher than one's adversary also carries obvious tactical advantages. The problem is that aircraft engines tend to choke for lack of oxygen in the thin air at high altitudes. The Materiel Division therefore spent a great deal of attention on engine superchargers—extra blowers that pressurize the air before it enters the combustion chamber, and thus restore some of the engine power otherwise lost at high altitudes.[48]

Another area ripe for general improvement was propeller technology. While in the air, the optimal pitch of the propeller blades varies from one flight profile to another; one pitch bites the right amount of air for takeoff, another for high speed at sea level, and others still for different altitudes. Through World War I, propellers consisted of a single piece of solid wood; the permanent blade pitch was necessarily a compromise between the various optimal pitches, and thus degraded performance under different flight conditions. In the mid-1920s, Frank Caldwell of the Hamilton Standard Company began experimenting with a propeller hub and removable metal blades that permitted the ground crew to change the pitch before takeoff, set in anticipation of the plane's most likely maneuvers for that flight. In 1928, Caldwell produced a two-position hub that allowed the pilot to switch between a high and low pitch setting during flight. And, in 1934, Caldwell's group devised a feedback governor that automatically varied the pitch to maintain a constant number of revolutions per minute; this kept the propeller at nearly the optimum speed for all maneuvers. A few years later, this same device was modified to allow "full feathering"; if an engine should fail on a multiengine aircraft, the blades of that propeller could be rotated so that they would ride edge-on into the wind, almost eliminating their drag and making the job of the remaining engines a little easier.[49] Virtually every military aircraft from the early 1930s through World War II benefited from the performance of Hamilton Standard propellers.

This sort of development work, including other all-purpose innovations like wing flaps and gear brakes, consumed the majority of the Engineering Division's resources during the 1920s. From 1920 to 1929, the division devoted an average of 52.9 percent of its "Experimental Development" budget toward all-purpose developments, while spending an average of 33.7 percent on specific new airplane models.[50]

The specific airplanes that the Air Corps purchased during the 1920s left a lot to be desired. Most of the models, designed and produced by private aircraft companies like Martin and Curtiss, were externally braced biplanes and triplanes with wooden frames and fabric skins. Despite some fascinating novelties, none of the aircraft produced during this decade possessed the speed, range, or bomb load to enable the Air Corps to mount the devastating bolt from the blue that ACTS theorists envisioned.[51] The Air Corps' standard bomber as of 1928, for example, could carry its 2,500 pounds of bombs for 860 miles at a speed of only 114 miles per hour.

Still, the technical outlook was improving by the late 1920s. Biplane designs, for example, were clearly on the way out; their struts and braces created too much drag for the extra lift they delivered. Multiple engines, though much more expensive to procure and maintain, held out the promise of greater range and speed, as well as improved chances of making it home should an engine fail in flight. Moreover, these early biplane bombers served the bombing enthusiasts in one crucial respect. Flying out of airfields throughout the country, pilots, bombardiers, and gunners were training daily in the use of machines and techniques for strategic bombing. The 2nd Bombardment Group, the Air Corps' primary operational bombing wing, developed a small cadre of airmen with groundbreaking experience in finding their targets, flying the approach, dropping their bombs, and protecting one another with defensive fire.[52] To be sure, neither the technology nor the doctrine was yet up to the challenge of enemy fighters, or even of enemy cities, but it was a start, and these aircraft kept the idea of strategic bombing bureaucratically viable.

The Bombsight

Getting the bombs to their target was only half the job; delivering them accurately onto their targets was the other. This was an extremely difficult technical problem, one that was not truly solved until the development of "smart" ordnance that is guided by radar, laser, or video. For conventional "dumb" bombs, like all of the ordnance used through World War II, the challenge consisted of finding a course that would bring the airplane directly in line with the target, and then determining precisely when to release the bombs so that they fell directly on the target.

Theoretically, the "bombing problem" might seem trivial. Given the aircraft's altitude and ground speed, the range to target, and the acceleration due to gravity, Galilean calculations provide a perfect solution. Under real, and particularly wartime, conditions, however, the problem is nearly impossible, in part because it is extremely difficult to measure the necessary parameters to sufficient precision.

The most difficult variable to measure is ground speed. Because ground speed is actually the resultant vector of true air speed and wind, one way to calculate ground speed would be to measure its component vectors. But, while true airspeed is relatively easy to measure (by sampling the air rushing past the aircraft and adjusting for altitude), the precise influence of wind in the vicinity of the target is extremely difficult to determine.

Bombsight development also suffered during the 1920s for institutional reasons. For much of the decade, the Air Corps devoted little attention or resources to the problem, far more interested instead with the more exciting issues of aircraft design. An Air Corps Bombardment Board complained in 1928,

> Unfortunately, in the past the bomb sight has been considered a mere accessory. The fact that a bombing plane or bombing formation is of no more value than the bomb sight installed there has not been recognized.... [I]t matters not one whit whether the plane costs $50,000 and the sight $1,000, or whether the sight costs $50,000 and the plane $1,000. It is the combination of bomb sight and airplane which makes the hit.... As it is now, our most destructive weapon is impotent at service altitudes; and at the altitudes at which we now operate is handicapped at least 50 per cent by the crude sights employed.[53]

Moreover, what had been true for bombardment aircraft was also true for bombsights. While the Air Corps' vision of bombing was still under debate during the early 1920s, its demands for bombsight accuracy were also unclear. From the experience of World War I, bombsight designers could draw some suggestions but little encouragement. Most bombing in the Great War had been conducted at relatively low altitudes and speeds, and thus made relatively low demands on bombsight accuracy. Bombing "low and slow" also left a great deal of discretion to the bombardier; with practice, bombardiers learned to judge when to release the bombs at least as accurately as any mechanical bombsight.[54]

The machines in use during the Great War to aid the bombardier's judgment were extremely rudimentary. The earliest bombsights consisted of little more than a pair of nails along the fuselage, set at the correct "dropping angle" to the vertical. Flying at a predetermined altitude and speed, the bombardier simply let the bombs drop when the target was lined up with both nails.

These sights were clearly not up to the task of realizing the Air Corps' interwar vision of strategic bombing. In addition to relying greatly on the personal skill of the individual bombardier, these early sights required the aircraft to drop the bombs from a predetermined altitude and velocity. Their inability to correct for drift (the effect of crosswinds) also forced the aircraft to approach the target either directly with or against the wind.

Sights developed by war's end, and improved during the early 1920s, used a more direct and reliable method of determining ground speed, thus allowing bombers to fly at variable altitudes and speeds. By pointing a swiveling telescope directly at the target, the bombardier could determine ground speed by measuring how the telescope's angle to the vertical changed over a set period of time. This became known as the "timing method" of determining the dropping angle. The bombsights Georges Estoppey designed in the early 1920s for the Materiel Division employed the timing method.[55]

These early bombsights suffered from several sources of error. In addition to the inaccuracies that could result from the optics or mechanical drives, the bombs could be thrown off target by the pilot's failure to direct the aircraft directly over the target; even the best of pilots were able to "eyeball" a flight path that took them only within several degrees of the correct dropping point.[56] Even worse, determining ground speed by measuring angles completely placed the accuracy of the drop at the mercy of the bombardier's ability to compare the line from the aircraft to the target against the vertical. If, at inopportune moments during the timing interval, the aircraft pitched, yawed, or accelerated, the bombardier's angular measurements, and thus the bomb load, would be thrown far off. At the low altitudes and speeds of World War I, such calculational errors might not have translated into large errors in where the bombs fell, but at the higher altitudes and speeds envisioned in the later 1920s, they certainly would; at only 120 miles per hour and 1,000 feet, a discrepancy of 10 miles per hour in the ground speed measurement would only throw a bomb off target by about 100 feet; but that same discrepancy would translate into a 400-foot miss when bombing from 10,000 feet. Rigidly mounted bombsights simply would not permit a sufficiently accurate determination of ground speed for anything more precise than area bombing; for even a hope of hitting individual buildings, the bombsight would have to be independently stabilized.

So, for much of the 1920s and into the 1930s, the Air Corps' conception of strategic bombing was simply beyond its technological ability. Neither the aircraft nor the bombsights were up to the task of delivering the aerial devastation that Air Corps leaders envisioned. Nor (perhaps more importantly) was the technology capable of providing the bureaucratic armament necessary to help the Air Corps convince the rest of the military community, much less the rest of the government, that strategic bombing was a job that was both practicable and the sole responsibility of the Air Corps.

Watershed

By the mid-1930s, however, the Air Corps' future with strategic bombing began to brighten. Political, doctrinal, and technological developments during those years converged to place the bomber at the center of the Air Corps' existence.

Politics

A variety of political developments during the mid-1930s served, sometimes inadvertently, to advance the cause of strategic bombing. First, as part of the New Deal, the Roosevelt Administration diverted $15 million of Public Works Administration (PWA) money to military aviation in 1933, divided evenly between the Navy and the Air Corps (amounting to roughly thirty percent of the annual Air Corps budget at the time).[57] Over the next few years, the Air Corps spent almost all of that windfall on development and procurement of bombers and attack aircraft.[58]

Second, a long-standing tension between the Air Corps and the Navy's Bureau of Aeronautics came to a head in 1933. Since the early 1920s, both services had laid claim to the role of defending the nation's coasts from aerial assault. The conflict had been temporarily defused by an informal agreement between Army Chief of Staff General Douglas MacArthur and Chief of Naval Operations Admiral William Pratt in 1930, which essentially gave the mission to the Air Corps.[59] For several years, the coast defense mission not only provided the Air Corps with a raison d'être but also with a justification for long-range bomber development; the airmen had often put forth the intriguing argument that, in order to defend either coast, they needed a bomber with the range to fly from coast to coast without refueling.

But when MacArthur and Pratt left their positions as service chiefs in 1933, the new Navy leadership decided to rescind the agreement.[60] Despite numerous attempts by the Air Corps to avoid losing this crucial bureaucratic foothold, the coast defense mission was back "in play," forcing the Air Corps to reinforce its claims on other justifications for its existence, especially strategic bombing.

Finally, the Air Corps unexpectedly became involved in a frustrating venture that made its misfortunes front-page news. In a complex counterattack against his Republican critics, Franklin Roosevelt instructed the Air Corps to begin transporting air mail for the Post Office in 1934.[61] The ensuing fiasco, which resulted in over sixty-six crashes and a dozen deaths, publicly demonstrated the Air Corps' deficiencies in long-distance and night flying—crucial military capabilities.

Ironically, the air mail fiasco became an expected boost to the Air Corps. For several months, the Air Corps' dearth of experienced pilots and up-to-date equipment was front-page news, and almost no one was willing to blame all of this on the Air Corps itself. Aviation proponents were quick to argue that the difficulties in flying the mail were a direct result of insufficient funding and support from the War Department. In the wake of the disaster, the War Department and the Roosevelt administration launched special investigations into Air Corps matters.

These investigations unanimously recommended increases in Air Corps funding (especially for aircraft), and further operational autonomy for the Air Corps within the Army.[62] Although not truly emancipated from its War Department masters, the Air Corps acquired its own, unified, combat arm—the General Headquarters (GHQ), Air Force—in 1935, thus giving the Air Corps greater freedom to develop air power doctrine independent of concerns on the ground.

Doctrine—The Image Refined

It was also during the mid-1930s that the Air Corps worked out in detail precisely how strategic bombing was supposed to work. The first commander of the GHQ Air Force, bomber advocate Brigadier General Frank Andrews, explained that aerial warfare was like exterminating insects.

> We do not wait until the enemy ground forces are ashore and able to maneuver, nor do we wait for his airplanes to take the air before attacking them. In the former case they are too scattered and too well protected to be dislodged easily. In the latter case they are in three dimensional space and are elusive. As mosquitos are more effectively eradicated at their breeding places than in flight, enemy forces are more susceptible to Air Force action when they are concentrated than when they are deployed and in position to fight.[63]

But before the Air Corps could begin eradicating the enemy in their nests, it had to have a clear idea precisely where those nests were. At the ACTS, where the idea of daylight precision bombing was already entrenched, the next theoretical problem was to work out precisely what should be bombed.

How can bombing paralyze a city, and ultimately an entire nation's will to resist? What buildings, products, or services need to be denied to a population in order to destroy the structure that distinguishes a city or a nation from a chaotic mass of humanity? The targeting problem thus became the purview of industrial economics, or even of social psychology—disciplines that seldom yield hard and fast answers and were, in any case, poorly represented at the ACTS. After World War II, Major General Haywood Hansell, Jr., recalled how First Lieutenant Hansell had struggled with the problem at the Tactical School from 1935 to 1938.

> It was essentially a problem for industrial economists, but no economists were available and no money was available to hire them, in view of the War Department's attitude toward such an approach. So the School did the best it could. It reasoned that other great nations were not unlike our own, and that an analysis of American industry would lead to sound conclusions about German industry, or Japanese industry, or any other great power's industry.[64]

Following this line of reasoning, ACTS bombardment theorists imagined how major American cities could be neutralized. They conducted a large study, for example, on how to bomb New York City, by analyzing maps of the metropolitan area's power grid, water supply networks, transportation infrastructure, and even the city's methods of importing and distributing food.[65]

This investigation of city crippling led to discussions of how to paralyze the war effort of an entire nation, again furthered by studying the example of the United States. Recalled Hansell,

> Our economy is highly specialized. For instance, the New England states make the great majority of our brass and copper items.... Likewise, almost all the shoes in the country are made in one locality. Most automobiles are made in one locality. Within each of these industries, there are in turn specializations.... An analysis of this great complexity indicates that munitions industries are especially sensitive to a relatively small number of plants, which make specialized parts, or systems which provide specialized service. The classic example of the type of specialization, and hence, vulnerability, literally fell into our laps. We discovered one day that we were taking delivery on new airplanes, flying them to their points of reception, removing the propellers, shipping the propellers back to the factories, and ferrying out additional airplanes. The delivery of controllable pitch propellers had fallen down. Inquiries showed that the propeller manufacturer was not behind schedule. Actually it was a relatively simple but highly specialized spring that was lacking, and we found that all the springs made for all the controllable pitch propellers of that variety in the United States came from one plant and that that plant in Pittsburgh had suffered from a flood. There was a perfect and classic example. To all intents and purposes a very large portion of the entire aircraft industry in the United States had been nullified just as effectively as if a great many airplanes had been individually shot up, or a considerable number of factories had been hit. That practical example set the pattern for the ideal selection of precision targets in the United States Tactical doctrine for bombardment. That was the kind of thing that was sought in every economy.[66]

Again, it is easy to see how this image of warfare suited the Air Corps' high-tech, futuristic, and highly professionalized self-perception. Although the search for "choke-point" industries continued into World War II, the idea that the precise destruction of wisely chosen targets—such as oil refineries or ball-bearing plants—could bring entire industries to a standstill was mainstream thinking at the Tactical School by 1937. This articulation, coupled with its earlier vision of the devastating, precise, and unstoppable bolt from blue, completed the Air Corps' strategic bombing doctrine.

Flying Fortress—Engineering the Strategic Bomber

By the mid-1930s, the Air Corps' continuing interest in strategic bombing was effecting technological developments that made the mission appear more feasible. In both aircraft and bombsights, the Air Corps developed and acquired the machines that made precision bombing a bureaucratic success.

The dramatic improvements in military aircraft design during the middle 1930s have been well documented, and need only cursory description here.[67] Driven both by Air Corps desires and the demands of the civilian air transport market, aircraft producers had moved toward larger, multiengine, all-metal designs by the mid-1930s.[68] The historian Eric Schatzberg has argued that the move from wood to metal was driven more by ideology than technical imperatives. While metal designs do have certain technical advantages (especially in military aircraft, which should, as much as possible, maintain their aerodynamic surfaces even when bullet-ridden—something a metal surface will do better than a fabric one), there can be little doubt that metal's appeal was at least partly because of its identification with progressive, high technology.[69]

A similar romance with high technology was evident in the Air Corps' bombers of the middle 1930s. The continuing quest for the ultimate bombing machine had its interwar culmination with the Boeing B-17 "Flying Fortress," first evaluated in 1935. Capable of carrying over a ton of bombs for two thousand miles at well over two hundred miles per hour, the sleek aircraft was a perfect match for the Air Corps' self-image. Submitted as an entry in an Air Corps bomber design competition, the B-17's four engines and all-metal construction gave it a technological appeal that bomber advocates found irresistible (all of the other entries were two-engine designs). Even before the competitive flight tests were underway, the Air Corps considered the B-17's victory foregone. Even before the prototype (designated Boeing Model 299) was delivered to Dayton, the enthralled *Air Corps Newsletter* practically declared it the winner.

> Hailed as the fastest and longest range Bomber ever built, a giant four-engined all-metal airplane, today was brought to light by the Boeing Aircraft Company of Seattle after more than a year of work on the project.
>
> Known merely as the Boeing 299, the huge craft shortly will undergo test

flights before being submitted to the United States Air Corps [*sic*] in open competition with other types at Dayton Ohio. These tests, it was announced, are expected definitely to stamp the plane as the most formidable aerial defense weapon ever offered this country, with far more speed and a substantially greater cruising range than any bomber ever before produced.

Military secrecy necessarily shrouds many details of the Model 299.[70]

Unfortunately for these bomber advocates, the B-17 technically lost the design competition when the prototype crashed and burned during tests (killing two pilots and wounding three others) and was unable to complete the trials. Although the accident was later attributed to ground crew error, the Boeing design was forced to withdraw from the contest.[71] The official winner of the design competition was the B-18, a much less expensive, two-engine model from Douglas.

Although the B-18 was, by all accounts, a perfectly competent aircraft, it was not the technological marvel of which the Air Corps dreamed.[72] Permitted to purchase thirteen of the defeated Boeing design, Air Corps leaders continuously lobbied the War Department to allow it to buy more. Realizing the large airplane's potential as a crowd pleaser (and thus as a potential weapon in the Air Corps' political and bureaucratic struggle), the Air Corps placed the B-17 at the center of its public relations campaign. The very first production model B-17, delivered in March 1937 after the long procurement battle with the War Department, spent several days on public display at Bolling Field within a week after arriving from Boeing; it attracted hundreds of spectators from the Washington, D.C., area. Four of the precious thirteen spent May 16, 1937, cruising a great circle over Langley, Augusta (Maine), Cleveland, Pittsburgh, and Richmond—in all, the bombers made appearances over fifteen states and twenty cities in eleven hours. That fall, six B-17s flew in formation over the American Legion convention in New York City.[73] The Air Corps was particularly pleased to have a B-17 on display for almost a year for the duration of San Francisco's Golden Gate International Exposition in 1939. When the fair ended, the Air Corps was proud to announce that some 5 million people had "stood in the shadow of her wings or touched her gleaming silvery sides."[74] As always, the airplane had been celebrated as the acme of American air power, and the public displays succeeded in wedding the Air Corps' public image to that of the large, high-tech bomber.

Pickle Barrel—Engineering Precision Bombsights

But the bomber was only half of the bombing machine. A central element of the Air Corps' vision of futuristic bombing was its pinpoint precision. Any military with large, fast airplanes could drop bombs indiscriminately on enemy cities. What made the Air Corps different was its mission of destroying only those facilities that underlay the enemy's ability to wage war—the individual buildings that house airplane or munitions factories, ball-bearing plants, railway centers, or oil refineries. This kind of precision in bombing, when coupled with the Tactical School's doctrine of high altitudes and high speeds, required extremely precise mechanical bombsights.

The Air Corps' vision of strategic bombing had profound implications for the development of this particular technology. While several other nations engaged in high-altitude strategic bombing during World War II, no other nation sought the level of technical precision of the U.S. Army Air Corps. Consequently, no other military went to such great lengths to acquire bombsights that could theoretically place bombs on individual buildings. The Air Corps did not succeed in this quest, of course, but this was not well known until after the war was over. What is important is that the quest for precision, even if imaginary, was manifested clearly in the Air Corps' machines.[75]

The experiments in bombsight development during the 1920s had demonstrated very clearly that even the best pilots were unable to fly an accurate enough course over the target, nor to keep the aircraft steady enough to drop the bombs with the desired precision. The technical solutions to these problems were evident early on: the pilot would have to be aided by some sort of mechanical autopilot, and the bombsight would have to be independently stabilized.

Autopilots were developed in the United States during the 1920s, and generally centered around high-speed gyroscopes and servos that kept the aircraft on a constant course and at a constant altitude. Probably the greatest concentration of expertise in the industrial uses of gyroscopes was in the Sperry Gyroscope Company, which developed many of the commercially successful autopilots during the interwar years.[76] By the mid-1930s, it was not too difficult for Air Corps engineers to link the autopilot to the bombsight itself. As long as the bombardier was able to keep the cross-hairs stably on the target, the autopilot could direct the aircraft directly over that spot, and, eventually, even compensate for the effects of wind.[77]

The greatest difficulty was in reliably stabilizing the bombsight. During the 1920s, the Materiel Division contracted for several experimental bombsights that were stabilized by either damped pendulums or gyroscopes. For the latter, which generally proved more successful, the Air Corps contracted mostly with Sperry. In particular, two bombsight designers, the Swiss émigré Georges Estoppey and Russian émigré (and later well-known airplane designer) Alexander Seversky, worked with Sperry Gyroscope and the Materiel Division's Armament Branch developing stabilized bombsights for the Air Corps; for most of the 1920s, the division's bombsight development was supervised by Captain H. B. Inglis (who eventually left for a position at Sperry).[78]

Despite numerous legal and financial tensions (often concerning possible sales to foreign governments), Seversky, Estoppey, Inglis, and Sperry Gyroscope developed several series of bombsight designs during the latter 1920s that employed not only gyroscope stabilization but also a new method of computing ground speed. The earlier timing method required the bombardier to keep the cross-hairs on target for a set amount of time in order to triangulate ground speed. But theoretically, the calculation could be done almost instantaneously; if the bombsight could measure the rate at which the bombardier needed to swivel the telescope to keep the reticule on target, only a few seconds of tracking should be necessary to measure the target's apparent angular velocity, and thus the airplane's ground speed. The dropping angle could then be calculated as quickly as the bombardier could synchronize the target's apparent motion with a variable rate drive gauge. This "synchronous method" of determining the dropping angle was incorporated into Sperry designs in the late 1920s.[79]

Unfortunately for bomber proponents, none of these designs proved completely satisfactory. The units were often too large and heavy to be practical in combat. They also were fragile and in need of constant (and expert) maintenance. Still, by the early 1930s, the Air Corps had three bombsight models, all independently stabilized and employing the synchronous method of determining dropping angle; the radial error of bombs dropped from the altitudes anticipated in combat (about fifteen thousand feet) were generally a respectable two hundred to three hundred feet.[80]

There was one other contender, however, which came, oddly enough, from the U.S. Navy. Since 1928, Air Corps bomber advocates had been hearing rumors about a gyro-stabilized bombsight, developed under the auspices of the Navy's Bureau of Ordnance, which yielded unprecedented accuracy. In 1932, the Air Corps was able to convince the Navy to let it purchase a few of these bombsights from its designer, a former Sperry engineer named Carl Norden.[81]

The Materiel Division's tests of the Norden bombsight (called the Mark XV by the Navy and the M-1 by the Air Corps) were both delightful and dismaying for Air Corps bomber advocates. The Air Corps was pleased to find that this new sight was the most accurate sight yet examined. Norden's design could use either the timing or synchronous methods of calculating dropping angle, had very well-crafted optics, and employed an extremely precise variable-speed motor that swiveled the telescope; by varying the speed of the telescope motor, the bombardier could keep the cross-hairs very precisely on the target.[82] By linking the bombsight to an autopilot (which Norden also designed), the system yielded a bombing accuracy far superior to any of the Air Corps sights.[83] The Air Corps officially adopted the Norden as standard in 1934.

The difficulty, of course, lay in the fact that the Norden bombsight was the exclusive property of the U.S. Navy. The bureaucratic dimension of the Air Corps' quest for strategic bombing is particularly evident here. It was simply intolerable for Air Corps leaders to further their struggle to make strategic bombing the bread and butter of the Air Corps by relying on Navy equipment. Even worse, the Navy insisted on maintaining its exclusive contract with Norden, thus requiring the Air Corps to purchase any Norden bombsights through the Navy. Airmen had hoped that the strategic bombing mission would be the road to freedom from the Army; they were now exasperated to find the road leading back to a subservient position, this time with the Navy.

For much of the mid-1930s, the Air Corps tried desperately to secure an independent contract with Norden, to no avail. The Navy refused to relinquish its own contract, and Norden, who had worked with the Navy since World War I, refused to allow any subcontracting or licensing of his design.

The situation was made even worse by the impression of many within the Air Corps that Norden was personally biased toward the Navy. Air Corps requests for improvements went unheeded, and Air Corps personnel visiting Norden's New York facility often received, they felt, a "cold shoulder."[84] Even into World War II, Air Corps officers felt shunned by Norden. Grumbled one Materiel Division representative after a visit,

> [A]s a result of this last trip, insofar as I am concerned, if I never enter the Norden factory again and deal with their high executive personnel, it will be too soon. It is not that I am rank conscious or ever stand on same, but in reality my reception at that Company was less than is offered to an ordinary seaman. It is my firm belief that the Army Air Forces can never expect any cooperation from this Company and it is my recommendation that we break all relations with this company insofar as possible and utilize Army facilities entirely. [85]

By 1936, the situation had become intolerable. Having to procure bombsights through the Navy had been humiliating enough; but now, as Air Corps demands increased, Norden's output of the largely handmade sight was falling behind schedule. In January, the Navy suspended all Norden deliveries to the Air Corps until the Navy could get its own orders filled.[86]

Faced with this very substantive reminder of its bureaucratic dependence, the Air Corps immediately started casting about for alternative bombsight sources—sources that would be exclusive and loyal to the Air Corps. The obvious place to turn, of course, was back to Sperry Gyroscope, which had continued to work on new bombsights at its own expense. Desperate to free itself from the Navy-Norden cartel, the Materiel Division contracted with Sperry for a new sight, designated S-1.

Unfortunately, Sperry was simply unable to reproduce the performance of the Norden.[87] The Sperry sight was less accurate, required a longer bombing run (thus exposing the bomber to greater enemy fire), and had poorer optics. Its electrical system was also more fragile than that of the Norden; small voltage or current surges (common in combat situations) caused the unit to malfunction.[88]

Significantly, despite the inferior performance of the Sperry bombsight, the Air Corps made it standard equipment alongside the Norden; the bureaucratic benefits of having an independent supplier of bombsights was, in the judgment of Air Corps leaders, "sufficiently important to warrant some degree of such concessions."[89] The Norden was not officially declared superior to the Sperry until the Air Corps was able to secure its own sources of Norden bombsights (sub-contracted to the Victor Adding Machine Company) in 1943.[90]

The Norden, of course, went on to become one of the most celebrated pieces of U.S. technology during World War II. Again, the mystique surrounding the bombsight, carefully cultivated by the Norden Company, fit wonderfully with the Air Corps' high-tech self-perception. The bombsight's "top secret" reputation; its supposed ability to put a bomb in a pickle barrel from twenty thousand feet; the rumor that the reticule was so fine that it required the especially delicate, blonde hair from one Mary Babnick of Colorado; all of these images, like those of the sleek and shiny B-17, reflected the Air Corps' bomber culture in a way that wedded the institution to those machines.[91]

Conclusion

The Air Corps' insistence on keeping the inferior Sperry bombsight as standard illustrates once again the complex relationship between military doctrine, culture, technology, and politics. It might at first appear puzzling that the Air Corps would, in the calm of peacetime, deliberately standardize a bombsight that it considered technically deficient to another. But this presumes that the Air Corps' only goal in developing strategic bombing was narrowly military or strategic. Although the Air Corps during the interwar years certainly pursued the strategic bombing mission because of its potential to enhance the military capabilities of the United States, it also pursued that mission for clearly bureaucratic reasons. This multipurpose pursuit, moreover, had deep and occasionally conflicting influences on the evolution of technology for strategic bombing. If the Navy had not had exclusive rights to the Norden bombsight, for example, it seems unlikely that the Sperry S-1 would ever have gone into production.

It is thus possible to provide a different kind of answer to a much-debated issue of military history and the history of technology: Was American strategic bombing successful in World War II? This is still a question that centers on military, economic, and technical considerations. However, the locus of those considerations should be the United States as much as Germany or Japan. Strategic bombing's bureaucratic function, including its role in shaping the institutional culture of the Air Corps itself, is finally evident in the creation, largely on the basis of the importance and uniqueness of the strategic bombing mission, of an independent U.S. Air Force in 1947. In that sense, strategic bombing—including the culture, doctrine, politics, and technology that made it possible—was completely successful.

Notes

1. What became the U.S. Air Force in 1947 went through various incarnations during the interwar years. It began as the Army Air Service during World War I, became the Army Air Corps in 1926, and the Army Air Forces during World War II.

2. Joseph J. Corn, *The Winged Gospel: America's Romance with Aviation, 1900–1950* (New York: Oxford University Press, 1983), 11.

3. George H. Quester, *Deterrence Before Hiroshima: The Airpower Background of Modern Strategy* (New York: John Wiley & Sons, 1966), 44; James P. Tate, "The Army and Its Air Corps: A Study of the Evolution of Army Policy Towards Aviation, 1919–1941" (Ph.D. diss., Indiana University, 1976), 3. For an example of the conversion from tons to pounds, see Robert Frank Futrell, *Ideas, Concepts, Doctrine: A History of Basic Thinking in the United States Air Force, 1907–1964* (Maxwell Air Force Base, Ala.: Air University, 1971), 25.

4. The Air Service began the war as part of the Army Signal Corps, a manifestation of the belief that the primary use of airplanes was for reconnaissance. In 1918, President Wilson, in response to widespread reports of the Air Service's disarray, reconstituted it directly below the Army General Staff.

5. I. B. Holley, *Ideas and Weapons: Exploitation of the Aerial Weapon by the United States during World War I: A Study in the Relationship of Technological Advance, Military Doctrine, and the Development of New Weapons* (1953; reprint, Washington, D.C.: Office of Air Force History, 1983), 37; David Eugene Johnson, "Fast Tanks and Heavy Bombers: The United States Army and the Development of Armor and Aviation Doctrines and Technologies, 1917 to 1945" (Ph.D. diss., Duke University, 1990), 75.

6. Congress, House, Committee on Military Affairs, *Hearings, Aeronautics in the Army,* 63rd Congress, 1st session (Washington, D.C.: GPO, 1913), 77, 83; Johnson, 63.

7. William Mitchell, *Memoirs of World War I: From Start to Finish of Our Greatest War* (New York: Random House, 1960), 59. Most of these memoirs appeared in the 1920s in *Liberty Weekly* magazine.

8. William Mitchell, *Winged Defense: The Development and Possibilities of Modern Air Power—Economic and Military* (New York: G. P. Putnam and Sons, 1925), 8.

9. Mitchell, *Winged Defense,* 97–119.

10. See Alfred F. Hurley, *Billy Mitchell: Crusader for Air Power* (New York: Franklin Watts, 1964).

11. It is worth noting that bureaucratic well-being does not necessarily require bureaucratic independence. One response to Mitchell's embarrassing crusade for independence was a compromise hammered out by Chief of Air Service Major General Mason Patrick and Secretary of War John Weeks in 1926: the creation of the Army Air Corps. The Air Corps Act of 1926 expanded the air arm and gave military aviators some measure of autonomy in staffing and planning. In a sense, this made the Air Corps' status within the Army comparable to the Marine Corps' status within the Navy.

12. Mitchell, *Winged Defense,* xv–xviii.

13. Mitchell, *Memoirs,* 3–4.

14. Mitchell, *Memoirs,* 105–7.

15. Thomas H. Greer, *The Development of Air Doctrine in the Army Air Arm, 1917–1941* (1955; reprint, Washington, D.C.: Office of Air Force History, 1985), 49.

16. H. H. Arnold, *Global Mission* (New York: Harper and Row, 1949), 157–58.

17. See Robert T. Finney, "History of the Air Corps Tactical School, 1920–1940," Air Historical Studies Number 100, USAF Historical Division, 1955. Microfilm copy at Center for Air Force History, Bolling Air Force Base, Washington, D.C. Although the official name of the school changed over these years, I refer to it throughout as the ACTS.

18. William Mitchell, "Tactical Application of Military Aeronautics," February 5, 1920; as quoted in Greer, 37.

19. Air Service Tactical School, Bombardment text, 1926, 72, as quoted in Johnson, 108; Greer, 41.

20. Max Hastings, "The Bomber as the Weapon of Choice" (paper delivered at the National Air and Space Museum Symposium on the Legacy of Strategic Bombing, Washington, D.C., January 11, 1990).

21. Major Oscar Westover, Commanding ACTS, to Chief of Air Service Mason Patrick, July 14, 1925; as quoted in Johnson, 210.

22. Finney, 31.

23. Bombardment text, 1930–1931; as quoted in Johnson, 212.

24. Finney, 31.

25. Finney, 32.

26. First Lieutenant Kenneth Walker to Assistant Commandant, ACTS, September 24, 1932; as quoted in Johnson, 398.

27. Bombardment text, 1933; as quoted in Johnson, 399.

28. Futrell, iv. Futrell dedicates the book to Walker, who died in 1943, and uses the axiom as an epigram for the entire book.

29. Martin P. Claussen, "Material Research and Development in the Army Air Arm, 1914–1945," Air Historical Study Number 50, Army Air Forces Historical Division, 1946, 14–17, 42. Copy available at the Center for Air Force History, Bolling AFB, Washington, D.C.

30. Brigadier General Benjamin Foulois, Chief of Training and Operations, to Chief of Air Corps, January 7, 1929, Record Group 18, Enter 166, File 400.112C, Box 806, National Archives.

31. Benjamin S. Kelsey, *The Dragon's Teeth? The Creation of United States Air Power for World War II* (Washington, D.C.: Smithsonian Institution Press, 1982), 43–44.

32. There exists a considerable literature on the creation and administrative operation of NACA. See Alex Roland, *Model Research: The National Advisory Committee for Aeronautics, 1915–1958* (Washington, D.C.: Scientific and Technical Information Branch, NASA, 1985); and Norriss S. Heatherington, "The National Advisory Committee for Aeronautics: A Forerunner of Federal Governmental Support for Scientific Research," *Minerva* 28: 2 (spring 1990), 59–80.

33. See Record Group 18, Entry 166, File 334.8, "NACA," Box 546, National Archives; Roland, 431–35.

34. Captain D. F. Stace, Materiel Liaison Section, to General H. H. Arnold, February 10, 1936, Record Group 18, Entry 166, File 334.8, Box 545, National Archives.

35. See Record Group 18, Entry 166, File 400.112A, "Tests & Experiments," Boxes 806–807, and Entry 166, File 334.8, "NACA," Box 545, National Archives.

36. Major General Mason Patrick, Chief of Air Service, to Secretary of War, December 16, 1925 [penciled note at top reads, "Prepared by JFV—sent forward by Gen. Patrick"]; "Report of Special Committee on Proposed Consolidation of the National Advisory Committee for Aeronautics with the Bureau of Standards," December 15, 1932; General Oscar Westover, Acting Chief of Air Corps, to Representative Clifton A. Woodrum, January 12, 1933; Secretary of War Hurley to Senator Hale, January 31, 1933; all in Record Group 18, Entry 166, File 334.8, "NACA," Box 546, National Archives.

37. Colonel L. W. McIntosh, Chief of Engineering Division, to Office of the Chief of Air

Service, February 21, 1924, Record Group 18, Entry 167, File 452.1, "Airplanes—General," Box 21, National Archives.

38.   Glenn L. Martin to Department of State, March 15, 1934, Record Group 18, Entry 167, File 452.1, "Sales of Planes Abroad, 1923–1935," Box 22, National Archives.

39.   Major General B. D. Foulois, Chief of Air Corps, to the Adjutant General, April 4, 1934, Foulois Papers, Box 21, Library of Congress; and Record Group 18, Entry 167, file 452.1, "Sales of Planes Abroad, 1923–1935," Box 22, National Archives.

40.   Foulois to Adjutant General, April 4, 1934. The phrases "Though I am loathe to recommend it," and "and to keep these facilities available for national emergency" were stricken from the final version.

41.   Robert Gross, Treasurer, Lockheed Aircraft Corporation, to Secretary of War, June 28, 1934; Captain G. Harris to Chief of Inspection Branch, Wright Field, November 22, 1934; Chief of Air Corps to Chief of Materiel Division, December 12, 1934; all in Record Group 18, Entry 167, File 452.1, "Sales of Planes Abroad, 1923–1935," Box 22, National Archives. Captain Harris even claimed that Fokker's representative backdated the plane's drawings and smeared them with grease to make them appear older than they were. I have been unable to verify these accusations.

42.   Richard P. Hallion, "Philanthropy and Flight: Guggenheim Support of Aeronautics, 1925–1930," *Aerospace Historian* 28: 1 (spring 1981), 11.

43.   Hallion, 12–13.

44.   Captain A. F. Hegenberger to Chief of Air Corps, June 24, 1934, Foulois Papers, Box 23, Library of Congress.

45.   Claussen, 46–47.

46.   Even as a lieutenant colonel, Arnold sometimes complained that his technical suggestions were not receiving sufficient attention; Lieutenant Colonel H. H. Arnold to Brigadier General H. C. Pratt, Chief of Materiel Division, October 24, 1933, Spaatz Papers, Box 6, Library of Congress.

47.   Kelsey, 72.

48.   Kelsey, 85.

49.   Kelsey, 83–84.

50.   Chief of Air Corps to Adjutant General, March 12, 1929, "Funds spent for 'Research and Development' and Limited Rearmament, fiscal years 1920–1929 inclusive," Record Group 18, Entry 167, File 400.112, Folder "Test, development, research of supplies, equipment, 1923–1935," National Archives. These "all-purpose" developments consisted of development of structures and aerodynamics, propellers, power plants, armament, materials, aircraft equipment, and work contracted to NACA.

51.   Probably the most unusual of these early types was the Barling bomber, an underpowered triplane behemoth with a 120-foot wingspan. Designed by a British bomber designer, the aircraft's six engines (four tractor and two pusher) proved unable to lift it high enough to clear the Appalachians on its first voyage from Wright Field to Washington, D.C. See Earl H. Tilford, Jr., "The Barling Bomber," *Aerospace Historian* 26: 2 (summer 1979), 91–97.

52.   Haywood S. Hansell, "The Keystone Bombers: Unhonored and Unloved," *Air Force Magazine* 60: 9 (September 1977), 130–36.

53.   Major Hugh J. Knerr, President, Bombardment Board, to Chief of Materiel Division, February 7, 1928, Record Group 18, File 471.6 "Bomb Sights," Entry 166, Box 1143, National Archives.

54.   H. B. Inglis, "Report on Bombsight Development since the Armistice," Air Service Engineering Division, January 8, 1926, 3–4. Copy in file "Bombsights, USA #3," File number S2009401, National Air and Space Museum Archives and Branch Library.

55.   Brigadier General W. S. Pierce, Assistant Chief of Ordnance, to Chief of Air Service,

January 4, 1921, Record Group 18, Entry 166, File 471.6, "Bomb Sights—Estoppey," Box 1143, National Archives.

56. Over 90 percent of skilled pilots were over five degrees off of vertical line terminating at the target; Inglis, 5.

57. Colonel Oscar Westover to Chief of Air Corps Foulois, November 10, 1933, Record Group 18, Entry 167, File 452.1, Box 21, National Archives.

58. John F. Shiner, *Foulois and the U.S. Army Air Corps* (Washington, D.C.: Office of Air Force History, 1983), 167.

59. Wesley Frank Craven and James Lea Cate, *The Army Air Forces in World War II,* vol. 1 (1948; reprint, Washington, D.C.: Office of Air Force History, 1983), 62.

60. Westover to Foulois, November 10, 1933; see note 57.

61. The best source on the air mail fiasco is Shiner, 125–49. The Hoover Administration had contracted with private air carriers to transport mail. The Roosevelt Administration found evidence of corruption in these contracts, very publicly canceled them, and turned the job over to the Air Corps.

62. Shiner, 198–99.

63. Brigadier General Frank Andrews, "The GHQ Air Force," n.d. [1935], Andrews Papers, File: GHQ Air Force Directives, Box 9, Library of Congress.

64. Haywood S. Hansell (Major General, USAF), "The Development of the U.S. Concept of Bombardment Operations," lecture at Air War College, Maxwell, Ala., September 19, 1951; quoted in Greer, 80–81.

65. Air Corps Tactical School, "Study of New York City," 1935, 249.211–28, Parts 1–11, in USAF Collection, Air Force Historical Research Agency, Maxwell Air Force Base, Montgomery, Ala.

66. Hansell, "The Development of the U.S. Concept of Bombardment Operations," quoted in Greer, 81.

67. See Maurer Maurer, *Aviation in the U.S. Army, 1919–1939* (Washington, D.C.: Office of Air Force History, 1987), and Jean H. DuBuque and Robert F. Gleckner, "Development of the Heavy Bomber, 1918–1944," Air Historical Study Number 6, USAF Historical Division, 1951. Copy available at the Center for Air Force History, Bolling AFB, Washington, D.C.

68. The Air Corps' first heavy bomber was the metal, two-engined Martin B-10, adopted in 1932.

69. See Eric Schatzberg, "Ideology and Technical Choice: The Decline of the Wooden Airplane in the United States, 1920–1945," *Technology and Culture* 35 (January 1994), 34–69.

70. "Boeing Test Bomber, Model 299," *Air Corps Newsletter* 18: 13 (July 15, 1935), 18.

71. Maurer, 354.

72. See Walter R. Close, "The B-18—A Reminiscence," *Aerospace Historian* 29: 2 (summer 1982), 90–92.

73. Maurer, 355.

74. "'Flying Fortress' on Exhibition at Golden Gate Fair," *Air Corps Newsletter* 22: 5 (March 1, 1939), 9; "Much Viewed Bomber Resumes Normal Role," *Air Corps Newsletter* 22: 22 (November 15, 1939), 19.

75. A useful comparison is again that of the British version of strategic bombing, which made no real (or even rhetorical) effort to target individual buildings or sets of buildings; Bomber Command generally targeted entire cities. Consequently, strategic bombing meant something very different to the British, and British technology differed accordingly.

76. See Thomas Parke Hughes, *Elmer Sperry: Inventor and Engineer* (Baltimore, Md.: Johns Hopkins University Press, 1971).

77. The Historical Office of the Air Corps' Materiel Division, later re-named the Air

Technical Services Command, compiled several useful, internal overviews of bombsight and autopilot development at the end of World War II. See "Case History of the Norden Bombsight and C-1 Automatic Pilot," January 1945, call number 202.2–35; "The Development of Bombing Equipment," May 1945, call number 201–13; and "Case History of S-1 and A-5 Automatic Pilot," June 1945, call number 202.2–14. All three are from the Air Technical Service Command, and are available on microfilm at the Center for Air Force History, Bolling AFB, Washington, D.C. In addition, the Navy compiled its own internal history of the Norden bombsight: Robert Vance Brown, "The Navy's Mark 15 (Norden) Bomb Sight: Its Development and Procurement, 1920–1945," Office of the General Counsel, U.S. Navy, April 1946; manuscript in Navy Department Library, Washington Navy Yards, Washington, D.C.

78. "The Development of Bombing Equipment," 30, 32, 43. For documents concerning Inglis's move to Sperry, see Record Group 342, Sarah Clark Files, 371.63 "Bombsights," RD 3312, Box 872, and RD 3416, Box 1282, Washington National Records Center, National Archives, Suitland, Maryland.

79. Brigadier General William E. Gillmore, Chief of Materiel Division, to Chief of Air Corps, January 19, 1928, Record Group 18, Entry 166, File 471.6, Box 1143, National Archives.

80. The three best Air Corps sights as of 1931 were the L-1 (Sperry-Inglis), C-4 (Sperry-Severksy), and D-7 (Estoppey). See "Comparative Tests of Bombsights," February 3, 1932, and "Progress of C-4 Bombsight Tests," December 23, 1932, Record Group 342, Sarah Clark Files, File 371.63, "Bombsights," RD 3222, Box 531, Washington National Records Center, National Archives, Suitland, Maryland.

81. Major General Benjamin D. Foulois, Chief of Air Corps, to Deputy Chief of Staff, November 23, 1934, document 5 in "Case History of the Norden Bombsight."

82. The Norden rate mechanism centered around two rapidly spinning disks, mounted at right angles to one another. The larger of the two spun at a constant rate; the second was driven by the first, its edge rolling along the surface of the larger disk. By varying the distance between the point of contact and the center of the large disk, the rate of the second disk could be varied very precisely. See Loyd Searle, "The Bombsight War: Norden vs. Sperry," *IEEE Spectrum* 26: 9 (September 1989), 60–66.

83. Foulois to Deputy Chief of Staff, November 23, 1934; see note 81.

84. Brigadier General F. M. Andrews, Commanding GHQ Air Force, to Chief of Air Corps, January 21, 1936; document 13 in "Case History of the Norden Bombsight."

85. Colonel R. E. Jarmon, Materiel Division, "Recent Visit to the C. L. Norden Company," December 29, 1943; document 176 in "Case History of the Norden Bombsight."

86. Andrews to Chief of Air Corps, January 21, 1936; see note 84; "The Development of Bombing Equipment," 57–58.

87. "Development of Bombing Equipment," 59–62. Searle (note 82) argues that the Sperry did perform as well as the Norden; but, based on contemporaneous documents, this opinion was clearly not widespread in the Air Corps during the 1930s and into World War II.

88. "Development of Bombing Equipment," 70–71.

89. Major General Oscar Westover, Chief of Air Corps, to Chief of Materiel Division, January 20, 1936, Record Group 18, Entry 166, File 471.6, Box 1143, National Archives.

90. At that time, the Norden was declared the Air Corps' only standard bombsight, and all remaining contracts with Sperry for the S-1 were canceled; "Development of Bombing Equipment," 71–73.

91. Searle, 64.

"Peace Is Our Profession"

The Bombers Take Over

H. Bruce Franklin

> When he had exhausted all possibilities in the letters, he began attacking the
> names and addresses on the envelopes, obliterating whole homes and
> streets, annihilating entire metropolises with careless flicks of the wrist as
> though he were God.
>
> —Joseph Heller, *Catch-22*

In 1938, Secretary of State Cordell Hull claimed to be "speaking for the whole American people" when he denounced the Fascist bombardment from airplanes of Barcelona, declaring, "No theory of war can justify such conduct."[1] On September 1, 1939, the day World War II started in Europe, President Roosevelt communicated an "urgent appeal to every Government which may be engaged in hostilities publicly to affirm its determination that its armed forces shall in no event, and under no circumstances, undertake the bombardment from the air of civilian populations." Alluding to Axis air assaults on Ethiopia, China, and Spain, he declared that "the ruthless bombing from the air of civilians ... which has resulted in the maiming and in the death of thousands of defenseless men, women and children, has sickened the hearts of every civilized man and woman, and has profoundly shocked the conscience of humanity." He warned that "hundreds of thousands of innocent human beings" would be victimized if the warring nations were to sink to "this form of inhuman barbarism."[2]

Yet, in the next six years, the United States participated in the aerial devastation of most of the cities of Germany as well as cities occupied by Axis forces in France, China, Vietnam, and elsewhere, virtually destroyed all but four Japanese cities (employing incendiaries specifically designed to create unquenchable firestorms in the residential neighborhoods), and cremated two of the remaining four with atomic bombs delivered without warning so that civilian casualties would be maximized. The American people enthusiastically supported all these actions.

Somehow in an eyeblink of historical time, American culture transformed from one that abhorred the bombing of civilians to one that not only accepted it as a military norm but viewed it with the kind of enthusiasm formerly reserved for football games. Then, in the postwar years, the warplane led to an equally astonishing cultural metamorphosis, less blatant but with even more

The Strategic Air Command of the U.S. Air Force was considered the ultimate Cold War instrument of nuclear deterrence. The irony of its slogan, "Peace Is Our Profession," becomes starkly evident in Stanley Kubrick's cult film *Dr. Strangelove: Or How I Learned to Stop Worrying and Love the Bomb*. The entrance to SAC headquarters in Omaha, Nebraska, proudly displayed its slogan for visitors. (U.S. Air Force, courtesy National Air and Space Museum (NASM 00149212), Smithsonian Institution.)

radical implications. First the nation successfully dedicated itself to deploying a nuclear-armed strategic air force designed to wipe out the entire population of the nation's designated major adversary. Predictably—and it was predicted—this invoked a reciprocal strategy from this adversary, thus creating a menace to the existence of the American nation and every person living in it. And then the United States committed itself to a doomsday strategy accurately labeled MAD—Mutual Assured Destruction.

The World War II enthusiasm for strategic bombing can perhaps be somewhat comprehended as an extreme form of the murderous frenzy that often possesses warring societies. More difficult to diagnose is the doomsday culture that could accept, and even celebrate, making the potential suicide of the species into the highest political and economic priority of the nation. Any analysis of these two cultural metamorphoses must confront the central role of the warplane.

Although the post–World War II U.S. air war armada never got to consummate Armageddon, it did manage to slaughter hundreds of thousands, if not millions, of civilians in North Korea, Vietnam, Laos, and Cambodia. But, during this process, especially in the 1960s and early 1970s, major segments of American culture began to manifest once again the earlier revulsion against what President Roosevelt had called "this form of inhuman barbarism." Yet, by the early 1990s the World War II ethos had reasserted its dominion as the nation seemed to accept the death of many thousands of civilians in Baghdad as insignificant "collateral damage" from an aerial assault ballyhooed as "surgically clean." Indeed, the vehicles that carried out this carnage became the icons of a virtual cult of high-tech aerial weaponry.

The cultural artifacts that expressed and produced these enormous social changes include speeches, newsreels, treatises, toys, essays, newspapers, magazines, songs, plays, radio and TV broadcasts, jokes, novels, advertisements, and so on. But perhaps the most revealing symptoms of these metamorphoses are Hollywood movies.

Prior to World War II, the rejection of the bombing of cities was virtually universal in American fiction and film. Only a handful of the most bizarre future-war novels and stories projected scenes of American bombing of cities. Movies made before the nation entered the war contained, as far as I am aware, not a single image of the United States engaging in such conduct.

Looking backward at American culture during the World War II bombing offensives, one can easily detect the fantasies that veiled and romanticized the bomber. The virtually unmitigated public approval of these aerial assaults is not surprising, in the light of their public images. What was seen and heard of the bombers was almost as innocuous and recreational as their scale models that millions of young boys (and even some girls) were gluing together. Missing from the verbal and cinematic pictures of the bombers was the world of the bombed, which appeared only in stories about our side, especially England, under Axis attack. After all, it was the Nazis who bombed civilians, while the English and Americans bombed military targets. Warner Brothers' 1941 *International Squadron* expressed this perfectly: while holding the body of a young girl killed in a raid on London, the American hero—played by Ronald Reagan—decides to enlist in the RAF; he gives his own life bombing a Nazi ammunition dump.

Hollywood's images of bombers cannot be separated from certain material facts of the movie industry. Making a commercial film about bombers is difficult without two things: large financial resources and the cooperation of the Air Force. This tends to limit the product to what is at least acceptable to both financial and military interests. Even before the United States entered the war, collaboration among the Army Air Corps, airplane manufacturers, and major film studios began to condition the public's responses to the bomber. World

War II–era movies forged a crucial link between Billy Mitchell's early use of the silver screen to propagandize the cult of the bomber and postwar movies designed to make the Strategic Air Command's bombers the emblem of the nation.

Back in 1935, amid the deep Depression, the Boeing Company was awarded its first production order for what was then called the XB-17, presaging a future U.S. economy dependent on the "aerospace" industry. The senators from the state of Washington, known even then as "the gentlemen from Boeing," later argued on the Senate floor that the Fascist bombings in Spain actually proved that the United States needed a fleet of bombers capable of carrying out similar actions.[3] Hollywood's role in glamorizing the bomber was established in 1938 in MGM's *Test Pilot,* with Clark Gable and Spencer Tracy flying a wondrous experimental plane, actually the YB-17, Boeing's prototype of the Flying Fortress. The Army Air Corps, in the midst of a massive publicity campaign aimed at winning congressional approval for full production, assigned all twelve existing YB-17s and their crews directly to the MGM film crew.[4] *Test Pilot* succeeded splendidly for all the collaborators. The movie was one of the biggest box-office attractions of 1938, and was nominated for three Academy Awards, including Best Picture and Best Original Story. The Air Corps and Boeing got their contract.

So in 1939, while the president was so eloquently denouncing the bombing of cities, Boeing's assembly lines had already begun mass production of the B-17. By 1940, what was needed was propaganda designed to recruit the men to fly the bombers. The bill was filled by Paramount's *I Wanted Wings,* a romantic semi-documentary about the training of aircrews. The Air Corps provided more than a thousand airplanes, including a squadron of B-17s, for the production, helping it become Paramount's top moneymaker in 1941 and an archetype for the genre.[5]

The paradigmatic movie image of the bomber was established by *Air Force,* a 1943 box-office smash produced by Warner Brothers at the suggestion of Air Corps General "Hap" Arnold and directed by Howard Hawks. The sexy star of the movie is "Mary Ann," a B-17 Flying Fortress endowed with awesome powers and passionately loved by her crew. *Air Force* concludes with a portentous prophecy of the strategic bombing of Tokyo and a hint of a future dominated by invincible U.S. bombers.

Feature films about the air war in Europe focused on the Nazi bombing of Britain and offered only rare glimpses of the strategic bombing of German cities, which was projected as precise attacks on specific military targets (dramatized only in documentaries such as the War Department's 1944 *Memphis Belle*). The bombing of Japan, however, was glorified not only in such purportedly realistic films as *Bombardier* (1943), *The Purple Heart* (1944), and *Thirty Seconds over Tokyo* (1944), but also in the most unbridled and prophetic of World War II bomber movies, *Victory Through Air Power,* Walt Disney's 1943 animated appeal for future unrestrained bombing to exterminate the Japanese people.

Back in 1932, Billy Mitchell had published his sublime vision of American strategic bombers raining incendiaries on "the greatest aerial targets the world has ever seen"—Japanese cities "built largely of wood and paper." His prediction that such attacks "would burn the cities to the ground in short order" would prove accurate as U.S. bombers carried out the systematic cremation of the cities of Japan.[6]

By 1943, the frenzy to burn Japan matched the genocidal fantasies of future-war fiction about the Yellow Peril common between 1880 and 1914.[7] Article after article echoed Mitchell in emphasizing the flammability of Japanese cities.[8] Some justified mass attacks on Japanese civilians as a means to save American lives. A piece in the January 1943 *Harper's* entitled "Japan's Nightmare: A Reminder to Our High Command" put it in terms that would become even more familiar in August 1945: "It seems brutal to be talking about burning homes. But we are engaged in a life and death struggle for national survival, and we are therefore justified in taking any action which will save the lives of American soldiers and sailors."[9] Some went even further. A professor of geology at Colgate proposed in the January 1944 *Popular Science* that we wipe out not just the Japanese people but also all the islands of Japan by using high-explosive bombs to initiate volcanic eruptions. After the firebombing of Japan's cities began, even more voices clamored for the extermination of the Japanese. The March 1945 U.S. Marine monthly *Leatherneck,* for example, featuring a cartoon of the Japanese as a hideous buck-toothed louse, acknowledged that the "flame throwers, mortars, grenades and bayonets" of the Marines alone could not complete "the gigantic task of extermination" of "Louseous Japanicas"; "the origin of the plague, the breeding ground around the Tokyo area, must be completely annihilated." The following month, the chairman of the War Manpower Commission, Paul V. McNutt, announced that he favored "the extermination of the Japanese people in toto."[10]

The most effective propagandist for implementing Mitchell's total air war on Japan was his long-time associate, the Russian émigré Alexander de Seversky, then president of Republic Aviation Corporation. In 1942, de Seversky gathered his articles from *American Mercury, Atlantic Monthly, American Magazine, Flying and Popular Aviation, Look, Coronet, Reader's Digest,* and *Town and Country* into his exceptionally influential book *Victory Through Air Power,* which sold hundreds of thousands of copies through the Book of the Month Club alone. In the first chapter, he uses the rhetorical strategy that Mitchell had adopted from future-war fiction, painting a lurid picture of what enemy bombers will do to America's cities if America doesn't do it to theirs first. The airplane has brought the age of "total war," and "the very ease with which a machine-age country can be blasted into chaos from on high is an invitation to the war of annihilation." In this war of "total destruction" and "extermination," the enemy's goal is to "destroy our civilization." Our goal then must be "to eliminate rather than take over Japan," and so we must base our strategy on "a war of elimination."[11]

Walt Disney was so impressed by de Seversky's book that he decided to turn it into an animated feature film. His 1943 *Victory Through Air Power* opens with an old newsreel clip of Billy Mitchell enunciating his doctrine of the bomber. Disney's animation turned out to be an ideal medium for this message. Gigantic American bombers blacken the sky as omnipotent machines, then magically transmute into an American eagle that claws the Japanese octopus to death. In what James Agee's review called "the gay dreams of holocaust at the end," Japan is bombed and burned into ruins with no human image of suffering, terror, or death on the screen. As the audience beholds the smoldering remains of this cartoon nation, it hears the swelling strains of "America the Beautiful." Then across the screen is emblazoned VICTORY THROUGH AIR POWER.[12]

Preparations were already under way to carry out these genocidal fantasies. Scientists from corporations and universities constructed models of typical Japanese dwellings and urban residential neighborhoods to determine how to generate the most relentless firestorms.[13] In Hollywood, First Lieutenant Ronald Reagan was taking part in what he refers to in his autobiography as one of the major "secrets of the war, ranking up with the atom bomb project": creating a complete miniature of Tokyo, so authentic in detail that even top Air Corps generals could not distinguish films of it from films of the real city. Footage of fake bomb runs on the toy city were then used to brief bombing crews, who were taken by Reagan's voiceover narrative all the way to his dramatic "Bombs away." As areas of Tokyo were burned out, Reagan tells how the Hollywood team would "burn out" their counterparts in "our target scene," obliterating, along with the city, boundaries between illusion and reality.[14]

In January 1945, the commander of XXI Bomber Command, Brigadier General Haywood S. Hansell, Jr., protested when ordered to conduct saturation firebombing of whole cities. Hansell was quickly removed, to be replaced on January 20 by Major General Curtis LeMay. Within a few months, LeMay's campaign to incinerate Japan produced more casualties among Japanese civilians than their armed forces suffered throughout the entire war.[15]

The grand finale of the global war waged against Fascism and Nazism—forces epitomized by rampant militarism and wanton slaughter of civilians—turned out to be dropping atomic bombs from B-29 Superfortresses on the cities of Hiroshima and Nagasaki. The bomber and the bomb were now to become crucial in U.S. military strategy, the postwar economy, the political process, and the nation's culture. Boeing's preparations for the new era might be detected in its final wartime ads, which assigned a new name to its B-29 Superfortress: the Peacemaker.

During the four years when it was the only nation in the world with nuclear weapons, the United States engaged in full-scale, unrestrained production and stockpiling of atomic bombs. U.S. forces encircled the former Soviet Union with a noose of more than four hundred major military bases and almost three thousand secondary bases, stretching from Greenland and Iceland through Europe, the Middle East, southwest Asia, the Pacific Ocean, Alaska, and Canada.

In March 1946, just seven months after the end of World War II, the Strategic Air Command (SAC) was formed; two months later, it was assigned the mission of preparing to carry out nuclear attacks anyplace on the planet.[16] Billy Mitchell's goal of an independent Air Force was reached in 1947. And preeminent within the Air Force was SAC, whose nuclear-capable B-29s and Boeing B-50s were now stationed at forward bases throughout the northern hemisphere within striking range of every major Soviet city. Soon these were superseded by true intercontinental bombers. Boeing's gigantic B-36, designed for the just-formed Strategic Air Command, first flew on August 8, 1946, one year after the Hiroshima and Nagasaki bombings and two weeks after the second Bikini bomb. In 1947 came SAC's B-47 jet bomber, precursor of the B-52, both produced by Boeing and each capable of reaching any target in the world, thanks to in-flight refueling provided by another Boeing product, the KC-97 tanker.

In the prewar Depression, peacetime markets could not consume the output of American industry's enormous capacity. Then this capacity was bloated far beyond its prewar limits by the Herculean tasks of wartime production. So, after a brief binge of pent-up consumer demand, only one kind of appetite could gobble up the productive excesses of postwar American heavy industry: the ever-growing, insatiable bulimia induced by war or the threat of war. Hence the permanent conversion of the great warmaking capacity achieved during World War II into what President Eisenhower in 1961 labeled the "military-industrial complex." At its core was a network of airplane manufacturers and related enterprises, now styling themselves "the aerospace industry," with an ongoing propaganda campaign and organizational structure designed to guarantee that their most technologically advanced products would seem obsolescent as soon as they began to roll off the assembly lines.

Mass-produced culture helped create an environment congenial to the needs of the aerospace industry. Before it was superseded by ever more futuristic weapons, the main vehicle to carry the new message was the multiengined bomber.

In the late 1940s, as the Air Force became preeminent in the Cold War strategy based on a constant threat of a U.S. nuclear attack, movies and novels about World War II bombers became vehicles for glorifying not just aerial combat but also top-down social control. The central characters were no longer the men flying the missions but the officers who commanded them. As if by coincidence, the terrific burden borne by high-ranking Air Force officers became the subject of popular and acclaimed works: William Wister Haines's 1947 novel *Command Decision,* made into a long-running Broadway play and a 1948 film; the 1949 film *Twelve O'Clock High;* and James Gould Cozzens's 1948 novel *Guard of Honor,* awarded the Pulitzer Prize for 1949. Both novels are unabashed apologetics for a ruling military elite; the two movies are a bit less overt. The subtext of all these works, although each ostensibly concerns World War II, celebrates the commanders of the nuclear-armed Air Force of the Cold War.

The movies *Command Decision* and *Twelve O'Clock High* are both set at British bases from which U.S. bombers were conducting the "daylight precision bombing" offensive against German forces. Each focuses on the grave responsibilities of a commanding general (Clark Gable in the first, Gregory Peck in the second) who must direct missions that he knows will lead to terrible losses among his men. Both seek to show how the commanders' vision transcends the limited view of their subordinates, forcing them to assume the anguish of ordering acts that might seem inhuman to less highly positioned observers. The giant World War II bomber offensive here becomes a totem for postwar corporate-military supremacy.[17]

From 1949 on, endless propaganda sought to convince the American people that they were living in peril of an imminent nuclear attack from the Soviet Union. The truth was that before 1957 the Soviet Union lacked any physical capability (not to mention the will) to launch even a small retaliatory attack. Indeed, as a KC-97 navigator and intelligence officer in SAC throughout 1957 and 1958, my main duties—when not engaged in mid-air refueling of B-47 and B-52 bombers on routine espionage and provocation overflights of the Soviet Union—were helping to conceal from the American people, particularly our own SAC flight crews, the fact that the Soviets still had neither operational intercontinental bombers nor missiles.

Yet, 1955 to 1957 was the period of the infamous "bomber gap," a public-relations coup successfully engineered by politicians, generals, and industrialists to scare up many more billions of dollars for SAC, the aerospace corporations, and related military-industrial interests. The United States was pictured lying almost defenseless under the menace of a vast Soviet bomber armada, which, as U.S. intelligence well knew, actually consisted of ten prototype Bisons, none either operational or based within range of the United States.[18]

Whatever private feelings people may have had, public cultural works opposed to the arms race were banished by the frenzied anticommunist repression. Hollywood illustrates the process dramatically.

The first two movies overtly against the arms race both appeared in 1951: the classic *The Day the Earth Stood Still,* in which an extraterrestrial federation, concerned about human violence being extended into space, threatens to destroy the planet if we do not cease our weapons buildup; and *Five,* the earliest Hollywood film set after an atomic holocaust. But these two would also be the last for several years. In the spring of 1951, the House Un-American Activities Committee began its yearlong mass hearings on the film industry, which resulted in the blacklisting of dozens of Hollywood figures deemed insufficiently anticommunist (in addition to the "Hollywood Ten" previously blacklisted or imprisoned). The effects on the social content of films were immediate.

A more acceptable attitude toward the atom bomb was dramatized in the 1952 semidocumentary *Above and Beyond.* Here the real tragedy of Hiroshima is that it spoiled the marriage of the B-29 pilot, Colonel Paul Tibbets (Robert Taylor), because he couldn't tell his wife (Eleanor Parker) about the secret weapon he was being trained to drop on the city. Besides turning the story into a soap opera, *Above and Beyond* presents a subtext urging civilians to accept secrecy, avoid meddling with military concerns, and be grateful for the bomb. Almost without exception, movies openly dealing with atomic weapons from 1952 through 1958 were Cold War propaganda tracts, such as *The Atomic City, Invasion USA, Hell and High Water, Strategic Air Command,* and *Bombers B-52.*[19]

By the mid-1950s, the strategic bomber had become a major icon of American culture. Hollywood's veneration went all the way back to the primitive church, featuring Gary Cooper as the martyred prophet in the 1955 *The Court Martial of Billy Mitchell.* The persecuted cult of the 1920s was now a state religion. SAC's nuclear-armed bombers no longer needed to be camouflaged as the revered Flying Fortresses that had blasted the cities of the Third Reich. Films like *Strategic Air Command* (1955) and *Bombers B-52* (1957), directed by Gordon Douglas (who five years earlier had made *I Was a Communist for the FBI*), could openly glorify the Cold War union of the strategic bomber and the nuclear bomb. Gone were the clanking, awkward, propeller-driven craft that had supposedly defeated fascism. In their place were gleaming, streamlined multijet beauties, each carrying a load of destruction equal to hundreds of World War II bombers. These were superweapons that men could love with an ardor surpassing anything inspired by a woman or even by a Flying Fortress. In *Strategic Air Command,* Jimmy Stewart's commanding general enthuses about the hydrogen bomb and the latest SAC bomber: "With the new family of nuclear weapons, one B-47 and a crew of three carries the destructive power of the entire B-29 force we used against Japan." Reverentially ushered into the presence of the B-47 he will pilot, Stewart ecstatically blurts out, "She's the most beautiful thing I've ever seen in my life."[20] Within a decade, *Strategic Air Command*'s perverted love affair with this deadly machine, its characteristic and potentially catastrophic confusion between eros and thanatos, would inspire the bomber movie to end all bomber movies, *Dr. Strangelove: Or How I Learned to Stop Worrying and Love the Bomb.*

After years spent trying to conceptualize a film on the cult of the nuclear bomb and bomber, poring over dozens of books and his subscriptions to the *Bulletin of the Atomic Scientists* and *Aviation Week*, Stanley Kubrick saw that the subject was too bizarre for realism. He discovered that only the blackest and wackiest comedy could project the grotesque antics of our insane love affair with our apocalyptic warplanes.

Dr. Strangelove, Or How I Learned to Stop Worrying and Love the Bomb is far less implausible than it might seem to those unfamiliar with the real SAC. Its milieu, characters, and situations are no fantasies. One of the movie's most jaundiced detractors, the film critic Andrew Sarris, offered this as his prime example of what he called its "blatant overstatement": "The sign reading 'Peace Is Our Business' has an ironic kick, however obvious, the first time it is shown in a strife-torn Air Force base, but when repeated a half dozen times more, the effect crosses the thin line between satire and propaganda."[21] Sarris seems unaware that the sign in *Dr. Strangelove*, which actually reads "Peace Is Our Profession," is a piece of realism, a precise replica of the sign gracing the entrance of every SAC base. Well, I, too, didn't know that this was the motto of the Strategic Air Command until I first encountered such a sign as I drove up to the main gate of a SAC base to report for duty in February 1957. But by the time, seven years later, when I saw *Dr. Strangelove*, I almost mistook Kubrick's absurdism for realism.

The main mission of both squadrons in my wing, as I soon discovered on our arctic and subarctic flights, was refueling SAC bombers on both espionage and provocation missions over the Soviet Union. Three times during my two years in SAC, it launched its bombers on full-scale attacks against the Soviet Union and recalled them only at the last moment. Once was supposedly when a flight of geese crossing our DEW (Distant Early Warning) and Pine Tree radar lines was interpreted as a flight of Soviet bombers, which SAC knew could not be the case. Once was when a guard was shot and killed at a "Special Weapons" (i.e., thermonuclear bomb) storage site, suggesting that SAC did actually believe in the myth of a communist fifth column prepared to destroy America's nuclear arsenal whenever Moscow gave the order. The third time even those of us in combat intelligence were never informed of the cause.

If General Jack Ripper's plan to dispatch his bombers to the Soviet Union in *Dr. Strangelove* seems preposterous, is it any less believable than SAC's routine provocation missions by B-47s and B-52s, which by 1964 had resulted in twenty-six U.S. planes being shot down over the Soviet Union? Or than the CIA's 1960 U-2 overflight of the Russian heartland, successfully designed to torpedo the Eisenhower-Khrushchev summit scheduled for two weeks later? Or than the Gulf of Tonkin incidents seven months after *Dr. Strangelove* opened, when a naval battle that never took place was used to get congressional approval for the longest war in U.S. history, all as part of top-secret plan NSAM 273 to turn the "covert war" into full-scale hostilities while maintaining "plausibility of denial"? Even the firefight between the Burpelson security force and the attacking U.S. Army unit has a basis in the surprise seizures of SAC bases by SAC's own infiltration and combat teams.[22]

Of course the most improbable and irrational feature of *Dr. Strangelove* is the Doomsday Machine deployed by the Soviets, and envied by ex-Nazi Dr. Strangelove and SAC General Turgidson. Yet, by 1964, both the United States and the Soviet Union, which had barely flinched at the brink of thermonuclear war during the 1962 Cuban missile crisis, were each frantically constructing their Doomsday Machine. For isn't that just another name for Mutual Assured Destruction?

Dr. Strangelove derives its most disturbing effects from its audience's upbringing in the cult of the strategic bomber, most especially through the bomber movies of World War II and the early years of the Cold War. The lone bomber, manned by its all-American heroic crew, winging inexorably toward its target though crippled by enemy defenses, flies straight out of a line of Hollywood productions extending back to the 1943 *Air Force,* starring "Mary Ann," the emblematic B-17 that must be defended from a treacherous attack on a U.S. base so that it can go on to win the war and save the world. *Dr. Strangelove*'s music soars along with the graceful bomber and the stirring drumbeat quickens our pulses as the determined and ingenious crew overcomes one hazard and obstacle after another. Part of our being, so conditioned by our bomber culture, *wants* the B-52 to get through and bomb its target, while another part of our being is forced to recognize that if it succeeds civilization will be destroyed. What we are thereby experiencing is the destruction of civilization already implicit in our construction and deployment of these doomsday devices.

The richest and most complex theme in *Dr. Strangelove,* as its title suggests, is the alienation of human love and sexuality in the cult of the bomber and the bomb. Sexual perversion permeates every scene, including: the midair copulation of the B-52 and KC-135, accompanied by the sweet strains of "Try a Little Tenderness"; General Ripper's devastating obsession with his own "precious bodily fluids"; General Turgidson's call from the War Room urging Miss Scott to "start her countdown" so when he returns she will be ready to "blast off"; Miss Scott's reappearance as Playmate of the Month (clothed only by a strategically placed copy of *Foreign Affairs*) in the *Playboy* ogled by Major Kong on the fatal B-52; Dr. Strangelove's ecstasy when contemplating his proposed future life in a deep shaft surrounded by women "selected for their sexual characteristics, which will have to be of a highly stimulating order!"; and, of course, the final orgy of blossoming nuclear mushrooms.[23]

Dr. Strangelove did not invent this strange love that invested superweapons with intense eroticism, making us want to learn "How to Stop Worrying and

Love the Bomb." It does force us to behold in a mirror the sickness and perversion of a culture that produced and participates in that passionate exclamation by Jimmy Stewart about a bomber in which he will carry "destructive power" equal to all the incendiaries, high explosives, and atomic bombs dropped on Japan: "She's the most beautiful thing I've ever seen in my life."

The main announced purpose of the thousands of U.S. nuclear-armed bombers was to "deter" the alleged plan of the Soviet Union and its "satellites"—such as China—to overrun the world with hordes of communist fanatics. These warplanes were supposedly the "peacekeepers" of their era, preventing war by making it too horrific to wage. Yet, in the decades after World War II, the United States became involved in almost unending warfare—warfare that disclosed the true meaning of Victory through Air Power.

In World War II, U.S. strategic bombing concentrated on what Billy Mitchell and the other theorists referred to as "industrial targets" (cities), "transportation centers" (cities), "communication complexes" (cities), and "nerve centers" or "vital centers" (cities). Using the manned bomber as an ultimate weapon of strategic warfare on predominantly peasant nations such as Korea and Vietnam would reveal new dimensions of its genocidal capacity, but also expose its very limited military effectiveness.

By September 1950, just three months after the Korean "police action" began, U.S. warplanes annihilated all the cities of North Korea. Even the smallest villages were targets of saturation attacks with high explosives, rockets, and napalm. Flight crews were complaining, "It's hard to find good targets, for we have burned out almost everything."[24] North Korea was bombed so intensively that for years afterward, trees that survived were marked with commemorative signs designating them "prewar trees." Moreover, U.S. tactical air supremacy over the battlefield was unchallenged. Nevertheless, despite the numerical superiority of U.S. and allied forces (contrary to contemporaneous propaganda about "hordes" of Chinese communists), the war ended in stalemate.

Meanwhile, total rule of the skies by France's U.S.-equipped air force was not saving the French from military defeat in Indochina. Replacing France, the United States unleashed on Vietnam, Laos, and Cambodia the longest and most devastating air assault in history.

In February 1965, just a few days before the sustained air offensive against North Vietnam began, appeared *Design for Survival* by General Thomas S. Power, recently retired head of SAC. General Power explained how easily air power could bring U.S. victory in Vietnam:

> Let us assume that, in the fall of 1964, we would have warned the Communists that unless they ceased supporting the guerrillas in South Vietnam, we would destroy a major military supply depot in North Vietnam. . . . If the Communists

failed to heed our warning and continued to support the rebels, we would have gone through with the threatened attack and destroyed the depot. And if this act of "persuasive deterrence" had not sufficed, we would have threatened the destruction of another critical target and, if necessary, would have destroyed it also. We would have continued this strategy until the Communists had found their support of the rebels in South Vietnam too expensive and agreed to stop it. Thus, within a few days and with minimum force, the conflict in South Vietnam would have been ended in our favor.[25]

This fantasy of the bomber's omnipotence was exposed by the reality of the U.S. air war against Vietnam.

During all of World War II, the United States dropped a total of about two million tons of bombs in all theaters, including the strategic bombing of Europe and Japan. From 1965, when General Power gave his prescription for painless victory through air power, through 1973, the United States dropped between 7.8 and 15 million tons of bombs on Indochina. To get some perspective on what even the lower number means, compare it to the total tonnage Germany inflicted on Great Britain from 1940 through 1945, including the Battle of Britain, the Blitz, and the V-bombs: 74,172 tons. According to the conservative estimate of 7.8 millions tons, the explosive force of the U.S. bombardment was equivalent to approximately 640 Hiroshima-size atomic bombs. Great swaths of Vietnam came to resemble the lunar landscape, with more than 21 million bomb craters just in South Vietnam, which the United States was allegedly defending; the total area cratered by high explosives in Vietnam is estimated to be approximately 122,000 square miles, about the size of New Mexico.

High explosives were not the whole story. Newly engineered incendiary, chemical, and antipersonnel fragmentation weapons were used with unprecedented concentration. The napalm and phosphorus bombs that had burned out the cities of Japan and North Korea were refined into improved incendiaries designed to stick better to human skin and burn more intensely. Cluster bombs were carefully crafted to maximize internal body wounds with plastic flechettes that would escape detection by surgeons' X rays. The poisoning and defoliation of Vietnamese cropland and forests with Agents Orange, White, Blue, and Purple lasted from at least 1961 through 1971; about half of South Vietnam's coastal mangroves were wiped out; over a third of the tropical hardwood forests were destroyed; and six million acres of farmland were inundated with toxic chemicals known to have severe mutagenic effects.[26]

Despite this unprecedented assault from the air, the United States was militarily defeated in Vietnam. And it was through this war that growing numbers of Americans became aware of the significance of America's most advanced weapons.

The cities and villages of Vietnam were perceived by the U.S. military as legitimate military targets because that is where the enemy—that is, the people— could be located. The American people were appalled once they learned that U.S. ground troops were massacring and burning whole villages, such as My Lai. Why was this more reprehensible than massacring and burning countless villages from the air? Because one of the distinguishing features of the warplane as an instrument of genocide is the dissociation it offers from its own effects. The interior of the plane does not even seem to be in the same universe as the victims on the ground. Divorced from the carnage it wreaks, the warplane becomes an icon of power, speed, beauty, and technological ritual.

When the dissociation between these icons and the human suffering they inflicted began to break down during the Vietnam War, the most potent symbols of American technological might—such as the carrier-launched supersonic fighter-bomber and the giant eight-jet B-52—became objects of revulsion for many Americans. While many other Americans still responded with thrills and veneration to their roar and flash, the reality of the aerial superweapon was beginning to pierce the fantasy.

In the midst of the changing consciousness about America's wars and weapons appeared the two most popular and influential American works of literature about the bombing offensive of World War II: Joseph Heller's *Catch-22* and Kurt Vonnegut's *Slaughterhouse-Five*. These two novels contributed to the new awareness, which at the same time helped provide their wide audience. It is no coincidence that both books waited until the 1960s to be born, although both authors had been personally involved in the World War II bombing, which had been crucial in shaping the creative vision of each.

Kurt Vonnegut, Jr., was a prisoner of war in Dresden during the Anglo-American raids that turned the city into an inferno, inflicting what he labeled "the greatest massacre in European history."[27] Dresden surfaced first in Vonnegut's fiction in the mid-1960s. The title character of *God Bless You, Mr. Rosewater* (1965), who is erotically aroused by images of fire, becomes so excited by a graphic description of the Dresden firestorms in Hans Rumpf's *The Bombing of Germany* (an actual book) that he hallucinates a gigantic phallus-shaped firestorm consuming Indianapolis. But it was not until 1969, twenty-four years after the Dresden raids, that Vonnegut finally was able to finish a novel expressing the inferno at the center of his tormented imagination, *Slaughterhouse-Five; or, The Children's Crusade: A Duty-Dance with Death.*

In the opening chapter, the author tells of wrestling with the Dresden experience ever since he returned from World War II. At first he thought that simply narrating the story would generate a "masterpiece": "all I would have to do would be to report what I had seen." His first attempts were in the late 1940s, before any of his fiction was published: "Even then I was supposedly writing a book about Dresden. It wasn't a famous air raid back then in America. Not many Americans knew how much worse it had been than Hiroshima, for instance. I didn't know that, either. There hadn't been much publicity" (10). Before *Slaughterhouse-Five* could be composed, much had to happen to America and to Vonnegut's fiction.

The warplane, that characteristic weapon of America's endless postwar wars, had to be perceived as a loathsome machine. By 1969, Vonnegut was able to assume that many of his readers would respond to the aerial killing machines not with wonder but disgust and revulsion. Thus, they could comprehend the ironies of a story embedded in *Slaughterhouse-Five*—attributed to Vonnegut's mythical science-fiction writer Kilgore Trout—about napalm dropped by a robot with bad breath:

> It was dropped on them from airplanes. Robots did the dropping. They had no conscience, and no circuits which would allow them to imagine what was happening to the people on the ground.
>
> Trout's leading robot looked like a human being, and could talk and dance and so on, and go out with girls. And nobody held it against him that he dropped jellied gasoline on people. But they found his halitosis unforgivable. But then he cleared that up, and he was welcomed to the human race. (168)

Abandoning the straightforward narrative that had proved inadequate for Dresden, Vonnegut constructed a fiction composed of wildly diverse modes of narrative reality. The autobiographical opening introduces what seems at first to be more or less realistic fiction about Billy Pilgrim, an oafish American prisoner of war at Dresden, who eventually becomes a well-to-do, apparently complacent optometrist—that is, a person whose job is to make people see things more clearly and accurately. In the novel, actual and imaginary books about the Anglo-American bombing offensive and the Dresden raids offer other narrative modes. Another layer of reality is composed of fictions by Billy's favorite author, Kilgore Trout, who appears as a character on still another level. Billy's view of time, life, and death is radically altered by experiencing a Trout-like science-fiction adventure: a flying saucer from the planet Tralfamadore kidnaps him, installs him in a zoo, and provides him with a movie-star sex mate so that the Tralfamadorians can ogle the earthling pair.

Just before being captured and sent to Dresden, Billy becomes "unstuck in time," so that he ricochets around erratically in his personal history like a dented Ping-Pong ball in a maze of air hoses. Without volition he aimlessly bounces among events: being captured by the Germans, bombed by the Allies, kidnapped by the Tralfamadorians, and absorbed passively into middle America. He is thus the perfect protagonist for this novel that strips the romance and glamour from war, that offers no John Wayne, no Jimmy Stewart, no Sylvester Stallone, no character the audience might want to be. As the narrator explains, since this is a novel about war, "There are almost no characters in this story, and almost no dramatic confrontations, because most of the people in it are so sick and so much the listless playthings of enormous forces" (164).

The Tralfamadorians advise Billy to forget about war and think only about pleasant events, a message opposed to the *danse macabre* of the novel. In his usual listless, almost autistic way, Billy goes along far enough with this Pollyanna philosophy to blind himself to the reenactment in the late 1960s of the massacre he had witnessed in 1944.

Whereas novels and movies of the late 1940s drew on the popular support of World War II to legitimize the Cold War, *Slaughterhouse-Five* draws on the popular revulsion against the Vietnam War to expose its continuity with World War II. Shuttling back and forth in history, Billy merges Dresden with Vietnam. As a prelude to the ghastly scene in which Billy and the other prisoners of war dig for corpses in the bombed-out shell of Dresden, Vonnegut reminds the readers that "every day my Government gives me a count of corpses created by military science in Vietnam" (210).

In 1967, Billy drives through a burned-out black ghetto, which reminds him of Dresden, on his way to a luncheon at the local Lions Club, of which he is a past president. The speaker, a major in the Marines, regales them with anecdotes about the Vietnam War and advocates "bombing North Vietnam back into the Stone Age" (60)—the famous words of General Curtis LeMay, who became commander of SAC and Air Force Chief of Staff after directing the incineration of Japan. The optometrist fails to see any connections: "Billy was not moved to protest the bombing of North Vietnam, did not shudder about the hideous things he himself had seen bombing do" (60). Billy agrees with the major that he is very proud of his son, a Green Beret sergeant in Vietnam, who is undoubtedly doing "a great job" (61). He thus ignores the one clear lesson Vonnegut had drawn from Dresden: "I have told my sons that they are not under any circumstances to take part in massacres. . . . I have also told them not to work for companies which make massacre machinery, and to express contempt for people who think we need machinery like that" (19).

Yet Billy's "unstuck" perspective on time offers unique visions of the aerial superweapons that superimpose Dresden on Vietnam. He watches on television an archetypal World War II bomber movie glorifying the entire military-industrial process that ends in burning down cities. Played backward in Billy's mind, the movie turns into its opposite: the bombers put out the fires and suck up the bombs, the German fighters repair the bombers and heal the wounded crewmen, the bombs are unloaded at the base and disassembled in factories, from which their mineral contents are shipped to specialists in remote areas whose job is "to put them into the ground, to hide them cleverly, so they would never hurt anybody ever again" (75).

Juxtaposed to the fantasy is the reality of being bombed, pieced together in kaleidoscopic chips of the Dresden experience. The British officer who briefs the American POWs tells them: "You needn't worry about bombs, by the way. Dresden is an open city. It is undefended, and contains no war industries or troop concentrations of any importance." "The loveliest city that most of the Americans had ever seen," Dresden was "jammed with refugees." "About one hundred and thirty thousand people" die when this "voluptuous and enchanted and absurd" city, which looks like "a Sunday school picture of Heaven," is consumed by "one big flame" that "ate everything organic, everything that would burn." U.S. fighter planes fly under the smoke to strafe any survivors, firing at but missing Billy and the other American POWs. Like the genocidal bombing of Vietnam, "The idea was to hasten the end of the war" (146–80).

This was also the rationale for dropping atomic bombs on Japanese cities, as explained in President Truman's August 1945 announcement. Truman's words are inserted here amid extended quotations from David Irving's *The Destruction of Dresden* (185–88), including the forewords by two key figures in the Anglo-American bombing offensive, U.S. Air Force General Ira C. Eaker and British Air Marshal Sir Robert Saundby. Eaker offers a calculus and an ideology to justify the bombing: "I deeply regret that British and U.S. bombers killed 135,000 people in the attack on Dresden, but I remember who started the last war and I regret even more the loss of more than 5,000,000 allied lives in the necessary effort to completely defeat and utterly destroy nazism" (187). Saundby (who engineered the saturation firebombing of Hamburg) admits that the bombing of Dresden was "a great tragedy" for which there was no military necessity: "Those who approved it were neither wicked nor cruel, though it may well be that they were too remote from the harsh realities of war to understand fully the appalling destructive power of air bombardment in the spring of 1945" (187–88). Then Saundby uses Dresden to argue in favor of nuclear weapons: "The advocates of nuclear disarmament seem to believe that, if they could achieve their aim, war would become tolerable and decent. They would do well to read this book and ponder the fate of Dresden, where 135,000 people died as the result of an air attack with conventional weapons" (188).

Billy encounters these published statements while sharing a hospital room with Harvard Professor Rumfoord, a retired brigadier general, apostle of Theodore Roosevelt's cult of strenuous manhood, and now "the official Air Force Historian" working on a history of the Army Air Corps in World War II. At first Rumfoord refuses to believe that Billy, whom he considers a "repulsive non-person," was actually in Dresden during the raids. When finally forced to confront this unpleasant fact, Rumfoord insists on a deterministic—that is, perfectly Tralfamadorian—rationalization, to which Billy blandly assents:

"It *had* to be done," Rumfoord told Billy, speaking of the destruction of Dresden.

"I know," said Billy.

"That's war."

"I know. I'm not complaining." (198)

Rumfoord concedes that "It must have been hell on the ground," which Billy verifies in two words: "It was." Then the official Air Force historian offers his only words of sympathy: "Pity the men who had to *do* it."

One of the men who did do the bombing of Europe was Joseph Heller, a bombardier with sixty combat missions over France and Italy. It took sixteen years of postwar personal and American history for Heller to publish his first book, *Catch-22,* the most widely read work of American literature to come out of the war, and arguably the single most influential American novel of the twentieth century.

Catch-22 goes much further than those historians who deride the military effectiveness of the Anglo-American bombing offensive in defeating the Nazi–Fascist Axis. The novel suggests that the bombers actually helped the enemy win the war.

The enemy in *Catch-22* is "they," all those who embody forces inimical to life, love, freedom, and other values for which the American people thought they were fighting. The ultimate interpretation of the novel's title comes from an old woman in Rome: "Catch-22 says they have a right to do anything we can't stop them from doing."[28] By this point in the story, and in the history it interprets, "they" have very few constraints on their power.

World War II, everybody knew back then, was to be the final victory over fascism. American bombs were defeating the would-be conquerors of the world, with their storm troopers, secret police, armed gangs of thugs, torturers, and rapists, war profiteers, militaristic madmen, demagogues, big lies, anticommunist crusades, fiendish scientists creating diabolical new weapons for giant cartels, and corporate states determined to make their war economy and culture permanent and universal. Yossarian discovers in 1944 what many more Americans later surmised: that these forces might achieve their global empire draped in red, white, and blue. Even President Eisenhower, several months before the publication of *Catch-22,* had warned the American people in his January 1961 Farewell Address:

Now this conjunction of an immense military establishment and a large arms industry is new in the American experience. The total influence—economic, political, even spiritual—is felt in every city, every state house, every office of the federal government. . . . In the councils of government, we must guard against the acquisition of unwarranted influence, whether sought or unsought, by the Military/Industrial Complex.

At the end of *Catch-22,* power is being consolidated by all the forces that at first seemed to be just bad jokes. The competing war profiteers and military bureaucrats have all merged into one giant cartel: M & M Enterprises. Like the "M.M.," the storm troopers who take over America in Sinclair Lewis's 1935 *It Can't Happen Here!,* M & M Enterprises is as American as apple pie. The syndicate's slogan, "What's good for M & M Enterprises is good for the country," echoes the famous declaration by Charles E. Wilson, President of GM, "What's good for General Motors is good for the country." M & M's most implausible and outrageous acts, such as contracting with both sides to maximize war profits, are no more outlandish than GM's construction of weapons for both sides throughout the war.[29]

Gestapo-like secret police, embodied by the Criminal Investigation Division (CID) men, have become ubiquitous and indistinguishable from their Nazi and Fascist counterparts. This is one of the meanings hidden in the metaphor of *déjà vu,* as the chaplain learns when he is arrested and interrogated by American officers in a torture room replete with rubber hose and blinding spotlight. Those who oppose these fascists are "disappeared," a transitive verb coined in the novel and soon absorbed into everyday American usage. Frenzied "loyalty" campaigns foreshadow the repression of the late 1940s and 1950s, part of the background of the novel.

Yossarian gets part of the message during his walk in Rome, which has fallen again, this time to a mob of "vandals," the hordes of U.S. military police terrorizing the civilian population. The cry "Help! Police!," Yossarian realizes, is no longer meant "as a call for police but as a heroic warning" to "everyone who was *not* a policeman with a club and a gun and a mob of other policemen with clubs and guns to back him up" (425). He sees the outcome of the war: "Mobs of policemen were in control everywhere" (426). And then he, too, is seized by MPs with clubs, "icy eyes," and "unsmiling jaws," each apparently "powerful enough to bash him to death with a single blow" (429), who haul him back to submit to Colonels Cathcart and Korn.

Colonel Cathcart, whose murderous ambitions cause the deaths of almost all of Yossarian's friends, is manipulated by Colonel Korn, whose "brown face with its heavy-bearded cheeks," bearing "deep black grooves isolating his square chin from his jowls" (436, 441) gives him more than a coincidental resemblance to Mussolini. In Yossarian's crucial confrontation with the colonels, they announce that they have become America: "'You're either *for* us or against your country. It's as simple as that'" (433). The logic of the colonels is as flawless as the corporate slogan of M & M Enterprises, for they are in command.

Crucial to the novel's structure and meaning is the mission against an undefended Italian mountain village, which we encounter shortly after learning of the arrival in Italy of Colonel Scheisskopf.[30] When last heard of, Scheisskopf was a mere lieutenant obsessed with parades and frustrated because he couldn't turn all the men into precision marching machines. Thanks to events flowing from this mission, Scheisskopf, who embodies the aesthetics of Nazi and Fascist militarism, will end up "in charge of everything" (400).

Among the most notorious tactics responsible for prewar American outrage against the bombing of civilians was the Italian bombardment of undefended Ethiopian villages. Especially infamous was the aesthetic ecstasy expressed about these raids by one of the pilots, the dictator's son Vittorio Mussolini, who enthused about the beauty of groups of tribesmen "bursting out like a rose after I had landed a bomb in the middle of them."[31] For the Fascists, beautiful images were only a bonus. But in *Catch-22* the sole purpose of the American annihilation of the undefended Italian village is to produce publicity photos of tight bomb patterns.

General Peckem, the power-mad officer who designs the raid, secretly acknowledges that bombing this "tiny undefended village, reducing the whole community to rubble" is "entirely unnecessary," but it will allow him to extend his power over the bombing squadrons. He has convinced them that he will measure their success by "a neat aerial photograph" of their "*bomb pattern*—a term I dreamed up," he confides, that "means nothing." The ostensible purpose of destroying the village is to create a roadblock to delay German reinforcements, although there is no evidence that any will be traveling on the road. The planned annihilation of a village filled with friendly civilians disgusts almost all the fliers.

"What the hell difference will it make?" demands Dunbar, pointing out that it would take the Germans only a couple of days to clear the rubble. McWatt and Yossarian want to know why the people in the village can't be warned. "They won't even take shelter," Dunbar argues, "They'll pour out into the streets to wave when they see our planes coming. . . ." (335–36). When Colonel Korn demands to know why the men don't want to bomb the village, Dunbar replies, "It's cruel, that's why." Colonel Korn responds with the argument used to legitimize the firebombing of Dresden and Tokyo, the nuclear attacks on Hiroshima and Nagasaki, and the aerial slaughter of Asian peasants:

> "Cruel?" asked Colonel Korn. . . . "Would it be any less cruel to let those two German divisions down to fight with our troops? American lives are at stake, too, you know. Would you rather see American blood spilled?" (336)

Korn quells the mutiny with two additional arguments: a threat to send the men on a more dangerous mission and a reminder that "we didn't start the war and Italy did." He of course does not mean this to remind anyone that air war began with Italy's 1911 imperial war in Libya, that the Anglo-American bombing offensive put into practice the theory of the Italian Fascist General Douhet, or that the raid on this undefended village is a grotesque reenactment of Italy's air war on the villages of Ethiopia, now carried out by B-25 Mitchells, bombers named for Douhet's principal disciple in America.

Yossarian is habitually slow in comprehending and acting. He bandages the wrong wound on Snowden, the dying gunner. He literally throws away his one opportunity for redemptive love with a woman, casually tossing out the address of Luciana, not realizing that "his heart cracked, and he fell in love" with her when he learned that it was an air raid by "*Americani*" that had deeply scarred her body (163). Not until the very end does he understand Orr's crafty plan for survival; in fact he furtively connives to avoid being assigned to fly with him. He vacillates until too late before accepting Dobbs's proposal to kill Colonel Cathcart, and fails to fathom or follow Dunbar's revolt. Thus he misses the alternatives offered to him by his comrades before they are dead or gone: escape (Orr), direct action (Dobbs), and resistance (Dunbar). All that is left for him is his existential, absurdist final flight from what his nation has become.

When we first met Yossarian, in the hospital, he was amusing himself by censoring mail as perversely as possible, "attacking the names and addresses on the envelopes, obliterating whole homes and streets, annihilating entire metropolises with careless flicks of his wrist as though he were God" (8). The joke of course is that he is annihilating only verbal symbols of homes, streets, and metropolises. But the joke turns inside out when we discover that Yossarian is a bombardier, whose duty requires him to obliterate actual towns and people. Yossarian escapes from the Air Force before he becomes part of the machinery designed to turn the joke into the central fact of human life. *Catch-22* shows the bombers of World War II helping to forge a world in which people live in terror of those who may annihilate entire metropolises with careless flicks of the wrist.

Six years after *Catch-22,* Yossarian's joke expanded to become Heller's play *We Bombed in New Haven:* actors playing Air Force crews wait to learn which cities their script has them annihilate. Tired of this piecemeal approach, some of them wish to blow up the whole globe: "That's what I would do if I were in charge, instead of picking it apart so slowly, piece by piece and person by person. Why don't we just smash the whole fucking thing to bits once and for all and get it over with?"[32] Some of the actors keep insisting that this is all make-believe, just a verbal construct. The play ends with the main character insisting to the audience that "There is no war taking place here now!" that "There has never been a war. There never will be a war." *We Bombed in New Haven* was first performed in December 1967, to an audience beginning to learn from the Vietnam War just what kind of victory was being achieved through air power.

Since then, American bombers have celebrated their triumph by bombing nations in Asia, Africa, the Middle East, Central America, the Caribbean, and Europe. How bizarre it would seem to Americans today if the Secretary of State were to declare that "no theory of war can justify" the bombing of cities and the president were to label such conduct "inhuman barbarism."

Notes

1. "Barcelona Horrors," *Time* 31 (March 28, 1938), 13; quoted in George E. Hopkins's superb account of the metamorphosis of official and public attitudes toward the bombing of cities, "Bombing and the American Conscience During World War II," *Historian* 28 (May 1966), 451–73. Hopkins's meticulous research, which begins with 1935, finds virtually universal condemnation of bombing cities prior to 1938. Much of the present essay is adapted from H. Bruce Franklin, *War Stars: The Superweapon and the American Imagination* (New York: Oxford University Press, 1988).

2. Franklin D. Roosevelt, "The President Appeals to Great Britain, France, Italy, Germany, and Poland to Refrain from Air Bombing of Civilians," *The Public Papers and Addresses of Franklin D. Roosevelt: 1939 volume* (New York: Macmillan, 1941).

3. Hopkins, "Bombing and the American Conscience," 455.

4. Bruce W. Orriss, *When Hollywood Ruled the Skies* (Hawthorne, Calif.: Aero Associates, 1984), 6–8.

5. Orriss, 23–24.

6. Mitchell, "Are We Ready for War with Japan?" *Liberty* (January 30, 1932), 12.

7. See *War Stars,* chapter 2.

8. Hopkins, 463. For extended analysis of the racism in the bombing of Japan, see Michael Sherry, *The Rise of American Air Power: The Creation of Armageddon* (New Haven: Yale University Press, 1987), 245–51 *et passim* and J. W. Dower, *War Without Mercy: Race and Power in the Pacific War* (New York: Pantheon, 1986), chapters 4–7.

9. Homer C. Wolfe, "Japan's Nightmare: A Reminder to Our High Command," *Harper's* 186 (January 1943), 187.

10. Harold O. Whitnall, "Can We Blast Japan from Below?" *Popular Science* 144 (January 1944), 103–4. *Leatherneck* drawing and caption, Dower, 184; McNutt quotation, Dower, 55.

11. Major Alexander P. de Seversky, *Victory Through Air Power* (Garden City, N.Y.: Garden City Publishing Co., 1943), 11, 101, 103, 117; this bestselling reprint used the plates of the original 1942 edition.

12. Richard Schickel, *The Disney Version: The Life, Times, Art and Commerce of Walt Disney* (New York: Simon and Schuster, 1968), 273–75; Sherry, 130–31. James Agee's review in the *Nation,* July 3, 1943, contains other insights into the "sexless sexiness" of Disney's animated "machine-eat-machine" version of war; reprinted in *Agee on Film: Reviews and Comments* (New York: McDowell, Obolensky, 1958), 43–44.

13. Wesley Frank Craven and James Lea Cate, eds., *The Army Air Forces in World War II,* 7 volumes (Chicago: University of Chicago Press, 1948–1958), v, 610; Sherry, 226–27, 397; Ronald Schaffer, *Wings of Judgment: American Bombing in World War II* (New York: Oxford University Press, 1965), 108–9.

14. Ronald Reagan with Richard G. Hubler, *Where's the Rest of Me?* (New York: Elsevier-Dutton, 1965), 118–19.

15. Craven and Cate, v, 564, 754.

16. *Fundamentals of Aerospace Weapons Systems* (Washington, D.C.: Air University, 1961), 275. On Boeing's ads, see Sherry, 126.

17. See Peter Biskind, *Seeing Is Believing* (New York: Pantheon Books, 1983), 70–77, for an excellent discussion of *Twelve O'Clock High* as exaltation of the corporate ethos attaining dominance in the late 1940s and 1950s.

18. Allen Dulles, *The Craft of Intelligence* (New York: Harper & Row, 1963), 149; H. Bruce Franklin, *Back Where You Came From* (New York: Harper's Magazine Press, 1975), 107–12.

19. On the 1951 House Un-American Committee (HUAC) hearings, see John Cogley, *Report on Blacklisting: I. Movies* (n.p.: The Fund for the Republic, 1956), 92–117; an appendix by Dorothy B. Jones, "Communism and the Movies: A Study of Film Content," quantifies the dramatic changes in film content, with at least thirteen militantly anticommunist films released in 1952 (231). On movies advocating nuclear weapons, including the government-sponsored documentaries made by Hollywood, see A. Costandina Titus, "Selling the Bomb: Hollywood and the Government Join Forces at Ground Zero," *Halcyon* 7 (1985), 16–29.

20. See Biskind, 67–68, for an analysis of this dialogue and its context.

21. Andrew Sarris, "Dr. Strangelove," *Village Voice,* February 13, 1964, as reprinted in his *Confessions of a Cultist: On the Cinema, 1955–1969* (New York: Touchstone Books, 1971), 121.

22. John M. Carroll, *Secrets of Electronic Espionage* (New York: E. P. Dutton, 1966), 134–35; David Wise and Thomas B. Ross, *The U-2 Affair* (New York: Random House, 1963), *passim;* Marvin E. Gettleman, Jane Franklin, Marilyn Young, and H. Bruce Franklin, *Vietnam and America: A Documented History* (New York: Grove Press, 1995), 241–52; *Back Where You Came From,* 107–19.

23. For discussions of the significance of sex in the film, see F. Anthony Macklin, "Sex and Dr. Strangelove," *Film Comment* 3 (summer 1965), 55–57; Norman Kagan, *The Cinema of Stanley Kubrick* (New York: Holt, Rinehart and Winston, 1972), 136–37; Thomas Allen Nelson, *Kubrick: Inside a Film Artist's Maze* (Bloomington: Indiana University Press, 1982), 89–95.

24. On the aerial devastation of Korea, see: Bruce Cumings, *The Origins of the Korean War: Volume II, The Roaring of the Cataract, 1947–1950* (Princeton: Princeton University Press, 1990), 705–7, 753–55; Cullum A. MacDonald, *Korea: The War Before Vietnam* (New York: Free Press, 1986), 234–36; I. F. Stone, *The Hidden History of the Korean War* (New York: Monthly Review Press, 1971), 256–57.

25. General Thomas S. Power, *Design for Survival* (New York: Coward-McCann, 1965), 224–25.

26. The statistics on German bombing of Britain are from R. J. Overy, *The Air War: 1939–1945* (New York: Stein and Day, 1982), 120. For figures on the explosives dropped on Indochina, comparisons with U.S. bombing during World War II, and an estimate of the cratered area, see James P. Harrison, "History's Heaviest Bombing" in *The Vietnam War: Vietnamese and American Perspectives,* ed. Jayne S. Werner and Luu Doan Huynh (Armonk, N.Y.: M. E. Sharpe, 1993), 130–39. James William Gibson, *The Perfect War: Technowar in Vietnam* (Boston: Atlantic Monthly Press, 1986), 320, 495, gives the basis for the conservative figure of 7.8 million tons of bombs and suggests that the actual total may have been over 15 million tons; Gibson's analysis shows in detail how the doctrine of victory through air power led to the nightmarish theory and practice of the American aerial devastation of Indochina. For documentation and details of the ecological impact of the air war on Indochina, see Ralph Littauer and Norman Uphoff, *The Air War in Indochina* (Boston: Beacon Press, 1972) and *Vietnam and America,* 462–70.

27. Kurt Vonnegut, Jr., *Slaughterhouse-Five; Or, The Children's Crusade: A Duty-Dance with Death* (New York: Delacorte Press/Seymour Lawrence, 1969), 101.

28. Joseph Heller, *Catch-22* (New York: Simon and Schuster, 1961), 416.

29.   Bradford C. Snell, "American Ground Transport," *Hearings before the Subcommittee on Antitrust and Monopoly of the Committee of the Judiciary, United States Senate, 93rd Congress, Second Session on S. 1167* (Washington, D.C.: U.S. Government Printing Office, 1974).

30.   Clinton Burhans, Jr., "Spindrift and the Sea: Structural Patterns and Unifying Elements in *Catch-22,*" *Twentieth Century Literature* 19 (1973), 239–50, meticulously charts the interrelations between the chronology of the novel and the chronology of the war and first pointed out the crucial importance of the mission against the village.

31.   *Voli sulle ambe* (Florence 1937), a book Vittorio Mussolini wrote to convince Italian boys they should all try war, "the most beautiful and complete of all sports"; as quoted in Denis Mack Smith, *Mussolini's Roman Empire* (New York: Viking, 1976), 75.

32.   Joseph Heller, *We Bombed in New Haven* (New York: Alfred A. Knopf, 1968).

Stick and Rudder University

Training and the Creation of the Flight Suit Officer

JOHN DARRELL SHERWOOD

> Some people sat down when the Air Force became a new service and decided
> that hey, we are the Air Force. We are not the Army's airborne cavalry, we do
> not have centuries and centuries of traditions to hamper our progress, we're
> going to do things our way. And they deliberately set out at Nellis to produce
> the best-trained, best-equipped fighter pilots in the world. And they did!
> —FRANK TOMLINSON[1]

Until quite recently, the literature of military aviation consisted of two forms
of historical writing: operational histories and memoirs. Operational histories, written primarily by official historians, served primarily to catalog the accomplishments of various air power institutions and as a result tended to be chronological and technical in their methodology. Robert Futrell's official history, *The Air Force in Korea,* typifies this approach. Although the book does delve into issues such as technology, logistics, and leadership, most of the work is devoted to descriptions of various air campaigns performed by the U.S. Air Force during the Korean War. For future war planners such material may be of great interest but, for the scholarly historian, it offers few connections with the general historical enterprise. The professional historian wants to understand the institutional culture of the American Air Force and how it relates to American culture writ large. Who were the people who joined the Air Force? Where did they come from? What did they believe in? How did major historical currents of the time influence them and their institution? Memoirs such as James Salter's *Burning the Days* or his fictional account, *The Hunters,* partially fill this gap in the historiography, but these works are highly subjective and narrow in scope.

The book *Officers in Flight Suits* goes a step further. Using the methodology of oral history, the book analyzes the war through the eyes of actual participants and then corroborates those findings where possible with statistics from official documents. The book examines the life experiences of a group of Korean aviators from birth through their postwar careers all in an attempt to define, in general terms, the institutional culture of American air power in Korea. Perhaps the most seminal chapter of the book is "Stick and Rudder University."

This chapter investigates a little-explored element of the military aviation experience—training. In particular, it explores how flight training proved inte-

Lt. William E. "Earl" Brown Jr., an African American fighter pilot in the U.S. Air Force during the Korean War, when African Americans in the Air Force were rare, was typical of the so-called flight suit officer. In this scheme of things, leadership was measured by how well one could pilot an aircraft in combat rather than how well educated or capable a commander he was. Brown went on to other positions, including NATO Air Commander in the Mediterranean. He retired as a lieutenant general. (U.S. Air Force, courtesy National Air and Space Museum, Smithsonian Institution [SI 99-15482].)

gral in shaping the institutional culture of the Air Force officer corps during the Cold War period. This culture I define as "flight suit culture." Flight suit culture, in its basic form, was a sense of self-confidence and pride that verged on arrogance. For a flight suit officer, the aircraft of preference was the high-performance, single-seat fighter, although one could find him in almost any model (particularly forward air control aircraft and rescue helicopters). This culture placed a premium on cockiness and informality. A flight suit officer spent more time in a flight suit than a uniform, and preferred conducting business in the ready room or better yet the bar at the O Club rather than in an administrative office. This type abhorred nonflying, "collateral" duties, and lived for one thing—flying. In his world, status was based on flying skills, not degrees, rank, or officer skills. Nor surprisingly, the flight suit officer greatly resented attempts by the burgeoning Air Force bureaucracy to "raise the bar" for promotion during the Cold War by requiring university degrees, disciplined "officer-like" behavior, and administrative skills for advancement. Most entered into the Air Force without a college degree and expected to get ahead in the service by living up to the Air Force motto of the period, "To Fly and Fight." In fact, during the 1950s, only 37 percent of the Air Force officer corps possessed baccalaureate degrees, compared to 75 percent for the Navy and 63 percent for the Army.

For the officer candidate without a college degree, the main route to an Air Force commission was Aviation Cadets—a program that combined officer candidate school with pilot training. Fully two-thirds of all Air Force officers received their commissions from this program during the Korean War period. Only one short four-week segment of the sequence focused exclusively on military indoctrination and training. The remaining three longer phases of training were primarily flight oriented. In short, pilot training defined the Air Force officer and presented him with skills and values necessary to flourish within the Air Force environment. In both a physical and psychological sense, it lifted him from the ground and transformed him into an "air-minded" individual and a member of the Air Force's "flying elite."[2]

At the same time, training was also a grueling initiation process complete with hazing, washouts, accidents, and even death. An average of only 61.6 percent of those who entered the training program earned their wings.[3] Furthermore, a majority of the washouts were due to "flying deficiencies" rather than academic or disciplinary problems.[4] So difficult was the process of learning to fly military aircraft that the Air Force Training Command, despite its dual mission to create officers and flyers, actually emphasized the latter more so than the former. Half of each training day was spent on the flight line or in the air, one-on-one, with instructors who often were civilian contractors with no prior military experience.[5] While on the line, students wore flight suits and were told not to salute officers or worry about standard military discipline: flying and all that goes with it, they were told, were to be their only concerns.[6]

The end result of this intensive, flight-oriented program was a more casual officer than the average Army second lieutenant or Navy ensign. "The impression of the Air Force that I had in the late '40s and early '50s," recalls Robert Pomeroy, "was a guy with a crushed hat and a cavalier attitude. In those days, flying was riskier than it is now: we learned to eat, drink, and be merry because tomorrow you may die."[7] In short, to survive flight training, one had to be "cockpit-minded": technique had to take precedence over military discipline, leadership, and hierarchy. A flight suit attitude was not simply an expression of machismo, it was a means of psychological survival in a danger-filled environment.

Pilot training defined the young Air Force officer of the 1940s and 1950s and created the flight suit persona. As much an initiation ritual for these men as a place to develop practical skills, pilot training was a critical indoctrination period for the young officer. If a trainee could overcome the various barriers to becoming a pilot (washouts, accidents, fear of flying, and the possibility of death), he could enter the brotherhood of the flight suit. Ancestry, education, and prior military training or military academy experience had very little to do with one's status in the Air Force: wings, the flight suit, and eventually, the one hundred combat mission Distinguished Flying Cross was what truly defined one as "elite" in this service. Training tested a young man's skill and courage; it also taught him that he would "sink or swim" in the Air Force based on his ability to fly, and that life outside the "flight suit" was secondary.

Selection and Testing

The process of choosing pilots was hardly a science in the 1950s, but it was not as random as it had been in earlier years. During World War I, applicants were "spun in a spin chair to test their equilibrium," and men "who could ride well, sail a fast boat, and handle a motorcycle were considered good prospects."[8] It was not until 1941 that the Army decided to implement a more "scientific" test, known as the "Standard Nine," or "stanine" for short. Because this test dictated who would become a pilot in an organization dominated by pilots, it played a crucial role in shaping the entire nature of the Air Force officer corps during its early history.

The "stanine," which changed little from World War II to the Korean War, tested a pilot on a broad range of intellectual and physical skills. But because flying was considered a mechanical skill, above all else, the test emphasized hand-eye coordination, excellent vision, and sound motor skills more than any other abilities.[9] Those who passed tended to he athletic but not necessarily intelligent in the traditional academic sense. Training Command studies suggested that "other than perhaps increasing self-confidence, education and academic attainment could not . . . improve [a pilot's] chances of finishing training." Consequently, the humanities and social sciences sections of the test were "rated next-to-last, just ahead of vocational skills."[10] A pilot could be deficient in both of those areas and still pass. When this factor is combined with the low educational requirements for aviation training (i.e., two years of college), it becomes clear that the Air Force had the least-educated officer corps in the 1950s. This was a serious problem for a service that took pride in its ability to field some of the most technologically advanced weapons in the military.

At the heart of the problem was the fact that demand for pilots was outstripping the supply. When the Aviation Cadet program reopened in 1947 after a postwar hiatus, it had to train only 3,000 pilots annually; in 1950, this number had increased to 4,000; and by 1952, with demands brought on by the Korean

War, the Air Force needed 7,200 pilots a year.[11] To meet these large production goals, the Air Force sent twelve traveling Aviation Cadet selection teams around the country in an attempt to recruit college students. Local Air Force bases also arranged base tours for high school seniors and college students. Recruitment letters were even sent out to all acquaintances of cadets, officers, and instructors.[12] These efforts were not enough: between 38 percent and 50 percent of those accepted into the program in the early 1950s were washing out.[13] The Air Force needed more pilot recruits. One of the major problems with college recruitment was that initially college students used the Aviation Cadet program as a loophole to avoid the draft. Before 1951, the Air Force granted immunity from further military service to all aviation washouts in an attempt to make pilot training more attractive to civilian recruits. This policy encouraged many young men to sign up for Aviation Cadets, and then resign after the first week or two of training. Between 1949 and 1950, for example, 18 percent of Aviation Cadets resigned during this initial period. Although this number might reflect the initial shock cadets felt on entering a rigorous training program, the Air Force suspected draft avoidance as the primary cause.[14] Consequently, General Gabriel P. Disosway, the Air Staff Director of Training, "ordered all civilian Aviation Cadet applicants enlisted as privates, USAF, for a period of four years."[15] Cadets who resigned after February 1951 would serve out the rest of their military time as Air Force privates.

Despite the efforts of Disosway and others, cadet shortages persisted during the Korean War. The following list describes the efforts of the Air Force to rectify the problem.[16] Clearly, the knee-jerk reaction of the Air Force to cadet shortages was to lower the entrance requirements—a solution which served to further water down the intellectual caliber of its officers.

Responses to the Aviation Cadet Shortage, August 1951–May 1952

September   Men with prior service who were eliminated from training excused from further service
            Minimum qualifying aircrew battery (stanine) test score reduced from six (out of nine) to five
November   Requirement that enlisted men serve eighteen months before applying for flight training waived
December   Applicants with two or more years of college obligated to only two years of enlisted service if eliminated from training
January   Time between testing and notification of the applicant of test results was streamlined and reduced
            Flight training applicants given priority handling
            Minimum educational level for enlisted applicants *reduced to high school diploma*

February   Minimum age for applicants lowered from twenty to nineteen
    April   Number of Aviation Cadet selection teams increased
            Minimum qualifying stanine score reduced to three

Another deficiency which the Air Force had difficulty addressing in the selection process was its lack of black pilots. When it integrated in 1949, 7.2 percent of the enlisted personnel were black, but the percentage of black officers was far lower: only 368 of 25,523, or 0.6 percent. In flight training, the numbers were equally low: only 11 of 1,356 (0.8 percent) Reserve Officer Training Corps (ROTC) student officers and 22 of 2,085 (1.1 percent) Aviation Cadets were black in 1949.[17]

These numbers did not improve much as educational standards were lowered for the program. By the end of 1952, blacks still represented only 1 percent of the Air Force officer corps.[18] Of the 93 cadets and student officers in pilot George Berke's class 53-E at Hondo AFB, only one student (an Aviation Cadet) was black and all the instructors were white; at Williams AFB, his basic school, 2 of the 106 students were black, as were 4 of 64 instructors.[19]

Clearly, the Air Force was not working hard enough to recruit blacks during this period. When it became a separate service in 1947, only 247 (0.4 percent) of its 49,529 officers were black.[20] By 1950, that number increased to 411, but black officers still represented only 0.6 percent of a total Air Force officer corps of 69,901.[21] In fact, black officers did not reach the 1 percent mark until 1953, and remained under 2 percent of the officer corps even as late as 1972.[22]

A 1948 study by the Industrial College of the Armed Forces (ICAF), entitled "Training and Utilization of Manpower," theorized that this racial disparity stemmed from the lower educational and health levels of blacks—factors it blamed on discrimination. It went on to argue that it was not the military's responsibility to promote racial justice: "Only as society changed could the military employ more blacks." Furthermore, "a division into white and Negro units was not the answer," nor was placing blacks in service and mess units.[23] In the end, the ICAF report recommended that nothing more should be done except additional studies.[24]

Although educational deficiencies may have barred blacks from many high-skill military jobs, pilot training should not have been greatly affected given that the stanine ranked academic achievement in its second-lowest category. A far more plausible reason for the deficiency is the Air Training Command's quota system. In a move designed to decrease racial tensions at its many southern training facilities during the 1949 Air Force integration, the ATC "on its own instituted a 10 percent quota to prevent bases from becoming overpopulated with blacks." The ATC attempted to further appease white civilian contractors and the white communities surrounding these bases by only sending them blacks of the "highest caliber" to "ease the shock of integration."[25] According to the ATC history: "A nucleus of high type, well trained and properly oriented Negro air-men would serve as a forerunner in establishing the confidence necessary to fa-cilitate increased assimilation of Negro personnel."[26]

Preflight

The basic curriculum of flight training changed little between the end of World War II and the Korean War. Aviation Cadets were given four weeks of "Pre-flight" officer training at Lackland AFB and then sent to one of ten "Primary" schools, where they were joined by ROTC and military academy graduates.[27] Primary lasted eighteen weeks and consisted of ground courses in basic naviga-tion and instruments plus 120 hours of elementary flying. After Primary, stu-dents attended an eighteen-week "Basic" course that consisted of jet transition for fighter pilots and two-engine transition for bomber pilots. Pilots were also introduced to the dangerous but crucial art of formation flying and given ad-vanced instruction in instruments and navigation. The final stage of prerated training was "Advanced," a twelve-week course that trained the pilot in his spe-cialty area—fighter tactics, gunnery, rocketry, bombing, and so forth.[28]

Of all these stages, Primary was the greatest hurdle: the pressures of learning to fly for the first time strained even the best students. Eighty-six percent of those who washed out in training did so in Primary.[29] "It was a common sight after a hard day of training to return to the barracks and find another cadet packing his bags," remembered Paul Turner. "It was murder."[30] Paradoxically, rather than assigning its top military instructors to these schools, the Air Force chose to staff nine out of ten with civilian contractors.[31] Originally, the contractor schools were set up during World War II as a means of conserving military pilots for war duty. However, when the Aviation Cadet program reopened in 1947, the Air Force reinstated many of these schools as a cost-cutting measure.[32] Hence, civil-ians not only became significant "gatekeepers" in the pilot training program, but also played a very important role in shaping the values and ideas of the young pilot. Not surprisingly, these values tended to relate more to the art of flying than to the profession of arms. A report written by the Air Training Command sum-marized the situation well:

> Contractors are too prone to emphasize the flying phase and minimize the im-portance of the others [i.e., the military and academic phases] to the extreme of being uncooperative and unsympathetic to the problems of the military and ac-ademic training organization. Many of these men do not actively support and respect the individual objectives of all of the phases of training [and] are not re-ally cognizant of their jobs at the Primary schools.[33]

As civilians, though, how could these men be expected to impart to cadets and student officers military values and officer skills? Most had neither the training nor the interest to accomplish such a mission. As professional pilots, their only concern was with flying and all that went with it.

Initially, the Air Force attempted to cope with the problem by setting up a Preflight program at Lackland AFB in 1949 for Aviation Cadets.[34] Actually, preflight training dates back to November 1940, when the Air Corps established four-week boot camps for pilot trainees at reception centers at Maxwell Field, Alabama; Kelly Field, Texas; and Santa Ana Field, California. These programs, however, were eliminated along with Aviation Cadets in 1946, and *did not* resume in 1947 when Aviation Cadets reopened. Apparently the Air Force, in its initial haste to build up its Cold War–rated force, did not consider military indoctrination to be a priority for pilots. It set up a "stopgap" four-week program in 1949 only after two separate panels recommended an extensive program.[35]

For the four-week Preflight program, the Aviation Cadet did not fly or even take classes on flying. Instead, he was processed into military life and taught all the basic military skills: "Drills, Ceremonies, and Inspection, Physical Training, and Effective Expression."[36] It was here that the cadet began to learn about the many rituals of military life. He was told to address his classmates not by their first names but by "Mister" followed by their last name. He also was instructed to maintain an impeccable appearance at all times or face demerits: shoes and buttons, for example, had to be shined before each breakfast formation. Finally, he was subjected to a host of stringent rules. The following are a sample:

- Cadets, upon leaving the barracks to go anywhere except to a scheduled formation or to meals, will sign the sign-out book with the exact time of departure and the exact time of return to the barracks, no matter where the destination.
- Cadets will not read or loiter in the latrines.
- Cadets will not proceed through the barracks in the nude or be in the latrine nude unless taking a shower.
- Cadets will not hang pictures on the walls, make any changes or additions to their rooms or barracks.
- Cadets will not create a disturbance or make unnecessary noise at any time.
- Cadets will not short-stop food being passed to another Aviation Cadet, without that Aviation Cadet's specific permission.[37]

The Aviation Cadet also had to adhere to a strict honor code. Under the code, anyone caught "cheating, stealing, or lying" was tried by the Honor Council, a collection of officers and generally at least one cadet. The code also stipulated that "anyone who withholds the knowledge of any honor code violations . . . will receive the same penalty as the person who actually committed the offense"—generally dismissal from the program.[38] The same honor code also applied to cadets and student officers in the Primary, Basic, and Advanced schools.[39]

Overall, the honor code, the other regulations, and the general military discipline of Preflight were supposed to "provide cadets with the fundamental knowledge required for their later development as Air Force officers," and "eliminate those students at once who were mentally, physically, or emotionally unsuited" to be Air Force officers.[40] In practice, Preflight training was too short to do either. Most of the pilots I spoke with either did not attend or did not remember this phase of the training. To a man, the pilots considered Primary to be the most memorable initiation experience. As Tomlinson pointed out, "It was where the rubber met the road."[41]

It was in Primary that cadets were first exposed to the discipline and hazing of "upperclassmen," a far more incorrigible group than the drill instructors at Preflight. More important, Primary blended the rigors of military initiation with those of flight initiation. In Primary, cadets and student officers learned all the basics of flight: how to take off, land, and fly simple maneuvers. It was there that they first discovered the joy and fear of flying.

Primary

The metaphor that Pomeroy used to describe the social composition of Primary is a three-cornered hat: on one corner were the military academy graduates, on the second, the ROTC officers, and, on the third, the Aviation Cadets. Flying officers (the ROTC and military academy graduates) represented about a third of the Primary class. They lived and ate separately from the Aviation Cadets, earned about $90 extra a month, were allowed to drink alcohol at the local officers' clubs, and were not "required to spend so much time in drills, ceremonies, and inspections as were the cadets."[42] Furthermore, if a student officer washed out, he would still be an officer, but if the same occurred for the Aviation Cadet, his Air Force career was essentially finished: before 1951, he would be discharged; after that date, he would be compelled to serve out his term as an enlisted man. Not surprisingly, the relationship between Aviation Cadets and student officers tended to be tense at first. However, as time went by and the men got to know each other, a more casual flight suit relationship developed. While on the flight line, military rank distinctions and discipline were minimized: saluting was forbidden and hazing was an absolute "no-no." As fellow students, Aviation Cadets and student officers needed all the support and camaraderie they could muster from one another; they could ill-afford to jeopardize the relationship with traditional military rigmarole. "You shared successes and failures," claims Pomeroy, "and after a while some cadets and officers even began referring to each other by their first names."[43] The fear, the challenges, and dangers of learning to fly, in the end, would enable these men to transcend distinctions in military status and become a unified band of brothers. Symbolizing this unity were the silver wings each man would receive at the end of Advanced training.[44]

In spite of the casual nature of the flight line, the Aviation Cadet still had to undergo a certain amount of traditional military initiation in Primary. Some of it consisted of drills and formations described in the Preflight section, but another part of it was the hazing they inevitably received from upper-class Aviation Cadets in the barracks and the mess halls. The most common form of hazing was the "brace," an exaggerated and highly uncomfortable form of attention that junior cadets were forced to assume for a long period of time. Crockett, a Tuskegee airman, remembers how upperclassmen would often turn on the lights in the middle of the night and brace the junior cadets or make them run in place. He also recalled how one upperclassman, Price D. Rice, "called him into his room and made him sit on an imaginary stool with his arms out against the wall, like wings, while he studied navigation." As Crockett's examples reveal, hazing was actually quite mild in Primary. In fact, the most pernicious form of hazing was the "square meal"—a practice whereby a cadet was forced to eat his meal at attention in a rigidly prescribed format. However, when it became so severe that cadets were unable to eat and were constantly seen rummaging for food during their spare time, ATC eliminated it in September 1950, along with excessive bracing.[45]

Perhaps more serious than standard hazing was the abuse some students received because of their religion, sexual preference, or race. "Nobody wanted to be ethnic in the military," claimed Berke, a Jewish American who even went to Christian chapel in an attempt to fit in. Nevertheless, he was still "made fun of a lot." Part of the problem was that as the senior student officer, Berke had to march other student officers, including some West Point and Annapolis men, to class, but he also believes that his religion was partly to blame. "The guys in my class set up a washout pool, and were betting that I would wash out first."[46]

Like religion, racial differences also could pose problems for the young cadet. At many of the contract fields in the South, blacks simply could not leave base because of fears of being attacked by the local white population. Tomlinson remembers that black pilots were told to stay on base at his civilian contractor school at Bainbridge, Georgia, because it was "cracker country" back then.[47] Crockett, for instance, never left the Tuskegee training base during his entire training period in the early 1940s.[48] Even as late as the 1960s, at nearby Maxwell AFB in Montgomery, Alabama, home of the Air Command and Staff School and the Air War College, black students were officially discouraged from socializing in white homes: "Students who still desired to entertain or study with Negro classmates were told to inform their neighbors that a fellow student, a

Negro, was coming to call, and were advised to be sure that whites knew just who he is and why he is coming."[49] Abuse, incidentally, was not confined to the off base activities of black trainees. At Tuskegee, Crockett remembers one civilian instructor who would not pass a single black student for six months. White instructors at Tuskegee also refused to eat in the same dining room with blacks.[50] Even after integration in 1949, there were still noncommissioned officers' clubs, officers' clubs, and other facilities where blacks were not welcome.[51] According to historian Alan Gropman, "The practice was introduced to establish branch clubs on the same base and it was tacitly understood that one club was for whites and the other for blacks. Such arrangements have persisted to 1985.[52]

Although students of different racial and religious backgrounds often suffered from various forms of harassment while on and off base, their presence in training was officially tolerated—but such was not the case for gay men. Homosexuality was banned by the Uniform Code of Military Conduct, but enforcement was not always standard or uniform. When a gay man made an advance to another cadet in Turner's class, vigilante justice prevailed: cadets forcefully removed the suspected gay man from the barracks in the middle of the night while he was sleeping. The cadets were never punished for their behavior and the gay man was quietly kicked out of the program.[53]

Hazing and other forms of emotional and psychological harassment could indeed be excessive in certain cases, but for most pilots, it was a minor aspect of the overall training experience. If one could survive the rigors of flight training, one could certainly endure a bit of hazing and military discipline. In fact, as Berke recalls: "You simply didn't have time to worry about that kind of stuff. In training, you were always under the gun, and there was always an instructor in the flight. You were interested in mechanical types of things, and you were always being evaluated on that. They didn't teach you management or officer skills, they were only interested in turning out cannon fodder for the war."[54]

The basic trainer in Primary was the North American AT-6 Texan, "a single-engine, propeller-driven, two-place trainer" with a top speed of 210 mph.[55] When Tomlinson first sat in the cockpit, what struck him was how many dials and switches there were in this "relatively simple aircraft." He did not have too much time to think about it because his instructor then got in the back seat, and the next thing he knew he was up in the air. "Gee, this is absolutely marvelous," he recalled. "This is the funnest thing I've ever done in my life. I always thought it was gonna be fun, and you bet, it was fun."[56] For others, like Earl Brown, flying took some getting used to:

> After looking forward to my first flight for so long, I was devastated when I got airsick. Fortunately, we had been warned by the upperclassmen, so I had an

empty potato chip bag in my pocket into which I deposited my breakfast. After the second time I got sick, my instructor pilot (IP) said, "Brown, it's that damn bag you carry. You expect to get sick and so you do. Leave that bag behind and you won't get sick." So I left the bag behind and on the next flight, I had to throw up in my hat.[57]

Brown, in the end, conquered his sickness problem and became a very proficient fighter pilot, but he was fortunate to have had a sympathetic instructor, an Air Force officer named Philip Plotkin. Captain Plotkin volunteered to take four of the six black pilots in class 51-H because he was "a little guy and had some idea what these guys were going through." Despite Plotkin's best efforts, though, Brown was the only black pilot to graduate in class 51-H.[58]

Although many pilots had fond memories of their instructors, not all did. For Berke, "The instructor was not your friend: every ride was a check ride, and they were trying to wash you out the entire time." Pomeroy's second instructor was an extremely overbearing person who would yell at a cadet over the intercom for the entire flying lesson: "If you did something right, it was just luck." This instructor washed out five students, and Pomeroy claims he would have been one of them if it had not been for West Point: "You had to have rocks in your head to enjoy the academy, but it did give you an emotional reserve and teach you how to let verbal abuse roll off your back!"[59] On one memorable training flight, Pomeroy was placed under a hood and told to fly with instruments only, a standard but very stressful exercise. As the flight progressed, his instructor got increasingly riled at him over a series of small errors, and in the end the instructor forgot to put down the landing gear, forcing Pomeroy to make an unplanned belly landing. Fortunately, this incident was an instructor error, and Pomeroy was not washed out. In retrospect, recalled Pomeroy, it was "a nice learning experience."[60] Pomeroy was lucky, but others were often not.

Because the Air Force wanted to eliminate people early to save time and money, it granted its Primary instructors tremendous latitude to wash out candidates. In 1952, for instance, the Training Command planned to wash out a total of 29 percent of the pilots, 25 percent in Primary. In the end, it washed out 36.5 percent, 30.8 percent in Primary.[61] Given the candidate shortages for aviation training, washing out large numbers of cadets appears to be a somewhat contradictory policy. The "washout," however, was a fundamental barrier to entry into the rated Air Force and very much a part of the practical Social Darwinism that defined pilot training.

The majority (approximately 57 percent) of all washouts in Primary were for flying deficiencies. Only an average of 1.5 percent washed out for academic reasons, and it was believed that these pilots failed the ridiculously simple academic tests on purpose.[62] Inevitably, flying proved to be the greatest hurdle. But flying was also the hardest skill to judge—evaluation standards tended to be capricious at best and arbitrary at worst.[63] Instructors could fail a pilot for everything from very straightforward criteria like not knowing procedures to very subjective ones such as "how well you control the aircraft or the aircraft controls you."[64] Gaining the proper "feel" for the aircraft made all the difference, as one cadet explained:

> As the plane climbed, he [the instructor] explained about coordinating rudder and aileron pressures in turns, about the "feel" of the airplane, about how too much rudder without aileron control made the airplane skid to the outside of the turn and too much aileron control without rudder made it slip to the inside. Demonstrating, he told me how to feel it in the seat of my pants when we slipped or skidded, and to note how the wind came through the side of the cockpit when a turn was uncoordinated. Hanging on grimly, with increasing queasiness, I tried to feel what I should.[65]

During the first phase of the eighteen-week Primary program, a pilot learned how to "shoot" normal and forced landings, how to turn, and how to recover from stalls and spins. In the second phase, he learned figure eights and "chandelles, or abrupt climbing turns."[66] The third phase, or "accuracy phase," emphasized precision, power on, power off, and short-field landings, and the last phase, "the diversified stage," stressed "loops, turns, and rolls."[67] The flying curriculum was forever being refined by the Training Command headquarters in Waco, Texas, but no matter how much headquarters attempted to micromanage the course, it was the individual instructor in the end who had the most control over standards. He was the one who decided whether your performance on various maneuvers was "above average, average, below average, or failing."[68] These grades, in turn, went into a folder that followed a pilot for his entire career, and, in many cases, determined his entire future as an Air Force officer. According to Tomlinson, "If in later life you decide you want to fly such and such a plane, they go back and look at your basic grades to see if you had trouble with any of the characteristics deemed necessary for that plane."[69]

Getting a bad grade was one thing, but a "washout" was tantamount to complete and utter failure. As one airman put it, "It sounded as though you turned colorless and just faded away, like a guilty spirit." Another explained the process in Social Darwinist terms: "If you were a flier, you passed; if you weren't, you washed out—fell out of the air, and became a lower order of being."[70] Pomeroy remembers vividly the day when one of the cadets in his group of four washed out: "When he got out of the cockpit that day, he looked completely beaten." Like a pariah, anyone washed out was immediately isolated from the group and transferred to another base.[71] Berke explained that "if you could fly, we accepted you, and if you couldn't, out!!! We didn't want you around."

Clearly, washing out was an emasculation of sorts, but who tended to wash out? Tomlinson speculated that some "either couldn't hack it or found that they didn't really have that initial desire."[72] A World War II pilot divided washouts into two groups: "First, there were those who had previous civilian flight training, who evidently had trouble flying the Army way." The second group were the ROTC and West Point graduates who "did not seem as motivated as were Aviation Cadets."[73] Berke, who fell squarely into the first group, in some respects fits this former characterization. "Everything to me was unfair and chicken shit; I considered myself a superior pilot from the word go, and as far as the niceties went, I let it all slide." Slide or not, Berke not only made it through the program, but graduated second in his class. If anything, prior flying experience appeared to improve a cadet's chances of making it through the program. However, when the Air Force set up a course in light plane training in late 1952 to provide cadets with some flying experience before Primary, attrition rates still hovered around 38.4 percent, a much higher figure than the planned 29 percent. The Air Force, in the end, blamed the continued high attrition on the lower stanine score of its applicants.[74]

A better example of a group that may have benefited from prior flight training was service academy graduates. An Air Training Command analysis of class 53-E found that while 149 out of 773 Aviation Cadets (19.3 percent) were eliminated, only 9 out of 109 Naval Academy students (8.3 percent), and 13 out of 111 West Pointer cadets (11.7 percent) washed out.[75] Pomeroy, who bitterly rejected the contention that West Point graduates were not as motivated as Aviation Cadets, claimed that service academy graduates performed better because they had already "been through a pressure-filled indoctrination."[76] When other officer groups accustomed to military life are examined, however, Pomeroy's argument appears specious. The same study of 53-E found that 23.5 percent (19 out of 81) of ROTC and Officer Candidate School officers in the class washed out, compared to 19.3 percent of the Aviation Cadets.[77] A more plausible explanation for the better performance of the academy types was the flying indoctrination program that all Air Force–bound West Point and Naval Academy cadets attended during the summer of their junior year. During this introductory course, cadets not only received academic instruction on flying but also were given actual flying time on T-6 and T-33 (jet) aircraft.[78] Pomeroy received ten hours of T-6 training during his tour and even dropped dummy bombs from an AT-8 into the Quaban Reservoir—Massachusetts's chief freshwater source![79]

All other factors being equal, additional flight training may have marginally improved some pilots' chances of graduating from Primary, but in the end, as the Air Force's experience with the stanine test suggests, one's ability to succeed, more than any other factors, rested on individual motor skills and a capacity to cope with the stress of flying. The stress of flying, in particular, was a rude awakening for many a young Aviation Cadet. Occasionally, those who began to fear climbing into the cockpit would approach their commanders and declare "lack of motivation" as their reason for resigning. Paul Turner's brother washed himself out in just such a manner. One day, he simply went to the base commander and told him: "I don't enjoy going down to the flight line, and I don't enjoy flying planes." More often, though, flying anxiety manifested itself in a rather bizarre condition known as fear of flying, or FOF. Air Training Command analyses of classes 52-E, F, and G reveals that an average of 7.5 percent of those eliminated were washed out due to FOF. More significantly, these same studies reveal that FOF was the third greatest cause of eliminations after flying deficiencies and physical deficiencies.[80]

FOF was not a new psychological condition in the 1950s; in fact, documented cases can be found as early as World War I. H. G. Anderson, a World War I Royal Air Force flight surgeon, was one of the first physicians to study the phenomenon extensively. He defined FOF, or "aeroneurosis" as he labeled it, as "unhappiness in the air, introspection, and morbid thoughts." Aeroneurosis, he claimed, could be caused by the stress of flight training, the shock of an aviation accident, or the anxiety of combat flying. Through his experiences in treating patients at a British flight training center, he concluded that "experienced pilots were the most likely to overcome aeroneurosis."[81]

During World War II, more investigations of FOF were undertaken, but general definitions remained vague. Douglas D. Bond, a psychiatrist with the Eighth Air Force in Europe, posited that FOF patients fell into three distinct groups:

> (1) fliers with childhood predispositions to phobic behavior that resulted from unresolved oedipal conflicts—their phobic symptoms grew and (if untreated) eventually rendered them unable to perform their duties; (2) fliers who exhibited a more restricted phobic pattern—noting that one could find a neurotic pattern in anyone if one looked deeply enough, he said the reluctance of his second group to fly was precipitated by more personal and intense circumstances than the first group; and (3) fliers who were simply physically exhausted, and treatable with a week's rest.[82]

P. F. Eggerston, disputing Bond's claims about unresolved oedipal conflicts, argued that FOF related to a propensity for suicide in pilots, or a "suicidal dynamic."[83] Finally, R. R. Grinker and J. P. Spiegel, two doctors who worked with AAF fliers during the North African campaign, described the phenomenon as "the anticipation of danger, experienced by the ego, which led the flier to behave as if formerly experienced dangers were present." They also drew a distinction between pilots suffering from simple exhaustion and those suffering from the FOF neurosis.[84]

During the Korean War, Dr. Lucio Gatto conducted what would become a widely cited study of FOF. He identified two forms of FOF: "Basic Universal," and "Fear of Flying Syndrome." Basic Universal FOF, he believed, was the "inherent fear of being maimed, mutilated, or killed by falling through space and hitting the ground with great force." By comparison, FOF Syndrome was "a complex reaction occurring among previously adjusted flying personnel, and characterized by various defensive and maladaptive behavioral processes which express anxiety over various external and internal conflicts, frustrations, insecurities, and dangers."[85] FOF Syndrome, in other words, was a form of anxiety that manifested itself as FOF but was not necessarily linked to any particular aspect of it. Flyers who developed FOF later on in their careers generally suffered from FOF Syndrome, whereas those who developed FOF during their first training flights in all likelihood suffered from Basic Universal FOF.

While Gatto's definition of FOF is somewhat vague, his understanding of FOF's symptoms is much clearer.[86] They included sleeplessness, nervousness, agitation, somatic complaints, nightmares, passive and or aggressive reactions, claustrophobia, alcoholism, and phobic responses to planes.[87] In short, they included symptoms that directly interfered with a pilot's ability to operate aircraft. The Air Force hierarchy, however, tended to treat FOF as a personnel problem rather than a medical condition.[88]

At the beginning of the war, officers or those who expressed a fear of flying were immediately grounded and compelled to face a review board, consisting of their squadron commander, their base commander, and other officers at their local base or training facility. Although a discharge from flying duties was practically guaranteed, the board, to discourage others from using FOF as a means to avoid flying, would subject the officer to a series of humiliating questions relating to the individual's patriotism and self-worth before reassigning him to a nonrated job.[89]

In order to ensure impartiality, decisions of local boards were then reviewed "all the way up the chain of command with the final decision made by Headquarters, USAF. "Higher officers tended to be even less sympathetic than the local boards. SAC commander Curtis LeMay's reaction to FOF, in many respects, typified the attitude of the Air Force leadership. He had no use for pilots who could not "cut the mustard," and believed anyone professing FOF was a "contaminating influence" who should immediately be court-martialed and dismissed from the service.[90] Air Force Chief of Staff Hoyt Vandenberg similarly favored some form of punishment, and believed that FOF represented a desertion from a "sworn duty." Vandenberg's views began to soften somewhat as more and more experienced pilots, including combat veterans, began to complain of FOF. It was one thing to court-martial Aviation Cadets but quite another to try an officer who had already served his country honorably in a war.[91]

When Vandenberg finally issued a policy directive in April 1952, he rejected LeMay's draconian suggestions and opted instead for a new two-category FOF policy. A flier declaring FOF would receive a medical examination, and "if diagnosed as having a psychoneurosis that manifested itself as FOF, he would be treated as a patient, grounded, and given proper psychiatric care."[92] Interestingly, the treatment would focus on specific symptoms of FOF because the policy did not recognize FOF as a medical condition.[93]

By contrast, if a flight surgeon found that the flier did not have a "disabling psychoneurosis," the entire matter would be handled administratively. Trainees and pilots with less than ten years of service were automatically given a general discharge "for the convenience of the government": a "general" discharge was "neither honorable or dishonorable."[94] For those with more than ten years of service, exceptions to this discharge policy could be made, but "only in unusual instances and where the individual possessed a critically needed non-rated skill."[95]

It is hard to know the exact number of trainees who opted out of flying by professing FOF. What is clear is that, between June 1950 and November 1952, over 880 cases were reported.[96] Of this number, only a small group of 134 lieutenants and captains was thoroughly analyzed by the Air Training Command. One hundred and thirty-one were recalled reservists, three were regulars, and none were "green" Aviation Cadets. Most of the men (101) were "observers undergoing training for assignments to the Strategic Air Command and crew duties in the B-29," and at least eighty-one had flown combat missions in World War II. Finally, a majority had wives and children.[97] Clearly, these veteran airmen understood war and its many dangers. As Vance Mitchell writes in *Personnel Policy History of the Air Force Officer Corps, 1944–1974,* "Now older, more settled, and faced with the prospect of combat in an unpopular war, they had neither the emotional reserves nor the will to face again the threat of violent death."[98] Gatto, similarly, discovered that about 50 percent of the FOF patients he treated in Korea were World War II veterans, and most "were married men with definite home responsibilities."[99] His belief was that these men felt a degree of conflict over their combat duties and were therefore highly susceptible to stress reactions.[100]

Despite the considerable numbers of cases of FOF in Primary and Basic training (approximately twenty-one per class in 1952), however, neither Gatto nor the ATC attempted systematically to analyze FOF cases at this level.[101] Part of the problem, according to a 1952 ATC Conference report, was that flight surgeons found "it hard to evaluate fear of flying at this stage of the game, particularly if the individual has never flown before." Another problem was that the ATC believed that FOF was simply a "made-to-order" excuse for men wishing to reduce their tour from four years to two. Finally, Aviation Cadets and student officers could resign from aviation training at any point in their program with very few questions asked; consequently, the Air Force was not compelled to investigate or review them in a systematic way—they were simply cast out into a nonrated or an enlisted job and forgotten about.[102] In all likelihood, therefore, the number of FOF cases in training was larger than ATC records suggest. However, insufficient follow-up investigation makes it difficult to characterize the type of individual who might have been particularly susceptible.[103]

What we do know is that FOF is the clearest manifestation of the stress from which every cadet and student officer suffered. Primary's emphasis on solo flying guaranteed that each aviation student, at some point, would have to confront all of his innermost fears and insecurities. Alone in a small airplane, he would have to take off, land, and perform a myriad of technical functions, all without losing his nerve—one small mistake could result in washout or even death. Not surprisingly, many men did not make it: Turner's brother "didn't see flying as worth the risk." Another friend of Turner's took drugs to help him get through, but eventually smashed his aircraft into a mountain at Nellis AFB. Those pilot trainees who did make it, however, could loosen up a bit and begin to assume the swaggering ways of a USAF pilot. After all, they had conquered the discipline of Primary, its host of often hostile instructors, and, most important, flying itself. Although silver wings were for the future, the Primary graduate knew in his heart he could fly an airplane.

Basic

In one respect, Basic was very similar to Primary: fundamental flying maneuvers and techniques were still emphasized. However, Basic differed in several significant respects. First, the elimination rate dropped precipitously. The average attrition rate for class 52-E, F, G, and H in Primary was 26.75 percent, but in Basic, it was only 8.08 percent. Similarly, 27.5 percent of classes 53-A, B, C, and D washed out in Primary, compared to only 11.38 percent in Basic.[104] Second, the accident rate increased: during the first six months of 1952, seven pilots were killed in Primary, compared to thirty-two in Basic.[105] Very few pilots went through Basic without seeing at least one colleague killed. It was a place where young men just beginning to cope with the exhilaration of flying began to understand its many dangers.

At the heart of the "accident problem" were the jet aircraft. For most of these pilots, Basic was their first initiation to jets. Although some pilots destined for the Korean War attended multiengine Basic schools to learn the rudiments of bomber flying, the majority attended jet transition Basic schools. In September 1952, for instance, the Air Force had 2,392 students enrolled in jet transition schools, and only 987 in multiengine schools.[106] The difficulty with jets in the 1950s was that they were neither easy to fly nor particularly safe. For the young student aviator, they were also alien. "Prop planes," remembered Berke, "had all the good smells and were familiar . . . [but] jets were uncomfortable, and smelled lousy." They were also famous for killing pilots who did not pay close attention to what they were doing.[107]

The aircraft used in the transition of students from propeller-driven planes to jets was the Lockheed T-33, a two-seat version of the Lockheed F-80 Shooting Star (famous for killing six test pilots, including America's number-one World War II ace, Richard Bong).[108] The T-33, or T-Bird as it was called, was powered by a General Motors Allison engine and could fly 600 miles per hour, about 150 miles per hour faster than top-rated prop planes like the F-51.[109] Besides being somewhat unstable in level flight, the T-33 could not fly straight up and had an extremely tricky throttle. Unlike a T-6 or an F-51, where one could "move the throttle rapidly from idle to full power" and get a decent response, recalls Brown, "this engine had to be carefully and *slowly* coaxed to full-power level, [and] if the pilot advanced the throttle too quickly, the sudden addition of fuel would cause the engine temperature to rise above limits" and explode.[110] Sudden throttle movement, in flight, could also cause a compressor stall—a dangerous situation which often required the pilot to bail out if he could not restart the engine or if he was simply too close to the ground. Brown described the "bailout" as follows:

> [The bailout] presented the pilot with an array of possibilities. Ejection seats were a necessary feature because the speeds at which jets flew made manual bailouts *extremely* risky. Ejection seat bailouts were only . . . risky. For taller pilots, ejection raised the hazard of knees hitting on the windshield rail while leaving the plane, which would really smart. Pilots could wear two types of parachutes in the T-33; either the back pack, which fit between the pilot's back and the back of the seat, or the seat pack, on which the pilot would sit, leaving more room to push back in the seat. The length of the pilot's thigh was measured, and if it went beyond a certain length, he had to wear the seat pack. This gave him a few extra inches to keep them from striking his knees as he ejected. But in the early days, I never knew a fighter pilot to turn down a chance to fly simply because the right parachute was not available. Some guys were so big that even with the seat chute, there was no room for a safe ejection.[111]

In addition to confronting the T-33's mechanical idiosyncrasies, a student flying it for the first time also had to adjust to much higher G forces than in the T-6. Six Gs were routine in combat maneuvers—a state that made "your ten-pound head weigh sixty pounds."[112] Pilots had to wear inflatable G suits to prevent "blood from pooling in the lower part of the body and make it easier for your heart to work."[113] Nevertheless, a pilot unaccustomed to the strain of constant Gs could easily lose his orientation in the air, as did one of Brown's classmates. It was toward the end of the day and the sun was visible at altitude, but not at ground level. In an effort to conserve fuel, Brown's flight was letting down at a horrendously fast rate. Everyone was becoming disoriented from the G forces and changing light conditions, but one pilot became so disoriented that he flew his plane right into the ground. According to Brown, "This put a damper on things for a while, but we were soon back at training with added motivation to learn all we could to prevent something like this from happening to us."[114] The Air Force did not give pilots an opportunity to grieve: "You were thrown from one lesson to the next without much reflection, and never given time to work out problems."[115]

Partly responsible for the frenetic state of affairs that Brown describes were the instructors. Basic instructors insisted on pushing students to their limits. "The whole philosophy of flight school was sink or swim," recalled Turner. "They threw you into the melee without much instruction."[116] Berke, who lost 4 of his class of 106, could not believe how instructors could demand tight patterns for landing—a practice that enabled them to see students better but also "increased the possibility of a low-altitude stall."[117] Instructors also insisted on very tight formations—a difficult skill to acquire for the novice flyer, as Charles Watry described in his World War II aviation training memoir:

> Beginners in formation flying always over control, fighting to hold the proper formation position with wild bursts of power, followed by sudden frantic yanking the throttles rearward when it appears that the wing of the lead plane is about to be chewed up by the propeller of the airplanes flying the wing position. Beginners also try to hold lateral position using only rudders. The airplane is likely to wallow through the air like a goose waddling to its pond.[118]

Although not in a jet at the time, Crockett's first accident occurred in just such a manner. He was flying close formation on a final approach in P-39s and getting closer and closer until a classmate named Othel Dixon reported that Crockett's prop was coming into his cockpit.[119] Crockett immediately "dumped the stick forward, broke off his vertical fin underneath" Dixon's airplane, and sliced Dixon's wingtip off. Both pilots survived, with Dixon receiving a mild cut above his right eye.[120] Crockett and Dixon were lucky, but other pilots were not; in fact, midair collisions during formation flights and traffic patterns were the most common form of training accidents.[121] Accidents during takeoffs and landings were also common. One of Berke's worst training memories was trying desperately to get a classmate out of a plane that crashed during a takeoff, being overcome by the heat and fumes, and finally watching his friend burn up.[122] Painful experiences like these tested even the strongest, but they also bonded and unified the men.

A good example of this bonding was the warm relationships the pilots developed with foreign students. The Air Force Training Command trained students from a number of allied countries, including Belgium, the Netherlands,

Denmark, France, Italy, and Thailand. Class 52-E, for example, had 188 foreign students out of a total of 745.[123] George Berke's section of 53-E at Williams had 21 foreign students out of a total of 108 students.[124]

Earl Brown formed a lasting friendship with his roommate in Basic, a French Air Force Academy cadet named Pierre Claude. Later in their careers, the two would serve side by side in Europe: Brown as the NATO Air Commander in the Mediterranean, and Pierre Claude as commander of the French Air Forces in southeastern France.[125] Although Paul Turner did not bunk with a foreign student, he "befriended them because they were a lot of fun." Turner even invited a Danish cadet to spend Christmas with his family after the Danish student washed out: "He was in my group," declared Paul, "and I felt responsible for him."[126] Student solidarity, in short, could even transcend differences of nationality.

Language differences, by contrast, were more difficult to bridge. The instructor pilots tried to speak in short sentences to facilitate communication, but that did not always help. One day during Brown's training, a French student forgot to perform a standard T-6 test known as the GUMP check:

- Gas: to the fullest tank
- Undercarriage: down
- Mixture: full rich
- Prop: full forward

Well, the instructor yelled "GUMP" several times over the radio net to remind him, and the French student bailed out.[127]

Despite language barriers, there is very little evidence suggesting that foreigners were more likely to wash out than cadets. In fact, an analysis of class 52-E by the ATC even suggests that, as a group, foreigners performed better than Aviation Cadets. In all, 32.2 percent of the allied students washed out in Primary and Basic, compared to 41.2 percent of the Aviation Cadets.[128]

At the conclusion of Basic, Aviation Cadets received their commissions as second lieutenants, but the trials of training did not end there. Future pilots still had to endure another twelve grueling weeks of Advanced before they were fully certified as Air Force pilots and could wear the coveted silver wings. Top-ranked students went on to Nellis to learn to fly and fight in the top-of-the-line F-86 Sabre fighter-interceptor; others went to Luke AFB, near Phoenix, Arizona, to become F-84 fighter-bomber pilots, and the rest went to bases such as Wichita Municipal Airport to become bomber pilots.

Advanced

Each dawn Nellis AFB, Nev., comes to life with a roar—the roar of jets taking off for the first day's many scheduled missions. In nearby Las Vegas, many a red-eyed

gambler is still pressing his luck at a gaming table. But at Nellis the men jockeying the F-80s or the F-86s are clear-eyed, aggressive, and alert. They have less need for artificial stimulus to lighten their lives.[129]
  —Everett Dodd, "The Tale of 'Tiger'"

Air Force Magazine and other popular aviation journals glorified the Nellis training program in advanced fighter tactics. Nellis gave pilots an unprecedented opportunity to practice aerial tactics with actual "aggressor" aircraft: a tremendously costly and dangerous method of training, but one which gave U.S. fighter pilots a clear advantage in dogfights over MiG Alley in Korea. "Although the F-86 was a splendid fighter," writes Air Force historian Wayne Thompson, "its overwhelming success against the MiG in Korea resulted in large measure from its superior pilots."[130] Nellis, however, was not the only Advanced training program, nor was it the only one where pilots confronted realistic and dangerous training conditions. At the Luke AFB Advanced Gunnery school, pilots also lost their lives on a regular basis practicing dive-bombing and other tactics in the F-84. Overall, jets like the F-86 and the F-84 were complicated planes that required a great deal of practice to fly properly. Unfortunately for the novice trainees, Advanced did not give them much time to get acquainted with new aircraft; instead, it emphasized the advanced aerial techniques a pilot needed to know in order to perform his given role in combat. In short, Advanced, although part of the basic training cycle, was more of a graduate program for the various flying disciplines than a course in fundamentals. The only thing the various Advanced schools had in common was their flight suit orientation, aggressive pace, and hazardous nature.

When George Berke got to Luke, for example, he received no instruction on the Republic F-84: he was simply told to get in the airplane and fly it. The F-84, like the T-33, was a temperamental and underpowered aircraft. The 586-mile-per-hour plane was designed to be a fighter-interceptor, but because of its slow speed relative to the MiG 15, it ended up being used primarily as a fighter-bomber. Pilots had to "carefully calculate the temperature, barometric pressure, and length of the runway before flying," and on hot days, no planes could take off.[131] Nevertheless, many pilots failed to follow the directions and crashed as a result. Students also had trouble dive-bombing with it. In dive-bombing practice, you would line up a certain target on the ground with your gun sight and when they matched, you would "pickle off your bombs." But if you got distracted, the target would never line up, and you could end up flying your plane into the ground, still trying to line up your target—a situation known as target fixation.[132] Despite these risks and dangers, Berke fell in love with the plane after his first takeoff. Unlike the conditionally stable T-33, "the F-84 felt like a stable rock—it was a real fighter."

Like the F-84, the F-86 was also a complicated plane to fly, but certainly not underpowered like the F-84. The fastest models could fly over 712 miles per hour.[133] The F-86 also had many unique features that pilots appreciated, such as a large bubble canopy for enhanced visibility, and a movable horizontal stabilizer for improved control at high speeds (a first for a production-line aircraft).[134]

At Nellis, F-86 pilots spent most of their time practicing the combat formation known as "fluid four" or "finger four." During the Korean War, it was discovered that four was the optimum number for a combat formation of high-speed jet fighters. Formations greater than four tended to get separated too easily in combat, and smaller formations were not as mutually protective. In a flight of four, the flight leader was the shooter, and all other planes protected him and acted as additional eyes.[135] Although the leader of the second pair was allowed to shoot if for some reason the formation split up, the two wingmen were never supposed to shoot, and the wingmen never left the shooters.[136] This is one reason why only 4.8 percent of the Sabre pilots accounted for over 38 percent of the kills in Korea.[137]

As pilots transitioned to faster and more sophisticated aircraft, not only did their flying skills improve but so did their self-esteem. Without the constant fear of being washed out, pilots in Advanced could begin to assume the swagger of the Air Force pilot. By the time Turner got to Advanced, he believed he was as good a pilot as many of the instructors: "People just didn't seem to realize that there were different ways of flying this airplane [the F-86]." Tomlinson, likewise, thought he was entering an elite club: "Everybody that wanted to fly a fighter wanted to fly the hottest, fastest, best thing, and that was the F-86 at that time. And we had a number of people that, uh, did get sent to F-84s, and F-80s, but they were trash haulers, you know, I mean we were the elite. We were the creme de la creme. Everybody wanted to be a jet pilot. I mean you go to the bar downtown in Las Vegas, you know. . . ."[138] At Advanced, pilots not only had enough liberty time to explore local social venues, but were also generally stationed in cities such as Las Vegas and Phoenix, which were very "accommodating." "Chasing women," declared Berke, "was one of the things you did as a fighter pilot—it was part of the cache [sic] and mark of things."[139] According to Tomlinson, "All the girls wanted the jet pilots, absolutely!"[140] But what kind of girls did pilots want? A 1950 article, entitled "Sarge Looks at Today's Cadet," in the Air Force Times attempted to answer this question:

> He's 22 years old, and pretty well set on what he expects of a girl. Brunettes with light blue eyes and healthy tans have a slight edge, but physical characteristics are not so important to him as, first, a sense of humor, and second, the ability to mix well. . . . One characteristic of the pilot of yesteryear he will retain—he's

something special. Something unique—and he wants his date to match him. He wants to have her have, for him, something no one else has or could have, and he wants to be proud—even a little vain—of her. That's not too much to expect for a young man with worlds to conquer, is it?[141]

As the popular Air Force literature suggests, not only did training constantly stress "aggressiveness and confidence," it also made these men feel special by smothering them with arresting, masculine compliments. Adjectives used to describe them in *Air Force Magazine* and the *Air Force Times* included "unique," "special," "different," and "hard living."[142] They also were told that they were "conquerors of new worlds"; the "thin blue line that stands between worldwide tyranny and freedom"; and "the answers to the dark hints that America's youth isn't fulfilling its obligations, that youths are afraid to fly."[143] Not surprisingly, men such as Tomlinson who considered themselves shy before becoming pilots emerged from training as the men "all the girls wanted."[144] After all, if they could overcome fear of flying and "conquer" the air, they could certainly conquer the American woman.

This flight suit cockiness that training produced did have a downside as far as the Air Force was concerned: it did not necessarily serve these men well in their role as professional officers in the U.S. Armed Forces. In 1952, the Air Force Training Command, after conducting a series of base inspections, interviews with students, and reviews of reports by elimination boards, concluded that the average student in the training program was "not properly motivated" and "not willing to accept his full responsibility as an officer, leader, and a fighter."[145] The investigation also found that more than 75 percent of Primary graduates wanted to be assigned to propeller-driven aircraft rather than jets.[146]

To counteract this trend, the Air Force implemented a program called Project Tiger. Starting at Nellis in early 1953 and later spreading to thirty-six other training bases, Tiger attempted to instill students with officer skills by "emphasizing crew, weapon, and firepower philosophy" at every stage of recruitment and training.[147] Old recruitment posters luring cadets with promises of golf and swimming in the afternoon were replaced with ones featuring jet fighters and the caption: "Can you take it?"[148] Preflight was extended from four weeks to three months and more emphasis was placed on "leadership and discipline, the development of a competitive spirit, and publicity of outstanding combat and training accomplishments."[149] Throughout all phases of training, students were constantly "steeped in Air Force lore, history, and customs": a bit of a paradox given that the Air Force was only six years old at the time.[150] Other measures included improving instructor quality, indoctrinating Primary instructors in jet aircraft operation, giving all pilots in Primary a "9-hour review in which single-engine jet training was emphasized," and building "esprit de corps and competitive spirit" through the following:

- Flight rooms were converted into "war rooms."
- Student flights were assigned areas in the dining hall as a unit.
- Student quarters were assigned according to flight.
- Academic subjects were attended by flight units.
- Distinctive insignia was developed and publicized.[151]

Finally, Advanced courses were staffed with as many Korean War veteran pilots and aces as possible.[152]

Although Tiger might have appealed to men such as SAC commander Curtis LeMay or General Jack D. Ripper, the fictional general in Stanley Kubrick's *Doctor Strangelove,* the program ended up being more hot air than substance. Instructors reacted to the program by placing more pressure on students to perform in-flight maneuvers and making training more of a "sink or swim routine."[153] More aggression and competition in training, in turn, did little to turn students into better officers. If anything, Project Tiger encouraged them to embrace the cocky pilot persona even more. Berke, who graduated from a Tiger program at Luke, sums it up well: training produced an "Air Force full of fighter pilots who were absolute guerrillas when it came to anything else and whose careers ended in disgrace."[154]

When the student pilot finally graduated from Advanced training, he gained more than the title of Air Force "pilot," he gained immeasurable status as well. Only he had the "rated" title; all other officers were "nonrated," in other words, insignificant. Symbolizing his new status were the silver wings he received on graduation. He would wear these wings on every uniform for the rest of his career, including his shirts and flight suits. Furthermore, as the pilot advanced in the Air Force, these wings, like badges of rank, would change. After seven years, a "senior pilot" star would be affixed to the top of the wings. Eight years later, a "command pilot" wreath would encircle that star. Command, in short, was directly linked to piloting: only pilots could have the prefix, "command," in their official titles because only they could control operational units such as squadrons, wings, and groups.[155] Navigators with fifteen years of experience, by comparison, were called "master navigators." So important were wings that if you walk into the home of any former Air Force pilot (as I have done on numerous occasions) and ask to see his first set of wings, inevitably he will produce them for you. Sometimes they will be framed in the den, sometimes mounted on a desk, but, more often than not, they will be hidden away in a top desk drawer where they can be easily accessed but never lost.

With wings, a pilot also acquired a collection of attitudes, ideas, and values that made him different from other types of officers. Unlike Peter Karsten's "naval aristocrat," the Air Force pilot did not enter a "social" elite on being rated. Military ancestry and institutional traditions were irrelevant to him; instead, elitism in the Air Force was defined by skill, courage, and plane type. If one could overcome the various barriers to becoming a pilot—washouts, accidents, fear, death—one could define oneself as elite, and be a part of the team. Within the Air Force flying elite, the degree of one's elitism then depended on the plane one flew: F-86 pilots were the most elite, followed by F-84s, F-80s, F-51s, B-26s, and so forth.

Unlike Samuel Huntington's or Morris Janowitz's "professional soldier," training also did not create an anti-individualistic, "corporate spirit," or an "organization man" in uniform; instead, it brought out the reverse. Bureaucratic concerns had little meaning for a pilot struggling to master the complexities, dangers, and fears associated with flight. That civilians played an integral role in the training process did not help matters, nor did the egalitarianism of the flight line. Like his flight suit (a jump suit with lots of zippers and pockets but few military markings of any kind), the pilot graduating from training was specialized, informal, and thoroughly functional. Military regimentation and institutional concerns had little meaning. Yes, he had to discipline himself while in the air, but while on the ground, he could let things slide a bit and assume a more casual demeanor. Training had taught him that he would "sink or swim" based on his ability to fly, and that life outside the flight suit was secondary.

Notes

Originally published in a slightly different form in John Sherwood, *Officers in Flight Suits: The Story of American Air Force Fighter Pilots in the Korean War* (New York: New York University Press, 1996). Reprinted with the permission of the publisher.

1. During the Korean War, Nellis AFB was the home of the Air Force's advanced single-engine fighter and aerial gunnery schools. In short, it was the final stop in the fighter pilot training cycle—the place where the Air Force transformed pilots into MiG killers. For more on the early history of Nellis, see Thomas A. Manning, *History of Air Training Command, 1943–1993* (Randolph AFB, Texas: Office of History and Research, Headquarters, Air Education and Training Command, 1993), 18, 19, 26, 31, 32, 39, 43, 46, 47, 63.

2. Vance Mitchell, "The First Generation: A Personal Policy History of the Air Force Officer Corps, 1944–1974" (unpublished manuscript, Center for Air Force History, Washington, D.C., 1992), 736, 183–84, 767.

3. Historical Division, Flying Training Air Force, "History of the Flying Training Air Force," January 1–June 30, 1953, vol. 1, Waco, Texas, September 10, 1953, Center for Air Force History, Washington, D.C., 83.

4. Mitchell, "First Generation," 733.

5. Civilian contractors were trained as flight instructors at Craig Air Force Base. See "History of the Flying Training Air Force," July 1–December 31, 1952, vol. 1, 80–85.

6. Pomeroy interview.

7. Ibid.

8. Mitchell, "First Generation," 731–32.

9. Ibid., 733.

10. Mitchell, "First Generation," 733–34.

11. "History of the Flying Training Air Force," July 1–December 31, 1952, vol. 1, 41; Mitchell, "First Generation," 203.

12. "History of the Flying Training Air Force," July 1–December 31, 1952, vol. 1, 65.

13. Mitchell, "First Generation," 205.

14. Ibid.

15. Ibid., 205–6.

16. Ibid., 208.

17. Alan Gropman, *The Air Force Integrates 1945–1964* (Washington, D.C.: Center for Air Force History, 1985), 121. The percentage of blacks in the general population in 1949 was approximately 10 percent.

18. Mitchell, "First Generation," 784.

19. Personal Papers of George Berke, Reston, Virginia. Berke completed this analysis with the help of *Hondo Final,* 53-E and *Contrails,* 53-E, Williams AFB, Arizona (his class yearbooks).

20. Director of Statistical Services, *United States Air Force Statistical Digest* (Washington, D.C.: Office of Statistical Services, 1947), tables 8, 11.

21. Statistical Services, *United States Air Force Statistical Digest* (Washington, D.C.: Office of Statistical Services, January 1949–June 1950), tables 20, 21, 23.

22. See Gropman, *Air Force Integrates,* Appendix I, table 2, 223.

23. Ibid., 132.

24. Ibid., 132.

25. Ibid., 135–36.

26. "History of the Air Training Command," July 1–December 31, 1949, 29–31, as cited in ibid., 136.

27. These schools were located at the following bases: Bainbridge, Bartow, Columbus, Goodfellow, Greenville, Hondo, Malden, Marana, Spence, and Stallings. See "Flying Training Air Force Statistical Digest," July 31, 1952, in Records of the Flying Training Air Force, Center for Air Force History, Washington, D.C.

28. "History of the Flying Training Air Force," July 1–December 31, 1952, vol. 1, 49–57, and vol. 2, 484–549.

29. "History of the Flying Training Air Force," July 1–December 31, 1952, vol. 1, 61.

30. Turner interview.

31. They included Bainbridge, Bartow, Columbus, Greenville, Hondo, Malden, Marana, Spence, and Stallings. Only the Primary school at Goodfellow AFB was staffed by military instructors. "History of the Flying Training Air Force," July 1–December 31, 1952, vol. 2, 670.

32. "History of the Flying Training Air Force," July 1–December 31, 1952, vol. 2, 45–46.

33. "Report of Conference, Primary Training, Headquarters Flying Training Air Force, Roosevelt Hotel, Waco, Texas, 4–5 December 1952," in "The History of the Flying Training Air Force," July 1–December 31, 1952, vol. 2, 579.

34. It was assumed that ROTC, West Point, and Annapolis graduates were already familiar with military ways and did not need this additional training. When these officers joined the Aviation Cadets in Primary, they lived apart from the Aviation Cadets and participated only in flight training and ground school with them.

35. In October 1947, the Aviation Cadet Examining Board at Randolph AFB, Texas, recommended a one- to five-month preflight training program, and the Flying Division of the Air Training Command recommended a twelve-week program in December 1948. "The History of the Flying Training Air Force," July 1–December 31, 1952, vol. 1, 46.

36. This segment was later increased to twelve weeks in October 1952. "History of the Flying Training Air Force," January 1–June 30, 1953, vol. 1, 38.

37. Ibid., vol. 2, 375–400.

38. Ibid., 375–400.

39. According to George Berke, military academy graduates took the code much less seriously than the Aviation Cadets. Although Pomeroy vehemently disagrees with this claim, Berke remembered seeing West Point graduates passing test answers back and forth. "The motto of these guys was cooperate and graduate," Berke claimed. "To them the Honor Code was like the tax code—you look for loopholes." Berke interview; Pomeroy interview.

40. "History of the Flying Training Air Force," January 1–June 30, 1953, vol. 1, 38; "History of the Flying Training Air Force," July 1–December 31, 1952, vol. 1, 46–47.

41. Tomlinson interview.

42. "History of the Flying Training Air Force," January 1–June 30, 1953, vol. 1, 40.

43. Pomeroy interview.

44. Pomeroy interview.

45. Mitchell, "First Generation," 206.

46. Berke interview.

47. Tomlinson interview.

48. Crockett interview.

49. Gropman, Air Force Integrates, 156.

50. Crockett interview.

51. Gropman, Air Force Integrates, 135.

52. Ibid.

53. Turner interview.

54. Berke interview.

55. Brown, "A Fighter Pilot's Story," 5.

56. Tomlinson interview.

57. Brown, "A Fighter Pilot's Story," 5–6.

58. Brown interview.

59. Pomeroy interview.

60. Pomeroy interview.

61. "History of the Flying Training Air Force," July 1–December 31, 1952, vol. 2, 670.

62. Mitchell, "First Generation," 733.

63. Rebecca Hancock Cameron, "To Fly: Military Flight Training, 1907–1945" (draft, historical manuscript, Center for Air Force History, Washington, D.C., 1993), 449.

64. Tomlinson interview.

65. Cameron, "To Fly," 446–47.

66. A chandelle is an abrupt and steep climbing turn made in an airplane, in which the airplane's momentum provides additional acceleration for the climb. The purpose of the candela is to change the direction of flight and change altitude at the same time.

67. Cameron, "To Fly," 450.

68. "History of the Flying Training Air Force," July 1–December 31, 1952, vol. 1, 84.

69. Tomlinson interview.

70. Cameron, "To Fly," 446, 454.

71. Such was not the case at the segregated World War II Tuskegee field. Because of the lack of other black AAF facilities, many washouts were made privates and stationed at Tuskegee, "depressing morale." See Stanley Sandler, Segregated Skies: All-Black Combat Squadrons of World War II (Washington, D.C.: Smithsonian Institution Press, 1992), 32.

72. Tomlinson interview.

73. Cameron, "To Fly," 453.

74. The plane used for this training was the Piper PA-18. "History of the Flying Training Air Force," January 1–June 30, 1953, vol. 1, 83.

75. "History of the Flying Training Air Force," July 1–December 31, 1952, vol. 1, 78.

76. Pomeroy, in general, was very sensitive to any critical remarks about the U.S. Military Academy. "West Pointers," he claimed, "wanted their wings just as much as the next guy; one of my classmates washed out and he was not a happy camper—he knew his military career was over with, and just marked time until he could get out." Pomeroy interview.

77. "History of the Flying Training Air Force," July 1–December 31, 1952, vol. 1, 78.

78. Ibid., 77.

79. Pomeroy interview.

80. "History of the Flying Training Air Force," January 1–June 10, 1952, vol. 2, 600–660.

81. Timothy Strongin, "A Historical Review of the Fear of Flying among Aircrewmen," *Aviation, Space, and Environmental Medicine* 58, no. 2 (1987), 264.

82. Ibid., 265.

83. Ibid., 264.

84. Ibid., 264–65.

85. Lucio Gatto, "Understanding the 'Fear of Flying' Syndrome," *U.S. Armed Forces Medical Journal* 5, no. 8 (1954), 1100.

86. Even today, the condition is poorly understood. In "Flying and Danger, Joy and Fear," *Aviation, Space, and Environmental Medicine* 57, no. 9 (February 1986), 131–36, Dr. David Jones of the Neuropsychiatric Branch of the USAF School of Aerospace Medicine, Brooks AFB, Texas, defined FOF as a "complex phenomenon, mixing elements of mental health and neurotic roots, childhood dreams and fears, real dangers and imaginary threats, and all the varieties of life experiences which may befall a flier as he or she ages." In short, FOF could be almost anything: all that is clear from this definition is that it is a complex psychiatric condition.

87. Lucio Gatto, "Understanding the 'Fear of Flying' Syndrome," *U.S. Armed Forces Medical Journal* 5, no. 8 (1954), 1100. Timothy Strongin, a researcher at the Neuropsychiatry Branch of the USAF School of Aerospace Medicine, offered the following symptomatic definition of FOF in a 1987 historical review of FOF in *Aviation, Space, and Environmental Medicine:*

> Its clearest manifestation is the frank refusal to fly or fear of the plane or the possible consequences of flying. More subtle is the case of a flier who says he would be willing to fly, if only he were able to concentrate, relax, get some sleep, or overcome some other manifestation of inner turmoil. Depending on the fliers personality, one observes that dissociative symptoms (sleepwalking, amnesia), restlessness, substances abuse (drugs, food, and alcohol), emotional regression, somatization (ulcers, gastritis, colitis, headaches, dermatitis), or conversion (hearing loss, back pain, weakness) may also indicate underlying anxiety.

Clearly, agreement between these specialists not only exists with respect to the primary symptom of FOF, a refusal to fly, but also with other symptoms, including anxiety and a range of psychosomatic conditions. Furthermore, Gatto's and Strongin's symptomatic descriptions are nearly equivalent: the jargon is somewhat different but the basic symptoms are the same. See Strongin, "Historical Review," 264.

88. Jones suggests that many cases of FOF could have been cured through basic therapy. See Jones, "Flying and Danger," 131–36.

89. Mitchell, "First Generation," 185.

90. Ibid., 190–91.

91. Ibid., 191–92.

92. Ibid., 193.

93. Ibid., 193.

94. Ibid., 192.

95. Ibid.

96. Ibid., 186.

97. Ibid., 187–88.

98. Ibid., 189.

99. Lucio Gatto, "Understanding the 'Fear of Flying' Syndrome, II: Psychosomatic Aspects and Treatment," *U.S. Armed Forces Medical Journal* 5, no. 9 (1954), 1285.

100. Strongin, "Historical Review," 265.

101. An analysis of classes 52-E, F, and G, reveals that an average of 7.5 percent of those eliminated were washed out because of fear of flying. "History of the Flying Training Air Force," January 1–June 30, 1952, vol. 2, 627–70.

102. Report of the Conference, Primary Pilot Training, Headquarters Flying Training Air Force, Roosevelt Hotel, Waco, Texas, in "History of the Flying Training Air Force," July 1–December 31, 1952, vol. 1, 578–85.

103. A more recent study by the Naval Aviation Medical Institute in 1964 suggests that aviation students afflicted with FOF do not want to fly "not so much because of a fear of death but because of their inability to deal with conflicts precipitated by the more mundane aspects of learning to fly (e.g., frequent tests, and relationships with instructors). These students often expressed their FOF overtly through motion sickness." Strongin, "Historical Review," 266.

104. "History of the Flying Training Air Force," July 1–December 31, 1952, vol. 1, 63; "History of the Flying Training Air Force," January 1–June 30, 1953, vol. 1, 83.

105. "History of the Flying Training Air Force," July 1–December 31, 1952, vol. 1, 98.

106. Headquarters Flying Training Air Force, "Statistical Digest," September 30, 1952, 16, in "History of the Flying Training Air Force," July 1–December 31, 1952, vol. 2, 765.

107. Berke interview.

108. Brown, "A Fighter Pilot's Story," 8.

109. Ibid.

110. Ibid., 9; Berke interview.

111. Brown, "A Fighter Pilot's Story," 10.

112. Ibid., 11.

113. Ibid.

114. Although this accident actually occurred at Brown's Advanced training at Nellis, I included it here because it is a good example of how G forces can kill a novice pilot. Brown interview; Brown, "A Fighter Pilot's Story," 16.

115. Berke interview.

116. Turner interview.

117. Berke papers, "Williams Analysis"; Berke interview.

118. Charles Watry, *Washout: The Aviation Cadet Story* (Carlsbad: California Aero Press, 1983), 118.

119. Dixon was later killed in a plane crash at Rametelli in Italy. Crockett interview.

120. Crockett interview.

121. "History of the Flying Training Air Force," July 1–December 31, 1952, vol. 1, 99; "History of the Flying Training Air Force," January 1–June 30, 1952, vol. 1, 62.

122. Berke interview.

123. "History of the Flying Training Air Force," January 1–June 30, 1952, vol. 2, 634.

124. Thirteen French, three Dutch, and two British; Berke papers.

125. Brown interview.

126. Interestingly, this same cadet later became the head of the Danish FAA. Turner interview.

127. Brown, "A Fighter Pilot's Story," 6–7.

128. Management Analysis Division, Air Force Training Command, "Analysis of Class 52-E," in "The History of the Flying Training Air Force," January 1–June 30, 1952, vol. 2, 629.

129. Everett Dodd, "The Tale of 'Tiger,'" *Air Force Magazine,* July 1953, 72.

130. Wayne Thompson, "The Air War in Korea," in Bernard Nalty, ed., "History of the United States Air Force 1907–1982" (unpublished manuscript, Center for Air Force History, Washington, D.C., 1992), 279.

131. Berke interview.

132. Ibid.

133. Brown, "A Fighter Pilot's Story," 14.

134. Ibid.

135. Mike Spick, *The Ace Factor: Air Combat and the Role of Situational Awareness* (Annapolis, Md.: Naval Institute Press, 1988), 128.

136. Brown, "A Fighter Pilot's Story," 14.

137. Spick, "Ace Factor," 128.

138. Tomlinson interview.

139. Berke interview.

140. Tomlinson interview.

141. J. G. Potter, "Sarge Looks at Today's Cadet," *Air Force Times,* September 16, 1950, 16.

142. Dodd, "Tale of 'Tiger,'" 72–79; Potter, "Sarge," 16.

143. Ibid.

144. Tomlinson interview.

145. "History of the Flying Training Air Force," July 1–December 31, 1952, vol. 1, 74–75.

146. Dodd, "Tale of 'Tiger,'" 75.

147. "History of the Flying Training Air Force," July 1–December 31, 1952, vol. 1, 75.

148. Dodd, "Tale of 'Tiger,'" 76.

149. "History of the Flying Training Air Force," July 1–December 31, 1952, vol. 1, 76.

150. Dodd, "Tale of 'Tiger,'" 75.

151. "History of the Flying Training Air Force," July 1–December 31, 1952, vol. 1, 75–76.

152. Dodd, "Tale of 'Tiger,'" 75.

153. Berke interview.

154. Ibid.

155. Mitchell, "First Generation," 728–30.

Bibliographic Essay

DOMINICK A. PISANO

General Secondary Materials

As time goes on, and there is more interest in the study of aviation from a scholarly perspective, the historiography of the subject will develop more fully. As this happens, aviation's social-cultural underpinnings—the assumptions, attitudes, behaviors, myths and ideologies that underlie the technology—will come to light. Eventually, the writing of the history of aviation will open itself up to a variety of methodologies, embrace interdisciplinarity, and be willing to include a multiplicity of source materials—photography, art, film, material culture—as well as more traditional primary source material. In 1998, Wright State University in Dayton, Ohio, held a major meeting of aerospace historians called The National Aerospace Conference: The Meaning of Flight in the Twentieth Century that marked a beginning toward the achievement of that goal. One of the thematic areas, "Flight, Culture, and Society," included a variety of papers on art, film, literature, popular culture, gender, and representation.[1]

The experience of the National Aerospace Conference indicates that the cultural history of aviation has become accepted into the mainstream of scholarship in the subject. Another encouraging sign is that more and more graduate students in American history, American Studies, and art history, among other areas, are choosing dissertation topics in the history of aviation. In fact, *The Airplane in American Culture* features material from recent doctoral dissertations. Although the historiography is somewhat limited, in the essay that follows I have tried to identify briefly the most important secondary sources that contain social and cultural interpretations of aviation or touch on important themes.

Suitable models for writing the social and cultural history of aviation in the United States exist among books and monographs that relate to European aviation. Peter Fritzsche, *A Nation of Flyers: German Aviation and the Popular Imagination* (Cambridge, Mass.: Harvard University Press, 1992), is an excellent study of aviation in Germany to the beginning of World War II. Robert Wohl, *A Passion for Wings: Aviation and the Western Imagination, 1908–1918* (New Haven: Yale University Press, 1993), is the groundbreaking first volume of a multiple-volume cultural history of aviation in Europe in the early twentieth century.

Joseph J. Corn, *The Winged Gospel: America's Romance with Aviation, 1900–1950* (New York: Oxford University Press, 1983) is perhaps the most complete statement of aviation in American culture to date. Roger Bilstein (a contributor to this volume), *Flight Patterns: Trends of Aeronautical Development, 1918–1927* (Athens: University of Georgia Press, 1983) and *Flight in America: From the Wrights to the Astronauts* (Baltimore: Johns Hopkins University Press, 1984), contain useful sections on the significance of the airplane in American culture. See especially chapter 7, "Symbolism and Imagery" in *Flight Patterns,* and chapter 8, "Folklore, Fantasy and Artifacts" in *Flight in America.*

Overview: The Airplane and the American Experience

Roger Bilstein's essay in this volume alerts the reader to a number of areas in which the airplane has had an effect on the American experience, including film, industrial design, education, and the comics. Although there is not yet a satisfactory scholarly treatment of aviation and film, Stephen Pendo, *Aviation in the Cinema* (Metuchen, N.J.: Scarecrow, 1985), James H. Farmer, *Celluloid Wings: The Impact of Movies on Aviation* (Blue Ridge Summit, Pa.: TAB, 1984), and Michael Paris, *From the Wright Brothers to Top Gun: Aviation, Nationalism and Popular Cinema* (Manchester, England: Manchester University Press, 1995), are useful introductions to the subject. Dominick A. Pisano, "*The Dawn Patrol* and the World War I Air Combat Film Genre: An Exploration of American Values," in Peter C. Rollins and John E. O'Connor, eds., *Hollywood's World War I* (Bowling Green, Ohio: Bowling Green State University Popular Press, 1997), 59–79, analyzes an influential aviation film in the light of its relationship to American values in the 1930s. The airplane's influence on industrial design in the United States is discussed in Donald J. Bush, *The Streamlined Decade* (New York: G. Braziller, 1975), Jeffrey Meikle, *Twentieth Century Limited: Industrial Design in America, 1925–1939* (Philadelphia, Pa.: Temple University Press, 1979), *Streamlining America: A Henry Ford Museum Exhibit* (Dearborn, Mich.: Henry Ford Museum & Greenfield Village, 1986), and Dominick A. Pisano, "The Airplane and the Streamline Idiom in the United States," in *Aerospace Design* (London: Merrell Publishers, forthcoming). Claude Lichtenstein and Franz Engler, eds., *Streamlined: A Metaphor for Progress* (Zurich: Lars Müller Publishers, n.d.), contains essays on streamlining the railways, aerodynamics in Italy and its influence on the streamlined automobile, and streamlined design at the Chicago (1933–1934) and New York World's Fairs Century of Progress Exposition (1939–1940) Corn, *The Winged Gospel,* and Dominick A. Pisano, *To Fill the Skies with Pilots: A History of the Civilian Pilot Training Program* (Urbana: University of Illinois Press, 1993), discuss Air Age Education, an attempt to employ aeronautics in elementary and secondary school curricula N. L. Engelhardt, Jr., *Education for the Air Age* (New York: Macmillan, 1942), and the Air Age Education series, published by Macmillan, and sponsored by the Institute of the Aeronautical Sciences in cooperation with the Civil Aeronautics Administration, are representative of the Air Age Education movement. James Silke, "Aviation Comic Strips," *Air Progress/Aviation Review* (August 1980), 18–23, Al Flick, "Flying in the Funnies," *Aviation Quarterly* 8 (1985), 4–47, and "Thrills and Glamor in the Funny Papers," in Sterling Seagrave, *Soldiers of Fortune,* The Epic of Flight Series (Alexandria, Va.: Time-Life Books, 1981), 66–71, are useful tidbits on flying in the comics.

The Airplane: Public Perception

Public acceptance of the airplane and the industry's attempt to promote aviation to the public are two important themes in the cultural history of aviation. Roger Bilstein, "The Airplane, the Wrights, and the American Public" in Richard P. Hallion, ed., *The Wright Brothers: Heirs of Prometheus* (Washington, D.C.: Smithsonian Institution, 1978), 39-51, discusses public perceptions and acceptance of aviation by Americans before and after the Wright brothers' invention of the airplane. This essay is a distillation of Bilstein's master's thesis, "The Public Attitude toward the Airplane in the United States, 1910–1925" (Ohio State University, 1960). See also, "'The Moment of Miracle': Americans Greet the Airplane" in Corn, *The Winged Gospel,* 3–27.

In its early history, aviation was known to the public as sport and as a means of providing entertainment for spectators. This tradition, despite the emphasis on the airplane's utility as a conveyance for passengers and as a weapon, continues to this day. Courtney G. Brooks's "American Aeronautics as Spectacle and Sport" (Ph.D. diss., Tulane University, 1969), is a well-argued analysis of aviation as sport in American culture. Brooks devotes a considerable amount of space to the ballooning era, but he also discusses the pioneer or "birdman" era (see chapter 5, "Pioneers with Wings), as well as barnstorming and air racing.

On ballooning as sport, see "The Sport of Kings," in Tom D. Crouch (a contributor to this work), *The Eagle Aloft: Two Centuries of the Balloon in America* (Washington, D.C.: Smithsonian Institution Press, 1983), 531–60. On the Wright brothers' exhibition flying team, see "The Montebank Game" in Tom D. Crouch, *The Bishop's Boys: A Life of Wilbur and Orville Wright* (New York: W. W. Norton, 1989), 424–39. On the Curtiss team, see "The Exhibitionists," in C. R. Roseberry, *Glenn Curtiss, Pioneer of Flight* (Garden City, N.Y.: Doubleday, 1972), 281–307. On barnstorming and the barnstorming era, see Hart Stilwell and Slats Rodgers, *Old Soggy No. 1: The Uninhibited Story of Slats Rodgers* (New York: Julian Messner, 1954, and New York: Arno Press, 1972); Bill Rhode, *Bal-*

ing Wire, Chewing Gum, and Guts: The Story of the Gates Flying Circus (Port Washington, N.Y.: Kennikat Press, 1970). Paul O'Neil, *Barnstormers and Speed Kings,* Epic of Flight Series (Alexandria, Va.: Time-Life Books, 1981), is a colorfully illustrated capsule history of barnstorming and air racing. Thomas G. Foxworth, *The Speed Seekers* (New York: Doubleday, 1976), is a comprehensive analysis of air racing in the 1920s. Carroll V. Glines, *Roscoe Turner: Aviation's Master Showman,* Smithsonian History of Aviation Series (Washington, D.C.: Smithsonian Institution Press, 1995), provides a glimpse into the life of one of the most colorful figures of the air race era.

On aviation's transition from sport-entertainment to commerce, see Bill Robie, *For the Greatest Achievement: A History of the Aero Club of America and the National Aeronautic Association* (Washington, D.C.: Smithsonian Institution Press, 1993). On the formation of the aircraft industry, see Jacob A. Vander Meulen, *The Politics of Aircraft: Building an American Military Industry* (Lawrence: University Press of Kansas, 1991). William M. Leary, ed., *Aviation's Golden Age: Portraits from the 1920s and 1930s* (Iowa City: University of Iowa Press, 1989), presents scholarly essays on key figures in the development of aviation, including Henry Ford, William P. MacCracken, Jr., and Herbert Hoover, among others.

Charles A. Lindbergh is the most recognizable name in that pantheon of heroic pilots and one of the most important cultural figures in molding public perception of aviation in the interwar years. Lindbergh's transatlantic flight in 1927 fixed widespread attention on aviation in the United States. Of the many biographies of Lindbergh, Kenneth S. Davis, *The Hero: Charles A. Lindbergh and the American Dream* (Garden City, N.Y.: Doubleday, 1959), despite its age, is an excellent analysis of the Lindbergh phenomenon and the culturally determined processes that helped to create Lindbergh's celebrity. John William Ward's "The Meaning of Lindbergh's Flight," in *Studies in American Culture: Dominant Ideas and Images,* ed. Joseph J. Kwiat and Mary C. Turpie (Minneapolis: University of Minnesota Press, 1960), 27–40, explains the significance of Lindbergh in cultural terms. Perry D. Luckett, "Lindbergh in Popular Culture," in *Charles A. Lindbergh: A Bio-Bibliography* (Westport, Conn.: Greenwood Press, 1986), contains a unique look at the public reaction to Lindbergh as seen in newsprint journalism, films, photographs, recordings, musical composition, songs, poems, and memorabilia. (Luckett is also useful for bibliographic information on Lindbergh.) Susan M. Gray, *Charles A. Lindbergh and the American Dilemma: The Conflict of Technology and Human Values* (Bowling Green, Ohio: Bowling Green State University Popular Press, 1988), is a thoughtful analysis of Lindbergh and of his relation to technology and American values. John Lardner, "The Lindbergh Legends," in *The Aspirin Age,* ed. Isabel Leighton (New York: Simon and Schuster, 1949), 190–213, is a corrective to the adulatory accounts of Lindbergh. Dominick

A. Pisano and F. Robert van der Linden, *Charles Lindbergh and the Spirit of St. Louis* (New York: Harry N. Abrams, 2002), examines the complex relationship between Lindbergh and the aircraft that helped to make him an international celebrity. Joyce Milton, *Loss of Eden: A Biography of Charles and Anne Morrow Lindbergh* (New York: HarperCollins, 1993), is one of the latest entries in the series of biographies on Lindbergh. A. Scott Berg, *Lindbergh* (New York: G. P. Putnam's Sons, 1998), makes good use of the Charles A. Lindbergh Collection and Anne Morrow Lindbergh Collection at Yale University's Sterling Memorial Library to probe more deeply into Lindbergh's personal life and motivation than previous writers on the subject. Lindbergh's own writings provide windows on the culture of aviation, especially *Of Flight and Life* (New York: Charles Scribner's Sons, 1948), *The Spirit of St. Louis* (New York: Charles Scribner's Sons, 1953), *The Wartime Journals of Charles A. Lindbergh* (New York: Harcourt Brace Jovanovich, 1970), and *An Autobiography of Values* (New York: Harcourt Brace Jovanovich, 1977).

The Airplane: Race and Gender

Public acceptance of the airplane was predicated on its projection of a democratic image. In its most important period of development, however, mere lip service was paid to including blacks and women in aviation's mostly white male-dominated world. Scholars have not adequately explored the social and cultural history of African Americans in aviation in the 1920s and 1930s. Jill Snider (a contributor to this work), "Flying to Freedom: African-American Visions of Aviation, 1910–1927" (Ph.D. diss., University of North Carolina, 1995), examines black attitudes toward aviation in the 1920s and 1930s, and thus provides an important glimpse at the reasons for black interest in aviation during its formative period. "Beginnings," the first chapter in Stanley Sandler, *Segregated Skies: All Black Combat Squadrons of World War II* (Washington, D.C.: Smithsonian Institution Press, 1992), 1–23, is illuminating, as is "The Black Public Becomes Air-minded," chapter 3 in Robert J. Jakeman, *The Divided Skies: Establishing Flight Training at Tuskegee, Alabama, 1934–1942* (Tuscaloosa: University of Alabama Press, 1992), 53–68. Chapter 1, "First Flight," in Benjamin O. Davis, Jr., *Benjamin O. Davis, Jr., American: An Autobiography* (Washington, D.C.: Smithsonian Institution Press, 1991), 1–20, gives an idea of how important flying was to the leader of the first all-black group of military pilots in the U.S. Army Air Forces. Although the work of Sandler, Jakeman, and Davis is primarily about military aviation, it contains valuable information about the cultural milieu for black aviators in the years between the wars.

The scholarly literature on women in aviation is surprisingly scarce considering strong interest in academia in women's studies and gender studies. Suzanne

L. Kolm (a contributor to this work), "Women's Labor Aloft: A Cultural History of Airline Flight Attendants in the United States, 1930–1978" (Ph.D. diss., Brown University, 1995), examines women's issues in relation to flight attendants and the commercial airline industry. Susan Ware, *Still Missing: Amelia Earhart and the Search for Modern Feminism* (New York: W. W. Norton, 1993), is the model for cultural history of an important woman in aviation. Ware sees Earhart as "an influential figure in the development of mass culture and the merchandising of popular figures [who] participated in the emergence of aviation as a major transportation industry [and] symbolized the new opportunities for women in modern life." Nancy Porter's film, *Amelia Earhart* (Nancy Porter, prod., for The American Experience, 1993), deals with Earhart's significance as a created celebrity, aviation pioneer, role model for women, and with her life as tragedy. Doris L. Rich, *Queen Bess, Daredevil Aviator* (Washington, D.C.: Smithsonian Institution Press, 1993), is a useful chronicle of the life of Bessie Coleman, an important African American aviatrix and symbolic figure in African American aspirations to become pilots. Molly Merryman, *Clipped Wings: The Rise and Fall of the Women Airforce Service Pilots (WASPs) of World War II* (New York: NYU Press, 1998), analyzes the failure of the most ambitious wartime program for women pilots." Katherine Sharp Landdeck (a contributor to this volume), "Pushing the Envelope: The Women Airforce Service Pilots and American Society," (Ph.D. diss., University of Tennessee, 2003), disagrees with Merryman's assessment and argues forcefully that the WASP program was a qualified success.[2]

The Airplane: Perceptions of the Landscape, Literature, and Art

A thoughtful analysis of the handful of aviators who have recorded their flying experiences in writing has yet to be written. George L. Mosse, *Fallen Soldiers: Reshaping the Memory of the World Wars* (New York: Oxford University Press, 1990), has some brief but interesting observations about two aviator-writers, Charles A. Lindbergh and Antoine de Saint-Exupéry. See also David McCullough, "Aviation Authors: Saint-Exupéry's 'Wartime Writings' Recalls a Remarkable Body of Work," *New York Times* Magazine, October 12, 1986, 50, 81–83, 85. McCullough also discusses Charles and Anne Lindbergh and Beryl Markham.

Laurence Goldstein (a contributor to this work), *The Flying Machine and Modern Literature* (Bloomington: Indiana University Press, 1986), is a comprehensive treatment of the airplane's influence on literature. Richard T. Dillon examines aviation's effect on literature and culture in "The Sound of Wings: Aviation in Twentieth-Century Literature" (Ph.D. diss., University of California, Berkeley, 1970). (See also Wohl, "Poets of Space," in *A Passion for Wings,* 97–122.)

Aviation's relationship with art begins in Italy in 1909 with the beginning of the Futurist movement and its leader Filippo Tommaso Marinetti. Twenty years later, the Futurists launched a movement called *Aeropittura Futurista* [Futurist aero painting], in which artists were exhorted to celebrate in their work "the immense visual and sensory drama of flight." On Aeropittura, see Wohl, "Painters Take Flight," in *A Passion for Wings,* 199 ff. (Wohl also discusses Kazimir Malevich and Robert Delaunay) and Gerald Silk (a contributor to this work), "Flight; Futurism; Aeropittura" in *Futurism Aeropittura* (Rome: Stilgraf, 1989). Although aviation had less influence on painting in the United States than in Europe, it did influence American muralists. On this subject, see Ruth Bowman, *Murals without Walls: Arshile Gorky's Aviation Murals Rediscovered* (Newark, N.J.: The Newark Museum, 1978), and Greta Berman, "Does 'Flight' Have a Future?" *Art in America* (September–October 1976), 97–99.

The Airplane and the Culture of War

Although a great deal of recent scholarship has been produced on the use of the airplane in combat, the role of air commanders, and architects of military aviation, very little work has been done on the cultural foundations of the airplane's place in conceptions of national power and of waging total war. This area has not yet been well defined but could include, among other things, the relationship between the military and the technology of aviation, military aviation and conceptions of national power and nationalism, the role of popular culture in supporting military aviation and its technology, the institutional culture of military aviation, the role of minorities in military aviation. The sources cited in this section touch on some of these aspects.

The closest anyone has come to an examination of the nationalistic symbolism with which the airplane was endowed in the United States is Michael S. Sherry, *The Rise of American Air Power: The Creation of Armageddon* (New Haven: Yale University Press, 1987). Robert Wohl, *A Passion for Wings,* sees the tension between the airplane's capacity to inspire wonder and nationalistic fervor at the same time as two sides of the same coin. (See "Towards a High Culture," 253–88, for Wohl's discussion of the rise of Mussolini in Italy and its relationship to aviation's assumption of a persona of power.) Peter Fritzsche, *A Nation of Flyers: German Aviation and the Popular Imagination,* details the airplane's role in the rise of German nationalism before and after World War I.

Typical of the relatively new scholarship on the air war in World War I are Lee Kennett, *The First Air War, 1914–1918* (New York: Free Press, 1991), and John H. Morrow, *The Great War in the Air: Military Aviation from 1909 to 1921* (Washington, D.C.: Smithsonian Institution Press, 1993). Dominick A. Pisano, Thomas J. Dietz, Joanne M. Gernstein, and Karl S. Schneide, *Legend, Memory and the Great War in the Air* (Seattle: University of Washington Press, 1992), a catalogue based on an exhibition at the National Air and Space Museum, discusses how government, the military, and the mass media molded public perceptions of aviation in World War I.

In the United States, the relationship between aviation technology and the military was firmly established during the interwar years. H. Bruce Franklin (a contributor to this work), "Billy Mitchell and the Romance of the Bomber," from *War Stars: The Superweapon and the American Imagination* (New York: Oxford University Press, 1988), 91-100, discusses air power advocate Mitchell's penchant for self-promotion and his quest to meld what Franklin terms a "superweapon" with the airplane. Timothy Moy (a contributor to this work), *War Machines: Transforming Technologies in the U.S. Military, 1920–1940* (College Station: Texas A&M University Press, 2001), examines how the institutional culture of the U.S. Army Air Service/U.S. Army Air Corps influenced its belief that technological progress was essential to its existence and produced the doctrine of strategic bombardment. Tami Davis Biddle, *Rhetoric and Reality in Air Warfare: The Evolution of British and American Ideas about Strategic Bombing* (Princeton, N.J.: Princeton University Press, 2002), examines why strategic bombing doctrine in the United States and Great Britain often was based on erroneous assumptions and insufficient evidence.

Although air power was employed on a massive scale by the United States in World War II, there was a great deal of controversy over the claims made for its effectiveness in winning the war. Lee Kennett, *A History of Strategic Bombing* (New York: Scribner's, 1982), and Sherry, *The Rise of American Air Power,* discuss the successes and failures of strategic bombing during the war. Ronald Schaffer, *Wings of Judgment: American Bombing in World War II* (New York: Oxford University Press, 1985), assesses how concern for bombing civilians from the air became less a factor as the war went on.

On the postwar period, John T. Greenwood, "The Emergence of the Postwar Strategic Air Force, 1945–1953," 215–44, and David A. Rosenberg, "American Postwar Air Doctrine and Organization: The Navy Experience," 245–78, in Alfred F. Hurley and Robert C. Ehrhart, eds., *Air Power and Warfare: The Proceedings of the 8th Military History Symposium, United States Air Force Academy, 18–20 October 1978* (Washington, D.C.: Office of Air Force History and U.S. Air Force Academy, 1979), analyze the development of postwar air doctrine and national security. Jeffrey G. Barlow, *Revolt of the Admirals: The Fight for Naval Aviation, 1945–1950* (Washington, D.C.: Naval Historical Center, Department of the Navy, 1994), examines the contentious struggle between the Air Force and the Navy over supremacy in aerial delivery of nuclear weapons during the early years of the Cold War. The institutional culture of the U.S. Air Force in the Cold War is explored in John D. Sherwood (a contributor to this work), *Officers in* books, including *The Automobile and American Culture* (1983), and published three volumes of poetry.

Suzanne L. Kolm thanks the Smithsonian Institution's National Air and Space Museum, the American Historical Association, the National Aeronautics and Space Administration and the history department at Brown University for support for her dissertation on the cultural history of flight attendants. Dr. Kolm lives in Wakefield, Massachusetts.

Katherine Sharp Landdeck is Assistant Professor of History at Texas Woman's University in Denton, Texas, home of the WASPs archives. She received a Guggenheim Predoctoral Fellowship from the National Air and Space Museum, Smithsonian Institution, in 2000. Landdeck has written numerous articles for aviation publications and is currently working to revise her dissertation, "Pushing the Envelope: The Women Airforce Service Pilots and American Society," into book form.

Timothy Moy is Associate Professor of History at the University of New Mexico, specializing in the history of science and technology. He is the author of *War Machines: Transforming Technologies in the U.S. Military, 1920–1940* (2001), which examines the interaction between technology, institutional culture, and military doctrine in the Army Air Corps and the Marine Corps between the wars. He is currently working on a study of the impact of nuclear weapons on institutional culture in the military in the early Cold War period.

Dominick A. Pisano is a curator in the Aeronautics Division at the National Air and Space Museum, Smithsonian Institution, Washington, D.C. During more than two decades at the museum, he has been involved in numerous research and writing projects, as well as in collections management, exhibitions, and service to the public. He is the author of *To Fill the Skies with Pilots: The Civilian Pilot Training Program, 1939–1946* (1993), and coauthor of *Legend, Memory and the Great War in the Air* (1992), and *Charles Lindbergh and the Spirit of St. Louis* (2002).

Charles L. Ponce de Leon is Assistant Professor of History at Purchase College, SUNY. He received his Ph.D. from Rutgers University and is the author of *Self-Exposure: Human-Interest Journalism and the Emergence of Celebrity in America, 1890–1940* (2002).

Flight Suits: The Story of American Air Force Fighter Pilots in the Korean War (New York: New York University Press, 1996).

After Korea, aerial warfare went off in other directions; namely, ballistic missiles and space, but air power in the traditional sense of the term was applied during the Vietnam War. Mark Clodfelter, *The Limits of Air Power: The American Bombing of North Vietnam* (New York: Free Press, 1989), argues that overestimation of air power based on preconceptions of its success in World War II and Korea caused it to be misapplied in the Vietnam War. Marshall L. Michel III, *Clashes: Air Combat over North Vietnam, 1965–1972* (Annapolis, Md.: Naval Institute Press, 1997), examines the role the Air Force and the Navy played in the air war over North Vietnam. Michel concludes that an institutional failure to evaluate and reevaluate training, air-to-air missile development, and tactics caused the Air Force to lose more aircraft than it shot down during Operation Rolling Thunder, the first phase of the air war over Vietnam. The Navy, on the other hand, paid close attention to improving all phases of its air offensive capabilities. As a result, it founded the Top Gun program in 1968 to improve its fighter pilots' skills and thus achieved a higher ratio of aircraft shot down to aircraft lost than the Air Force, particularly during Operation Linebacker, the second phase of the air offensive during the Vietnam War. Finally, John D. Sherwood, *Fast Movers: America's Jet Pilots and the Vietnam Experience* (New York: Free Press, 1999), continues the line of investigation carried on in his previous work, *Officers in Flight Suits* (see earlier), but this time he presents a hard-hitting assessment of the institutional culture of fighter pilots during the Vietnam War.

Notes

1. See Dominick A. Pisano, "Flight, Society, and Culture Program Opening Remarks," in *Proceedings of the National Aerospace Conference* (Dayton, Ohio: Wright State University Press, 1999), 6–7.

2. Ware, 12.

Contributors

Roger Bilstein is recently retired from his position as Professor of History at University of Houston–Clear Lake, where he was a member of the Charter Faculty of the university, which was established in 1974. He is the author of numerous books, including *Flight Patterns: Trends of Aeronautical Development in the United States, 1918–1929* (1983), *Flight in America: From the Wrights to the Astronauts* (3d ed., 2001), *Enterprise of Flight: The American Aviation and Aerospace Industry* (2001), and *Testing Aircraft, Exploring Space: An Illustrated History of NACA and NASA* (2003), and many scholarly articles, book chapters, and entries in encyclopedias and other reference works.

Tom D. Crouch is Senior Curator in the Aeronautics Division at the National Air and Space Museum, Smithsonian Institution, Washington, D.C. A Smithsonian Institution employee since 1974, he has served both the National Air and Space Museum and the National Museum of American History (NMAH) in a variety of curatorial and administrative posts. He is the author or editor of a number of books and many articles for both popular magazines and scholarly journals. His authored books include *The Bishop's Boys: A Life of Wilbur and Orville Wright* (1989), *Eagle Aloft: Two Centuries of the Balloon in America* (1983), and *A Dream of Wings: Americans and the Airplane, 1875–1905* (1981).

H. Bruce Franklin is the author or editor of eighteen books on culture and history including *War Stars: The Superweapon in the American Imagination* (1988), *M.I.A. or Mythmaking in America* (1992), and *Vietnam and Other American Fantasies* (2000). Before his academic career, he served three years as a navigator and intelligence officer in the Strategic Air Command. He is currently the John Cotton Dana Professor of English and American Studies at Rutgers University, Newark.

Laurence Goldstein is Professor of English Language and Literature at the University of Michigan, where he has edited *Michigan Quarterly Review* since 1977. He is the author of three books of literary criticism: *Ruins and Empire: The Evolution of a Theme in Augustan and Romantic Literature* (1977); *The Flying Machine and Modern Literature* (1986); and *The American Poet at the Movies: A Critical History* (1994). In addition, he has edited or coedited seven other

John Darrell Sherwood holds a Ph.D. in history from the George Washington University and is the author of *Officers in Flight Suits: Story of American Air Force Fighter Pilots in the Korean War* (1996), and *Fast Movers: America's Jet Pilots and the Vietnam Experience* (1999). His most recent book, *Afterburner: Naval Aviators and the Vietnam War, 1968–1972,* will be published in 2004.

Gerald Silk is Professor of Art History at Tyler School of Art, Temple University. He has written widely on modern and contemporary art and been a curator and essayist for numerous exhibitions. He has taught at Columbia University and the University of Pennsylvania, and been a Senior Fellow at Center for Advanced Studies in the Visual Arts at the National Gallery and an American Academy in Rome Prize Fellow. He has served as an Associate Editor at *Artsmagazine* and been on the editorial board of *Art Journal.* His books include *The Automobile and Culture* and *Museums Discovered: The Wadsworth Atheneum.*

Jill D. Snider is an independent historian who lives and works in Chapel Hill, N.C. She earned her doctorate in U.S. history from the University of North Carolina at Chapel Hill in 1995. Having been a postdoctoral fellow at the National Air and Space Museum in 1995–96 and the American Historical Association in 1996–97, she is currently working on a manuscript on African American visions of aviation.

Index